# Business Basics
# for Law Students

# Business Basics for Law Students

## Essential Concepts and Applications

### Third Edition

**Robert W. Hamilton**

Minerva House Drysdale Regents
Chair in Law
University of Texas

**Richard A. Booth**

Professor of Law & Faculty Editor—The Business Lawyer
University of Maryland

ASPEN LAW & BUSINESS
A Division of Aspen Publishers, Inc.
New York        Gaithersburg

Permissions
Aspen Law & Business
1185 Avenue of the Americas
New York, NY 10036

Printed in the United States of America.

1 2 3 4 5 6 7 8 9 0

ISBN 0-7355-2558-7

**Library of Congress Cataloging-in-Publication Data**

Hamilton, Robert W., 1931-
  Business basics for law students : essential concepts and applications
/ Robert W. Hamilton, Richard A. Booth. — 3rd ed.
    p. cm.
  Includes index.
  ISBN 0-7355-2558-7
  1. Business law—United States. 2. Business enterprises—Law and legisla-
tion—United States. I. Booth, Richard A., 1950-    . II. Title.
KF889 .H238   2002
346.7307—dc21                                              2002018320

# About Aspen Law & Business
# Legal Education Division

With a dedication to preserving and strengthening the long-standing tradition of publishing excellence in legal education, Aspen Law & Business continues to provide the highest quality teaching and learning resources for today's law school community. Careful development, meticulous editing, and an unmatched responsiveness to the evolving needs of today's discerning educators combine in the creation of our outstanding casebooks, coursebooks, textbooks, and study aids.

**ASPEN LAW & BUSINESS**
**A Division of Aspen Publishers, Inc.**
**A Wolters Kluwer Company**
*www.aspenpublishers.com*

# SUMMARY OF CONTENTS

# ◆ CONTENTS

Contents

CHAPTER 4

# ANNUITIES AND RETIREMENT PLANS　69

CHAPTER 5

# INSURANCE　87

CHAPTER 6

# ACCOUNTING AND FINANCIAL REPORTING　113

## CHAPTER 7

# ◆ VALUATION OF A GOING BUSINESS — 161

## CHAPTER 8

# ◆ FEDERAL TAXATION — 199

Contents

CHAPTER 9

# ◆ INSOLVENCY AND BANKRUPTCY 225

CHAPTER 10

# ◆ BUSINESS ORGANIZATIONS 237

CHAPTER 11

◆
# CORPORATE SECURITIES 279

Contents

CHAPTER 12

# DIVIDENDS AND DISTRIBUTIONS                                         301

CHAPTER 13

# MERGERS AND ACQUISITIONS                                            317

CHAPTER 14

# TRADING IN STOCKS AND BONDS                                    355

CHAPTER 15

# OPTIONS, FUTURES, AND DERIVATIVES                              407

Contents

# ◆ PREFACE AND ACKNOWLEDGEMENTS

This book is written primarily for the benefit of law students who have little or no business background and who feel they need additional help in connection with financial matters. Topics covered include modern business forms, securities regulation and trading, income taxation, investments (including real estate), insurance, bankruptcy, and similar matters. The book describes the fundamentals of business law and practice that are important to business lawyers and the practice of business law itself, including relationships between business lawyers and sophisticated clients.

The focus of this book is on business and finance and not primarily on legal concepts. Thus, it is not a substitute for standard law school texts in traditional courses. Rather, it is intended to be a supplement to be used in connection with those texts. It is designed to demystify business concepts for law students who may feel intimidated by the subject matter (or by the apparent sophistication of fellow students). It is also designed to overcome a fear of numbers that is common among law students with social science or liberal arts backgrounds. In the modern practice of business law, an understanding of numbers and (relatively simple) financial concepts is essential.

The book emphasizes vocabulary that may be unfamiliar to readers. Words or acronyms such as *amortize*, *discount rate*, *hedge fund*, *naked put*, *OID*, and *zero coupon bond* may strike fear in the heart of an English major. This book explains and demystifies these terms by defining and using them in the context of the business settings in which they arise. The terms are boldfaced when they are first used, and are also included in a list at the end of the book, which provides the pages on which each initial explanation or definition may be found.

Many readers will find some of the material in this book to be elementary, but it is unlikely that everyone will find all of it so. Indeed, we think that the book will be quite useful to practicing lawyers and judges who need a ready source to refresh their recollection as to the meaning of specific terms. The book may also be useful for business students and business people generally, who may not understand the legal reasoning and policy behind specific rules that confine their activities. For example, every developer understands that a person usually cannot borrow all of the money necessary to fund a project, but few may have actually thought through why that should be so.

In addition, this book may be used quite successfully as the primary text in courses that are now offered at many law schools in conjunction with programs involving concentration in business law. These courses may be called Basic Business Concepts, Quantitative Methods, Fundamentals of Business Practice, Business Planning, or something similar.

This is the third edition of this book, which was first published under the title *Fundamentals of Modern Business* (Student Edition) by Professor Robert W. Hamilton of the University of Texas School of Law in 1989. The original book aged well, but the business world changes rapidly. Thus, Professor Richard A. Booth of the University of Maryland School of Law undertook to revise and update the original work (in collaboration with Professor Hamilton) in a second edition that appeared in 1998. The current edition will bear the date 2002.

Portions of the current edition are somewhat condensed as compared with earlier editions. We have combined former chapters on accounting and financial statement analysis into a single chapter. The chapters on insurance and taxation have also been significantly tightened. On the other hand, in the opposite direction, we have expanded the chapter on valuation to include a discussion of the capital asset pricing model, and the chapter on real estate to include a discussion of residential as well as commercial transactions. We have also added a new chapter on insolvency and bankruptcy. Other chapters dealing with financial markets and investing have been reorganized and updated to reflect developments such as decimal pricing of securities. We have also revised the chapter on the practice of law to describe the "bust cycle" that unexpectedly followed the long boom period of the 1990s.

Finally, we would like to thank the staff of Aspen Law & Business for their faith in the book, their superb editorial skills, and their remarkable attention to detail. Many thanks also to our assistants, Judy Dodson and April Cropper for their help in keeping the manuscript moving and keeping us generally on schedule.

*Robert W. Hamilton*
Austin, Texas

*Richard A. Booth*
Baltimore, Maryland

April 2002

# Business Basics
# for Law Students

# CHAPTER 1

# DEBT AND INTEREST

## §1.1  Introduction

The concept of **interest** is one of the most fundamental ideas in all of business. At its simplest, interest is the amount charged for the use of some amount of money for some period of time. Although the question might sound quite elementary, it helps at the outset to ask why it is routine (at least in most cultures) to charge interest on a loan. Perhaps the simplest answer is that one charges interest because one can. Other lenders receive interest, so it is foolish —at least in commercial transactions—not to insist on the going rate of return. Obviously, that answer is circular, but that does not make it invalid. A more sophisticated but still circular reason for charging interest is that rather than lending some sum to another, one could put the money in the bank and receive interest on it. To lend it without a comparable rate of return is to lose the money that one could have made. In other words, interest is compensation for the opportunity cost of allowing someone else to use your money. Forgone interest is not only lost interest; it is in effect interest paid. Although this answer is better than the first one, it is still circular because it depends on the fact that a bank or other financial institution pays interest on amounts deposited (which they only do because they can lend money to those who want to borrow). Perhaps the best answer to the puzzle of interest is that money can be used to buy things that can be used for production and consumption. A lender must forgo consumption while the borrower enjoys its benefits. Interest is thus compensation for opportunity costs.

If lenders routinely insist on interest, then why does anyone invest in something that pays no interest? Why do people take their savings out of the bank to start a business? Why do investors put their money in so-called growth stocks that pay no dividends? The simple answer is that people make these investments because they expect the eventual returns on such risky investments to be even greater than the interest they could receive from a bank account, savings bond, or other similar investment.

Thus, interest is only a subset of the even more basic concept of **return on investment (ROI)**. Although people do not usually think of returns from investments such as small businesses and stocks in terms of an equivalent interest rate, all investment returns are in fact part of a single continuum with lower rates of return (interest) paid in connection with safer investments (such as a **bond** or other debt instrument) and higher rates of return (**profits** or **dividends**) paid on riskier investments such as **stock** or other forms of **equity**. The line between interest and other forms of return is quite fuzzy, although the distinction can be quite important for tax and other purposes. Generally speaking, however, interest refers to the return paid on an enforceable obligation to pay money. With other forms of investment, the return tends to be much more variable, and the investor has no promise of either the payment of a return or the repayment of the amount invested. Assume, for example, that an investor agrees to purchase a 50 percent ownership interest in a small business for $500,000. Such a purchase (an **equity** investment) entitles the investor to 50 percent of all distributions by the business and 50 percent of the proceeds when the business is sold or dissolved. The transaction is not a loan to the business, because there is no promise of periodic payments and no promise of repayment at a definite time. The risk being taken by such an investor is greater than that taken by a bank lending funds, and the investor naturally expects a greater return. After all, if the business merely breaks even, the investor will receive no distribution at all, while a bank would still need to be paid.

Debt is often considered a bad thing—potentially dangerous and a drag on future earnings and assets. While it is certainly true that excessive debt may lead to undesirable consequences, the careful use of debt may be highly beneficial. Indeed, debt is central to most complex modern business transactions and may be of critical importance to personal transactions such as buying a new residence or automobile, or creating a new business from scratch. For most persons, such transactions would be impossible without the use of debt financing.

Successful businesses analyze decisions to undertake new projects by comparing the potential return from the project with the cost of capital necessary to fund the project. Capital for a new project may come from borrowing, from diversion of internally generated funds to the project, and from contributions by investors. The cost of borrowed capital is the interest charged by the lender; businesses also usually assign a reasonable cost to the diversion of internally generated funds to a new project. The return that investors expect depends on the circumstances, particularly representations made by the business to those investors. If the new project can be expected to generate returns that equal or exceed these costs, the project makes economic sense.

Many established businesses assume that a new project should generate at least a 15 percent return, roughly the historical average return on stocks. This calculation is complicated somewhat if the project is to be financed partly with debt. Moreover, there may be situations in which an inferior return is better than any alternative use for the money. After all, even a meager return is better than none at all. But the point for present purposes is the concept that an investment usually makes sense only if the expected return exceeds the cost of the funds invested. And this is as true for an individual deciding to invest in stocks as for a business investing in a new factory.

To be sure debt can be dangerous. Failure to make payments when due can have dire consequences. By the same token, however, debt also generates discipline. A business that must meet a payment on its debt cannot simply choose not to pay without facing litigation and bankruptcy. On the other hand, to the extent that the business has raised capital through the sale of stock, it may withhold dividends from the shareholders if the business finds itself in a tight spot. And it may be tempting for management to play it safe even if there is only a slight possibility that the business may need cash. On the other hand, shareholders might well prefer that the business pay generous dividends, so that it must come back to the market or the investors if it needs additional capital.

Similar reasoning applies at the consumer level. No one likes to be in debt. But it often makes sense to borrow money. Whether one borrows to buy a house, a car, a computer, or an education, the key consideration is whether the utility to be derived from the purchase equals or exceeds the interest cost. Here too, debt engenders discipline, in effect forcing the consumer to save. In the case of a house, there is also the possibility of monetary gain if the house can be sold for a higher price down the road. If one buys a house for $100,000 and sells it for $120,000, the return is 20 percent. If one borrows $80,000 of the purchase price, however, one starts out with $20,000 in equity and ends up with $40,000 in equity for a return of 100 percent. That is the basic concept of **leverage**, the use of debt to increase the return on an investment by borrowing funds at a lower interest rate than the return on the investment. On the other hand, if the house declines in value to $80,000, the homeowner who bought with all cash will have a 20 percent loss, while the homeowner who borrowed will have lost 100 percent of the equity investment. In other words, leverage can increase returns but it also increases risk, whether one borrows to buy a house, invest in stock, or build a new factory.

## §1.2 Simple Interest and Compound Interest

Interest is the cost of a loan to a borrower and the return to the lender. The amount of interest that a borrower pays is a function of three variables: (1) the amount borrowed, (2) the period for which it is borrowed, and (3) the rate of interest. In addition, to determine how much interest is to be earned on a specific loan, one must know the periods over which interest is to be computed, and, if the loan is to continue for more than one interest period, whether the interest is to be calculated as simple interest or compound interest.

The most common practice is to quote interest rates on an annual basis. The manner in which the actual computation is to be made, however, is not uniform. Interest quoted at the rate of 6 percent per year may actually mean interest calculated at 0.5 percent per month due at the end of each month, or it may mean interest at the rate of 1.5 percent per quarter due at the end of every three-month period, 3 percent semiannually due at the end of six months, or 6 percent due at the end of a year. Usually, these different calculations lead to different results. The times when payments are to be made on a loan may or may not coincide with the times when interest is calculated.

The computation of interest over several periods also involves an assumption as to whether the earned interest is in effect withdrawn every period so that each period's interest is computed on a stable principal, or whether the earned interest from the previous period is left with the borrower and treated as principal thereafter, itself to earn interest in the future period. The former is called **simple interest** and the latter **compound interest**.

A good example of compound interest involves the deposit of money with a bank. In this transaction, the depositor is the lender and the bank is the borrower who pays the lender interest at a specified rate. Let us assume that you have $10,000 that you deposit with a bank that advertises that it pays 8 percent per year, compounded quarterly. The word "quarterly" means that although the bank quotes its interest rate as 8 percent per year, it actually calculates interest at the rate of 2 percent for each accounting period of three months and adds that amount of interest to your account at the end of that period. Thus, if you left your $10,000 with the bank for three months, you would be credited with $200 (2 percent of $10,000), which you could withdraw without reducing your account below $10,000.

Suppose you let the bank keep (use) your money for another three months. If the bank computed its obligation on a simple interest basis, you would simply earn another $200 during the second three months. If the bank computed its obligation on a compound interest basis (as most banks do and as your bank expressly promised to do when it advertised that its 8 percent rate was "compounded quarterly"), it would consider that you had $10,200 on loan to it throughout the second quarter, and interest would be calculated on this amount at the end of six months, so that you would earn $204 during this period rather than simply $200. This is compound interest. The additional $4 reflects interest on the last period's interest. Over several accounting periods, the difference between compound and simple interest becomes increasingly significant. If you left your compound interest investment with the bank for a full year, you would have an account worth $10,824.32; at the end of two years, it would be worth $11,716.59. If only simple interest were paid, the investment would be worth $10,800 after one year and $11,600 after two years. At the end of ten years, your investment will be $22,080.40 at compound interest; if only simple interest were paid, the account would be worth $18,000. The compounding of interest thus significantly increases the growth rate of capital. If the interest rate is 6 percent (compounded quarterly), the investment doubles in 11.75 years; at 8 percent, in about 9 years; at 10 percent, in about 7 years. (A trick for determining roughly when an amount of money will double from compounding of interest is the Rule of 72. If one divides 72 by the interest rate, the resulting number is the approximate number of years it takes to double the amount deposited or invested.)

If the bank had calculated the interest it owed you on a simple interest basis, in effect it would be ignoring the interest earned in previous periods in calculating the current period's interest. To put it another way, the bank would assume that you had withdrawn the interest earned at the end of each accounting period even though you had not in fact done so. Presented in this way, it seems clear that compound interest more accurately reflects the reality of loan transactions over several accounting periods than does simple interest. The continued existence of simple interest computations here and there in the economy probably reflects a lack of sophistication by some lenders, the somewhat greater complexity of compound interest calculations as compared with simple interest calculations, and possibly an illogical remnant of the historical antipathy to the payment of interest at all. One can imagine, for example, a creditor making a two-year, 6 percent loan, and concluding that he should receive the original principal of the loan plus an aggregate of 12 percent in interest at the end of two years. The creditor may not realize that he is in fact charging less than 6 percent per year; or in other words that he is worse off setting up the transaction this way than if he made a one-year loan at 6 percent for that year and then "rolled over" that entire loan—principal and interest—at the end of that year into a second one-year loan at 6 percent for the second year.

The apparent complexity of compound interest transactions may have been a serious problem when calculations were made with paper and pencil, and some lenders may have concluded that the additional interest was just not worth the trouble. This calculation problem, however, has been entirely eliminated by the development of compound interest tables and inexpensive calculators and computers.

One of the peculiarities of compound interest calculations is that whenever interest is compounded more frequently than the quoted annual rate, the actual interest rate earned for the year is more favorable to the lender than the quoted rate. If, for example, the quoted rate is 8 percent, the actual rate of return for the first year is 8.243 percent. The quoted rate is sometimes also called the **nominal rate**, while the actual rate earned is usually called the **effective rate** of interest or the **annual percentage rate (APR)**. Some advertisements set forth both rates in seeking to attract potential depositors.

Interest is usually compounded for periods of less than one year, though rates are usually quoted on an annual basis. Many financial institutions advertise that their interest is compounded daily, meaning that interest is computed each day and is added to principal to compute the following day's interest. Because compound interest rate calculations rapidly approach a limit as the interest rate and the time period are divided into smaller and smaller segments, the daily compounding of interest increases the productivity of money only slightly compared with quarterly compounding. For example, if you invest $10,000 with a borrower offering to pay 8 percent per year compounded daily, your investment after three years will be worth $12,712.14. If the interest had been compounded quarterly, your investment would be worth $12,682.42. If it were compounded only annually, it would have been worth $12,597.12. If it were compounded hourly, every day and night for the three years, it would be worth $12,712.36, almost exactly the same as it would on the basis of daily compounding.

Bankers also distinguish between **ordinary interest** and **exact interest**.

These terms arose in connection with the computation of interest for periods of less than one year. When calculations were made by paper and pencil, and many loans were for days, weeks, months, or fractions of years, it greatly simplified matters to consider a year as 360 days based on 12 months of 30 days each. Interest computed on the basis of these simplifying assumptions is ordinary interest and is still used by many banks, and in the computation of interest on corporate, agency, and municipal bonds. Exact interest treats the year as consisting of 365 or 366 days, as the case may be, and ignores months. Finally, when calculating interest, it is customary to exclude the day the loan is made and include the day in which it is repaid.

## §1.3  Formulas Used to Calculate Compound Interest

The examples so far make one important point about compound interest problems: The calculation of compound interest appears to be complex because it involves more than simple arithmetic or multiplication. Indeed, if one were to compute the interest at the end of each period, add it to the previous balance, and then compute the interest for the next period, the calculation would be quite laborious. There is, however, a formula for computing compound interest:

$$FV = P \times (1 + i)^t$$

where i is the interest rate, t is the number of time periods, P is the principal and FV is the future value after t periods.

For many years, lenders used printed tables that set forth compound interest computations. Table 1-1 is an example of a compound interest table. It shows the future value of $1 (including return of principal) at various interest rates for 50 time periods. Assume you deposit $1,000 in a bank that pays 8 percent per year compounded quarterly. If you leave the money there for ten years, how much will be in the account after ten years? Because the interest is compounded quarterly, the question involves a calculation over 40 periods at 2 percent per period. Looking in the "40" row and "2%" column, we see that $1 will grow to $2.2080 after 40 periods. Hence, $1,000 will have grown to $2,208. Another question: Assume you will need $10,000 in five years for law school tuition. If a bank will guarantee a 6 percent rate compounded semiannually, how much must you deposit today to have $10,000 in five years? This requires a calculation over 10 periods at 3 percent. Using the "10" row and "3%" column, we find that $1 deposited today will have grown to $1.3439 in five years. Hence you must deposit $10,000/1.3439 = $7,441.03. Note that these hypotheticals are not entirely realistic. First, no account is taken of the income tax that would be due on the periodic interest earned. Second, most banks today will not guarantee a fixed interest rate over time, although other financial devices exist that may permit "locking in" a fixed rate.

Calculators are available with compound interest and other calculations built into their memories. One has only to enter any three of the four variables:

Table 1-1
## Future Value After n Periods of $1 Invested Today

| No. of Periods | 2% | 3% | 4% | 5% | 6% | 7% | 8% |
|---|---|---|---|---|---|---|---|
| 1 | 1.0200 | 1.0300 | 1.0400 | 1.0500 | 1.0600 | 1.0700 | 1.0800 |
| 2 | 1.0404 | 1.0609 | 1.0816 | 1.1025 | 1.1236 | 1.1449 | 1.1664 |
| 3 | 1.0612 | 1.0927 | 1.1249 | 1.1576 | 1.1910 | 1.2250 | 1.2597 |
| 4 | 1.0824 | 1.1255 | 1.1699 | 1.2155 | 1.2625 | 1.3108 | 1.3605 |
| 5 | 1.1041 | 1.1593 | 1.2167 | 1.2763 | 1.3382 | 1.4026 | 1.4693 |
| 6 | 1.1262 | 1.1941 | 1.2653 | 1.3401 | 1.4185 | 1.5007 | 1.5869 |
| 7 | 1.1487 | 1.2299 | 1.3159 | 1.4071 | 1.5036 | 1.6058 | 1.7138 |
| 8 | 1.1717 | 1.2668 | 1.3686 | 1.4775 | 1.5938 | 1.7182 | 1.8509 |
| 9 | 1.1951 | 1.3048 | 1.4233 | 1.5513 | 1.6895 | 1.8365 | 1.9990 |
| 10 | 1.2190 | 1.3439 | 1.4802 | 1.6289 | 1.7908 | 1.9672 | 2.1589 |
| 11 | 1.2434 | 1.3842 | 1.5395 | 1.7103 | 1.8983 | 2.1049 | 2.3316 |
| 12 | 1.2682 | 1.4258 | 1.6010 | 1.7959 | 2.0122 | 2.2522 | 2.5182 |
| 13 | 1.2936 | 1.4685 | 1.6651 | 1.8856 | 2.1329 | 2.4098 | 2.7196 |
| 14 | 1.3195 | 1.5126 | 1.7317 | 1.9799 | 2.2609 | 2.5785 | 2.9372 |
| 15 | 1.3459 | 1.5580 | 1.8009 | 2.0789 | 2.3966 | 2.7590 | 3.1722 |
| 16 | 1.3728 | 1.6047 | 1.8730 | 2.1829 | 2.5404 | 2.9522 | 3.4259 |
| 17 | 1.4002 | 1.6528 | 1.9479 | 2.2920 | 2.6928 | 3.1588 | 3.7000 |
| 18 | 1.4282 | 1.7024 | 2.0258 | 2.4066 | 2.8543 | 3.3799 | 3.9960 |
| 19 | 1.4568 | 1.7535 | 2.1068 | 2.5270 | 3.0256 | 3.6165 | 4.3157 |
| 20 | 1.4859 | 1.8061 | 2.1911 | 2.6533 | 3.2071 | 3.8697 | 4.6610 |
| 21 | 1.5157 | 1.8603 | 2.2788 | 2.7860 | 3.3996 | 4.1406 | 5.0338 |
| 22 | 1.5460 | 1.9161 | 2.3699 | 2.9253 | 3.6035 | 4.4304 | 5.4365 |
| 23 | 1.5769 | 1.9736 | 2.4647 | 3.0715 | 3.8197 | 4.7405 | 5.8715 |
| 24 | 1.6084 | 2.0328 | 2.5633 | 3.2251 | 4.0489 | 5.0724 | 6.3412 |
| 25 | 1.6406 | 2.0938 | 2.6658 | 3.3864 | 4.2919 | 5.4274 | 6.8485 |
| 26 | 1.6734 | 2.1566 | 2.7725 | 3.5557 | 4.4594 | 5.8074 | 7.3964 |
| 27 | 1.7069 | 2.2213 | 2.8834 | 3.7335 | 4.8223 | 6.2139 | 7.9881 |
| 28 | 1.7410 | 2.2879 | 2.9987 | 3.9201 | 5.1117 | 6.6488 | 8.6271 |
| 29 | 1.7758 | 2.3566 | 3.1187 | 4.1161 | 5.4184 | 7.1143 | 9.3173 |
| 30 | 1.8114 | 2.4273 | 3.2434 | 4.3219 | 5.7435 | 7.6123 | 10.0627 |
| 31 | 1.8476 | 2.5001 | 3.3731 | 4.5380 | 6.0881 | 8.1451 | 10.8677 |
| 32 | 1.8845 | 2.5751 | 3.5081 | 4.7649 | 6.4534 | 8.7153 | 11.7371 |
| 33 | 1.9222 | 2.6523 | 3.6484 | 5.0032 | 6.8406 | 9.3253 | 12.6760 |
| 34 | 1.9607 | 2.7319 | 3.7943 | 5.2533 | 7.2510 | 9.9781 | 13.6901 |
| 35 | 1.9999 | 2.8139 | 3.9461 | 5.5160 | 7.6861 | 10.6766 | 14.7853 |
| 36 | 2.0399 | 2.8983 | 4.1039 | 5.7918 | 8.1473 | 11.4239 | 15.9682 |
| 37 | 2.0807 | 2.9852 | 4.2681 | 6.0814 | 8.6361 | 12.2236 | 17.2456 |
| 38 | 2.1223 | 3.0748 | 4.4388 | 6.3855 | 9.1543 | 13.0793 | 18.6253 |
| 39 | 2.1647 | 3.1670 | 4.6164 | 6.7048 | 9.7035 | 13.9948 | 20.1153 |
| 40 | 2.2080 | 3.2620 | 4.8010 | 7.0400 | 10.2857 | 14.9745 | 21.7245 |
| 41 | 2.2522 | 3.3599 | 4.9931 | 7.3920 | 10.9029 | 16.0227 | 23.4625 |
| 42 | 2.2972 | 3.4607 | 5.1928 | 7.7616 | 11.5570 | 17.1443 | 25.3395 |
| 43 | 2.3432 | 3.5645 | 5.4005 | 8.1497 | 12.2505 | 18.3444 | 27.3666 |
| 44 | 2.3901 | 3.6715 | 5.6165 | 8.5572 | 12.9855 | 19.6285 | 29.5560 |
| 45 | 2.4379 | 3.7816 | 5.8412 | 8.9850 | 13.7646 | 21.0025 | 31.9204 |
| 46 | 2.4866 | 3.8950 | 6.0748 | 9.4343 | 14.5905 | 22.4726 | 34.4741 |
| 47 | 2.5363 | 4.0119 | 6.3178 | 9.9060 | 15.4659 | 24.0457 | 37.2320 |
| 48 | 2.5871 | 4.1323 | 6.5705 | 10.4013 | 16.3939 | 25.7289 | 40.2106 |
| 49 | 2.6388 | 4.2562 | 6.8333 | 10.9213 | 17.3775 | 27.5299 | 43.4274 |
| 50 | 2.6916 | 4.3839 | 7.1067 | 11.4674 | 18.4202 | 29.4570 | 46.9016 |

Table 1-1 (*cont.*)
Future Value After n Periods of $1 Invested Today

| No. of Periods | 2% | 3% | 4% | 5% | 6% | 7% | 8% |
|---|---|---|---|---|---|---|---|
| 1 | 1.0900 | 1.1000 | 1.1100 | 1.1200 | 1.1300 | 1.1400 | 1.1500 |
| 2 | 1.1881 | 1.2100 | 1.2321 | 1.2544 | 1.2769 | 1.2996 | 1.3225 |
| 3 | 1.2950 | 1.3310 | 1.3676 | 1.4049 | 1.4429 | 1.4815 | 1.5209 |
| 4 | 1.4116 | 1.4641 | 1.5181 | 1.5735 | 1.6305 | 1.6890 | 1.7490 |
| 5 | 1.5386 | 1.6105 | 1.6851 | 1.7623 | 1.8424 | 1.9254 | 2.0114 |
| 6 | 1.6771 | 1.7716 | 1.8704 | 1.9738 | 2.0820 | 2.1950 | 2.3131 |
| 7 | 1.8280 | 1.9487 | 2.0762 | 2.2107 | 2.3526 | 2.5023 | 2.6600 |
| 8 | 1.9926 | 2.1436 | 2.3045 | 2.4760 | 2.6584 | 2.8526 | 3.0590 |
| 9 | 2.1719 | 2.3579 | 2.5580 | 2.7731 | 3.0040 | 3.2519 | 3.5179 |
| 10 | 2.3674 | 2.5937 | 2.8394 | 3.1058 | 3.3946 | 3.7072 | 4.0456 |
| 11 | 2.5804 | 2.8531 | 3.1518 | 3.4785 | 3.8359 | 4.2262 | 4.6524 |
| 12 | 2.8127 | 3.1384 | 3.4985 | 3.8960 | 4.3345 | 4.8179 | 5.3503 |
| 13 | 3.0658 | 3.4523 | 3.8833 | 4.3635 | 4.8980 | 5.4924 | 6.1528 |
| 14 | 3.3417 | 3.7975 | 4.3104 | 4.8871 | 5.5348 | 6.2613 | 7.0757 |
| 15 | 3.6425 | 4.1772 | 4.7846 | 5.4736 | 6.2543 | 7.1379 | 8.1371 |
| 16 | 3.9703 | 4.5950 | 5.3109 | 6.1304 | 7.0673 | 8.1372 | 9.3576 |
| 17 | 4.3276 | 5.0545 | 5.8951 | 6.8660 | 7.9861 | 9.2765 | 10.7613 |
| 18 | 4.7171 | 5.5599 | 6.5436 | 7.6900 | 9.0243 | 10.5752 | 12.3755 |
| 19 | 5.1417 | 6.1159 | 7.2633 | 8.6128 | 10.1974 | 12.0557 | 14.2318 |
| 20 | 5.6044 | 6.7275 | 8.0623 | 9.6466 | 11.5231 | 13.7435 | 16,3665 |
| 21 | 6.1088 | 7.4002 | 8.9492 | 10.8038 | 13.0211 | 15.6676 | 18.8215 |
| 22 | 6.6586 | 8.1403 | 9.9336 | 12.1003 | 14.7138 | 17.8610 | 21.6447 |
| 23 | 7.2579 | 8.9543 | 11.0263 | 13.5523 | 16.6266 | 20.3616 | 24.8915 |
| 24 | 7.9111 | 9.8497 | 12.2392 | 15.1786 | 18.7881 | 23.2122 | 28.6252 |
| 25 | 8.6231 | 10.8347 | 13.5855 | 17.0001 | 21.2305 | 26.4619 | 32.9190 |
| 26 | 9.3992 | 11.9182 | 15.0799 | 19.0401 | 23.9905 | 30.1666 | 37.8568 |
| 27 | 10.2451 | 13.1100 | 16.7386 | 21.3249 | 27.1093 | 34.3899 | 43.5358 |
| 28 | 11.1671 | 14.4210 | 18.5799 | 23.8839 | 30.6335 | 39.2045 | 50.0656 |
| 29 | 12.1722 | 15.8631 | 20.6237 | 26.7499 | 34.6158 | 44.6931 | 57.5755 |
| 30 | 13.2677 | 17.4494 | 22.8923 | 29.9599 | 39.1159 | 50.9502 | 66.2118 |
| 31 | 14.4618 | 19.1943 | 25.4104 | 33.5551 | 44.2010 | 58.0832 | 76.1435 |
| 32 | 15.7633 | 21.1138 | 28.2056 | 37.5817 | 49.9471 | 66.2148 | 87.5651 |
| 33 | 17.1820 | 23.2252 | 31.3082 | 42.0915 | 56.4402 | 75.4849 | 100.6998 |
| 34 | 18.7284 | 25.5477 | 34.7521 | 47.1425 | 63.7774 | 86.0528 | 115.8048 |
| 35 | 20.4140 | 28.1024 | 38.5749 | 52.7996 | 72.0685 | 98.1002 | 133.1755 |
| 36 | 22.2512 | 30.9127 | 42.8181 | 59.1356 | 81.4374 | 111.8342 | 153.1519 |
| 37 | 24.2538 | 34.0039 | 47.5281 | 66.2318 | 92.0243 | 127.4910 | 176.1246 |
| 38 | 26.4367 | 37.4043 | 52.7562 | 74.1797 | 103.9874 | 145.3397 | 202.5433 |
| 39 | 28.8160 | 41.1448 | 58.5593 | 83.0812 | 117.5058 | 165.6873 | 232.9248 |
| 40 | 31.4094 | 45.2593 | 65.0009 | 93.0510 | 132.7816 | 188.8835 | 267.8635 |
| 41 | 34.2363 | 49.7852 | 72.1510 | 104.2171 | 150.0432 | 215.3272 | 308.0431 |
| 42 | 37.3175 | 54.7637 | 80.0876 | 116.7231 | 169.5488 | 245.4730 | 354.2495 |
| 43 | 40.6761 | 60.2401 | 88.8972 | 130.7299 | 191.5901 | 279.8392 | 407.3870 |
| 44 | 44.3370 | 66.2641 | 98.6759 | 146.4175 | 216.4968 | 319.0167 | 468.4950 |
| 45 | 48.3272 | 72.8905 | 109.5302 | 163.9876 | 244.6414 | 363.6791 | 538.7693 |
| 46 | 52.6767 | 80.1795 | 121.5786 | 183.6661 | 276.4448 | 414.5941 | 619.5847 |
| 47 | 57.4176 | 88.1975 | 134.9522 | 205.7061 | 312.3826 | 472.6373 | 712.5224 |
| 48 | 62.5852 | 97.0172 | 149.7970 | 230.3908 | 352.9923 | 538.8065 | 819.4007 |
| 49 | 68.2179 | 106.7190 | 166.2746 | 258.0377 | 398.8818 | 614.2395 | 942.3108 |
| 50 | 74.3575 | 117.3909 | 184.5648 | 289.0022 | 450.7359 | 700.2330 | 1083.6574 |

the interest rate per period, the number of periods, the original principal amount, and the future value. The calculator supplies the missing variable.

One common question is how much of a payment on a loan is interest and how much is principal. The question obviously arises if one desires to pay off a loan early. The straightforward method is to calculate the interest due on the unpaid balance at the time each payment is made, and the excess part of the payment is credited to principal. This is usually called the simple interest method and is undoubtedly the fairest way to determine the unpaid balance.

Another method widely used in many states is the **Rule of 78** or **sum of digits** method of calculating interest. This method of calculating is much more favorable to the creditor than the simple interest method. Using a 12-month loan as an example, assign the numbers 1 through 12 to the months the loan is outstanding and add the numbers together. The total is 78. If the borrower pays off or refinances the mortgage after one payment, he or she is assumed to have paid 12/78th of the total interest owed; after two payments, 23/78th of the interest has been paid off, and so forth. On a 2-year loan, the digits 1 through 24 would be added together to form the denominator. This method allocates a significantly higher portion of the total payments to interest in the early months than the simple interest method, and therefore increases the amount of principal that remains unpaid under the simple interest method. Thus, the Rule of 78 is widely viewed as unfair to consumers, and its use is barred in many states. When negotiating a loan in a state in which its use is permitted, it is sometimes possible to insist that a simple interest calculation be incorporated in a new loan.

## §1.4 The Variety of Interest Rates

How are interest rates established in the real world? If one compares banks and other lending institutions and reads the financial press, it quickly becomes apparent that a jungle of inconsistent rates all simultaneously exist side by side. For example, the following table lists nineteen different rates prevailing on a single day, and some of those listed display internal variations.

Several factors help to explain the diversity. First, interest rates have varied widely during different historical periods. For example, long-term treasury bonds paid 15.34 percent at the end of 1981, and just 1.94 percent at the end of 1940. Many financial transactions—such as many loans to purchase a house —involve fixed interest rates, even though they may be outstanding for 30 years. Much of the diversity of rates simply reflects the historical level of rates when the transaction giving rise to the loan occurred. In recent years, devices that permit periodic adjustment of interest rates have been used increasingly, though many long-term, fixed-rate obligations continue to be written. Fixed rates add an element of gambling to transactions. For example, a homeowner may have a 5 percent loan on his house when current market rates for new loans are 7 percent or more. The below-market-value loan is itself a valuable asset that enhances the value of the home—especially if the owner can convey the benefits of that loan to a purchaser. On the other hand, the homeowner's asset is the lending institution's albatross. If the bank could get the homeowner

# MONEY RATES

**Friday, October 19, 2001**

The key U. S. and foreign annual interest rates below are a guide to general levels but don't always represent actual transactions.

**PRIME RATE:** 5.50% (effective 10/03/01). The base rate on corporate loans posted by at least 75% of the nation's 30 largest banks.

**DISCOUNT RATE:** 2.00% (effective 10/02/01). The charge on loans to depository institutions by the Federal Reserve Banks.

**FEDERAL FUNDS:** 2 7/16% high, 2 3/8 % low, 2 3/8 % near closing bid, 2 7/16% offered. Reserves traded among commercial banks for overnight use in amounts of $1 million or more. Source: Prebon Yamane(U.S.A) Inc. FOMC fed funds target rate 2.50% effective 10/02/01.

**CALL MONEY:** 4.25% (effective 10/03/01). The charge on loans to brokers on stock exchange collateral. Source: Reuters.

**COMMERCIAL PAPER:** Placed directly by General Electric Capital Corp.: 2.39% 30 to 32 days; 2.33% 33 to 40 days; 2.25% 41 to 59 days; 2.22% 60 to 77 days; 2.25% 78 to 96 days; 2.20% 97 to 149 days; 2.17% 150 to 270 days.

**EURO COMMERCIAL PAPER:** Placed directly by General Electric Capital Corp.: 3.71% 30 days; 3.62% two months; 3.58% three months; 3.51% four months; 3.46% five months; 3.43% six months.

**DEALER COMMERCIAL PAPER:** High-grade unsecured notes sold through dealers by major corporations: 2.40% 30 days; 2.31% 60 days; 2.29% 90 days.

**CERTIFICATES OF DEPOSIT:** Typical rates in the secondary market, 2.41% one month; 2.28% three months; 2.24% six months.

**BANKERS ACCEPTANCES:** 2.43% 30 days; 2.32% 60 days; 2.30% 90 days; 2.25% 120 days; 2.27% 150 days; 2.26% 180 days. Offered rates of negotiable, bank-backed business credit instruments typically financing an import order. Source: Reuters

**LONDON LATE EURODOLLARS:** 2.44% - 2.31% one month; 2.44% - 2.31% two months; 2.38% - 2.25% three months; 2.38% - 2.25% four months; 2.38% - 2.25% five months; 2.31% - 2.19% six months.

**LONDON INTERBANK OFFERED RATES (LIBOR):** 2.4450% one month; 2.36625% three months; 2.32125% six months; 2.5025% one year. British Banker's Association average of interbank offered rates for dollar deposits in the London market based on quotations at 16 major banks. Effective rate for contracts entered into two days from date appearing at top of this column.

**EURO LIBOR:** 3.75763% one month; 3.60213% three months; 3.44825% six months; 3.34913% one year. British Banker's Association average of interbank offered rates for euro deposits in the London market based on quotations at 16 major banks. Effective rate for contracts entered into two days from date appearing at top of this column.

**EURO INTERBANK OFFERED RATES (EURIBOR):** 3.761% one month; 3.607% three months; 3.451% six months; 3.353% one year. European Banking Federation-sponsored rate among 57 Euro zone banks.

**FOREIGN PRIME RATES:** Canada 5.25%; Germany 3.75%; Japan 1.375%; Switzerland 4.25%; Britain 4.50%. These rate indications aren't directly comparable; lending practices vary widely by location.

**TREASURY BILLS:** Results of the Monday, October 15, 2001, auction of short-term U.S. government bills, sold at a discount from face value in units of $1,000 to $1 million: 2.200% 13 weeks; 2.160% 26 weeks. Tuesday, October 16, 2001 auction: 2.280% 4 weeks.

**OVERNIGHT REPURCHASE RATE:** 2.54%. Dealer financing rate for overnight sale and repurchase of Treasury securities. Source: Reuters.

**FREDDIE MAC:** Posted yields on 30-year mortgage commitments. Delivery within 30 days 6.32%, 60 days 6.41%, standard conventional fixed-rate mortgages: 3.375%, 2% rate capped one-year adjustable rate mortgages. Source: Reuters.

**FANNIE MAE:** Posted yields on 30 year mortgage commitments (priced at par) for delivery within 30 days 6.38%, 60 days 6.47%, standard conventional fixed-rate mortgages; 4.25%, 6/2 rate capped one-year adjustable rate mortgages. Source: Reuters.

**MERRILL LYNCH READY ASSETS TRUST:** 2.80%. Annualized average rate of return after expenses for the past 30 days; not a forecast of future returns.

**CONSUMER PRICE INDEX:** September, 178.3, up 2.6% from a year ago. Bureau of Labor Statistics.

---

to pay off the balance of his mortgage, the money could be reinvested at 7 percent by lending to a new buyer.

Second, some interest rates are established by government fiat and reflect statutory policies rather than market rates. For example, the government might choose to favor government-designated groups, such as veterans buying homes.

Third, wide variations occur because of differences in risk. Other things being equal, an investor demands a higher return from more risky investments than from investments that are less risky. The difference in rates may reflect a difference in risk, although the probability of default by either is slight. More likely, the difference is attributable to the length of time over which the loan will be outstanding and the risk that interest rates will rise in the meantime. In most cases, longer term rates are higher than shorter term rates, as is illustrated by the comparison of various treasury securities. This is the normal pattern. The relationship between rates and time to maturity is often called the **yield curve** as illustrated in the following table.

Ordinarily, investors demand more return to tie up their money longer. But if investors expect rates to fall and are more eager to lock in current at-

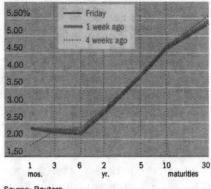

## Treasury Yield Curve
Yields as of 4:30 p.m. Eastern time

Friday
1 week ago
4 weeks ago

Source: Reuters

# YIELD COMPARISONS

Based on Merrill Lynch Bond Indexes, priced as of midafternoon Eastern time.

|  | 10/19 | 10/18 | 52 WEEK HIGH | 52 WEEK LOW |
|---|---|---|---|---|
| Corp.-Govt. Master ...... | 4.74% | 4.71% | 6.74% | 4.69% |
| **Treasury** | | | | |
| 1-10yr ........................ | 3.36 | 3.33 | 6.05 | 3.30 |
| 10+yr ......................... | 5.27 | 5.22 | 6.09 | 5.21 |
| **Agencies** | | | | |
| 1-10yr ........................ | 3.75 | 3.72 | 6.71 | 3.69 |
| 10+yr ......................... | 5.83 | 5.79 | 6.78 | 5.79 |
| **Corporate** | | | | |
| 1-10 yr High Qlty ........ | 4.56 | 4.55 | 7.10 | 4.52 |
| Med Qlty .......... | 5.77 | 5.75 | 7.80 | 5.69 |
| 10+yr High Qlty ......... | 6.75 | 6.69 | 7.74 | 6.68 |
| Med Qlty ......... | 7.44 | 7.40 | 8.38 | 7.29 |
| Yankee bonds (1).......... | 5.48 | 5.45 | 7.49 | 5.45 |
| **Current-coupon mortgages** (2) | | | | |
| GNMA 6.00% ............. | 6.02 | 5.98 | 7.54 | 5.96 |
| FNMA 6.00% .............. | 6.04 | 6.00 | 7.59 | 5.95 |
| FHLMC 6.00% ........... | 6.05 | 6.00 | 7.61 | 5.97 |
| High-yield corporates... | 13.10 | 13.07 | 14.17 | 12.01 |
| **Tax-Exempt Bonds** | | | | |
| 7-12-yr G.O. (AA) ....... | 3.91 | 3.91 | 4.85 | 3.87 |
| 12-22-yr G.O. (AA) ..... | 4.82 | 4.82 | 5.49 | 4.67 |
| 22+yr revenue (A)....... | 5.06 | 5.06 | 5.76 | 4.96 |

Note: High quality rated AAA-AA; medium quality A-BBB/Baa; high yield, BB/Ba-C.
(1) Dollar-denominated, SEC-registered bonds of foreign issuers sold in the U.S. (2) Reflects the 52-week high and low of mortgage-backed securities indexes rather than the individual securities shown.

tractive rates, they may bid up the price of long-term debt and thus force down the yield even below short-term rates. If longer term rates are lower than shorter term rates, there is said to be an inverted yield curve.

The possibility that a borrower will not be able to repay the obligation when it matures is called **default risk**. There are independent rating services that determine the default risk for many publicly traded debt securities. Bond ratings provided by Moody's and Standard & Poor's are the most widely followed. These ratings assign alphabetical designations to risk categories. AAA refers to the strongest and most secure securities, sometimes called gilt-edged securities. More speculative debt securities are assigned successively lower designations, such as AA, A, BBB, BB, B, CCC, and so forth, down to C and D (to use the Standard & Poor's designations). The latter ratings are assigned to highly speculative securities that may already be in default or seem unlikely to be repaid. The classification of a debt security in one risk category or another materially affects the interest rate that the borrower has to pay. Obviously, a guarantee of repayment by the federal government significantly reduces the risk that a borrower will default, and therefore reduces the interest cost to the borrower.

Fourth, debt securities that state or municipal borrowers issue are usually exempt from federal income tax. This favored tax status of state or municipal borrowers largely explains why they may borrow at a significantly lower rate than large corporations.

There is an active market for lendable funds. Interest is the factor that balances the supply and demand for money in this market, in which the sellers of money are commercial banks and other financial institutions and the buyers are individuals and commercial enterprises. This is a retail market for money to distinguish it from the market in which commercial banks obtain funds—a wholesale market (in which individuals and businesses may themselves be sellers). The basic interest rate in the retail market is called the **prime rate**. That is the rate that is usually (although not accurately) defined as the rate large commercial banks charge the biggest and safest borrowers for whom there is little risk of default. Competition requires large commercial banks throughout the United States to maintain a largely uniform prime rate; however, the rate often changes, and there may be periods of transition in which some banks quote the old rate while others quote the new. If the demand for funds appears to be increasing, one or more banks may announce a quarter-point or even a half-point increase in the prime rate. If other banks believe the higher rate is supportable by the market for funds, they also announce an increase, and the movement becomes nationwide. If other banks do not go along, the innovative banks will probably rescind the increase in order to ensure that their large borrowers do not go elsewhere for funds. A similar pattern appears when the demand for lendable funds appears to be slack and a decline in the prime rate is being considered.

Many borrowers are not candidates for a prime rate loan. However, all such borrowers are affected by changes in the prime rate, because interest rates for less secure commercial borrowers are usually tied to the prime rate.

For example, a retail bookstore with sales of $10,000,000 per year may have a **line of credit** of $1,000,000 to finance inventory from a local bank at three quarters of a point above the prime rate. A line of credit is a very common kind of open arrangement between a bank and a customer by which the customer—in this case the bookstore—may borrow money as needed up to the stated limit of $1,000,000. To take care of the possibility that there are slightly different prime rates being quoted on the last day of the month, such agreements usually specify which bank's quotations of prime rates should be looked to. In this arrangement, of course, the interest rate is flexible and over time varies with the prime rate—and therefore the market price for bank-made commercial loans also varies. If the business is cyclical, the store may need the line of credit for only part of each year. If not, the store may have loans under the line of credit close to or at the maximum all year round.

Similarly, a small store owner may obtain a signature loan of, say, $5,000. A **signature loan** is also a very common arrangement between a commercial bank and an individual with a good credit rating: It is simply an unsecured loan made solely on the borrower's signature. Two years ago, the store owner borrowed the same amount and was charged 7.5 percent interest. This time, the interest rate is 11 percent. "After all," the friendly banker apologetically explains, "two years ago the prime rate was 6.5 percent; today it is 10 percent." The store owner is in effect being charged one point over the prime rate.

The federal government uses interest rates and the supply of money in commercial banks as devices to fight inflation and unemployment and to encourage a high level of economic activity. (The fact that these may be partially conflicting goals need not detain us.) This control is exercised principally by the Federal Reserve Board (the Fed) through several devices, the most important of which are (1) open market transactions in federal securities, (2) reserve requirements, (3) federal debt management transactions, and (4) the discount rate.

A detailed discussion of how reserve requirements, open market transactions, and similar devices influence the supply of money and the prime rate is beyond the scope of this book. These devices all operate generally by increasing or decreasing the amount of funds banks have available to lend to customers. The fourth, the discount rate, is more visible because it is an interest rate that the Federal Reserve System charges on loans to commercial banks. The discount rate is set by the Federal Reserve System partly on political and partly on economic considerations. Changes in this rate receive even more publicity than changes in the prime rate and can dramatically affect prices in the stock and bond markets. From a bank's perspective, the discount rate is a wholesale rate and the prime rate is a retail rate for money. The spread between the discount and prime rate is usually about 2 percentage points. Thus, if the Fed raises the discount rate, the prime rate also usually rises.

## §1.5 Formalities of Debt

There is more to lending and borrowing money than calculating interest payments. When one person (the creditor) lends money to another (the debtor), one question that arises is what evidence of that debt the creditor should demand. Small noncommercial loans are frequently evidenced simply by a cancelled check, or acknowledged by a handshake, or a simple "thank you." Of course, a debt exists any time there is a loan, even if it is not evidenced by any writing or formality, and the creditor may enforce the repayment obligation upon proving that a loan was in fact made and not repaid.

A slightly more formal arrangement might be for the debtor to give a written acknowledgment that a debt exists. Such acknowledgment is called an **IOU**. (The initials "IOU" simply stand for "I owe you.") An IOU may simplify the evidentiary requirements otherwise imposed on a creditor seeking to enforce a debt but it is not, by itself, a promise to repay the debt on any particular terms.

A higher level of formality and potentially greater legal consequences occur when the debtor is required to sign a **promissory note**. A promissory note states that the debtor promises to pay the creditor the amount of the debt, usually together with interest. Sometimes a promissory note is made payable **on demand**, in which case it is almost equivalent to a check. Such a **demand note** may not bear interest precisely because the term is indefinite.

A promissory note may be made payable to the order of a specific person or to the "bearer." A **bearer note** is payable to whoever has physical possession of the piece of paper; the debt is transferred simply by physical transfer of the paper. A promissory note payable to the order of a person is usually transferred by **endorsement**. The payee of the note writes on the back of the note "Pay to the order of Y," signs his or her name, and delivers the note to Y. Y can then enforce the note as though he or she were the payee, or may endorse the note to Z by following the same process.

Debts may be freely sold, assigned, or traded without the prior consent of the debtor. A person purchasing or otherwise acquiring a debt is known as an assignee and may enforce the creditor's claim against the debtor, subject to whatever defenses arising out of the same transaction the debtor may have against the original creditor. The debtor, however, may also agree in the original transaction to waive defenses he or she may have in a suit brought by an assignee, and such a waiver will be given effect in most circumstances.

A promissory note is said to be in **negotiable form** if it meets minimal statutory requirements: It must (1) be signed by the maker (the debtor), (2) contain only an unconditional promise to pay a certain sum in money, (3) be payable on demand or at a definite time, and (4) be payable to order or bearer. Most notes used in commercial transactions are in negotiable form. The advantage of a note in this form is that, if the person acquiring the note is a **holder in due course** (i.e., is a person who acquires the note for value and without knowledge of possible defenses), he or she is able to enforce the promise of payment set forth in the note free of certain defenses that the debtor might have had if suit had been brought directly by the creditor on the underlying transaction. The negotiation of a promissory note to a holder in due course results in a debt becoming an article of commerce largely freed from the underlying transaction that gave rise to it: The debt ceases to be a personal obligation between the creditor and debtor.

To illustrate: Assume that a seller of certain computer equipment originally received cash for a portion of the purchase price and lent the buyer the balance, taking a negotiable promissory note that the buyer executed. The buyer, however, has stopped making payments on the ground that the equipment did not perform as warranted. Obviously, if the seller directly seeks to enforce the buyer's promise to pay the balance of the purchase price, the defense of breach of warranty will be raised. It may not be completely ethical, but if the seller can negotiate the promissory note to a holder in due course, for example, a bank, the buyer will not be able to assert the defense of breach of warranty against the holder in due course. In other words, in the hands of a holder in due course, the promissory note is enforceable in and of itself without regard to the underlying commercial transaction that gave rise to it. If the buyer is forced to pay the holder in due course in full, he or she may then turn around and sue the seller for breach of warranty, so that at least theoretically, the wrongdoer—the seller whose product did not conform to his or her warranties —ends up ultimately being held responsible. In the process, however, the innocent purchaser of the promissory note is permitted to enforce it in accordance with its terms, and the defense of breach of warranty can only be asserted against the other party to the original transaction in a separate lawsuit.

It is, of course, possible in the preceding hypothetical that the holder in due course will be unable to get satisfaction from the buyer even though he or she obtains a judgment. The seller, who endorsed the note to the holder in due course, is then liable to take back the note from the holder in due course and return any consideration paid, because an endorser warrants that the instrument will be honored when it is presented. Other persons in the chain of transfer may also be liable if they transferred the instrument with knowledge of the maker's insolvency. In other words, if the buyer refuses to pay and the holder in due course is compelled to seek satisfaction from the seller/endorser or earlier transferees on their warranties, the same result is reached—the wrongdoer ends up holding the bag.

The cutting-off of defenses described in the previous paragraphs does not apply to certain **real defenses**, such as forgery or duress. Also, if the person acquiring the note is not a holder in due course or if the transaction is cast as an **assignment** of a note rather than as a **negotiation**, no defenses are shut off (unless the maker agrees to waive them) and the holder of the note stands in precisely the same shoes as the original lender. The difference between assignment ("I hereby assign the attached note to Z") and negotiation ("pay to the order of Z") may seem to be mere semantics; however, different legal consequences often flow from different words. The detailed rules about the negotiation of promissory notes and other types of commercial paper, who qualifies as a holder in due course, and the rights of such a holder all appear in Articles Three and Four of the Uniform Commercial Code and are covered in detail in advanced law school courses in commercial law.

Almost all commercial loan transactions are evidenced by promissory notes. Most of them are in negotiable form. Forms for negotiable promissory notes can readily be found in form books, and printed promissory notes in negotiable form with blanks to be filled in can be obtained from a legal stationer.

**Bonds** and **debentures** are gussied-up promissory notes that corporations use to borrow long-term funds. Such instruments are often publicly held and widely traded. These are discussed in more detail in the chapter on corporate securities.

## §1.6 Secured and Unsecured Loans

Creditors often are not satisfied with the simple right to sue for payment even as a holder in due course of negotiable commercial paper. For example, if the creditor has made a simple **signature loan**, the right to collect on the claim depends on the debtor being able to pay the amount due when a judgment is obtained. The time when collection is sought is more critical than the time the transaction occurred: A debtor may have numerous assets when the debt is created but business reverses or unwise transactions may make the debt uncollectible when enforcement is sought. A holder in due course is no better off than the original creditor in this regard, because even if the holder gets a judgment on the promissory note, the holder still has to collect on the judgment. Not even a holder in due course can squeeze blood from a turnip.

Creditors increase the likelihood of repayment by requiring, at the time of the transaction, that the debtor grant an interest in some or all of his or her property to secure the repayment of the loan. If the transaction involves the sale of goods on credit, the seller will normally take a **security interest** in the goods sold. In other types of transactions, the security interest may involve various kinds of tangible or intangible property or rights. Typically, the property or assets remain in the control of the debtor until a default on the loan occurs, when the creditor may take judicial steps or self-help to seize the property or rights in order to satisfy the debt. Historically, these creditor-owned interests in debtors' property were called **liens** or **chattel mortgages**. Under the Uniform Commercial Code, they are called **security interests** or **purchase money security interests**, though references to liens still regularly appear in cases involving personal property. Basically, a lien or security interest is an intangible property interest that allows the creditor, if the loan is not repaid, to seize the property subject to the lien to satisfy the unpaid loan; usually the property is sold and the proceeds are applied against the unpaid loan.

Notice of a security interest in the debtor's property is publicly made by filing with a public office to perfect the security interest against claims of subsequent creditors. (There are some important exceptions to the filing requirement for **perfection**. Where an exception is applicable, the security interest is perfected either by other means, such as taking possession of the collateral, or automatically.) A failure to perfect means that subsequent creditors may obtain competing security interests senior to the unfiled interest or that a bankruptcy trustee may be able to avoid the unfiled security interest, reducing the creditor to unsecured status.

The process by which a secured creditor realizes upon the security is usually described as **foreclosure**, though in the case of consumer goods it may involve **repossession**. Typically, the seized property is sold and the proceeds applied to the payment of the debt. If the proceeds of the sale of seized property are not sufficient to discharge the loan (as is usually the case), the creditor continues to have an unsecured claim against the debtor for the balance, usually called a **deficiency** or **deficiency judgment**. If the proceeds exceed the loan balance, unpaid interest, and allowable fees or charges (often including attorney's fees), the debtor is entitled to the balance.

Everyone has heard of hard-hearted creditors repossessing automobiles or washing machines from luckless debtors or the equipment and land of farmers being put up for sale at auction at the direction of one or more creditors. Although such events do obviously happen with some regularity when debtors are individuals, most enforcement efforts involve something less than foreclosure. For one thing, as a device to encourage payment, creditors often take security in property of dubious value but of personal value to the debtor. Second-hand furniture probably will not bring very much upon resale, but the threat of foreclosure could mean the potential loss of a family's cherished items and only furniture, and payment of the secured loan may be made to ensure that the furniture is not lost. Many secured creditors threaten and cajole: They may make numerous threatening telephone calls or even post property for foreclosure. Foreclosure, however, is not free of cost and is usually a last resort. Automobile repossession in many areas is an exception because of the relative mobility and ease of marketability of the collateral.

Even though substantial businesses that raise capital by borrowing are also often required to pledge machinery and other business assets as security for the loans, foreclosure is even less common in the case of businesses than in the case of individuals. A business is typically worth more as a going enterprise than it is broken up and sold in parts. Thus, when a substantial business runs into financial difficulty and secured creditors begin making threatening noises to seize the railroad's freight cars or the manufacturer's machinery and equipment, the debtor usually seeks protection from foreclosure in the federal bankruptcy courts by filing a petition for reorganization so its operating assets can be preserved as a single unit. Although secured creditors holding liens on operating assets are in a better position than unsecured creditors in a reorganization proceeding, there is no assurance that in bankruptcy a secured creditor will be able to realize directly upon his or her security.

Much of the law relating to obtaining and perfecting security interests appears in Article Nine of the **Uniform Commercial Code (UCC)**. Legal problems relating to security interests also arise under bankruptcy law, real estate law, securities and banking law, and matters of corporate finance.

## §1.7  The Importance of Interest in Commercial Transactions

There are numerous vehicles for investment available to persons with excess capital. Many of these investment vehicles permit the earning of interest on a daily basis. In reflecting on the concept of interest as compensation for the use of funds, it should be apparent that it is uneconomic to leave large amounts of capital in non-interest-bearing form for any period of time. The most common example of a non-interest-bearing form is the simple checking account. Other examples are cash in a mattress or safe deposit vault, or investments in jewels, works of art, or gold. Of course, one needs to retain cash in a checking account to pay current bills and to avoid bank service charges, but in this day of electronic fund transfers and flexible investment vehicles, excess cash should generally be earning interest rather than lying idle in some form. It is not uncommon for businesses to have an average daily balance in the tens or hundreds of thousands of dollars. In such cases, more effective cash management may permit a steady interest income to be developed where none presently exists.

It is also important to recognize that even one day's interest on a large sum of money involves enough dollars to dictate careful planning. Assume, for example, that your client has successfully negotiated the sale of his solely owned business for $25,000,000 in cash, payable by bank certified check at the closing. The closing should be scheduled early enough in the day to permit investment of the $25,000,000 the same day. Something like $5,000 in interest for one day will be lost if a closing is scheduled at 4:00 p.m. after local banks are closed. That may sound astonishing, but it is true: Large sums generate an appreciable amount of interest each day. Similarly, to set up an escrow account for $10,000,000 without providing for investment of the escrowed amount and a clear statement as to who is entitled to the interim interest is so negligent as to border on malpractice. Of course, clients with large sums of money are usually well aware of the cost of leaving funds idle for even short periods of time and will insist on appropriate investment provisions.

When very large sums are involved, even payment schedules are apt to become a matter of negotiation, because interest may be earned on interest payments. The creditor will usually seek payments quarterly or even monthly to take advantage of this fact. Correspondingly, the debtor may opt for semi-annual or even annual payments, if he or she can. Assume, for example, that your client owns a large hotel and apartment complex on the beach, complete with swimming pool and 18-hole golf course. He has negotiated a sale of the entire property for $100,000,000 on the following terms: $25,000,000 down with the balance payable over 5 years, $15,000,000 per year at 6 percent compound interest per year. Your client proposes that payments of principal and interest be made quarterly each year; the buyer is equally adamant that there be a single $15,000,000 payment plus interest payable on each anniversary date only. If your client can earn more than 6 percent on alternative investments, quarterly payments permit investment at the higher rate sooner than an annual payment. Even a one percent additional yield on investments above the 6 percent rate makes the quarterly payment plan worth $30,000 more than the annual payment plan in the first year alone. Because the purchaser can also earn more than 6 percent per year on alternative investments, it is to his or her decided advantage to place the funds to be used to make payments in these alternative investments, leave them there as long as possible, and make payments as late as possible. In a very real sense, time is money.

# PRESENT VALUE

## §2.1  Introduction

One of the most fundamental financial concepts is that money to be paid or received in the future is not worth as much as money to be paid or received today. Relatively simple formulas permit a direct comparison of the value of amounts to be paid at different times. This chapter discusses this concept, which underlies much of financial theory and much of current business practice. The process by which amounts payable at different times are made comparable is usually referred to as discounting future payments to **present value**. The word **discounting** in this context simply means reducing. Another phrase that describes this concept is **time value of money**.

What is the right to receive $1,000 a year from now worth today? Assuming that there is no risk that the payer will default, it is clear that the right is worth something less than $1,000. If one had $1,000 today, one could invest it for a year in a riskless investment and thereby earn one year's interest in addition to the original $1,000. Thus, $1,000 payable a year from now has to be worth somewhat less than $1,000 in hand today. How much less? One way to answer such a question is to approach it from the point of view of a hypothetical investor: If that investor can make 12 percent per year on his or her money in a riskless investment, how much should the investor pay today for the right to receive that $1,000 in a year? So phrased, the issue becomes an algebraic calculation:

$$x + .12x = \$1,000$$

$$1.12x = \$1,000$$

$$x = \frac{\$1,000}{1.12} = \$892.86$$

To such an investor, the right to receive $1,000 a year from now is worth precisely $892.86. But, it may be rejoined, why choose a 12 percent return? Why not, say, an 8 percent return, in which case the calculation becomes:

$$x + .08x = \$1,000$$

and the value of the right to receive the $1,000 in 12 months becomes $925.93? The difference between these two amounts is significant. Of course, there is no one single rate of return that is correct in an absolute sense. But that element of uncertainty as to what the correct value is should not hide certain basic truths that these simple examples reveal: (1) because interest rates are positive, a dollar in the future is always worth less than a dollar today, and (2) the higher the interest that can be earned on a riskless investment, the lower is the current value of a right to receive a future payment. In other words, there is an inverse relationship between interest rates and current values of future payments. This leads to yet a third basic truth: (3) the riskier the investment, the lower the current value of a right to receive the future payment. Why? Because the riskier the investment, the higher the rate of return on which the investor will insist.

The present value of a future sum is the reverse of the **future value** of a present sum invested at the same interest rate. For example, assume that one plans to buy a $1,000 stereo a year from now; how much do you have to put aside today in an account earning 12 percent per year to have $1,000 in one year? The answer, of course, is the now familiar amount, $892.86; determining that the present value of $1,000 payable one year from now is $892.86 is simply looking at the same transaction from a different perspective.

When speaking of the earning power of a present amount over time, one usually speaks of the interest rate. When going the other way and computing the present value of a future payment, one usually speaks of the discount rate. However, it is the same rate, because the present value of a future sum and the future value of a present sum involve precisely the same calculation, examined from opposite perspectives.

## §2.2 Present Value Calculations Over Multiple Periods

Following the same line of reasoning, what is $1,000 payable two years in the future worth today? If we again assume a 12 percent interest rate, it turns out that a $797.19 investment today grows to $892.86 after one year and to precisely $1,000 after two years. Thus, the present value of $1,000 payable two years from today is $797.19 at 12 percent interest. This involves a compound interest calculation, because the comparison is with a $797.19

investment today that is left untouched until the end of the two-year period. A formula to determine present values of future payments over multiple periods, derived from the formula for compound interest, is:

$$PV = \frac{FV}{(1 + i)^n}$$

where PV = present value; FV = future value; i = the interest rate; and n = the number of periods. The calculations of one-year present values set forth earlier are simply special applications of this formula.

Despite the apparent mathematical certainty of the formula, it is important to recognize that the precise calculation of the present value of a future sum over a specified period depends both on the applicable interest or discount rate and the number of subperiods within the period over which interest is compounded. In other words, in order to get mathematical precision, one must know both the applicable discount rate and whether interest is compounded quarterly, annually, or over some other set of subperiods during the two-year period in question. In the foregoing calculations, it is assumed that interest is compounded only annually so that the number of periods is two. In most calculations like this, involving relatively short time periods, the number of subperiods used does not change the results significantly. For example, if one calculates a 12 percent discount rate compounded quarterly over the two-year period, interest is compounded eight times at 3 percent per quarter, and the present value of $1,000 payable two years from now is $789.41 as compared with the $791.19 obtained above on the assumption that interest is compounded only annually. Do you see why increasing the number of subperiods reduces the present value of a future payment?

Table 2-1 indicates what $1,000 payable at various times in the future is worth today at 12 percent and at 6 percent. Several fundamental relationships described in this table should be emphasized:

First, the longer the period before the payment is to be received, the smaller the value.

Second, the present value of the right to receive even large sums of money in the far distant future is not worth very much, if anything. For example, how much should you pay for the right to receive $100,000 in a lump sum 100

**Table 2-1**

| Number of years | Value of $1,000 at 12% | Value of $1,000 at 6% |
|---|---|---|
| 1 | 892.90 | 943.40 |
| 2 | 797.20 | 890.00 |
| 3 | 711.80 | 839.60 |
| 4 | 635.50 | 792.10 |
| 5 | 567.40 | 747.30 |
| 10 | 322.00 | 558.40 |
| 25 | 58.80 | 233.00 |
| 50 | 3.50 | 54.30 |
| 100 | 0.01 | 2.94 |

years from now? Not very much: According to the above tables, you should pay no more than one dollar at a 12 percent discount rate and $294 at a 6 percent rate.

Third, in making these present value computations, the discount rate that is chosen has a tremendous effect on the outcome of the calculation. One can manipulate answers obtained by minor changes in that number.

Table 2-2 shows the present values of one dollar payable at various time periods in the future at most plausible interest rates. Note that the numbers in Table 2-2 are all decimals less than one, while in Table 1-1 all the entries are one or larger. That is because each entry in Table 2-2 is the reciprocal of each entry in Table 1-1. In other words:

$$\text{present value} = \frac{1}{\text{future value}}$$

A simple illustration of the use of Table 2-2 might involve a person planning to set aside a sum of money today to provide $10,000 of law school tuition five years from now. Suppose that an investment earns interest at the rate of 6 percent compounded semiannually. One simply has to look up the discount factor for 3 percent over 10 periods in Table 2-2, which yields 0.7441, and multiply by $10,000 to get $7,441.

One of the most egregious examples of failure to recognize the time value of money can be seen in the advertising for lottery jackpots. A prize may be quoted as $1,000,000 although it is paid out at the rate of $50,000 per year for 20 years. If so, the prize is not in fact $1,000,000 but some lesser number depending on the appropriate rate of interest. The higher the rate of interest the lower the lump sum value of the payment.

The decimal numbers in Table 2-2 are sometimes called **discount factors**, because they can be added together to determine the present values of future payments as the following section illustrates.

## §2.3 Annuities

An **annuity** is a stream of constant payments to be made at fixed intervals. This section provides a preliminary examination of the underlying concept. Annuities are treated in detail in Chapter 4.

The present value of the right to receive $1,000 each year, beginning next year and continuing for five years at 12 percent compounded annually can be computed in several ways. First, one may simply add up the present values of each of the first five payments in Table 2-1 ($892.90 + $797.20 + $711.80 + $635.50 + $567.40). The sum $3,604.80 is the present value of the right to receive an aggregate amount of $5,000 in increments of $1,000 per year over the next five years. It seems odd that the right to receive $100,000 in a lump sum 100 years from now, also discounted at 12 percent, is worth only one dollar, while the right to receive only $1,000 per year over the next five years is worth thousands of times as much. Yet that is the magic of the time value of money.

## Table 2-2
### Present Value of $1 Payable After n Periods in the Future

| No. of periods | 2% | 3% | 4% | 5% | 6% | 7% | 8% |
|---|---|---|---|---|---|---|---|
| 1 | .9804 | .9709 | .9615 | .9524 | .9434 | .9346 | .9259 |
| 2 | .9612 | .9426 | .9246 | .9070 | .8900 | .8734 | .8573 |
| 3 | .9423 | .9151 | .8890 | .8638 | .8396 | .8163 | .7938 |
| 4 | .9238 | .8885 | .8548 | .8227 | .7921 | .7629 | .7350 |
| 5 | .9057 | .8626 | .8219 | .7835 | .7473 | .7130 | .6806 |
| 6 | .8880 | .8375 | .7903 | .7462 | .7050 | .6663 | .6302 |
| 7 | .8706 | .8131 | .7599 | .7107 | .6651 | .6227 | .5835 |
| 8 | .8535 | .7894 | .7307 | .6768 | .6274 | .5820 | .5403 |
| 9 | .8368 | .7664 | .7026 | .6446 | .5919 | .5439 | .5002 |
| 10 | .8203 | .7441 | .6756 | .6139 | .5584 | .5083 | .4632 |
| 11 | .8043 | .7224 | .6496 | .5847 | .5268 | .4751 | .4289 |
| 12 | .7885 | .7014 | .6246 | .5568 | .4970 | .4440 | .3971 |
| 13 | .7730 | .6810 | .6006 | .5303 | .4688 | .4150 | .3677 |
| 14 | .7579 | .6611 | .5775 | .5051 | .4423 | .3878 | .3405 |
| 15 | .7430 | .6419 | .5553 | .4810 | .4173 | .3624 | .3152 |
| 16 | .7284 | .6232 | .5339 | .4581 | .3936 | .3387 | .2919 |
| 17 | .7142 | .6050 | .5134 | .4363 | .3714 | .3166 | .2703 |
| 18 | .7002 | .5874 | .4936 | .4155 | .3503 | .2959 | .2502 |
| 19 | .6864 | .5703 | .4746 | .3957 | .3305 | .2765 | .2317 |
| 20 | .6730 | .5537 | .4564 | .3769 | .3118 | .2584 | .2145 |
| 21 | .6598 | .5375 | .4388 | .3589 | .2942 | .2415 | .1987 |
| 22 | .6468 | .5219 | .4220 | .3418 | .2775 | .2257 | .1839 |
| 23 | .6342 | .5067 | .4057 | .3256 | .2618 | .2109 | .1703 |
| 24 | .6217 | .4919 | .3901 | .3101 | .2470 | .1971 | .1577 |
| 25 | .6095 | .4776 | .3751 | .2953 | .2330 | .1842 | .1460 |
| 26 | .5976 | .4637 | .3607 | .2812 | .2198 | .1722 | .1352 |
| 27 | .5859 | .4502 | .3468 | .2678 | .2074 | .1609 | .1252 |
| 28 | .5744 | .4371 | .3335 | .2551 | .1956 | .1504 | .1159 |
| 29 | .5631 | .4243 | .3207 | .2429 | .1846 | .1406 | .1073 |
| 30 | .5521 | .4120 | .3083 | .2314 | .1741 | .1314 | .0994 |
| 31 | .5412 | .4000 | .2965 | .2204 | .1643 | .1228 | .0920 |
| 32 | .5306 | .3883 | .2851 | .2099 | .1550 | .1147 | .0852 |
| 33 | .5202 | .3770 | .2741 | .1999 | .1462 | .1072 | .0789 |
| 34 | .5100 | .3660 | .2636 | .1904 | .1379 | .1002 | .0730 |
| 35 | .5000 | .3554 | .2534 | .1813 | .1301 | .0937 | .0676 |
| 36 | .4902 | .3450 | .2437 | .1727 | .1227 | .0875 | .0626 |
| 37 | .4806 | .3350 | .2343 | .1644 | .1158 | .0818 | .0580 |
| 38 | .4712 | .3252 | .2253 | .1566 | .1092 | .0765 | .0537 |
| 39 | .4619 | .3158 | .2166 | .1491 | .1031 | .0715 | .0497 |
| 40 | .4529 | .3066 | .2083 | .1420 | .0972 | .0668 | .0460 |
| 41 | .4440 | .2976 | .2003 | .1353 | .0917 | .0624 | .0426 |
| 42 | .4353 | .2890 | .1926 | .1288 | .0865 | .0583 | .0395 |
| 43 | .4268 | .2805 | .1852 | .1227 | .0816 | .0545 | .0365 |
| 44 | .4184 | .2724 | .1780 | .1169 | .0770 | .0509 | .0338 |
| 45 | .4102 | .2644 | .1712 | .1113 | .0727 | .0476 | .0313 |
| 46 | .4022 | .2567 | .1646 | .1060 | .0685 | .0445 | .0290 |
| 47 | .3943 | .2493 | .1583 | .1009 | .0647 | .0416 | .0269 |
| 48 | .3865 | .2420 | .1522 | .0961 | .0610 | .0389 | .0249 |
| 49 | .3790 | .2350 | .1463 | .0916 | .0575 | .0363 | .0230 |
| 50 | .3715 | .2281 | .1407 | .0872 | .0543 | .0339 | .0213 |

Table 2-2 (*cont.*)
Present Value of $1 Payable After n Periods in the Future

| No. of periods | 2% | 3% | 4% | 5% | 6% | 7% | 8% |
|---|---|---|---|---|---|---|---|
| 1 | .9174 | .9091 | .9009 | .8929 | .8850 | .8772 | .8696 |
| 2 | .8417 | .8264 | .8116 | .7972 | .7831 | .7695 | .7561 |
| 3 | .7722 | .7513 | .7312 | .7118 | .6931 | .6750 | .6575 |
| 4 | .7084 | .6830 | .6587 | .6355 | .6133 | .5921 | .5718 |
| 5 | .6499 | .6209 | .5935 | .5674 | .5428 | .5194 | .4972 |
| 6 | .5963 | .5645 | .5346 | .5066 | .4803 | .4556 | .4323 |
| 7 | .5470 | .5132 | .4817 | .4523 | .4251 | .3996 | .3759 |
| 8 | .5019 | .4665 | .4339 | .4039 | .3762 | .3506 | .3269 |
| 9 | .4604 | .4241 | .3909 | .3606 | .3329 | .3075 | .2843 |
| 10 | .4224 | .3855 | .3522 | .3220 | .2946 | .2697 | .2472 |
| 11 | .3875 | .3505 | .3173 | .2875 | .2607 | .2366 | .2149 |
| 12 | .3555 | .3186 | .2858 | .2567 | .2307 | .2076 | .1869 |
| 13 | .3262 | .2897 | .2575 | .2292 | .2042 | .1821 | .1625 |
| 14 | .2992 | .2633 | .2320 | .2046 | .1807 | .1597 | .1413 |
| 15 | .2745 | .2394 | .2090 | .1827 | .1599 | .1401 | .1229 |
| 16 | .2519 | .2176 | .1883 | .1631 | .1415 | .1229 | .1069 |
| 17 | .2311 | .1978 | .1696 | .1456 | .1252 | .1078 | .0929 |
| 18 | .2120 | .1799 | .1528 | .1300 | .1108 | .0946 | .0808 |
| 19 | .1945 | .1635 | .1377 | .1161 | .0981 | .0829 | .0703 |
| 20 | .1784 | .1486 | .1240 | .1037 | .0868 | .0728 | .0611 |
| 21 | .1637 | .1351 | .1117 | .0926 | .0768 | .0638 | .0531 |
| 22 | .1502 | .1228 | .1007 | .0826 | .0680 | .0560 | .0462 |
| 23 | .1378 | .1117 | .0907 | .0738 | .0601 | .0491 | .0402 |
| 24 | .1264 | .1015 | .0817 | .0659 | .0532 | .0431 | .0349 |
| 25 | .1160 | .0923 | .0736 | .0588 | .0471 | .0378 | .0304 |
| 26 | .1064 | .0839 | .0663 | .0525 | .0417 | .0331 | .0264 |
| 27 | .0976 | .0763 | .0597 | .0469 | .0369 | .0291 | .0230 |
| 28 | .0895 | .0693 | .0538 | .0419 | .0326 | .0255 | .0200 |
| 29 | .0822 | .0630 | .0485 | .0374 | .0289 | .0224 | .0714 |
| 30 | .0754 | .0573 | .0437 | .0334 | .0256 | .0196 | .0151 |
| 31 | .0691 | .0521 | .0394 | .0298 | .0226 | .0172 | .0131 |
| 32 | .0634 | .0474 | .0355 | .0266 | .0200 | .0151 | .0114 |
| 33 | .0582 | .0431 | .0319 | .0238 | .0177 | .0132 | .0099 |
| 34 | .0534 | .0391 | .0288 | .0212 | .0157 | .0116 | .0086 |
| 35 | .0490 | .0356 | .0259 | .0189 | .0139 | .0102 | .0075 |
| 36 | .0449 | .0323 | .0234 | .0169 | .0123 | .0089 | .0065 |
| 37 | .0412 | .0294 | .0210 | .0151 | .0109 | .0078 | .0057 |
| 38 | .0378 | .0267 | .0190 | .0135 | .0096 | .0069 | .0049 |
| 39 | .0347 | .0243 | .0171 | .0120 | .0085 | .0060 | .0043 |
| 40 | .0318 | .0221 | .0154 | .0107 | .0075 | .0053 | .0037 |
| 41 | .0292 | .0201 | .0139 | .0096 | .0067 | .0046 | .0032 |
| 42 | .0268 | .0183 | .0125 | .0086 | .0059 | .0041 | .0028 |
| 43 | .0246 | .0166 | .0112 | .0076 | .0052 | .0036 | .0025 |
| 44 | .0226 | .0151 | .0101 | .0068 | .0046 | .0031 | .0021 |
| 45 | .0207 | .0137 | .0091 | .0061 | .0041 | .0027 | .0019 |
| 46 | .0190 | .0125 | .0082 | .0054 | .0036 | .0024 | .0016 |
| 47 | .0174 | .0113 | .0074 | .0049 | .0032 | .0021 | .0014 |
| 48 | .0160 | .0103 | .0067 | .0043 | .0028 | .0019 | .0012 |
| 49 | .0147 | .0094 | .0060 | .0039 | .0025 | .0016 | .0011 |
| 50 | .0134 | .0085 | .0054 | .0035 | .0022 | .0014 | .0009 |

A second way to calculate the present value of the same annuity is to add up the first five discount factors in Table 2-2 under 12 percent (.8929 + .7972 + .7118 + .6355 + .5674 = 3.6048) and multiply the product by $1,000.

An even simpler method exists. Table 2-3 is a table of the present values of annuities (payable at the end of each period). To get the present value of the 12 percent, five-year annuity, one simply looks up the "five year" row and "12 percent" column to find the number 3.6048. Obviously, Table 2-3 may be obtained from Table 2-2 by a process of systematic summing of amounts.

For those mathematically inclined, a nice complex formula to derive the present value of a stream of constant payments in the future is:

$$PV = \frac{P(1 - (1 + i)^{-n})}{i}$$

where P = the recurring payment; PV = the present value; i = the interest rate; and n = the number of periods.

Many calculators have been programmed to compute present and future values of annuities directly, but one should understand the underlying theory. No matter how one calculates it, however, the assumption that the payments are identical in amount and evenly spaced should be kept in mind.

## §2.4  The Value of a Perpetual Annuity

Assume that an annuity will continue to pay $1,000 per year forever. One might think that such an annuity must be worth an infinite amount because both the number of payments and the total amount paid are infinite. Not so.

For simplicity, let us assume that an appropriate discount rate is 12 percent, so that we know that the first five years of the annuity is worth $3,604.80. If you turn back to Table 2-2, it appears that the "infinity" answer may be wrong because the present value of future payments drops off dramatically. Similarly, if one looks at Table 2-3 under the 12 percent column, the present value of a 45-year annuity is $8,282.50, while the present value of a 50-year annuity is $8,304.50. In other words, from the 45th to the 50th year, the five years of $1,000 payments increase the present value by only $22. By extension, it is clear that the value of a perpetual annuity is not infinite.

The present value of a perpetual stream of fixed payments is precisely equal to the reciprocal of the discount rate multiplied by the payment. To state the formula in algebraic terms:

$$PV = \frac{1}{i} \times P$$

In the hypothetical, $1/.12 = 8.333$. The reciprocal of the discount rate is often called the **multiplier**. To calculate the present value of a perpetual annuity, one simply multiplies the payment by the appropriate multiplier. Plugging in the numbers from the hypothetical:

# Table 2-3
## Present Value of an Annuity of $1 Payable at the End of Each Period
### for n Periods

| No. of Periods | 2% | 3% | 4% | 5% | 6% | 7% | 8% |
|---|---|---|---|---|---|---|---|
| 1 | .9804 | .9709 | .9615 | .9524 | .9434 | .9346 | .9259 |
| 2 | 1.9416 | 1.9135 | 1.8861 | 1.8594 | 1.8334 | 1.8080 | 1.7833 |
| 3 | 2.8839 | 2.8286 | 2.7751 | 2.7232 | 2.6730 | 2.6243 | 2.5771 |
| 4 | 3.8077 | 3.7171 | 3.6299 | 3.5460 | 3.4651 | 3.3872 | 3.3121 |
| 5 | 4.7135 | 4.5797 | 4.4518 | 4.3295 | 4.2124 | 4.1002 | 3.9927 |
| 6 | 5.6014 | 5.4172 | 5.2421 | 5.0757 | 4.9173 | 4.7665 | 4.6229 |
| 7 | 6.4720 | 6.2303 | 6.0021 | 5.7864 | 5.5824 | 5.3893 | 5.2064 |
| 8 | 7.3255 | 7.0197 | 6.7327 | 6.4632 | 6.2098 | 5.9713 | 5.7466 |
| 9 | 8.1622 | 7.7861 | 7.4353 | 7.1078 | 6.8017 | 6.5152 | 6.2469 |
| 10 | 8.9826 | 8.5302 | 8.1109 | 7.7217 | 7.3601 | 7.0236 | 6.7101 |
| 11 | 9.7868 | 9.2526 | 8.7605 | 8.3064 | 7.8869 | 7.4987 | 7.1390 |
| 12 | 10.5753 | 9.9540 | 9.3851 | 8.8633 | 8.3838 | 7.9427 | 7.5361 |
| 13 | 11.3484 | 10.6350 | 9.9856 | 9.3936 | 8.8527 | 8.3577 | 7.9038 |
| 14 | 12.1062 | 11.2961 | 10.5631 | 9.8986 | 9.2950 | 8.7455 | 8.2442 |
| 15 | 12.8493 | 11.9379 | 11.1184 | 10.3797 | 9.7122 | 9.1079 | 8.5595 |
| 16 | 13.5777 | 12.5611 | 11.6523 | 10.8378 | 10.1059 | 9.4466 | 8.8514 |
| 17 | 14.2919 | 13.1661 | 12.1657 | 11.2741 | 10.4773 | 9.7632 | 9.1216 |
| 18 | 14.9920 | 13.7535 | 12.6593 | 11.6896 | 10.8276 | 10.0591 | 9.3719 |
| 19 | 15.6785 | 14.3238 | 13.1339 | 12.0853 | 11.1581 | 10.3356 | 9.6036 |
| 20 | 16.3514 | 14.8775 | 13.5903 | 12.4622 | 11.4699 | 10.5940 | 9.8181 |
| 21 | 17.0112 | 15.4150 | 14.0292 | 12.8212 | 11.7641 | 10.8355 | 10.0168 |
| 22 | 17.6580 | 15.9369 | 14.4511 | 13.1630 | 12.0416 | 11.0612 | 10.2007 |
| 23 | 18.2922 | 16.4436 | 14.8568 | 13.4886 | 12.3034 | 11.2722 | 10.3711 |
| 24 | 18.9139 | 16.9355 | 15.2470 | 13.7986 | 12.5504 | 11.4693 | 10.5288 |
| 25 | 19.5235 | 17.4131 | 15.6221 | 14.0939 | 12.7834 | 11.6536 | 10.6748 |
| 26 | 20.1210 | 17.8768 | 15.9828 | 14.3752 | 13.0032 | 11.8258 | 10.8100 |
| 27 | 20.7069 | 18.3270 | 16.3296 | 14.6430 | 13.2105 | 11.9867 | 10.9352 |
| 28 | 21.2813 | 18.7641 | 16.6631 | 14.8981 | 13.4062 | 12.1371 | 11.0511 |
| 29 | 21.8444 | 19.1885 | 16.9837 | 15.1411 | 13.5907 | 12.2777 | 11.1584 |
| 30 | 22.3965 | 19.6004 | 17.2920 | 15.3725 | 13.7648 | 12.4090 | 11.2578 |
| 31 | 22.9377 | 20.0004 | 17.5885 | 15.5928 | 13.9291 | 12.5318 | 11.3498 |
| 32 | 23.4683 | 20.3888 | 17.8736 | 15.8027 | 14.0840 | 12.6466 | 11.4350 |
| 33 | 23.9886 | 20.7658 | 18.1476 | 16.0025 | 14.2302 | 12.7538 | 11.5139 |
| 34 | 24.4986 | 21.1318 | 18.4112 | 16.1929 | 14.3681 | 12.8540 | 11.5869 |
| 35 | 24.9986 | 21.4872 | 18.6646 | 16.3742 | 14.4982 | 12.9477 | 11.6546 |
| 36 | 25.4888 | 21.8323 | 18.9083 | 16.5469 | 14.6210 | 13.0352 | 11.7172 |
| 37 | 25.9695 | 22.1672 | 19.1426 | 16.7113 | 14.7368 | 13.1170 | 11.7752 |
| 38 | 26.4406 | 22.4925 | 19.3679 | 16.8679 | 14.8460 | 13.1935 | 11.8289 |
| 39 | 26.9026 | 22.8082 | 19.5845 | 17.0170 | 14.9491 | 13.2649 | 11.8786 |
| 40 | 27.3555 | 23.1148 | 19.7928 | 17.1591 | 15.0463 | 13.3317 | 11.9246 |
| 41 | 27.7995 | 23.4124 | 19.9931 | 17.2944 | 15.1380 | 13.3941 | 11.9672 |
| 42 | 28.2348 | 23.7014 | 20.1856 | 17.4232 | 15.2245 | 13.4524 | 12.0067 |
| 43 | 28.6616 | 23.9819 | 20.3708 | 17.5459 | 15.3062 | 13.5070 | 12.0432 |
| 44 | 29.0800 | 24.2543 | 20.5488 | 17.6628 | 15.3832 | 13.5579 | 12.0771 |
| 45 | 29.4902 | 24.5187 | 20.7200 | 17.7741 | 15.4558 | 13.6055 | 12.1084 |
| 46 | 29.8923 | 24.7754 | 20.8847 | 17.8801 | 15.5244 | 13.6500 | 12.1374 |
| 47 | 30.2866 | 25.0247 | 21.0429 | 17.9810 | 15.5890 | 13.6916 | 12.1643 |
| 48 | 30.6731 | 25.2667 | 21.1951 | 18.0772 | 15.6500 | 13.7305 | 12.1891 |
| 49 | 31.0521 | 25.5017 | 21.3415 | 18.1687 | 15.7076 | 13.7668 | 12.2122 |
| 50 | 31.4236 | 25.7298 | 21.4822 | 18.2559 | 15.7619 | 13.8007 | 12.2335 |

Table 2-3 (*cont.*)
Present Value of an Annuity of $1 Payable at the End of Each Period
for n Periods

| No. of Periods | 2% | 3% | 4% | 5% | 6% | 7% | 8% |
|---|---|---|---|---|---|---|---|
| 1 | .9174 | .9091 | .9009 | .8929 | .8850 | .87723 | .8696 |
| 2 | 1.7591 | 1.7355 | 1.7125 | 1.6901 | 1.6681 | 1.6467 | 1.6257 |
| 3 | 2.5313 | 2.4869 | 2.4437 | 2.4018 | 2.3612 | 2.3216 | 2.2832 |
| 4 | 3.2397 | 3.1699 | 3.1024 | 3.0373 | 2.9745 | 2.9137 | 2.8550 |
| 5 | 3.8897 | 3.7908 | 3.6959 | 3.6048 | 3.5172 | 3.4331 | 3.3522 |
| 6 | 4.4859 | 4.3553 | 4.2305 | 4.1114 | 3.9975 | 3.8887 | 3.7845 |
| 7 | 5.0330 | 4.8684 | 4.7122 | 4.5638 | 4.4226 | 4.2883 | 4.1604 |
| 8 | 5.5348 | 5.3349 | 5.1461 | 4.9676 | 4.7988 | 4.6389 | 4.4873 |
| 9 | 5.9952 | 5.7590 | 5.5370 | 5.3282 | 5.1317 | 4.9464 | 4.7716 |
| 10 | 6.4177 | 6.1446 | 5.8892 | 5.6502 | 5.4262 | 5.2161 | 5.0188 |
| 11 | 6.8052 | 6.4951 | 6.2065 | 5.9377 | 5.6869 | 5.4527 | 5.2337 |
| 12 | 7.1607 | 6.8137 | 6.4924 | 6.1944 | 5.9176 | 5.6603 | 5.4206 |
| 13 | 7.4869 | 7.1034 | 6.7499 | 6.4235 | 6.1218 | 5.8424 | 5.5831 |
| 14 | 7.7862 | 7.3667 | 6.9819 | 6.6282 | 6.3025 | 6.0021 | 5.7245 |
| 15 | 8.0607 | 7.6061 | 7.1909 | 6.8109 | 6.4624 | 6.1422 | 5.8474 |
| 16 | 8.3126 | 7.8237 | 7.3792 | 6.9740 | 6.6039 | 6.2651 | 5.9542 |
| 17 | 8.5436 | 8.0216 | 7.5488 | 7.1196 | 6.7291 | 6.3729 | 6.0472 |
| 18 | 8.7556 | 8.2014 | 7.7016 | 7.2497 | 6.8399 | 6.4674 | 6.1280 |
| 19 | 8.9501 | 8.3649 | 7.8393 | 7.3658 | 6.9380 | 6.5504 | 6.1982 |
| 20 | 9.1285 | 8.5136 | 7.9633 | 7.4694 | 7.0248 | 6.6231 | 6.2593 |
| 21 | 9.2922 | 8.6487 | 8.0751 | 7.5620 | 7.1016 | 6.6870 | 6.3125 |
| 22 | 9.4424 | 8.7715 | 8.1757 | 7.6446 | 7.1695 | 6.7429 | 6.3587 |
| 23 | 9.5802 | 8.8832 | 8.2664 | 7.7184 | 7.2297 | 6.7921 | 6.3988 |
| 24 | 9.7066 | 8.9847 | 8.3481 | 7.7843 | 7.2829 | 6.8351 | 6.4338 |
| 25 | 9.8226 | 9.0770 | 8.4217 | 7.8431 | 7.3300 | 6.8729 | 6.4641 |
| 26 | 9.9290 | 9.1609 | 8.4881 | 7.8957 | 7.3717 | 6.9061 | 6.4906 |
| 27 | 10.0266 | 9.2372 | 8.5478 | 7.9426 | 7.4086 | 6.9352 | 6.5135 |
| 28 | 10.1161 | 9.3066 | 8.6016 | 7.9844 | 7.4412 | 6.9607 | 6.5335 |
| 29 | 10.1983 | 9.3696 | 8.6501 | 8.0218 | 7.4701 | 6.9830 | 6.5509 |
| 30 | 10.2737 | 9.4269 | 8.6938 | 8.0552 | 7.4957 | 7.0027 | 6.5660 |
| 31 | 10.3428 | 9.4790 | 8.7331 | 8.0850 | 7.5183 | 7.0199 | 6.5791 |
| 32 | 10.4062 | 9.5264 | 8.7686 | 8.1116 | 7.5383 | 7.0350 | 6.5905 |
| 33 | 10.4644 | 9.5694 | 8.8005 | 8.1354 | 7.5560 | 7.0482 | 6.6005 |
| 34 | 10.5178 | 9.6086 | 8.8293 | 8.1566 | 7.5717 | 7.0599 | 6.6091 |
| 35 | 10.5568 | 9.6442 | 8.8552 | 8.1755 | 7.5856 | 7.0700 | 6.6166 |
| 36 | 10.6118 | 9.6765 | 8.8786 | 8.1924 | 7.5979 | 7.0790 | 6.6231 |
| 37 | 10.6530 | 9.7059 | 8.8996 | 8.2075 | 7.6087 | 7.0868 | 6.6288 |
| 38 | 10.6908 | 9.7327 | 8.9186 | 8.2210 | 7.6183 | 7.0937 | 6.6338 |
| 39 | 10.7255 | 9.7570 | 8.9357 | 8.2330 | 7.6268 | 7.0997 | 6.6380 |
| 40 | 10.7574 | 9.7791 | 8.9511 | 8.2438 | 7.6344 | 7.1050 | 6.6418 |
| 41 | 10.7866 | 9.7991 | 8.9649 | 8.2534 | 7.6410 | 7.1097 | 6.6450 |
| 42 | 10.8134 | 9.8174 | 8.9774 | 8.2619 | 7.6469 | 7.1138 | 6.6478 |
| 43 | 10.8380 | 9.8340 | 8.9886 | 8.2696 | 7.6522 | 7.1173 | 6.6503 |
| 44 | 10.8605 | 9.8491 | 8.9988 | 8.2764 | 7.6568 | 7.1205 | 6.6524 |
| 45 | 10.8812 | 9.8628 | 9.0079 | 8.2825 | 7.6609 | 7.1232 | 6.6543 |
| 46 | 10.9002 | 9.8753 | 9.0161 | 8.2880 | 7.6645 | 7.1256 | 6.6559 |
| 47 | 10.9176 | 9.8866 | 9.0235 | 8.2928 | 7.6677 | 7.1277 | 6.6573 |
| 48 | 10.9336 | 9.8969 | 9.0302 | 8.2972 | 7.6705 | 7.1296 | 6.6585 |
| 49 | 10.9482 | 9.9063 | 9.0362 | 8.3010 | 7.6730 | 7.1312 | 6.6596 |
| 50 | 10.9617 | 9.9148 | 9.0417 | 8.3045 | 7.6752 | 7.1327 | 6.6605 |

$$PV = 8.333 \times \$1,000 = \$8,333.33$$

Although many find it more convenient to calculate the multiplier first, the formula can be considerably simplified to: $PV = P/i$. Again, plugging in the numbers from the above hypothetical: $PV / \$1,000/.12 = \$8,333.33$.

Either way, the present value of the right to receive $1,000 per year forever (at a 12 percent discount rate) is $8,333.33. This should become intuitively obvious when you realize that $8,333.33 invested at 12 percent yields almost $1,000 per year ($8,333.33 × .12 = $999.99), year after year, forever. Because the present value of a 50-year annuity on those terms is $8,304.50, it follows that the present value of the right to receive every payment, from the 51st year on to infinity, is only $25.50. When one values a long-term annuity, for example, one for 15 years or more, a simple way to approximate its value is to assume that it is infinite, and multiply by the reciprocal of the discount factor.

## §2.5 Valuing Variable Future Payments

Skill in discounting future payments to present value is useful in a variety of contexts. Clients are sometimes faced with selecting the most attractive of several offers that involve payments at different times and in different amounts, or choosing between two or more strategies that involve payments of various amounts at various times under various assumptions. To avoid the common mistake of comparing oranges and apples, that is, of comparing dollars payable at different times without taking into account the time value of money, it is necessary to reduce all future payments to current values. In doing this, one must select one or more discount rates. If all the payments are to be made by the same entity under apparently constant circumstances, it is customary to use a single discount rate for all calculations. Consider the following example: Your client owns a valuable piece of real estate. He is considering three offers that involve the following terms:

a) $90,000 cash;
b) $10,000 down, $1,000 per month for 120 months; and
c) $25,000 down, $1,200 per month for 72 months.

The total payments to be received under the first offer are $90,000. Under the second, the total payments to be received are $130,000 ($10,000 plus 120 times $1,000). The contract presented by the hopeful purchaser to your client ignores the interest component entirely and states, as the purchase price, the full $130,000. Under the third alternative, the total payments are $111,400 ($25,000 plus 72 times $1,200). However, because of the time value of money, this comparison of gross amounts to be received is misleading. Calculation shows that at a 9 percent interest rate, and ignoring income taxes, the present value of $1,000 per month for 120 months is $78,941.69 and the present value of $1,200 per month for 72 months is $66,572.22. Thus, the present values of the three offers are:

a) $90,000;
b) $88,941.69; and
c) $91,572,22.

Even though the second alternative yields the largest gross amount, it has the smallest present value. This occurs because the immediate down payment in alternative b is rather small and periodic payments continue over ten years rather than six years as in the third alternative. On the other hand, because the present values of the three offers are very close, most people would probably recommend that the all-cash offer be accepted on the theory that there is some advantage in being immediately disentangled from a property. However, it certainly is not intuitively obvious that this is the most sensible solution.

In this hypothetical, different conclusions may be reached if a different discount rate is chosen. For example, if one computes the present value of the three payment options using a discount rate of 6 percent rather than 9 percent, the results are as follows:

a) All cash — $90,000;
b) $10,000 down, $1,000 per month over 120 months — $100,073 and
c) $25,000 down, $1,200 per month over 72 months — $97,407.

Suddenly, the payments to be spread out over a period of time have become more attractive, because the present value of future payments is higher at lower discount rates, so that at the lower discount rate the future payments become relatively more valuable compared with the down payments than when a higher discount rate is used. As noted before, there is an inverse relationship between value and discount rates: The higher the rate, the less a future payment is worth.

## §2.6 Choosing a Discount Rate

Why was the interest rate of 12 percent used in most of the above calculations? In the last example comparing three different payment schedules, why were the rates compared unexpectedly changed to 9 percent and 6 percent? Where do rates in the real world come from anyway?

Unfortunately, there is no simple answer to the question of which discount rate to use in all circumstances in the real world. The choice depends on the current level of market interest rates, the investment alternatives available to the parties, and the risk in the loan or investment to be made. As described above, the differences in results reached vary significantly depending on the rate chosen, though the differences between choosing a 6 or a 6.5 percent rate are nowhere near as substantial as the difference between choosing between 6 and 12 percent, as Table 2-1 illustrates. However, that does not give much guidance as to whether a 6 or a 12 percent rate should actually be used.

Most real-life problems in determining present values come down to a choice among one of the four following rates:

1. The market interest rate for essentially risk-free investments (e.g., the yield on short-term debt securities issued by the federal government).
2. The highest interest rate that a person could obtain for a deposit within his or her means at a local financial institution.
3. The lowest interest rate that a person would be charged in order to borrow funds of the same magnitude as the transaction involves.
4. The return that a business has determined it must make on an investment in order to be willing to enter into a transaction.

When a person of doubtful wealth has the obligation to make a future payment, an appropriate upward adjustment may be made to the discount rate. Of course, the greater the risk, the higher the discount rate (and the lower the present value of that payment) will be. In most instances, however, the calculations are made using one of the four basic rates set forth above without express adjustment in the discount rate for the risk of nonpayment. Indeed, most readily ascertainable rates already include some adjustment for the possibility of default. Where the risk of default is higher than normal, however, that risk is usually taken into account in a subjective way in deciding whether to enter the transaction at all, even if the calculation shows the value of the transaction to be attractive.

## §2.7 Capital Budgeting by Businesses

Traditional books on finance used in business schools present considerably more sophisticated models for financial decision-making by businesses than those described here. The problem is generally addressed in terms of a business facing alternative investment choices, each of which involves certain outflows (or payments) and inflows (or receipts). The problem addressed is for the business to select, on a rational basis, which projects it should pursue and which it should not. The size of outflows and inflows may be fixed or they may be uncertain (though some way must be found to quantify the uncertainty).

If outflows and inflows occur over various periods of time, the calculation of capital budgeting can become complex even if the element of uncertainty is absent. However, the underlying theory is directly based on the time value of money described in this chapter. There are two widely accepted methods of capital budgeting.

The **internal rate of return (IRR)** is defined as a discount rate that equates the present value of the expected cash outflows with the expected cash inflows. Assume, for example, that a business is faced with an immediate cash outlay of $20,000 that is expected to yield inflows of $6,000 per year over each of the next five years thereafter. The internal rate of return is that discount rate that makes the present value of the future inflows equal to the present value of the outflow. In this instance, that rate is approximately 15 percent. If similar calculations are made for each of the alternative projects the business is considering, the business should select those with the highest internal rate of return. The calculation of internal rates of return may involve successive estimations, or iterations, of the appropriate rate when done by hand, but here again, calculators and computer programs are readily available that perform such calculations. Comparison of internal rates of returns of alternative ventures provides a useful means of determining which ventures are most attractive for a business.

The net present value technique involves establishing a minimum rate of return on projects that the business has determined is necessary for its financial health. When this discount rate is established, all outflows and inflows are reduced to present values using this discount rate and outflows are subtracted from inflows: The project is attractive if the net present value is positive; if it is zero or negative, the project is unattractive.

These capital budgeting theories, as well as many other present value calculations, often contain a hidden assumption that may affect the accuracy of the calculation. That assumption is that interim payments to be received may be reinvested at the same interest rate that was applicable when the transaction was originally entered into. The following simplified example makes this point: Assume that you are the financial vice president of an insurance company with $100,000 to invest. You know that five years from now you must have on hand $190,000 to pay anticipated life insurance claims. A reliable borrower offers to borrow that $100,000 for five years, with annual interest payments at 14 percent per year. In other words, each year the borrower will pay you the amount of the interest due for that year. If one simply calculates the future value of $100,000 at the end of five years at an interest rate of 14 percent, that value is $192,541. There is, however, a critical assumption hidden in this example: this calculation assumes that your company will be able to invest consistently the $14,000 annual interest payment each year, also at the steady rate of 14 percent per year. That assumption, of course, may not be correct; if interest rates decline, you may be able to invest some interest payments at only 8 percent, say, and your company then will not have the $190,000 available as expected. Although this problem of reinvesting interim payments may seem to be self-evident after it is pointed out, it is an implicit assumption in many capital budget calculations that is not always fully appreciated.

# CHAPTER 3

# REAL ESTATE

## §3.1 Introduction

This chapter focuses on transactions in real estate, including both residential and commercial transactions. Although the purchase of a residence is not usually motivated primarily by the prospect of profit (as is almost always the case with a commercial transaction), the transaction and the financing arrangements are quite similar in many respects to those of a large commercial real estate transaction, and they illustrate in a familiar (and homey) way the application of many basic business principles.

The discussion that follows generally assumes that the property is a freestanding house on a parcel of land that will be conveyed free and clear in the transaction. There are, of course, many other forms of ownership. With a **condominium (condo)**, the property is the airspace. With a **cooperative (coop)**,

33

the property is shares in a company that owns the building together with a lease to a particular unit attached to those shares. And even with a free-standing house, it is possible that all rights may not be conveyed. For example, it may be that the land is owned by a condominium association (even though the house is owned by the homeowner) or that someone has retained the mineral rights under the property. These variations in forms of ownership generate interesting legal questions, but they are not the focus here. Rather, this chapter focuses on transactions.

In most cases involving the sale of an existing home, the seller lists the property with a **real estate agent** (also called a **real estate broker**) who will receive a **commission** (usually 5 to 7 percent of the price) if an acceptable offer is obtained. It is also possible for the owner to sell the house without the help of a broker, but the broker offers services, such as advertising and showing the house, that may be difficult for the owner to replicate. Moreover, many buyers may be reluctant to buy a house without the help of a broker for fear that the price may have been set too high. In other words, the broker, who as a repeat player has a reputation to protect, in effect vouches for the fairness of the price. Although the prospective buyer may contact the listing broker directly as a result of a sign or advertisement, it is probably more common for a buyer to contact another agent who undertakes to identify several properties for the buyer to view. If a transaction takes place, the two brokers typically split the commission. Thus, the seller nevertheless pays the entire commission out of the proceeds of the sale, and technically speaking both agents are working for the seller. (There are some real estate agents who hold themselves out as agents for the buyer (**buyer's brokers**) and who are paid a fee by the buyer over and above the commission paid by the seller.)

Once a buyer has decided to buy a particular house, the broker assists the buyer in preparing a written offer. In most larger cities, offers are made using a standard form by which the specific terms of the offer are spelled out. In smaller towns, where the volume of transactions is less, the offer may be drafted by a lawyer. The seller may then accept or reject the offer or may make a counteroffer, usually by marking out the terms to be changed and writing in new terms by hand. (After the parties have agreed on all the terms, it is common to execute a clean copy of the contract.)

The contract does not itself effect the sale of the property. Rather, it binds the parties to execute or close the transaction at some specified date in the future if the conditions set forth in the contract are met. For example, the contract may make closing contingent on an acceptable report from an inspector to be hired by the buyer, although in some states (notably California) sellers are required to warrant the condition of the property. The buyer may make the deal contingent on obtaining a loan of some minimum amount. And the lender may require that the house be appraised. Clearly, it takes time to satisfy these conditions.

Although the foregoing description is typical of most sales of existing homes, it is not the only pattern. There are significant variations if one purchases directly from a builder and even more significant variations if one undertakes to construct a home.

In some parts of the country homes are sold by means of an installment sale (often called a **contract for deed** or a **land contract**). In such cases, the buyer gains immediate possession and use of the residence, but title does not pass until all payments have been made. In contrast, with a conventional sale, title passes immediately to the buyer even though in some cases the seller may have helped the buyer to finance the transaction by taking back a note and agreeing to accept payment over time.

Most commercial real estate transactions and indeed most large business transactions follow similar patterns. There are numerous agents involved. A contract is typically executed in advance of the closing of the deal. There are usually numerous contingencies to be satisfied. And the money usually comes from several sources. Some comes from the buyer, and some (often most) comes from a lender (or other investors) who expect periodic payments in return. But there are additional factors to be considered in connection with a commercial transaction to which we turn in the later sections of this chapter.

## §3.2 Source of Funds for Acquiring Residential Real Estate

Relatively few people have the money to purchase a home with cash. Unlike commercial real estate, residential real estate does not produce a cash flow from which payments on loans may be made in the future. Rather, the payments must come from the future earnings of the owner, and eligibility for a loan is largely based on the earning capacity of the purchaser. A relatively large down payment is required for residential property because the lender relies on the resale value of the property as security for its loan and wants to have a cushion between the amount of the loan and the value of the property securing it. The minimum down payment required for a loan to purchase residential property varies with the type of lender and the economic conditions at the time of the transaction, but the amount required is much more standardized than the down payment for commercial real estate.

There are two traditional sources for residential real estate financing: conventional loans made by banks, **savings and loan associations (S&Ls)** and other financial institutions and government-guaranteed loans (usually guaranteed by the **Veterans' Administration (VA)** or the **Federal Housing Administration (FHA)**).

Most conventional mortgages are limited to 80 percent of the value of the property. This is often called the **loan to value (LTV)** ratio. In other words, the down payment (or equity) required to be contributed by the buyer is traditionally 20 percent of the purchase price. In some circumstances lenders may accept a somewhat smaller down payment. For example, if **private mortgage insurance (PMI)** is available, lenders will usually accept a 10 percent down payment, but the purchaser must pay a monthly insurance premium. As a result, mortgage insurance is available only for those who can afford a higher monthly payment.

In concrete terms, to purchase a $100,000 residence using a conventional loan, the purchaser must make a $20,000 down payment in cash. Although the down payment may itself be borrowed, most lenders prohibit it. In some cases, the lender will require proof of the source of the down payment.

The terms of VA and FHA loans are largely dictated by federal regulation. They typically are available only for less expensive properties, and the down payment may be as low as 5 percent of the purchase price. Because of the governmental guarantee of payment, the lender does not have the same concern about default.

In addition to the down payment, the purchaser must pay a variety of additional **closing costs** that may easily add several thousand dollars to the amount of cash that is required "up front." These costs may include *points*, a concept discussed further below.

A potential purchaser may have enough cash for a larger down payment and yet be concerned whether her income can comfortably support the monthly payments required by the mortgage. In this situation, the purchaser may reduce the size of the mortgage by increasing the down payment, thereby reducing future monthly payments.

On the other hand, even in the rare case where a purchaser of a residence has the capital necessary to pay all cash, she often prefers to borrow a substantial part of the purchase price. First, it is important for every individual to retain readily available funds for emergencies or contingencies, and capital invested in a home cannot be withdrawn quickly. In a word, capital invested in a residence is **illiquid**. For another, rational investors **diversify**. They do not put all of their financial eggs in one basket. To do so is risky, because a single asset may decrease in value quite unexpectedly. Diversification reduces risk, but investing a large proportion of one's wealth in a single residence increases risk. Third, the purchaser may prefer to borrow most of the purchase price of the residence, leaving more capital available for other investments. A loan secured by residential real estate may be on more attractive terms than the purchaser could obtain if the owner were to invest the capital in a residence and then borrow against it for outside investments.

Although the rate of interest paid on a mortgage tends to be lower than the rates on other consumer loans, it is not usually possible for an individual to invest at a similar rate of return without assuming additional risk. Thus, it makes no sense (from an investment point of view) to take out a big mortgage and then invest one's spare cash in a certificate of deposit (CD) or government securities.

Finally, and probably most important, interest payments on a mortgage are **deductible** for income tax purposes whereas most other forms of interest are not deductible by individuals. Thus, mortgage interest is paid in **pre-tax dollars** and reduces taxable income. This means that the effective rate of interest on a mortgage loan is lower than that on other loans. For example, for someone in the 40 percent tax bracket (combined federal, state, and local), a 10 percent mortgage is the same as a 6 percent loan, because a dollar paid for mortgage interest would be worth only 60 cents in **after tax dollars** if retained by the borrower as income.

It is often possible after purchasing a house to arrange for a home equity loan or line of credit. A home equity loan is in effect a second mortgage and interest paid on it is deductible as with a first mortgage if the total debt outstanding against the property does not exceed the cost of the house plus improvements. Home equity loans are readily available up to 85 percent LTV and in some cases 100 percent or more, but the interest rate tends to be somewhat higher than on first mortgages, because the holder of the first mortgage has priority over the home equity lender in the event of default. With a home equity line of credit, the homeowner may borrow simply by writing checks against the line of credit up to a total of the maximum amount approved. As with first mortgages, home equity loans and lines typically involve closing costs. The lender also usually charges an annual fee for maintaining the account.

Of course, the purchase of a residence is also an investment. Many people own several homes during their lifetimes, typically selling one home in order to purchase the next one. The sales proceeds from the old home usually provide all or most of the purchase price of the new one. In the past, residential real estate values have generally risen in most areas, so that people usually profit from buying a residence, living in it a few years, and then selling it in order to buy a new one.

The sale of a residence may give rise to a taxable gain. Generally, in the event of a **sale or exchange** of a capital asset, one must pay tax on the **capital gain** (or may take a **capital loss**, reduce taxable income, and thus reduce tax to be paid). There is, however, a special rule in §121 of the **Internal Revenue Code (IRC)** that grants an exclusion of up to $500,000 in gain on a joint return in connection with the sale of a principal residence, defined as a residence in which one has resided for at least two of the last five years.

## §3.3 Mortgages

A loan made to enable the borrower to purchase or develop real estate is represented by a promissory note that is usually on a standard printed form. The promissory note is usually secured by a lien on the real estate that is the subject of the transaction. The lien is usually created in a separate document, either a **mortgage** or **deed of trust**, which is executed simultaneously with the note at the closing. The terms of these documents are so standardized that printed forms are usually used with a few blanks filled in. (Typed-in clauses referring to special terms such as prepayment privileges are also sometimes added.) These standardized forms are typically prepared by the lender, who usually resists making changes in them. A deed of trust differs from a mortgage in only minor respects: The type of instrument used in a particular state or community depends more on tradition or convention than on the differences between the two forms of instruments. Hereafter, the word "mortgage" will be used to refer to both types of instruments.

The lien created by a mortgage covers the entire property that is the subject of the transaction. It covers the improvements as they are constructed as well as the land itself. Liens have both a geographic and a temporal aspect. If the transaction involves a commercial development that includes the installation of streets and utilities followed by a sale of lots, it is necessary to arrange, in the mortgage, a procedure by which the developer can obtain the release of individual lots from this lien when they are sold. Otherwise, the purchasers of the lots purchase subject to the lien of the mortgage covering the whole project and will be unable to arrange first lien financing to construct improvements on the lot. Similarly, temporal rights, such as the rights of a lessee under a ten-year lease, are subject to the lien of the mortgagee, although in the event of a default the mortgagee usually will not want to dispossess tenants. In some cities, rent control laws may limit the power of owners to dispossess tenants even when they wish to do so.

The promissory note secured by a real estate mortgage is, of course, a promise by the person signing it to pay the amount set forth. In most commercial (and practically all residential) real estate transactions, the developers or owners are required to sign the note individually so that they will be personally liable if a default occurs. That is, in addition to losing the property, the developer or owner will be liable for any further amount that may be owed to the lender after the property is sold. In commercial real estate, however, it is not unknown for the lender to agree to look solely to the property as the source of payment and not require the developer to assume personal liability. This may be done by having some third person—a straw party—or a corporation without substantial assets sign the note. The same result may be reached by a non recourse loan in the note that limits the power of the holder to recover from the maker in the event of default. In the case of such a loan, if there is a default, the developer is faced with the loss of the property, including whatever equity he or she has in the property, but is not personally liable for the debt.

Even where the developer is personally liable on the note, individual investors may not be. It is quite common for developers to sell participations in a project through the medium of a corporation or a limited partnership in which the individual investors risk their original investments but have no personal liability in excess of that amount.

Finally, individual liability on real estate notes may be discharged through the bankruptcy process if the individual is insolvent.

A traditional real estate mortgage is for a long term—25 or 30 years—at a fixed interest rate established at or close to the market rate of interest at the time the loan is made. Monthly payments are required, and interest is computed on the unpaid balance each month. The loan is amortized over the period of the loan by these monthly payments, which are fixed in advance and remain constant throughout the life of the mortgage. The words **amortize** and **amortization** are fancy terms that simply mean the loan is set up so that a portion of each monthly payment is applied to principal as well as interest: In the classic mortgage of this type, the monthly payment is computed so that the final level payment—the 360th in a 30-year mortgage—reduces the loan balance to zero.

The first payment on a traditional mortgage represents virtually all interest with a few dollars being applied to principal; the second payment consists of a tiny bit less interest (because the first payment reduced the principal slightly) and therefore a tiny bit more is available to be applied to reduce principal. This process continues over the life of the mortgage, with each payment representing a somewhat larger amount of principal and smaller amount of interest than the previous one.

To illustrate: on a $75,000 loan at 9 percent, the level monthly payment is $603.47 over the 30 years. The first payment reduces principal by $40.97 (the remaining $562.50 is interest); the second payment reduces principal by $41.27 (the remaining $562.19 is interest); and so on. The 12th payment reduces principal by $44.48; after this payment, the principal has been reduced to $74,487.60. The payment made on the 5th anniversary of the mortgage (the 60th payment), reduces principal by $63.66 and the mortgage then has been reduced to $71,910.10. Obviously, only a small amount of the unpaid balance is amortized in the early years of the mortgage. After 10 years, the principal has been reduced to $67,072.31; after 15 years, it has been reduced to $59,497.86; after 20 years to $47,638.70; after 25 years to $29,071.04. During the last five years, most of each payment is principal, and upon making the 360th payment, the principal is reduced to zero. As with compound interest, tables, calculators, and computer programs are readily available that give the level payment amount per dollar borrowed at various rates of interest over various periods.

The fixed-interest, level-payment loan described here is so common and so widely used that it is sometimes referred to as a **conventional loan**. (The term conventional is also sometimes used in a different context to describe residential real estate loans made by a savings and loan association or other lender in contrast to loans guaranteed under federal programs such as those administered by the FHA or VA.) Until the late 1970s, the level-payment loan was the only mortgage arrangement available for residential real estate and was used almost universally in commercial real estate as well. With the very high interest rates that prevailed in the late 1970s, a number of alternative mortgages were created that departed from the level-payment structure. Some of these alternative mortgages are widely used today in connection with commercial real estate mortgages.

The basic premises underlying the level-payment mortgage appear to be (1) that the person making payments on the mortgage has a level income over the term of the mortgage, (2) that interest rates are going to remain relatively stable over the term of the mortgage, and (3) that there is no inflation in the system. These premises obviously have not been true in the recent past, and they seem particularly inappropriate for commercial real estate with its open-ended potential for producing cash flow. Indeed, a very common cash flow pattern in commercial real estate is relatively small gross receipts in early years followed by gradual improvement as the project becomes established and successful. It would seem sensible to structure mortgage payments for commercial loans not on a fixed level over the term of the mortgage, but on a basis that increases over time. Once lenders escaped from the traditional thinking underlying the level-payment mortgage, several variations were commonly offered:

1. The simplest pattern involves interest-only payments for a period of several years followed by an increase in the payments to permit amortization of the principal over the balance of the mortgage when the interest-only period ends. This results in an abrupt increase in the size of the payments when amortization of the principal begins.

2. There is no reason why the initial payments must fully cover the interest costs of the initial years as long as the payments are thereafter increased sufficiently to pay off the whole mortgage when it is due. So-called **negative amortization** loans provide initial payments below the interest-only level with the unpaid interest added to principal so that the

outstanding balance of the mortgage increases in the early years of the mortgage. Later payments obviously must increase in amount to cover both the negative amortization in the early years and the regular amortization of the principal in the remaining years. Payments often increase gradually to ease the impact on cash flow in later years.

3. There is also no reason why the interest rate on a mortgage must be fixed for the life of the mortgage. The **adjustable rate mortgage (ARM)** provides for adjustments to the effective interest rate on the mortgage periodically based on changes in a specified market interest rate.

4. Another real estate financing technique involves balloon notes. A **balloon note** is a simple idea: It is a note that requires periodic payments, but the unpaid balance comes due long before the payments amortize the borrowed amount. In the real estate context, a balloon note might come due in 5 or 10 years, but the periodic monthly payments are computed based on a 25-year or 30-year amortization schedule. Such a note might be described as a 5-year balloon with payments based on a 25-year 10 percent amortization schedule. This means that monthly payments are computed on the 25-year 10 percent table, but the loan itself comes due in 5 years. Of course, when it comes due, there is a huge final payment that is due—the balloon—because monthly payments have mostly gone to the payment of interest and the principal has been reduced only slightly. Because most borrowers do not have the funds to pay the balloon in cash when it comes due, the property is often resold or refinanced. **Refinancing** may involve a second balloon note, which in turn may lead to a third. If interest rates have risen or fallen when the balloon comes due, the new mortgage covering the balloon is written at the then-current market rate. A balloon note, in other words, is not unlike the ARM discussed above in ultimate economic effect. The difference is that with a balloon note, the burden is on the borrower to find substitute financing. Most balloon notes are probably carried by sellers of property, though a number of financial institutions also accept short-term balloon notes. Many balloon notes appear as part of second mortgages in creative financing transactions discussed below.

5. A wide variety of short-term mortgages known as **bridge loans, mezzanine financing**, or simply short-term **interim financing** exist. Such loans usually provide for interest-only payments with no reduction of principal for periods as short as one year, but often running three to five years. Like the balloon note, such loans usually result in refinancing of the project when the note comes due. Sometimes these short-term loans may be unsecured.

## §3.4  Valuation and Appraisal

A person thinking about the purchase or sale of residential real estate must consider how much the residence is worth. Although valuation of commercial real estate usually involves estimates of future cash flows, this technique is generally not appropriate for residential real estate. A single family house is usually worth more for purposes of owner occupancy than it is as a rental property. In other words, it is not usually possible to buy a house and then rent it out for enough to cover expenses, at least during the first few years of ownership. This suggests that people usually pay a premium for their own residence or, in other words, that single family owner occupancy is the **highest and best use** of a property. For this reason, it is usually not appropriate to determine the value of a residence based on the value of a similar rental house. One must resort to other methods.

Of course, the owner of real estate is familiar with the property, its advantages, its idiosyncracies, and its defects, and usually has some idea as to its value. When the property is put up for sale, the owner must put an asking price on that property. That price, however, is not a reliable indication of value because an owner often inflates the asking price. It is quite common to negotiate over price in connection with residential real estate, and setting a slightly inflated asking price may be justified in the owner's mind as providing some room to negotiate. Not all sellers use this tactic. Some simply set what they view to be an acceptable price and refuse to negotiate. As a result, an asking price is not a reliable indication of value.

A second source of information is the appraised value of the residence for local real estate taxation purposes. Taxing authorities maintain an appraisal office, the function of which is to estimate the value of properties within the jurisdiction for purposes of taxation. These valuations may usually be obtained simply by a telephone call, but the usefulness of this information is limited. Tax appraisals are often not current. They may be redetermined once every few years (or even less frequently), with some kind of automatic adjustment made in the intervening years. More seriously, however, many jurisdictions do not appraise properties for tax purposes at 100 percent of market value. Assessments may be set at two-thirds, one-half, or some smaller fraction of estimated value. In the absence of specific knowledge about the practices followed by the local assessment office, these tax valuations should not be viewed as reliable indicators of value.

The most reliable method of estimating value is to employ an independent appraiser who is familiar with properties in the community. The most widely used method estimates the market value of the residence based on recent sales of similar nearby properties—**comparables**. This comparison is obviously best suited to appraising homes that are substantially similar to other homes in the immediate neighborhood and is less reliable for residences that are unique. Examination of sale prices of other homes creates a range of prices and terms. The appraiser must then adjust these figures, either up or down, to take into account the specific features and deficiencies of the property. Most residential real estate valuations are based on this method.

Another method of appraisal involves an estimate of the replacement cost of the residence. Appraisers estimating the replacement cost of a residence usually rely on appraisal handbooks that give current construction costs for various materials. This approach often involves long and complicated calculations. Replacement cost is the principal method of valuation used if the property is unique and there are no comparable properties for which independent sales data are available.

Finally, the appraiser may consider the sales history of the property in question. If the present owner purchased the property in the recent past, the price paid may be indicative of the current value. This information, however, may not always be easy to obtain. Further, it is always possible that the present owner obtained the property at a bargain price or that recent market trends show that the historical price is no longer an accurate estimate of current value. As a result, most appraisers place less weight on historical data than on recent sales of similar properties in the community.

In making a formal appraisal, an appraiser may estimate value on more than one basis and then compare values obtained by using different approaches. In some cases, the appraiser may average the values obtained by these different methods, but a more accepted practice is to select a value that appears to be representative and ignore other approaches that lead to divergent values.

These methods of valuation may be considered in the appraisal of commercial properties along with cash-flow projections. In other words, in estimating the value of a commercial apartment building, an appraiser may consider the prices paid for other comparable buildings in the area and the estimated cost of replacing the current structure, as well as cash-flow data.

The two variables that determine how expensive a house one can afford are (1) the amount of the down payment one can or is willing to make and (2) the size of the loan that a lender will make based on the expected income of the purchaser. Lenders typically use guidelines to determine the size of a loan for which a borrower may qualify. One common rule is that monthly mortgage payments for principal and interest should not exceed 25 percent of monthly gross income. Another common rule is that aggregate monthly housing costs and payments on other loans should not exceed 35 percent of gross monthly income, though many families have demonstrated that one can survive a much higher percentage—over 50 percent—if there are no unexpected emergencies. There is usually some flexibility in close cases, depending on the market and the demand for real estate loans. Often, a lender will decline to make a loan at the lowest market interest rate but will offer to make the loan at a somewhat higher rate to compensate for the perceived riskiness of the loan.

## §3.5  The Structure of a Real Estate Purchase

The purchase of real estate is usually a two-step process that is quite similar to a commercial transaction. The first step is the execution of a **contract** of sale, setting forth the terms of the transaction. There then follows a period, often lasting a month or more, during which each party prepares to perform under the contract. Usually, the most important responsibility of the purchaser during this period is to arrange the necessary financing. Another important matter (which may be the responsibility of either the purchaser or the seller depending on the conventions followed by local realtors) is establishing that the seller has **marketable title** satisfactory to the purchaser. Marketable title is a title that a reasonable attorney in the community should accept. The second step is the **closing**, at which the formal steps required to complete the transaction take place. Upon the execution of the contract, the parties are legally bound to complete the transaction. The closing is where this actually occurs.

## §3.6 Real Estate Brokers

Most purchases and sales of real estate involve **real estate brokers** (also called **real estate agents** or **realtors**). Often, neither the purchaser nor the seller of real estate is familiar with the details of such transactions. In addition, the parties to a residential real estate transaction often do not consult a lawyer. Real estate brokers routinely guide persons through the intricacies of buying and selling properties. In contrast, purchasers and sellers of commercial real estate typically have considerably greater sophistication, are accustomed to dealing with lawyers, and may deal directly with each other, limiting the role of brokers.

The first question that a potential seller must face is whether to list the property with a broker or to seek a purchaser directly. The major disadvantage of using a broker is the commission, which typically is 5 to 7 percent of the aggregate selling price and in the case of unusual properties or difficult market conditions may be higher. The commission is payable independently of the amount of effort exerted by the broker and is computed on the aggregate selling price, not on the amount of cash that changes hands. For example, on a $100,000 property for which the purchaser is to pay $20,000 in cash and take out a $80,000 mortgage, a 6 percent commission is $6,000, exactly the same as if the purchaser were paying all cash for the property. In this example, the commission is 30 percent of the buyer's equity (though it is paid by the seller). It is sometimes possible to negotiate with a broker over the amount of the commission, particularly if there is reason to believe that the property will sell quickly.

Many owners of residential property initially seek to sell their properties on their own to avoid paying the broker's commission. They may advertise in local newspapers and place signs on the property. This is often unsuccessful because the seller may be unfamiliar with the real estate market and may set an unrealistic price on the property even without a commission. Also, most brokers refuse to show unlisted properties, and many potential purchasers immediately contact a real estate broker rather than trying to first find a suitable unlisted property. Sometimes, a prospective seller will specify that brokers are welcome or **brokers protected** in advertising the property, which means that the seller is willing to pay the customary portion of the commission that would be earned by a showing broker or that some other amount will be negotiated. Many properties initially offered **for sale by owner (FSBO)** are later listed with a broker.

Properties listed for sale with a real estate broker are referred to as **listings**. Real estate brokers in most communities have a **multiple listing system (MLS)**, a centralized system that gives all participating brokers access to current listings that have been placed with other participating brokers.

A potential purchaser usually consults a broker to help locate a suitable property. The broker may happen to be the same broker that has the original listing (as when the prospective buyer calls the telephone number on the sign posted on the property) in which case the broker earns the entire commission. If different brokers are involved, they will usually share the commission equally. Commissions are typically paid solely by the seller out of the proceeds of the sale. The purchaser may not be aware that the friendly broker who shows the purchaser numerous houses, seemingly out of graciousness, is motivated primarily by the fact that the broker will receive part of the commission payable by the seller.

It is not unusual to hear stories of brokers who earn a full commission with little effort. The broker accepts the listing one morning, and that afternoon an eager buyer calls. One must balance stories about such windfalls with stories about the broker that conducts an open house every weekend for six months, advertises the property in the newspaper at the broker's own expense, and takes unusual steps to try to sell a property. Also, a broker assisting a purchaser may show a potential purchaser fifty different houses and then fail to earn even a partial commission when the purchasers stumble onto the perfect house on their own.

## §3.7 Negotiation of the Contract of Sale

After locating a suitable property, the potential purchaser makes an offer on the property. This usually takes the form of a proposed written contract of sale, which in the case of residential real estate is usually prepared by the purchaser's broker on a standard form contract, setting forth the terms on which the purchaser hopes to purchase the property. This contract covers the basic terms of the sale, including the price, the terms of financing to be obtained, the time possession is to be transferred, what personal property is included in the sale, and so forth. Many unsophisticated purchasers may not appreciate the potential binding effect that this document has on their rights in connection with the proposed purchase. If the seller simply accepts the proposed contract, the purchaser is bound in accordance with its terms. Because this initial document is so important, a lawyer should always examine it on behalf of the purchaser before it is submitted. But brokers usually do not suggest this, and the purchaser may not be sophisticated enough to insist on it. After the proposed contract is completed and signed by the prospective purchaser, it is typically presented by the purchaser's broker to the seller's broker, and then by the seller's broker to the seller. A nominal down payment known as **earnest money** is usually enclosed with the proposed contract. The seller may make a counteroffer by changing the terms of the contract of sale, perhaps by increasing the price or by requiring the buyer to increase the size of the down payment, and the revised form of contract is returned to the purchaser's broker who then presents this counteroffer to the purchaser. In the process, the brokers may act as facilitators, sometimes urging the seller to accept less or the purchaser to offer more, rather than as true agents of one party or the other. Brokers usually prefer to act as intermediaries between the potential purchaser and seller rather than to allow them to negotiate directly. (One concern is that a direct confrontation may lead to a breakdown in the negotiations. There is also the possibility that the purchaser and seller will get along too well and try to work out a private deal to avoid the commission.)

If the purchaser is represented by an attorney, that attorney prepares a formal contract of sale that is usually not based on the standardized contract of sale used by real estate brokers. This contract probably represents the purchaser's interests more effectively than does the standard contract. Indeed, one might argue that real estate brokers routinely engage in the **unauthorized practice of law (UPL)**, but the role of realtors appears to be well established and to raise few such controversies.

## §3.8 The Closing

The final step of a typical real estate deal is the closing, which occurs after the title has been examined and the necessary financing arranged. The contract of sale usually specifies a time period during which the closing is to occur, but in practice the date is usually dictated by the financing commitment and the convenience of the parties.

The closing usually occurs at the offices of a title company. At the closing, deeds, promissory notes, mortgages, and other documents are executed, and the cash to be contributed by the purchaser and the lender is paid. Checks are usually made payable to the title company. Usually, the executed documents and checks are placed **in escrow** which means that the documents and money have been delivered to a disinterested third person with instructions to deliver documents and disburse funds to specified persons only upon the occurrence of specified conditions or events. Escrow is a convenient device for any type of closing transaction that requires a series of steps to be taken in specific sequence and more or less simultaneously. Pursuant to the escrow instructions, the closing officer first makes sure that all checks have cleared and the funds deposited in a special trust account. The escrow officer then records in the local land records, in the proper sequence, the release of the old mortgage, the new deed, and the new mortgage. Funds are then disbursed to the various parties in accordance with the settlement sheet, and the recorded documents are delivered to the persons entitled to them. The seller receives the balance of the purchase price, and the brokers receive their shares of the commission. The old mortgagee receives the unpaid balance of its loan. The promissory note originally executed by the sellers is marked paid and returned to them. The purchaser receives the deed, and arrangements are made for the purchaser to make the required periodic payments on the new mortgage.

Although escrow is a well-established practice, it is probably more common nowadays for the purchaser and lender to deliver certified checks at the closing or to have the funds transferred electronically.

Possession of the property may be transferred at the closing by the delivery of keys, but that is a matter of local custom and agreement between the parties, and possession may be transferred either before or after the closing.

## §3.9  Allocation of Closing Costs

The closing officer must prepare a **settlement statement (HUD-1)** show-ing charges allocable to the purchaser, charges allocable to the seller, and the disposition of the remaining cash. Federal law requires copies of this statement to be distributed to the purchaser and seller for their review before the closing.

Examination of a settlement statement shows that a number of charges are imposed on the purchaser and a number imposed on the seller. Some of the charges relate to the costs of preparing and filing the basic documents in the public land records. Others relate to items required by the lender, such as an appraisal, a credit report, loan origination fees, points, and other charges. Still others relate to the costs of obtaining title assurance and a survey. These charges may add up to a substantial amount.

At first glance, the allocation of certain charges to the purchaser and others to the seller appears arbitrary. But a careful reading of the contract usually reveals that it allocates most of the costs to one party or the other. The line between custom and contract in this connection is rather blurred because of the widespread use of standard form contracts. Theoretically, the purchaser or seller can include provisions shifting costs to the other party. But this rarely happens because it must be done at the time the original contract is prepared, and the preparer (whether broker or lawyer) may be reluctant to change the customary allocation of costs. After all, the amounts are usually relatively small compared to the purchase price of the house, and an attempt to shift them may create controversy or even make the contract unacceptable to the seller.

It is important to recognize that practices with respect to the allocation of closing costs vary widely. For example, it is the custom in some areas for title insurance to be a charge to the seller on the theory that the seller should provide acceptable proof of title. In other places, it is customary for the purchaser to pay for title insurance on the theory that it is part of the cost of obtaining the loan. On the other hand, in most communities it is common to prorate taxes according to the number of days of the year that purchaser and seller will each have owned the house. Because property taxes are usually paid at the end of the tax year, this payment will usually run from seller to purchaser.

## §3.10  Title Insurance

Documents relating to interests in land are binding on third persons only if publicly filed and recorded in the land records of the county or other local government unit. Public land records are usually filed in the order in which they are received, and the filing office usually maintains **grantor-grantee** and **grantee-grantor** indexes. Unfortunately, it is virtually impossible to find out the status of the title to a piece of real estate using records in this form unless the records have been computerized. Instead, in these states **title companies** or **abstract companies** maintain summaries of the same records organized on a much more useful tract index basis. In smaller communities, a leading real estate lawyer may also own and operate a title company. To obtain a current and accurate picture of the title of a tract without incurring excessive search costs, one must use the services of a title company that updates its records daily to reflect all documents filed in the public land records. In most communities **title insurance** is provided (**written**) by private companies that assume the risk that there may be a defect in (**cloud on**) the title to a property. In many rural communities, the older practice of providing title assurance through a legal opinion prepared by an attorney still flourishes, while in a few urban areas governmental title registration plans have been adopted.

In most areas today, title insurance is written by these specialized companies that maintain tract indexes. (Companies involved in writing life or casualty insurance usually are not involved in title insurance.) Title insurance is an unusual type of insurance. First, there is only a single premium, and a title insurance policy written on behalf of an owner theoretically remains outstanding forever to protect against claims asserted by others. It is more similar to an indemnification agreement than to an insurance policy. Second, title insurance companies generally do not take known risks. If the title search shows that a risk exists, the company will exclude that risk from the coverage of the policy. If a title search reveals a trivial potential defect (**flyspeck**), the company is nevertheless likely to include an express exception. It is in the interest of both the purchaser and the lender to persuade a title company to eliminate as many exceptions of this nature as possible. It is sometimes possible to do this by arguing, for example, that the excepted defect was cured by the statute of limitations or that an exception for an unconveyed dower interest arising from a marriage that took place in 1912 is unlikely to be a real defect today simply because of the passage of time. A third unusual aspect of title insurance is that the premium is based solely on the purchase price of the property and is not dependent on problems with the title. A major problem in the title will be excepted from the coverage if it is known, though a title company will decline to issue a policy at all if it concludes that the potential seller probably does not have title to the property.

Title insurance does protect against forged deeds, misfiled deeds, and the like. As a practical matter, however, these risks are not significant, though occasionally one hears of cases where the title company is compelled to acquire land or cover losses incurred by insureds.

Before issuing a title policy, a title company sets forth the results of its title search in the form of a **binder, commitment to insure**, or **title report**. This is an important document that every purchaser should examine carefully, because title is subject to the exceptions set forth in that document. A nonlawyer may have difficulty determining whether express exceptions are important. Thus, review by a lawyer at this stage is often useful. A lawyer may also have experience dealing with the title company in removing relatively minor exceptions. If a substantial defect appears, the purchaser may reject the title and refuse to complete the transaction on the ground that the title is not marketable. Even if the defect is trivial, it may be unwise to ignore it, because the same defect will reappear when the purchaser tries to resell the property in the future, and the new purchaser may take a less charitable attitude toward the problem and reject the title. Where a defect is trivial, the purchaser may be able to negotiate a reduction in the purchase price.

Title companies offer both a **mortgagee policy** and an **owner's policy**.

The first protects the lender to the extent of the unpaid balance of the mortgage. The second protects the purchaser both with respect to his or her equity in the property and, more importantly, against claims that may be made by the title company against the owner if a claim is made by the mortgagee. If the title company must pay the mortgagee, it has a right of **subrogation** against the owner. Subrogation means stepping into the shoes of another: The title company pays off the mortgage, takes an assignment of the mortgage note, and then sues the owner for the unpaid balance of the mortgage note as **subrogee**. The cost of the owner's policy is not great when purchased in connection with the mortgage policy, and a purchaser should always be advised to acquire an owner's policy as well as the mortgagee policy.

In a few urban communities, the practice of having local public registries maintain records on a tract-index basis may obviate the need for title companies and title insurance. In Illinois and a handful of other states, a novel method of title registration called the **Torrens System** provides for direct title registration by a governmental agency. The Torrens System does not appear to offer significant advantages over more traditional title assurance systems, and has not been widely copied. Title insurance written by large and well-financed title companies, on the other hand, does appear to provide significant advantages over the older practice of lawyer's title opinions, and the use of such insurance has grown steadily over the years.

A final word should be added about warranties of title in deeds. There are three basic types of deeds: **general warranty deeds, special warranty deeds**, and **quitclaim deeds**. The first, as its name implies, includes a general warranty by the seller that title is valid as against the world. The second warrants title as against any act of the seller but does not warrant good title against the world. The third simply conveys whatever title the seller possesses without any warranty of any kind. These title warranties may serve as a basis for litigation by the grantee against the grantor if there is a title defect. (This is an additional reason to insist that purchasers acquire an owner's title policy, which insures against such warranty claims made by a subsequent purchaser as well.)

The type of warranty deed to be tendered at the closing of a routine real estate transaction is a matter of **custom in the community**. In most areas, general warranty deeds are the custom. If a seller refuses to give the customary type of deed used in the community, that is a powerful warning that there is some title defect somewhere. In particular, if a seller is willing to give only a quitclaim deed in a community in which warranty deeds are customary, that is almost a guarantee that there is something fundamentally wrong with the title to the property.

In addition to title insurance, lenders usually require a survey of the property as a condition for making the loan. This typically modest cost is usually allocated to the purchaser. Even where a current survey is not required by the lender, lawyers often recommend that the purchaser obtain a new survey for his or her own protection. If it should turn out that the fence at the back of the lot was put up after the last survey and is six inches onto the neighbor's land, the purchaser typically has no recourse. Title warranties and title policies are based on whatever state of facts an accurate survey would show.

## §3.11 Points

A **point** (or **discount point**) is a charge equal to 1 percent of the loan amount. For example, a lender who charges 3 points on a $100,000 loan is paid a $3,000 fee at closing. Originally, points were charged to the borrower in order to keep real estate loans from exceeding state **usury laws** or to keep the stated interest rate in line with other published rates. So, if a purchaser of real estate borrows $100,000 at 11 percent for 30 years but then is immediately required to pay 3 points (or $3,000) back to the lender at closing, the borrower is really borrowing only $97,000, but is paying back $100,000 on the regular amortization schedule for that amount. The effect of charging three points on this loan is to increase the effective interest rate on the $97,000 actually borrowed from the quoted 11 percent figure to 11.38 percent without calling attention to it. A similar practice in the business world is for a bank to require a corporate borrower to maintain a **compensating balance** in an non-interest-bearing account. The borrower pays interest on the funds but does not have their use, while the bank is free to relend the funds and earn additional interest.

The economic effect of charging points against the borrower is so obvious that the federal government in its guaranteed loan programs generally prohibits the evasion of maximum ceiling rates on interest by charging points. But both the VA and the Department of Housing and Urban Development (**HUD**) generally permit points to be charged against the *seller* on the theory that this does not increase the borrowing cost to the purchaser. Nevertheless, the probable effect of charging the seller points is to cause sellers to increase the price of the property. If so, points charged against the seller are indirectly paid by the purchaser over the lifetime of the loan through larger payments.

The practice of charging points is practically universal today in both commercial and residential real estate transactions. It is usually possible to avoid paying points, however, by agreeing to a slightly higher interest rate. It makes particular sense to do this if one does not expect to live in the house for the entire term of the loan. Moreover, although points may be deducted as interest for income tax purposes at the time they are paid if the loan is in connection with a purchase of a home, the points may only be deducted over the life of the loan if the loan is a refinancing. Thus, it may take as long as 30 years to get the full tax benefit of an up-front payment. Many additional fees that may not be described as points are economically equivalent to points if they are received by the lender and do not reflect the actual cost of providing services. For example, many lenders charge a 1 percent **loan origination fee** in addition to other direct charges.

## §3.12 Insurance and Taxes

For reasons discussed earlier, lenders who make residential real estate loans rely on the value of the property as security. Thus, lenders must assure themselves that real estate taxes are paid when due and that property insurance against various forms of physical damage is kept up. Taxes and insurance may be a significant expense. To ensure that these bills are paid when due, lenders usually require the purchaser to pay an additional monthly amount to cover the estimated cost of insurance and taxes. These amounts are held **in escrow** by the lender and disbursed directly to the insurer and the taxing authorities when due.

The internal treatment of these escrow funds varies from area to area (and in several states the issue whether interest must be paid on escrowed funds has been the subject of litigation). In some areas, lenders collect escrow payments, but do not pay interest on them. Because a lender may have hundreds or thousands of mortgages outstanding, the amount of interest-free money may be quite substantial and provides a significant additional return to the lender who invests these funds until they are needed. If it is possible to negotiate with the lender, one may be able to eliminate the tax and insurance escrows completely or to work out an arrangement by which escrow payments earn interest. On the other hand, the handling of these escrowed funds and paying taxes and insurance involves a cost to the lender (though this cost is probably far less than the amount earned on these funds) and in a sense is a convenience to the borrower. Moreover, if the escrow account is too small to pay taxes or insurance, the lender will often advance the necessary funds to make up the shortfall in which case the borrower effectively enjoys the interest on the difference. In some cases, excess escrow payments are treated as reducing the principal of the mortgage, and payments of taxes or insurance premiums as increasing the mortgage. In effect, interest is being paid on escrow funds at the mortgage rate.

The monthly payment needed to amortize the borrowed amount is referred to as the **PI (principal and interest)** payment. The full payment including tax and insurance escrows is referred to as the **PITI** payment. When monthly mortgage costs are discussed with prospective purchasers, the PI amount is usually quoted because the TI portion of the payment is unknown. Some naive purchasers have relied on a PI quotation as the monthly cost of a mortgage and later discovered to their dismay that PITI is considerably larger than PI.

## §3.13 The Market for Residential Real Estate Loans

Before the 1980s, banks and S&Ls usually held mortgage loans as permanent investments. In common parlance, they retained the mortgages in their own **portfolio** as **portfolio loans**. This practice gave rise to a series of crises in real estate lending in the 1970s and 1980s when interest rates rose sharply and S&Ls suffered massive withdrawals by depositors who found that they could invest their money elsewhere at high rates of return (a phenomenon known as **disintermediation**). The S&Ls had committed a classic banking error: borrowing short and lending long. When a bank receives a deposit it is in effect borrowing from depositors to whom it pays interest. Thus as far as a bank is concerned, a deposit is a liability, and a loan is an asset. During the early 1980s, many banks that found themselves short of deposits actually *bought* deposits by (for example) arranging with a brokerage house to sell high yield certificates of deposit to distant investors. In many cases, the banks defaulted on these instruments, which in turn placed a strain on the **Federal Deposit**

**Insurance Corporation (FDIC)** and called into question the wisdom of deposit insurance generally.

Disintermediation also led to adjustable rate mortgages and other new financing devices described earlier in this chapter. It also led to the deregulation of S&Ls and arguably to the S&L crisis of the early 1990s, because many S&Ls abused their new found freedom and invested in risky commercial ventures.

Disintermediation also led to the creation of an entirely new financial network: the mortgage trading business. It is uncommon today for a bank to hold in its portfolio the mortgages it creates. Rather, a bank creates a mortgage, retains a small fee, and immediately frees up its capital to make additional loans. Its mortgages are combined with many others and then split up and reformed into new types of securities known generally as **collateralized mortgage obligations (CMOs)**. The purchasers of CMOs are typically institutional investors (such as insurance companies and pension funds) that have immense pools of cash to invest. To them, CMOs are attractive because the risks of default are low and the return is higher than can be obtained from other traditional debt securities.

This process is administered primarily by two quasi-governmental agencies, the **Federal National Mortgage Association (FNMA** or **Fannie Mae)** and the **Federal Home Loan Mortgage Corporation (FHLMC** or **Freddie Mac)**. These agencies buy vast amounts of home mortgage loans, combine them into standardized pools, and resell interests in the pools to institutional investors who are thus relieved from scrutinizing the credit-worthiness of individual mortgages that form part of the pool. These investors own interests in real estate mortgages without ever knowing whose mortgages are involved. Similarly, the homeowner whose mortgage loan is resold into this massive secondary market may never know that the loan is not owned by the friendly local bank or S&L.

In addition to Fannie Mae and Freddie Mac, the **Government National Mortgage Association (GNMA** or **Ginnie Mae)** issues securities based on pools of VA and FHA guaranteed mortgages. (The original name of Ginnie Mae was simply the National Mortgage Association but the name was changed because of the nickname that ensued.) A similar organization, the **Student Loan Marketing Association** or **Sallie Mae** packages and resells student loans.

Fannie Mae and Freddie Mac are private corporations chartered by the federal government. (Fannie Mae was originally partly owned by the federal government, but became completely private in 1968.) Nevertheless, most investors think of these corporations as agencies of the federal government. Indeed, the securities they issue are called **agency bonds** or simply **agencies** in the financial press. Indeed, Fannie Mae and Freddie Mac enjoy certain privileges that are unavailable to potential competitors. They have special tax status and a line of credit from the Treasury Department and do not register the securities they issue with the SEC. Many observers believe that FNMA and FHLMC are "too big to fail" and that the federal government will bail them out in the event of failure as it did with the S&Ls. Moreover, although the securities originally issued by Fannie Mae and Freddie Mac were simply undivided interests in the mortgage pool, the 1986 tax act permitted the creation of complex pass-through vehicles called **real estate mortgage investment conduits (REMICs)**. REMICs are exotic securities on individual parts (**tranches**) of return. For example, one might issue a bond whose return depends entirely on late payment fees. Thus, Fannie Mae and Freddie Mac have been among the most aggressive issuers of derivative securities. It is not surprising that they are controversial.

Yet another effect of the 1979-1982 interest rate spike was that many potential homeowners with relatively good incomes found themselves unwilling or unable to take on the high monthly payments required by market rates. This in turn meant that existing homeowners found it difficult to sell their homes. One alternative under such circumstances if the seller has an **assumable mortgage** is for the buyer to take over the payments on the old low-rate mortgage of the seller. (Clearly the original lender will have an interest in knowing who the new obligor is and may have retained the right to run a credit check, though the fact that the mortgage is assumable suggests that the lender probably relied more on the value of the property than on the creditworthiness of the borrower.)

One problem with mortgage assumption is that if the value of the house has increased significantly, the old mortgage may represent a relatively small percentage of the purchase price. If so, another lender might be willing to lend additional amounts on a second mortgage and have the borrower make a single payment to the new lender who in turn makes the payment to the original lender. Such an arrangement is called a **wraparound mortgage** and may roll several mortgages into a single payment.

A second alternative is for the seller to finance the transaction by receiving some amount of cash plus a note and mortgage (a **takeback mortgage**) from the buyer at a below market rate of interest. In most cases, such loans were balloon notes required to be paid in full within three to five years. A loan at less than market rate can raise thorny tax issues. Although the lender may claim that the rate is (say) 12 percent when market rates are 18 percent, the IRS may argue that the rate is actually 18 percent and the note is simply worth less than its face amount. Thus, the IRS may conclude that the lender is really receiving (in part) a deferred interest payment when the loan is paid off. The borrower may be happy with this treatment because it means higher interest deductions. In any event, the widespread use of below market rate loans in the early 1980s led to elaborate new provisions in IRC §§1271-1275 designed to define the situations in which the terms of such loans will be recast.

Although assumable mortgages were quite common before the 1980s, virtually all mortgages today contain a **due on sale** clause that not only prevents formal assumption of the mortgage but also precludes seller financing in which the seller continues to make payments under the old mortgage. Wraparound mortgages are also largely a thing of the past. Assumable mortgages would likely have disappeared on their own simply because of the interest rate spike and the concomitant advent of adjustable rate mortgages. But equally important factors are the growth of the secondary market in general and Fannie Mae and Freddie Mac in particular. These agencies have become so vital that few banks would consider making anything other than a **conforming** loan that complies with the terms required by them. A nonconforming loan simply cannot be sold. For the same reason, mortgage lenders insist on enforcing the terms of a loan to the letter. For example, a lender may waive a late fee only once during the life of a loan.

Borrowers are not necessarily worse off than they were in the days of the assumable mortgage. Aside from the fact that mortgage rates are kept low because lenders are able to diversify and minimize risk, the secondary market also makes it possible for borrowers to **refinance** with ease. For example, if interest rates are high at the time of purchase, one might opt for an ARM that carries a lower rate of interest (because the borrower does not assume the risk that rates may go up in the future). If rates thereafter go down, the borrower has the choice of keeping the ARM (the rate on which may have also gone down) or refinancing at a lower rate and paying off the higher rate loan with the proceeds. Also, if the value of the house has increased in the meantime (or if the borrower's income has increased), it may be possible to obtain a bigger loan and use the excess cash for other purposes. In the days when banks held most loans in their portfolio, they were reluctant to refinance these loans. Why give up an existing high rate loan simply because the borrower wants to make a lower payment? Indeed, it was common to impose a **prepayment penalty** to discourage borrowers from refinancing loans through another lender. Now that banks pools most of their loans, they make their money on fees rather than on interest. And the more loans they make (whether original or refinancing), the more money they make. Indeed, it has become quite unusual for lenders to impose a prepayment penalty.

Another effect of the development of a secondary market in mortgages is that borrowers do not need to shop around for a mortgage. Terms have become so standardized that a borrower can readily determine the size of a loan for which the borrower can qualify usually with a single phone call or web visit. As a result, most real estate brokers advise potential buyers to prequalify for a loan. And sellers may refuse to deal with buyers who have not done so. Thus, it has become less common, especially in a seller's market, for a seller to agree to a contract that is subject to a financing contingency.

## §3.14 Commercial Real Estate Transactions

The following sections consider real estate from the standpoint of a developer or owner. (They do not discuss the relationship of landlords and tenants or the rights and duties of tenants.) Although this discussion deals primarily with the financing of commercial real estate transactions, many of the matters discussed here also apply to commercial transactions involving the purchase and sale of whole businesses, of components or segments of businesses, of individual business assets, of controlling shares of stock in corporations, and of valuable personal property.

Commercial real estate transactions differ in several respects from residential transactions. For one, commercial transactions tend to be much larger than residential transactions, often involving large tracts of land and construction of large and expensive buildings involving millions of dollars. However, the most important difference by far is that commercial real estate generates funds on a recurring basis, usually in the form of rent from commercial or residential tenants or by the subdivision and sale of parts of the tract. Homeowners receive no such income.

Some commercial real estate investments, however, do not fit into this general pattern. For example, a person speculating in commercial real estate may purchase a tract of land and simply hold it, hoping for appreciation in value; such an investment usually has no positive cash flow until the property is sold. Or a person may buy land and build houses, apartments, or other structures, planning to resell the real estate as improved. Houses or apartment complexes built on this basis are usually referred to as built **on spec** (for "speculative" or "speculation"); the cash flow in this situation is likely to be sporadic and unpredictable. Or a business may buy or develop a commercial real estate tract to use for its own purposes—say, as its manufacturing plant or to house its own offices—thereby, it is hoped, reducing costs that the business would otherwise incur if it rented equivalent space. Such an investment does not create an identifiable cash flow, because the benefits that a business generates through the use of its own real estate are usually not segregated on the books of the business as arising specifically from the use of the commercial real estate. Rather, these benefits are viewed as part of the overall profitability of the business.

The return that a commercial real estate project generates is referred to as its **cash flow**. If the project produces more cash inflow than the cash outflow necessary to operate the project, it is said to have a positive cash flow. If disbursements exceed receipts, the project has a negative cash flow. A negative cash flow means that the cash being generated by the project is not sufficient to cover its cash needs—and that is usually bad. In some new ventures, however, a negative cash flow may be anticipated in the first few years of operation, and provision may be made for the additional capital infusions in the original planning. In other words, it is entirely possible for a good investment, one with net positive **income** over time, to have a negative cash flow for a while. The situation in which a positive cash flow is projected but does not materialize is most serious, because the investor then faces the painful and unexpected choice of making an additional unplanned capital investment or permitting the project to go into default.

Consider the following investment in a rental house. The purchase price is $120,000 to be financed with a $100,000 mortgage loan. Closing costs are estimated at $4000. Table 3-1 shows the anticipated cash flow following purchase of the property.

Table 3-2 shows how the income tax saving line of Table 3-1 is calculated. (The assumption of a 50 percent tax bracket may be somewhat high for many investors, but is close to the maximum rate that the highest bracket investors pay if one considers federal, state, and local income taxes.) Table 3-3 reconciles the entries for mortgage payments in Table 3-1 and mortgage interest in Table 3-2. Net operating income in Table 3-2 is calculated in the third line of Table 3-1. In Tables 3-1 and 3-3, "Mortgage Payments (PI)" is the monthly payment on the mortgage. ("PI" means simply principal and interest.)

Most investors are accustomed to income or profit-and-loss statements that show the earnings (or lack thereof) of a venture on an annual or monthly basis. Such statements are discussed in some detail in later chapters. The net

Table 3-1
Cash Flow

|  | Year 1 | Year 2 | Year 3 |
|---|---|---|---|
| Gross receipts | $10,260 | $10,773 | $11,312 |
| Less expenses | 2,500 | 2,625 | 2,756 |
| Net operating income (NOI) | 7,760 | 8,148 | 8,555 |
| Less mortgage payments (PI) | 11,850 | 11,850 | 11,850 |
| Cash flow before tax | (4,090) | (3,702) | (3,294) |
| Income tax saving (from Table 3-2 below) | 8,351 | 7,595 | 6,826 |
| Cash flow after tax | $ 4,261 | $ 3,893 | $ 3,532 |

Table 3-2
Calculation of Tax Saving

|  | Year 1 | Year 2 | Year 3 |
|---|---|---|---|
| Net operating income (NOI) | $ 7,760 | $ 8,148 | $ 8,555 |
| Mortgage interest | (11,501) | (11,457) | (11,407) |
| Depreciation | (12,960) | (11,880) | (10,800) |
| Net gain (loss) (NOI − interest depreciation) | (16,701) | (15,189) | (13,652) |
| Tax saving on other real estate income (50% bracket) | $ 8,351 | $ 7,595 | $ 6,826 |

Table 3-3
Mortgage Analysis

|  | Year 1 | Year 2 | Year 3 |
|---|---|---|---|
| Mortgage payments (PI) | $11,850 | $11,850 | $11,850 |
| Interest | 11,501 | 11,457 | 11,407 |
| Principal reduction | $ 349 | $ 393 | $ 443 |

cash flow statement set forth in Table 3-1 is not an income or profit-and-loss statement in the traditional sense (though the calculation of taxable income in Table 3-2 is a form of income statement). Rather, it is a cash-in and cash-out analysis that simply compares the dollars coming in with the dollars going out. The net cash flow statement differs from a profit-and-loss statement in several respects.

First, principal payments on a mortgage (the amount that each monthly payment reduces the balance due on the mortgage) reduce the cash available from the venture and therefore negatively affect the cash flow statement for that period. However, these payments do not affect the income statement, because the repayment of a loan, in the eyes of an accountant, is a reduction in a liability but not an expense of doing business. Thus, the reduction of principal of $349 in Year 1, $393 in Year 2, and $443 in Year 3 all affect the cash flow statement but not the income statement.

Second, some expense items such as **depreciation** are considered to be

55

expenses for profit-and-loss purposes, but because they do not involve any cash payments by the project, they do not affect the net cash flow statement. Depreciation may be thought of for this purpose as amounts subtracted from income in order to reflect the gradual using up of the building. It may be an expense appropriately taken into account in determining profit and loss, but it does not involve any payment of cash.

The hypothetical investment above reflects a common pattern of commercial real estate projects. It shows a loss on the income statement but a positive cash flow after taxes. An investor in a project with negative income (loss) can, for tax purposes, use the negative income on his or her federal income tax return as a tax deduction to shelter the taxable income from other real estate projects from tax. Before the 1986 tax act, such negative income could be used to shelter income of all types from tax. This led to numerous real estate investments (like that in the hypothetical) by high-income individuals to get tax deductions without additional investment, a practice that was sharply limited by the 1986 tax act.

In the hypothetical, the investment is attractive only because the income tax savings significantly exceed the negative cash flow. It assumes that the owner is consistently in the 50 percent tax bracket each year. Of course, the investor has invested $24,000 and the total after-tax cash flows from Year 1 through Year 3 do not equal that amount. However, the investor owns the property (subject to the mortgage) and should recoup all or most of this investment when the property is sold. Strictly speaking, this outflow and inflow of capital should also considered in deciding whether to make the investment.

To repeat, "cash flow" and "income" are not synonymous. Income assumes there is some matching of income and expense in an accounting sense, while cash flow is a pure checkbook concept. Any kind of cash receipt increases cash flow and any kind of cash payment decreases it.

## §3.15  The Purchase of Commercial Real Estate

The goal of a person purchasing commercial real estate differs from that of a person purchasing residential real estate. The goal in purchasing resi dential real estate is largely personal satisfaction—finding a good place to live given the constraints of the person's financial resources. In contrast, the goal of a person purchasing commercial real estate is usually purely economic, based on the hoped-for financial return in light of the required investment, and is usually (though not always) unrelated to personal considerations of taste or aesthetics.

The ability of commercial real estate to generate gross cash flows sometimes makes a **bootstrap acquisition** possible. By borrowing most of the cost of the land and improvements, the developer of the property may use the later cash flows to repay the loans and thereby pay for the land and improvements with no further personal investment. When commercial real estate is being acquired, a developer often persuades a lender to finance the project by generating estimates of the later cash flow that show that it will be sufficient to repay the loan. These estimates may be in the form of computer-generated spreadsheets or documents with titles such as **projected cash flow** or **pro forma cash pro-**

**jections**. The hypothetical cash flow pro jection set forth in the previous section might well have served to convince a lender.

Because commercial real estate loans are typically made or refused primarily on the basis of projected cash flows, analysis of these projections is usually vital to the success of a contemplated project. The question that a commercial real estate developer asks is not primarily "Is this a good project?" but rather "Can I persuade a lender to make a large loan on it?" To a very substantial extent, decisions regarding whether or not projects will go forward are made by the sources of possible financing, not by the developer itself. For this reason, the developer of commercial real estate often seeks to obtain letters of intent from potential tenants—particularly the major tenants or **anchor tenants**—in order to improve the reliability of the cash flow projections in the eyes of possible lenders. Such letters are usually not binding in a legal sense, but are indications of interest in the project.

No traditional minimum cash down payment is required for a commercial real estate project. If the cash flows are high enough, a developer may be able to persuade one or more lenders to lend 100 percent, or even more, of the acquisition and development cost of the project. Generally, it is in the interest of the developer to obtain the largest loan possible in order to make the project self-sufficient and reduce the amount of personal capital the developer must invest in the project. After all, the investor in the previous section needed to come up with $24,000 in cash. He doubtless would have preferred to invest a smaller amount. The way to do that is to get a larger mortgage. If a loan for 80 percent of the purchase price is desirable, then a 90 percent loan is usually preferable, and a 100 percent loan may be ideal from the investor's standpoint. In the 100 percent mortgage case, of course, the developer owns a project with essentially a zero capital investment. But even when a capital investment is required of the developer, if the cash flows develop as planned or, even better, if they exceed the original estimates, the developer may be able to recoup his or her original investment in a relatively brief period of time. The developer will then own a project (subject of course to the lender's interest) that may be worth millions of dollars with a zero capital investment. It is like magic— making money for oneself using other people's money. Many real estate fortunes have been made on the basis of the simple principle of borrowing as much as possible and then making the project a success.

Most lenders are concerned that the developer not get a totally free ride, and they therefore do not usually give 100 percent mortgages. On the other hand, projected cash flows from a commercial project are often sufficient to justify more than a single mortgage on the project. Junior mortgages from different sources, often called second or third mortgages depending on their priority, may permit a developer to approach or exceed 100 percent financing in specific situations even if the senior lender refuses to fund more than 70 or 80 percent of the project's anticipated cost. Because junior mortgages are risky, a junior lender may insist on receiving a percentage of the ownership as a condition of making the loan.

The fact that a developer may be able to justify loans exceeding the cost of a project illustrates that the project's real value lies in its cash flow. It is quite possible, of course, that the cash flow of a project will be less than expected and that the cost of development will be greater than the project's value. Obviously, such projects should be avoided, but anticipated cash flows must be estimated long in advance of completion of the project, and it is easy to be overly optimistic or to fail to anticipate some event that greatly reduces the anticipated cash flow. The trick to real estate development is finding projects in which the value of cash flows is greater than the cost of development and avoiding those in which the opposite is true.

Even if a lender is confident that a project's value will exceed the cost of development, however, many lenders prefer that a developer invest some equity in the project, that is, some value over and above the amount of the loans against the project. This equity investment will be lost if the project fails, and it therefore creates an incentive for the developer to make the project a success and to pay back the lender. The lender will be concerned not only about the loan it has made but also about all other loans that the developer may obtain that are secured by the project. Even though the primary lender has retained the right to be paid first in the event the project goes under, the primary lender has additional default risk foisted on it by virtue of subsequent junior loans that reduce the incentives for the developer. For this reason, loan agreements typically contain numerous covenants that are designed to restrict further borrowing as well as many other potential courses of business and that require that periodic reports about the project be sent to the lender.

The foregoing discussion assumes that the developer is personally responsible to repay the loan. In some cases, however, a lender will agree in connection with real estate loans not to hold the developer personally liable in the event of default and to look only to the property for repayment. Such a loan is called a **nonrecourse loan**. Even when the developer has a nonrecourse loan, however, the developer still has an interest in maintaining his or her reputation with lenders. If the developer walks away from an unsuccessful project, the developer will find it difficult to find favorable loans in the future. In a sense, the developer's reputation is an additional asset that has been pledged as security, though a developer may be willing to sacrifice this asset if the cost is too great or if the developer does not anticipate any future projects.

The only safe generalizations are that down payments on commercial real estate purchases usually comprise a lower percentage than that required on residential real estate purchases, that the amount of capital that a developer must invest in a commercial project is inversely dependent on the attractiveness of the cash-flow projections, and that nonrecourse financing may be available in whole or in part to commercial developers if a project is sufficiently attractive.

The possibility that the cash that a project generates may not cover the costs of the loans, leading to default, and the possible personal liability of the developer on these various mortgages, is discussed further below.

## §3.16 Permanent and Interim Loans for Real Estate Development

In many situations, a person plans to use the proceeds of a loan to construct improvements on the raw land already owned. In other instances, a single loan may cover both the acquisition of the raw land and the construction of the improvements. In this case, the lender will usually advance the land acquisition cost separately from the funds needed to construct the improvements.

Where loan proceeds are to finance construction, it is quite common for two different lenders that provide basically different services to participate in the transaction. These two lenders are usually called the **construction lender** and the **permanent lender**, respectively.

The construction lender advances funds as construction proceeds to enable the contractor to complete the construction; in advancing these funds, the construction lender relies on architects' or engineers' certificates as required by the construction loan agreement to ensure that work to date has been performed properly and that a designated stage or percentage of completion has been attained. Payments made by that lender are called **progress payments**. When the project is completed, the construction loan is usually paid off in full with the proceeds of the permanent loan. The construction lender therefore usually makes no investigation of the economics of the completed project; rather, it relies on the reputation and credit of the developer or the commitment of the permanent lender to make the permanent loan upon the project's completion.

The permanent lender in effect agrees to make the long-term loan on the property when the project is completed. In other words, the permanent lender examines the cash flow projections submitted with the loan application and determines the project's viability. It performs the functions of the lender described in the preceding sections in assessing the long-term economics of the project and the financial strength of the borrower. In the balance of this chapter, "lender" refers to the permanent lender and not the interim lender.

In some instances, the same lending institution may serve as both the interim and the permanent lender. Typically, however, such a lending institution has two staffs, one skilled in the responsibilities of an interim lender and the other skilled in the responsibilities of a permanent lender.

## §3.17  Junior Mortgages and Their Economic Equivalents

Many commercial real estate transactions involve second, third, and sometimes even more **junior mortgages**. The rights of junior mortgages in case of default are described below. This section describes why purchasing commercial real estate often involves such financing.

Many lenders are constrained by statute, regulation, or internal policy to make only **first mortgages** up to a designated LTV ratio. These first mortgage lenders are commercial banks, savings and loan associations, and other lenders subject to some degree of state or federal regulation. The usual pattern of commercial real estate financing is to obtain a first mortgage from one of these lenders. This mortgage may be a traditional fixed-interest rate, level-payment mortgage, or it may be an ARM or some other type of innovative financing. Nevertheless, it is for a long term and provides only a substantial portion of the needed financing. The difference between the amount of the mortgage and the estimated cost of the project must come either from the developer as a large capital investment or from other lending sources.

Junior mortgages usually provide most of the remaining financing needed to develop the project. The junior mortgages carry significantly greater risk of nonpayment if the project does not work out as well as the developer projects. As a result, they usually carry higher interest rates. In addition, the most risky of these mortgages may carry an equity kicker, the right of the holder to purchase a portion of the developer's interest in the project, usually at a bargain price. Two somewhat similar variations are deals (1) in which the lender receives a specified amount to be applied against the loan or as additional compensation for making the loan and (2) in which the lender shares in the increase in value upon the sale or refinancing of the project but does not participate in the cash flow.

An example might be helpful. Assume that Jones, a real estate speculator and developer, owns land that is suitable for apartment development: She bought the land two years ago for $15,000 cash and now has an independent appraisal that the current value of the land is $26,000. She plans to build a 45-unit apartment that she estimates will cost $950,000 after making due allowance for all contingencies. After discussions with lenders, Jones works out the following financing arrangements:

1. A 75 percent (of $950,000) first mortgage from a savings and loan association for 30 years at 10 percent. This first mortgage provides $712,500 of the cost.
2. A $150,000 second mortgage, from a commercial lending company engaged in speculative but not unduly risky investments, for 10 years at 14 percent, adjustable after 3 years on the basis of an index based on the average discount rate on 26-week Treasury bills as announced by the U.S. Treasury Department following sale of these securities. (Treasury bills and discount rates are discussed in a later chapter; simply assume for present purposes that this average rate is a reliable indication of market interest rates for commercial first mortgage loans.)

These two mortgages leave Jones $87,500 short of the $950,000 she needs ($950,000 − 712,500 − 150,000 = $87,500), well within striking distance. She obtains a bridge loan for this amount from a privately owned investment firm that specializes in high-risk loans. The bridge loan carries an interest rate of 16 percent, with monthly payments of interest only for three years. At the end of three years, the $87,500 of principal is due. In addition, Jones is required to give the investment firm the option to purchase a 25 percent interest in the project for $87,500 at that time. If the project is successful, the holder of the third mortgage will probably exercise its option, which will precisely cancel the principal payment due on the third mortgage. The holder thereafter will not get interest but will have a substantial equity participation in the project. If the project is not sufficiently successful, the holder of the third mortgage will not exercise its option and Jones will (1) have to come up with $87,500 cash, (2) negotiate with the holder of the third mortgage for an extension of that mortgage, or (3) suffer a default and likely foreclosure on that mortgage. If the option is not exercised, the renegotiation alternative is probably the most likely.

On the basis of the foregoing, Jones has invested $26,000 in the form of the value of the land and has borrowed $950,000 to finance the improvements. Her equity investment is therefore about 3 percent, a not unusual figure for commercial projects in real life.

Calculations will reveal that for the first three years after the completion of the project the required monthly cash flow to service the indebtedness is $9,748.35: $6,252.70 on the first mortgage, $2,329.00 on the second, and $1,166.67 on the third. This is only $216.63 per apartment. Of course, there are other items of disbursement in addition to debt service, and it is possible that if the discount rate on Treasury bills rises, the second mortgage payments may increase. If the project appears to be successful and the holder of the third mortgage exercises its option to purchase 25 percent of the project, the payments will drop to $8,581.70 per month after three years, or about $190.70 per apartment. To continue with the mathematics of this example, at the end of three years the first two mortgages will have been paid down to $699,330.48 and $124,279.50 respectively or a total of $823,610. The decision by the holder of the third mortgage whether to exercise its option must be based on an estimate of the difference between the value of the project and this indebtedness.

A complicating factor in real estate financing is that there are many different interests in land that are not formally designated as mortgages but that have the same economic effect as mortgages. For example, a person planning to develop a tract of land might sell the land to an investor for a lump sum and take back a long-term ground lease for 99 years. The lump sum that the developer receives is similar to mortgage proceeds, and the obligation to pay rent for 99 years on the ground lease is analogous to monthly payments on a mortgage. In the event of nonpayment, cancellation of the lease is analogous to foreclosure of a mortgage. (Undivided interests in the ownership of the land subject to the ground lease may even be sold to investors who participate in the yield from cash flow as well as possible appreciation in the value of the land.) The developer may thereafter place one or more conventional mortgages on his or her interest in the ground lease; these mortgages in effect are second or third mortgages (because the lease payments on the ground lease are superior to the rights of the nominal first mortgage on the interest in the leasehold).

If the property has existing improvements, the owner may be able to sell the land but not the improvements to one investor and the improvements but not the land to a second investor, in both cases taking back long-term leases. One or more conventional mortgages may then be placed on the leaseholds. Transactions in which interests are carved up among several layers or tiers of sales and leasebacks and then mixed with traditional mortgages on the developer's interests may be exceptionally complex and difficult to analyze. Indeed, it may sometimes be difficult to establish the precise priorities of various lenders.

In the following sections, the possibility that one or more layers of financing may be represented by sale and leaseback interests is ignored; for simplicity, the assumption is that only traditional mortgages are involved.

## §3.18  Default and Foreclosure

What happens when there is a **default** on a mortgage? The answer can be best developed by considering what might happen if the apartment development described above does not work out as projected.

It is important to recognize that not all defaults lead immediately to foreclosure on the property and lawsuits brought to recover missed payments. Loan instruments often provide for **grace periods** in which missed payments may be made up, often upon the payment of an additional fee or charge. In addition, legal action is expensive, and taken only as a matter of last resort. It is not uncommon for lenders to threaten foreclosure, and even post property for sale under the procedures set forth in the mortgage without completing the threatened action. As will be seen in more detail below, foreclosure may well lead to the lender purchasing the property at the foreclosure sale. What does the lender do with the property then? If the developer could not make a go of it, will the lender be able to do any better? Probably not, and it may very well do even worse. Also, a lender must worry about its own bottom line. If a lender forecloses on property that cannot be resold at a high enough price to cover the unpaid portion of the loan, the lender must recognize the difference as a loss. A troubled lender may therefore prefer to retain problem loans or noncurrent loans in its portfolio rather than closing them out by foreclosure. For these various reasons, defaults often lead to negotiation between the lenders and the developer in an effort to work out a revised schedule of payments that is realistic under the circumstances. Indeed, many lenders maintain work out groups that may try to avoid foreclosure by temporarily assuming control over a project and supervising disbursements to persons other than the lender. The final steps of foreclosure, described below, usually occur only after all these preliminary solutions prove unworkable.

An uncured default usually permits the lender to declare the entire unpaid balance due. A default on a mortgage may lead to foreclosure and ultimately public sale of the property by auction after public announcement. The procedures to be followed for sale of the property are set forth in the mortgage itself; usually no judicial order is required before the sale. The proceeds of the sale, after deduction of expenses, are applied to the mortgages in default. Two critical rules about the effect of a foreclosure of one mortgage on other mortgages are (1) a foreclosure of a junior mortgage does not affect a senior mortgage and the purchaser at the foreclosure sale takes the property subject to the senior mortgage, and (2) the sale of the property following foreclosure of a senior mortgage automatically extinguishes the liens of all junior mortgages. Thus, if Jones defaults only on the third mortgage, the rights of the first two mortgagees are unaffected, and the purchaser at the foreclosure sale takes the property subject to the prior rights of the holders of the first and second mortgages. If that purchaser fails to make the payments necessary to keep those mortgages current, another foreclosure may occur. However, if Jones defaults on the first mortgage, all junior mortgagees are in imminent danger of losing their interest in the apartment building. Thus, a default on a senior mortgage is typically also a violation of covenants in junior mortgages, so that a default on a senior mortgage usually triggers defaults on junior mortgages.

Assume that the apartment project fails to meet the cash-flow projections, and that after one year Jones does not have the necessary cash to make all three payments. Knowing that she is going into default, she does not make any further payments on any of the mortgages. At this time, the unpaid principal balances on the three mortgages are approximately as follows:

| | |
|---|---|
| First Mortgage | $708,500 |
| Second Mortgage | 142,500 |
| Third Mortgage | 87,500 |
| Total Loans | $938,500 |

Assume further that the holder of the first mortgage declares a default and that the property is put up for sale. What happens at the sale depends on the value of the property after deduction of foreclosure expenses. At the public foreclosure sale, each of the creditors and Jones herself may bid on the property. In addition, third persons hoping to find a bargain may also enter bids. If we assume that the value of the property is $950,000 (exceeding the sum total of the three mortgages of $938,500), the foreclosure of the first mortgage should lead to some spirited bidding at the sale. The holder of the first mortgage, knowing that the value of the property exceeds its interest in the property, bids the amount of the unpaid balance of the first mortgage: $708,500. If this holder bids any higher than the amount of its debt, the surplus goes not to it but to holders of the inferior mortgages or to Jones. The holder of the second mortgage bids up to $851,000 in order to protect its interest in the property. If it acquires the property, it will need to pay the first mortgagee $708,500 to pay off the first mortgage, and therefore it should bid another $142,500 to cover its own debt. If the holder of the second mortgage bids any more, the surplus goes not to it but to the holder of the third mortgage or to Jones. The holder of the third mortgage has a similar motivation to bid up to $938,500 but no more: $708,500 to pay off the first mortgage, $142,500 to pay off the second, and up to $87,500 to protect its own interest. If it bids any more, the surplus simply goes to Jones.

Because Jones has a positive equity in the property of $11,500 (the hypothetical value of the property, $950,000, minus the unpaid balances on the mortgages, $938,500), in theory she should bid on the property to preserve her equity (i.e., the difference between the mortgages and the market value of the project). Of course, if Jones could not meet the monthly payments, she probably will not be able to raise $938,500 to pay off the loans at the foreclosure sale in cash. As a result, whatever equity she has in the project is, as a practical matter, probably gone. A third person could theoretically bid $938,501 and get Jones's $11,500 equity for $1. It would be unusual, however, for someone to invest $938,501 in a problematic venture in order to secure the equity ownership of an interest worth $11,500. Where the owner's equity is larger, however, it is quite possible that a third person or the defaulting owner may be able to raise the necessary funds through a short-term loan that may be paid off when the purchaser refinances or resells the property. One thing is clear: If the owner has a substantial equity in the foreclosed property, she must scramble: If she does not, someone else—either one of the lending institutions or some opportunistic third person—will obtain a bargain at her expense.

If the hypothesized market value is only $650,000, no one other than the holder of the first mortgage will bid, because the value of the property is less than the first lien balance of $708,500. The security for the second and third mortgages as well as Jones's equity is simply gone upon the foreclosure sale. If the hypothesized market value is $750,000, the holder of the second mortgage should end up purchasing the project.

These examples are somewhat unrealistic because it is difficult to estimate the fair market value of a defaulted project. It is therefore not uncommon for bidders to make mistakes. Some things can, however, be said with confidence. Although it is theoretically possible to find bargains, in the real world secured debts usually exceed the market value for projects in foreclosure. Thus, because in the typical case there is no positive equity, the only bidders are the representatives of the lenders. After all, if there were any significant equity in the project, the owner probably could have paid on time or could find substitute financing.

Although many foreclosure sales involve bidding only by existing creditors, deciding how much to bid is not necessarily a simple matter. Assume that the property is worth $650,000 and the balance on the first lien is $708,500. How much should the first lien holder bid? The fair market value of the property, the amount of the loan, or something in between? If the lender hopes to collect the deficiency from the developer, the lender probably should bid low in order to preserve its rights against the developer. When the developer is not personally liable on the mortgage, or is insolvent, the lender is likely to bid the full amount of the mortgage. As long as the bid is less than $708,500, in one sense it does not matter if the bid is above market value because the holder of the first lien is in effect paying itself back out of the purchase price. However, estimates of fair market value are always uncertain, and the lender may wish to defer recognition of any loss on its own financial statements until the property is finally disposed of. The most likely scenario therefore is that the lender would bid precisely $708,500 even though it believes the property is worth less.

Once the holder of the first lien acquires the property, what happens to it? The new owner is unlikely to dispose of it at a fire sale price; after all it has $708,500 invested in it and does not want to take a loss. It may manage the apartment complex on its own or it may try to find someone willing to buy it for $708,500 or more. This may be practical because the new owner is itself a financial institution and may grant a new purchaser favorable financing terms (e.g., no money down or interest deferred for some period of time) in order to persuade the potential purchaser to take over the project. Favorable financing in effect lowers the price, although such sales might not always need to be recognized as losses by the lender for accounting purposes. If things do not work out, the original holder of the lien might need to foreclose again, but it is not significantly worse off than if it owns the defaulted project. And in the meantime it does not have the headache of managing an apartment complex.

As far as our developer Jones is concerned, it is possible that she may not be personally liable on the mortgages; if she is not, she can walk away from the project, sacrificing only her initial investment. If, as is more commonly the case, Jones is personally liable on the mortgages, she may be insolvent or judgment-proof. Often, if one project that a developer owns goes bad, other projects have gone bad or will do so in the near future. The developer's liabilities therefore may greatly exceed her assets. In addition, if Jones is pursued vigorously in an effort to collect from her personal assets, she may always take refuge in the federal bankruptcy courts. Further, as a practical matter, Jones is liable only for any deficiency between the realized value of the collateral (the apartment building project) and the amount of the indebtedness. Foreclosure may take several months, and suit must then be brought on the **deficiency** (the amount by which the proceeds of the sale after expenses of collection are less than the unpaid balance on the mortgage). Only then must a developer be concerned about his or her liability on the promissory notes.

## §3.19   Debt and Leverage

Developers of commercial real estate usually want to finance their projects with the largest possible loan. The use of debt may be prompted simply by the developer's lack of funds to invest in a larger equity interest. A more important reason for using debt, however, is **leverage**.

Jones's apartment building described in the preceding sections provides a clear illustration of the concept of leverage. The total cost of the apartment house, including the land contributed by Jones, is $976,000. Assume that under Jones's cash-flow projections, the apartments should rent for $400 each, and that (for simplicity) 100 percent occupancy can be expected. There are 45 units, the monthly gross revenue is $18,000, and the annual revenue is $216,000, from which operating expenses, real estate taxes, insurance, upkeep, and similar items must be deducted. Assume that Jones projects that these expenses (exclusive of mortgage loan payments) will be approximately $27,000 per year. Accepting their accuracy, however, one can investigate the cash-flow return Jones will receive on the basis of various assumptions about financing:

1. If Jones builds the project entirely with her own cash and obtains no loans at all, she will have invested a total of $976,000, from which there will be a positive annual cash flow of $189,000 per year ($216,000 gross cash flow minus $27,000 of expenses, real estate taxes, insurance, etc.). On the $976,000 that she invested, Jones will receive a return of about 19 percent on a cash-flow basis before income taxes.
2. If Jones builds the project with only the first mortgage as financing (face amount of $712,500 and monthly payments of $6,252.70), she will have invested a total of $263,500 and the expected cash flow will be reduced to $113,967.60 for a yield on each dollar that Jones invests of about 43 percent on a cash-flow basis. (The $263,500 figure is obtained by subtracting from $976,000 the amount of the first mortgage ($712,500); the $113,967.60 cash flow is obtained by taking the

$189,000 cash flow from an all-cash investment and subtracting the annual payments on the first mortgage; again no account is taken of income taxes.)

3. If Jones builds the project with both the first and second mortgages as financing, her cash investment will be reduced to $113,500 ($263,500 minus $150,000 for the second mortgage) and her annual cash flow will be reduced to $86,019.60 ($113,967.60 minus $27,948, the total annual payment on the second mortgage). Even so, this increases the yield on Jones's cash investment to 76 percent on a cash-flow basis.

4. If Jones builds the project with all three mortgages, as she originally contemplated, her cash investment is reduced to $26,000 (the fair market value of the land), and the cash flow will be reduced to $72,019. This is a 277 percent return; while Jones has a large payment coming due on the third mortgage in a couple of years, the cash flow should be ample to cover it.

Leverage reflects the fact that the more Jones borrows, the higher the percentage return is on each dollar that she has invested. In the foregoing example, every dollar invested in the project yields a cash flow of about $0.19 each year. When Jones borrows on the first mortgage, she is borrowing a dollar at an interest cost of $0.10 per year and receiving $0.19 on that dollar. The additional $0.09 is additional return on the dollars that Jones herself invests. Hence, her return on each dollar she invests is improved by each additional dollar she borrows. No wonder borrowing is attractive under such circumstances. Indeed, if Jones can obtain loans for 100 percent of her cost at an interest rate of less than 19 percent per year, she should do so; she then has a zero investment in the project and an infinite return on that investment.

The secret of leverage is that if a borrowed dollar yields a greater cash flow than the cost of borrowing it, you should borrow it. The excess is then allocable to the dollars you do invest, increasing the return, often dramatically. Leverage, in short, involves the productive use of other people's money. As we shall see, the concept of leverage applies to virtually all aspects of finance, not just real estate.

Leverage is a two-edged sword. By increasing the number of borrowed dollars working for the developer, the rate of return on the developer's equity investment may be greatly increased. As long as the per dollar return from the venture exceeds the interest cost, it appears to be sensible to borrow. On the other hand, these assertions take no account of the possibility that the developer might miscalculate and the per dollar return might be less than the interest cost. If this occurs, the leveraged transaction may be a disaster for the investor, because the fixed interest costs must still be met in any event. Indeed, most of the spectacular collapses of real estate ventures have been the result of excessive leverage and a miscalculation by the developer of the return from a venture.

In the hypothetical based on Jones's apartment complex, a number of calculations were based on optimistic cash-flow projections: rents of $400 per apartment, out-of-pocket costs of $27,000 per year, and 100 percent occupancy rates. Assume, however, that because of an unexpected economic downturn in the local economy a large surplus of apartments develops, and Jones finds that she actually has a 60 percent occupancy rate and an average rent of $360 per month per apartment. Costs other than financing, furthermore, turn out to be $3,000 per month, or a total of $36,000 per year rather than the $27,000 projected. These are dramatic shortfalls in the projections, but in real life it is not uncommon for rosy cash-flow projections to turn bleak in such a dramatic fashion. These misfortunes bring the net cash flow from the project before financing costs to $77,400 per year rather than the projected $189,000.

In the unleveraged transaction (Jones investing all $976,000 in cash) the result is extremely disappointing but not disastrous: Rather than the project showing the expected 20 percent return on a cash-flow basis, the return is a little under 8 percent. Similarly if Jones takes out the first mortgage and invests capital of $263,500, the result is again disappointing but not disastrous: The interest payments on the first mortgage consume virtually the entire cash flow, reducing it to only $2,367 per year, and Jones is receiving a cash-flow return of less than one percent on her $263,500 investment. If, however, she has "leveraged up" the project, the results become increasingly disastrous. If she takes out the first two mortgages and invests $113,500 in cash, the project has a negative cash flow after financing costs of over $25,000 per year. In other words, she has the choice of watching her $113,500 disappear without a trace or coming up with an additional $25,000 per year, with no end in sight unless the apartment rental market improves dramatically. If she takes out three mortgages involving monthly cash payments of over $9,000 per month, both she and the project are in deep trouble: The negative cash flow increases to nearly $40,000 per year. At this point, the critical question becomes whether Jones is personally liable on those three mortgages. If she is, Jones's personal wealth may well be drawn down the drain. If she is not, she can walk away from the project losing only the original land value she contributed to the project.

In the remaining chapters of this book, we will encounter the concept of leverage in a number of different guises. In many transactions involving securities, for example, a portion of the purchase price may be borrowed. Such transactions are leveraged because the investor buys (or sells) a larger amount of the security in question than he or she could without borrowing. The investor is in effect gambling that the price movement (and cash return if any) will more than offset the interest cost of the borrowing. As a result, any change in the price of the security has a correspondingly greater effect on a borrowing investor than on one who invests the same amount of capital but does not borrow in order to increase the size of the investment. Similarly, a corporation uses leverage whenever it finances expansion of its productive capacity by borrowing funds at fixed interest rates rather than by selling additional shares of common stock. There are many other examples of business transactions involving the borrowing of capital in order to improve the profitability of the transaction to equity holders.

## CHAPTER 4

# ANNUITIES AND RETIREMENT PLANS

## §4.1  Introduction

A stream of payments payable at specified intervals in the future is called an **annuity**. Annuities affect the lives of most people in the United States at some time, even though many may not even know what the word means. Annuities are an essential part of pensions and retirement plans, often supplementing social security and related public benefit programs. This chapter introduces the annuity in a logical but indirect way, dealing first with simple and somewhat artificial examples, and then progressing to retirement annuities.

Some annuities are purchased by individuals, usually from life insurance companies. If payments are of fixed amounts for a fixed period, the determination of the present values of such payments is a straightforward application of the time value of money, that is, the principle of discounting future payments to present values, applying an appropriate discount rate to each payment to determine the present value of each payment, and then adding up those present values (as explained more fully above in the chapter on present value).

Most annuities are designed not to make payments for a fixed period but rather to continue for the lifetime of one or more persons. The pricing of such annuities requires an estimate of the probable lifespans involved, which in turn involves reliance on mortality or life expectancy tables. Indeed, if the word "annuity" conjures up any image at all to the average person, it is probably one of an elderly person receiving a payment each month for the balance of his or her life. Mortality and life expectancy tables are discussed briefly in the chapter on insurance. Retirement programs often rely on commercial annuities, usually by the purchase of a lifetime annuity shortly before the employee's retirement. An annuity for the life of a person is in a sense the converse of life insurance on the life of that person: The annuity pays for the lifetime of the person and ends upon that person's death, while life insurance becomes due and payable on death and provides for the period following the death of the person.

In the discussion of commercial annuities below, the person creating the annuity is referred to as the **contributor.** The person receiving the annuity is referred to as the **annuitant;** the annuitant and the contributor can, of course, be the same person. The person or entity agreeing to make the payments is referred to as the **writer** of the annuity: As noted, many life insurance companies are also in the business of selling annuities.

## §4.2  Single-Premium Fixed Annuities

The simplest kind of annuity does not involve any mortality calculation. For example, suppose that your client, a 55-year-old widow, is considering the purchase of an annuity. For $100,000 paid to a large life insurance company, the company will agree to pay $1,200 per month each year for 10 years to her or her estate. The theory behind the 10-year provision is that in 10 years she will begin receiving retirement income from other sources: social security payments and a lifetime annuity from an employee pension plan. The 10-year annuity is thus a stopgap. There is no gambling on the death of your client in this example; payments are guaranteed for 10 years, whether or not your client is alive. If she dies within the 10 years, the payments will continue to be made to her estate, or to whomever she directs in her will, for the balance of the 10-year term. At the end of ten years, the obligation of the writer of the annuity ends.

It should be obvious in this example that each monthly payment that your client receives consists partly of return of her principal and partly of interest earned on the balance of the money. Without taking into account the time value of money, it appears that she is investing $100,000 and receiving back a total of $144,000 ($1,200 per month times 120 months). The reason that this is economical from the standpoint of the life insurance company is that each month it is earning interest on that portion of the $100,000 that it has not yet repaid to your client. In other words, each payment except for the last has an interest component as well as a return of principal component. A computation (difficult with pencil and paper but easy with a calculator) reveals that your client is actually receiving a 7.75 percent return on her $100,000 investment over 10 years. In other words, the sum of the present values of the 120 payments of $1,200 each computed at 7.75 percent is almost precisely $100,000. Mathematically, at 7.75 percent, the first monthly payment of $1,200 (the first annuity payment) constitutes $645.83 of interest on the $100,000 and $554.17 return of principal. The second payment consists of $642.25 of interest (one month's interest on $99,445.83 ($100,000 − $554.17)) and $557.75 return of principal; the third payment consists of $638.65 of interest (one month's interest on $98,888.08 ($99,445.83 − $557.75)) and $561.35 of principal.

And so on, for each of the remaining payments until the last $1,200 payment, which consists almost entirely of principal and finally exhausts the original $100,000 of principal. In each month, the remaining principal is calculated by subtracting the amount of principal repaid the previous month. (If these figures look vaguely familiar, compare the analysis of the conventional level-premium mortgage in the chapter on real estate. From the mortgagee's perspective, an "annuity" is being received from the mortgagor.)

If the current market rate for riskless investments is 9 percent at the time of the proposed purchase, this annuity at first glance does not appear to be a very attractive deal. Your client would apparently be better off simply investing the money in a federally insured bank account at the higher market interest rate of 9 percent, and withdrawing each month the accumulated interest and a portion of principal necessary to yield her $1,200 per month, a do-it-yourself annuity. The economic difference between the life insurance company's product and the do-it-yourself annuity can be made graphic by considering the composition of the first few payments. If the same amount were invested at 9 percent, the first month's interest would have been $750, and only $450 would have had to be drawn from principal to make the $1,200 payment. The life insurance company only gave your client credit for interest of $645.83 and repaid her $554.17 from her principal. At 9 percent, the interest for the second month would be $746.63 and the amount of principal that would have to be drawn out would be $453.38. Corresponding figures for the life insurance company annuity are $642.25 of principal and $557.75 of interest. In each month thereafter the performance of the do-it-yourself annuity is superior, reflecting the fact that the dollars are invested at a 9 percent annual rate rather than at a 7.75 percent annual rate. At the end of the 10-year pay-out period, the bank account would still have $12,918 in it, while the commercial annuity would have been exhausted.

Why might a person be interested in buying a commercial annuity at apparently disadvantageous terms rather than simply investing the money in a bank? There are several possible advantages. For one thing, it is more convenient simply to receive a check each month, rather than to visit the bank and withdraw $1,200. There is also the matter of self-discipline. Does your client have the mental resolve to follow the routine each month without taking out "a little extra, just this time"? Third, an elderly person with a large bank account may be defrauded by a smooth-talking swindler; investment of funds in an annuity provides protection to the annuitant against such unwise dissipations of assets. These factors may not appear to be of great importance in this simple example, but in individual cases they may well justify the decision to purchase a commercial annuity rather than to simply turn over a large sum of money to someone who must rely on that sum over a long period of time to provide his or her livelihood. In other words, an annuity can be rather like a spendthrift trust.

A much more substantial advantage of the life insurance company annuity from the standpoint of your client is that the return of 7.75 percent is guaranteed for the next 10 years. Someone opening the bank account implicitly assumes that the 9 percent market rate will remain stable for that period. If the market rate of interest were to drop to 6 percent a year after the annuity arrangement was created, your client would have been considerably worse off electing to "do-it-herself." Correspondingly, if interest rates go up, the life insurance company gets fat from investing your client's funds at (say) 15 percent while continuing to make fixed payments at a rate of 7.75 percent. It obviously suffers if interest rates drop and the insurance company earns 5 percent on invested funds while being required to pay your client 7.75 percent. In effect, the insurance company takes the risk of market fluctuations in the interest rate. The company is able to do this profitably because it can diversify against this risk. It enters into many different arrangements and many different investments of varying maturities and varying yields at different times. It probably would be difficult or impossible for your client to find a riskless 10-year investment that would be guaranteed to continue to pay 9 percent and would also permit monthly withdrawals. The insurance company provides an important service in packaging the investment to meet your client's needs.

A countervailing factor is the possibility of insolvency. The do-it-yourself annuity is invested in insured savings accounts, but the right of your client to receive payments from the insurance company under the commercial annuity is not secured in any way and is dependent on the continued solvency of the insurance company. This may seem to be theoretical because life insurance companies rarely go under, but major companies writing single-premium annuities have been known to become insolvent after promising annuity payments at higher interest rates than could be maintained. On the other hand, banks and thrifts also become insolvent, and although funds on deposit are typically insured, interest payments are not.

A second countervailing factor to consider is the possibility that your client may become ill and need a significant portion of her principal back immediately rather than in bits of $1,200 per month. This, of course, is not a problem with the do-it-yourself annuity. Most commercial single-premium annuities, however, allow cancellation of the annuity and a refund of most of the remaining unpaid principal. Although cancellation may entail a significant penalty, it at least permits most financial emergencies to be met.

On balance, it appears that a fixed-return annuity can provide a considerable amount of convenience and security at the cost of some loss of yield. One way of looking at this transaction is that for a premium of 1.25 percent, the insurance company is assuming the administrative costs of handling the transaction as well as the risk that interest rates may decline during the next 10 years. There are other arrangements that may be close substitutes for annuities. For example, one might consider creating a trust that would invest and disburse the $100,000. The relatively small amount involved, and the attendant fees probably would make this alternative unattractive.

Moreover, insurance companies are able to pay higher rates of return on annuities because they contain an insurance component. That is, the agreed return is paid only to those who survive until the time of each payment. Because some number of people who buy annuities can be expected to die prematurely, the returns that would have been paid to those who die can in effect be transferred to those who survive. This is not to say that annuities are a bad deal. Indeed, they may be a very good deal particularly if you are a survivor. The fact that an annuity diverts the returns of those who die to those who survive explains the favorable rates paid on them.

## §4.3  Single-Premium Deferred Annuities

The example set forth in the preceding section involved payments to the annuitant commencing immediately upon purchase of the annuity. It is also possible, however, to purchase a single-premium annuity that does not begin to make payments to the annuitant for a period of years.

Assume that a contributor makes a single, lump-sum payment of $100,000 when he is 35 years old for an annuity commencing at age 65. The contributor may be seeking to fund or supplement retirement by making a long-term investment. Traditionally, most annuities of this type provided a fixed-dollar return beginning at the age of 65. In other words, both the interest rate being paid on the $100,000 contribution over the 30 years before the first payment comes due and the interest rate that determines the amount of the annuity to be paid each month thereafter were set forth in the original contract. Nowadays, it is more typical for a series of elections to be provided so that before the annuitant reaches the age at which the first payment is due to be made, the annuitant may select a payment option. Typical options are payments for the balance of the contributor's life, for the lives of the contributor and his or her spouse, or for the contributor's life with a guaranteed period of payments in the event the contributor dies shortly after retirement.

The growth that naturally occurs over the 30-year period between the time the annuity is purchased and the time the first payment is due is called the buildup. Mathematically, the buildup over 30 years on $100,000 is very substantial: If the insurance company agrees to pay 4 percent per year, the amount available at age 65 would be $331,349.80; at 6 percent, it is $602,257.22; and at 8 percent, $1,093,572.96. Thus, if the contributor can afford to put aside a substantial sum at a relatively young age, there is quite a pot at the end of the rainbow.

Thirty years is, of course, a long time. A similar investment over 10 years shows results that are not as spectacular, but are still substantial. A $100,000 investment made at age 55 with payments to begin in ten years grows to $149,083.27 at 4 percent; to $181,939.67 at 6 percent; and to $221,964.02, at 8 percent.

## §4.4  The Concept of Tax Deferral

If our hypothetical 35-year-old contributor were to try to create a do-it-yourself annuity, he might open a savings account and deposit $100,000 in it, planning to allow it to accumulate for 30 years. However, he would be required to pay income taxes each year on the interest earned on that account, whether or not any amount was withdrawn. Assuming that the depositor was in the 28 percent bracket, the interest income each year would need to be reduced by 28 percent when evaluating the do-it-yourself annuity. As a practical matter, if the depositor created a do-it-yourself annuity, it is likely that he would not actually reduce the account by the 28 percent tax but would simply pay the taxes out of other earnings or other assets, allowing the account to grow unconstrained. However, it should be obvious that from a total net worth standpoint, these tax payments must be viewed as part of the cost of the do-it-yourself alternative.

In the case of the commercial annuity, no income tax is due from the contributor on the interest on the $100,000 until the annuitant actually begins to receive payments at age 65. In other words, a **deferred annuity** offers **tax deferral**, whereas the savings account does not. Because of the 28 percent tax rate differential, an 8 percent do-it-yourself deferred annuity accumulates at about the same rate as a 6 percent commercial deferred annuity. This advantage, however, is not permanent. The tax deferral under the annuity continues only during the period of the buildup. Once payments on the annuity commence, a significant portion of each payment becomes subject to income tax. On the other hand, the person creating the do-it-yourself annuity has been paying taxes all along, and a much smaller proportion of each subsequent payment will be subject to tax.

The underlying concept of tax deferral (which applies to many different kinds of transactions) does not mean that the 30 years of buildup escapes tax forever. Tax is merely put off until the time the contributor receives his or her first payment under the annuity after reaching the age of 65. At that time, taxation of the buildup begins. Each payment under the annuity is viewed as having two different components: Part of the payment is a refund of a portion of the $100,000 contribution that the contributor makes and part of the payment represents a distribution from the buildup. The first portion of each payment is viewed as a tax-free return of capital and the second portion is taxed as ordinary income. The ratio is called the exclusion ratio and the Internal Revenue Code and the regulations issued thereunder contain precise rules for calculating it. That ratio, however, is calculated only once at the time of the first payment and is thereafter applied to each payment. Assuming that the exclusion ratio is properly computed, that all the contemplated payments are made as scheduled, that the annuity is for the lifetime of the contributor, and that the contributor lives precisely to his or her life expectancy, then the annuitant ultimately pays income taxes on every dollar of the buildup.

The advantages of tax deferral lie in part in the time value of money. When tax deferral is available, the contributor has the use of the funds otherwise needed to pay taxes in order to earn additional interest for an extended period. A dollar today is always worth more than a dollar in the future. A dollar not paid in tax today is worth more than the same dollar paid in tax in 30 years. For this reason alone, tax deferral is almost always advantageous. Furthermore, because the tax deferral in an annuity usually extends over several years, the buildup occurs at an accelerated rate because subsequent earnings on prior years' tax deferrals are also tax deferred. Tax deferral offers other possible advantages as well. For example, tax rates may be lower by the time the tax payments begin than they were during the buildup. Another possible advantage is that after retirement, persons may be in a lower tax bracket than they were when employed, and thus the deferral may again result in the application of lower tax rates.

There is nothing inherent in the concept of an annuity that requires it to be tax-deferred. Indeed there are many investments such as zero-coupon bonds that pay no return until maturity but that nonetheless generate taxable income during their life. Although the favored tax-deferral treatment of annuities is usually justified as a way to encourage private savings and private arrangements to provide retirement income, there are many other investment vehicles that could be made tax deferred for the same reason. Thus, the favored treatment of annuities may be more a reflection of the influence of the insurance industry in Congress than anything else.

## §4.5 Variable Annuities

Fixed-rate annuities lost much of their attractiveness during the period of high interest rates in the late 1970s and early 1980s. Even with the advantage of tax deferral, an investment yielding perhaps 4 percent per year is unattractive when compared with riskless market investments yielding 12 or 14 percent per year, as was the case in the early 1980s. A person who has invested in such a fixed annuity will naturally seek to suspend or terminate the annuity in order to invest the remaining proceeds at the higher market interest rate. Moreover, the relatively high level of inflation during this period made fixed-rate annuities extremely unattractive. The contributor had made a payment with, say, 1965 dollars but received an annuity in deflated dollars starting in 1995. These two problems are related because higher inflation levels tend to cause higher interest rates. Together they make any long-term fixed-payment investment relatively unattractive.

There is no inherent reason why one must gamble on interest and inflation rates. The gamble arises from the decision to calculate interest at a fixed rate established in advance. Why not let the company put all payments for future annuities into an investment fund and have the amount of the ultimate annuity depend on how much the company actually earns from this fund? This proposal eliminates much of the gamble on interest rates that inevitably occurs whenever a long-term investment is made at a fixed interest rate. On the other hand, this arrangement makes retirement planning less precise, because the amount of the ultimate annuity to be paid becomes expressly dependent on the fund's investment success. Commercial annuities based on this novel but sensible approach are called **variable annuities**.

The earliest versions of variable annuities date back to the 1950s. They eliminated the fixed-return feature, but assumed that the premium would be invested in traditional fixed income investments. The "variable" feature resulted only from changes in yields of such fixed investments over the years. However, once the variable annuity concept was recognized, it was a relatively small additional step to relax the requirement that investments be in long-term interest-yielding investments. Any kind of investment might be appropriate for the fund. Further, it took only a series of relatively small additional steps (1) to create several different funds with different investment goals, (2) to permit contributors to designate funds, and (3) to allow for changes in the investment mix from time to time. The final step in increasing flexibility was to allow contributors to borrow back a portion of their initial contribution whenever they wanted. Now that the amount of the ultimate annuity was not fixed but was dependent on investment results, such borrowing became essentially a matter of indifference to the writer of the annuity. If the loan was never repaid, the annuity was simply reduced appropriately. If the loan was repaid, it reduced principal for the period it was outstanding, which reduced the amount of the buildup but did not affect the company's long-term obligation.

At this point, it is useful to step back and look at what the annuity has become. The power to make decisions regarding the investments to be made during the buildup period and the power to withdraw contributions makes the plan not terribly different from an income-producing bank deposit or an investment in a mutual fund. Yet tax deferral is still available. During the 1970s, the Internal Revenue Service (IRS) resisted without success the argument that such an account should be subject to deferred taxation as an annuity. As a result, earnings on variable annuities remain tax-deferred.

Of course, there are administrative costs associated with all annuities. It has been estimated that the yearly administrative costs associated with the management of a variable annuity are about two percent. In addition, heavy **surrender charges** may be applicable upon early withdrawal. These charges typically decline over time and disappear entirely after the annuity contract has been in existence for a specified period. Annuity contracts also carry insurance-related charges that reduce the earnings. In order to qualify for favorable tax treatment, an annuity must include some insurance feature. At a minimum, this means that the issuer must guarantee that all contributions will be paid back to a named beneficiary in the event the contributor dies before payout begins. The charge for this bare bones benefit is quite small, and can be as little as .005 percent per year of the market value of the investments in the account (including accumulated returns). Some companies offer more extensive insurance protection, but it is doubtful that this benefit is of much real value in that the tax-free accumulation of value in the account (which is payable to the beneficiary in any event) will usually exceed the death benefit within a few months after opening the account.

Variable annuities are often sold as tax-deferred mutual fund investments, which in some ways they resemble. There are, however, important differences: Variable annuity fees are higher, the alternative investments that are available are fewer, and one is locked in, as a practical matter, for a much longer time. Advertisements for variable annuities regularly compare the growth of a tax-deferred annuity with a taxable certificate of deposit or other fixed-income investments. This comparison is potentially misleading, because no account is taken of the deferred tax obligation on the buildup.

Because a variable annuity is an interest in a fund, there is probably little default risk in the purchase of such an investment. If the investor elects to take a lifetime annuity, the interest in the fund disappears and the continued payment of that annuity depends on the continued solvency of the insurance company.

Although fixed annuities waned in popularity during the 1980s because of extremely high interest rates, their popularity increased dramatically when interest rates declined. Many investors found that the rates of return available on these investments were higher than on investments of supposedly comparable risk—such as certificates of deposit (CDs).

It is not entirely clear that the default risk in these two products is comparable. Although the risk with an annuity may be small, it is nonetheless real. The principal on a CD, on the other hand, is typically insured—up to $100,000 per depositor per institution—by federal deposit insurance (and in practice the Federal Deposit Insurance Corporation (FDIC) has generally made good on all deposits even in excess of that amount). On the other hand, interest payments are not insured by the FDIC. Annuities are generally not insured at all, although some protections comparable to federal deposit insurance are provided at the state level when an insurer becomes insolvent. In the end, the relative safety of insurance companies, together with state-level protections, may roughly balance out with the somewhat limited scheme of deposit insurance available at banks and savings and loans.

## §4.6 Multiple-Premium Annuities

Consider the situation of a 35-year-old man who lacks the resources to make a $100,000 investment but who desires to make some provision for retirement in 30 years. Insurance companies have long offered annuity plans that are designed to meet the needs of such a person. They involve monthly payment plans under which the contributor gradually builds up a nest egg. The payments accumulate and are converted into an annuity shortly before retirement.

Perhaps this person can contribute $5,000 per year toward retirement. Traditionally, a fixed interest rate was involved, so that the amount accumulated after the 30 years of payments can be calculated mathematically. For simplicity, let us assume that each payment is made at the end of the year, that the person plans to retire at the end of the 30th year, that interest is compounded annually, and that the insurance company guarantees a 7 percent annual return. The value in 30 years of the stream of $5,000 payments is then equal to the future value of $5,000 over 30 years plus the future value of $5,000 over 29 years plus the future value of $5,000 over 28 years, and so forth. This calculation is made much simpler by tables showing the future value of annuities. To determine the amount that will be available in this example for the purchase of an annuity in 30 years, one need merely look in the 30 row and 7 percent column of Table 4-1. The number (94.4608) is simply multiplied by $5,000 to determine that the amount available for the retirement annuity will build up to $472,304 in 30 years.

Three important points should be made about the accumulation aspects of this kind of transaction. First, any kind of regular contribution made over a long period of time builds up to a large amount in absolute terms over 30 years. Whether or not this is considered advantageous, however, depends on what assumptions one makes about inflation over 30 years. If inflation remains low, a comfortable retirement may be expected; under the worst inflation sce-

## Table 4-1
### Future Value of a Stream of $1 Payments
### Made at the End of Each Period After n Periods

| No. of Periods | 2% | 3% | 4% | 5% | 6% | 7% | 8% |
|---|---|---|---|---|---|---|---|
| 1 | 1.0000 | 1.0000 | 1.0000 | 1.0000 | 1.0000 | 1.0000 | 1.0000 |
| 2 | 2.0200 | 2.0300 | 2.0400 | 2.0500 | 2.0600 | 2.0700 | 2.0800 |
| 3 | 3.0604 | 3.0909 | 3.1216 | 3.1525 | 3.1836 | 3.2149 | 3.2464 |
| 4 | 4.1216 | 4.1836 | 4.2465 | 4.3101 | 4.3746 | 4.4399 | 4.5061 |
| 5 | 5.2040 | 5.3091 | 5.4163 | 5.5256 | 5.6371 | 5.7507 | 5.8666 |
| 6 | 6.3081 | 6.4684 | 6.6330 | 6.8019 | 6.9753 | 7.1533 | 7.3359 |
| 7 | 7.4343 | 7.6625 | 7.8983 | 8.1420 | 8.3938 | 8.6540 | 8.9228 |
| 8 | 8.5830 | 8.8923 | 9.2142 | 9.5491 | 9.8975 | 10.2598 | 10.6366 |
| 9 | 9.7546 | 10.1591 | 10.5828 | 11.0266 | 11.4913 | 11.9780 | 12.4876 |
| 10 | 10.9497 | 11.4639 | 12.0061 | 12.5779 | 13.1808 | 13.8164 | 14.4866 |
| 11 | 12.1687 | 12.8078 | 13.4864 | 14.2068 | 14.9716 | 15.7836 | 16.6455 |
| 12 | 13.4121 | 14.1920 | 15.0258 | 15.9171 | 16.8699 | 17.8885 | 18.9771 |
| 13 | 14.6803 | 15.6178 | 16.6268 | 17.7130 | 18.8821 | 20.1406 | 21.4953 |
| 14 | 15.9739 | 17.0863 | 18.2919 | 19.5986 | 21.0151 | 22.5505 | 24.2149 |
| 15 | 17.2934 | 18.5989 | 20.0236 | 21.5786 | 23.2760 | 25.1290 | 27.1521 |
| 16 | 18.6393 | 20.1569 | 21.8245 | 23.6575 | 25.6725 | 27.8881 | 30.3243 |
| 17 | 20.0121 | 21.7616 | 23.6975 | 25.8404 | 28.2129 | 30.8402 | 33.7502 |
| 18 | 21.4123 | 23.4144 | 25.6454 | 28.1324 | 30.9057 | 33.9990 | 37.4502 |
| 19 | 22.8406 | 25.1169 | 27.6712 | 30.5390 | 33.7600 | 37.3790 | 41.4463 |
| 20 | 24.2974 | 26.8704 | 29.7781 | 33.0660 | 36.7856 | 40.9955 | 45.7620 |
| 21 | 25.7833 | 28.6765 | 31.9692 | 35.7193 | 39.9927 | 44.8652 | 50.4229 |
| 22 | 27.2990 | 30.5368 | 34.2480 | 38.5052 | 43.3923 | 49.0057 | 55.4568 |
| 23 | 28.8450 | 32.4529 | 36.6179 | 41.4305 | 46.9958 | 53.4361 | 60.8933 |
| 24 | 30.4219 | 34.4265 | 39.0826 | 44.5020 | 50.8156 | 58.1767 | 66.7648 |
| 25 | 32.0303 | 36.4593 | 41.6459 | 47.7271 | 54.8645 | 63.2490 | 73.1059 |
| 26 | 33.6709 | 38.5530 | 44.3117 | 51.1135 | 59.1564 | 68.6765 | 79.9544 |
| 27 | 35.3443 | 40.7096 | 47.0842 | 54.6691 | 63.7058 | 74.4838 | 87.3508 |
| 28 | 37.0512 | 42.9309 | 49.9676 | 58.4026 | 68.5281 | 80.6977 | 95.3388 |
| 29 | 38.7922 | 45.2189 | 52.9663 | 62.3227 | 73.6398 | 87.3465 | 103.9659 |
| 30 | 40.5681 | 47.5754 | 56.0849 | 66.4388 | 79.0582 | 94.4608 | 113.2832 |
| 31 | 42.3794 | 50.0027 | 59.3283 | 70.7608 | 84.8017 | 102.0730 | 123.3459 |
| 32 | 44.2270 | 52.5028 | 62.7015 | 75.2988 | 90.8898 | 110.2182 | 134.2135 |
| 33 | 46.1116 | 55.0778 | 66.2095 | 80.0638 | 97.3432 | 118.9334 | 145.9506 |
| 34 | 48.0338 | 57.7302 | 69.8579 | 85.0670 | 104.1838 | 128.2588 | 158.6267 |
| 35 | 49.9945 | 60.4621 | 73.6522 | 90.3203 | 111.4348 | 138.2369 | 172.3168 |
| 36 | 51.9944 | 63.2759 | 77.5983 | 95.8363 | 119.1209 | 148.9135 | 187.1021 |
| 37 | 54.0343 | 66.1742 | 81.7022 | 101.6281 | 127.2681 | 160.3374 | 203.0703 |
| 38 | 56.1149 | 69.1594 | 85.9703 | 107.7095 | 135.9042 | 172.5610 | 220.3159 |
| 39 | 58.2372 | 72.2342 | 90.4091 | 114.0950 | 145.0585 | 185.6403 | 238.9412 |
| 40 | 60.4020 | 75.4013 | 95.0255 | 120.7998 | 154.7620 | 199.6351 | 259.0565 |
| 41 | 62.6100 | 78.6633 | 99.8265 | 127.8398 | 165.0477 | 214.6096 | 280.7810 |
| 42 | 64.8622 | 82.0232 | 104.8196 | 135.2318 | 175.9505 | 230.6322 | 304.2435 |
| 43 | 67.1595 | 85.4839 | 110.0124 | 142.9933 | 187.5076 | 247.7765 | 329.5830 |
| 44 | 69.5027 | 89.0484 | 115.4129 | 151.1430 | 199.7580 | 266.1209 | 356.9496 |
| 45 | 71.8927 | 92.7199 | 121.0294 | 159.7002 | 212.7435 | 285.7493 | 386.5056 |
| 46 | 74.3306 | 96.5015 | 126.8706 | 168.6852 | 226.5081 | 306.7518 | 418.4261 |
| 47 | 76.8172 | 100.3965 | 132.9454 | 178.1194 | 241.0986 | 329.2244 | 452.9002 |
| 48 | 79.3535 | 104.4084 | 139.2632 | 188.0254 | 256.5645 | 353.2701 | 490.1322 |
| 49 | 81.9406 | 108.5406 | 145.8337 | 198.4267 | 272.9584 | 378.9990 | 530.3427 |
| 50 | 84.5794 | 112.7969 | 152.6671 | 209.3480 | 290.3359 | 406.5289 | 573.7702 |

Table 4-1 (*cont.*)
Future Value of a Stream of $1 Payments
Made at the End of Each Period After n Periods

| No. of Periods | 2% | 3% | 4% | 5% | 6% | 7% | 8% |
|---|---|---|---|---|---|---|---|
| 1 | 1.0000 | 1.0000 | 1.0000 | 1.0000 | 1.0000 | 1.0000 | 1.0000 |
| 2 | 2.0900 | 2.1000 | 2.1100 | 2.1200 | 2.1300 | 2.1400 | 2.1500 |
| 3 | 3.2781 | 3.3100 | 3.3421 | 3.3744 | 3.4069 | 3.4396 | 3.4725 |
| 4 | 4.5731 | 4.6410 | 4.7097 | 4.7793 | 4.8498 | 4.9211 | 4.9934 |
| 5 | 5.9847 | 6.1051 | 6.2278 | 6.3528 | 6.4803 | 6.6101 | 6.7424 |
| 6 | 7.5233 | 7.7156 | 7.9129 | 8.1152 | 8.3227 | 8.5355 | 8.7537 |
| 7 | 9.2004 | 9.4872 | 9.7833 | 10.0890 | 10.4047 | 10.7305 | 11.0668 |
| 8 | 11.0285 | 11.4359 | 11.8594 | 12.2997 | 12.7573 | 13.2328 | 13.7268 |
| 9 | 13.0210 | 13.5795 | 14.1640 | 14.7757 | 15.4157 | 16.0853 | 16.7858 |
| 10 | 15.1929 | 15.9374 | 16.7220 | 17.5487 | 18.4197 | 19.3373 | 20.3037 |
| 11 | 17.5603 | 18.5312 | 19.5614 | 20.6546 | 21.8143 | 23.0445 | 24.3493 |
| 12 | 20.1407 | 21.3834 | 22.7132 | 24.1331 | 25.6502 | 27.2707 | 29.0017 |
| 13 | 22.9534 | 24.5227 | 26.2116 | 28.0291 | 29.9847 | 32.0887 | 34.3519 |
| 14 | 26.0192 | 27.9750 | 30.0949 | 32.3926 | 34.8827 | 37.5811 | 40.5047 |
| 15 | 29.3609 | 31.7725 | 34.4054 | 37.2797 | 40.4175 | 43.8424 | 47.5804 |
| 16 | 33.0034 | 35.9497 | 39.1899 | 42.7533 | 46.6717 | 50.9804 | 55.7175 |
| 17 | 36.9737 | 40.5447 | 44.5008 | 48.8837 | 53.7391 | 59.1176 | 65.0751 |
| 18 | 41.3013 | 45.5992 | 50.3959 | 55.7497 | 61.7251 | 68.3941 | 75.8364 |
| 19 | 46.0185 | 51.1591 | 56.9395 | 63.4397 | 70.7494 | 78.9692 | 88.2118 |
| 20 | 51.1601 | 57.2750 | 64.2028 | 72.0524 | 80.9468 | 91.0249 | 102.4436 |
| 21 | 56.7645 | 64.0025 | 72.2651 | 81.6987 | 92.4699 | 104.7684 | 118.8101 |
| 22 | 62.8733 | 71.4027 | 81.2143 | 92.5026 | 105.4910 | 120.4360 | 137.6316 |
| 23 | 69.5319 | 79.5430 | 91.1479 | 104.6029 | 120.2048 | 138.2970 | 159.2764 |
| 24 | 76.7898 | 88.4973 | 102.1742 | 118.1552 | 136.8315 | 158.6586 | 184.1678 |
| 25 | 84.7009 | 98.3471 | 114.4133 | 133.3339 | 155.6196 | 181.8708 | 212.7930 |
| 26 | 93.3240 | 109.1818 | 127.9988 | 150.3339 | 176.8501 | 208.3327 | 245.7120 |
| 27 | 102.7231 | 121.0999 | 143.0786 | 169.3740 | 200.8406 | 238.4993 | 283.5688 |
| 28 | 112.9682 | 134.2099 | 159.8173 | 190.6989 | 227.9499 | 272.8892 | 327.1041 |
| 29 | 124.1354 | 148.6309 | 178.3972 | 214.5828 | 258.5834 | 312.0937 | 377.1697 |
| 30 | 136.3075 | 164.4940 | 199.0209 | 241.3327 | 293.1992 | 356.7868 | 434.7451 |
| 31 | 149.5752 | 181.9434 | 221.9132 | 271.2926 | 332.3151 | 407.7370 | 500.9569 |
| 32 | 164.0370 | 201.1378 | 247.3236 | 304.8477 | 376.5161 | 465.8202 | 577.1005 |
| 33 | 179.8003 | 222.2515 | 275.5292 | 342.4294 | 426.4632 | 532.0350 | 664.6655 |
| 34 | 196.9823 | 245.4767 | 306.8374 | 384.5210 | 482.9034 | 607.5199 | 765.3654 |
| 35 | 215.7108 | 271.0244 | 341.5896 | 431.6635 | 546.6808 | 693.5727 | 881.1702 |
| 36 | 236.1247 | 299.1268 | 380.1644 | 484.4631 | 618.7493 | 791.6729 | 1014.3457 |
| 37 | 258.3759 | 330.0395 | 422.9825 | 543.5987 | 700.1867 | 903.5071 | 1167.4975 |
| 38 | 282.6298 | 364.0434 | 470.5106 | 609.8305 | 792.2110 | 1030.9981 | 1343.6222 |
| 39 | 309.0665 | 401.4478 | 523.2667 | 684.0102 | 896.1984 | 1176.3378 | 1546.1655 |
| 40 | 337.8824 | 442.5926 | 581.8261 | 767.0914 | 1013.7042 | 1342.0251 | 1779.0903 |
| 41 | 369.2919 | 487.8518 | 646.8269 | 860.1424 | 1146.4858 | 1530.9086 | 2046.9539 |
| 42 | 403.5281 | 537.6370 | 718.9779 | 964.3595 | 1296.5289 | 1746.2358 | 2354.9969 |
| 43 | 440.8457 | 592.4007 | 799.0655 | 1081.0826 | 1466.0777 | 1991.7088 | 2709.2465 |
| 44 | 481.5218 | 652.6408 | 887.9627 | 1211.8125 | 1657.6678 | 2271.5481 | 3116.6334 |
| 45 | 525.8587 | 718.9048 | 986.6386 | 1358.2300 | 1874.1646 | 2590.5648 | 3585.1285 |
| 46 | 574.1860 | 791.7953 | 1096.1688 | 1522.2176 | 2118.8060 | 2954.2439 | 4123.8977 |
| 47 | 626.8628 | 871.9749 | 1217.7474 | 1705.8838 | 2395.2508 | 3368.8380 | 4743.4824 |
| 48 | 684.2804 | 960.1723 | 1352.6996 | 1911.5898 | 2707.6334 | 3841.4753 | 5456.0047 |
| 49 | 746.8656 | 1057.1896 | 1502.4965 | 2141.9806 | 3060.6258 | 4380.2819 | 6275.4055 |
| 50 | 815.0836 | 1163.9085 | 1668.7712 | 2400.0182 | 3459.5071 | 4994.5213 | 7217.7163 |

narios, $472,304 may be only the cost of a haircut in 30 years. Second, the interest rate that is used in the accumulation phase has an immense impact on the amount of the ultimate annuity. Third, if the buildup phase involves monthly payments and monthly compounding of interest (rather than annual payments and compounding, as in the previous hypothetical), the amount of the buildup is significantly increased.

Again, a fixed interest rate is not an essential aspect of the multiple-premium annuity. The multiple-payment annuity can readily be a variable annuity dependent on the investment results obtained through actual experience in the manner described in the previous section. Indeed, variable annuity plans usually permit contributors to make discretionary payments from time to time.

## §4.7  Retirement Plans

In the preceding example, the plan was financed with after-tax dollars. This means simply that the contributor must pay income tax and then must make the contribution to fund the annuity out of the dollars that remain. In other words, an employee who is in the 28 percent bracket must earn about $1.39 in order to make a $1 contribution to the retirement plan (and even that does not reflect other income or payroll taxes that may apply).

If the contributor's employer has created a pension or profit-sharing plan that meets the requirements of the federal **Employee Retirement Income Security Act (ERISA)** and the Internal Revenue Code (IRC), contributions may be made by the employer and the employee without being included in the employee's tax return and without affecting the deductibility of the contributions as business expenses of the employer. A plan that meets the requirements of these federal statutes is referred to as a **qualified plan**. Such a plan provides for a much greater degree of tax deferral than a plan financed with after-tax dollars, because no tax is imposed on either the contributions or the buildup until the employee retires (unless the funds are withdrawn before retirement).

Federal law imposes a number of very specific requirements on qualified retirement plans. These requirements include **vesting** (which deals with the question whether the **retirement benefits** will be paid if the employee quits before retirement) and **nondiscrimination** (which ensures that lower paid as well as higher paid employees are covered by the plan).

The justification for the significant tax benefits of qualified plans is that they provide employers with an incentive to make adequate provision for the retirement of their employees, supplementing the social security system. And, indeed, qualified retirement plans are an important source of retirement income for most working people today.

Qualified retirement plans are divided into defined benefit plans and defined contribution plans. In a **defined benefit plan**, the size of the contribution is determined on an actuarial basis to provide employees with designated benefits: An example might be a defined retirement benefit equal to 2 percent of the employee's average salary over the last 3 years of his or her employment multiplied by the number of years of employment. Thus, an employee with 30 years of service would receive a retirement benefit equal to 60 percent of his or her average 3-year preretirement salary.

A **defined contribution plan**, on the other hand, does not establish the amount to be paid by the employer on the basis of the benefits ultimately to be conferred on employees. Rather, the amount is established by reference to extrinsic information during each period, such as the employer's profits, or the actual salary paid to the employee during the period in question. For example, a defined contribution plan might provide an annual contribution by the employer equal to 7 percent of the employee's salary each year. The employee receives 100 percent of his or her salary. The employer contributes an additional 7 percent of this amount to the qualified plan and claims as a deduction for tax purposes 107 percent of the employee's salary. The 7 percent each year builds up in a fund until retirement. The amount in that fund upon retirement cannot be ascertained until retirement: Whatever the amount is, it will then be used to purchase an annuity for the life of the retired employee. The amount of that annuity is determined solely by the amount in that employee's fund.

Some qualified plans are funded by contributions defined by reference to the contributing company's profits or to the value of a specified number of shares of the company's stock. These plans are called **profit-sharing plans** or **stock bonus plans** (respectively), but in the end they are simply special types of defined contribution plans.

Somewhat confusingly, a retirement plan that is funded by the employer is called a **noncontributory plan**, whereas a plan that is funded by deductions from the employee's pay is called a **contributory plan**. Most plans are mixed in the sense that an employee in a retirement plan funded by the employer may usually elect to have some additional amount periodically withheld and added to the account.

In addition to the more traditional retirement plans discussed above, several new types of plans have emerged since 1980 that may eventually replace traditional plans altogether. These new types of plans include the **individual retirement account (IRA)**, the **Keogh plan, 401(k) plans**, and **403(b) plans**. Generally speaking, IRAs are available to employees who are not covered by a retirement plan, while Keogh plans are available to self-employed individuals, and 401(k) and 403(b) plans (which are named for the Internal Revenue Code sections authorizing them) may be set up by employers in lieu of traditional plans and may allow for employees to make additional pretax contributions up to certain limits. (The 401(k) plan is available to private sector employers, while the 403(b) plan is available to public sector employers.) IRAs may also be used on a limited basis by individuals otherwise covered by a retirement plan, but contributions are made in after-tax dollars. Such plans differ from traditional plans in that they vest immediately and therefore are not lost if the employee changes jobs.

Finally, brief mention should be made of a device that has some limited usefulness in certain family-related or tax-oriented transactions. A **private annuity** is created by the transfer of property to a person in exchange for a promise by that person to make fixed periodic payments for the life of the transferor. The rights must be unsecured and the transferor cannot be in the business of writing annuities. In other words, it is an annuity based on the credit of a private individual not in the business of writing annuities. Private annuities may offer tax benefits by deferring the taxation of the transaction.

## §4.8  Annuities for One or More Lifetimes

Most annuities are payable for the life or lives of one or more persons. They involve actuarial calculations as well as the time value of money. Actuaries calculate average life expectancies on the basis of mortality records that show numbers of persons of various ages and occupations who die each year. These records form the basis for widely used tables of life expectancies of persons of various ages that in turn form the backbone of both the life insurance industry and the annuity industry. The IRS has also published a table of life expectancies to be used for the calculation of the tax consequences of transactions involving annuities and lifetime interests.

Assume that an employee has reached the age of retirement after participating for many years in a tax-deferred noncontributory defined contribution plan and that the amount in the employee's account is $200,000. Now 67, the employee has decided to retire. He must now choose what to do with the $200,000 nest egg. The plan provides the following alternatives upon retirement:

1. Take the total accumulation in cash.
2. Elect a single life annuity payable for his life.
3. Elect a life annuity for the life of the employee with payments for 10 years guaranteed. (If he dies within 10 years, payments will continue to be made to his beneficiary.)
4. Elect a life annuity for the combined lives of the employee and his spouse. The payments are to continue while either the employee or his spouse are alive.
5. Elect a life annuity for the combined lives of the employee and his spouse with a guaranteed 10-year period.
6. Elect a life annuity for the combined lives of the employee and his spouse with a further election that if the employee dies first, (i) the annuity drops to two-thirds of the level at which it was paid while both are alive, or (ii) the annuity drops to half of the level at which it was paid while both are alive.

The election must be made before the date of retirement, and once payments have commenced, it is usually irrevocable.

Choice 1 is obvious and the simplest, though often not the most advantageous. Because the plan was noncontributory, the employee has made no contributions into the plan and the entire amount of $200,000 will be taxable to him upon the date of receipt. Moreover, if the employee elects this option, he then faces the problem of providing for himself and his spouse. There is always some risk with a do-it-yourself retirement plan that the money may run out while one or both of the beneficiaries are still alive.

Choice 2 requires knowledge of two factors: the life expectancy of a 67-year-old man and the interest rate used by the commercial insurance company in calculating the amount of a lifetime annuity for a single person of a specified age. Table 4-2 is a pre-1986 IRS table showing the expected return on an ordinary life annuity. The term **multiple** as used in the table refers to the number of years a

**Table 4-2**
**Pre-1986 Internal Revenue Code Table**
**Ordinary Life Annuities — One Life — Expected Return Multiples**

| Age | | | Age | | | Age | | |
|---|---|---|---|---|---|---|---|---|
| Male | Female | Multiple | Male | Female | Multiple | Male | Female | Multiple |
| 6 | 11 | 65.0 | 41 | 46 | 33.0 | 76 | 81 | 9.1 |
| 7 | 12 | 64.1 | 42 | 47 | 32.1 | 77 | 82 | 8.7 |
| 8 | 13 | 63.2 | 43 | 48 | 31.2 | 78 | 83 | 8.3 |
| 9 | 14 | 62.3 | 44 | 49 | 30.4 | 79 | 84 | 7.8 |
| 10 | 15 | 61.4 | 45 | 50 | 29.6 | 80 | 85 | 7.5 |
| 11 | 16 | 60.4 | 46 | 51 | 28.7 | 81 | 86 | 7.1 |
| 12 | 17 | 59.5 | 47 | 52 | 27.9 | 82 | 87 | 6.7 |
| 13 | 18 | 58.6 | 48 | 53 | 27.1 | 83 | 88 | 6.3 |
| 14 | 19 | 57.7 | 49 | 54 | 26.3 | 84 | 89 | 6.0 |
| 15 | 20 | 56.7 | 50 | 55 | 25.5 | 85 | 90 | 5.7 |
| 16 | 21 | 55.8 | 51 | 56 | 24.7 | 86 | 91 | 5.4 |
| 17 | 22 | 54.9 | 52 | 57 | 24.0 | 87 | 92 | 5.1 |
| 18 | 23 | 53.9 | 53 | 58 | 23.2 | 88 | 93 | 4.8 |
| 19 | 24 | 53.0 | 54 | 59 | 22.4 | 89 | 94 | 4.5 |
| 20 | 25 | 52.1 | 55 | 60 | 21.7 | 90 | 95 | 4.2 |
| 21 | 26 | 51.1 | 56 | 61 | 21.0 | 91 | 96 | 4.0 |
| 22 | 27 | 50.2 | 57 | 62 | 20.3 | 92 | 97 | 3.7 |
| 23 | 28 | 49.3 | 58 | 63 | 19.6 | 93 | 98 | 3.5 |
| 24 | 29 | 48.3 | 59 | 64 | 18.9 | 94 | 99 | 3.3 |
| 25 | 30 | 47.4 | 60 | 65 | 18.2 | 95 | 100 | 3.1 |
| 26 | 31 | 46.5 | 61 | 66 | 17.5 | 96 | 101 | 2.9 |
| 27 | 32 | 45.6 | 62 | 67 | 16.9 | 97 | 102 | 2.7 |
| 28 | 33 | 44.6 | 63 | 68 | 16.2 | 98 | 103 | 2.5 |
| 29 | 34 | 43.7 | 64 | 69 | 15.6 | 99 | 104 | 2.3 |
| 30 | 35 | 42.8 | 65 | 70 | 15.0 | 100 | 105 | 2.1 |
| 31 | 36 | 41.9 | 66 | 71 | 14.4 | 101 | 106 | 1.9 |
| 32 | 37 | 41.0 | 67 | 72 | 13.8 | 102 | 107 | 1.7 |
| 33 | 38 | 40.0 | 68 | 73 | 13.2 | 103 | 108 | 1.5 |
| 34 | 39 | 39.1 | 69 | 74 | 12.6 | 104 | 109 | 1.3 |
| 35 | 40 | 38.2 | 70 | 75 | 12.1 | 105 | 110 | 1.2 |
|  |  |  |  |  |  | 106 | 111 | 1.0 |
| 36 | 41 | 37.3 | 71 | 76 | 11.6 | 107 | 112 | 0.8 |
| 37 | 42 | 36.5 | 72 | 77 | 11.0 | 108 | 113 | 0.7 |
| 38 | 43 | 35.6 | 73 | 78 | 10.5 | 109 | 114 | 0.6 |
| 39 | 44 | 34.7 | 74 | 79 | 10.1 | 110 | 115 | 0.5 |
| 40 | 45 | 33.8 | 75 | 80 | 9.6 | 111 | 116 | 0.0 |

person of a given age may be expected to live on average and thus to the number of annual payments that can be expected to be made under an annuity. Table 4-2 expressly takes the sex of an annuitant as well as age into account as do most nongovernmental mortality tables. Because females live longer than males (on the average), a contribution of a fixed amount made for the benefit of a female annuitant leads to a smaller monthly payment under this table than if the same payment were made for the benefit of a male. In 1986, the IRS adopted a revised unisex table (Table 4-3) that now governs annuity calculations.

Table 4-3
1986 Internal Revenue Code Table
Ordinary Life Annuities—One Life—
Expected Return Multiples

| Age | Multiple | Age | Multiple | Age | Multiple |
|---|---|---|---|---|---|
| 5 | 76.6 | 42 | 40.6 | 79 | 10.0 |
| 6 | 75.6 | 43 | 39.6 | 80 | 9.5 |
| 7 | 74.7 | 44 | 38.7 | 81 | 8.9 |
| 8 | 73.7 | 45 | 37.7 | 82 | 8.4 |
| 9 | 72.7 | 46 | 36.8 | 83 | 7.9 |
| 10 | 71.7 | 47 | 35.9 | 84 | 7.4 |
| 11 | 70.7 | 48 | 34.9 | 85 | 6.9 |
| 12 | 69.7 | 49 | 34.0 | 86 | 6.5 |
| 13 | 68.8 | 50 | 33.1 | 87 | 6.1 |
| 14 | 67.8 | 51 | 32.2 | 88 | 5.7 |
| 15 | 66.8 | 52 | 31.3 | 89 | 5.3 |
| 16 | 65.8 | 53 | 30.4 | 90 | 5.0 |
| 17 | 64.8 | 54 | 29.5 | 91 | 4.7 |
| 18 | 63.9 | 55 | 28.6 | 92 | 4.4 |
| 19 | 62.9 | 56 | 27.7 | 93 | 4.1 |
| 20 | 61.9 | 57 | 26.8 | 94 | 3.9 |
| 21 | 60.9 | 58 | 25.9 | 95 | 3.7 |
| 22 | 59.9 | 59 | 25.0 | 96 | 3.4 |
| 23 | 59.0 | 60 | 24.2 | 97 | 3.2 |
| 24 | 58.0 | 61 | 23.3 | 98 | 3.0 |
| 25 | 57.0 | 62 | 22.5 | 99 | 2.8 |
| 26 | 56.0 | 63 | 21.6 | 100 | 2.7 |
| 27 | 55.1 | 64 | 20.8 | 101 | 2.5 |
| 28 | 54.1 | 65 | 20.0 | 102 | 2.3 |
| 29 | 53.1 | 66 | 19.2 | 103 | 2.1 |
| 30 | 52.2 | 67 | 18.4 | 104 | 1.9 |
| 31 | 51.2 | 68 | 17.6 | 105 | 1.8 |
| 32 | 50.2 | 69 | 16.8 | 106 | 1.6 |
| 33 | 49.3 | 70 | 16.0 | 107 | 1.4 |
| 34 | 48.3 | 71 | 15.3 | 108 | 1.3 |
| 35 | 47.3 | 72 | 14.6 | 109 | 1.1 |
| 36 | 46.4 | 73 | 13.9 | 110 | 1.0 |
| 37 | 45.4 | 74 | 13.2 | 111 | 0.9 |
| 38 | 44.4 | 75 | 12.5 | 112 | 0.8 |
| 39 | 43.5 | 76 | 11.9 | 113 | 0.7 |
| 40 | 42.5 | 77 | 11.2 | 114 | 0.6 |
| 41 | 41.5 | 78 | 10.6 | 115 | 0.5 |

In the present example, one may determine the life expectancy of a 67-year-old under the current IRS expected return schedule. From Table 4-3 one sees that the employee's life expectancy is an additional 18.4 years. If we assume that an interest rate of 6 percent is used, a $200,000 payment for 18.4 years yields a monthly payment of $1,495.54. It is important to recognize that the payments in this amount continue for the balance of the employee's life, no matter how long or how short that life in fact turns out to be. A particularly long-lived annuitant causes a loss to the insurance company, while one who dies tomorrow gives the company a gain. From the standpoint of the insurance company, if many annuities are written, longer-lived annuitants are balanced and cancelled out by the shorter-lived ones. In other words, the insurance company has diversified away the risk that would attend writing a single annuity. As will be seen, the concept of diversification, like time value of money and leverage, has application in many other contexts and especially in investment strategies.

Choice 3 is like Choice 2 except that payments are guaranteed for 10 years. This also involves an actuarial computation. A moment's thought should reveal that the $200,000 payment will purchase a smaller monthly payment under Choice 3 than under Choice 2. The reason is that the premature death of the annuitant under Choice 3 does not benefit the writer of the annuity as it does under Choice 2; as a result, the total obligation of the writer of the annuity is increased. In the above example, the monthly payment under Choice 3 will be approximately $1,400 per month. The $95 difference from the annuity payable under Choice 3 compensates the writer of the annuity for the possibility that the annuity must continue for a full 10 years even if the annuitant dies before then.

Choice 4 is obviously somewhat more complicated, because payments are to continue while either the annuitant or his spouse are alive. In order to ascertain the amount of the monthly payment if this choice is elected, one must know the age of the spouse as well as of the principal annuitant.

Choice 5 is a compromise between preserving current lifestyles in the immediate postretirement period and not leaving a surviving spouse in dire straits.

The selection of any of these options must take into account the peculiar needs of the retiree and spouse, their ages, their general health, other available assets, and insurance.

Retirement plans that offer a variety of lifetime annuity arrangements sometimes describe the effect of the various arrangements as a percentage of a standard benefit. A plan widely used by institutions of higher education to provide retirement benefits for faculty and administrators, for example, estimates the benefit that would be payable on the basis of a life annuity with 10-year guaranteed payments as 100 percent. If the annuitant is 65 at the age of retirement, the election of a lifetime annuity with a 20-year guaranteed payment pays 93 percent of the base annuity. A single life annuity without guaranteed payments pays 104 percent of the base annuity. An annuity for the life of both a 67-year-old husband and his 60-year-old wife, and the survivor of them, with a guaranteed 10-year payment, pays 85 percent of the base amount. These percentages are sometimes more meaningful in the eyes of a person selecting irrevocably among these bewildering choices than dollar figures based on a hypothetical example.

# CHAPTER 5
# INSURANCE

## §5.1 Introduction

This chapter deals with the subject of insurance. The bulk of the chapter is devoted to life insurance, addressing first the basic concept of life insurance, the relationships among the parties to life insurance contracts, the actuarial process, and some of the peculiar tax aspects of insurance. The last few sections of the chapter address other forms of insurance. As will be seen, life insurance companies depend on time value of money in order to offer the products they do. But they also depend on diversification of risk. Other forms of insurance, such as property and casualty insurance, automobile insurance, and health insurance, depend much less on time value of money and much more on diversification. Finally, this chapter briefly addresses the importance of insurance in business and the effect that the availability of insurance has had on legal rules.

In thinking about insurance, one should keep in mind the peculiar treatment that insurance enjoys under federal tax law. Generally speaking, one pays for insurance with taxable dollars and collects benefits tax free. This pattern is, of course, precisely the opposite of the pattern found in many of the retirement plans discussed in the last chapter. But the logic of tax law as it relates to insurance makes sense considered in isolation. Congress is generally reluctant to grant deductions, and it is thus not surprising that no deduction is allowed for insurance premiums (unless they constitute business expenses). Moreover, insurance benefits are, in many cases, merely compensation for a loss of some sort and should thus not be seen as income. The same thing is generally true with tort damages. Insurance benefits have traditionally been viewed primarily as a way of putting the insured back in his or her original position, although it is clear that many consumers use insurance as a substitute for savings. Thus, innovations such as the variable annuity have been able to offer tax-free growth of sums invested, because they grew at least partially out of the idea of insurance.

## §5.2 Life Insurance Generally

Life insurance is one of the most familiar applications of the concept of time value of money. For example, a 45-year-old might agree to pay a premium of $1,000 per year for a life insurance policy that pays $100,000 in the event of death. How can the insurance company afford to enter into such a deal? One answer is that on the average 45-year-olds live an additional 34.1 years to the age of just over 79 (see Table 5-1). Thus, assuming the insurance policy calls for level premiums over the entire life of the insured and assuming the insured continues to make these payments as required, on the average the insurance company will enjoy 34 years of receiving $1,000 per year in exchange for the obligation to pay $100,000 whenever the insured dies. Looking back at Table 4-1, one can determine the value to the insurance company of each dollar received for a given period of years into the future at a given interest rate. As it turns out, at a 6 percent interest rate, the value of one dollar per year to the insurance company will be $104.1838 at the end of 34 years, and the value of $1,000 per year will be $104,183.80. Thus, assuming that the insurance company's costs in administering the policy do not exceed $4,183.80 by the end of 34 years, the insurance company at least breaks even in the deal if it can earn 6 percent on the premiums received from the insured.

There is, however, more to insurance than simply the time value of money. The insurance company assumes a significant risk in writing the policy as described. If the insured dies at any time before the end of 34 years, the insurance company loses money. Of course, if the insured lives beyond 34 years the insurance company makes money. But insurance companies, like other businesses, are risk averse. The possibility of loss weighs more heavily in deciding whether to enter into a particular deal than does the possibility of gain. After all, if the insurance company writes only the one policy described, there is a 50-50 chance that the company will lose money on the policy.

So how does the insurance company protect itself against this risk? The answer is diversification. By selling many policies to many 45-year-olds (or indeed many people of differing ages), the insurance company can reduce and actually eliminate the risk that premium payments will be insufficient to meet the demand for benefits. For example, if the insurance company sells 1,000 policies such as the one described above, it will take in $1,000,000 in premiums in the first year. As long as fewer than ten policy holders die during the first

Table 5-1
Expectation of Life and Expected Deaths by Race, Sex, and Age: 1997

| Age (years) | Expectation of life in years | | | | | Expected deaths per 1,000 alive at specified age [1] | | | | |
| | | White | | Black | | | White | | Black | |
| | Total | Male | Female | Male | Female | Total | Male | Female | Male | Female |
|---|---|---|---|---|---|---|---|---|---|---|
| At birth | 76.5 | 74.3 | 79.9 | 67.2 | 74.7 | 7.23 | 6.67 | 5.36 | 15.49 | 12.83 |
| 1 | 76.1 | 73.8 | 79.3 | 67.2 | 74.7 | 0.55 | 0.53 | 0.45 | 1.05 | 0.80 |
| 2 | 75.1 | 72.8 | 78.4 | 66.3 | 73.8 | 0.36 | 0.36 | 0.27 | 0.69 | 0.55 |
| 3 | 74.1 | 71.9 | 77.4 | 65.3 | 72.8 | 0.29 | 0.29 | 0.23 | 0.58 | 0.39 |
| 4 | 73.2 | 70.9 | 76.4 | 64.4 | 71.8 | 0.23 | 0.23 | 0.17 | 0.39 | 0.32 |
| 5 | 72.2 | 69.9 | 75.4 | 63.4 | 70.9 | 0.21 | 0.20 | 0.16 | 0.38 | 0.33 |
| 6 | 71.2 | 68.9 | 74.4 | 62.4 | 69.9 | 0.20 | 0.19 | 0.15 | 0.35 | 0.31 |
| 7 | 70.2 | 67.9 | 73.4 | 61.4 | 68.9 | 0.19 | 0.19 | 0.14 | 0.32 | 0.29 |
| 8 | 69.2 | 66.9 | 72.4 | 60.5 | 67.9 | 0.17 | 0.17 | 0.13 | 0.28 | 0.26 |
| 9 | 68.2 | 66.0 | 71.4 | 59.5 | 66.9 | 0.15 | 0.15 | 0.12 | 0.23 | 0.24 |
| 10 | 67.2 | 65.0 | 70.5 | 58.5 | 66.0 | 0.14 | 0.13 | 0.12 | 0.18 | 0.23 |
| 11 | 66.2 | 64.0 | 69.5 | 57.5 | 65.0 | 0.14 | 0.14 | 0.12 | 0.18 | 0.22 |
| 12 | 65.3 | 63.0 | 68.5 | 56.5 | 64.0 | 0.19 | 0.20 | 0.15 | 0.28 | 0.23 |
| 13 | 64.3 | 62.0 | 67.5 | 55.5 | 63.0 | 0.28 | 0.33 | 0.20 | 0.49 | 0.27 |
| 14 | 63.3 | 61.0 | 66.5 | 54.5 | 62.0 | 0.41 | 0.50 | 0.26 | 0.79 | 0.32 |
| 15 | 62.3 | 60.0 | 65.5 | 53.6 | 61.0 | 0.55 | 0.68 | 0.34 | 1.11 | 0.38 |
| 16 | 61.3 | 59.1 | 64.5 | 52.6 | 60.1 | 0.68 | 0.85 | 0.41 | 1.40 | 0.44 |
| 17 | 60.4 | 58.1 | 63.6 | 51.7 | 59.1 | 0.78 | 0.99 | 0.46 | 1.67 | 0.50 |
| 18 | 59.4 | 57.2 | 62.6 | 50.8 | 58.1 | 0.85 | 1.07 | 0.47 | 1.92 | 0.54 |
| 19 | 58.5 | 56.3 | 61.6 | 49.9 | 57.1 | 0.89 | 1.13 | 0.46 | 2.15 | 0.59 |
| 20 | 57.5 | 55.3 | 60.7 | 49.0 | 56.2 | 0.93 | 1.18 | 0.45 | 2.41 | 0.64 |
| 21 | 56.6 | 54.4 | 59.7 | 48.1 | 55.2 | 0.98 | 1.24 | 0.45 | 2.68 | 0.70 |
| 22 | 55.6 | 53.4 | 58.7 | 47.3 | 54.3 | 1.01 | 1.28 | 0.44 | 2.87 | 0.76 |
| 23 | 54.7 | 52.5 | 57.7 | 46.4 | 53.3 | 1.01 | 1.28 | 0.45 | 2.94 | 0.83 |
| 24 | 53.8 | 51.6 | 56.8 | 45.5 | 52.3 | 1.01 | 1.26 | 0.46 | 2.92 | 0.89 |
| 25 | 52.8 | 50.6 | 55.8 | 44.7 | 51.4 | 1.00 | 1.24 | 0.47 | 2.85 | 0.96 |
| 26 | 51.9 | 49.7 | 54.8 | 43.8 | 50.4 | 0.99 | 1.22 | 0.48 | 2.81 | 1.04 |
| 27 | 50.9 | 48.8 | 53.8 | 42.9 | 49.5 | 1.00 | 1.22 | 0.50 | 2.81 | 1.11 |
| 28 | 50.0 | 47.8 | 52.9 | 42.0 | 48.5 | 1.03 | 1.26 | 0.52 | 2.85 | 1.18 |
| 29 | 49.0 | 46.9 | 51.9 | 41.1 | 47.6 | 1.08 | 1.32 | 0.56 | 2.94 | 1.26 |
| 30 | 48.1 | 45.9 | 50.9 | 40.3 | 46.7 | 1.14 | 1.39 | 0.59 | 3.04 | 1.33 |
| 31 | 47.1 | 45.0 | 49.9 | 39.4 | 45.7 | 1.19 | 1.46 | 0.63 | 3.14 | 1.41 |
| 32 | 46.2 | 44.1 | 49.0 | 38.5 | 44.8 | 1.26 | 1.53 | 0.68 | 3.27 | 1.53 |
| 33 | 45.2 | 43.1 | 48.0 | 37.6 | 43.8 | 1.33 | 1.60 | 0.73 | 3.43 | 1.68 |
| 34 | 44.3 | 42.2 | 47.0 | 36.8 | 42.9 | 1.40 | 1.68 | 0.78 | 3.62 | 1.85 |
| 35 | 43.4 | 41.3 | 46.1 | 35.9 | 42.0 | 1.49 | 1.75 | 0.84 | 3.83 | 2.04 |
| 36 | 42.4 | 40.4 | 45.1 | 35.0 | 41.1 | 1.57 | 1.83 | 0.90 | 4.06 | 2.22 |
| 37 | 41.5 | 39.4 | 44.2 | 34.2 | 40.2 | 1.67 | 1.94 | 0.97 | 4.31 | 2.40 |
| 38 | 40.5 | 38.5 | 43.2 | 33.3 | 39.3 | 1.78 | 2.06 | 1.04 | 4.60 | 2.57 |
| 39 | 39.6 | 37.6 | 42.2 | 32.5 | 38.4 | 1.92 | 2.21 | 1.13 | 4.94 | 2.75 |
| 40 | 38.7 | 36.7 | 41.3 | 31.6 | 37.5 | 2.06 | 2.38 | 1.23 | 5.29 | 2.93 |
| 41 | 37.8 | 35.8 | 40.3 | 30.8 | 36.6 | 2.22 | 2.56 | 1.34 | 5.68 | 3.14 |
| 42 | 36.9 | 34.8 | 39.4 | 30.0 | 35.7 | 2.39 | 2.76 | 1.45 | 6.15 | 3.37 |
| 43 | 35.9 | 33.9 | 38.5 | 29.1 | 34.8 | 2.57 | 2.97 | 1.57 | 6.72 | 3.64 |
| 44 | 35.0 | 33.0 | 37.5 | 28.3 | 33.9 | 2.78 | 3.19 | 1.69 | 7.38 | 3.94 |
| 45 | 34.1 | 32.1 | 36.6 | 27.5 | 33.1 | 3.00 | 3.44 | 1.83 | 8.15 | 4.29 |
| 46 | 33.2 | 31.2 | 35.6 | 26.8 | 32.2 | 3.25 | 3.72 | 2.00 | 8.97 | 4.65 |
| 47 | 32.3 | 30.4 | 34.7 | 26.0 | 31.4 | 3.52 | 4.02 | 2.19 | 9.74 | 5.02 |
| 48 | 31.5 | 29.5 | 33.8 | 25.3 | 30.5 | 3.80 | 4.35 | 2.41 | 10.40 | 5.37 |
| 49 | 30.6 | 28.6 | 32.9 | 24.5 | 29.7 | 4.11 | 4.71 | 2.67 | 10.98 | 5.73 |
| 50 | 29.7 | 27.7 | 32.0 | 23.8 | 28.8 | 4.44 | 5.12 | 2.96 | 11.61 | 6.13 |
| 51 | 28.8 | 26.9 | 31.0 | 23.1 | 28.0 | 4.82 | 5.57 | 3.27 | 12.38 | 6.61 |
| 52 | 28.0 | 26.0 | 30.1 | 22.3 | 27.2 | 5.24 | 6.05 | 3.61 | 13.25 | 7.15 |
| 53 | 27.1 | 25.2 | 29.3 | 21.6 | 26.4 | 5.71 | 6.59 | 3.96 | 14.22 | 7.73 |
| 54 | 26.3 | 24.4 | 28.4 | 20.9 | 25.6 | 6.23 | 7.19 | 4.36 | 15.26 | 8.34 |
| 55 | 25.4 | 23.5 | 27.5 | 20.3 | 24.8 | 6.85 | 7.90 | 4.82 | 16.30 | 8.96 |
| 56 | 24.6 | 22.7 | 26.6 | 19.6 | 24.0 | 7.55 | 8.74 | 5.36 | 17.40 | 9.63 |
| 57 | 23.8 | 21.9 | 25.8 | 18.9 | 23.3 | 8.33 | 9.68 | 5.95 | 18.72 | 10.42 |
| 58 | 23.0 | 21.1 | 24.9 | 18.3 | 22.5 | 9.16 | 10.68 | 6.56 | 20.34 | 11.36 |
| 59 | 22.2 | 20.3 | 24.1 | 17.6 | 21.8 | 10.05 | 11.76 | 7.20 | 22.25 | 12.46 |
| 60 | 21.4 | 19.6 | 23.2 | 17.0 | 21.0 | 11.01 | 12.91 | 7.91 | 24.43 | 13.71 |
| 61 | 20.6 | 18.8 | 22.4 | 16.4 | 20.3 | 12.08 | 14.20 | 8.71 | 26.64 | 15.00 |
| 62 | 19.9 | 18.1 | 21.6 | 15.9 | 19.6 | 13.21 | 15.65 | 9.56 | 28.53 | 16.18 |
| 63 | 19.1 | 17.4 | 20.8 | 15.3 | 18.9 | 14.39 | 17.24 | 10.45 | 29.81 | 17.10 |
| 64 | 18.4 | 16.7 | 20.0 | 14.8 | 18.2 | 15.60 | 18.94 | 11.37 | 30.63 | 17.85 |
| 65 | 17.7 | 16.0 | 19.3 | 14.2 | 17.6 | 16.79 | 20.63 | 12.29 | 31.09 | 18.42 |
| 70 | 14.3 | 12.7 | 15.5 | 11.5 | 14.3 | 25.65 | 32.00 | 19.24 | 44.61 | 28.83 |
| 75 | 11.2 | 9.9 | 12.1 | 9.3 | 11.5 | 38.43 | 47.96 | 30.21 | 62.78 | 40.68 |
| 80 | 8.5 | 7.4 | 9.1 | 7.3 | 8.9 | 59.38 | 74.08 | 49.39 | 85.45 | 58.43 |
| 85 and over | 6.3 | 5.4 | 6.6 | 5.7 | 6.7 | 1,000.00 | 1,000.00 | 1,000.00 | 1,000.00 | 1,000.00 |

[1] Based on the proportion of the cohort who are alive at the beginning of an indicated age interval who will die before reaching the end of that interval. For example, out of every 1,000 people alive and exactly 50 years old at the beginning of the period, between 4 and 5 (4.44) will die before reaching their 51st birthdays.

Source: U.S. National Center for Health Statistics, *Vital Statistics of the United States*, annual; and *National Vital Statistics Report*, Vol. 47, No. 28; and unpublished data.

year, the insurance company is ahead. In addition, the insurance company can control risk by varying the terms of the insurance contract. In the example of the 45-year-old man, the risk of death rises as he gets older while the value of premium dollars to be received in the future falls. Thus, the insurance company might try to sell a policy that lasts only for (say) five years, at which time it must be reviewed and may be renewed at a higher premium rate. Indeed, the insurance policy described in the above example would be quite unusual if it is available at all. It would be much more common for the amount of the insurance to decline or for the premiums to increase periodically, as is described more fully in the following section on term insurance.

## §5.3  The Business of Insurance

There are two types of insurance companies writing policies today: mutual companies and stock companies. A **mutual company** does not have shareholders. Its policyholders elect its board of directors, and excess earnings of the company are paid to its policyholders in the form of annual dividends. In a broad sense, the owners of a mutual life insurance company are the policyholders. One should not put too much weight on this ownership, however. Policyholders are widely scattered and unorganized and as a result have virtually no voice in how a mutual company is actually managed. Also, most policyholders are indifferent to management issues as long as their individual policies are not adversely affected. Management of a mutual company can therefore run the company with almost complete freedom from oversight by the owners, the only discipline being provided by the need to offer relatively competitive products compared with those offered by other insurance companies.

The second type of insurance company is a **stock company**. In form, it is a traditional corporation with shareholders who purchase stock in the company and who are entitled to elect the company's board of directors. Dividends in a stock company are paid to the shareholders, not to the policyholders as in a mutual company. In a stock company, policyholders are more analogous to customers of the corporation than to owners.

Policies that are entitled to share in dividends are called **participating policies**, and such policies are usually written by mutual companies. In effect, each year when the premium notice is sent, the amount of the dividend is set forth and the owner of the policy may elect to have the dividend credited against the amount of next year's premium. In mutual companies, dividends may be paid on all types of life insurance outstanding or only on specified classes or types of policies. Policies written by stock companies are usually nonparticipating, that is, they are not entitled to receive dividends. The amount of the annual premium is fixed and is not subject to reduction by a dividend. In making comparisons between various life insurance policies and the costs of similar policies issued by different companies, it is necessary to take into account whether the proposed policy is participating or nonparticipating. Although the amount of a dividend on a participating policy is apt to be rather small in contrast with the amount of a premium, it tends to be stable and reasonably predictable.

Even though a mutual company pays dividends to policyholders while stock companies pay dividends to shareholders, one should not assume that mutual companies usually offer cheaper products. Both types of companies compete vigorously for the same insurance dollar. It is not uncommon for a stock company to offer a cheaper policy even after the mutual company dividend is taken into account.

A few insurance companies offer **low load** or **low commission insurance** without the services of an insurance agent. Distribution costs of ordinary policies run 20 to 25 percent over the full life of a policy; they run 5 to 10 percent in the case of low load policies. Low load policies include universal and whole life insurance and annuity contracts. Companies offering low load policies tend to be small. It may not be easy to locate them, because life insurance agents, for obvious reasons, do not tout them.

Until the 1970s, life insurance companies sold a limited number of products, primarily **term insurance** and **whole life insurance**. There are a number of subvariations of these basic types of insurance. Together they are often described as **ordinary life insurance**. These traditional products were designed basically to provide protection against the unexpected death of wage earners and their spouses and, in the case of whole life policies, to encourage savings in low-yielding investments in the guise of providing lifetime life insurance protection. The twin factors of high inflation and high interest rates in the period between the late 1960s and early 1980s shook up the life insurance industry. The traditional policies became less attractive, and new types of life insurance were developed: **flexible premium life insurance** (often called **universal life insurance** or **adjustable life insurance**), and more importantly, **variable life insurance** (often called **single premium insurance**), a type of policy that contains significant tax shelter benefits. Even though tax legislation has generally attempted to eliminate or minimize tax shelter and tax-deferral devices, the tax benefits of variable life insurance were not affected by this legislation, and it remains as one of the few legitimate tax shelter devices to survive the Tax Reform Act of 1986. Much of the recent growth in the purchase of life insurance products has been fueled by these new, tax-oriented policies.

In addition to the life insurance company that writes the policy, every life insurance policy involves three actors: the **insured**, the **beneficiary**, and the **policy owner**. The insured is the person whose death triggers the obligation of the insurance company to pay the face value of the policy, and the beneficiary is the person to whom the face value is paid. The beneficiary of the policy is often the insured's spouse or children, but it may also be the insured's estate or persons unrelated to the insured. The owner of the policy is the person who has the power to exercise a number of options with respect to the policy: to name or change the designation of the beneficiary, to borrow against the policy or pledge it as security for a loan (if it has a cash surrender value), and to surrender the policy or decide to let it lapse for nonpayment. Usually, the owner of the policy is the person who pays the premiums. The owner and the insured may be the same person, but they need not be, and indeed it is often advantageous from a tax standpoint for them to be different persons. Under the federal estate tax law, if the insured has retained the incidents of ownership (e.g., the right to change beneficiaries or to pledge the policy as security for a loan) at the time of death, the policy is includable in his or her estate. This is true even if the beneficiary of the policy is a spouse, other family member, or another individual.

Life insurance that is payable to the decedent's estate is, of course, available for the payment of estate obligations, while life insurance that is payable to an individual usually is not. However, the proceeds of an insurance policy are includable in the estate of the decedent for federal estate tax purposes if the policy is payable to the estate of the decedent, no matter who owns the policy. The use of life insurance to improve the liquidity of the estate may therefore increase the taxes imposed on the estate.

The rules about when life insurance must be included in the taxable estate of the decedent for federal estate tax purposes are not as important today as they were a few years ago. Changes in federal tax laws have greatly reduced the impact of this tax, and it now affects only the most wealthy individuals.

## §5.4  The Value of Insurance

Death may strike a person at any age. The most serious family crises are likely to arise from the unexpected death of a person who is the sole or principal income producer for young and dependent children and a spouse who lacks salable job skills. Life insurance obviously provides essential benefits in this type of situation, and as a result it is not surprising that traditionally most life insurance was sold to "breadwinners" in the classic sense. Today, it is not uncommon for both spouses to work even when the children are relatively young, but life insurance may still provide essential protection because the loss of one income may have devastating consequences. Even when one spouse remains home to care for young children, it is increasingly recognized that his or her services are also essential to the family unit and costly to replace. Thus, life insurance protection is often purchased for both spouses.

Even when the death of the insured does not create an immediate financial crisis, life insurance is often a desirable component of financial planning, because it provides liquidity upon the death of the insured. Many persons have assets that may have substantial value if they can be disposed of in an orderly way but relatively little value if they must be sold immediately at "fire sale" or "distress" prices. Good examples of such assets include real estate such as the family home, a closely held business, or shares of stock in a family corporation. In addition, a person's heirs may desire to retain certain assets for their own use after the death of the insured, such as the family home, a cabin in the mountains, or an art collection. Whether this is practical may depend on whether the estate has other liquid assets sufficient to cover taxes, expenses, cash bequests, and outstanding indebtedness. If the estate does not, something must be sold and what is most salable is often precisely what the heirs desire to keep for their own use. Life insurance provides liquidity in the form of ready cash that may be of inestimable value in simplifying the immediate post-death affairs of the deceased person's estate and his or her heirs.

Some people undoubtedly view life insurance (and perhaps other types of insurance as well) as a form of ghoulish gambling. In this view, the person buying life insurance is betting that he or she will not live beyond his or her life expectancy, while the insurance company is betting that the insured will live to a ripe old age. There are, however, limitations on such gambling. In order to purchase an insurance policy on someone else's life, the purchaser must have an **insurable interest** in that other person's life. Needless to say, one spouse has an insurable interest in the other. A corporation may also have an insurable interest in its high-level managers. Thus corporations sometimes purchase **key person** insurance policies. But one cannot purchase a life insurance policy on some randomly selected individual, in part precisely because such agreements are viewed as gambling and in part because the availability of insurance in such circumstances could lead to many forms of advantage-taking that insurers could not control.

It is important to recognize that from the life insurance company's standpoint, life insurance is not gambling at all. Consider, for example, the situation where a new insured, Jane Doe, aged 30 with three small children, pays her first premium but is hit and killed by a truck ten minutes later while leaving the insurance agent's office. The face amount of the policy is almost certainly due in this situation, because an insurance company typically gives its agents authority to bind the company on prospective policies while the company assesses the risk and decides whether to issue a permanent policy. (A **binder**, in other words, is a kind of temporary insurance policy.)

The unexpected demise of Jane Doe does not mean that the insurance company writing the policy lost a gamble. The foundation of life insurance is the existence of reliable **mortality tables** for members of the population as a whole. The earliest such tables date from the late 1600s and early 1700s, and data have been collected on a regular basis ever since. **Actuarial science** (a branch of statistics) focuses on the translation of this information into tables that permit the determination of theoretical premiums to be charged an average person for a life insurance policy in a specified amount on his or her life. The principal variable is, of course, age, but other more controversial variables (such as sex and race) have been used by **actuaries** in predicting mortality rates. In addition to relying on actuarial tables, insurance companies diversify and reduce risk by writing many policies on many different people in many different situations. As long as the population of insureds drawn from a specific risk group that a specific company covers resembles the population of that risk group as a whole, and the premiums are established on an actuarial basis to cover not only the risk but also the insurance company's costs and expenses, the element of gambling is eliminated. Indeed, in this perspective, the premature death of our unfortunate Jane Doe is not an unexpected event at all. The mortality tables build in the fact that on average a certain number of 30-year-old women of Jane Doe's race will die in motor vehicle accidents each year. From the perspective of the actuary, this tragedy is a predictable statistic.

Although insurance is often depicted as one of the most boring topics conceivable, it is important to understand how beneficial it can be. From the consumer's point of view, untimely death is a significant risk. Although the chances may be slim, the consequences may be devastating. But the insurance company does not itself assume risk when it writes a policy protecting a consumer from the financial consequences of untimely death. It can eliminate its risk altogether through diversification. Just as with leverage, the process seems almost like magic. By combining numerous discrete risks, the insurance company can avoid risk and provide a valuable service to society.

Even when a person lets an insurance policy lapse and never collects a dime from it, the insured has received a benefit. Insurance must be viewed from what economists call the **ex ante** perspective, that is, from the point of view of someone who does not know how things will turn out, rather than from the **ex post** perspective of hindsight. The value of insurance is that it reduces uncertainty. It has nothing to do with how things turn out other than to the extent that the likelihood of various future events and their consequences must be assessed in deciding whether and how much insurance to buy.

As long as the individuals being insured by a life insurance company reflect the mortality experience of the population from which they are drawn, premiums may be safely calculated on the basis of available statistics on average mortality tables or life expectancies. Of course, insurance companies must assess individual risks to make sure that the risk is an average one and not unique in some way. An insurance company must always be careful that risks are randomly obtained and are not self-selected. For example, a life insurance company could easily go broke if it wrote standard insurance policies on a disproportionately large number of persons with serious heart disease and persons engaged in ultrahazardous activities like motorcycle racing, skydiving, and bomb disposal. For exactly the same reason, property casualty companies generally refuse to write flood insurance, because only persons living in flood-prone areas are likely to request such insurance, while persons living on top of the hill realize that they do not need the insurance and do not apply for it. In other words, it is impossible when writing flood insurance to avoid **adverse selection**).

The process by which an insurance company determines whether or not to write a policy and thus assume a particular risk in return for a particular premium is called **underwriting**. The term is also sometimes used to refer to the business of insurance generally. It is also used in the mortgage business to refer to the process of approving the terms of a particular loan and in the securities business to refer to buying securities from an issuer for redistribution to individual investors. Although these may seem like very different uses of the word, all relate in some way to the assumption of risk for a fee.

The major ways used by an insurance company to ensure that risks are randomly selected are physical examinations (which are often but not always required) and questions on the application form relating to medical histories, occupations, and hobbies. A person who can demonstrate that he or she is in reasonably good health and engages in activities of average risk is said to be **insurable**, while a person who cannot is said to be **uninsurable**. These are not black-and-white categories, however. Insurance companies often write **extra-risk insurance** policies for persons with known medical problems, such as apparently controlled cardiovascular disease or cancer that has been successfully treated. Such policies carry higher premiums, of course, and are written only after careful assessment of the applicant's medical condition. A person with controlled high blood pressure is insurable on an extra-risk basis, because insurance companies have had sufficient experience with mortality rates of persons with that medical condition to permit the writing of actuarially sound insurance.

Persons engaged in hazardous occupations may also often obtain life insurance only upon the payment of a higher premium. Many insurance companies now give discounts for nonsmokers; a discount in this situation is simply a reduction in premiums for nonsmokers or, phrased differently, the establishment of a somewhat higher premium rate for insurance applicants who smoke.

Questions on the application form for life insurance are carefully devised to provide the insurer accurate information as to the risks involved. Questions usually relate not only to medical histories and known medical conditions but also involve open-ended inquiries that may lead to further investigation, such as whether the applicant has been denied life insurance in the past or whether the applicant has recently been under the care of a physician for any reason. An applicant for life insurance has every incentive to fudge on the application form or to omit reference to medical facts or hazardous activities in order to obtain insurance at favorable rates (or in some cases, to obtain insurance at all). Material omissions or misstatements constitute fraud and, if discovered, usually lead to the cancellation of the policy. On the other hand, insurance companies may be tempted to renege on policies that have been in effect for a long period of time for nondisclosure of material facts in the original application form. Such a practice may deprive insureds of benefits even though they have dutifully paid premiums for years and have not sought substitute insurance because they thought the original policy was valid. Life insurance regulation (which is a matter of state law) prevents insurance companies from cancelling policies for nondisclosure after the lapse of a specified period of time. These **incontestability clauses** are a kind of statute of limitations. They permit life insurance companies only a limited time to raise defenses; after that time has expired, the obligation to insure is binding and cannot be avoided for misrepresentation or nondisclosure in the application. These clauses are mandated by state law. The Texas statute, for example, states that each life insurance policy must contain provisions that state that it and the application form "shall constitute the entire contract between the parties and shall be incontestable after it has been in force during the lifetime of the insured for two years from its date, except for nonpayment of premiums, and which provisions may, at the option of the company, contain an exception for violation of the conditions of the policy relating to naval and military service in time of war."

In addition to the judicious evaluation and acceptance of individual risks, insurance companies may diversify their portfolio of risks by **reinsurance,** through which an insurance company may transfer certain risks to other insurance companies in exchange for a sharing of premiums. Through this process, imbalances of risks may be distributed throughout the life insurance industry. A specific insured is unlikely to be aware that his or her policy has been transferred through reinsurance to another company.

A somewhat similar insurance company practice is the transfer of hundreds of thousands of policies from one insurer to another, with the acquirer taking on the entire insurance obligation of each assigned policy. Insureds are usually notified that their policies have been transferred and are directed to make future premium payments to the acquiring company. This practice is known as **assumption reinsurance**. Policy transfers of this type affect the insureds if the acquiring life insurance company becomes insolvent and disclaims further responsibility on the policies. The original issuing company in these circumstances is likely to argue that its liability under the policy ended with the assumption. The standard legal argument made by policy holders in response is that they did not consent to the assignment or the release of the original insurer who therefore remains liable on its original obligation. There is also a practice known as **indemnification reinsurance** by which a reinsurance company will agree to pay some specified portion of claims arising under one or more policies. This practice, which is sometimes called **syndication,** is similar to the practice among large banks and brokerage houses that agree to share the risk of a large loan or securities offering by assuming responsibility for some specified fraction of the risk.

Assumption reinsurance may be subject to regulation by state insurance regulatory agencies. Insureds who are adversely affected may also have claims against state insurance guaranty funds. However, until the rights of insureds in this situation are adequately protected, it may be sensible to object to any assignment of policies in writing, stating that the insured will make payments to the assigning company but does not release the assigning company from liability under the policy. This precaution seems particularly justified where the credit rating of the assuming company is lower than the credit rating of the assigning company.

As Mark Twain said, "There are lies, damn lies, and statistics." It is important in dealing with all statistics to understand their limitations and to consider all factors that might affect the data. For example, why have life expectancies increased steadily during the last century? The obvious factors are improvements in medical care, the development of antibiotics, and the like. However, much of the increase in the life expectancy of a white male (which was less than 50 years if he was born in 1900 and 74.3 years if he was born in 1997) is due to decreases in infant and child mortality rather than improvements in adult health care.

Another contentious statistical issue: Is it appropriate (or constitutional) for life insurance companies to use sex-based and race-based tables? The accumulated statistics that support these distinctions provide valid predictors, but they have come under increasing criticism. The reason for this is more political than economic, because sometimes the use of separate tables benefit women and minorities and sometimes they do not. In 1997, a 65-year-old white male had a life expectancy of 16.0 years, while a white female of the same age had a life expectancy of 19.3 years. If we assume that both the male and the female retire at the same time and have precisely $100,000 to invest in a lifetime retirement annuity that is based on their respective life expectancies, the male would receive monthly payments that are significantly higher than the female. On the other hand, if the transaction contemplates the purchase of life insurance, on the same assumptions the female would be charged a significantly lower premium for the same amount of insurance, because she will, on average, be paying premiums for several more years and the insurance company will have the use of her money for a longer period.

It may seem unfair to charge different rates to persons who cannot control the factors that cause them to be more or less at risk. On the other hand, it is sometimes difficult to draw the line between what can and cannot be controlled. Single male drivers under the age of 25 generally pay the highest rates for auto insurance. Clearly they cannot control their sex or age, though they can in theory decline to drive until they get older or married. On the other hand, a recent study found that single male drivers under 25 tend to drive many more miles per year than female drivers and in fact pay less per mile driven than female drivers.

Similar issues arise in connection with health insurance. Is it appropriate for insurance companies to deny coverage for preexisting conditions or to charge much higher rates to the elderly because they are more likely to get sick? If it is not, what is to keep the younger and healthier from simply not buying insurance until they get older and sicker or indeed from forming their own insurance company? One solution to these problems may be to require insurance companies to accept all applicants, but it may then also be necessary to require everyone to be insured.

Yet another controversy: someone with a terminal illness arguably should be able to use life insurance benefits to cover medical and housing expenses before death. Thus a number of companies offer to buy the life insurance policies of terminally ill patients so the patients can use the cash that will become payable upon their inevitable death. These companies pay the patient anywhere from 50 to 90 percent of the face value of the policy, depending on how long the patient is expected to live. This arrangement is sometimes called a **viatical settlement** and is similar in many ways to the old practice of selling one's expectancy.

Some of these companies have raised funds by arranging to sell life insurance policies or participations therein. The ultimate return depends on how soon a specific patient dies. The sooner the patient dies, the more profitable the arrangement is from the investor's standpoint. Some companies, moreover, provide a selection of patients to choose from, along with medical information on each. Although many at first had doubts about the legality of these arrangements (ranging from whether the investor has an insurable interest to whether the investment is a security), many insurance companies have been induced to offer plans by which benefits can be paid to terminally ill patients who have been certified by their doctor as likely to die relatively soon.

## §5.5 Term Insurance

**Term insurance** is a traditional type of life insurance that provides basic life insurance protection. It provides solely death protection for a fixed period of time such as one, five, or ten years. The face amount of the policy is paid only if the insured dies within the time or term stated in the policy. Term insurance is pure insurance, based on actuarial data on the probability of death occurring within the fixed period of the policy. There is no cash value buildup, and hence there is no savings or investment component as there is with some other forms of insurance. As the insured gets older, the probability of his or her death during the current time period obviously increases; thus the cost of term insurance increases with the age of the person involved. At about age 65, the cost of pure term insurance becomes prohibitive. However, for a 35-year-old breadwinner with a nonworking spouse and two or three young children to support—perhaps the prototypical individual needing life insurance—term insurance provides a very large degree of temporary protection at a relatively modest cost.

Even though term insurance is based on actuarial principles, there may be wide variations in price quotations, based on different assessments of risk, different premium structures, different commission rates payable to agents, and so forth. In addition, a variety of options may be offered in connection with a term policy: double payment in the event of accidental death, for example, or an option to convert term insurance at a later date into other types of insurance without a new medical examination.

Term insurance policies usually require a medical examination, though some companies may write term policies for younger persons solely on the basis of written health-related questions. Persons in certain risky occupations or having risky avocations may not be able to obtain term insurance at all, or may be able to obtain it only by paying an additional premium. Term insurance policies are usually renewable for additional terms (at higher premiums) without another medical examination or questionnaire. Many policies provide for level premiums for periods of up to five years, with the level premium during this period being approximately equal to the average of annual premiums over the period for a person of the age in question. Term insurance is also often sold at bargain prices in connection with or as a sweetener for other types of life insurance.

Employers often provide **group life insurance**, a type of term insurance, for their employees. It is also often offered by membership organizations, such as fraternal organizations, trade associations, social clubs, and investment clubs. The premium for group life insurance is usually lower than the premium for the equivalent amount of term insurance that could be purchased individually. There are several reasons for this. The administrative costs of insuring a group may be significantly lower than the cost of insuring members individually: selling and advertising costs are usually nominal and the employer or organization arranging for the group insurance may assume some of the administrative costs. Second, the risk characteristics for the group in question may be more favorable than for the population generally. For example, a group of accountants may be able to obtain term insurance at more favorable group rates than as individuals because the accountants as a group have a better life expectancy than the population as a whole: They eat better, they are not subjected to employment-related risks that most blue collar workers face, and they are probably less likely to engage in hazardous activities such as motorcycle racing or skydiving. Third, in some cases the insurer may be willing to quote lower rates because the volume of term policies generated improves its diversification of risk or because it wishes to retain important business relationships with the employer. Finally, by selling to groups, insurance companies avoid some of the risks of self-selection.

Term insurance may be either **face amount insurance** (in which event the face amount is constant and the premium increases periodically) or **declining balance** (in which event the premium remains constant but the face amount of insurance coverage declines as the person gets older). A very common kind of declining balance insurance is mortgage insurance, sold in connection with a mortgage on a home, or credit insurance, offered by many lenders when they make small consumer loans. The theory behind such mortgage and credit insurance is that for a small additional monthly payment, life insurance equal to the unpaid balance of the loan is maintained to make sure the loan is repaid in the event the borrower dies before the indebtedness is paid. The charges for this type of insurance are often significantly higher than the cost of a straight term policy. Moreover, the insured or his or her estate has no power to determine how the proceeds of such policies will be used. It should come as no surprise that many consumer loan organizations maintain relationships with insurers and try to have these insurers write all of this lucrative type of insurance.

Declining balance term insurance is also sold through magazine or newspaper advertisements that promise small amounts of insurance and claim that premiums will not increase before a person reaches some specified age. These policies are usually extremely expensive for the coverage provided. A giveaway that declining balance term is being advertised is usually that the amount of the insurance is either not set forth or is described as up to some specified amount.

## §5.6  Whole Life Insurance

The most common type of traditional life insurance sold today is **whole life.** These policies, unlike the tax-oriented variable or universal life insurance policies described in later sections, provide a fixed benefit on the death of the insured. Further, unlike term insurance, the premiums remain level from the date of the inception of the policy until the maturation of the policy upon the death of the insured. They differ significantly from term insurance in three important, indeed fundamental, respects.

First, the premiums for whole life policies for relatively young adults (or rarely, young children) are initially much higher than for term insurance for the amount of insurance protection for a person of the same age. For example, a 35-year-old man will typically pay an annual premium of $15 or $20 per $1,000 of coverage for a whole life policy, while a comparable one-year renewable term policy would cost somewhere between $2 and $5 per $1,000. To be sure, the premiums on term insurance increase with the age of the insured. But if our hypothetical 35-year-old man retained the same amount of term insurance year after year, he would be in his early 60s before the annual term insurance premium equaled the annual premium for his whole life policy.

Second, even though the premiums remain constant, the face amount of insurance that a whole life policy provides also remains constant. Whole life insurance is unlike declining balance term insurance in this respect.

Third, whole life policies develop cash values or cash surrender values each year after the policy has been in existence for a specified initial period. Much of the initial excess premium over the cost of term insurance goes to building up this value.

The logic underlying a whole life policy is simple. The premiums during the early years of such a policy are much higher than the amount needed to buy only death protection (i.e., term insurance). A portion of this excess is set aside in a kind of savings account for later use by the owner of the policy. A whole life policy, unlike a term policy, thus combines a savings element as well as a life insurance element. This savings element gradually increases as the years go by and more premiums are paid. As described below, the owner of the policy may borrow this cash value, and it will be paid to him or her if the policy is surrendered and the insurance lapses. When the insured dies, however, the company pays only the face value of the policy, not the face value plus the cash value. Thus, the payment of the face value of the whole life policy upon the death of the insured in part comes from the savings account inherent in the cash value concept and in part from true life insurance. As the years go by and the cash surrender value increases, the company needs to provide a decreasing amount of pure life insurance protection. At some point when the insured reaches a ripe old age, the savings account reaches the amount of the face value of the policy and the obligation to pay premiums ends. Such a policy is fully paid up, because the savings account equals the face value of the policy and there is no remaining component of life insurance to be paid from premiums.

This description is in some ways an oversimplification. Typically, cash values in a whole life policy build very slowly: There is usually no cash value after one or two years of premiums, and it may be three or four years before the entire cash value equals the amount of the premium due in any single year. Thereafter, the cash value builds more rapidly, fueled in part by the premium payments and in part by earnings on the money already invested. Cancellation of the policy during its first years therefore may involve a substantial financial penalty. Furthermore, if a policy lapses and an attempt is made to replace it at a later date, the insured will find that the premium is increased because he or she is placed in an older age group when applying for the new insurance. These costs are often used by insurance agents as arguments against cancelling a whole life policy, or allowing it to lapse, when they learn that an insured is having difficulty making the payments.

At first glance, it may seem backward that the buildup of cash value in the earliest years is the lowest, given that the pure insurance cost for protection in the earliest years is also the lowest. Several factors help to explain this structure: the administrative costs of writing a policy (including the cost of a medical examination); the commission structure for the life insurance agent (typically one half or more of the first year's premium goes to the agent as a commission for selling the policy); and the desire to establish a premium structure that encourages retention of a policy rather than surrendering it.

As indicated above, the cash value of a whole life policy increases gradually each year after the first year the policy is in effect. A whole life policy is an investment, an asset of the owner of the policy, much like a bank account or a deposit in a mutual fund. A whole life policy may be assigned to a creditor as security for a loan; the creditor may name itself as beneficiary so that it will receive the proceeds from the policy upon the death of the insured and repay the loan from the proceeds. The remaining balance, if any, presumably belongs to the estate of the insured or his or her heirs. During the lifetime of the insured, the creditor may also surrender the policy for its cash surrender value if a default on the obligation occurs. Although loans secured by assignments of life insurance are not uncommon, it is a mark of some desperation by the borrower, because he or she may be depriving the family of needed insurance protection in order to arrange a loan.

While alive, the owner of the policy can also borrow all or part of the cash value from the insurance company. A loan of the cash surrender value does not increase the insurance risk from the standpoint of the insurer, because if the insured dies while a loan is outstanding, the insurer simply subtracts the outstanding loan from the face amount of the policy and pays the beneficiary the difference. Traditionally, the interest rate on such loans is very low, often 5 percent in the case of older policies. It is important to recognize that this is a very peculiar loan because the insurance company is already holding the cash surrender value in order to make a death payment at some future time. Thus loans of the cash surrender value are more like advances than loans. In one respect, loans of the cash surrender value may adversely affect the insurance company. Its cash flow comes from two sources: premium payments and the return from investments. Loans of cash surrender values reduce the amount available for investment by the insurance company and may reduce its cash flow. This occurs on every such loan whenever the market interest rate on investments is higher than the interest rate charged to the policy owner.

After a whole life policy has been in effect for several years, loans from the cash surrender value may be used to pay future premiums. This practice may permit an insured to keep a policy in effect over long periods without paying premiums, but subject to a gradual reduction of the death benefit that will ultimately be paid.

In addition to the traditional whole life policy, many other life insurance policies are offered that combine savings and life insurance protection in varying degrees. For example, an **endowment policy** involves premiums for a specified period, perhaps 20 or 30 years; at that point the cash value equals the policy face amount and the insurance is fully paid up. Obviously, substantially higher premium payments are required for endowment or **paid-up policies** than for a whole life policy. As a result, these policies enjoy limited attractiveness.

A study prepared by the Federal Trade Commission in 1979 attempted to estimate the rate of return on a whole life policy viewing its cash value as an investment. This is not a simple computation, because a portion of each premium must be allocated to the insurance feature of the whole life policy. The study concluded that the return was negative—that is, the cash value was less than the amount invested—for over 10 years; after 20 years the rate of return was only 2 percent. Thus as a savings vehicle, the whole life policy is inferior even to an insured savings account. Indeed, a strategy of "buy term and invest the rest" (a phrase used by critics of the traditional insurance industry) usually yields a significantly larger investment after 20 years than buying a whole life policy. This strategy is somewhat similar to the do-it-yourself annuities discussed in the previous chapter, and both suffer from some of the same problems. For example, while the buying term and investing the difference yields superior results, the specific results are based on the assumption that a savings account will yield a definite return, and this cannot be guaranteed. A decline in the rate of interest on the savings component may make the differences much less dramatic. Also, savings through life insurance premium payments is convenient and there is a built-in incentive not to let the insurance lapse. Many persons might lack the discipline to make the same payments into a savings account without the need to preserve their insurance. Whole life policies also contain some significant options that cannot be replicated in a do-it-yourself plan: A waiver of premiums in the event of disability, for example, is generally available at no additional cost and is tremendously valuable in the rare situation where disability occurs. Other valuable rights may include such options to purchase annuity rights and the ability to use the cash surrender value to buy additional paid-up insurance without a medical examination. Finally, accumulations in a "buy term and invest the rest" plan are subject to federal income taxes each year, while the growth of cash value within a whole life policy is tax deferred.

An argument can be made that it is unrealistic to analyze a whole life policy as being divided into an insurance component and a savings component. One can argue that the whole life insurance contract should be viewed as an undifferentiated whole, and that it consists of buying insurance protection on a level-premium installment plan, in which young people prepay their premiums in the earlier years for protection they will receive many years later when the actual insurance costs greatly exceed the premium then being paid. One basic problem with this analysis is that it gives little weight to the phenomenon of the growth of the cash value within a whole life policy, which is a central feature of whole life insurance. Furthermore, this approach toward whole life raises new questions: It ignores the time value of the money that is prepaid, and also gives no weight to the possibility of inflation and increased earning capacity in later years. If this were the sole explanation of whole life insurance offered to most persons, it is likely that they would opt for term insurance and invest the difference.

## §5.7  Comparing Insurance and Other Investment Vehicles

Traditional life insurance (such as a whole life policy) is a combination of true insurance coverage and an investment vehicle or savings plan of some sort. Although many insurance companies pay adequate returns on the investment portion of such plans, it is extremely difficult to obtain accurate information about such investments that is comparable to information about other similar investments (e.g., mutual funds). And even if one obtains such information, the investment component of a policy is tied to the insurance component. Thus, one component of a plan may be attractive while the other is not, and the task of finding the optimal package can be complicated. Indeed, the optimal package may not even be available in the sense that the best deal on insurance may be from a source wholly different from the best deal on investment (even though many insurance companies offer a variety of different investment funds that are typically managed in-house).

Another basic problem is that insurance is governed by state law, which varies from state to state, while most comparable investment vehicles (e.g., mutual funds) are regulated by federal law and thus are subject to standardized disclosures. Some states have attempted to require disclosure of investment performance by insurance companies, but these steps in the direction of full disclosure fall far short of the information available on free-standing mutual funds and other investment companies.

For these reasons, the market for the various forms of insurance with cash value is much less competitive than the market for insurance alone or investments alone, and the consumer is usually the loser. Perhaps the primary reason that such forms of insurance continue to be purchased is that they may (but do not always) offer tax deferral on investment returns. Now that other methods of tax-deferred investment (such as individual retirement accounts (IRAs)) are available, traditional insurance is far less important as an investment vehicle.

On the other hand, insurance products such as variable annuities and single premium life insurance offer the advantage of tax-deferred investing without the limits on contributions that go with IRAs and similar plans. The problem is that such investments necessarily come in a package with insurance, because, as a matter of law, if the investments do not contain a significant insurance component, they will be classified as mutual funds and become subject to federal disclosure and tax regulations covering investment companies.

California requires that insurers disclose a yield comparison index for whole life and universal life policies. The index is meant to give consumers some idea of what their return would be if the policy was surrendered a given number of years in the future, taking into account returns in the form of possible death benefits as well as investment returns. Although the index appears to be useful as a way of comparing one policy with another, especially insofar as commissions affect the value of the policy, the payoff's hybrid nature makes it useless for purposes of comparison to other investment vehicles.

The excessive trading of securities to generate commissions for the broker is called **churning**. The practice of churning may also be a problem in life insurance. Specifically, insurance agents may urge consumers to trade in policies with high cash value primarily in order to generate commissions. Often, insureds will not be aware that a portion of the cash value of the old policy is used to pay a commission to the agent selling the new policy. Indeed, the insureds may not learn of it at all unless they attempt to take out a loan against the policy or otherwise gain access to the cash value. (And where a loan is already outstanding and the policy is traded in and the loan forgiven, there may be taxable income to the insured without any distribution of cash with which to pay the tax.) State regulators have attempted to monitor such practices.

## §5.8 Other Forms of Insurance

There are many forms of insurance other than life insurance. Automobile insurance, homeowners insurance, liability insurance, and health insurance are just a few examples. Other less familiar kinds of insurance include product liability insurance, malpractice insurance for professionals (sometimes called errors and omissions insurance), and **directors and officers liability insurance (D&O insurance)**.

These other forms of insurance differ from life insurance in that they do not depend primarily on life expectancy for the insurance company to determine premium rates to be charged to various insureds. To be sure, many of the events that give rise to the payment of benefits under such insurance policies may involve a death. For example, the estate of someone killed in an automobile accident may receive benefits under an accident policy and may also receive payments from insurance policies carried by other motorists involved in the accident. If the accident was caused by some sort of mechanical defect, the estate may ultimately receive payment from an insurer of the manufacturer. The estate may, of course, also receive payment under a life insurance policy on the life of the deceased, which in fact may be doubled as benefits often are in the event of accidental death.

The rates charged for some of these other types of insurance are based on actuarial models about the likelihood of certain kinds of accidents or other events. For example, premiums for health insurance are based on models that attempt to predict the frequency with which certain diseases or medical conditions are likely to strike the insured. These other forms of insurance, however, are based almost purely on risk diversification as opposed to being based in part on the time value of money, as is life insurance. (Of course, insurance companies writing these other forms of insurance will still invest their available funds at the highest possible rate between the time premiums are received and benefits are paid out.)

Perhaps the most basic difference between life insurance (at least whole life) and other forms of insurance is that with other forms of insurance, most policyholders do not collect as much in benefits as they pay in premiums. This does not mean, however, that other forms of insurance are bad deals. Indeed, quite the contrary is true. People buy insurance to protect themselves against catastrophic events for which individual wealth is likely to be inadequate. For example, a homeowner is unlikely to have $100,000 in cash to rebuild a house if it is destroyed by fire. Homeowners insurance allows many homeowners, in effect, to pool their money in order to compensate those few homeowners whose houses actually do burn down. And the insurance company profits by facilitating the transaction.

These types of insurance are a **zero sum game** (except for the expenses of administering them and the profits earned by the insurance company). The monetary value of insurance to a homeowner is the amount of the benefit times the probability of fire or other damage. Assume that one is only worried about fire and that the chances of fire are 1 in 1,000. If the house in question is worth $100,000, the strictly monetary value of the insurance benefit is $100, that is, the value of the benefit times the probability that it will be received. Nevertheless, most homeowners would quite willingly spend more than $100 per year to protect against the possibility of fire. Indeed, one can well imagine that a homeowner might be willing to pay $150 or even $200 per year for such protection.

The fact that people purchase insurance suggests that they perceive a gain from buying insurance. What is the source of the gain? The answer is the elimination of risk. Many insurance company tout the "peace of mind" that comes from being insured. That is just a colloquial way of saying that people tend to be **risk averse**. The possibility of a significant loss, particularly one that is so large that the individual could not soon regain the same lifestyle, tends to weigh more in deciding what to do with $100 per year than does the possibility of using the same money to somehow enhance one's life in the present (say) by buying a new tennis racquet or installing a skylight. There is no real financial gain to the insured who gets precisely what is paid for—or actually a little less —that is, a 1 in 1,000 chance for a payment of $100,000. Still, because the insured has eliminated a worrisome risk, it is a good deal. What is magical about insurance is that the risk is simply gone. By pooling their small annual contributions through the insurance company, the participating homeowners have simply eliminated the risk of financial loss by fire. Of course, one could also argue that the insureds have collectively just figured out a way to pay for the damage in advance and, in effect, have assumed that the worrisome event will occur somewhere sometime. But in fact statistics indicate that it will, and accurately predicting the likelihood and consequences of such events is how insurance companies make money. The value of insurance, from the point of view of any given homeowner, is eliminating the possibility that such random-seeming events will happen to him or her. This view of insurance suggests that premium payments should be made deductible from income for tax purposes in the same way that the benefits of insurance are viewed as not being taxable income, that is, merely a way of making the insured whole. After all, casualty losses are deductible. Nevertheless, insurance premiums are not deductible, and the policy behind the casualty loss deduction is apparently limited to minimizing the devastating effects of larger losses on uninsured or partially insured tax payers.

The benefits of some types of insurance extend beyond the insured's simply receiving a check for the amount of a loss. Where someone else is or may be legally responsible for the loss, the insurance company will typically pay the insured victim promptly and then seek to recover that amount from the wrongdoer. Thus, insurance offers convenience and prompt payment, as well as avoiding the risk that a lawsuit may not succeed. Because insurance companies thus depend to some extent on getting back amounts they have paid out from wrongdoers (if any), insurance policies routinely provide for **subrogation**. Subrogation means that the insurance company obtains the right to sue in the name of the insured when it pays a claim. The insured must also undertake to cooperate with the insurance company in pursuing the case. However, from the point of view of a defendant, the insured remains the plaintiff, partly because in most cases the defendant may not introduce evidence of insurance because of the effect it might have on the jury's deliberations.

Where the insured is a defendant (in a case in which there is coverage for the harm done), most liability policies require the insurance company to provide a defense at its expense. It is, of course, in the interest of the insurance company to do so, given that the insured would prefer to settle for the amount of the coverage just to avoid the inconvenience of the lawsuit. Nevertheless, the provision of a defense has some value even to the insured in that the insurance company may often avoid the award of damages exceeding the limits of the policy.

## §5.9  Common Coverage Issues

Many individuals purchase **umbrella policies** that protect against awards that exceed the limits on auto or homeowners insurance policies. Umbrella policies also provide for some additional coverage (as President Clinton discovered when his insurance company agreed to provide a defense in connection with sexual harassment claims made against him). In some cases, especially in connection with umbrella policies and professional malpractice coverage, the insurance company will deduct the cost of providing a defense from the coverage available under the policy. Thus, if one has a $1 million umbrella policy and it costs $200,000 in attorney fees and court costs to defend a case, the amount available under the insurance policy to pay an award of damages will be reduced to $800,000. In most cases, umbrella policies provide the face amount of coverage for the policy year and do not cover multiple claims once the policy is depleted. Automobile insurance, on the other hand, tends to have only per-occurrence limits.

One of the issues that arises in connection with umbrella policies and more often with professional malpractice and product liability policies is how to determine which claims are covered. For example, a claim made in 1997 may be the result of events that occurred in 1995. Is the claim covered by a 1997 or a 1995 policy? For a variety of reasons, many umbrella policies and almost all malpractice policies and product liability policies are written on a **claims-made basis**, that is, they cover the insured for claims formally made during the policy year irrespective of when the events giving rise to the claims occurred. Claims-made policies avoid controversy about precisely when the claim arose and the problem of claims arising years after a policy has expired. On the other hand, a claims-made policy, rather than some sort of **occurrence coverage**, requires that the insured continue to buy insurance against claims that may have arisen in the past, and it requires the insurance company to cover risks that may not be currently evident or indeed may be unknown to the insured. Although these problems may not be serious in the case of an insured who renews with the same company year after year, they create difficulties in certain settings. For example, a company that has stopped manufacturing a particular product may need to continue to buy insurance for claims that may be made in connection with the old product at least until the statute of limitations has run. In many states, the statute of limitations on claims based on injuries caused by defective products does not begin to run until the injury occurs. Insurance against these later arising claims, called **tail insurance**, may be available in some instances but may be difficult or impossible to obtain.

In the context of malpractice insurance, a claims-made policy means that a lawyer who leaves a law firm will usually cease to be covered for claims made in connection with his or her practice at the former firm and, if the lawyer moves to another firm, claims may be asserted against the new firm's policy for conduct while at the former firm. The end result has sometimes been that an aggrieved client may recover from both firms for the value of both policies (to the extent they have not been depleted by other claims, of course). A lawyer or other professional who leaves a firm should be aware of the need for continuing protection, and a professional firm that takes on a new partner or employee should be aware that he or she may sometimes carry along liabilities. Tail coverage is sometimes available to cover these types of risks.

## §5.10 Overinsurance, Self-Insurance, and Moral Hazard

The primary rationale for buying insurance (including term life insurance) is to spread the risk of various catastrophic events that one cannot afford to cover out of pocket. It should therefore be apparent that in some situations, insurance makes little or no sense even though an insurance company may urge you to buy it. Extended warranties on products are a good example, although they may not be usually thought of as insurance. Anyone who ever attempts to make a claim under an extended warranty quickly discovers that such plans operate very much like insurance policies. Extended warranties for relatively cheap household goods usually make little sense given the cost, the contractual limitations, the difficulties in collecting under them, and, most important, the fact that the item thus "insured" can be repaired or replaced with little financial disruption. If a person purchased an insurance policy against all the minor losses that he or she might suffer in any given year, assuming that these losses could even be catalogued, the cost of the insurance would far exceed the cost of paying out of that person's own pocket for the random events that actually occur.

Separate insurance to pay debt obligations (mortgage insurance is the best example) seldom makes economic sense. To be sure, the mortgage needs to be paid if one dies (assuming that the family home is not to be sold), but if one is adequately insured through other policies, there is nothing peculiar about the need to pay the mortgage that constitutes a unique risk. Indeed, it is arguable that insurance companies create confusion about what constitutes risk as a way of selling more insurance. (It should be emphasized that the mortgage insurance described here is not the same thing as **private mortgage insurance (PMI)** that lenders sometimes require as a condition for making a loan. PMI is a separate guaranty of payment that lenders require for their own benefit if they consider the risk of default to be high.)

For similar reasons, many large businesses **self-insure** in connection with risks for which individuals rationally buy insurance. For example, many large employers do not actually purchase health insurance for their employees. Instead, they simply pay for medical care as the need arises, because there are so many employees that the likelihood of certain conditions arising is roughly the same as it is in the population as a whole. Because the company only covers its employees and is not in the business of selling insurance, there is little risk that persons who know that they are more at risk than the average person will seek out jobs with the company in order to take advantage of its health insurance.

From the employee's perspective, employer self-insurance of health care is usually indistinguishable from an insurance plan purchased from an independent insurance company. In most cases, a self-insuring employer contracts with an insurance company to administer the plan. Thus, the employee may be required to fill out the same forms that are required of others who are in fact insured by an independent company. The only difference is that when a bill is paid, it comes out of the employer's account rather than that of the insurance company.

It should be obvious that the gains from buying insurance are limited to the value of the property at risk. It makes no sense to buy more insurance than one needs. Indeed, insurance companies refuse to insure for amounts that exceed the value of the property insured, and if the insured attempts to buy policies from more than one company in order to double-cover a risk (and in effect bet on the destruction of the property), insurance contracts generally provide that each insurer will pay only a pro rata share of the claim (which is also the reason that medical insurance forms typically ask if there is other coverage).

If one were able to overinsure (and collect), it would create perverse incentives to engage in reckless behavior and even to destroy the insured property, for example, through arson. The insurance industry depends to a great extent on the natural tendency of insureds to avoid the events insured against anyway. Few people are indifferent to being involved in an automobile accident just because they are insured. And indeed, insurance companies are quite active in campaigning for insureds to engage in safer behavior. A basic concern in writing all kinds of insurance is that it should not somehow increase the risk of the event insured against. Thus, life insurance policies routinely exclude claims arising from suicide. On a subtler level, most liability policies exclude coverage for awards of punitive damages against the insured. Why? Punitive damages typically arise because of some form of intentional bad behavior on the part of the defendant from which the defendant hoped to gain (such as various forms of fraud). Such claims thus involve risks created by the insured and are excluded, although most insurance policies cover punitive damages assessed purely vicariously against an employer who did not participate in or induce the misdeeds of the employee. (Ironically, insurance companies themselves have been the frequent target of punitive damages claims in connection with failure to pay claims. The courts have recognized that one way an insurance company might make a bit more money is to refuse to pay or delay paying legitimate claims.)

There are generally no limitations on the amount of life insurance one may buy or the number of different insurance companies with whom one may deal. Of course, when it comes to life insurance, it may seem difficult to say how much a life is worth. But insurance cannot compensate for the personal and intangible loss of life. The point of life insurance is to protect not only against financial losses (usually the loss of earning power) but also other sorts of financial losses as well. If one thinks rationally about life insurance, it is possible to determine the amount of life insurance one should have. If, for example, one is living comfortably on $50,000 per year, including paying the mortgage and various bills as they become due, then adequate life insurance would be in an amount that would allow for a return of $50,000 per year if it is invested. Of course, there may be extraordinary expenses that should be considered, such as sending the children to college a few years hence or even paying for excess medical expenses or funeral expenses. And it may be that one would want to provide for a better standard of living for one's survivors in order to make the loss of a life a bit more bearable. It is entirely possible, however, to estimate these numbers. Having estimated the cash needs of one's survivors and having taken into account other sources of potential income, such as income from existing investments and social security benefits, deciding how much insurance to buy becomes in essence a simple present value calculation: How much of a lump sum is necessary to generate the needed amount per year? The urge to buy any more insurance than that should be resisted, because the cash that is used to buy insurance could also be used to live better in the present, or simply be saved. For similar reasons, it makes little sense to purchase insurance on someone who is not earning a living or providing services on which others depend. Thus, it makes little sense for a retired person to buy life insurance or for a parent to buy life insurance on a child.

## §5.11  Insurance and the Law

In many situations, insurance is required either by law or contract. For example, all auto owners are required to carry insurance (although there is usually an exemption for owners who can demonstrate that they have sufficient personal wealth to pay damages up to a specified amount). And, as a usual condition of obtaining a mortgage on a personal residence, the homeowner must insure the property against fire and other sorts of sudden damage. In the case of both auto insurance and homeowners insurance, the concern is that drivers and homeowners will be unable or unwilling to make good on their obligations. An automobile accident can result in hundreds of thousands of dollars of claims. The responsible individual would need to work for many years to pay off a large claim if indeed he or she would ever be able to pay it off. An obvious alternative is simply to declare bankruptcy and walk away from the obligation (if the claim is one that can be discharged in bankruptcy).

An individual is said to be **judgment proof** if he or she has no significant personal wealth with which to pay legal judgments. For example, most mortgages on individual residences specify that the mortgagor is personally liable on the note, but personal liability is not worth much if the person is not worth much. For this reason, many insurance policies require that a property be insured for at least 80 percent of its value. An insurance company may also make large checks payable jointly to the insured and the mortgagee. Both of these restrictions are designed to ensure that the proceeds of insurance are used for their intended purpose and not diverted for other purposes.

Insurance companies face the possibility that as a result of insurance, the insured will be less careful than he or she might otherwise be (a form of so-called moral hazard), or that the insured will make claims for very minor events that cost more in time and effort to administer than they are worth. One way of dealing with claims for minor events is to specify a deductible or require co-payment. With a deductible, the insured must pay the first $100, $250, $500, or other specified amount in connection with the claim. This is a very common arrangement in connection with **collision insurance** for automobiles, the in-surance that protects the auto owner against damage to the insured's own car. There are, however, no deductibles in connection with liability coverage, that is, coverage for damage done to others. Why? Because insurance does not make one any less vigilant about avoiding accidents involving other automobiles or property. But one may be tempted to make a claim for minor dents and dings that could be avoided through a bit more care.

A **co-payment** is slightly different in that it requires the insured to pay some percentage of every claim. This is much more common in connection with health insurance, which also often specifies some deductible amount (e.g., $100 per year per individual). A typical health insurance policy (at least one that operates by reimbursement of the insured) might cover medical care only after the insured has paid out the first $100 and only then to the extent of 80 percent of further expenses.

Although liability insurance is not generally mandatory for businesses, there are certain risks for which insurance is required, such as unemployment and workers compensation. And, of course, there are certain lines of business that require special forms of insurance, such as deposit insurance for banks, or simple accident insurance for a trucking company. The availability (or not) of insurance has affected the development of the law dramatically in recent years. For example, one of the arguments that underlies the growth in consumer rights to sue for injuries suffered from defective products is that the manufacturer is in a better position either to spread the cost of such accidents by obtaining insurance (or self-insuring) and increasing the price of the product somewhat to offset the increased cost. If the availability of insurance is a factor to be considered in deciding whether a business is liable for a particular harm, the practical effect is to require the business to buy insurance or self-insure (which is to say pay the claim out of its own pocket).

Similarly, the law has long held that an employer is liable for damages that an employee causes while acting within the scope of employment. This doctrine is sometimes called by its original Latin name **respondeat superior** and is a kind of **vicarious liability**. Although many arguments have been advanced his-torically for why employers should be held liable for the accidents caused by their employees, one economic argument is that employers and employees would usually agree that the employer is in a better position to spread the cost by paying for accidents and reducing wages a bit to make up for it or by buying insurance. In effect, there is a hypothetical agreement by which the employer agrees to insure the employee in exchange for a lower wage or salary. As with commercial insurance, it is a matter of indifference to the employer whether it pays a lower wage and pays out a claim now and then or whether it pays a higher wage and lets the employees pay their own claims, assuming, of course, that the employer has an adequate number of employees performing more or less repetitive tasks so that the employer can accurately assess the risk. Indeed, the employer may gain from such an arrangement, because the employer may be able to assess risks more accurately than employees or even an outside in-surance company and may be able to take steps to control these risks through various safety incentives and so forth that would not be instituted by the em-ployees on their own. Thus, it may be argued that the law of employer liability mandates the agreement that ordinarily employer and employee would freely enter into unless they were conspiring to avoid responsibility altogether. One problem with this theory is that the law gives the employer the right to seek indemnification (reimbursement) from the employee in most situations, though few employers ever do. One notable exception is the federal government, which has by statute given up the right to sue its own employees for indemnification in connection with accident claims.

Another example of how insurance affects the law relates to the benefit of limited liability when doing business in the form of a corporation or limited liability company. With these forms of business, the owners of the business are not personally responsible for debts of the business. But in the case of corporations at least, the courts, in situations in which they conclude that the corporate form has somehow been abused, may **pierce the corporate veil** and hold the shareholders of the corporation personally liable. One of the factors that courts cite in piercing cases involving torts is that the corporation was undercapitalized in the sense that there were insufficient funds available to pay claims that should have been foreseen as likely in the line of business in question. Many courts have noted that the purchase of insurance obviates the **undercapitalization** argument in such cases. The net effect is that, practically speaking, a business that fails to insure against likely harms it may cause runs an enhanced risk of personal liability for its owners in cases of tortious conduct, although not in cases of contractual liability.

## §5.12 No Fault Insurance Systems

Where both parties to an accident are insured, any legal action that arises out of the accident will involve one insurance company suing another. One may question whether such lawsuits make much sense, given that over large numbers of insureds, automobile accidents (like mortality) become quite predictable. Indeed, in many cases an insurance company may end up on both sides of the same accident, in which case it becomes apparent that the company will pay no matter how the lawsuit turns out. Why bother? It is this logic that has led to the institution of **no fault insurance**. The fact that the involved motorists may be insured by different insurers makes little difference in the end in that as far as each insurance company is concerned, it will be on the winning and losing side of cases a predictable number of times. Thus, it would seem eminently sensible for all insurance companies to get together and simply agree to pay the legitimate claims of their own insureds and agree not to sue each other for reimbursement. Of course, no single company will unilaterally give up the right to sue, for to do so would put it at a competitive disadvantage. In the language of economists, there is a **barrier to contract** or **market failure** that requires an act of the legislature, that is, a statute, if the parties are to enjoy the benefits of a rational bargain.

Ironically, a no fault insurance system in which one's own company pays for most claims gives rise to the need for a residual form of coverage against the possibility that someone involved in the accident may not have bought insurance and may seek to sue the driver who is covered. Such **uninsured**

**motorist coverage** is now required in most states, but it is quite cheap because it only applies in rare circumstances.

Unfortunately, the phrase "no fault" has been appropriated for use in other contexts (such as no fault divorce laws) in which much of its original sense is lost. The logic of no fault automobile insurance is that litigation is wasteful in a setting in which accidents are highly predictable and recoveries between insurance companies net out over time. There is no such logic that seems to apply in the context of divorce law.

# CHAPTER 6

# ACCOUNTING AND FINANCIAL REPORTING

## §6.1   Introduction

As business transactions occur, they are recorded in financial books and records. The results of the operation of the business are periodically communicated through financial statements that are based on these financial books and records. Accounting thus involves the collection, summarization, and reporting of financial data by a business, as well as the computation of profit and other measures of a business's financial health. The creation and maintenance of financial records is the responsibility of the accountant, and the language in which the results are communicated is the language of the accountant. Every lawyer should have working familiarity with this language.

In addition, in order to understand what is being communicated in financial statements, one has to understand not only the underlying principles on which modern accounting systems are based but also the major limitations on, or more accurately, the major policy decisions that underlie, these accounting systems. Because financial statements can be prepared on any number of different accounting systems, one also has to know what principles were followed in the creation of the specific financial statements under consideration, whether they depart from accepted accounting principles, and if they do, the extent to which the differences affect the results being reported. The standard set of accounting principles that forms the norm for financial reporting in the United States is known as **generally accepted accounting principles (GAAP)**. These principles must be followed by most publicly held corporations in the United States in publicly reporting the results of their operations. GAAP is not officially set down anywhere in the form of a code. Instead, GAAP is a loose set of rules and principles that outlines a range of reasonable and permissible treatments of many transactions.

GAAP has a hierarchy of principles, standards, and practices. First, the most authoritative of these principles are standards published by the **Financial Accounting Standards Board (FASB)**, a panel created by the **American Institute of Certified Public Accountants (AICPA)** with the cooperation of the **Securities and Exchange Commission (SEC)** to review accounting issues and promulgate GAAP standards. (In earlier times, the **Accounting Principles Board (APB)** performed a similar function, and many of its pronouncements remain valid standards to the extent that they have not been overruled by subsequent statements by the FASB.) Next in the hierarchy come other accounting standards published by AICPA, followed by general principles that pervade the practice of accounting and the accounting literature, and finally prevalent customs and usages in the practice of accounting. The SEC has legal authority to prescribe mandatory accounting standards that reporting publicly held companies must follow, but the magnitude of accounting issues has led the SEC to rely primarily on the FASB to establish principles. In other words, the accounting profession is largely self-regulated. In recent years, however, the FASB has been criticized as being too beholden to the businesses whose books they monitor, and the SEC has threatened to assume greater control. At the same time, businesses have complained that the FASB is too regulatory and disclosure-oriented in approach. These controversies are likely to intensify in the wake of the collapse of Enron in late 2001.

Some knowledge of the accounting process is essential for lawyers in a corporate or business practice, and indeed is useful for all lawyers without regard to the nature of their practice. Furthermore, there is an art to the process of analyzing financial statements that should be familiar to every lawyer. Law students without business or financial backgrounds may have irrational—almost primordial—fears about accounting principles and concepts. It is true that accounting can become very complex and esoteric; after all, accounting itself is a subject in which people regularly receive advanced graduate degrees and then spend productive lifetimes. On the other hand, one can readily understand the fundamental principles of accounting and learn to read and understand financial statements without becoming enmeshed in these complexities. This chapter describes the principles that underlie accounting statements.

It deals with the accepted methods of treating commonly recurring accounting problems in a complex enterprise.

## §6.2  The Functions of Accounting

Accounting in a large business involves two basic functions: the entering of records of transactions as they occur and the subsequent determination and reporting of results of operations on a periodic basis. In a large publicly held corporation, unaudited financial results are usually reported quarterly to the public and audited results are reported annually. Financial reports are widely publicized and are used and relied on by investors, creditors, regulatory agencies, employees, and others. The preparation of these public reports is usually described as financial accounting as contrasted with management accounting. A major goal of financial accounting is to ensure that the financial reports are prepared honestly and in accordance with GAAP so that they are comparable with earlier reports and the reports of other companies. Innumerable investment and commercial decisions are made on the premise that such reports are comparable with the same company's reports for earlier periods and with published reports of other companies in the same or different industries. Nevertheless, perfect comparability cannot be achieved, because in any complex organization numerous discretionary accounting judgments make variations in treatment inevitable.

Financial information about corporate affairs is also essential if management of a publicly held corporation is to make informed internal decisions. For internal purposes, financial results may be reported to top management and the board of directors on a weekly or even a daily basis. Financial analyses of specific business alternatives or strategies will also be prepared as the need arises. These internal reports and analyses are usually not prepared in accordance with GAAP, and they are not publicly available. Their preparation is sometimes called management accounting to distinguish this area from the publicly oriented financial accounting described in the preceding paragraph.

The routine recording and summarization of transactions is also essential to ensure that the business always has the proper inventory of raw materials and finished goods on hand. This permits the manufacturing operations of the business to continue smoothly and to actually produce what customers have ordered or are willing to buy. The two functions of accounting—keeping track and reporting—are related in that the records used in the process of recording transactions as they occur are also used as the basis for the compilation of the results of operations. Modern accounting is a continuing process that permits transactions that are numerous, large, and complex to be accounted for on a routine basis involving relatively low-paid and marginally skilled employees. Of course, the original creation of the bookkeeping process for a specific business, the oversight of that process, and decisions as to how specific significant transactions are to be accounted for within that process require the participation of persons who have a broad view of the whole accounting process.

Persons unfamiliar with the accounting process are apt to believe that accounting is a precise science, or at least that there is general acceptance of basic principles as to how transactions should be handled for financial accounting purposes. Financial accounting gives a deceptive aura of accuracy. Amounts are entered in precise dollars-and-cents figures. Accountants state that accounting principles require a specific treatment of an item. This appearance of accuracy and specificity should not be permitted to hide the fact that there is often room for differences of opinion as to how matters should be treated and presented.

Within the accounting profession, and to a large extent in general business publications, discussions of the most appropriate treatment of specific transactions or of classes of transactions are often heated and the conclusions are controversial. For example, the seemingly arcane issue of whether the grant of stock options should be treated as an expense went on for several years and made front page news in many major papers. And a 1996 Supreme Court decision as to how a savings bank should account for the purchase of another bank resulted in an apparent increase of several billion dollars in the cost to the federal government in connection with settling certain claims by failed savings banks.

These controversies are fueled by the underlying fact that the success or failure of an enterprise is largely measured by its reported financial results, and any change in GAAP that significantly affects the reported results of operations of publicly held companies may have significant and wide-ranging repercussions, even though only the manner of reporting the transaction—rather than the transaction itself—has changed. In a fundamental sense, accounting is a language that (like most languages) allows considerable variation in expression; it is not a matter of right and wrong so much as what is useful and comparable and what is not.

Indeed, there is considerable disagreement as to whether the entire edifice of accounting principles described in this and the following chapters is built on quicksand and should be scrapped in favor of a discounted cash-flow analysis. Again, the collapse of Enron in late 2001 is likely to add fuel to this fire.

## §6.3  The Basic Accounting Equation

The starting point of the whole subject of accountancy is a very simple equation:

$$equity = assets - liabilities$$

Equity in this equation has nothing to do with the historical courts of equity or with notions of fairness or simple justice: It means ownership or net worth. This equation simply states that the net worth of a business is equal to its assets minus its liabilities.

A balance sheet is in many ways the most fundamental financial statement: It is simply a restatement of this fundamental equation in the form:

$$assets = liabilities + equity$$

A balance sheet simply is a presentation of this equation in a chart form.

| Assets | Liabilities |
|--------|-------------|
|        | Equity      |
| Total  | Total       |

Every balance sheet, whether it is for General Motors or the smallest retail grocery store, is based on this format.

The asset side of a balance sheet is sometimes referred to as the left-hand side, even though it is sometimes printed above rather than to the left. Similarly, the liability/equity side is sometimes called the right-hand side, even though it is sometimes printed below rather than to the right.

There are four fundamental premises underlying financial accounting that can readily be grasped from this simple introduction. First, financial accounting assumes that the business that is the subject of the financial statements is an entity. A person may own several different businesses; if each business maintains its own records, it will be on the assumption that each is independent from the person's other businesses. The equity referred to in that business's balance sheet will be limited to the person's investment in that single business. If a person owns two businesses that keep separate financial records, a debt that one business owes to the other will be reflected as an asset on one balance sheet and a liability on the other.

Second, all entries must be in terms of dollars (at least in the United States). All property, tangible or intangible, and obligations shown on a balance sheet must be expressed in dollars, either historical cost or fair market value or some other method of valuation. Many "assets" or "liabilities" of a business, however, are not reflected at all. A person's friendly smile may be an asset in a sense, but will not appear on a balance sheet because a dollar value is not normally given to a smile. Assets, such as a debt owed to the company or rights to a patent, on the other hand, do appear in balance sheets. Similarly, a company may have a reputation for sharp practices or questionable dealing. Although that reputation is doubtless a liability in a sense, it is not the type of liability that appears on a balance sheet. A liability in the balance sheet sense is a recognized debt or obligation to someone else, payable either in money or in something reducible to money. Not all liabilities that in the legal or lay sense meet this test are recognized as liabilities in the accounting sense.

Third, a balance sheet must balance. The fundamental accounting equation itself states an equality: The two sides of the balance sheet restate that equality in somewhat reorganized form. A balance sheet therefore is itself an equality, and the sum of the left-hand side of the balance sheet must precisely equal the sum of the right-hand side. Indeed, when accountants are involved in auditing a complex business, they take advantage of this characteristic by running trial balances on their work to make sure they have not inadvertently transposed or omitted figures: The mathematical equality of the two sides of the balance sheet provides a check on the accuracy of the accountant's labors. In short, if a balance sheet doesn't balance, there is a mistake somewhere.

Fourth, every transaction that a business enters into must be recorded in at least two ways if the balance sheet is to continue to balance. This last point underlies the concept of that mysterious (and somewhat illicit sounding) subject, double entry bookkeeping, and is the cornerstone on which modern accounting is built.

Assume that we have a new business that is just starting out, in which the owner has invested $10,000 in cash (for this purpose it makes no difference whether the business is going to be conducted in the form of a proprietorship, partnership, or corporation; all that is important is that it will be accounted for as an entity separate from the owner). The opening balance sheet will look like this:

| Assets |  | Liabilities | -0- |
|---|---|---|---|
| Cash | 10,000 | Equity | 10,000 |
| Total | 10,000 | Total | 10,000 |

Now let us assume that the owner buys a used truck for $3,000 cash. The effect of this transaction is to reduce cash by $3,000 and create a new asset on the balance sheet:

| Assets |  | Liabilities | -0- |
|---|---|---|---|
| Cash | 7,000 |  |  |
| Used Truck | 3,000 | Equity | 10,000 |
| Total | 10,000 | Total | 10,000 |

Voila! The balance sheet still balances. Next, let us assume that the owner goes down to the bank and borrows an additional $1,000. This also has a dual effect: It increases cash by $1,000 (because the business is receiving the proceeds of the loan) and increases liabilities by $1,000 (because the business thereafter must repay the loan). Yet another balance sheet can be created showing the additional effect of this second transaction:

| Assets |  | Liabilities |  |
|---|---|---|---|
| Cash | 8,000 | Debt to Bank | 1,000 |
| Used Truck | 3,000 | Equity | 10,000 |
| Total | 11,000 | Total | 11,000 |

Further insights should be evident from these two examples: First, a balance sheet records a situation at one instant in time. It is a static concept, an equilibrium that exists at one point in time rather than a record of change from an earlier period. Put another way, every transaction potentially creates a different or new balance sheet when the transaction is recorded. Second, the bottom line of a balance sheet—$11,000 in this example—is not itself a meaningful figure, because transactions such as the bank loan that do not affect the real worth of the business to the owners may increase or decrease the bottom line.

## §6.4 Accounting for Profits and Losses

The two transactions described above—the purchase of a used truck and a short-term bank loan—involve a reshuffling of assets and liabilities. From an accounting standpoint, the owner of the business is neither richer nor poorer as a result of them. However, most transactions that a business enters into are of a different type: They involve ordinary business operations leading to a profit or loss in the current accounting period. Consider a simple example. Suppose the business described above involves hauling things in the truck for customers. Thus, the company hires a truck driver at a cost of $200 per day to drive the truck and pick up and deliver for it. During that first day the truck driver works very hard and for long hours making deliveries for which the business is paid $500. It is simple to create a profit and loss statement or income statement for the business for the one day of operation. "Profit and loss" and "income" are synonyms for this purpose. The basic formula is:

$$income = revenues - expenses$$

Obviously, the business had income of $300 ($500 of revenue minus $200 of expense for the truck driver) for its first day of operation. There may have been other expenses as well that arguably should be charged to that first day of operation, but for simplicity we are ignoring that possibility.

At first glance, the income statement appears to have nothing to do with the balance sheet described in the previous section. It is possible, however, to create a new balance sheet to reflect each of these transactions.

First, the payment of the $200 to the truck driver involves a cash payment of $200 by the business; it is easy to record that. But where should the offsetting entry be? The balance sheet cannot look like this:

| Assets | | Liabilities | |
| --- | --- | --- | --- |
| Cash | 7,800 | Debt to Bank | 1,000 |
| Used Truck | 3,000 | Equity | 10,000 |
| Total | 10,800 | Total | 11,000 |

Something is obviously wrong, because this balance sheet does not balance. There must be an offsetting entry. It certainly should not be a reduction of liabilities (because the amount of the bank loan is unchanged) or an increase in value of the truck. Perhaps one could view the services as an asset something like the truck, but that does not make much sense, because the services are simply gone. One could perhaps argue that no balance sheet should be created until the payment to the truck driver is offset by whatever the driver earns during the rest of the day, but that cannot be correct either, because the balance sheet should balance after every transaction, not just at the end of a sequence of transactions. By process of elimination, the only possible solution is to reduce "owner's equity" by the payment:

| Assets | | Liabilities | |
|---|---|---|---|
| Cash | 7,800 | Debt to Bank | 1,000 |
| Used Truck | 3,000 | Equity | 9,800 |
| | 10,800 | | 10,800 |

Second, the $500 payment for the services rendered:

| Assets | | Liabilities | |
|---|---|---|---|
| Cash | 8,300 | Debt to Bank | 1,000 |
| Used Truck | 3,000 | Equity | 10,300 |
| | 11,300 | | 11,300 |

Admittedly, these two balance sheets are not very helpful in showing the relationship between the balance sheet and the income statement. What is needed is a segregation of income items within the equity account so that the permanent investment and the transient changes are shown separately. Thus, the following balance sheet at the end of the period is much more illuminating:

| Assets | | Liabilities | |
|---|---|---|---|
| Cash | 8,300 | Debt to Bank | 1,000 |
| Used Truck | 3,000 | Equity | |
| | | Original Capital | 10,000 |
| | | Earnings | 300 |
| | 11,300 | | 11,300 |

The important point at present is that profit and loss items are reflected on the balance sheet as changes in owner's equity.

The balance sheet is a static concept showing the status of a business at a particular instant in time, while the income statement describes the results of operations over some period of time: daily, monthly, quarterly, or annually. In a sense, the balance sheet is a snapshot, and the income statement is a motion picture. The income statement also serves as the bridge between the balance sheet at the beginning of the period and the balance sheet at the end of the period, because positive income items (revenues) increase owner's equity while negative income items (expenses) reduce it. Most investors and creditors look first at the bottom line of the income statement when evaluating financial statements, because the income statement reflects the operations of the business. The balance sheet usually plays a lesser role in financial analysis.

The concept of profit and loss and accounting periods rests on additional fundamental postulates. First, accounting assumes the continuing existence and activity of the business enterprise as a going concern. In other words, it is assumed that the business will be around for an indefinite number of future accounting periods. If a business is in such dire straits that its continued existence is unlikely, a totally different set of accounting principles must be adopted. Second, each business must adopt a fiscal or accounting period and must report the results of operations for that period as a separate accounting unit. The unit usually chosen is a year—either a **calendar year** or a **fiscal year**. (A fiscal year is a reporting period that the business chooses that ends on a date other than December 31 and may vary somewhat in length from a period of precisely 12 months.) Third, in determining the results of operations during an accounting period, some kind of logical relationship must be created between the revenues and expenses that are taken into account in determining profit or loss for that period. The principle usually followed is that costs allocable to the creation of revenue should be matched with that revenue. Other costs arising from the passage of time are allocated to the accounting period on the basis of that time and not the time of receipt. Fourth, some principles must be established as to when revenue is realized. Usually, the rule that is adopted is that revenues are realized when the business becomes unconditionally entitled to their receipt, not when payment is received. In the case of a contract for the sale of goods, for example, revenue may be realized when the goods are shipped, not when the contract was entered into or when payment is made. As a corollary, property of the business that may have appreciated in market value does not give rise to revenue until the gain in value is realized by sale or disposition of the property.

This concept is known as **accrual accounting**, and most businesses follow it. Indeed, most businesses of any size are required to use accrual accounting even though **cash basis accounting** might seem simpler. Most individuals use cash basis accounting for tax purposes (even if they do not know it). Accrual accounting, however, tends to give investors and creditors a better sense of the financial health of a business.

At this point, it is necessary to go back and introduce the way in which the double entry bookkeeping system is used to record transactions as they occur and to permit the development of balance sheets and income statements from those records.

## §6.5 Journal Entries

The essence of double-entry bookkeeping is the systematic recordation of every transaction in the offsetting ways described above. For many centuries, the process of recordation involved the manual entry of transactions by bookkeepers wearing green eye shades. In larger businesses, many transactions need to be entered each day. The development of the computer has automated the bookkeeping process as it has so many other areas: In most businesses today, the process involves relatively small inputs of human labor. Computerized accounting programs, however, largely follow the logic of the earlier manual system. In the following discussion, it is assumed that all transactions are entered manually so that the structure can be examined.

A business does not normally create a new balance sheet after each transaction; in any business with even minimal activity numerous entries are made each day and a balance sheet is created only periodically. The bookkeeper records each transaction in a **journal** to reflect both sides of each transaction. For example, **journal entries** to reflect the truck purchase and the bank loan transactions would look something like this:

| Description of Transaction | Debit | Credit |
|---|---|---|
| 1/1   Cash |  | $3,000 |
|         Vehicles | $3,000 |  |
| To record purchase of truck |  |  |
|  |  |  |
| 1/2   Cash | $1,000 |  |
|         Current Liabilities |  | $1,000 |
| To record 90-day loan from bank |  |  |

There may not seem to be any relationship between these two entries and the two balance sheets previously set forth. But because of accounting conventions, they are reflections of the same transactions, and an accountant can readily go from the journal entries to the balance sheets.

First of all, a word needs to be said about the words **debit** and **credit** in the titles to the foregoing journal entries (titles, incidentally, that are so well understood that they do not usually appear on real journal pages). The word debit simply means "left hand" and the word credit means "right hand." There is widespread popular confusion over the meaning of these two terms. In a lay sense, debit is probably associated with reduction, while credit is associated with increase. Once the notion of double entry bookkeeping is introduced, however, it is clear that the words require more careful elaboration, because every transaction, in a sense, involves both an increase and a decrease. Further, all journal entries by conventional understanding are positive. The basic accounting convention that ties journal entries to balance sheet items can be simply stated but is rather confusing: A debit journal entry increases left-hand items on the balance sheet and decreases right-hand items, while a credit journal entry reduces left-hand items and increases right-hand items. Thus, in the foregoing examples, an experienced accountant looking at the two entries knows at a glance that the business reduced its cash account by $3,000 when it bought the truck and increased it by $1,000 when it entered into the bank loan. Similarly, an accountant knows at a glance that the credit reflecting the bank loan increased the business's liabilities, because "liabilities" is a right-hand account.

Because the income statement may be viewed as part of the right-hand side of the balance sheet, journal entries are also used to enter transactions involving the income statement. The basic concept is that revenue items are credits and expense items are debits. (Recall that credits increase right-hand items and debits reduce them.) Thus, the journal entries for the salary payment to the truck driver and the receipt of the fee look like this:

| Description of Transaction | Debit | Credit |
|---|---|---|
| 1/1   Current salaries—expense | $200 |  |
|         Cash |  | $200 |
| To record truck driver's salary |  |  |
|  |  |  |
| 1/2   Cash | $500 |  |
|         Fees earned—income |  | $500 |
| To record fee for truck driver's services |  |  |

The "current salaries" account is an income statement item (an expense item that reduces earnings, as all debits must do), while the cash account to which it is joined in the journal appears only on the balance sheet; similarly the "fees earned" account is also an income statement item (a receipt item that increases earnings, as all credits must do), while the balance sheet item cash is increased.

The genius of the double entry system is that a single set of entries permits the development of both types of financial statements and provides the internal controls that are essential for any large business.

## §6.6 The Balance Sheet

Before turning to a discussion of some of the major issues in accounting, it is useful to present a balance sheet and income statement for a relatively complex business and briefly describe the items in each statement. The relationship of these two statements to the simple examples used in previous sections should be evident. The purpose of this exercise is primarily to familiarize the reader with the traditional language used in financial statements and give an example of what financial statements look like.

As is customary, the balance sheet shown in Table 6-1 is as of the close of business on the last day of the accounting period covered by the income statement. The left-hand side of the balance sheet reflects the various **assets** of the business. It is usually subdivided into two categories: current assets and non current assets.

**Current Assets** consist of cash plus other assets that normally may be expected to be turned into cash within a year (or, in a few cases, in a longer period constituting the business's normal operating cycle):

**Cash** includes not only funds on deposit in checking accounts, but also cash equivalents. As described in earlier chapters, large sums of money are not normally left idle for even short periods of time. In most publicly held companies, temporarily excess funds are conservatively invested short-term in riskless securities that are usually not subject to swings in value. Such investments may include United States Treasury bills or notes, certificates of deposit, commercial paper, bankers' acceptances, and so-called money market accounts.

**Marketable Securities** includes longer term investments. Businesses may have excess or idle cash available for longer periods of time that may be temporarily invested in longer-term marketable securities. The funds may be set aside for business purposes such as long-term capital improvements or real estate acquisition, or they may simply be excess cash that the company does not want to distribute to shareholders in the form of dividends.

**Accounts Receivable** are amounts due from customers. Accounts receivable typically arise from the sale of goods on credit. An allowance for bad debts (somtimes more elegantly referred to as an allowance for doubtful accounts) is subtracted from accounts receivable. The amount of this item is usually estimated based on the prior collection history of the business.

**Inventories** include several types of goods needed by the business in production of its end product: raw materials, partially finished goods in pro-

### Table 6-1
### ABC Incorporated
### Balance Sheet as of December 31

|  | Last Year | This Year |
|---|---|---|
| **ASSETS** | | |
| **Current Assets** | | |
| Cash | $250,000 | $300,000 |
| Marketable Securities | 460,000 | 460,000 |
| Accounts Receivable (net) | 1,750,000 | 1,900,000 |
| Inventories | 2,800,000 | 3,000,000 |
| Total Current Assets | $5,260,000 | $5,660,000 |
| **Noncurrent Assets** | | |
| Fixed Assets | | |
| Land | 450,000 | 450,000 |
| Buildings | 3,600,000 | 3,600,000 |
| Machinery | 545,000 | 850,000 |
| Office Equipment | 95,000 | 95,000 |
| Less Accumulated Depreciation | (1,225,000) | (1,500,000) |
| Total Fixed Assets | $3,465,000 | $3,495,000 |
| Prepayments and Deferred Charges | 40,000 | 40,000 |
| Intangible Assets | | |
| Patents and Copyrights | 75,000 | 75,000 |
| Goodwill | 25,000 | 25,000 |
| Other Assets | 50,000 | 50,000 |
| **Total Assets** | $8,915,000 | $9,345,000 |
| **LIABILITIES** | | |
| Current Liabilities | | |
| Accounts Payable | 903,000 | 940,000 |
| Notes Payable | 900,000 | 1,000,000 |
| Accrued Expenses Payable | 590,000 | 590,000 |
| Total Current Liabilities | $2,393,000 | $2,530,000 |
| Long Term Liabilities | | |
| 5% Debentures (due 2016) | 2,700,000 | 2,700,000 |
| **Total Liabilities** | $5,093,000 | $5,230,000 |
| **STOCKHOLDERS' EQUITY** | | |
| Capital Stock | | |
| Preferred Stock (60,000 Shares / Par Value and Liquidation Preference $10) | 600,000 | 600,000 |
| Common Stock (300,000 Shares / Par Value $5) | 1,500,000 | 1,500,000 |
| Additional Paid in Capital | 700,000 | 700,000 |
| Retained Earnings | 1,022,000 | 1,315,000 |
| Total Stockholders' Equity | $3,822,000 | $4,115,000 |
| **Total Liabilities and Stockholders' Equity** | $8,915,000 | $9,345,000 |

cess of manufacture, and finished goods ready for shipment. The inventory of a retail operation may consist almost solely of finished goods. There are several methods of reporting inventory, and the choice of method can be controversial, as is discussed more fully below.

**Non current Assets** consist of all assets that are not classified as current and include a variety of quite different items:

**Fixed Assets** are traditionally defined as property, plant, and equipment. Such items are usually recorded at historical cost; plant and equipment is depreciated over its expected life. Hence, the negative item, **accumulated depreciation**, appears as an offset. This negative item is the total of all prior deductions for depreciation in earlier years. The truck in the simple illustration used earlier to describe basic bookkeeping techniques is an example of depreciable equipment. Land is a fixed asset that is not depreciable. The reporting of fixed assets and the depreciation concept is discussed below.

**Prepayments and Deferred Charges** are also sometimes described as **prepaid charges**. They are discussed below in connection with the concept of accrual.

**Intangible Assets** fall into various categories. Traditional intangible assets (those that are usually not controversial from the standpoint of accounting principles) include patents, trademarks, and franchises. These intangible assets are reported at acquisition or development cost. The presence of other intangible assets, particularly **goodwill, capitalized organizational cost**, or **capitalized research and development costs** on a balance sheet are a warning sign for careful analysis. These assets may reflect only balancing entries for prior transactions. For example, if a company buys a bundle of assets for more than the sum of their individual fair market values, the excess may be entered as "goodwill." Whether or not the purchase was desirable, not much weight can be given to goodwill as an asset. It is unclear on the face of the balance sheet what the "Goodwill— $25,000" entry represents; it is unlikely, however, that it is an asset in any realistic sense of the word.

**Other Assets** may include a variety of interests (e.g., debts owed to the company that mature in more than one year, minority interests in other businesses, and the like).

Companies in specialized fields may include additional asset items or different breakdowns of traditional items.

**Liabilities** in the accounting sense are obligations that probably will need to be paid in an amount that can reasonably be estimated when the balance sheet is prepared. Material litigation or claims that do not qualify as liabilities in this sense do not appear on the balance sheet itself but should be referred to in the accompanying notes to the financial statements as contingent liabilities.

**Current Liabilities** are those expected to be satisfied out of current assets, usually including all liabilities that will become due in the coming year. Their relationship to current assets can be an important one for evaluating the financial strength of the business. The most common current liabilities are usually broken down and listed separately:

**Accounts Payable** are amounts owed to suppliers based on deliveries of supplies and raw materials on credit.

**Notes Payable** are amounts due to banks and other lenders in connection with loans that mature during the following 12 months. The portion of a long-term loan payable in installments that is due to be paid within 12 months is also included within notes payable.

**Accrued Expenses Payable** is a catchall for amounts owed to other creditors that do not fall within the categories of accounts or notes payable. It may include amounts owed to employees for wages and salaries on the date of the balance sheet; interest on open accounts not reflected as promissory notes; amounts owed to federal, state, or local governments for taxes; fees owed to attorneys; insurance premiums; required pension plan contributions; and a variety of other current liabilities. Because accountants are conservative and interested in matching costs with revenues, accrued expenses payable may include items that are not yet enforceable legal liabilities.

**Long-term Liabilities** are liabilities due more than one year from the date of the balance sheet. The most common kinds of long-term liabilities are mortgages on real property or bonds and debentures that the company issues in order to raise working capital. The debentures shown in Table 6-2 are unsecured debt obligations of ABC carrying a 5 percent interest rate and not due for repayment for nearly 30 years. The payment date is so far in the future that such debt should realistically be viewed as part of the permanent capitalization of the company.

**Stockholders' Equity** is the balancing factor between assets and liabilities on the balance sheet. In the case of partnerships or proprietorships, this part of the balance sheet may be titled **owners' equity**, or simply **capital** or **capital contributed by partners**. Stockholders' equity consists basically of two parts: (1) the permanent non-debt capitalization of the business, and (2) **retained earnings**. Retained earnings is the accumulated income of the business (less any distributions to owners). It is also the item that ensures that the balance sheet balances. Specifically, the equity portion of the balance sheet usually contains the following categories:

**Preferred Stock** is usually a stock with a prior (but limited) claim to distributions ahead of the common shares. Preferred stock also usually has a prior (but limited) claim on liquidation. In the case of ABC, no information is given on the balance sheet as to the **dividend preferences** or **liquidation preferences** of this preferred stock.

**Common Stock** represents the residual ownership of the corporation. In many states, it is customary to assign a **par value** to common (and preferred) stock. Par value is an arbitrary amount, a relic of earlier corporation practices. When par value is used, the virtually universal practice is to specify a very low par value and to issue shares for a price higher than par value. Nevertheless, par value stock is entered as permanent capital on the balance sheet at its **aggregate par value**, an item that is sometimes called **stated capital**. The excess amounts that investors paid over par value when the stock was issued is shown separately as **additional paid in capital (APIC)**.

**Retained Earnings** is (as the name suggests) the accumulated income that the company has booked from operations and other sources. When a company makes a sale of an item of inventory at a profit and then either holds the cash or uses it to purchase more inventory, the inventory account will go up by the amount of the profit. The balance sheet will thus be out of balance unless some amount is added to either liabilities or stockholders' equity. Clearly, the addition to assets is not a liability nor was it received in exchange for stock. Retained earnings is the default account into which the difference goes. And when the business has a loss, retained earnings is reduced. Thus, retained earnings is in a sense a fudge factor. But it is an important fudge factor in that it reflects the ability of the business to make profits over time. As will be seen in more detail, retained earnings is the connection between the balance sheet and the income statement. When the business pays out dividends to its stockholders, retained earnings is reduced.

The following formulas should clarify the relationship between the balance sheet and the income statement:

$$\text{beginning owner's equity} + \text{net income} - \text{dividends declared} \\ + \text{stock issued} - \text{stock repurchased} = \text{ending owner's equity}$$

$$\text{beginning capital} + \text{stock issued} - \text{stock repurchased} = \text{ending capital}$$

$$\text{beginning retained earnings} + \text{revenues} - \text{expenses} \\ - \text{dividends} = \text{ending retained earnings}$$

The most important concept embedded in these formulas is that the owner's equity reported on the balance sheet will increase and decrease during the year by revenues and expenses (income statement items). In other words, if instead of using journal entries, we record transactions according to the impact they have on assets, liabilities, and owner's equity, the changes to owner's equity during the year (excluding changes due to stock transactions and dividends) will be the income statement.

## §6.7 The Income Statement

The items on the income statement are easier to understand than the items on the balance sheet. As described above, it is built on the fundamental notion that:

$$\text{revenues} - \text{expenses} = \text{net income}$$

This relationship should be immediately apparent from even a cursory examination of the income statement shown in Table 6-2.

Table 6-2
ABC Incorporated
Income Statement for Year Ended December 31

| | | |
|---|---|---|
| Net Sales | | $10,200,000 |
| Cost of Goods Sold | | 7,684,000 |
| Gross Margin | | 2,516,000 |
| Other Expenses | | |
| Depreciation | 275,000 | |
| Selling and Administrative Expense | 1,325,000 | |
| | | 1,600,000 |
| Operating Profit | | 916,000 |
| Other Income | | |
| Dividends and Interest | | 27,000 |
| Total Income | | 943,000 |
| Less Interest Paid on Debentures | | 135,000 |
| Income Before Provision for Federal Income Tax | | 808,000 |
| Provision for Federal Income Tax | | 365,000 |
| Net Profit for Year Before Extraordinary Items | | 443,000 |
| Extraordinary Gain—Settlement of Legal Action | 123,000 | |
| Less Applicable Taxes | 55,000 | 68,000 |
| Net Income for Year | | $511,000 |

The income statement set forth here is for a business primarily involved in manufacturing and selling some sort of tangible product. (In the case of a business not involved primarily in selling goods, the revenue side may be titled operating revenues and the expense side not broken down between costs of goods sold and other expenses.) It should be noted that there are six "bottom lines" in this rather elaborate income statement: (1) sales minus **cost of goods sold** equals **gross margin**; (2) gross margin minus **operating expenses** (expenses not allocable directly to the goods sold) equals **operating profit**; (3) operating profit plus other income (e.g., income from dividends, interest, or rent not connected with the entity's principal business) equals **total income**; (4) total income less interest on long-term debentures equals **income before provision for income tax**; (5) income before provision for income tax minus income tax equals **net income for year before extraordinary items**; and finally, (6) net income takes into account the extraordinary gain from the settlement of litigation, which is the bottom bottom line. The net income for year before extraordinary items is normally used to compare results with previous years or with other companies. Not all published income statements contain this degree of breakdown. For example, gross margin is primarily useful for internal control and projections by management and is not ordinarily separated out. Similarly, interest on bonds or debentures is often not separated out but included as a part of operating expenses as a single item interest expense, so that the distinction between total income and income before provision for federal income tax disappears.

Several items on this balance sheet merit further explanation:

**Net Sales** means gross sales minus returns. One of the expenses deducted as other expenses from net sales is **depreciation**. This reflects the portion of the original purchase price of each depreciable asset that is allocated to the current year as the cost of gradually using up that asset, and should be distinguished from the **accumulated depreciation** item on the balance sheet, which represents all prior deductions for depreciation of all depreciable property in the asset account.

**Extraordinary Items** are nonrecurring items that materially affect the operating results. Such items are usually separated out and shown at the very bottom of the income statement after calculating the operating profit, which represents the earnings capacity typical of the firm. Then, an estimate of the taxes that would be due on that profit is determined. Extraordinary items may or may not give rise to accompanying income tax adjustments. For example, an extraordinary item involving the writing off of assets no longer needed in business operations may not be deductible from federal income taxes. When an extraordinary loss item is deductible for tax purposes in the year in question, the extraordinary loss is shown below the net profit from operations line, reduced by the accompanying tax saving. As a result, taxes payable on regular operations are shown separately from those arising from the extraordinary item, for example:

| | |
|---|---|
| Extraordinary Loss from Confiscation of Iran Properties | $6,000,000 |
| Less Tax Saving | $2,800,000 |
| Net Extraordinary Loss | $3,200,000 |

## §6.8  Other Statements

The balance sheet and the income statement, the most fundamental accounting statements, are usually accompanied by two additional statements. The **Statement of Changes in Retained Earnings** makes explicit the link between the income statement and the balance sheet. Table 6-3 provides an illustration. This statement is based on the following formula:

retained earnings at beginning of period + income for period
− dividends declared = retained earnings at end of period

This formula makes explicit the common sense notion that earnings for the accounting period in question should be reduced by dividends declared during

**Table 6-3**
**ABC Incorporated**
**Statement of Changes in Retained Earnings**

| | |
|---|---|
| Balance January 1 | $1,022,000 |
| Net Income for Year | 511,000 |
| Total | 1,533,000 |
| Less: Dividends Declared | |
| On Preferred Stock | 30,000 |
| On Common Stock | 188,000 |
| Balance December 31 | 1,315,000 |

the period in computing the increment to retained earnings from the start of the period. If new shares are issued, this information will appear in a statement entitled **Statement of Changes in Stockholders' Equity** (which, of course, will also include the information presented in the Statement of Changes in Retained Earnings).

The **Statement of Cash Flows** is a reclassification of items that appear in the balance sheet and income statement. Its ostensible purpose is to show how a company acquired cash and what it did with it. A typical funds statement is shown in Table 6-4.

Table 6-4
ABC Incorporated
Statement of Cash Flows

| | |
|---|---|
| Net Income | 511,000 |
| Cash Flow from Operating Activities | |
| Depreciation | 275,000 |
| Increase in Accounts Payable | 37,000 |
| Increase in Accounts Receivable | (150,000) |
| Increase in Inventories | (200,000) |
| Cash Flow from Investing Activities | |
| Purchases of Machinery | (305,000) |
| Cash Flow from Financing Activities | |
| Bank Loan | 100,000 |
| Dividends Paid | (218,000) |
| Net Increase in Cash | 50,000 |

The typical presentation of this statement is curious. In effect it begins with the assumption that income is equivalent to cash and then proceeds to list all the ways in which it is not and to add or subtract appropriate amounts to arrive at a number equal to the change in cash. This is called the indirect method of reporting cash flows. A company may choose to report cash flows directly, by listing cash receipts and payments. And indeed accounting pronouncements encourage the direct method. But few companies use the direct method, possibly because they must then separately report changes in working capital accounts anyway.

## §6.9  The Concept of Accrual

Most individuals and households keep their accounts (such as they are) on a **cash basis**. Salaries and other income are entered into the checkbook when they are received; payments are entered when they are made. For most people, this method of accounting for personal income and expenses is reasonably satisfactory. Most businesses, however, find this method of accounting inadequate, and operate on an **accrual basis**. Indeed, accrual accounting is required by GAAP and by the Internal Revenue Service (IRS) for most businesses that sell goods.

The basic difference between the accrual and cash methods of accounting lies in the answer to the question, when should transactions be recognized? The cash method of accounting is based on the convention that transactions should be recognized when cash comes in or goes out. That system, however, is likely to lead to very erratic results and be subject to manipulation in businesses that maintain an inventory of goods. A large purchase of inventory at a very favorable price in one year should not be treated as an expense for that period. To do so may result in the business showing a loss for the accounting period for that year even though the purchase permitted the business to enjoy high profits in later years. If the accounting process is to reflect what is really happening, that inventory should be treated as an asset and taken into expense only when sales are made from it. Hence, the development of **accrual accounting**.

Second, emphasis on cash payments or receipts ignores the most significant event in the transaction, namely doing the work or committing oneself to pay for something that is used immediately but paid for later.

Third, it is relatively easy to manipulate accounting results if a transaction enters the accounting system only when cash comes in or goes out. One can defer receipt or put off paying, whichever happens to be in the interest of the management of the business. (This should not be construed as indicating that manipulation is not possible in the accrual system. It is, but it is not as easy.) Businesses in which inventories of physical goods are an important aspect of the operation almost universally operate on the accrual system to avoid distortions of income and expense caused by the timing of raw material purchases and sales on cash or credit. It is for this reason that the Internal Revenue Code requires accrual tax accounting for such businesses.

In any event, the accrual system assumes that transactions should be recognized and taken into account when they have their primary economic impact, not when cash is received or disbursed. On the revenue side, that time is usually the rendering of service or the sale of goods. In the case of revenue items dependent on the passage of time—say, rent or interest—the critical event is simply the passage of time. As a practical matter, that means such items are taken into account at the end of specific time periods: weekly, monthly, quarterly, or annually. Thus, revenue items may, and often do, accrue even though they have not been billed and even though there is no right to immediate payment.

Under the accrual system, costs or expenses are taken into account when the benefit occurs, which is typically when the revenues to which they relate are earned. In short, the goal of the accrual system is the matching of expenses with corresponding revenues wherever possible. However, a variety of indirect expenses cannot be allocated to specific revenues; these items are accrued over time and independent of revenues. Examples of indirect expenses are interest on borrowed funds or rent that must be paid on land.

Cash receipts or payments that relate to income or expenses for accounting periods other than the current period are viewed as creating assets or liabilities on the balance sheet; these assets or liabilities are **parked** on the balance sheet and **written off** (i.e., taken as expenses) in the year in which they are recognized for accounting purposes. A few examples of the accrual concept may be useful.

In the following examples, assume that the business's accounting period closes on December 31.

*(a) The business purchases inventory (goods for resale) on 12/15, paying $500 in cash.* This transaction affects only the balance sheet, increasing inventory by $500 and reducing cash by the same amount. Again, assets equal liabilities plus owner's equity. This equation holds true for every individual transaction. In other words, the balance sheet must remain in balance at all times. If an asset is increased, either another asset must be decreased or liabilities or owner's equity must be increased. Thus, a particular transaction may affect just one side of the balance sheet in offsetting ways, or it may affect both sides of the balance sheet by the same amount. If an increase in an asset is not offset by a decrease in another asset or an equal increase in a liability, then it must generate an increase in owner's equity. If there is an increase in owner's equity, it must be because the business made a profit. Profits must, of course, be reflected on the income statement, and accordingly it may take more than one set of journal entries to account for such a transaction. Nevertheless, the relationship between the balance sheet and the income statement can be appreciated if one simply keeps in mind that every transaction must leave the balance sheet in balance and that any net increase or decrease in assets or liabilities must affect owner's equity and must thus somehow be reflected on the income statement. Finally, it should also be clear that there are many transactions that involve cash flows that do not affect the income statement. Indeed, the above purchase of inventory for cash is just such a transaction.

*(b) On 1/6, the business sells to a retail customer from inventory goods that cost $300; the sales price for the goods is $600, to be paid within 90 days.* This transaction decreases inventory by $300 (the cost of the goods sold) and increases accounts receivable by $600 (the sales price that is now owed to the business). The $300 difference is the profit on the transaction and it increases retained earnings, which of course is a component of owner's equity. When the increase in retained earnings is reported on the income statement, it has two components: sales revenue ($600) and cost of goods sold ($300).

*(c) On 3/9, the customer pays her $600 bill.* Cash is increased by this amount and accounts receivable are reduced. Again, the transaction affects only the asset side of the balance sheet and thus has no impact on earnings, although it clearly constitutes cash flow.

The effect of these various transactions is that the sale of goods is taken into income in January when the sale takes place; the earlier purchase of inventory is parked in the inventory account on the balance sheet until the sale occurs, and then it is moved into the income statement as part of cost of goods sold. The corporation's income accounts would not be affected if the payment of the account had occurred in the following year, whether the transaction was a cash rather than a credit sale, or whether the customer had made a series of layaway payments in the prior year. In each event, the income statement would reflect the sales revenue of $600, in the year in which the sale itself was made.

*(d) The business opens a new store on 12/1 and is required by its new landlord to pay two years of rent in advance.* Transactions of this type require the

creation of a new balance sheet asset account, "prepaid rent." At the end of one month, $500 is deducted from the prepaid rent account, thus decreasing owners' equity by the same amount. When the decrease in retained earnings is recorded on the income statement, it is called "rent expense." During each month of the following year, the appropriate amount of rent is deducted from prepaid rent and retained earnings are reduced. The effect of this treatment is that the prepayment of rent is actually allocated to each time period during which the business has the use of the rented property for income statement purposes. Prepaid expenses are assets, while the receipt of prepaid income creates a liability.

*(e) The business owns an apartment house. It rents an apartment to X, who is required to pay the first and last month's rent of $800 (for a total of $1600) when he enters into the lease on the first day of the tenancy.* A new balance sheet liability, "unearned rent," is created to reflect the receipt of the rent for which services have not yet been provided. At the end of the first month, rental income is recognized for the first month's rent. Liabilities are reduced by $800, which means that retained earnings must increase by $800 in order for the balance sheet to remain in balance. When the increase in retained earnings is reported on the income statement, it is called "rental income." The unearned rent liability remains on the books of the business until the last month of the rental. It is eliminated when the last month's rent has been earned.

There is a common theme in all of these examples: Because revenue is not accounted for until the transaction occurs (or time passes, in the case of rental income), any receipts or payments of cash allocable to other accounting periods are treated purely as balance sheet entries. Prepaid expenses are treated as assets and unearned receipts are treated as liabilities. Although some people sometimes find it difficult to accept that the prepayment of an expense item creates an asset while the receipt of unearned income creates a liability, this treatment may be appreciated intuitively by noting that the prepayment of an expense is indistinguishable in principle from the purchase of an asset such as a truck. Indeed, in one sense, all assets on a balance sheet other than cash are expenses waiting to be written off (used up) in an appropriate future accounting period.

It should also be noted that in accrual accounting, income and expense items are not adjusted for many transactions that intuitively seem to be income-generating or expense-generating unless gain or loss is recognized. For example, no income is recognized upon the receipt of prepaid rent; that rent can be earned only by the passage of time.

The simple accrual system works best for businesses that have large numbers of profit-making or loss-creating transactions during each accounting period. In other types of businesses, however, traditional accrual accounting results in the bunching of income, making accounting results incomparable from one year to the next.

A classic example of this latter type of business is an airplane manufacturer with a contract that involves two years of design and construction work before the first plane is delivered. If the contract involves, say, a $60,000,000 payment when each plane is delivered, the airplane manufacturer, if it follows simple accrual accounting principles, will show no income during the two-year development phase and will record its first revenue with the sale of the first plane in the third year of the contract. If the airplane manufacturer follows conventional accrual principles, it will capitalize development expenses (i.e., treat them as an asset rather than as expenses) and will show zero income for the first two years, followed by profits in the years during which the planes are sold. However, if it appears likely from the outset that the project will be profitable, it is more realistic to allocate a portion of the ultimate profit to each of the two developmental years in which much of the work is done rather than show an erratic and unrealistic zero-profit income statement for two years, followed by years of high income when the airplanes are sold. Much the same pattern may be present in the development of software for computers, the production of motion pictures, heavy construction projects, and other business activities that involve development periods of more than one year.

The application of an accrual accounting system to such businesses is not without controversy. The accountant takes pride in treating recognition issues conservatively, and refusing to recognize income unless it is certain to be earned. The difficulty with our hypothetical airplane manufacturer is that it is usually not possible to determine that the airplane being developed will in fact be salable until after sales begin.

Accounting on a basis other than traditional accrual principles is nevertheless well accepted in some industries. For example, many companies engaged in commercial construction report income on a percentage-of-contract-completion basis that spreads anticipated profits over the lifetime of the contract. Sellers of large consumer or commercial equipment on credit may report income on the installment basis rather than using the point of sale as the time of realization of income. Deciding what is the most appropriate time for revenue recognition is often a matter of judgment.

## §6.10  Historical Cost

**Historical cost** has little or nothing to do with value. Value usually means the price established by transactions between willing buyers and sellers in a market. It might also mean the value of the asset to the user, or the cost of reproducing or replacing the asset. Usually, the one thing it most certainly does not mean is what the asset cost, perhaps years earlier. Yet, that is precisely the number from which most financial statements under GAAP are derived. The use of historical cost as the basis for accounting can be justified on several pragmatic grounds. It fits in easily with the intricate systems of accounts created under principles of double entry bookkeeping. It is also objective and easily verifiable.

Theoretically, one could develop an alternative accounting system that immediately recorded unrealized appreciation. Abstractly, such a system is neither right nor wrong. However, such a system would be risky, because asset values that go up can also go down. Moreover, there is a serious risk that such asset values might be intentionally overstated.

A couple of important qualifications to the historical cost principle are contained in GAAP. One qualification is that GAAP assumes that the business is a **going concern**. If an auditor concludes that the business is contemplating liquidation or is otherwise unlikely to survive, he or she should insist that the basis for reporting values be changed from historical cost to liquidation values. As a practical matter, that change usually results in a significant mark-down in reported amounts and the elimination of many assets from the balance sheet. For example, organizational expenses may be capitalized and viewed as an asset only if the business is a going concern: It is clear that these expenses have little or no inherent market value if the business is to be liquidated.

Another major qualification is embodied in the principle that assets the firm holds for resale should be reported at the **lower of cost or market**. In other words, if the market value of inventory is less than original cost, it should be immediately written down to current market value. In connection with inventory, this devaluation of assets may be made either on an item-by-item basis, or by classes of products.

The principles outlined in this section are sometimes cited as illustrating the conservatism of the accounting profession. Accountants may in fact be conservative, but it should be recognized that historical cost can just as easily overstate current value as understate it. To be sure, it seems likely that using historical cost understates assets more often than it overstates them. But although the accountant's conservatism is likely to hurt (say) sellers of shares, it is equally likely to help buyers of shares, assuming, of course, that either takes financial statements at face value.

## §6.11 Depreciation, Depletion, and Amortization

**Depreciation**, **depletion**, and **amortization** all refer to the allocation of the cost of a long-lived asset to consecutive accounting periods as expenses to reflect the gradual using up of the asset. Depreciation is associated with the process of writing off plant and equipment; depletion refers to the gradual exhaustion of natural resources. Amortization is used with intangible assets (such as copyrights or patents) and deferred charges (such as organizational expenses, research and development costs, or dry holes in oil and gas exploration). In a sense, the writing off or **expensing** of long-lived assets is similar to any prepayment of future expenses: The purchase of a truck, for example, can be seen as a prepayment to ensure the availability of the truck over the balance of its useful life in much the same way that the advance payment of two years' rent creates an asset—prepaid expenses.

One of the transactions discussed in this chapter was the purchase of a used truck for $3,000. This purchase led to an increase in the asset "truck" of $3,000, the truck's purchase price (historical cost). The following steps are required to calculate the depreciation of this asset following its acquisition: Someone (presumably an accountant) estimates (1) the useful life of the truck and (2) the scrap or resale value of the truck, if any, at the end of that period. Assuming that **straight line depreciation** is being followed, the difference between the original cost and the **scrap value** (or **salvage value**) is then divided by the number of years of the truck's estimated useful life. That amount is treated as the annual expense of using up the truck. For example, if the useful life of the truck is estimated to be five years, and the resale value of the truck at the end of that period is estimated to be zero, straight line depreciation accounting requires that the business include as an expense, in each of the next five years, ($3,000 − 0) / 5, or $600 per year. In each of those years, the asset truck will decrease by $600 and there will be a corresponding $600 decrease in retained earnings. When reported on the income statement, this decrease in retained earnings will be called **depreciation expense**. Often, a special account called a **contra account** will be added to the balance sheet to record the cumulative decrease in the depreciable asset. After two years of depreciation have been expensed, the balance sheet entry will look like this:

| | |
|---|---|
| Equipment (Truck) | $3,000 |
| Less: Accumulated Depreciation | $1,200 |
| | $1,800 |

There are several important points to make about this simple example. First, the balance sheet item **accumulated depreciation** is purely a bookkeeping item. There is no separate fund or separate account in the corporation's assets marked "depreciation account" or "depreciation reserve" that contains $1,200, and there are no funds set aside to help pay for the truck's replacement when it wears out. Rather, the $1,200 is simply the sum of two $600 items taken as expenses. Thus, in the example, instead of reducing the asset "truck" by $600, the contra account, "accumulated depreciation" would be increased by that amount. The offsetting charge to retained earnings remains the same.

Second, the truck will gradually wear out, and will presumably need to be replaced. Depreciation deductions do not affect this process in a direct way. The only real effect of depreciation expense is that it (1) reduces reported earnings without being a drain on the business's current cash flow, and (2) reduces the business's tax bill (assuming that the Internal Revenue Code permits the particular depreciation deduction to be calculated and claimed in the way proposed). This tax consequence arises because depreciation is a deductible expense for tax purposes, and larger depreciation deductions mean lower income subject to tax. Arguments for faster depreciation deductions are usually motivated to some extent by the prospect of larger tax deductions.

Third, after two years, the $3,000 amount reported for the truck has been reduced to $1,800 on the books of the business through two depreciation deductions of $600 each. This $1,800 figure is called the **book value** of the truck (because it is the value of the truck as shown on the books of the business). Is there any relationship between this book value and what the truck is actually worth after two years? Probably not. If the current market value of the truck is in fact $1,800, it is purely by chance. Trucks do not usually decline in value at a steady rate precisely equal to that originally estimated by an accountant. Furthermore, the starting value for the depreciation calculation was the cost of the truck two years ago. What has happened to the used truck market in the meantime? Indeed, there is no reason to believe that the business originally paid the truck's fair market value when it bought the truck: It could have paid too much or too little. For accounting purposes, however, the value of the truck when it is purchased is its cost. Certainly, the depreciation calculation takes none of these factors into account. When the business sells the truck, it probably will be at a price different from its book value; the gain or loss on that transaction is reflected in income or retained earnings at that time.

Fourth, does the truck disappear after it has been reduced to zero on the books of the business? Of course not. If the truck still has economic value it may continue to be used in the business. In this case, the original estimate of the truck's useful life was too conservative—the truck was written off more quickly than its useful life actually warranted. Once the truck has been fully depreciated (i.e., reduced to its estimated scrap or resale value) no further depreciation deductions are available to the business for that truck if it continues to be used in the business thereafter. But if the truck is sold to another business, it may be depreciated all over again to the extent of the sale price.

This traditional way of handling depreciation has one justification: It requires that costs of certain assets be allocated in an orderly and verifiable fashion to different accounting periods. Whether or not the specific allocations to specific periods are accurate may be less important than that they be done on a systematic basis that approximates the useful life span of the asset.

The foregoing discussion has assumed that annual depreciation deductions would be calculated by dividing the depreciable value of the property by its expected life. This type of depreciation is usually called **straight line depreciation**, because the amount of the deduction for depreciation each year is constant over the life of the asset. That is, a graph of the book value of the asset over time would be a downward sloping straight line.

Accelerated depreciation systems involve placing relatively larger amounts of the depreciation deductions in the early years of the asset's life. These systems are to a large extent tax-oriented, because the increased deductions that these systems generate in the early years of the life of the asset, if accepted for federal income tax purposes, create significant tax benefits. In some circumstances, however, these systems may be independently justified from an accounting standpoint, because taking most of the depreciation charges in the early years of the asset's life more closely approximates actual market values for assets such as automobiles or trucks, which typically depreciate in value very rapidly during their early years of use.

Perhaps the most popular accelerated depreciation system is the **sum of the digits method**. In this method, the depreciation deduction is calculated each year by creating a fraction, in which the numerator equals the number of years of useful life remaining and the denominator equals the sum of all the useful years of life of the asset. For example, for the truck with a five-year useful life expectancy, the denominator is $5 + 4 + 3 + 2 + 1$, or 15. In the first year, the numerator is five (and the fraction is 5/15 or 1/3); in the second year, the numerator is 4 (and the fraction is 4/15); in the third year, the numerator is 3 (and the fraction is 3/15 or 1/5), and so forth. The logic of this system is not as important as the accelerated pattern of deductions that it creates.

Another popular accelerated depreciation system is the **declining balance method**. In this method, a stable fraction or percentage is applied to the current book value of the asset (historical cost minus previous depreciation deductions), rather than to original cost less salvage value. (Salvage value is not considered when applying the declining balance method.) The fraction or percentage is usually a multiple of the straight line depreciation rate. Thus, if the asset has a five-year life, the straight line depreciation rate is 20 percent per year. The double declining balance method applies twice the 20 percent rate, or 40 percent per year. For example, a $3,000 truck depreciated over five years by the double declining balance method would lead to the following depreciation deductions in the first five years:

| Cost less depreciation | Rate | Depreciation deduction |
|---|---|---|
| $3,000 | 40% | $1,200 |
| (3,000 − 1,200) = 1,800 | 40% | $720 |
| (1,800 − 720) = 1,080 | 40% | $432 |
| (1,080 − 432) = 638 | 40% | $259.20 |
| (638 − 259.20) = 378.80 | 40% | $151.52 |

The **150 percent declining balance method** would entail the use of a 30 percent rate on a five-year asset. The declining balance method, like the sum of the digits method, results in very substantial deductions in early years. In the above example, the double declining balance method results in a write-off of 40 percent of the cost of the truck in the first year, compared with the 33 percent maximum write-off obtainable under the sum of the digits method.

*Depletion.* The calculation of depletion of natural resources is usually made on the basis of estimates of the total recoverable resources in the property in question. The original purchase price or cost of the asset is divided by the estimated recoverable resources in the oil field, ore body, timber reserve, or other property to determine the cost per unit. Then, as each unit is captured and recovered, the cost is shown less accumulated depletion much the same way as depreciation is shown. In effect, depletion allocates the investment's initial cost in accordance with the recovery from the asset itself rather than over an arbitrary period of years, as is done with depreciation. If the field or ore body contains more resources than estimated, recovery after full depletion of the original cost results in a zero deduction for depletion of the additional units. For many years, depletion of oil or gas reserves was on an income rather than cost basis. That is, a fixed percentage of income (depending on the nature of the asset) was written off as cost. However, that is now permitted only for smaller unintegrated firms.

*Amortization.* The amortization of intangible assets and deferred charges follows a similar pattern, though the issues are considerably more controversial. Relatively few problems are created by traditional intangible assets such as patents, copyrights, and trade names that are purchased or developed internally so that the cost of acquisition or development can be readily established. Serious problems, however, are created by the capitalization and amortization of **research and development (R&D)** costs—the drilling of dry holes in connection with the successful exploration of oil and gas, and start-up expenses for a variety of new businesses or enterprises. If a firm expends funds for R&D, for example, it generally must treat the expenditures as expenses in the year incurred unless it can show that the expenditures will lead to marketable products. If the firm can prove this connection, it may capitalize the expenditures and write them off in future years against those products. Although R&D expenditures directed toward a specific product or project probably should be capitalized, basic or general research often cannot be allocated with any precision, and it is usually **expensed** when incurred. The variety of treatment of R&D expenses among publicly reporting companies was so great that GAAP was revised in 1974 to require that most R&D expenditures be expensed currently. Although this treatment is not entirely consistent with the basic notion that expenses should be recognized when the revenue to which they relate is recognized, the possibility of manipulation and foul play in financial statements was so great that an objective and relatively bright-line rule was thought appropriate.

## §6.12  Accounting for Inventory

Inventory includes (1) **finished goods** awaiting sale, (2) goods in various stages of production including raw materials (**work-in-process**), and (3) goods on hand that are ultimately consumed in the production of goods (**raw materials**). Accounting for inventory is complex primarily because there is tremendous variation from business to business as to the nature and variety of items maintained in inventory.

Control of inventory costs is a major component in determining whether a business is successful. Problems of pilferage or shortages are most likely to involve inventory. Unaccountable losses of inventory—whether due to pilferage, failure to maintain adequate records, spoilage, or other causes—are also called, somewhat charitably, **shrinkage**.

Goods that are manufactured or purchased are usually stored (or parked) in the inventory account on the balance sheet until they are taken into the expense account of the income statement. Practical considerations, however, require most businesses to adopt artificial conventions for estimating inventory costs, because it is not practical for most businesses to keep track of each inventory item as it wends its way through the manufacturing process.

The most widely used inventory systems require businesses to record additions to inventory as they occur on the balance sheet, but to determine the cost of goods sold only at the end of each accounting period. The cost of goods sold for a period is determined at the close of the period by the following basic formula:

$$\text{cost of goods sold} = \text{opening inventory} \\ + \text{additions to inventory} - \text{closing inventory}$$

Both the opening inventory and the closing inventory are determined by taking physical counts of what is on hand at the end of an accounting period and then assigning it a dollar amount. In other words, an essential part of the year-end auditing process is a physical count of inventory. (The inventory amount at the end of one period (the **closing inventory**) is the inventory amount at the beginning of the next period (the **opening inventory**) so that only one physical count per year is necessary.) The manner of placing dollar amounts on the items counted when inventory additions occur at varying prices is the subject of the remainder of this section. Before turning to this question, however, a second formula should be introduced to make clear the importance of the physical inventory count and the manner of reporting that inventory in determining the profitability of the business:

$$\text{gross profit} = \text{net sales} - \text{cost of goods sold}$$

This formula reveals that every change in the number of dollars attributed to **cost of goods sold** leads to a dollar-for-dollar increase or reduction in the gross profit of the business. Further, these two formulas are obviously interrelated; one can substitute the first formula into the second formula to yield this:

$$\text{gross profit} = \text{net sales} - \text{value of opening inventory}$$
$$- \text{additions to inventory} + \text{value of closing inventory}$$

(Remember the effect of minus signs on other minus signs.) The implications to be drawn from formula (3) are these: First, every change in the number of dollars attributed to closing inventory also means a dollar-for-dollar change in gross profit. Second, the higher the closing inventory, the lower the cost of goods sold and the higher the gross profit. Correspondingly, the lower the closing inventory, the higher the cost of goods sold and the lower the gross profit.

That the closing inventory affects cost of goods sold is a result of the use of a formula to calculate the costs of goods sold: The calculation does not attempt to trace what specific inventory items were actually consumed during the period in question, but simply subtracts closing inventory from all inventory available to the business during the period (opening inventory plus additions to inventory for the period). Because the increase of closing inventory by one dollar increases gross profit by one dollar, while the decrease of closing inventory by one dollar decreases gross profit by that amount, the manner of assigning dollar amounts to closing inventory significantly affects reported earnings.

Before turning to methods of measuring closing inventory, it may be helpful to consider the nature of the inventory of three prototype businesses. To take the simplest case first, assume that the business involves only the retail sale of new automobiles. The number of inventory items is relatively small and each inventory item—each new car—is clearly identifiable by serial number, and the cost of each item in inventory is readily known. In effect, each inventory item can be "tagged" with its applicable cost, and the process of determining the value of the closing inventory for such a business involves merely identifying which cars are on hand at the close of the period and adding up their costs.

Second, consider a corn oil manufacturer whose inventory consists of raw corn to be crushed for oil. The corn is stored in a large bin. From time to time, additional corn is added, always to the top of the bin. Raw corn varies in price from day to day, although the amount and cost of all the raw corn added to the top of the bin can be readily calculated. When the manufacturing process needs more raw material, there are two alternatives: Either someone opens a valve and corn pours out of the bottom or someone opens a trap door and shovels some corn out from the top of the bin. Although one must question whether the use of corn from the bottom or from the top of the bin should be decisive in determining the value of closing inventory, there is clearly no way that the corn oil producer can physically tag raw corn and determine the cost of the raw materials on hand at the end of the accounting period. It must adopt a more general system.

Third, consider a large retail clothing store. It has on hand at any one time thousands of products in hundreds of sizes, styles, and colors. The number of units of each specific type, size, and style of product retained in inventory is relatively small for most items. Again, prices of individual items may vary over time so that, for example, two indistinguishable hats lying side by side may have originally cost different amounts. Although it may be theoretically possible to tag each item and determine its actual cost in closing inventory within the store, such a system is not very practical or cost-justified. With the development of computerized sales recording and reordering systems for many retail operations, tagging may become more feasible, but it is unlikely to supplant existing accounting methods of measuring closing inventory.

These last two prototypes are much more typical of the average inventory problems that businesses face than is the tagged inventory of the retail new car business. Indeed, when one considers the problems of the service department of the hypothetical retail new car business with an inventory consisting of replacement parts, boxes of spark plugs, bins of screws and bolts, barrels of motor oil or transmission fluid, and the like, it should be apparent that even a new car dealer must adopt generalized accounting procedures for much of its inventory.

*Specific identification inventory method.* Intuitively, the simplest method of assigning dollar amounts to closing inventory is to keep track of the cost of individual items. The new car inventory of the automobile dealer is a good illustration. This system, however, has basic problems. Assume that the information in Table 6-5 about one inventory item (all of which items are identical) is available. As in other examples used throughout this chapter, only a skeletal number of transactions is set forth to illustrate the basic principles.

If one can establish, by examining the "tags," that the 400 units on hand

Table 6-5

| Date | Purchases | | Sales |
| | No. units | Cost | No. units |
| --- | --- | --- | --- |
| On hand | 200 | $5 | |
| 3/1 | 100 | $6 | |
| 3/15 | | | 200 |
| 6/15 | 400 | $7 | |
| 7/15 | | | 300 |
| 8/15 | 200 | $8 | |
| 12/10 | | | 300 |
| 12/15 | 300 | $9 | |
| Close | 400 | ? | |

at the end of the accounting period consisted of (a) 200 units purchased on 8/15, (b) 100 units purchased on 3/1, and (c) 100 units carried over from the start of the year, one can determine the value of the closing inventory:

$$200 \times 8 + 100 \times 6 + 100 \times 5 = \$2,700$$

Of course, from this number, one can determine the cost of goods sold and the gross profit of the business from the formulas set forth earlier in this section.

One immediate problem with this method of measuring closing inventory is that it may encourage management to behave opportunistically. Management can increase or decrease gross profit by selecting which units are sold and which units are carried over into closing inventory. For example, if it wished to increase gross profit, management might sell all the cheaper items and keep in inventory only the items purchased on 8/15 and 12/15, so that the closing inventory value would be:

$$300 \times 9 + 100 \times 8 = \$3,500$$

Similarly if management wished to reduce gross profit, possibly to defer the profit to the next accounting period, it could sell the most expensive items and preserve the cheaper ones in closing inventory. It should be emphasized that even though gross profit may be manipulated in this fashion, the real worth of the business is unchanged.

*Weighted average method.* This method determines the weighted average price of every unit of inventory on hand at any time during the accounting period and assigns that average value to every unit. It is a "weighted" average because the number of units at each price is taken into account:

$$\frac{200 \times 5 + 100 \times 6 + 400 \times 7 + 200 \times 8 + 300 \times 9}{1,200 \text{ (the total number of units)}} = \frac{8,700}{1,200} = \$7.25 \text{ per unit}$$

The average cost per unit in the above example is \$7.25; the value of closing inventory is then $400 \times 7.25 = \$2,900$, and the cost of goods sold is $800 \times 7.25 = \$5,800$.

This method is not widely used in part because of its complexity in other than the simplest situations, and in part because the system creates its own anomalies. For example, the purchase of 300 units on 12/15 in the foregoing example increased the cost of all goods sold during the year even though all the actual sales of goods occurred before this final purchase.

*First-In First-Out Method.* One widely used method of computing closing inventory is to assume that the earliest items in inventory are always sold first. In the foregoing example, the sale of 800 units during the year is assumed to be composed of the earliest items acquired; the 200 items carried over from the prior accounting period and the purchases on 3/1, 6/15, and, in part, on

8/15. Closing inventory would then consist of 300 units at $9 and 100 units at $8, for a total of $3,500. This method of computing inventory is universally known as **FIFO**, which stands for first-in first-out.

FIFO has certain advantages. For one thing, it actually conforms with the physical inventory practices of many businesses, which follow the principle that because of spoilage, staleness, or obsolescence, the oldest items should always be sold first. That would be true, for example, for our corn oil producer if the corn was always poured from the bottom. Second, FIFO is relatively easy to administer. Third, it eliminates the possible manipulation of gross profit by management that is inherent in any system of assigning varying costs to specific inventory units. Under FIFO, it makes no difference whether the corn is taken from the bottom or from the top; in either case it is presumed that the oldest corn is used first. Finally, because inventory is always composed of the last-acquired items, the amount of closing inventory on the balance sheet is likely to reflect closely the current market value of inventory items. In this sense, FIFO improves the reliability of the balance sheet because the important inventory item reflects the most current prices at which inventory was actually purchased. But, as will be seen, it has the opposite effect on the income statement.

*Last-In First-Out Method.* The major alternative to FIFO proceeds on the opposite assumption, namely that the last items are always sold first, hence the acronym **LIFO**, which stands for last-in first-out. (When comparing LIFO with FIFO, it may be helpful to think of LIFO as FISH—first-in still-here.) In the foregoing example, the 400 units of closing inventory is assumed to consist of 200 units at $5,100 units at $6, and 100 units at $7, for a total value of $2,300. No account is taken of the sequence of actual subtractions from inventory in applying either FIFO or LIFO. If one chooses LIFO, it is assumed that corn is always taken from the top of the bin no matter what the actual practice is.

The advantages of LIFO over FIFO arise because of inflation. By generally increasing inventory replacement costs consistent with inflation, LIFO tends to decrease the value of closing inventories, thereby reducing reported income and federal income tax liability. (Since 1939, businesses have generally been permitted to use LIFO in calculating federal income tax.) Indeed, if one assumes that inventory costs increase steadily, FIFO maximizes the business's taxes, while LIFO minimizes them. Arguably, every business should shift from FIFO to LIFO simply because of this tax saving. Paradoxically, however, some companies continue to use FIFO despite the virtually universal view of accountants and financial management strategists that most companies would obtain significant tax benefits from adopting LIFO. One argument that is sometimes made for FIFO is that the stock market would react negatively to lower earnings figures. But studies of securities prices of businesses that shift from FIFO to LIFO indicate that the market does not reduce securities prices to reflect the reduced earnings caused by the shift to LIFO. In other words, markets apparently understand that the reduction in earnings caused by a change in accounting for inventory is not a real change in earnings.

The tax savings arising from LIFO are permanent as a practical matter.

Theoretically, tax savings arising from LIFO will be lost when the low-cost LIFO inventory is liquidated. Indeed, when inventory is totally liquidated, FIFO and LIFO should have led to the same total cost of goods sold. This, however, ignores the time value of money: The immediate reduction of taxes through LIFO is worth much more than the future increase in taxes when the LIFO inventory is consumed. Moreover, most companies go on for years or centuries without totally liquidating inventory. Thus, practically speaking, the tax benefits of the LIFO election are not only immediate, but they are also permanent.

A second advantage of LIFO is that it tends to cause reported earnings to reflect the cost of goods sold more accurately. LIFO uses more current inventory costs. FIFO tends to make the inventory number shown on the balance sheet relatively current, but it overstates earnings. LIFO emphasizes the accuracy of the income statement over that of the balance sheet—consistent with modern thinking about the relative roles of the two statements. The major disadvantage of LIFO is that the cost of inventory as shown on the balance sheet tends to become increasingly obsolete if, as is usually the case, the business maintains a stable or increasing inventory over several years. If a stable inventory is assumed, the LIFO inventory will always be reported at the cost it had as of the date on which the LIFO election was made. In other words, it is quite possible that a current balance sheet reflects inventory costs based on 1980 product prices.

A second major problem with LIFO arises when, by reason of a strike or shortage, for example, a LIFO inventory must be partially consumed to keep up current production or sales. The inventory so consumed, which is carried on the books at an artificially low price, causes earnings to be inflated solely because of the method of accounting for inventory costs.

A final observation may be made about the choice between FIFO and LIFO in inflationary periods. Irrespective of the inventory accounting system adopted, profits are going to be inflated during inflationary periods simply from price increases occurring during the period between the time of purchasing inventory and the time of recording it as an expense. The profit that the business records is in part its normal operating profit from whatever business it is in and in part an abnormal trading profit caused by price increases during the manufacturing or resale process. LIFO tends to minimize the amount of this artificial profit, but does not eliminate it entirely. Elimination would require a radical shift to a current value system for reporting inventory consumed during the accounting period similar to that discussed in the previous section relating to depreciable plant and equipment. For example, one might imagine a system based on a next-in first-out (NIFO) convention. Such a proposal has never been adopted. But LIFO is more sensitive to the effect of inflation on income statements than is FIFO.

Of course, not all goods appreciate in value over time, even during inflationary periods. Changes in technology may lead to price reductions even though prices generally have increased. A good example is the modern personal computer industry, which over the last decade has seen product prices decline as product quality and sophistication have improved steadily. Firms in such an industry have little or no tax reason to adopt LIFO accounting.

## §6.13 Uses of Financial Statements

When examining financial statements, one must always keep in mind the examination's purpose. What is the client proposing to do? The client may be considering (1) lending money to a business; (2) buying from, selling to, or otherwise dealing with a business; (3) making an investment in a business; or (4) buying a business outright. The attitude one takes toward financial statements depends on the nature of the proposed transaction and the client's exposure to loss should the other party run into unexpected financial difficulties or be unable to perform as contemplated.

If the proposed transaction involves lending money to or entering into commercial transactions with the business on a relatively short-term basis, an extended analysis of financial statements is seldom required. The question usually is simply whether the business is likely to be able to repay the loan or pay for the goods or services being provided. For this purpose, a credit check through one of the commercial credit reporting agencies may provide information about the bill-paying history of the business that is more useful than information garnered from financial statements. In addition, useful information about specific companies may be obtained from a variety of publications such as Standard & Poor's Corporation Records, Moody's Industrial Manual, and the Value Line Industrial Survey.

The risk of nonpayment may also be reduced or eliminated by simple protective measures: obtaining a lien or security interest in the debtor's property, requiring the principal shareholders of the debtor to guarantee personally the payment of the debt, or requiring the debtor to provide a letter of credit from a responsible financial institution that assures that payment will be made when required. If a personal guarantee is sought, it is essential to obtain financial statements of both the guarantors and the principal debtor.

In assessing the risk of nonpayment, the debtor's financial statements may be examined to determine whether the transaction is of such a magnitude that it may strain the debtor's normal resources. If so, a short-range cash-flow analysis may be done in order to determine how the debtor contemplates obtaining the necessary funds to complete the transaction. When the risk appears to be substantial, a client may structure the transaction in order to limit risk (e.g., by providing that performance may be suspended if payments are not made at specified intervals).

Decisions concerning long-term investment in another business (either of debt or equity) are almost always preceded by an investigation into the nature and quality of the business. Expert analysis of the financial statements (often referred to simply as financials) is generally a part of this investigation. Earning potential or longer-term cash flows should be evaluated. Financial statements, prepared on the basis of generally accepted accounting principles (GAAP) or otherwise, may be the principal source of information for this analysis.

In this situation, one must always be alert for danger signals indicating that the business is not as healthy as the financial statements might indicate. In making a financial analysis, one should always try to obtain financial statements for at least the last five years to study trends not apparent from current financial statements only. A declining rate of growth or a rate of growth smaller than the industry as a whole are signs of possible trouble. Many danger signals, however, cannot be detected solely from the financial statements themselves. They include unusual turnover of key personnel, changes in auditors, and a gradual slowdown in the rate of payment of liabilities. Additional factors are described in subsequent sections.

If a client proposes to acquire control of the business, a basic question is whether the client wants to acquire specific assets or the entire business. Matters of concern are whether the book value of assets significantly overstates their market value, whether the cash flows of the business appear to be sufficient to finance future growth, and whether the business has undisclosed or contingent or **off-book liabilities**, such as pending litigation, the probability of future product liability claims, tax claims, and the like. Obviously, whether such liabilities exist cannot be discovered solely from examining the financial statements.

When a business is purchased, risk can be reduced in various ways. For example, one may require the seller to warrant the accuracy of the financial statements and to represent that there are no material off-book liabilities. A right to rescind the entire transaction may be negotiated if these warranties and representations turn out to be false after the transaction is closed. It also may be possible to structure the transaction as an asset-purchase transaction that does not involve the assumption of contingent or undisclosed liabilities rather than as a stock-purchase transaction that leaves the purchased business subject to these liabilities. As a general rule, a purchaser of assets alone for fair value is not obligated to assume liabilities (unless, of course, the purchaser expressly agrees to do so). However, in some situations courts have ruled that an asset-purchaser must also take responsibility, for example, for product liability claims, despite express provisions that the purchaser does not assume such liabilities. And some claims, such as those for environmental harms, must effectively be assumed as a matter of statutory law no matter how the transaction is structured. When shares of stock in a corporation are acquired by purchase or the corporation itself is acquired by a merger, the business acquired (and quite possibly the acquirer as well) remains liable on preacquisition liabilities.

Negative factors, such as the existence of undisclosed or contingent liabilities, may affect only the amount of consideration being paid for the business. In some circumstances, however, the problems discovered may be so significant as to call into question the soundness of the entire transaction.

## §6.14 GAAP and Non-GAAP Financial Statements

Publicly held corporations registered under the Securities Exchange Act of 1934 are required to prepare public financial statements in accordance with GAAP. A major purpose of these mandatory principles is to ensure comparability of public financial statements. In addition, there are standards for auditor independence and the conduct of audits that permit a user to deal with such financial statements with some confidence. However, one should not overstate the degree of reliability of financial statements on the basis of an unqualified or **clean opinion** by an outside auditor.

Even though GAAP is designed to ensure that operating results that different publicly held businesses report have a large degree of comparability, it is important to recognize that GAAP, like accounting generally, is not a set of precise mathematical rules. Rather, it is a set of principles intended to make financial statements useful to persons who use them. There is considerable discretion as to how certain transactions are treated for accounting purposes. When transactions are material, a reference to the way they are treated should appear either in the auditor's statement or in the notes to the financial statements. Management, rather than the outside auditor, usually makes these discretionary decisions, though the outside auditor has a voice in the matter, and that voice may sometimes be decisive as discussed more fully below. Significant disagreements between a business and its outside auditors as to how a transaction should be treated under GAAP do not occur often, but the fact that they occur at all reveals that even fundamental accounting notions may be subject to challenge and that accounting principles are neither right nor wrong in any absolute sense. Like legal principles generally, the application of GAAP in a specific situation involves exercise of judgment.

Properly read and understood, financial statements created in accordance with GAAP can be used with some confidence. In any event, GAAP statements are the most that normally can be expected. The following sections of this chapter describe more or less standard methods of analysis of financial statements assuming the basic accuracy and comparability of the published figures. These methods of analysis usually may be applied to GAAP financial statements with relative confidence without making an extensive inquiry into what lies behind the figures.

Many smaller businesses and closely held corporations use professional accounting services but do not prepare financial statements on the basis of GAAP. Rather, such statements may incorporate GAAP treatment of some assets or transactions but depart from GAAP in other respects. Such statements may also be useful for analysis; indeed, there is no one right way to present the results of operations of a complex business. Statements that depart from GAAP, however, must be used with caution. Material adjustments may be necessary in a number of areas in order to reflect income accurately or to allow for comparison with businesses that follow GAAP. Of course, considerable variation also exists within GAAP statements in these respects as well.

It should not be assumed that there is a consistent bias in the direction of overstating assets or income in non-GAAP statements. Closely held corporations often adopt accounting principles in an effort to minimize income rather than to maximize it. For example, many closely held corporations follow a policy of **expensing** as many asset acquisitions as possible in order to reduce stated income and federal income taxes. Excessive salaries payable to the major equity owners of the business who control day-to-day operations may appear as expenses even though these salary payments should be treated as dividends. Similarly, expense accounts may reflect hidden compensation. In these instances, the reported earnings of the closely held corporation may be significantly understated. Moreover, even the assumption that a single accounting system has been consistently applied by a closely held corporation is open to question.

Finally, it is important to recognize that all accounting principles, whether or not GAAP, involve not only flexibility and discretion, but also conventions and assumptions about honesty and good faith which was dramatically illustrated by the collapse of Enron in late 2001. Financial statements are usually prepared to put the best possible face on management's performance, and, as discussed more fully below, management has considerable discretion as to which accounting conventions are adopted. No accounting system provides protection against outright fraud or theft. There are many dishonest ways to cook the books even if they are nominally kept on a GAAP basis. One major fraud, for example, was based on rigging the inventory count at the end of the accounting period by counting four boxes of sutures as 44, three boxes of gauze pads as 33, and so forth. Even though the auditor participated in the physical count of inventory, it did not notice these discrepancies. By overstating the closing inventory, the perpetrators sought to overstate gross profit. Thereafter, the scheme was to "destroy" the nonexistent inventory thus created. Because one of the conspirators went to the Securities and Exchange Commission (SEC) in an effort to avoid prosecution, the scheme collapsed. Obviously, even the finest GAAP financial statements cannot guarantee the honesty and probity of their creation.

Although the idea that a business might keep multiple sets of books may sound vaguely criminal, there are very good reasons for doing so, and the practice is indeed common. For most purposes, the books of a business should be kept according to GAAP. Tax accounting, as dictated by the Internal Revenue Code (IRC) and regulations and practices thereunder, may differ significantly from GAAP. For example, under tax law, depreciation and depletion allowances may be able to be taken at a faster rate than is economically realistic for a particular business. Thus, taxes may legitimately be reduced. (The discrepancy is what gives rise to the **deferred tax** account one sometimes sees on a GAAP balance sheet.) Yet another situation that might call for a third set of books arises because corporation law often allows distributions to be made to shareholders on the basis of accounting principles set down as a matter of state statute. Although a few states expressly incorporate GAAP into their corporation laws, most do not. On the other hand, most states afford corporate boards of directors the ability to rely on financial statements rendered by trusted accounting professionals. Thus, in practice many boards of directors find it desirable to forgo whatever flexibility may be available by following statutory accounting principles. Finally, for purposes of negotiations in connection with mergers and acquisitions and in many valuation proceedings, yet another method of accounting involving the calculation of cash flow, as opposed to accounting income, is generally followed.

## §6.15  Cash Flow Financial Projections

In recent years, an alternative method of analysis—a study of expected cash flows—has become popular. Many persons believe that cash-flow analysis is inherently more reliable than GAAP financial statements in estimating the risks presented by specific investments. This is particularly true with short-term extensions of credit where repayment is not dependent on long-term profitability.

Cash-flow statements are usually specific projections of what funds are likely to be available to the business in the future. GAAP statements, of course, reflect what happened in the past, and projections of earnings trends into the future must be provided by the user of the financial statements.

When one encounters a financial statement or financial analysis that includes projections or cash-flow analysis, they should be examined with care, particularly the bases or assumptions on which projections of cash flow are made. It is very easy to project continued growth and continued improvement in sales, rents, or fees indefinitely into the future, but these projections are rarely realistic. Cash-flow projections that extend far into the future are obviously less reliable than short-term cash-flow projections based on results of operations in the recent past and indeed may be inherently unreliable. Since the early 1980s, the SEC has permitted good-faith projections and estimates of future cash flow to appear in disclosure documents, but good faith is no guarantee of accuracy.

Cash-flow analysis is not always focused on the future. In some cases, a lender or other investor will want to know whether a profitable company in fact generates enough cash to pay back a loan or otherwise make good on an obligation or investment. After all, one of the basic problems with accrual accounting is that a company may record profits and losses well before the cash actually flows. Thus, one of the more important functions of cash-flow analysis is to assess the liquidity of the company in the absence of any concern about whether the business is growing or shrinking.

As cash-flow analysis has gained popularity, techniques of estimation from traditional financial statements have become more sophisticated. Further, cash flow may itself be categorized, depending on the objective of the person making the estimate. A potential bidder for control, for example, may attempt to analyze **operating cash flow**, while an investor may analyze **free cash flow**. These concepts may be defined as follows:

$$\text{cash flow} = \text{net income} + \text{depreciation} + \text{depletion} + \text{amortization}$$

$$\text{operating cash flow} = \text{cash flow} + \text{interest expense} + \text{income tax expense}$$

$$\text{free cash flow} = \text{cash flow} - \text{capital expenditures} - \text{dividends.}$$

The potential bidder works from operating cash flow because it plans to restructure the current capital structure of the target and eliminate income tax expense by dramatically increasing interest expense. The investor, on the other hand, is concerned with free cash flow, because the investor assumes that current operations and financial structure will remain unaffected.

For most investors, net income remains the handiest snapshot of a company's immediate future prospects. However, free cash-flow analysis may shed light on the quality of the earnings so projected: If profits appear to be improving but cash flow is not, the company's growth in earnings may be short lived.

## §6.16  Who Has the Responsibility for Preparing Financial Statements?

The reliability of financial statements is to some extent dependent on their being prepared by or under the direction of independent professionals. As a result, their reliability must be viewed as seriously compromised if they are prepared by persons who are employees of, or somehow dependent on, management.

The preparation of publicly available financial statements prepared in accordance with GAAP is generally viewed as the norm. The preparation of such statements is overseen by outside and independent **certified public accountants (CPAs)**, who must certify in an auditor's report that the statements have been prepared pursuant to GAAP principles. As a practical matter, in a large and complex business, "overseen" means "spot checked" and the reality is that management largely has the responsibility for preparing the financial statements.

Most large publicly held corporations use as their outside auditors one of the **big five accounting firms** that have offices in all major cities— PricewaterhouseCoopers, Deloitte & Touche, Ernst & Young, KPMG, and Arthur Andersen & Co. These accounting firms are immense partnerships with hundreds or thousands of partners, though some of them have attempted to segregate out operations in each country from potential liabilities arising from activities in other countries. Smaller accounting firms may be capable of serving as auditors for huge corporations, but most of these corporations stick with the big five.

The SEC views the selection of the auditor as an important factor in ensuring objectivity in financial statements. The SEC's regulations require the shareholders to ratify the selection of each independent auditor: The SEC has also expressed public concern over corporations that engage in **opinion shopping** by threatening to change auditors if the present auditors prove unwilling to accept the accounting treatment of transactions that management desires.

As indicated above, the actual role of outside auditors in preparing financial statements is more that of overseeing the audit than doing the audit. In a large, publicly held corporation, it is not practical for outside auditors to review all transactions or even to review a majority of them. The outside auditor's role is necessarily more limited: Typically, the outside auditors review the accounting systems used to generate the underlying data, test a sampling of the largest transactions to make sure that they are handled in an appropriate fashion, and participate to a limited extent in making physical counts of inventory, cash on hand, and other assets and liabilities. The AICPA has established auditing standards that deal with the manner in which CPAs carry out independent examinations of the financial statements of companies. These standards are often referred to as **generally accepted auditing standards (GAAS)**. Many auditing firms have developed audit manuals to provide guidelines in various areas and for various problems. Most auditing firms also routinely use forms and checklists in connection with audits. Other mechanisms may involve the periodic rotation of audit partners or peer review, either within the large accounting firms or by outside evaluators. Nevertheless, in the final analysis, much of the compilation of data used in the outside auditor's report is actually assembled by the company's own internal accounting staff.

Under these circumstances, it is not surprising that routine outside audits often do not catch fraud or theft, particularly fraud or theft hidden by an employee who is familiar with the accounting practices followed by the company. Again, this point is well illustrated by the Enron debacle. Congress has recently required outside auditors to make greater efforts to detect fraud or theft. In early 1996, a modest provision requiring auditors of publicly traded companies to adopt procedures designed to detect illegal acts and to report discovered acts to management and the board of directors or the SEC was adopted. It is possible that future legislation may stiffen auditing standards further. Of course, such proposals entail additional costs and greater exposure to personal liability on the part of the auditors. Auditing firms often argue that their principal function is to ensure that an acceptable system of accountability is in place and not to uncover fraud or theft. Despite this, auditing firms are often named as defendants in litigation to recover losses caused by undetected fraud or significant misrepresentations as to the prospects of the business. In these cases, the issue is whether the auditor performed its audit in accordance with accepted standards for performing audits, and if not, whether that audit would have prevented the losses if it had been performed with customary care. The law varies among the states as to whether an accountant owes a duty to exercise customary care to persons who rely on accounting statements, or whether claims are limited to those with a direct contractual relationship with the accountant. One complicating factor in the context of auditors for publicly held corporations is that the shareholders, who are often the ones misled by erroneous financial statements, are legally speaking the owners of the company.

In early 1993 the Auditing Standards Board of the AICPA issued Statement on Auditing Standards (SAS) No. 72 to provide guidance to accountants in issuing so-called **comfort letters** to underwriters and broker-dealers in connection with 1933 Act registrations. A comfort letter, sometimes also referred to as **cold comfort**, is a written representation falling short of a formal opinion, that the accountant or auditor is not aware of any adverse information. The new policy prohibits the issue of such a letter unless the requesting recipient represents that he or she has reviewed the underlying material. In other words, the policy is designed to limit the practice of using accountant comfort letters as a way for underwriters and broker-dealers to avoid due diligence as to financial statements.

As should be apparent, where publicly held corporations are concerned, the identity of the auditor is no guarantee that the financial statements accurately reflect the financial condition of the business or that a systematic examination has been made in an effort to detect fraud or misconduct. As one moves away from publicly held corporations, the relationship between auditor and corporation becomes even more critical. When considering financial statements for a small closely held corporation, one is likely to encounter financial statements prepared by local accounting firms of unknown reputation and quality. In addition, it is likely that the corporation has had close relationships with the auditor for many years, and the auditor's independence may be in serious question. In these situations, inquiry should normally be made about the auditor's local reputation as well as his or her connection with the corporation in question. Of course, one must consider whatever financial statements are available. Even financials that were prepared by a person under the control of the owner of the business are better than no financials at all. Issues of auditor independence, in other words, go only to the degree of confidence one places in the reliability of the financial statements. It is almost never practical to require a new audit, though it may be possible to request a second auditing firm to review the existing report.

## §6.17 The Importance of the Auditor's Opinion

The first step in reviewing financial statements is to read carefully the auditor's opinion, the signed statement that appears immediately before the financial statements. An **unqualified opinion** (a **clean opinion**) contains three paragraphs in approximately this language:

> We have audited the accompanying balance sheet of XYZ Company as of December 31 and the related statements of income, stockholders' equity and cash flows for the years then ended. These financial statements are the responsibility of the Company's management. Our responsibility is to express an opinion on these financial statements based on our audit.
>
> We conducted our audit in accordance with generally accepted auditing standards. Those standards require that we plan and perform the audit to obtain reasonable assurance whether the financial statements are free of material misstatement. An audit includes examining, on a test basis, evidence supporting the amounts and disclosures in the financial statements. An audit also includes assessing the accounting principles used and significant estimates made by management, as well as evaluating the overall financial statement presentation. We believe that our audit provides a reasonable basis for our opinion.
>
> In our opinion, the financial statements referred to above present fairly, in all material respects, the financial position of XYZ Company as of December 31 and the results of its operations and its cash flows for the years then ended in conformity with generally accepted accounting principles.

Explanation regarding any change or variation in accounting principles must be made in the form of exceptions in a separate paragraph. Because of the highly stylized nature of these opinion forms, any deviation from the standard language and particularly the inclusion of any additional statements in the opinion should be considered carefully and made the subject of further inquiry. Generally, if the auditor believes an item is important enough to mention in the opinion, it is important enough to be considered by users of the statements. Nevertheless, despite any uncertainty, the auditor must leave the third paragraph alone and conclude that the financial statements are fairly presented on the basis of the amounts recorded and the disclosures made concerning the uncertainties set forth in the footnotes. If an uncertainty is so significant that it may have a material impact on future financial statements, the auditor must red flag the item in an explanatory or emphasizing paragraph. When there is a material departure from GAAP, or when the company restricts the scope of the auditor's examination, the auditor's opinion in the third paragraph should state that the financial statements are fairly presented **except for** the effects of the matters described in the concluding explanatory paragraph, which would describe the significance of the departures from GAAP or the restrictions on the audit's scope.

A qualification of an opinion is a serious matter and is not made lightly by the auditing firm. It may well cause the company, if it feels the qualification is unjustified, to consider changing auditing firms. On the other hand, the failure to qualify an opinion may serve as the basis for subsequent litigation against the auditor by investors or creditors and may also lead to dismissal of the auditor as it did in the case of Enron and its auditor Arthur Andersen.

The additional information referred to in an auditor's opinion is often of fundamental importance. As auditor for Texaco, Arthur Andersen was faced with the issue of what should be said about the 1985 Pennzoil judgment for $10.53 billion arising out of the struggle for Getty Oil Company. Texaco was vigorously contesting liability under the judgment, and it was therefore not reflected as a liability on the balance sheet. Arthur Andersen decided to add a third paragraph to its opinion on Texaco's 1985 financial statements referring to the Pennzoil judgment. This paragraph stated that the "ultimate outcome of this litigation is not presently determinable," and that Arthur Andersen's certification of the Texaco financial statements was therefore "subject to the effect of . . . such adjustments, if any, that might have been required had the outcome of the litigation . . . been known." One can imagine that Texaco was not pleased with this **qualified opinion**, but its wisdom was attested to in 1987, when the Pennzoil judgment forced Texaco to file for reorganization under Chapter 11 of the Bankruptcy Code.

## §6.18 The Importance of Notes to the Financial Statements

A second source of important information about financial statements is the notes to the financial statements. Some financial statements contain the notation, "The notes are an integral part of these financial statements." Whether or not a statement of this type appears, notes should always be carefully read and their implications considered fully. This is not always easy to do, because the carefully prepared language that appears in notes to financial statements is often spare and concise, and the significance of what is being said may not always jump out at the reader. An important disclosure may be stated without any indication of its significance.

To illustrate the importance of notes, consider the following company, whose accounting period ends on December 31. The preparation of financial statements takes some time, and the statements may not actually be released until early March. A not unreasonable question is whether there were important adverse changes in the company's operations between December 31 and early March. If something important has happened after December 31—for example, the company's business has largely dried up and there is now imminent danger of insolvency—that information will not appear in the year-end financial statements themselves, but the essential facts should be set forth as the first note to the financial statements.

One problem with notes is that they are uneven: Some contain additional detail and information about the numbers, while others contain significant qualifications to the numbers. The latter is obviously more important than the former, but the notes mix the two together and do not always distinguish between them. In part this is because there is no clear line between explication and qualification. The following areas are usually covered in notes to financial statements:

1. Material adverse post-accounting period developments.
2. A summary of the discretionary accounting policies the company has elected to adopt (e.g., last-in first-out (LIFO) or first-in first-out (FIFO), depreciation schedules, and policies relating to revenue recognition and the capitalization of deferred expenses).
3. The accounting treatment of significant transactions entered into by the company. The notes should indicate, for example, whether the obligations that the company incurred in connection with its employees' pension plan are currently funded and the extent to which the obligation appears as a liability on the balance sheet.
4. Breakdowns of reported amounts that appear as single aggregated figures in the financial statements. A one-page balance sheet often requires the consolidation of numerous accounts into single entries; the notes provide a breakdown in somewhat greater detail. Examples might include breakdowns of long-term indebtedness that the company owes and categories of fixed assets that the company owns.
5. Outstanding commitments not included as liabilities in the financial statements. Certain commitments that the company enters into may be material but not treated as liabilities under GAAP. Examples include rent obligations for future years under leases that are not cancelable, promises to redeem preferred stock at the option of the holder, and obligations to issue stock pursuant to stock options issued to employees. Material commitments of these types are all usually described in the notes to the financial statements.
6. Contingent liabilities, prospective losses, and unresolved litigation not included as liabilities in financial statements. Under GAAP, contingent items are taken into the accounts only when the outcome of the matter and the amount of the liability can be predicted with a reasonable degree of certainty. (Texaco did not show the Pennzoil judgment as a liability on its financial statements even though the trial court had entered judgment against it, because Texaco was appealing and vigorously contesting the claim.) Obviously, some contingent obligations, if they materialize, may overwhelm the company as it did in the Enron case. The notes to the financial statements set forth the nature of material contingencies and an estimate of the possible range of loss. Ordinarily, the company's lawyers will be called on by the auditors to express an opinion as to the likelihood of an adverse judgment, and such inquiries can create difficult conflicts for lawyers who are bound to maintain client confidences.

7. The tax returns for specific years that have been audited by the Internal Revenue Service and the years that are currently open or in audit.

8. A 5-year or 10-year summary of operations to permit longer-term evaluations of the company.

9. Information on major lines of business and classes of products where the company is a conglomerate involved in activities in unrelated industries.

10. Information on the impact of changes in price and value (i.e., inflation accounting) by large companies. This information adjusts the financial statement's current replacement costs. It (a) restates the financial statement on a constant dollar basis to reflect changes in general price levels, and (b) reflects current replacement costs of inventory, property, plant, and equipment. Experience with inflation accounting reveals considerable divergence in approach from company to company, and many investors find this information to be confusing and complex and probably of limited value.

11. Management explanations and interpretations relating to favorable or unfavorable trends, changes in product mix, plans to acquire or dispose of major assets or lines of business, and the effect of unusual gains or losses.

## §6.19 Adjusting the Numbers in Financial Statements

It is often desirable to make adjustments in financial statements before (or as part of) the analysis of them. There is nothing magical or correct about numbers simply because they are written down in an official-appearing and certified set of financial statements. And the reliability and utility of financial statements is not improved merely because they appear in an attractive format in an annual report printed in four colors and containing a glowing report from management. It is surprising how reluctant many people are to subject attractively printed financial statements to the same skeptical scrutiny they would routinely give typed or handwritten financial statements. The gift wrapping is not important: It is what is inside that counts.

When financial statements are examined, it is important to consider the basis on which they were prepared. If the statements are not GAAP statements, both that fact and the manner in which they were prepared should be revealed in the financial statements or the notes. If the contemplated analysis involves comparisons with publicly available GAAP financial statements of comparable companies, adjustments sometimes may need to be made.

In deciding what adjustments should be made even to GAAP statements, one must always keep in mind the issue that is being addressed. For example, adjustments that entirely eliminate intangible assets such as goodwill from the balance sheet may be entirely appropriate when your client is considering the purchase of the business in order to acquire its physical assets and the question is how much to offer to pay. Similarly, if the financial statements treat as expenses amounts that should more appropriately be viewed as distributions to the shareholders, income should be increased and expenses decreased appropriately if one is using the earning capacity of the business as the basis for deciding how much to offer. Recurring types of adjustments to GAAP financial statements are described below.

*Current Market Value.* Assume that you are considering financial statements of a company that has been continuously in existence since 1923. On its balance sheet is the enigmatic entry "Land . . . . $300,000." Such an entry should be a red flag for further investigation and possible adjustment, because that $300,000 is a cost figure, and it may reflect either a purchase more than 50 years ago when land was selling for a fraction of what it is today or a purchase last week at or above current market values.

If the company owns marketable securities, the balance sheet should set forth by parenthetical notation a recent estimate of the current market value of the securities. It may be appropriate to substitute these market values for the cost figures for analytic purposes. It may also be appropriate to substitute up-to-date market values for those appearing in the parenthetical notation on the balance sheet (which states figures as of the close of the accounting period).

Other asset adjustments that should be considered include an upward adjustment in value if inventory is calculated on a LIFO basis and a readjustment of the machinery and equipment account if accelerated depreciation is used. If accelerated depreciation schedules are used, an upward adjustment to earnings may also be appropriate. On the down side, the machinery and equipment account may include obsolete assets that should be written off to zero because their usefulness is exhausted and their resale value is nonexistent. Inventory is theoretically valued at the lower of cost or market, but additional write-downs may also be appropriate for obsolete or stale items. Adjustments of these types usually require a fairly detailed investigation of specific asset accounts by a person intimately familiar with the type of business involved.

*Non-asset Assets.* Balance sheets often contain items that have zero realizable value. The most common items of this type appear in the intangible assets account: "goodwill," "organizational expense," "capitalized promotional expense," or "capitalized development costs." It may be appropriate to eliminate these items entirely from the balance sheet, reducing retained earnings by the same amount.

The problem of non-asset assets is not limited to these intangible asset accounts. Investments in subsidiary corporations or other businesses may also have a zero realizable value. Even traditional asset accounts such as fixed assets or inventory may contain positive values for property that are unrealistic. Usually, a detailed investigation is necessary to determine the extent of over-statement in these accounts.

*Off Balance Sheet Liabilities.* Most businesses have at least some material liabilities that are not reflected in the balance sheet. As the Enron case illustrates, it is possible that these liabilities may be massive. These items include future obligations under pension and profit-sharing plans, litigation in process, potential future product liability claims, commitments under fixed contracts such as long-term leases and employment contracts, and potential tax liabilities arising out of ongoing audits of operations of earlier years. Some of these items may be referred to in the notes to the financial statements. If not, it is usually difficult for an outsider to learn of their existence. It may be appropriate to increase book liabilities to reflect these off-book liabilities or to make an appropriate adjustment to the terms of the contemplated transaction to take account of their existence.

A separate inquiry is often made about possible future product liability claims arising from sales in earlier years. In many jurisdictions, such claims are not barred by the statute of limitations, which begins to run only when the injury occurs. The adequacy of insurance for such risks should also be investigated. Most insurance against liabilities of these types is written on a claims-made basis that may require insurance to be maintained indefinitely even if the portion of the business manufacturing the products in question is discontinued.

When a business is being purchased, it is customary to require the sellers to warrant specifically that material unknown liabilities (other than those specifically referred to in the financial statements and notes) do not exist. The absence of such liabilities may also be a condition of closing, so the purchaser may withdraw from the transaction if its investigation reveals the existence of material undisclosed liabilities.

Long-term liabilities are shown on financial statements at face value. In other words, a $10,000,000 bond issue is shown at $10,000,000 even though it may not be due to be repaid for another 20 years. Depending on the interest rate on these bonds, their market value may be significantly less than $10,000,000. If reacquisition of these bonds by market purchases is feasible, the liability item on the balance sheet may be reduced for analytic purposes to reflect the actual cost of reacquiring and retiring the bonds.

Because of the central role of the income statement in most analyses, it is important that recent changes in accounting principles or practices do not artificially inflate current earnings. For example, recent changes in the estimated lives of assets subject to amortization or depreciation might be examined for their possible effect on the income statement. Apparent reductions or deferrals of discretionary costs such as advertising or research might be reviewed, because that is a relatively easy way to preserve an earnings record despite increases in costs or declines in revenue. Of course, reduction or deferral of such items may be unwise from a longer-term perspective. Professional or expert analysis of the financial statements and the underlying accounting records is usually necessary to determine whether such changes have occurred, and whether they materially affect the results of operations.

In a closely held corporation, accounting policies are often adopted in an effort to minimize apparent income for tax or other purposes. Upward adjustments to reflect income consistent with GAAP principles may be appropriate. The most likely adjustments are to capitalize items that were treated as expenses in the financial statements, to restore to earnings amounts distributed to the owners of the business in the form of excessive salaries or fringe benefits and to eliminate the effects of excessively rapid depreciation.

## §6.20 Cooking the Books

Financial statements nominally prepared in accordance with GAAP are subject to manipulation and may involve outright fraud and misrepresentation. Fraud is often practiced by using fictitious transactions to hide thefts or by adopting non-GAAP accounting principles without disclosing them. Income statements may be blatantly overstated by rigging inventory counts, creating fictitious assets, or omitting liabilities from the balance sheet. Sales to wholly owned affiliates at attractive prices may be booked as sales to independent outside parties as they were in the Enron case. Sales may be booked immediately even though goods have been shipped on approval or subject to buy-back guarantees that are likely to be exercised as they were in the Sunbeam case. Depending on the sophistication of the persons engaged in the wrongful conduct, it may be difficult or impossible to discover that the books have been cooked without tracing specific transactions. Major thefts may often be hidden in the books of a large and complex business in a way that may escape detection for long periods of time. The development of computerized accounting systems does not prevent cooking the books; it simply requires a different kind and degree of sophistication to cook the books successfully. Of course, persons who misappropriate business assets or fraudulently misrepresent the financial condition of a business usually face criminal charges if they are apprehended.

At a higher level of social acceptability are discretionary decisions that have the effect of improving the appearance of profitability. Management's goal may be to improve the market price of the stock of the company by creating the appearance of a stable history of growing earnings. Erratic earnings are not as likely to be highly capitalized by the market as steady and predictable earnings. A fair amount of smoothing out and improving of earnings may be accomplished by discretionary decisions (e.g., by booking income at an early stage of the sales process even though additional costs may later be incurred).

Another common strategy is **taking a bath** during one bad accounting period. From the standpoint of securities prices and markets it is usually desirable, if a business is going to have a bad year anyway, to take as many **write-offs** in that period as possible so that a return to predictable increases in profits becomes possible in the following year. Obviously, it is no fun to issue a press release revealing losses of hundreds of millions of dollars in a single accounting period. But memories are short, and with potential losses eliminated, the reported earnings in the following accounting periods should show dramatic improvement. For publicly held companies, taking a bath in this fashion is a widely followed strategy.

Taking a bath involves discretionary decisions to take as many losses as possible within a single accounting period. Smoothing out income involves discretionary allocations of income and expense items to specific periods to stabilize reported earnings. Many of these decisions may be consistent with GAAP principles, because management has considerable discretion when to book transactions and when to recognize losses. For example, businesses often have assets or whole lines of business that can only be disposed of at a loss; the timing of the disposition is discretionary. Similarly, intangible assets or capitalized expenses that can never be fully recovered may be written off at a time that is to some extent at the discretion of management. Bad debts or obsolete inventory may similarly be written down or off when convenient. Whenever one reads about a company that unexpectedly announces very substantial losses despite a history of profitability, it is likely that the company is taking a bath.

Companies sometimes engage in transactions near the end of their fiscal year primarily to improve the closing figures and the various ratios described above. The company may make big shipments from inventories at bargain prices near the close of the accounting period in order to be able to book the sales. In effect, the company may be "borrowing" from next year's sales, effectively booking 13 months of sales in a single year. Manipulation of the mix of inventory between raw materials and finished products may increase closing inventory (thereby increasing gross margin) at the expense of the following year. A company that has cash-flow problems may borrow money on December 28 in order to show a large amount of cash on hand at the close of the fiscal year. Of course, that cash is only temporarily resident in the company's accounts and may disappear on January 3. These tactics are known as **window dressing** and shade off into actionable fraud or deception.

## CHAPTER 7

# VALUATION OF A GOING BUSINESS

## §7.1   Introduction

This chapter deals generally with the question of what a business is worth and what shares or interests in that business are worth. In this context "business" means any asset or group of assets that promises to produce a flow of cash or income in the future. It may include a piece of commercial real estate, a manufacturing business, a retail store, a consulting business, a barber shop, or a legal practice. The definition is broad enough to include a portfolio of securities, but the valuation of such securities usually presents few problems, because quotations for marketable securities are readily available from brokerage firms.

The words **valuation** and **appraisal** are virtually synonymous and are used interchangeably in this chapter. In corporation law, there also exists a narrow statutory **appraisal right** or **right of dissent and appraisal** designed to protect minority shareholders against certain types of potentially abusive transactions

specifically defined in the statutes. This statutory appraisal right is only incidentally involved in the issues discussed in this chapter.

Valuation of a business is a factual and business-related issue, not a legal
issue on which a lawyer will ordinarily opine, although valuation may often
arise as a factual issue in negotiations, transactions, and litigation. For example,
a lawyer may be required to prepare or examine or cross-examine an expert
witness in a matter involving valuation. Or the lawyer may be called upon to
advise a client who wants to buy or sell a small business. Valuation questions
also often arise in connection with tax matters. If a shareholder in a closely held
business dies, the value of the stock must be established to determine the estate
tax liability, if any. Similarly, if the owner gives shares to family members, the
value of the shares must be established for gift tax purposes.

As between shareholders in a closely held business, it is usually advisable
to set up a buy-sell agreement to cover the possibility that irreconcilable differences may arise as to the management of the business. Buy-sell agreements
usually contain provisions that either permit or require the corporation to purchase shares at a specified price or a price to be determined by a specified
formula. Clearly, a lawyer who sets up such an agreement must know something about valuation. Even in the absence of such an agreement, many states
now have statutes that allow a minority shareholder who has suffered some sort
of oppressive treatment at the hands of a controlling majority shareholder, to
seek dissolution of the corporation and that also allow the corporation or a
shareholder to purchase the shares of the complaining minority shareholder at
fair value. The determination of fair value is a fact issue that must be litigated.
Thus, a business lawyer must be familiar with the techniques of valuation.

## §7.2  Business Appraisers

Many individuals and firms hold themselves out as valuation or appraisal
experts. These persons are retained regularly to provide opinions or recommendations or to serve as expert witnesses in litigation on valuation questions.
However, valuation is not an exact science and the conclusions of even sophisticated "experts" can be suspect. Thus, although a business lawyer need not do
valuations in the first instance, he or she must be familiar with techniques of
valuation in order to understand the work of experts and translate it for clients
and courts, and sometimes in order to challenge the work of others' experts.

It is indeed easy to be cynical when discussing valuation experts. Every
person in business is familiar with stories in which valuation opinions were
given primarily on the basis of what the person paying for the opinion wanted
to hear. The necessary points of view are usually not conveyed by such crass
statements as "I want you to come out with a high value," or "I want an
opinion that this business is worth between $20,000,000 or $30,000,000," or
"I want an opinion that $21 per share is a fair price for the rest of the stock."
Rather, these points of view may be effectively communicated simply when the
proposed transaction or reason for the appraisal is described to the person
retained to give a valuation opinion. After all, it does not take a genius to realize
that sellers usually want high valuations and buyers usually want low valuations,

or that minimizing taxes is the goal of an estate seeking a valuation of a closely held business. It is also not unknown for a person dissatisfied with one opinion to commission a second opinion from a different, and perhaps more sympathetic, source.

Among the many individuals and firms that consider themselves competent in business valuation matters are the following:

1. Accountants and accounting firms. These firms regularly make recommendations on valuation issues. They may prepare studies and recommendations for the benefit of management decision-making on investment or divestment issues that involve substantial valuation questions. Suppose that a company has decided to sell off a line of business on which it is currently losing money but which it believes can be turned around with different management. The price to be placed on that line may be based on a report and recommendation by the company's outside auditors. Although the company's internal accounting staff probably has essentially the same expertise as the outside auditor and may also make a study and report, or may review the outside auditor's report and make an independent recommendation, the report of an outside accounting firm may be obtained as a check on the conclusions of the inside auditors or because an internal recommendation may be viewed as subject to the domination of management.

2. Investment banking firms. These firms also regularly make valuation recommendations or give opinions relating to value, particularly with regard to transactions involving the purchase or sale of interests to the general public. The expertise of investment banking firms in the valuation area arises from their historical role of establishing prices for the sale of stock to the general public. The establishment of such public issue prices is tricky. When the offering is an **initial public offering (IPO)**, setting the offering price involves the same difficulties faced in valuation of a closely held business. When the offering is of additional shares of a stock that is already publicly traded, the price must be low enough to attract outside capital and yet not so low as to anger existing shareholders because of the dilution caused by issuing new shares at bargain prices. Investment banking firms are also heavily involved in the takeover business, and often prepare fairness opinions on whether a proposed price for a business is a fair one. These opinions have sometimes been the subject of litigation.

3. Full-service securities brokerage firms. These firms, which provide a variety of advisory and related services in addition to the simple execution of securities transactions, offer similar valuation expertise. Such firms regularly provide investment advice that necessarily involves valuation questions, and business valuation is a natural extension of this function. In many cases, a full-service brokerage firm also maintains an investment banking operation.

4. Independent firms that describe themselves as management consulting firms. These firms, which also provide valuation services, may employ persons with experience in accounting and auditing as well as management decision-making.

5. Real estate brokerage firms or individual real estate brokers. These firms may prepare valuation or appraisals of specific income-producing properties such as commercial real estate. Persons actively engaged in buying and selling

commercial real estate in the community usually have a feel for the market and are likely to be familiar with prices being paid for other commercial properties in the area and the comparability of those other properties to the property in question.

6. Auction or brokerage firms. These firms may specialize in the purchase and sale of substantial commercial assets such as heavy construction equipment, and may provide valuation opinions in some situations. These values may be liquidation values, based on the assumption that the operating assets are to be broken up and sold or auctioned off individually. For some types of second-hand equipment, there may be published blue books or catalogues used in estimating value.

7. Business brokers who specialize in listing businesses for sale and in locating persons who are interested in acquiring businesses and who have the financial resources to do so. Most businesses listed with such brokers are relatively small, but some large firms may list themselves or specific lines of business with these brokers. These brokerage firms have extensive experience with business valuation matters, although their principal interest is usually the commission upon the completion of the sale.

## §7.3  The Standard of Value

There is general agreement that the fundamental goal of valuation is to determine the **fair market value (FMV)** of a business, which in turn is defined as the price that would be established by a buyer and a seller in an arm's-length negotiation for the purchase and sale of the business, with both parties ready, willing, and able to enter into the transaction, under no compulsion to enter into the transaction, and having complete information about the relevant factors.

Although this fundamental standard is relatively easy to state, it gives little guidance as a practical matter in cases in which the business is closely held by relatively few owners and there have been no recent sales of the business or a closely comparable business. Indeed, the "ready, willing, and able" test begs the question, because it gives no clue as to what techniques should be used by a hypothetical buyer and hypothetical seller in determining what price to offer and what price to accept.

In a publicly held business, there exists an active market for ownership interests—the stock market. The existence of a public market for ownership interests makes valuation of a publicly held business considerably easier than that of a closely held business, because there are always current market price quotations available. It should not be assumed, however, that there are no valuation problems in publicly held businesses.

Those unfamiliar with the valuation process often labor under the mistaken belief that businesses have a single determinable value, and that the goal of the valuation process is to find the holy grail of true value. Valuation is not an exact science. Basically, there is no objective answer to the question, "What is this business really worth?"

Valuation issues are interesting and challenging precisely because there is no single value of a business. At best, there is a **range of value**. At worst, there are wildly varying approximations regarding value with the approximations based on different but plausible approaches as to how value should be measured. Indeed, the uncertainties of the valuation process are often so significant that high or low valuations may plausibly be asserted on the basis of the same basic technique of valuation.

A number of different adjectives may be associated with the word "value." For example, financial analysts often use **fair value, fair market value, book value, asset value, liquidation value, replacement value,** and **going concern value**. Some of these phrases refer to specific and meaningful concepts. For example, book value, liquidation value, and replacement value all refer either to existing numbers or to a specific method of calculating a number in connection with a business. Other phrases, such as fair value, real value, true value, and actual value, have no well defined meaning at all. At best, these phrases are merely synonyms for the basic definition of value, namely the price on which a willing buyer and willing seller would agree.

Whatever the reason for the notion that a business has a single correct value, many people regularly rely on this notion when valuation issues are first discussed. One also finds traces of it in opinions of presumably sophisticated judges who argue, for example, that a transaction should be set aside because a price for shares of closely held stock was set entirely arbitrarily and did not reflect "real," "actual," or "true" value. Such reasoning is simply the assertion of a conclusion and not analysis.

The essential point is that there are many different techniques that may be used to analyze value, and each technique may yield significantly different numbers. Thus, it is considerably more accurate to envision the ultimate "value" of a business as a range than as a specific number. For the same reason, the valuation opinions of even sophisticated individuals with extensive backgrounds in valuation techniques usually may be impeached, or at least shaken, by a lawyer familiar with valuation techniques and their limitations. These various techniques are described in the following sections of this chapter.

## §7.4  Market Price

When valuing a business, one sometimes discovers that a negotiated sale of the entire business occurred at some earlier time. A sale of the entire business in the fairly recent past, in an **arm's-length transaction** between sophisticated individuals, is perhaps the best evidence of value as of the time of the sale. Indeed, when a retrospective valuation is involved, such as for tax purposes in connection with a gift made several years ago, an arm's-length sale occurring years after the gift will usually be seen as providing a reliable basis for going back and estimating the value of a business at the earlier time. Adjustments made to that negotiated sales price are limited to changes that occurred in the business between the time the sale took place and the earlier or later date on which the value is to be ascertained.

More commonly, prior transactions involve purchases and sales of shares of stock of the company rather than a sale of the entire company. Here, the difference between a closely held corporation and a publicly held corporation becomes critical. In the case of a publicly held company, purchases and sales of stock usually occur daily. Professional analysts keep up with the company and make recommendations about the stock. In closely held corporations, on the other hand, the sales are almost by definition isolated, infrequent, and few in number. Furthermore, transactions in shares in closely held corporations often occur in circumstances in which one party to the transaction is under financial compulsion to sell while the other party may be under little or no compulsion to buy.

When the common stock of a company is publicly traded on an exchange or in the over-the-counter market, the market price is often considered to be a reliable measure of value. But it is clearly not always so.

Many smaller companies are publicly traded on the over-the-counter market, but by reason of their size or the number of shareholders, the volume of trading does not approach that of companies listed on the major exchanges. These publicly held stocks are referred to as being **thinly traded** or having **thin markets**. Prices of trades in thin markets may need to be individually examined, because some thinly traded stocks may have more characteristics of closely held corporations than of publicly held corporations.

Even when a publicly traded stock has a broad market with numerous transactions, it does not necessarily follow that the total value of the business, if it were sold as a single entity, equals the current market price per share multiplied by the total number of shares outstanding. If this conclusion were correct, valuation of publicly held corporations would be relatively easy, because one could obtain the current value of the entire business simply by adding up the current market values of all outstanding shares. But the premiums typically paid to shareholders in corporate takeovers demonstrate that the value placed on a business by the securities markets is often significantly lower than the amount that a purchaser is willing to pay for the entire business (or all the outstanding stock). In other words, the market often appears to understate the value of the entire company. This phenomenon has been the subject of considerable speculation, because there is a great deal of evidence in other contexts that the public securities markets are efficient in the sense that the price reflects all currently available public information about the stock. Of course, it may be that the market is not efficient, or that it is efficient only in the sense that it processes information quickly even though some of the information may be false or somehow misconstrued. Nevertheless, the fact that investors and many others rely on the market not only to set prices, but also as a reliable indicator of value for innumerable other purposes, suggests that it is widely believed that the market is basically efficient.

One plausible explanation for the price variation in some takeovers is that the securities markets value the business only on the assumption that current management will remain in office, while bidders in takeovers set a higher value, because they plan to replace incumbent management with more effective management that justifies a higher price per share.

Another explanation is that the trading markets for securities are primarily markets for investments, not markets for controlling interests in companies. Almost all transactions on public securities markets involve minute fractions of the total outstanding shares of companies, and these transactions individually do not carry with them any meaningful opportunity to affect the company's business policies. However, where the transactions increase in size so that control of the company may be involved, the purchasers are willing to pay more — usually significantly more — than the prices for smaller blocks of shares that are traded solely as investments. Of course, if one person buys enough small blocks in a publicly held corporation, he or she will ultimately end up with a big block, and conceivably a majority block. But that is not the way things usually work, because only a few persons have the financial resources to assemble such a block of shares, and federal law requires public disclosure of a person who accumulates more than 5 percent of any public corporation's stock. The result is that the market for the whole corporation — the takeover market or market for control, as it is sometimes called — arguably is different from the regular market for investment securities.

Yet a third explanation is that the price offered for a controlling interest of publicly held corporations is dictated more by the availability of funds to finance the acquisition than considerations of value. Many acquisitions of publicly held corporations involve the extensive use of debt to finance the purchase. Usually, the business being purchased becomes the ultimate debtor whose cash flow is expected to discharge the debts incurred in the takeover. This type of acquisition is called a **bootstrap acquisition** (because the company is in effect purchased with its own assets) or a **leveraged buyout** (if incumbent management and outside financiers end up as the ultimate owners of the business). How is the price to be offered for such a transaction ascertained? Clearly, it must be set significantly higher than the current market price in order to be attractive to investors and to close out possible competitive offers from other sources. The decision as to whether such a transaction is feasible may be based on (1) a cash-flow analysis indicating the maximum amount of debt the business can possibly carry and (2) estimates of the amounts for which nonessential assets or peripheral lines of business can be sold for. In the most extreme case, most of the business's assets may be sold off to raise funds to reduce the outstanding indebtedness incurred to finance the purchase price: a **bust-up acquisition** in the true sense of the word. Although this description may seem to have little to do with the value of the target company, the fact that borrowed money is used to purchase target stock may mean that the potential cash flow of the target is higher than the market perceives or that the capitalization rate applied by the market is too high. This explanation is consistent with the facts that valuation is an art, that varying estimates and assumptions made by an appraiser may lead to very different results, and that valuation studies may lead to the discovery of important business opportunities.

There are other theories regarding why publicly traded companies are routinely bought and sold for more than the aggregate market value of their shares and how takeover premiums can be reconciled with the idea that the securities market is efficient. It is possible that bidders simply overpay for many target companies. It is also possible that investors disfavor diversified or under-leveraged companies. And it may be that the market is not perfectly efficient — that market prices are determined by a range of investor perceptions and tend to change with the changing supply of stock or in reaction to fluctuations in trading by successive groups of investors who see a stock as overpriced or underpriced as a result of trading by other investors with other opinions or pursuant to other strategies. In the end, there may be truth in all of these explanations. These forces, either individually or working together, may drive market prices for individual companies away from the value that would be set by a perfectly efficient securities market. The resulting fluctuations in market prices are sometimes called **market noise**.

Many courts and commentators have concluded that the substantial premiums paid in takeovers mean that the market routinely undervalues publicly traded companies. This difference is sometimes called an "imbedded discount" or "inherent discount." Thus, it is common in appraisal proceedings to look to premiums in comparable transactions as a way of adjusting market price. There are, however, potential problems with this approach. First, it may be the case that companies that are undervalued for some other reason tend to become targets and that the premium paid is simply a reflection of what the market price of the company should be. Second, the premium may reflect a shift in the use of assets and may thus be inappropriate in a case in which no shift is contemplated. Third, it is important to keep in mind that the addition of a premium is intended to adjust for the tendency of the market to assign too low a value to the subject company. It does not follow that the premium should be added to other measures of value such as going concern or asset value.

## §7.5  Asset Value

Valuation based on what the assets of the business would bring if they were sold may seem to be the simplest and most intuitive method of valuation of a business. An individual who asks, "What is my financial worth?" is likely to think in terms of what the various assets he or she owns would bring if sold. For example, many individuals have had the experience of selling a used car, where value means **resale value** that can be easily approximated simply by looking it up in the "blue book," by going to several used car dealers and asking for price quotations, or by advertising the car oneself and seeing what offers come in. These are appropriate ways to measure the value of goods that are reasonably standardized and are recognized objects of trade. The problem is that businesses are rarely like used cars. They are not at all standardized, each one is unique, there is no authoritative blue book, and there is not an active market with many buyers and sellers. A value may need to be assigned to a business where there are no sales that are even remotely comparable.

A second intuitive approach toward value is to assume that value really means **liquidation value**; that is, what the assets could be sold for if the business were closed down and the assets broken up and sold. For an individual, this would be the answer to the question, "What are my worldly assets worth?" or, in more pessimistic terms, "How large would my estate be if I died today?" A business can certainly be valued in this way. However, in almost every situation, liquidation of the business is not contemplated by anyone, and what is being valued is not a mass of isolated assets but something that has value because it produced income or cash flow in the past and has (presumably) greater potential of producing income or cash flow in years to come. The use of liquidation value in most situations is therefore illogical, because it values the business in a way that does not address the actual value-producing ability of the business.

In most circumstances, **asset valuation** is unrealistic, because neither the buyer nor the seller contemplates that the liquidation will in fact occur. Typically, what is being bought and sold is an entity that produces earnings or cash flow, not a string of individual, unrelated assets. In other words, asset valuation is often too low, because it assumes that the pieces of a business are being sold to someone other than the current owner. If the current owner is a competent manager, however, those assets should be being used in their highest and best use to produce as much income or cash flow as possible. Thus, in a sense, asset valuation assumes a sale to a second-best user and is naturally lower. It is for this reason that when a business is sold as a going concern, it is often sold for more than the value of the assets. The difference is sometimes referred to as **goodwill**, which may be thought of as a number that represents the intangible capacity of well-managed assets to generate more in income than the assets are worth separately.

Asset valuations nevertheless may enter into the calculation of the value of a business in many circumstances. The most obvious situation is one in which the purchaser's goal is in fact to liquidate the business—a **bust-up transaction**, as it is sometimes called. Bust-up transactions occur in publicly held corporations when the corporation's securities are depressed in price and the liquidation value of its assets exceeds its value as a going business as measured in the securities markets. Similar transactions may also occur in closely held corporations if the incumbent owners fail to recognize that the corporation is worth more liquidated than as a going entity.

Another situation in which liquidation values may enter into the valuation of a business arises when the purchaser's basic goal is to obtain the use of one asset or line of business and to dispose of the other assets after the sale is completed. In this situation, the buyer is likely to value the business by determining the value of the desired asset or line of business (based on its contemplated cash flow or income) and adding to it an estimate of the liquidation value of the remaining assets.

If the business being acquired has assets that the purchaser believes to be unnecessary for the successful continuation of the business (or if the assets duplicate underutilized property that the purchaser currently owns), the purchaser may again simply add the liquidation value of these assets to the value based on earnings to determine the total price he or she is willing to offer. Similarly, if the company being valued has cash or marketable securities in excess of its needs, the buyer may increase the price by the amount of the excess cash or cash equivalents, which, if the purchase is successful, may be withdrawn without adversely affecting the operation of the acquired business. In effect, the buyer pays cash for cash or cash equivalents. In many of these situations, the seller may be aware of the existence of the excess assets and will exclude them from the sale (or distribute them as dividends to the owners of the business before the sale takes place).

The calculation of liquidation value becomes very difficult on an asset-by-asset basis for any substantial business. In such situations, estimates of net asset value are usually made by using book values and making adjustments for assets such as land, marketable securities, and last-in first-out (LIFO) inventories. When lines of business are salable as units, income or cash-flow analysis may be applied to these lines with the resulting value being treated as net asset values for each particular line.

Assets may also be valued on the basis of what it would cost to replicate or replace the plant and operations of the business, rather than what the assets of the corporation would bring upon dissolution. **Replacement cost** is often used when a business is contemplating expanding into a new area of operation and is choosing between building a plant from scratch or buying an existing company. However, replacement cost, like liquidation value, is generally not an appropriate way to measure the value of an ongoing business, because the purchaser normally would not view the business as equal in value to what a brand-new plant created from scratch would cost. Indeed, in the case of many mature businesses, the replacement cost of a plant greatly exceeds the value based on future cash flow, which ultimately is the only reliable indication of value.

Probably the most common formulation of the standard is the willing-buyer / willing-seller test, which seeks to determine the value of assets where neither party is under any compulsion to buy or sell. The fair market value of assets less liabilities (however it may be measured) should usually be less than going concern value. If the assets are worth more sold off in pieces than they are worth as part of a going business, then presumably they should and would be sold off in pieces so as to maximize value for owners and investors. In other words, it should ordinarily be the case that assets at work in a business generate more return in that application than they would in some other application. That is, it should usually be the case that assets are devoted to their **highest and best use**. Indeed, the difference between going concern value and asset value is what is meant by **goodwill**, which is the intangible asset created when one business acquires another for more than the value of the acquired company's assets. This is not to say that assets are always devoted to their highest and best use, but only that they should be. Many if not most deals involve shifts in the use of assets to increase their productivity. But where the goal is to determine the value of a business in its current form, it should ordinarily be assumed that going concern value exceeds asset value. Thus, it is well settled in the context of appraisal proceedings that going concern value is the proper standard. On the other hand, asset valuation should arguably be used if the transaction involves a disposition of assets.

## §7.6  Book Value

**Book value** means **net worth** or **owners' equity** according to the financial records of the business. It is the amount that remains after subtracting liabilities from assets. Thus, book value is an accounting concept rather than a true measure of value. Financial records are normally kept on the basis of historical cost, and book value therefore usually does not reflect either the earning capacity of the business or the current value of its inventory and capital assets.

Despite these deficiencies, book value is almost always calculated as part of the valuation process. There are several reasons. First, it is always easy to calculate book value from the financial records of the business; second, book value tends to increase with the success of the business so that it is not automatically made obsolete simply by the passage of time; third, shareholders may view book value as a floor under the price for shares and resist proposed sales for less than book value. On the securities markets, a stock that is selling for less than book value is often viewed, somewhat irrationally, as a questionable investment. Even though these attitudes are not strictly logical, they do reveal that book value, based as it is on historical cost, is given some weight in the valuation process.

One problem with book value is that it may be significantly affected by accounting conventions that do not themselves affect the earning capacity or assets of the business. For example, if there are two identical companies, one using LIFO and the other using first-in first-out (FIFO) to reflect inventory costs, the book value of the FIFO company will usually be higher than the book value of the LIFO company. Thus, if book value is relied on, adjustments may be necessary to offset the use of these accounting conventions.

Another problem with book value is that a company that pays generous dividends will have a smaller book value, other things equal, than a company that retains more cash, even though the two companies may have identical earning power. Moreover, although the payment of a dividend reduces owners equity, the payment of a dividend is also the basic way in which investors receive their financial return (short of selling their stock or interest or of the company liquidating). Thus, book value may significantly understate the true value of a company that has adopted a policy of paying substantial dividends. Moreover, long-term liabilities may be overstated or understated depending (among other things) on whether the interest rate is higher or lower than current market rates and time to maturity. To be sure, it may be possible to adjust the figures shown on the balance sheet to reflect fair market value. Indeed, the accounting profession is currently studying how it might move toward fair value accounting and away from historical cost. But even if the balance sheet can be thoroughly adjusted to reflect fair market value, there are still problems with book value. Two otherwise identical companies may have radically different book values depending on dividend policy. A company that follows a policy of maximizing distributions to its shareholders will have a smaller book value than a company that retains all of its earnings. Yet from the shareholders' point of view, the company that maximizes payout may well be worth more. Despite these shortcomings, there is some evidence that the price-to-book-value ratio is reliably correlated with future returns. The lower the ratio, the higher the return going forward.

## §7.7 Going Concern Value

Usually, a business's value lies in its ability to provide a future stream of net cash. The most direct way of measuring value, therefore, is to estimate what this stream will be in the future and assign a value to it, using the techniques described in earlier chapters on discounting future payments to present value. But reliable estimates of future cash flows will usually not be available, and the only available information will be conventionally prepared income statements for prior accounting periods. Estimates of future income flows, based on prior income statements, are widely used instead of estimates of cash flows, simply because income numbers are usually easy to obtain directly from accounting statements. Indeed, this method of valuation is usually described as the **capitalization of income** or **capitalization of earnings**. It is a well-established method of estimating value.

As should be apparent from earlier chapters, however, income as determined by accountants is subject to numerous rules and discretionary choices in presentation that may cause the bottom line of income to diverge significantly from the amount of cash that is in fact available to the owner. The amount actually available to the owner is sometimes referred to as **free cash flow** and may be thought of as a firm's capacity to make distributions. An investor is primarily (and often only) interested in the cash return that a business will generate. Thus, although accounting income may come quite close to cash flow over the long haul, it is cash flow and not accounting income that is ultimately most important to investors. Although it is tempting to use the terms cash flow and income (or earnings) interchangeably, it should always be kept in mind that these terms have distinct meanings and that cash flow should be the focus of any rigorous valuation.

It will be recalled that the valuation of an annuity or a stream of cash payments in the future requires knowledge of two variables: the size of the payments each year and the appropriate discount or interest rate by which the future payments can be discounted to present value. This rate in turn is a function of two variables: the market interest rate for riskless loans and a **risk premium**, that is, an additional amount of interest dependent on the degree of risk presented by the specific transaction. When constant perpetual payments are involved—that is, the stream of payments is assumed to remain fixed in amount and continue permanently in the future—the present value of the stream is equal to the reciprocal of the interest rate multiplied by the payment:

$$\text{present value} = \text{payment} \times \frac{1}{\text{discount rate}}$$

The reciprocal of the **discount rate** (1/interest rate) is often called the **multiplier** or **capitalization factor**. Table 7-1 shows how one can quickly develop a table of reciprocals that show what the multiplier is for a variety of discount rates.

In the context of a going business, a value can be obtained simply by estimating the future income or cash flow of the business, selecting a discount

Table 7-1

| Discount Rate | Multiplier |
|---|---|
| 100% | 1 |
| 50% | 2 |
| 33.33% | 3 |
| 25% | 4 |
| 20% | 5 |
| 16.66% | 6 |
| 12.5% | 8 |
| 10% | 10 |
| 8% | 12.5 |
| 7% | 14 |
| 6% | 16.7 |
| 5% | 20 |

rate, and multiplying by the reciprocal set forth in Table 7-1. Thus, if a business's estimated future cash flow is $120,000 per year, and it is determined that an appropriate discount rate is 10 percent, that business is worth 10 × $120,000, or $1,200,000. If the estimated future cash flow is $90,000 per year, the value would be $900,000. If the business is considerably riskier and the appropriate discount rate is 20 percent, the company would be worth precisely half as much: 5 × $100,000 or $500,000. The riskier the business, the higher the discount rate, the smaller the multiplier, and the lower the value placed on the cash flow (or income). It is apparent that accurate assessments of both anticipated cash flow (or income) and discount rate are essential if the valuation so obtained is to be reliable. In real life, however, accurate information about both variables is difficult to find.

## §7.8 Estimating Income

For some businesses, future returns can be estimated with a fair degree of reliability. For example, the rental income of a shopping center may be based on long-term leases that provide a reasonable basis for estimating future returns (though the standard practice of charging rent based in part on a percentage of gross sales may be a complicating factor). Much the same thing may be true of a hotel or an apartment house in which vacancy rates can be estimated based on experience or historic patterns. The more common situation, however, is that future cash flows or income are highly erratic, uncertain and problematic.

As described in the chapters on accounting, in some instances projections of future income or cash flow prepared by management may be available. These estimates may be used as the projection of earnings into the future; there is a risk, however, that these estimates may be overly optimistic.

For most businesses, historical information is available as to how the business fared in the recent past. Table 7-2 is an example of information that may be available as to income for the previous five years.

Again a caveat is necessary: These are **book earnings** taken directly from the company's financial statements. Adjustments may be necessary to reflect the

Table 7-2

| Year | Net income after taxes |
|------|------------------------|
| Year 1 | $100,000 |
| Year 2 | $120,000 |
| Year 3 | $180,000 |
| Year 4 | $210,000 |
| Year 5 | $160,000 |

true capacity of the company to generate cash flow or income as discussed more fully in Chapter 6, which discussed the analysis of financial statements. For example, in the case of many small businesses, the earnings of the business may or may not include compensation to the owner. If the business is unincorporated and therefore not required to file a tax return that is separate from that of the owner, it may well be that the owner has viewed the income of the business and his or her personal income as one in the same. This may mask the fact that if the business needed to hire a manager, the investment return of the business would be somewhat smaller than the income figures indicate.

Another important consideration that may apply even in the case of relatively large and incorporated businesses is that income may reflect the way the business has been financed and the accounting choices that have been made in calculating the income. In many closely held businesses, the owners choose to lend significant sums of money to the business instead of investing it permanently in the company as part of its capital. The reason is that interest payments on debt are deductible by the corporation, and thus reduce corporate income for tax purposes. Moreover, lending money to the corporation, rather than contributing it in exchange for stock, may create additional protections in bankruptcy, permit control to be divided up in a different way from financial participation, and allow some investors to enjoy leveraged returns (though the same investor cannot leverage his or her own return by lending his or her own money to the business). In any event, it is quite common for stockholders in closely held corporations also to be creditors of the corporation, and such arrangements are generally respected for tax and other purposes as long as the amount of stockholder debt is not excessive in comparison to equity.

The point for present purposes is that when the income of a business is determined for valuation purposes, it is usually best to calculate **earnings before interest and taxes (EBIT)**, because deductible interest may in fact be an element of return to the owner and its deduction reduces the amount of tax owed. Some analysts extend the concept of EBIT also to exclude depreciation and amortization **(EBITDA)**. EBITDA is, however, really an effort to combine cash-flow analysis with adjustments for interest and taxes. The problem is that these two adjustments are conceptually very different and any effort to perform both at the same time may lead to confusion and even double counting. Moreover, there is more to cash-flow analysis than adding back depreciation and amortization. (Indeed, it is not entirely realistic to ignore these noncash expenses unless one in fact has no plans to replace aging assets.)

Assuming, however, that the income stream has already been suitably adjusted, can one draw an inference about what future income will be from this historical data? Referring back to Table 7-2, one might take the average earnings over these five years ($154,000) and conclude that this number is a reasonable estimate of the average earnings of the business in the future. One can then choose an appropriate discount rate and calculate the business's value. For example, at 12 percent, the multiplier would be 8.333 and the value of the business would be $1,283,282.

It is easy to raise objections to the reliability of this process. First of all, is it realistic to assume that the earnings will average $154,000 per year forever? What about the period beginning three years from now? Ten years from now? Certainly, as the time frame lengthens, the uncertainties and inaccuracies of present predictions must also increase. On the other hand, because of the time value of money, the contribution to value made by these later years is relatively small in contrast to the contribution of the next few years, where the estimate presumably is more reliable. In other words, most of the overall value is represented by the next five, more reliable years, and a relatively small amount is represented by the assumption that earnings will average $154,000 thereafter. Hence, one might conclude that the calculation should not be materially changed if the $154,000 assumption were extended to the infinite future or, alternatively, that a different assumption were made about the income in these later years. Moreover, although it is true that uncertainties increase further into the future, it also is as likely that the current estimate will understate future earnings as it is that it will overstate them. If the probability of upside error and downside error are roughly equal, the current estimate will not be materially changed. We are clearly engaged in an impressionistic and not a scientific inquiry, and there is a gamble in it from the perspective of both sides.

The seller of the contemplated business (who obviously wants a high valuation) might legitimately complain that the $154,000 average figure gives undue weight to the first two years, which are the most remote from the present. After all, in the last three years of the five-year period, earnings never were below $160,000 and yet future earnings are estimated at only $154,000. It is more reasonable, it might be argued, to use only the average earnings of the last three years, which places the estimated earnings at $183,333 per year. The overall value of the business, using a 12 percent discount rate, would then be $1,527,714. In response, it might be argued that the significant decline in earnings in the last year is a warning that conditions giving rise to the steady increase in earnings in prior years may have changed, and that the average earnings in the future should in no event be viewed as being greater than those in the last year ($160,000). Along the same line, earnings arguably should be less than $160,000 if the downward trend can be expected to continue. Obviously, analysis of causes of the decline is of central importance in this debate.

Let us assume a somewhat different pattern of earnings with no change in average earnings for the period:

| | |
|---|---|
| Year 1 | $100,000 |
| Year 2 | $120,000 |
| Year 3 | $160,000 |
| Year 4 | $180,000 |
| Year 5 | $210,000 |

This rather minor adjustment gives a dramatically different appearance to the business's future. The seller might well argue that the estimate of average income in the future should build in a growth factor. For example, the seller might argue that the trend of growth in current earnings should be extrapolated into the future, for example:

| | |
|---|---|
| Year 5 (actual) | $210,000 |
| Year 6 (estimate) | $240,000 |
| Year 7 (estimate) | $270,000 |
| Year 8 (estimate) | $300,000 |

If this analysis is accepted, and the average of these four projections ($255,000) is taken as the anticipated income or cash-flow stream, the value of this business at a 12 percent discount rate becomes $2,124,915. At the very least, the trend might justify the use of the results for the most recent year ($210,000) as estimated future income. If the 12 percent discount rate is applied to this figure, the value of the business is $1,749,930.

## §7.9  Valuation with Growth

When a constant rate of growth can be anticipated, the formula is:

$$\text{value} = \frac{\text{return}}{\text{capitalization rate} - \text{growth rate}}$$

For example, consider a business with income of $200,000 in the most recent year. This business is expected to grow at an annual rate of 10 percent. In other words, the income is expected to be $240,000 in the next year and $288,000 in the year after that, and so on. If the appropriate capitalization rate before growth is 12 percent, the value of the business would be:

$$\$200,000 \;/\; (.12 - .10) \text{ or } 200,000 \;/\; .02$$

Because of the extremely low (net) discount rate, the value of the business works out to a whopping $10,000,000 rather than a modest $1,666,666 million for the same business without growth.

It is extremely important in considering the effect of growth on valuation to think clearly about the source of the growth. How would a company make itself grow at 10 percent per year? Although it is possible that the company has happened onto a growth opportunity that requires little or no new investment, such opportunities will usually be subject to intense competition and will therefore be rare. It is much more likely that the business will grow by investing more in its current line of business. Assume that the company decides to plow back half of its income into investment in expanded facilities in order to make the company grow. Assuming that the $100,000 will generate a return of 12 percent (which is the current return on the value that investors currently have invested), the increase in earnings will be $12,000 or 6 percent. How much will the company now be worth according to the valuation with growth formula? Plugging the numbers into the formula:

$$\$200,000 - \$100,000 \ / \ (.12 - .06) = \$100,000 \ / \ .06 = \$1,666,666$$

In other words, the company is worth exactly what it was worth without growth. The reason is that one must subtract the amount that is reinvested in growth, because such funds are not in fact free cash flow available for distribution to the owners. To be sure, reinvested funds still belong to the owners and have the effect of increasing the value of the company's assets. And the funds could be used to pay dividends instead of financing growth. But to count the funds as available for distribution when they are being committed to the generation of more income in the future, and then to count the increased future income as well, is to count the same money twice. (Indeed, counting both has the effect of mixing asset valuation with going-concern valuation.)

In the real world, many companies continue to pay dividends and borrow to finance new growth. But borrowing creates a dollar-for-dollar increase in liabilities that cancels out the increase from growth unless the company can borrow at interest rates lower than its capitalization rate. The resulting growth is as much a result of an increase in leverage as it is of the discovery of a new opportunity for extraordinary profits.

The most important point about valuation with growth is that the value of the company turns out to be the same as without growth if one assumes that the rate of return on new investment is the same as the rate of return on existing business. The value of an additional $12,000 in income capitalized at 12 percent is $100,000, exactly the same as the amount invested.

How realistic is the assumption that new business will generate income at the existing capitalization rate? Quite. Clearly a business should never invest in new business with a rate of return less than its capitalization rate. To do so will depress the value of the business as a whole. (If the new business is significantly less risky than the existing business, however, investors may capitalize the new business at a lower rate, thus placing a higher value on smaller chunks of income and keeping the value of the business steady. That is why a business that retains some of its income in money market funds or government securities rather than paying dividends is generally not penalized in terms of market value.) On the other hand, if the business can find new business with a rate of return that exceeds its capitalization rate, then undertaking that business will generate more return percentagewise than existing business and will increase the aggregate value of the company. But how likely is it that such opportunities will regularly be found? Not very. If the business operates in a competitive environment, as most businesses do, competition for attractive opportunities will have the effect of reducing extraordinary returns to a market rate. To be sure, there are situations in which new business carries a higher rate of return. For example, the business may be able to take advantage of economies of scale. The business may have unused production capacity that can be exploited simply by investing in a few new salespeople. Needless to say, such opportunities tend to be exploited quickly and are thus not likely to be a permanent trait of the business. Still, it is crucial in doing a valuation to have some sense of where a business is in its life cycle.

One important implication of this discussion is that it is crucial for financial managers within a company to have a good sense of the company's capitalization rate. Indeed, it may be more important for those within the company than for anyone else. Management may otherwise be tempted to take on new business that will cause the value of the company to fall, possibly exposing the company to the threat of takeover. For any new business under consideration, management will typically calculate an **internal rate of return (IRR)** based on projected cash flows of the new business. If the IRR equals or exceeds the capitalization rate, then the new business is worth considering further. In practice, financial managers actually do use the capitalization rate (often referring to it as the cost of capital) to set goals in terms of the required rate of return that must be generated by any new business being considered.

The fact that the value of a business tends to be the same with or without growth makes the valuation process much easier in a way. It means that as long as one is careful to calculate the maximum amount that the business can distribute without compromising its ability to keep generating cash to make such distributions indefinitely into the future, it is unimportant to consider what the company is in fact doing with its money as long as the company is well managed. Thus, the exercise of calculating value with growth is a powerful argument for cash-flow analysis, because the central goal of the valuation process becomes a determination of the maximum return that the business can in fact pay to its owners indefinitely. The relationship between valuation without growth and valuation with growth makes it clear that one should focus on cash flow.

Although the previous example involves much guesswork, it gives a flavor of the process. In real life, a cash-flow valuation will often involve the assessment of likely future cash-flow outcomes, the assignment of probabilities to each outcome, and the weighting of all possible results with the probability that that result will occur. The end result of this process is a single number that represents the value of the probable outcome given the uncertainties worked into the analysis.

Consider the following simple example. In arriving at the above estimate that earnings for Year 6 would be $240,000, an analyst might attempt to predict results under a best case, average case, and worst case. (What constitutes each case could be any conceivable factor that is important to the business's success, ranging from interest rates, to corn prices, to ski conditions. And in most businesses there will be many such factors to be considered.) The analyst has come up with the following outcomes and probabilities (with the probabilities expressed as decimals):

|  | *Outcome* | *Probability* | *Expected Return* |
|---|---|---|---|
| Best Case: | $300,000 | (.25) | $ 75,000 |
| Average Case: | $230,000 | (.50) | $115,000 |
| Worst Case: | $200,000 | (.25) | $ 50,000 |
| Total (Weighted Average): |  |  | $240,000 |

The expected return column shows the product of the outcome multiplied by the probability of that outcome. In essence, each possible payoff is multiplied by the odds that it will happen to determine how much the bet is worth. By adding up the values of each of the outcomes, one can place a value on all of the outcomes in the aggregate. Such a **weighted average** is usually more accurate than an effort simply to choose a most likely outcome, because a weighted average values all outcomes in proportion to their likelihood. Indeed, it bears noting that in the above example, there is no situation in which the analyst really expects earnings to be $240,000, even though that turns out to be the best guess if one calculates a weighted average of possible outcomes.

Using a weighted average also allows for the quantification of risk. Consider the following, which is a different estimate of probable outcomes:

|  | Outcome | Probability | Expected Return |
|---|---|---|---|
| Best Case: | $400,000 | (.25) | $100,000 |
| Average Case: | $230,000 | (.50) | $115,000 |
| Worst Case: | $100,000 | (.25) | $ 25,000 |
| Total (Weighted Average): |  |  | $240,000 |

The expected return for this period is the same as in the earlier example. But are the two investments worth the same? Clearly not. The first is worth more because the **dispersion** of expected returns is narrower and therefore less risky than the second. The return has less **volatility**. (**Dispersion** and **volatility of returns** are the essence of risk.) To be sure, there is always the chance with the second investment that one would receive $400,000. But there is an equal chance that one would receive only $100,000. The potential gain on the upside is thus precisely offset by a potential loss on the downside. Yet, the same expected return is available in the first investment without wild swings in outcome. Intuitively, other things equal, the first investment is better because it is less risky. Although it is difficult to quantify the difference, it seems clear that if both investments were offered at the same price, that is, if both required a commitment of the same amount of capital, investors should choose to put their money in the first before turning to the second. In order to make the second investment equally attractive to investors, it must be offered at a lower price. For example, if the first opportunity could be sold to an informed investor for $2,400,000 (to generate a 10 percent return), the second investment might need to be offered at $2,000,000 (to generate a 12 percent return). A rational investor demands more return if he or she takes more risk.

By using a weighted average approach to valuation, it is possible to quantify to some extent the risk of the two investments. The traditional method of quantifying dispersion of outcomes is by calculating a **standard deviation**. (A standard deviation is the square root of the sum of the squares of the differences between the average outcome and each individual outcome each multiplied by the probability of that outcome.) Without belaboring the process here, the standard deviation of the first investment is about $37,000, whereas the standard deviation of the second is about $107,000. Note that the standard deviation is expressed in the same terms (dollars) as the outcomes. The chances are about two out of three that the actual outcome will be within one standard deviation of the mean, and about 95 percent that it will be within two standard deviations. Although the standard deviation gives some sense of risk, it is not especially useful in comparing different investments, because it varies in proportion to the amounts in question. In the examples given, this is no problem, because the average return is the same for both investments, and the two standard deviations may thus be directly compared. But an investor is often faced with two or more possible investments with very different weighted average returns. The solution to this problem is to calculate a **coefficient of variation (COV)**, which is the standard deviation divided by the mean. The COV for the first investment is 37,000/240,000 or about 15 percent, while the COV for the second investment is 107,000/240,000 or about 45 percent. One can also think of the COV as an expression of units of risk per dollar of return that allows different investments to be compared to each other.

The isolation of possible outcomes and the assignment of specific probabilities to each outcome gives a satisfying specificity to the entire operation. However, even if all major contingencies are isolated in the decision tree analysis (itself a dubious assumption), the assignment of probabilities to them usually involves so much guesswork and is so uncertain that it is doubtful that this technique's use in real life situations provides a materially improved estimate of future events than the much more impressionistic analysis based on a mixture of historical results and generalized predictions about future trends set forth above. And the danger of assigning hard numbers to estimates is that the conclusion may appear to be more specific, and therefore more reliable, than it actually is.

## §7.10 Discounted Cash Flow (DCF)

The previous sections estimated an average return based on GAAP earnings. Although this approach may be good enough for many purposes, in practice a somewhat more fine-grained approach is often used. The most widely accepted method of valuation is the **discounted cash flow (DCF)** method. Under this method, one seeks to determine the maximum dividend that can be paid by the company without affecting the company's ability to function as a going business and continue to make profits. This is sometimes also referred to as **free cash flow**. Typically, the appraiser seeks to determine year by year for the next five years, how much free cash the company is likely to generate, taking into account the company's plans for growth, new investment, replacement of aging equipment and facilities, and other uses of its available cash.

DCF differs from a valuation based on an average of accounting earnings in several ways. GAAP earnings are not cash. Therefore, GAAP earnings do not reflect the ability of the company to distribute cash to investors. GAAP earnings are reduced by numerous noncash charges such as depreciation and deferred taxes. But earnings are not reduced by many cash payments such as the purchase of new inventory. Indeed, in the case of a fast-growing company, it is entirely possible that the company will report increasing earnings and yet not have enough cash to pay its bills without borrowing.

The DCF method also has a different perspective than valuation based on GAAP earnings. The DCF method is forward-looking rather than backward-looking. It considers cash inflows and outflows as of the time they actually occur. Thus, if a particular factory must be replaced in five years, the DCF method treats that expenditure as an outflow five years from now while the accountant reduces reported income each year for the next five years to reflect the fact that the factory is depreciating in value. Similarly, the DCF method recognizes expenses for research and development as of the time they occur, while an accountant will capitalize them and recognize them over a period of years. Because of the time value of money, the two methods often lead to very different valuations. Sometimes, the DCF method gives a higher valuation, sometimes lower. It is almost always different, however, from valuation obtained using GAAP principles.

To summarize, the essential goal of DCF analysis is to determine how much cash *could* be distributed to investors consistent with plans for the business and its need for cash. Cash flow is calculated by determining:

projected net income after tax (as would be shown on the income statement)
+ noncash charges − projected capital expenses
− projected increases in net working capital (other than cash and equivalents)
+ interest expense (adjusted for tax effect) = cash flow

The resulting number is the amount of cash available to make payments to shareholders or debtholders. The result might be called the **unleveraged cash flow**. In other words, the resulting number is the cash available to pay all investors. The ratio of debt to equity is another matter entirely, though it may be important in setting the capitalization rate (as explained more fully below). It should also be emphasized that whether the business in fact distributes available cash to its shareholders is wholly independent of cash flow. That will depend on the investment opportunities available to the company and to some extent on the preferences of the shareholders.

It is now relatively easy to determine a firm's cash flow for past periods for firms whose financial statements are prepared according to GAAP by inspection of the Statement of Cash Flows. Although this statement does not predict the future any more than any other financial statement, it does reveal the precise ways in which cash and earnings differ for a given company and thus is a good starting point for projections.

An appraiser will often calculate projected values for the next five years.

That is, the appraiser attempts to determine how much cash will be available at the end of each year for the next five years and calculates the present value of a hypothetical dividend payment based on that amount. The value of the firm after that time (variously called **residual value**, **terminal value**, or **salvage value**) is typically based on the assumption that the firm will continue to operate indefinitely after five years at the level of the fifth. (The residual value of the firm so calculated is usually little different in practice from the value obtained by using accounting numbers. Nevertheless, residual value is usually a large proportion of the value of the firm.)

Finally, in the last step of the valuation process, the individual values for the five years and the residual value are added together to give the value of the firm.

Consider the business described in Table 7-2 (which is reproduced here for convenience).

### Table 7-2

| Year | Net income after taxes |
|------|------------------------|
| Year 1 | $100,000 |
| Year 2 | $120,000 |
| Year 3 | $180,000 |
| Year 4 | $210,000 |
| Year 5 | $160,000 |

Suppose that at the very beginning of Year 1 you are considering an investment in this business and that these numbers represent projections of the expected income over the next five years. The average income is $154,000 per year. At 12 percent, the present value of $154,000 per year for five years is $555,139. But if one discounts the returns from individual years, the present value is $536,897. The difference is attributable to the timing of the returns. If the best year had come earlier and the worst year had come later, it may be that the year-by-year approach would show that the investment is actually worth more than indicated by the average approach. The point is that if information about the timing of returns is available, it may significantly affect the calculation of value.

Although it is often difficult to predict variations in return, some can be predicted with relative certainty. Suppose that one is contemplating an investment in a business that returns an average of $154,000 per year. The business operates out of a building for which it paid $100,000. The building has a five-year useful life, and it is projected that replacement at the end of five years will cost $100,000. The accountants have used straight line depreciation in their *pro forma* projections. Thus, the income of $154,000 per year includes a $20,000 annual depreciation expense.

If one bases the valuation of this business on average annual income, the discounted present value of the first five years of return is $555,139. But we have better information. We know that the depreciation expense in the first four years does not represent an actual cash outlay, and that there will be a real expense of $100,000 in the fifth year. Thus, the annual cash flow is really $174,000 for each of the first four years, and $74,000 in the fifth year. The present value is $570,478. On the other hand, suppose that we also know that because of inflation it will probably cost $150,000 to replace the building in five years. Then the cash flow for the final year becomes $24,000, and the present value of the five years worth of return is $542,108.

The foregoing example illustrates the DCF method of valuation. In essence, this method considers the timing of individual returns (based on expected inflows and outflows) and neutralizes the effects of accounting conventions (as with depreciation in the example). In the real world, of course, this method will usually require many more adjustments than reflected in this simple example. For example, the business may have years in which cash flow is negative because of the need to increase inventory or purchase a new major asset. These assumptions would significantly affect the DCF analysis but would not affect GAAP earnings.

It is customary for appraisers to focus in detail on five years of operations. But few businesses plan to liquidate after five years. If the owners then decide to sell, they will likely sell the business to someone who will continue to run it. Thus, strange as it may sound, it is quite realistic to think of a business as having perpetual life. Indeed, this is the default approach of corporation law as opposed to that of many unincorporated business forms. In any event, one cannot realistically value a business based on just five years of cash flow. Years six and after have value too. Accordingly, the general practice is to do a detailed cash flow valuation for the first five years and add to that the residual value for the following years based on the assumption that the business will continue to generate returns at some uniform average rate thereafter. Although the use of averages after five years may seem imprecise, the variations year to year become increasingly less important because of the time value of money. Moreover, projected cash flows in the early years will often reflect specific business opportunities that will probably be dissipated by competition after five years.

This is not to say that terminal value is unimportant. Often, it is the greatest part of the value of a business. In the above example, the aggregate value of $154,000 per year for Year 6 and beyond is $728,194. On the assumption that the building in question will cost $100,000 to replace in five years, the business is worth $570,478 + $728,194 or $1,298,672 whereas the value of $154,000 in perpetuity is $1,283,333. Clearly, these are not major differences. But under different assumptions they might be. Moreover, in a business negotiation or takeover battle, a difference of a dollar a share may be enough to get a deal done.

## §7.11  Capitalization Rate

Recall that the interest rate used to discount future payments back to present values in effect describes a measure of the risk that the payments will not occur. The same process applies in connection with valuation of a going concern. Typically, the terms **capitalization rate** or **multiplier** are used in this context rather than **discount rate** or **interest rate**. The capitalization rate is the **rate of return** that an investor would demand in exchange for making the investment in question given other available investment opportunities. The multiplier is the reciprocal of the capitalization rate. Because investors demand more return when they take more risk, the capitalization rate varies directly with the riskiness of the venture. The higher the risk, the higher the capitalization rate, and the smaller the multiplier.

The determination of which capitalization rate or multiplier to use in valuing a business appears at first glance to involve variables even more uncertain than the determination of the anticipated income or cash flow of the business. Indeed, one might argue that the multiplication of one gross approximation by an even grosser approximation is a classic example of garbage in garbage out and results in a figure that is so unreliable that it should not be used at all.

The capitalization rate or multiplier used in valuing a business is usually established from the actual relationships between average earnings and sales prices of similar businesses in the recent past, and not from a market interest rate plus additional risk assessment. Those familiar with the purchase and sale of businesses usually are generally familiar with actual sales prices of businesses that have been sold in the recent past and the estimated earnings used in the negotiations leading to these sales. Statements such as "Companies in which the personal services of the owners are an important income-producing factor generally sell at two times earnings, or less," or "Steel companies generally sell for about eight times earnings," or "Companies developing computer software that have marketed at least one successful product generally sell for at least 15 times earnings," are all meaningful statements that provide useful signposts for the selection of an appropriate capitalization factor for a roughly comparable business in the same or related industry.

In addition, for publicly traded securities there is readily available information about the **price/earnings (P/E) ratio**. The P/E ratio is the ratio between the market price per share and the earnings per share during the previous year.

The P/E ratios for individual companies (and indeed for industry groups) can be highly misleading. Because the published P/E ratio is (necessarily) based on the previous year's earnings, it does not convey a sense of what investors expect in the future. Ultimately investors care only about the future. Thus, a company that had a loss in the most recent year will nevertheless have a positive stock price and therefore will have a P/E ratio of infinity (because the denominator—that is, the figure representing earnings—is less than zero). Clearly, no one should be misled by a P/E ratio of infinity, but a similar effect arises if a company has substantial prospects but only barely positive earnings in the past year. If a company had earnings of (say) 10 cents per share last year and a current stock price of $20, the P/E is 200. But it may be that the previous year was a transition year and investors expect earnings of $2 per share in coming years. If so, the multiplier should be seen as 10, not 200. Most newspapers do not publish P/E ratios of 100 or more, although clearly a P/E of 60 or 70 is likely to be as misleading. In any event, one should be careful in using the P/E ratio of a single stock for purposes of valuation. If the P/E ratio is not extremely high and has been reasonably stable over the last few years, it is probably a reliable indicator of the appropriate capitalization rate. In most industries, using an industry average will control for the differing fortunes of individual companies, though it is possible that even an industry average will be misleading if the entire industry had an unusually good or bad year.

Yet another reason why the P/E ratio is not a precise indicator of the appropriate capitalization rate or multiplier is because the P/E ratio of a publicly traded stock reflects a multitude of investment decisions for small blocks of stock not affecting the control of the business, while the capitalization rate or multiplier should reflect the fact that control of the business is being bought and sold. In other words, the P/E ratio of publicly held companies, as usually computed, reflects only the investment value of securities and not any premium that represents control. If takeover bids are any indication, control premiums average about 50 percent higher and may be as high as 100 percent above the market price. Use of P/E ratios as the capitalization factor for valuation purposes for closely held businesses therefore may considerably underestimate the value of the company being appraised.

In the end, however, the uncertainties inherent in the valuation of a closely held business may outweigh uncertainties about the accuracy of P/E ratios for publicly held businesses. Clearly, the two are closely related, and P/E ratios (with appropriate adjustments) are routinely used as estimates of capitalization rates.

In an ideal situation, one may be able to find a publicly held corporation that is similar in most important respects to the closely held business being valued. If the two businesses are roughly comparable, then the P/E ratio of the publicly held stock can be applied as a ballpark estimate of the appropriate capitalization rate for the closely held company being valued. Again, it must be remembered that we are not dealing here with precise scientific data but with an impressionistic analysis establishing a range of values.

Unfortunately, however, there is often no publicly held corporation that is a close match for the company being valued. The most common problem of noncomparability is that the publicly held corporation has substantial business operations in several different industries, while the closely held corporation being valued is active in only a single industry. In this situation, one may use a composite P/E ratio for all the publicly held companies in the industry, if that is available. That composite ratio may be an appropriate capitalization factor for a business active only in the same industry on the theory that the averaging of P/E ratios for different publicly held companies tends to cancel out the effect of different multiple operations in different industries. If the notes to the financial statements of one or more of the publicly held corporations contain sufficient breakdowns and information on the results of operations in the industry in question, it may also be possible to derive an estimate of a separate P/E ratio for those operations alone.

In selecting an appropriate capitalization rate, it may be appropriate to adjust an industrywide P/E ratio to reflect unique aspects of the company in question. For example, if the company appears to have a more obsolete plant than the comparable company or the industry average, it may be appropriate to reduce the capitalization rate. There are two problems with this type of adjustment, however. First, it is relatively easy to say that an "appropriate" adjustment should be made, but there is usually no criterion for determining what that adjustment should be. If the base rate is 9 times earnings, should the appropriate capitalization rate for the corporation with a somewhat obsolete plant be 8 times earnings? 8.5 times? 8.75 times? Such differences in the capitalization rate may have substantial effects on the business's overall value. The difference between 8.5 and 8 times earnings may easily involve millions of dollars. The second problem is the risk of double counting a negative factor. If the obsolete plant is used first to justify a reduction of anticipated future earnings or cash flow, and a second time to reduce the appropriate capitalization rate, it is likely that the double use of the same negative factor will overstate its importance.

Logically, an adjustment of this nature probably should be made in the expected cash flow or income determination rather than the discount rate, because changes in the capitalization rate affect all elements of cash flow and not just reductions that may be entailed by replacing an outdated plant.

Although it is clearly easier to refer to sales of comparable companies or to P/E ratios, both are short cuts for the process of assigning a capitalization rate. The capitalization rate is the rate of return that a rational investor would demand in exchange for making the investment in question given other investment opportunities available. Because investors demand more return when they take more risk, capitalization rates must vary directly with the riskiness of the venture. The higher the risk, the higher the capitalization rate. The capitalization rate may be estimated by taking the prevailing **riskless rate of return** and adding a premium for the riskiness of the venture in question. Thus, if the riskless rate of return is 6 percent and because of the risk involved in a given venture an investor would require an additional 12 percent, the capitalization rate should be 18 percent, which translates into a multiplier of about 5.6.

The beginning point for choosing a capitalization rate from scratch is the riskless rate of return, that is, the rate of return available on long-term government securities. (When valuing a business, it is usually appropriate to use long-term securities as a benchmark, because they will only mature in the distant future and thus come closest to matching the typical business situation in which no liquidation is contemplated.) In some cases, however, the riskless rate of return may in fact be too high, because some portion of it is attributable to inflation. Creditors, after all, understand that repayment in inflated dollars reduces the effective rate of return. The riskless rate of return actually has two elements: the so-called **real interest rate** and an inflation factor. In recent years the inflation factor has been very low, but it may increase again in the future. If so, it may be appropriate to base a going-concern valuation on the real interest rate without an inflation factor. Also, a business that is largely immune to the effects of inflation because the price of its product may be easily increased with inflation. (Indeed, such a business may make money from inflation to the extent that its inventory increases in value simply from the passage of time.)

Finding the appropriate **risk premium** is considerably more difficult than finding the appropriate base rate, but it helps to keep in mind that the goal of the process is to determine only the required rate of return. If one has estimated the cash flow or income from the business on the basis of a weighted average calculation, then to some extent risk can be quantified in at least relative terms by calculating the COV. The COV may then be compared with other investments of varying risk to get a sense of how much additional return is needed to compensate for additional risk.

Charts and tables that suggest risk premiums for various types of businesses are also available in business publications. One author suggests that risk premiums should range from 6 to 10 percent for established businesses with a large share of the relevant market, strong financing, stable earnings history, and depth of management to 26 to 30 percent for a one-person firm in a personal services business. With regard to larger businesses, it bears noting that research based on stock market prices does seem to indicate that the premium over the riskless rate is about 6 percent on the average.

What then should be said about capitalization of earnings or cash flow as a valuation method? It is the most popular method of valuation of closely held businesses that are being purchased because of their potential earnings or cash flow. It is also widely used in valuation disputes generally, such as those relating to the value of stock in a closely held business for gift and estate tax purposes. Indeed, despite its drawbacks, the capitalization of earnings or cash flow is generally believed to be the most reliable method of estimating the value of a business anticipated to be in existence indefinitely.

## §7.12  Capital Asset Pricing Model (CAPM)

Although it is common to estimate the capitalization rate by analysis of comparable companies and their market prices, it is also possible to derive the capitalization rate by comparison to the market as a whole. In essence this is the approach taken by the **Capital Asset Pricing Model (CAPM)**, probably the most widely accepted method for determining capitalization. The reasoning behind CAPM is relatively simple when taken one step at a time. Taken as a whole, however, it affords powerful insights.

As noted earlier, rational investors diversify in order to reduce risk. Accordingly, any individual investment is worth more as part of a diversified portfolio than as a stand-alone, all-your-eggs-in-one-basket, investment. If investors value investments as part of a portfolio, then the price of stocks (and other securities) will tend to move in concert. In other words, stock prices tend to rise and fall with the market, which (incidentally) is why investors pay attention to market indices such as the **Dow Jones Industrial Average (DJIA)** and the **Standard & Poor's 500 (S&P 500)**.

Although one can eliminate **company-specific risk** (also called **unsystematic risk**), one cannot eliminate **market risk** (also called **systematic risk**), the risk that the market as a whole will rise or fall. Nevertheless, some stocks tend to rise and fall more than the market, whereas other stocks tend to rise and fall less than the market. A stock that moves on the average twice as much as the market is said to have a **beta coefficient** (or simply **beta**) of 2.0, while a stock that moves half as much as the market is said to have a beta of 0.5. A stock that moves by the same percentage as the market has a beta of 1.0.

The relationship between beta and capitalization rate is shown in the chart on the following page. The curved line EF is called the **efficient frontier**. It represents the maximum return that can be achieved by combining risky

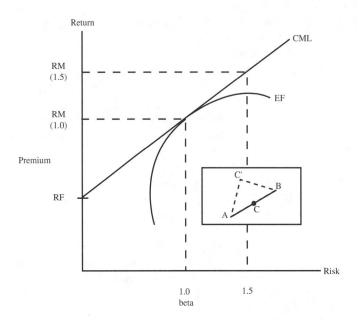

investments into portfolios. It bulges upward and to the left because with increasing diversification risk is reduced while return is maintained. (The inset
shows how this works with two investments A and B. Although a portfolio
consisting of equal amounts of these two stocks might be thought to have a
blended risk-return combination of C, the true risk-return combination is C'
because diversification has reduced risk.)

A line running from the risk-free rate RF on the vertical axis and tangent
to EF defines the optimum portfolio, which is presumed to be the market
portfolio. By definition, the market as a whole has a beta of 1.0 as shown by
the dashed vertical line. And the required rate of return for a portfolio with a
beta of 1.0 is RM as shown by the dashed horizontal line. The difference between RM and RF is the risk premium.

Because investors can achieve any combination of returns along the line of
tangency—the capital market line (CML)—by combining the market portfolio
with government securities (to the left of the vertical line) or by borrowing at
the risk-free rate (to the right of the vertical line), it follows that CML represents the rate of return that the market will demand for a given level of risk.
Moreover, because CML is defined by just two points it is a straight line.

As a result, one can derive the capitalization rate for a given company or
industry by determining the beta for the company or industry and adjusting
the risk premium proportionally. In other words, a company with a beta of 1.5
would have a risk premium equal to 1.5 times the market premium, whereas a
company with a beta of 0.5 would have a risk premium equal to 0.5 times the
market premium. For example, if the RF is 6.0 percent and RM is 14.0 percent,
then the risk premium is 8.0 percent, and stock with a beta of 2.0 would have
a risk premium of 16.0 for a total capitalization rate of 22.0 percent. Similarly,
a stock with a beta of 0.5 would have a risk premium of 4.0 for a total capitalization rate of 10.0 percent.

## §7.13 Problems with CAPM

There are several important qualifications to the Capital Asset Pricing Model.

First, it is not clear what index one should use to define the market and thus to determine the market rate of return. The most frequently used index is the S&P500, but arguably one should use an even broader index. (The various stock indices are discussed in the chapter on trading in stocks and bonds.) Presumably, the choice of index will affect the determination of the market rate of return for any given period, because narrower indices exclude smaller companies. On the other hand, if one can eliminate company-specific risk by investing in 20 to 50 stocks (as appears to be the case), then even the S&P500 may be overkill. Moreover, as the risk-free rate fluctuates so does the point of tangency and the slope of CML, which suggests that different portfolios may constitute the market portfolio at different times.

Second, CAPM appears not to work especially well for smaller companies, in that the predicted rate of return is systematically lower than the observed rate of return. This may be the result of using a too narrow index to define the market. In any event, it appears that small stocks yield more than they should under CAPM. For example, over the period 1926 to 2000, the ninth and tenth deciles of US listed stocks (microcap stocks) yielded 2.62 percent more than they should have on an average beta of 1.36 relative to the S&P500. And the tenth decile alone yielded 4.63 percent more on a beta of 1.42. Thus, it is common practice in valuing small companies to add a small company premium to an industry-based beta to adjust for this size effect. Although this anomaly has led some to question the model, it may be that *investor* use of narrower indices in constructing portfolios has led the market to ignore smaller companies. If investors use the S&P500 in combination with margin to achieve higher rates of return rather than buying a portfolio of higher-risk stocks, then it stands to reason that higher-risk stocks would trade at lower prices than indicated by the model. Indeed, the fact that the addition of a company's stock to the S&P500 leads to a bump up in its price tends to confirm this hypothesis. Moreover, it is not clear that investors can borrow at the risk-free rate to buy stocks on margin. Assuming that the going rate for margin loans is higher than the risk-free rate, investors will presumably insist on rates of return for riskier stocks that will compensate for the additional interest expense.

Third, it is not clear how one should calculate beta. Although beta figures are readily available from many investment advisory services, the calculations may differ according to the frequency of observations. There is no general agreement as to whether beta should be based on daily or weekly or monthly stock prices, although the most common method appears to be to use monthly closing prices over a five-year period. Arguably, one should exclude price movements that are attributable to company-specific news, but it is unclear that anyone attempts to do so. After all, the idea behind beta is to determine the tendency of a stock to move with the market when the stock is unaffected by company-specific news. To be sure, it may be that price movements caused by company-specific news cancel out over the long haul. But this also suggests that for some companies (presumably those with higher betas), the calculation of beta is based on more scattered observations and that the final answer is therefore less reliable than for other companies (presumably those with lower betas). Moreover, the typical 60-month (five-year) period over which data is gathered may be too long for some companies. Companies and indeed whole industries may change considerably in a five-year period. At the very least, one should give somewhat greater weight to more recent observations. It is unclear that anyone attempts to do so. Similarly, beta is inherently backward-looking and does not purport to value a company's prospects. Then again, returns in excess of the market rate are difficult to find, and a diversified investor is not focused on company-specific prospects anyway. Thus, the market as a whole (which is widely regarded as a leading indicator) is probably a much better measure of economic prospects than any company-specific information.

Fourth, it is not at all clear why individual stocks should move with the market in *varying* proportions. Indeed, the fact that they do is purely a matter of observation. Moreover, CAPM itself suggests that one could construct a portfolio containing half stocks with betas of 0.5 and half stocks with betas of 1.5 and end up with a portfolio with a 1.0 beta. Indeed, it appears that sophisticated investors such as mutual fund managers do engage in such strategies. But if market value is dictated by diversified portfolio investors, and if all stocks are potentially part of a benchmark market portfolio, then why should they not all have a beta of 1.0?

## §7.14  Adjusting for Capital Structure

As noted above in connection with the discussion of EBITDA, the best way to determine the value of a business is to look at cash flow before the payment of interest on long-term debt and taxes so as to control for the effect of discretionary financing choices. Ideally, one would determine the value of the firm before interest and taxes and then subtract the market value of debt and preferred stock to arrive at a value for the common stock interest in the company. In other words, the company as a whole should be valued, and that value should then be divided up among the various long-term interests including those attributable to long-term debt financing. The problem with this approach is that it complicates the determination of an appropriate capitalization rate. Whether one looks to P/E or beta, comparable companies presumably have some debt. Indeed, even the S&P500 is leveraged to the extent that the companies therein have debt. As of September 2001, it was reported that the average debt load of publicly traded companies in the United States was 28 percent of assets (up from about 17 percent in 1980).

There are two ways to handle this problem. One is to recalculate the capitalization rate for the comparable companies or index. The other is to determine the average level of debt in the comparable companies or index and then adjust the value of the target company accordingly. The latter method is presumably simpler. And on balance it is probably more accurate in that it is difficult to know for sure how the market would value the comparable companies with more or less debt. Thus, there is less chance of error in adjusting the target company valuation because it has more or less debt than comparable companies. Nevertheless, it is a common practice among appraisers to calculate the **unlevered beta** for a company (and comparable companies) by subtracting the beta of a company's debt from its observed levered beta. While this may make some sense in the context of a comparable company analysis (especially where companies in the same industry have varying levels of debt), it makes no sense in deriving a capitalization rate from the market as a whole (which is itself leveraged to some extent). Moreover, there is no central market for corporate debt and thus no reliable market data upon which to calculate the beta of the company's debt.

Note that it is usually important to use market value for debt in making any adjustment. If the debt is trading for less than par, presumably it may be repurchased at the market price. Moreover, it is presumably trading for less than par because it carries a below-market interest rate and is therefore a good deal for the issuing company. There may, however, be situations in which the company has allowed redeemable securities to trade at prices higher than the redemption price, in which case it may be appropriate to look to the lower redemption price if the company is in a position to redeem the securities. If the company cannot redeem the securities for some reason—as where the company has insufficient cash or is subject to some sort of covenant or where redemption would trigger conversion rights—the market value of the securities should presumably be used.

For purposes of determining the value of common stock, it is also important to consider any outstanding preferred stock. Again, the market price of the preferred should ordinarily be used rather than the face amount subject to the same considerations as noted above for debt securities.

## §7.15 Valuation Based on a Mixture of Methods

When valuing a business, it is customary to make estimates of value based on different approaches or assumptions. For example, a person preparing a valuation opinion might assemble the following estimates of value:

1. Straight book value, without adjustment for accounting conventions.
2. Adjusted book value, with adjustments for such items as LIFO inventory accounting, appreciation in marketable securities, and elimination of intangible assets.
3. Capitalized earnings, assuming average performance by the business.
4. Capitalized earnings, assuming a reasonable rate of growth.
5. Capitalized cash-flow assuming the current level of debt and, in the alternative, assuming an increased level of debt if available at attractive rates.
6. Estimated resale value of assets (obtained by using balance sheet assets excluding intangible assets and making adjustments for inventory valuation, marketable securities, land, and any excess depreciation taken in earlier years).

After making these six calculations, the results may be tabulated and the degree of disagreement among the various indicated values considered. If all are within a relatively narrow range, it is likely that a value within that range is appropriate. If the numbers vary widely, it is tempting to calculate an average and view the average as the best estimate of value. This is a somewhat muddled approach. The averaging process involves combining different numbers based on different assumptions. The decision to take the arithmetic mean of book value, liquidation value, and value based on capitalized earnings estimates, for example, has little theoretical justification.

There is, however, some judicial support for averaging different estimates of value. In statutory proceedings for the appraisal of the value of shares and in other cases in which share value must be determined, some courts apply a stylized valuation technique, known as the **Delaware Block Method** to measure value based on three different approaches, and then assign weights to each approach that reflect the court's judgment as to the reliability of the factor. In *Gibbons v. Schenley Industries, Inc.,* 339 A.2d 460 (Del. Ch. 1975), for example, the court-appointed appraiser valued shares of Schenley common stock as follows:

|  | Value factors | Weight | Assigned value |
|---|---|---|---|
| Market | 29.00 | 35% | 10.15 |
| Earnings Value | 52.78 | 45% | 23.75 |
| Asset Value | 49.83 | 20% | 9.97 |
|  |  |  | 43.87 |

The market value was based on actual trading of stock of Schenley. The earnings value was computed by averaging five years of earnings and applying a multiplier of 14 based on the average P/E ratio of comparable companies. The asset value was an estimate of the value of Schenley's plant, property, and equipment based on expert appraisals. On review by the Chancellor, the weight given to asset value was reduced to zero, the earnings per share were reduced by the exclusion of a nonrecurring transaction, and the capitalization rate was increased. The result was that the above table was revised as follows:

|  | Value factors | Weight | Assigned value |
|---|---|---|---|
| Market | 29.00 | 55% | 15.95 |
| Earnings Value | 39.79 | 45% | 17.91 |
| Asset Value | 49.83 | 0% | 0.00 |
|  |  |  | 33.86 |

This is obviously a highly stylized approach toward valuation in which the court's analysis is channeled in narrow directions. In a more recent decision, *Weinberger v. UOP, Inc.,* 457 A.2d 701 (Del. 1983), the Delaware Supreme Court rejected this long established approach toward judicial evaluation on the ground that "to the extent it excludes other generally accepted techniques used in the financial community and the courts, it is now clearly outmoded." The court adopted "a more liberal approach [which] include[s] proof of value by . . . techniques or methods which are generally considered acceptable in the financial community and otherwise admissible in court." Nevertheless, several states continue to use the Delaware Block Method of valuation.

## §7.16 Discounts for Lack of Marketability and Other Factors

Once the value of the entire business has been determined, the value per share would appear to be calculable simply by dividing the value of the business by the number of outstanding common shares. (This value per share is different from book value per share, which is obtained by dividing the net worth of the business, as ascertained from the balance sheet, by the number of outstanding shares.) Unfortunately, life is not that simple. When valuing shareholdings, there is no inherent reason why the value of a business must be allocated proportionately to each share. The usual manner of handling these differences between otherwise identical shares is by assigning discounts and premiums that reflect such characteristics as lack of marketability or ability to control the management of the company. A discount is simply a justification for knocking off a portion of the per-share value. A premium is an additional amount added to a block of shares.

There are several justifications for discounts that are recognized in the financial community as well as in case law.

A discount for **lack of marketability** may apply to shares that are otherwise publicly traded but that are subject to significant legal restraints on transferability. Sometimes publicly traded stock subject to legal restraint on transferability is called **letter stock** or **legend stock,** because as a matter of law a restriction on transfer can only be enforced against a buyer if the restriction appears in writing on the share certificate or other official evidence of ownership. Stock that may be freely sold or transferred is sometimes said to be **freely alienable**. Thus, stock that cannot be sold or transferred is sometimes said to lack alienability. Similarly, agreements applicable to shares of publicly held corporations that require the shares to be offered first to the corporation may justify a discount from the market price of shares not subject to the restrictive agreement. The value at which the shares must be offered is likely to be accepted as the maximum value of the shares for valuation purposes without regard to other valuation techniques. And even in the absence of some sort of imposed or agreed restriction, federal and state securities law may restrict the ability of a controlling shareholder to sell if the sale may be construed as a public offering.

In addition, large blocks may be more difficult to market than smaller blocks, though mutual funds and other institutional investors routinely buy and sell thousands of shares at a time. In a thinly traded market, the dumping of a large block of shares may depress the market significantly. A discount per share for large blocks of publicly traded shares may thus be warranted. Large blocks of shares are often sold through **block positioning firms** (i.e., specialized brokerage firms that assume the risks of selling unusually large numbers of shares). These firms command high per share fees for handling such transactions, and thus large blocks of shares tend to be priced somewhat lower than shares sold in more typical quantities. Large blocks of shares may sometimes need to be sold through a costly underwriting. These costs of distribution may be viewed as an estimate of an appropriate **block discount**. Sometimes buyers of large blocks of shares agree in advance with the issuer that the issuer will at some point foot the bill for underwriting a public offering in which the buyer's shares may be sold usually in conjunction with a new issue of stock by the company. A block trading discount is limited to non-control blocks of shares. If the block of shares are control shares, normally no discount is appropriate, and a premium may indeed be justified.

There are many other examples of discounts that may be applied to reflect risk factors, including discounts for the dependence of the business on a few key individuals for success, discounts for enhanced risk because of the small size of the business or its dependence on contracts with a small number of customers or suppliers, discounts for the inability to obtain financing, discounts for the need to rely on unaudited financial statements, discounts for political risks, and so forth. In some of these cases, the discount arises because the business itself is risky, while in other cases it arises because the information on which a valuation is based is thought to be somewhat unreliable. In most of these cases, however, the discount is one that will apply to the company as a whole. Although one often hears such factors cited as reasons for imposing a discount on the valuation of the business, it is probably more appropriate and informative to reflect such uncertainties in a higher capitalization rate or lower multiplier rather than by knocking off some arbitrary dollar amount from the calculated value of the business. After all, the capitalization rate is supposed to be the rate of return that an investor would require in exchange for assuming the risks of the investment. Thus, it makes sense to set the rate as accurately as possible. In short, the idea of a discount or premium should be reserved for valuations of blocks of shares with attributes that distinguish them from run of the mill shares of the same company.

In a closely held corporation, minority interests are unlikely to be saleable to outside investors at prices that reflect their allocable portion of the value of the business if sold as a unit. One reason for this is that closely held corporations rarely pay dividends; rather, they tend to disguise distributions as salary expenses and similar payments to shareholders. A minority shareholder, therefore, has no assurance of any return from his or her investment unless the majority shareholders permit the minority shareholder to be an employee of the corporation at a salary that is comparable with the salaries of other shareholder-employees. Because the minority shareholder cannot assure an outsider of employment with the corporation, even if the outsider would be interested in the job, it is unusual for a nonshareholder to negotiate independently with a minority shareholder to acquire a minority interest. When such negotiations occur, the nonshareholder is apt to demand a significant discount to reflect the lack of liquidity of the investment and the risk that the anticipated return may not be forthcoming.

Shares of closely held corporations are usually subject to **share transfer restrictions** or **buy-sell agreements** that require a shareholder who dies or who desires to dispose of his or her shares to offer (or sell) the shares to the corporation or to the other shareholders at a fixed or readily determinable price. A very popular price used in these agreements is book value. An option agreement commits the shareholder to sell but does not commit the corporation or other shareholders to purchase; a buy-sell agreement commits the purchaser as well as the seller to the transaction. Binding agreements of these types set a cap on the value that may be placed on the shares for most purposes. If the agreement is a buy-sell agreement that binds the purchaser as well as the seller, the shares are usually valued at the contract price (assuming that the purchaser is capable of making the purchase); if it is an option agreement in which the purchaser has the power to purchase at a designated price but is not committed to do so, the shares may be valued at or below the agreed upon price.

In the absence of a binding option or buy-sell agreement, a minority shareholder desiring to sell his or her shares usually cannot compel the corporation or other shareholders to purchase. The shareholder who desires to sell must instead seek voluntary transactions either with the corporation or with one or more other shareholders. In most cases, such sales will be negotiated with the corporation itself, rather than individual shareholders, because a purchase by the corporation does not affect the relative holdings of the remaining shareholders. Moreover, neither majority nor minority shareholders have a strong incentive to offer the selling shareholder a generous price: Other minority shareholders do not generally improve their position significantly vis-à-vis each other or the majority shareholder by becoming larger minority shareholders. The majority shareholder, on the other hand, by hypothesis already has a controlling position and does not need the additional minority shares to cement or preserve that control. However, the other shareholders collectively, and the majority shareholder individually, usually do desire to eliminate minority interests if they can do so on an acceptable basis: Minority shareholders are therefore usually able to liquidate their holdings by selling to the corporation or to the majority shareholder if they are willing to accept a low enough price. Even though the situation is not hopeless in terms of finding a buyer, it is certainly not the traditional willing buyer and willing seller exchange.

When three or more factions exist, and none of these factions individually has a majority of the outstanding shares, the dynamics are quite different. If the balance of power is represented by the shares owned by the shareholder who wishes to sell, spirited bidding by the remaining factions may occur as each seeks to obtain the **swing shares** necessary to acquire the controlling interest in the management of the business. The per-share value of the swing block may overstate the aggregate per share value of the business in this situation.

Although it is clear that when a minority shareholder desires to sell, the minority shareholder must often accept a lesser price, it does not necessarily follow that the majority shareholder can take advantage of the differential by (say) arranging to have the corporation repurchase the majority shareholders' shares at a higher price than that offered to the minority. The courts quite routinely rule against transactions in which the majority seeks to use its power over the corporation to obtain favored treatment, though the courts also recognize that there are some situations (e.g., where a majority shareholder desires to retire) in which the minority may not be entitled to strictly identical treatment. Similarly, the courts have been quite ready to review actions made by majority shareholders to remove minority shareholders from offices or jobs with the corporation. Although the courts recognize that one faction must prevail over another when there are genuine differences of opinion as to how to run the business, the courts also recognize that the power of the majority to eliminate the primary return enjoyed by most shareholders in closely held businesses (a paying job) can be used to pressure a minority shareholder to sell out to the majority at a bargain price.

When shares of a closely held business are subject to a buy-sell agreement or when the transaction in question is such that the majority would be precluded from using its power to exact favorable treatment from the corporation, it is arguable that neither a control premium nor a minority discount should be applied. Nevertheless, the Internal Revenue Service, always on the lookout for ways to maximize tax dollars, often argues for estate tax purposes that control shares should be valued more highly even though the corporation or other shareholders are contractually entitled to purchase such shares at the same price at which the minority would be required to sell. Moreover, as a matter of logic, any control premium assigned to one block of shares should be matched by a comparable minority discount for other blocks of shares. After all, the business as a business is only worth so much. Nevertheless, in matters of estate tax (as well as other areas of the real world) things do not always work out so neatly.

When valuing the overall business, what weight, if any, should be given to a sale of a minority interest—say, a 10 percent interest—that does not involve control considerations by a minority shareholder? This question has no fixed answer: It depends entirely on the circumstances. Such sales should be investigated to determine how closely they meet the valuation ideal (a ready buyer dealing with a ready seller). Thus, a sale between family members under circumstances indicating that a motive for the transaction may have been partially to make a gift is given little or no weight. A sale to the corporation, to the majority shareholder, to another minority shareholder, or conceivably to an outsider, that appears to be at arm's length and not entered into by the seller under financial exigency or pressure, may be presumptively accepted as an accurate valuation of at least a minority interest at the time of the sale. When the purchaser is the corporation or the majority shareholder, however, it is likely that the minority shareholder was under considerably greater compulsion to sell than the purchaser was to buy. Thus, the circumstances underlying each specific sale must be examined carefully.

For example, an arm's-length sale by a 10 percent shareholder to the majority shareholder at a price that was clearly bargained over would be given some weight even though it might appear that the seller was in some financial distress and needed cash for personal reasons. Absolute perfection in the bargaining process is not required. On the other hand, if it appears that in a similar transaction (1) there were unsuccessful attempts by the seller to find other potential purchasers, (2) the seller needed cash urgently for personal reasons or to avoid bankruptcy, or (3) the sale took place at a price set by the buyer on a take-it-or-leave-it basis, that sale is not a reliable indication of value. It all depends on an estimate of how close the actual transaction came to the theoretical ideal. In many other contexts, a price negotiated at arm's length is given some weight in assessing the fair market value of an asset even though defects exist in the negotiation process. One need only think of transactions taking place at rug bazaars, at country auctions, and in a host of everyday transactions in which it is unlikely that the ideal conditions of perfect knowledge and lack of compulsion are present. The same thing is true of isolated arm's-length sales of closely held securities to outsiders, to the corporation, to other minority shareholders, or to the majority shareholder.

When the value of an entire business is estimated from isolated sales of minority shares, an appropriate adjustment should be made to reflect the discounts normally applied to such shares for lack of marketability and the minority status of such shares. This subject is discussed more fully below.

Prior sales of controlling interests in closely held businesses, unlike sales of minority interests, are usually viewed as reliable indicators of value. The majority shareholder usually is reasonably sophisticated and knowledgeable about his or her business and is in a position to negotiate effectively. Further, controlling interests are more salable to outside persons than minority interests, because the purchaser obtains the power to manage the business rather than becoming a passive investor subject to the whim of the majority. As a result, a majority block of shares commands a significantly higher price per share than a minority block, even though the shares are formally indistinguishable. The majority shares are referred to as **control shares**. Minority shares that are not part of the control block sell at significant discounts from the price that control shares command, when they sell at all. It is not uncommon for a person seeking to buy all of the outstanding shares of a closely held corporation to offer a significantly lower price per share for the minority shares than for the control shares on a per-share basis. In the closely held corporation, this distinction between control shares and minority shares is easy to visualize, because ordinarily it is permanent: It is not possible for minority blocks of shares aggregating, say, 40 percent of the stock, ever to outvote the majority's 60 percent block.

## §7.17 Valuation Based on Subsequent Performance of the Business

When a business is being sold, differing valuations of the business may create an impasse. The gap between the lowest price the seller is willing to accept and the highest price the buyer is willing to offer may be unbridgeable by negotiation. This gap is usually traceable to differing assumptions about what the future holds for the business. The parties agree that the price should be 10 times future earnings but they disagree on what the future earnings are likely to be: The seller sees a high probability of continuing improvement in earnings or cash flow with relatively little risk, while the buyer, naturally more cautious, sees cloudier skies with greater probability of disappointing results. This impasse threatens to kill the deal entirely, and yet it involves the valuation issue exclusively.

One way to bridge the gap is to set the initial contract price at the buyer's price but defer the final determination of the sales price until after the post-sale operations of the business can be evaluated. The buyer commits to the conservative price he or she is willing to pay and agrees to pay an additional amount at the end of one or two years if earnings exceed an amount stated in the agreement (basically the buyer's conservative prediction). If the operations are more profitable than this stated amount, the seller is entitled to an addition to the purchase price computed on the actual post-sale earnings. This contingent payment based on actual post-sale results largely eliminates the impasse over valuation. If the buyer's more pessimistic forecasts turn out to be accurate, no further payment is due, while if the business is as profitable as the seller expects, the ultimate purchase price will be based on the seller's estimate. These devices are sometimes called **earnout agreements** or **workout agreements**, because a portion of the purchase price is earned or worked out after the transaction is closed. (They have nothing to do with workouts of businesses on the brink of insolvency.) Agreements of this type permit transactions to close immediately without requiring consensus on the value of the company at the time of the closing. The usual period for an earnout is three years or less following the closing, although longer periods are possible.

Earnout agreements involve complex negotiation and complex drafting, particularly where the parties have no reason to trust the other side's good faith. The seller may be unwilling to accept the unsecured promise of the buyer that the additional purchase price will be paid when it becomes due a year or two after the sale has closed. The seller may request that the workout payment be placed in escrow to assure the seller that the payment will be made promptly if it is earned. The buyer may resist this proposal if he or she proposes to use the cash flow generated during the workout period to pay the additional purchase price. And, of course, an escrow arrangement ties up independent funds for a significant period of time.

There may also be detailed negotiations over the terms on which the business is to be conducted during the workout period. The seller, of course, wishes to ensure that the purchased business has a fair shot at earning whatever amount is required by the workout agreement. The two parties must decide whether the buyer or the seller is to manage the business until the workout period ends, how much additional capital the buyer must provide during the workout period (if any) and at what times and in what amounts, and a host of other business issues such as limitations on salaries, on transactions the buyer may enter into with the purchased business, and so forth. Usually, the seller proposes to run the business during the workout period: If this is acceptable to the buyer, the buyer may nevertheless seek protection against artificial changes in business operations, such as reduction of deferrable expenses, which the seller may quietly institute in order to improve earnings during the workout period and thereby earn the workout payment.

Even though the development of a workout agreement may involve difficult negotiations and complex issues, the advantage of permitting negotiations to come to a settlement without requiring either party to accept the valuation assumptions of the other is obvious.

# CHAPTER 8

# FEDERAL TAXATION

## §8.1   Introduction

The federal income tax has a major influence on virtually all business and financial transactions. Indeed, the **Internal Revenue Code (IRC)** probably has a greater effect on business and financial transactions, than any other statute.

The federal income tax laws are administered by the **Internal Revenue Service (IRS)**, an agency within the United States **Department of the Treasury**.

The reasons for the importance of tax law can be set forth quite simply. The primary purpose of employment is to earn income. The purpose of business and financial transactions is to earn a profit. The federal income tax requires persons who earn income or profits to share a substantial portion—indeed, at times a very substantial portion—with the United States government. Further, the federal income tax is not, and never was, a **flat tax** imposing the same percentage tax on all income, but is composed of numerous distinctions imposing different levels of taxation on different amounts of income, different types of income, and different types of taxable organizations. Different tax rates are also applicable to individuals with identical incomes depending on their marital or filing status. During the period from World War II through 1986, some dollars of income were taxed at very high rates: as high as 90 percent at some periods shortly after World War II, and as high as 70 percent as late as

1980. Tax rates at these levels provide a powerful incentive for devising techniques to avoid their full impact wherever possible. For many years, ingenious minds have been devoted to creating and perfecting such techniques. For example, for **ordinary income (OI)** at the same time that the maximum rates of 70 percent or more were in effect, the maximum tax rate on a different form of income—long-term **capital gains** arising from the sale or exchange of capital assets—was only 25 percent. This dramatic difference in rates created strong incentives to structure transactions or establish long-term strategies so as to transform ordinary income into long-term capital gain in order to make the 25 percent rather than the 70 percent rate applicable.

The Tax Reform Act of 1986 (the 1986 Act) made dramatic changes in tax policy. The core ideas behind this dramatic change in tax policy were to (1) cut maximum tax rates; (2) expand the tax base; and (3) minimize or eliminate tax shelter transactions that are entered into primarily for their tax effect. A maximum tax rate of 28 percent was applied to both ordinary income and long-term capital gain. Congress has passed several major tax bills since 1986. In 1990, the maximum tax rate applicable to ordinary income was increased to 31 percent. In 1994, the maximum tax rate was increased to 36 percent with a special surtax being imposed on incomes in excess of $250,000 to increase the maximum tax rate to 39.6 percent. In 2001, the maximum rate was reduced to 39.1 percent, with further yearly reductions through 2006 to a maximum rate of 35 percent. As for capital gains, the maximum rate was reduced in most cases to 20 percent as of 1999, and to 18 percent as of 2001 for assets held five years or more. In addition, several further reductions to these rates have been added over the years, for example, a maximum rate of 10 percent for sales of small business stock held five years or more.

The income tax laws (including the regulations issued by the IRS to implement these laws) are exceedingly complex. Anyone attempting to read the thousand-plus page statute for the first time is almost immediately lost in numerous cross references, defined terms, and opaque and elliptical provisions that appear to form a seamless web with no beginning and no end. The regulations are in many ways even worse: they consist of multiple volumes of fine print that are, if anything, even more difficult than the statute.

Although the tax laws have increased steadily in their complexity since World War II, this complexity has increased significantly in recent years. Beginning in about 1975, new and often fundamental concepts were introduced into the tax laws almost every year. Regrettably, many of the recent changes in the IRC have added new layers of complex provisions over what was there before without repealing the old law. This is particularly true with respect to provisions relating to tax shelters, passive losses, the deductibility of nonbusiness interest, and the alternative minimum tax (a complex set of rules designed to prevent taxpayers from using special loopholes to eliminate all or most of their tax liability). As a result the present tax laws are longer, thicker, and more difficult to understand than ever before.

Of course, many Americans are relatively unaffected by this tax complexity. Most Americans are employed and are subject to the tax-withholding mechanism that in effect requires all employers to become tax collectors. For most Americans, paying taxes involves little discretion (at least if they are honest) and usually is relatively painless. Indeed, because many taxpayers whose sole incomes are salaries or wages end up being entitled to a refund, the process is often almost pleasant. And calculation of the tax due by these taxpayers is quite simple, because a standard deduction avoids the necessity of itemizing specific deductions and special tax tables usually require no calculation to determine the actual amount of tax due. Special tax return forms, the 1040A and 1040EZ reduce the reporting burden. Further, many low-income taxpayers today owe no federal income tax at all because the 1986 Act created much more generous personal exemptions and a larger standard deduction. One important consequence of the 1986 Act is that many individuals at or close to the poverty line are completely exempted from all liability for federal income taxes.

The natural consequence of complexity on important economic matters is the development of specialists to deal with problems and give advice. And so it has been with a vengeance in the tax area. Today, the tax laws are so complex that sometimes even tax specialists despair of understanding the entire tax structure and fear that they are becoming unable to provide prompt and accurate advice to clients. Thirty years ago, most taxpayers filled out their own tax returns: Many lawyers who were not tax specialists advised clients on tax matters and often prepared tax returns for valued clients, either for a nominal fee or as a favor. This work is increasingly being done by accountants, "store front" commercial tax return preparers, and lawyers who specialize in tax law. The complexity of the tax laws has increased so substantially that most taxpayers today obtain professional assistance in filling out their tax returns if they involve the use of **Form 1040**, the **long form** that is required of all individuals who do not qualify for the simpler forms **1040A** or **1040EZ**. Indeed, the reputation of the IRC leads many taxpayers who qualify for simpler forms to seek professional assistance as well.

Lawyers in general practice have become increasingly cautious about giving tax advice or preparing returns for clients. To be an effective tax lawyer today, one must usually specialize in that subject. This growth of specialization is in part a result of the increased specificity of IRC provisions defining how certain transactions are to be handled. A generation ago, much tax advice involved the application of general tax principles to a specific situation. Today, there are often very specific provisions that must be located and carefully parsed in connection with each specific situation.

## §8.2 Tax Planning and Tax Evasion

It is entirely proper to seek to minimize one's taxes by lawful means. Careful planning and judicious structuring and timing of receipts and transactions may permit the same income or gain to be taxed at much lower rates, to be deferred to a later tax year, or in some instances to escape income tax entirely. Thus, the tax attorney, tax planner, and tax adviser were born. All engage in essentially the same planning activity—to structure transactions and economic activities in a way that takes maximum legitimate advantage of the various provisions of the IRC—to structure transactions so as to minimize taxes due. Of course, these tax specialists engage in other activities as well. They may prepare returns or represent taxpayers before the IRS in administrative proceedings or in litigation against the IRS.

Every tax adviser must constantly be aware of the basic distinction between legitimate **tax planning** on the one hand and improper **tax evasion** on the other. Tax planning is the structuring of transactions so as to take legitimate advantage of the provisions of the IRC and the regulations existing thereunder. Tax evasion, on the other hand, involves improper or unlawful reduction of tax liabilities by omission, misstatement, misrepresentation, or fraud. To take simple illustrations: The special tax treatment for long-term capital gains is available only for capital assets held for more than one year. Gains from the sale or exchange of capital assets held for less than one year are taxed at the relatively higher rates applicable to ordinary income. A person planning to sell a capital asset at a profit might legitimately wait until the day after the twelve-month period expired to make the sale. That is simple tax planning: By deferring the sale, the taxpayer takes the economic risk that the value of the capital asset may decline during that period. On the other hand, say that the same transaction is agreed on eleven months and twenty days after the taxpayer originally acquired the asset, possession of the asset is transferred immediately to the purchaser, and both the sale contract and the payment check are dated and delivered so that the sale appears to have occurred after the expiration of the twelve-month holding period. In this case, there is a significant risk that the IRS, if the circumstances become known, will treat the sale as occurring within the one-year holding period. More serious examples of improper evasion are situations involving "forgetting" to include items of income at all or claiming exemptions for six children when in fact the taxpayer only has three. If such transactions are discovered, civil fraud penalties are usually imposed, and in extreme cases, there may also be criminal prosecution.

Often, however, the distinction is not as easy or sharp as these two hypotheticals suggest. Many transactions have as their principal purpose the reduction of taxes. The IRS may attack these transactions on very broad grounds: for example, that they are **sham transactions** without **business purpose** that should be ignored entirely, that they are **step transactions** that should be viewed as a single whole rather than as a series of independent transactions, or that the effect of the transactions should be recast so as to **clearly reflect income**. In some instances, a taxpayer may be able to obtain an advance ruling as to how a specific transaction should be treated for tax purposes (a **letter ruling**, as it is usually called), but the IRS declines to give rulings in many sensitive or fact-specific areas. Tax shelters have been a major target of the Service for many years. The tax returns of many thousands of taxpayers were ensnarled in this campaign during the late 1980s, and some are still ensnarled 10 years later.

The giving of tax advice is greatly affected by the fact that most returns are not fully audited, and the questionable treatment of a specific item may never be raised. Nevertheless, disclosure of the questionable item in the return is sensible in order to minimize the risk that the IRS may later attempt to impose a fraud penalty on the taxpayer or, conceivably, penalties on the attorney involved or on the person who prepared the return. Also, relatively high-income persons with complex or tax-planning-oriented transactions cannot rely on escaping an audit, because the probability of an audit increases substantially as the taxpayer's income increases.

## §8.3 Progressive Tax Rates

Before the 1986 Act, tax rates for individuals combined high-percentage tax rates with a highly progressive rate structure. A **progressive rate** structure is one in which the rates are fixed so that as taxable income increases, the tax rate on additional dollars also increases. Under a progressive rate structure, additional or last dollars earned by a higher-income person are taxed at a higher percentage rate than the same number of additional dollars earned by a lower-income person. Current tax rates have a degree of progressivity, but are less progressive than rate structures in the pre-1986 tax law. Tax rates for the 2001 tax year are shown in the table on the following page.

The different levels of income subject to different tax rates in the table are referred to as **tax brackets.** The percentage rates set forth in the table are called marginal rates because they apply only to the additional dollars earned above the previous bracket. The **marginal rate** must be distinguished from the **effective rate** of taxation, which is the percentage that the total tax is of one's total taxable income (or of one's gross income before exemptions and deductions).

For tax-planning purposes, the marginal rate is usually more important than the effective rate. For example, a strategy that defers tax on a transaction defers the tax that would be due if the gain from that transaction were added to all the other taxable income of the taxpayer. The bulk of the taxpayer's other income, and the tax that will be due on that income, is unaffected.

Under even a progressive tax rate structure with very high marginal rates, it always pays to earn another dollar (as long as the highest bracket is less than 100 percent). Prior to the 1986 Act, high-income taxpayers often complained that it was not worth it to earn more money because of the tax structure. Certainly, if one earns another dollar, one will always keep a part of it even under a progressive tax structure. A more subtle question is whether one will engage in risky, entrepreneurial conduct in an effort to earn an extra dollar when one is allowed to keep only 30 percent of it.

The rate structure before the 1986 Act also created significant anomalies in treatment for essentially indistinguishable taxpayers. For example, one major consequence of the rate structure described above was that for higher income taxpayers, splitting income among two or more different taxpayers would often reduce the total tax due. When high progressive rates were first imposed during World War II, most families consisted of a single, male income earner and a wife who remained at home to care for the family. The first major controversy arose when married couples with a single wage earner who resided in community property states argued successfully that the nonworking spouse should report one half of the community's earnings on the theory that one-half of the earnings was hers under state law. If the couple's income was substantial, this **income-splitting** created obvious discrimination between otherwise identical families who happened to live in community property and noncommunity property states. This dispute was resolved by the development of different tax schedules for single individuals and for married individuals filing a joint return,

# 2001 Tax Rate Schedules

**Schedule X-** Use if your filing status is **Single**

| If the amount on Form 1040, line 39, is: Over- | But not over- | Enter on Form 1040, line 40 | of the amount over- |
|---|---|---|---|
| $0 | $27,050 | ......... 15% | $0 |
| 27,050 | 65,550 | $4,057.50 + 27.5% | 27,050 |
| 65,550 | 136,750 | 14,645.00 + 30.5% | 65,550 |
| 136,750 | 297,350 | 36,361.00 + 35.5% | 136,750 |
| 297,350 | ......... | 93,374.00 + 39.1% | 297,350 |

**Schedule Y-1-** Use if your filing status is **Married filing jointly** or **Qualifying widow(er)**

| If the amount on Form 1040, line 39, is: Over- | But not over- | Enter on Form 1040, line 40 | of the amount over- |
|---|---|---|---|
| $0 | $45,200 | ......... 15% | $0 |
| 45,200 | 109,250 | $6,780.00 + 27.5% | 45,200 |
| 109,250 | 166,500 | 24,393.75 + 30.5% | 109,250 |
| 166,500 | 297,350 | 41,855.00 + 35.5% | 166,500 |
| 297,350 | ......... | 88,306.75 + 39.1% | 297,350 |

**Schedule Y-2-** Use if your filing status is **Married filing separately**

| If the amount on Form 1040, line 39, is: Over- | But not over- | Enter on Form 1040, line 40 | of the amount over- |
|---|---|---|---|
| $0 | $22,600 | ......... 15% | $0 |
| 22,600 | 54,625 | $3,390.00 + 27.5% | 22,600 |
| 54,625 | 83,250 | 12,196.88 + 30.5% | 54,625 |
| 83,250 | 148,675 | 20,927.50 + 35.5% | 83,250 |
| 148,675 | ......... | 44,153.38 + 39.1% | 148,675 |

**Schedule Z-** Use if your filing status is **Head of household**

| If the amount on Form 1040, line 39, is: Over- | But not over- | Enter on Form 1040, line 40 | of the amount over- |
|---|---|---|---|
| $0 | $36,250 | ......... 15% | $0 |
| 36,250 | 93,650 | $5,437.50 + 27.5% | 36,250 |
| 93,650 | 151,650 | 21,222.50 + 30.5% | 93,650 |
| 151,650 | 297,350 | 38,912.50 + 35.5% | 151,650 |
| 297,350 | ......... | 90,636.00 + 39.1% | 297,350 |

with the latter entitled to use a tax schedule that in effect gave all married couples the advantage of income-splitting that community property residents were entitled to for tax purposes. Today, there are schedules not only for married and single taxpayers but also for heads of households and married taxpayers filing separately.

With growth in the number of two income households, the income-splitting tax schedules for families created a new type of discrimination. If one spouse within a family was the sole wage earner, the rates applicable to married taxpayers filing joint returns provided a significantly lower tax than if that same wage earner were unmarried. However, if two persons had equal amounts of income, their total tax bill was significantly higher if they were married and required to file joint returns than it would have been if they were not married and were filing separately. This results from the fact that when the two taxpayers are married, the second income is added to the first, and is taxed only at the higher brackets. When the two taxpayers are not married, each gets to take advantage of the very low marginal rates on their first dollars of income. The difference can be viewed as a **marriage penalty** or a bonus for living in sin. This discrimination against marriage even led a few married couples to divorce but continue to live together, or to divorce on December 28 and remarry on January 3, in order to save on federal income taxes. (The filing category for "married couples filing separate returns" was created to ensure that couples filing separate returns were subject to the same tax brackets and rates as if they filed jointly; as a result the marriage penalty cannot be avoided simply by filing separate returns.)

High-income taxpayers also found it profitable from a tax standpoint to give income-producing property to infant children in order to permit the income to accumulate for college expenses at lower tax brackets than if the parent retained the property, paid tax on the income from the property, and then used the remainder to pay for college. This strategy was largely foreclosed in the 1986 Act by a provision that requires the **unearned income** of children under the age of 14 in excess of a minimal amount to be taxed at the parents' top rate.

The progressive structure of rates also has one other significant effect. It caused tax revenues to increase automatically during periods of inflation. As individual incomes increased along with price increases, taxpayers were pushed into higher marginal brackets, although the taxpayers were probably not better off economically from the increased wages. Eliminating or reducing **bracket creep** was also a major motivation for the 1986 Act.

The sharply progressive tax structure and relatively high marginal rates was a basic philosophical underpinning of tax policy until 1986. The notion that a person who makes more could afford to, and should be required to, pay a higher portion of the extra dollars earned seemed so obvious as not to require extended discussion. The resulting anomalies that were necessarily created between married and cohabiting taxpayers, or between single and married one-income taxpayers, were viewed as an inevitable cost of a progressive system. Although the 1986 Act radically reduced progressivity, it has gradually crept back into the system.

It is not surprising that various proposals have been put forward, suggesting either a different income tax rate structure or, more radically, the abandonment of the income tax entirely for a national sales tax, value added tax, or other tax structure.

It is important to recognize that some arguments against progressivity and the present federal tax structure are based on profound dissatisfaction with government in general, and the federal government in particular. Many people believe the federal government is too large, too heavily oriented toward ill-conceived welfare schemes, and too intrusive on individual citizens and local governments. One way to attack big government is based on the quite erroneous belief that reduction of tax revenues will automatically lead to a reduction in growth of governmental operations. In fact, reductions in the growth of tax revenues, when they did occur following the 1986 Act, did not produce a corresponding change in governmental activities, but rather simply inflated the federal deficit. A second argument is that high tax rates are undesirable because they have adverse effects on the economy. Lower tax rates, it is argued, spur economic activity and increase national wealth. Whether this is true is debatable from an historical standpoint.

A third argument attacks the basic premise of progressivity that it is fair to tax higher incomes at a higher rate than lower incomes. Fairness, it may be argued, requires a flat tax, with the same rate applicable to everyone. Rather inconsistently, proponents of a flat tax argue that a fair amount of proportionality is created automatically if there is a rather high basic exemption before any tax is imposed.

A more pragmatic argument is that the high and progressive rate structure prompts inexorable political pressure by interest groups for special deductions, special exceptions, and special credits for favored activity. One perverse result of this constant pressure was that prior to the 1986 Act the tax system enabled many high-income individuals quite legally to avoid paying taxes entirely or to pay only very small amounts — often less than a middle-class wage earner. Even today many large compaines end up owing no tax or even being entitled to refunds of tax from earlier years despite the fact that they may report substantial earnings to their investors. On the other hand, it also may be that the corporate income tax should be eliminated altogether, because corporate income is taxed when the stockholders receive distributions. In any event, what appears on the surface to be a progressive tax system may in fact hide a system of special benefits for the sophisticated and wealthy so that the tax burden falls disproportionally on the average wage earner who has no special benefits.

In addition, high progressive tax rates and complex rules tend to lead to the development of sophisticated planning techniques by affluent taxpayers. Congress has responded to many of these techniques over the years by special provisions designed to close off specific techniques. This, however, increases the IRC's complexity and does not solve the underlying problem, which is the motivation to create new techniques caused by high and progressive rates. New tax-planning devices are created about as rapidly as older ones are closed off.

Finally, there is the belief that the special tax treatment of long-term capital gains gives unwarranted tax benefits to high-income taxpayers who use complex strategies to transform ordinary income into capital gains. At the other extreme, it is also argued that a reduction or elimination of the tax on capital gains would lead to a higher level of economic activity.

Although complaints about the current tax structure are numerous and there are many suggestions for radical change, there is no consensus about what should be done.

Most of these radical new tax proposals would change the basis of federal taxation away from using income or earnings as the measure of taxation to using consumption or wealth or some related kind of measurement.

## §8.4  Individual Income Taxation

The current federal income tax is a tax on **income**, not **gross receipts**. Thus, a business must subtract its costs and expenses from receipts in order to arrive at an income figure on which income taxes are calculated. An individual engaged in an individual trade or business is entitled to these deductions to the same degree as a corporation. An individual who operates a retail hardware store as a sole proprietorship may deduct the costs of inventory, rent, advertising, and the like.

In addition to business expenses, individual taxpayers are entitled to a number of credits or deductions in the calculation of the amount of tax due in addition to the deduction of trade or business expenses. The process by which a taxpayer who receives salary or wages moves from gross receipts to the amount of income subject to tax (or **taxable income**) involves a series of discrete steps. These steps are set forth on Form 1040 (a copy of which is reproduced here). The steps involved are as follows:

First. One starts by adding up income from various sources.

Second. From total income, one subtracts certain specified adjustments to income, if any (for example, employee business and moving expenses, pension plan deductions, and alimony) in order to determine **adjusted gross income (AGI)**.

Third. From adjusted gross income, one subtracts allowable itemized personal deductions (or the **standard deduction** if one does not itemize) and an allowance for **personal exemptions** based on the number of individuals in the household. The resulting figure is **taxable income.**

Fourth. One calculates the tax due on the taxable income reflected in the return either from tax tables or by a calculation using formulas set forth in the tax rate schedule. This is the amount of tax due.

Fifth. Following the calculation of the amount of tax due, one goes through another set of calculations to determine the amount (if any) that must be remitted with the return. The amount of tax due is then reduced by certain allowable credits that may be treated as payments of tax and by payments made through withholding by employers or quarterly payments of estimated tax by persons who have taxable income that is not subject to withholding. The net result is the amount of the additional payment that is due from the taxpayer or the amount of refund the United States pays to the taxpayer.

**Form 1040**

Department of the Treasury—Internal Revenue Service
**U.S. Individual Income Tax Return** 2001 (99) IRS Use Only—Do not write or staple in this space.

For the year Jan. 1–Dec. 31, 2001, or other tax year beginning , 2001, ending , 20

OMB No. 1545-0074

**Label** (See instructions on page 19.) **Use the IRS label.** Otherwise, please print or type.

L A B E L   H E R E

Your first name and initial — Last name — Your social security number

If a joint return, spouse's first name and initial — Last name — Spouse's social security number

Home address (number and street). If you have a P.O. box, see page 19. — Apt. no.

City, town or post office, state, and ZIP code. If you have a foreign address, see page 19.

▲ **Important!** ▲ You **must** enter your SSN(s) above.

**Presidential Election Campaign** (See page 19.)

Note. Checking "Yes" will not change your tax or reduce your refund.
Do you, or your spouse if filing a joint return, want $3 to go to this fund? ▶

You: ☐Yes ☐No Spouse: ☐Yes ☐No

**Filing Status**

Check only one box.

1 ☐ Single
2 ☐ Married filing joint return (even if only one had income)
3 ☐ Married filing separate return. Enter spouse's social security no. above and full name here. ▶
4 ☐ Head of household (with qualifying person). (See page 19.) If the qualifying person is a child but not your dependent, enter this child's name here. ▶
5 ☐ Qualifying widow(er) with dependent child (year spouse died ▶ ). (See page 19.)

**Exemptions**

6a ☐ **Yourself.** If your parent (or someone else) can claim you as a dependent on his or her tax return, **do not** check box 6a
b ☐ **Spouse**
c **Dependents:**

| (1) First name    Last name | (2) Dependent's social security number | (3) Dependent's relationship to you | (4) ✓ if qualifying child for child tax credit (see page 20) |
|---|---|---|---|
| | | | ☐ |
| | | | ☐ |
| | | | ☐ |
| | | | ☐ |
| | | | ☐ |
| | | | ☐ |

If more than six dependents, see page 20.

No. of boxes checked on 6a and 6b ___
No. of your children on 6c who:
• lived with you ___
• did not live with you due to divorce or separation (see page 20) ___
Dependents on 6c not entered above ___
Add numbers entered on lines above ▶

d Total number of exemptions claimed

**Income**

Attach Forms W-2 and W-2G here. Also attach Form(s) 1099-R if tax was withheld.

If you did not get a W-2, see page 21.

Enclose, but do not attach, any payment. Also, please use Form 1040-V.

7 Wages, salaries, tips, etc. Attach Form(s) W-2 — 7
8a Taxable interest. Attach Schedule B if required — 8a
b Tax-exempt interest. Do not include on line 8a — 8b
9 Ordinary dividends. Attach Schedule B if required — 9
10 Taxable refunds, credits, or offsets of state and local income taxes (see page 22) — 10
11 Alimony received — 11
12 Business income or (loss). Attach Schedule C or C-EZ — 12
13 Capital gain or (loss). Attach Schedule D if required. If not required, check here ▶ ☐ — 13
14 Other gains or (losses). Attach Form 4797 — 14
15a Total IRA distributions — 15a — b Taxable amount (see page 23) — 15b
16a Total pensions and annuities — 16a — b Taxable amount (see page 23) — 16b
17 Rental real estate, royalties, partnerships, S corporations, trusts, etc. Attach Schedule E — 17
18 Farm income or (loss). Attach Schedule F — 18
19 Unemployment compensation — 19
20a Social security benefits — 20a — b Taxable amount (see page 25) — 20b
21 Other income. List type and amount (see page 27) — 21
22 Add the amounts in the far right column for lines 7 through 21. This is your **total income** ▶ — 22

**Adjusted Gross Income**

23 IRA deduction (see page 27) — 23
24 Student loan interest deduction (see page 28) — 24
25 Archer MSA deduction. Attach Form 8853 — 25
26 Moving expenses. Attach Form 3903 — 26
27 One-half of self-employment tax. Attach Schedule SE — 27
28 Self-employed health insurance deduction (see page 30) — 28
29 Self-employed SEP, SIMPLE, and qualified plans — 29
30 Penalty on early withdrawal of savings — 30
31a Alimony paid b Recipient's SSN ▶ — 31a
32 Add lines 23 through 31a — 32
33 Subtract line 32 from line 22. This is your **adjusted gross income** ▶ — 33

For Disclosure, Privacy Act, and Paperwork Reduction Act Notice, see page 72.    Cat. No. 11320B    Form **1040** (2001)

Form 1040 (2001)                                                                                        Page **2**

| | | | |
|---|---|---|---|
| **Tax and Credits** | 34 | Amount from line 33 (adjusted gross income) . . . . . . . . . . . | 34 |

**Standard Deduction for—**

- People who checked any box on line 35a or 35b **or** who can be claimed as a dependent, see page 31.
- All others:

Single, $4,550

Head of household, $6,650

Married filing jointly or Qualifying widow(er), $7,600

Married filing separately, $3,800

| | | |
|---|---|---|
| 35a | Check if: ☐ **You** were 65 or older, ☐ Blind; ☐ **Spouse** was 65 or older, ☐ Blind. Add the number of boxes checked above and enter the total here . . . . ▶ **35a** | |
| b | If you are married filing separately and your spouse itemizes deductions, or you were a dual-status alien, see page 31 and check here . . . . . . ▶ **35b** ☐ | |
| 36 | **Itemized deductions** (from Schedule A) **or** your **standard deduction** (see left margin) . | 36 |
| 37 | Subtract line 36 from line 34 . . . . . . . . . . . . . . . . | 37 |
| 38 | If line 34 is $99,725 or less, multiply $2,900 by the total number of exemptions claimed on line 6d. If line 34 is over $99,725, see the worksheet on page 32 . . . . . . . | 38 |
| 39 | **Taxable income.** Subtract line 38 from line 37. If line 38 is more than line 37, enter -0- . | 39 |
| 40 | **Tax** (see page 33). Check if any tax is from **a** ☐ Form(s) 8814 **b** ☐ Form 4972 . . . | 40 |
| 41 | **Alternative minimum tax** (see page 34). Attach Form 6251 . . . . . . . . | 41 |
| 42 | Add lines 40 and 41 . . . . . . . . . . . . . . . . . ▶ | 42 |
| 43 | Foreign tax credit. Attach Form 1116 if required . . . . | 43 | |
| 44 | Credit for child and dependent care expenses. Attach Form 2441 | 44 | |
| 45 | Credit for the elderly or the disabled. Attach Schedule R . | 45 | |
| 46 | Education credits. Attach Form 8863 . . . . . . | 46 | |
| 47 | Rate reduction credit. See the worksheet on page 36 . . | 47 | |
| 48 | Child tax credit (see page 37) . . . . . . . . | 48 | |
| 49 | Adoption credit. Attach Form 8839 . . . . . . . | 49 | |
| 50 | Other credits from: **a** ☐ Form 3800 **b** ☐ Form 8396 **c** ☐ Form 8801 **d** ☐ Form (specify) | 50 | |
| 51 | Add lines 43 through 50. These are your **total credits** . . . . . . . . | 51 |
| 52 | Subtract line 51 from line 42. If line 51 is more than line 42, enter -0- . . . . . ▶ | 52 |

| | | |
|---|---|---|
| **Other Taxes** | 53 | Self-employment tax. Attach Schedule SE . . . . . . . . . . . . . | 53 |
| | 54 | Social security and Medicare tax on tip income not reported to employer. Attach Form 4137 . | 54 |
| | 55 | Tax on qualified plans, including IRAs, and other tax-favored accounts. Attach Form 5329 if required . | 55 |
| | 56 | Advance earned income credit payments from Form(s) W-2 . . . . . . . . | 56 |
| | 57 | Household employment taxes. Attach Schedule H . . . . . . . . . . . | 57 |
| | 58 | Add lines 52 through 57. This is your **total tax** . . . . . . . . . . ▶ | 58 |

| | | |
|---|---|---|
| **Payments** | 59 | Federal income tax withheld from Forms W-2 and 1099 . | 59 | |
| | 60 | 2001 estimated tax payments and amount applied from 2000 return . | 60 | |
| If you have a qualifying child, attach Schedule EIC. | 61a | **Earned income credit (EIC)** . . . . . . . . | 61a | |
| | b | Nontaxable earned income . . **61b** | | |
| | 62 | Excess social security and RRTA tax withheld (see page 51) . | 62 | |
| | 63 | Additional child tax credit. Attach Form 8812 . . . . | 63 | |
| | 64 | Amount paid with request for extension to file (see page 51) . | 64 | |
| | 65 | Other payments. Check if from **a** ☐ Form 2439 **b** ☐ Form 4136 | 65 | |
| | 66 | Add lines 59, 60, 61a, and 62 through 65. These are your **total payments** . . . . ▶ | 66 |

| | | |
|---|---|---|
| **Refund** | 67 | If line 66 is more than line 58, subtract line 58 from line 66. This is the amount you **overpaid** ▶ | 67 |
| Direct deposit? See page 51 and fill in 68b, 68c, and 68d. | 68a | Amount of line 67 you want **refunded to you** . . . . . . . . . . . ▶ | 68a |
| | ▶ b | Routing number ☐☐☐☐☐☐☐☐☐ ▶ c Type: ☐ Checking ☐ Savings | |
| | ▶ d | Account number ☐☐☐☐☐☐☐☐☐☐☐☐☐☐☐☐☐ | |
| | 69 | Amount of line 67 you want **applied to your 2002 estimated tax** ▶ | 69 | |

| | | |
|---|---|---|
| **Amount You Owe** | 70 | **Amount you owe.** Subtract line 66 from line 58. For details on how to pay, see page 52 ▶ | 70 |
| | 71 | Estimated tax penalty. Also include on line 70 . . . . | 71 | |

| | |
|---|---|
| **Third Party Designee** | Do you want to allow another person to discuss this return with the IRS (see page 53)? ☐ **Yes.** Complete the following. ☐ **No** |

| Designee's name ▶ | Phone no. ▶ ( ) | Personal identification number (PIN) ☐☐☐☐☐ |
|---|---|---|

**Sign Here**

Joint return? See page 19.

Keep a copy for your records.

Under penalties of perjury, I declare that I have examined this return and accompanying schedules and statements, and to the best of my knowledge and belief, they are true, correct, and complete. Declaration of preparer (other than taxpayer) is based on all information of which preparer has any knowledge.

| Your signature | Date | Your occupation | Daytime phone number ( ) |
|---|---|---|---|
| Spouse's signature. If a joint return, **both** must sign. | Date | Spouse's occupation | |

**Paid Preparer's Use Only**

| Preparer's signature ▶ | Date | Check if self-employed ☐ | Preparer's SSN or PTIN |
|---|---|---|---|
| Firm's name (or yours if self-employed), address, and ZIP code ▶ | | EIN | |
| | | Phone no. ( ) | |

Form **1040** (2001)

## §8.5  Business Income

An individual who is the owner of a business must subtract the costs and expenses of the business from its receipts in order to determine income. These expenses are deductible on a separate schedule, **Schedule C,** that is similar to a profit and loss statement for any business. After deducting these expenses, only the net amount of income is transferred forward to the Form 1040. Much the same pattern of deduction of business expenses from gross receipts before the calculation of total income also appears in **Schedule E** (income from "rents, royalties, partnerships, trusts, etc.") and **Schedule F** (farm income). In effect, Schedules C, E, and F permit deduction of trade and business expenses before the calculation of total income. The test for whether specific trade or business, rental, or farming expenses are deductible is whether they are "ordinary and necessary" for the business and "paid or incurred" during the taxable year in question. Expenses that provide a benefit over several taxable years, (e.g., the purchase of a truck) must be capitalized and depreciated (or amortized) over the useful life of the asset. Depreciation schedules for most major assets are set by the statute rather than by individualistic estimates of useful life.

## §8.6  Adjusted Gross Income

A second category of business-related expenses that are treated differently from trade or business expenses includes **employee business expenses, expenses for the production of income,** and a limited number of other deductions.

First, expenses relating to the production of income or wages by an employee not directly related to a trade or business: unreimbursed moving expenses and employee business expenses such as union dues, uniforms (where required by the employer), unreimbursed travel expense, the expense of maintaining an office in the home, and unreimbursed entertainment expense. Many expenses that in a sense relate to a job, however, are viewed as personal and not deductible: for example, commuting expenses are not deductible, because they are viewed as arising from the employee's personal choice as to where to live. Educational expenses designed to improve the employee's job status also are not deductible, because they are not required for the employee's job. Also, many items deducted from the employee's salary check, such as payments on account of federal income taxes, social security, and health benefits, are also not deductible as expenses for the production of income, although some may be deductible on some other basis.

Second, expenses for the production of income, including rental fees for safe deposit boxes, accountants' fees for keeping books of income-producing property, insurance charges to protect merchandise held by the taxpayer for resale as an investment, investment advisers, and the like. These income-generating expenses are deductible only to the extent that they exceed two percent of total income. This calculation appears on Form 2106 rather than on the Form 1040. In other words, the amount entered on the Form 1040 has already been reduced by two percent of the amount shown on line 22. There are two justifications for this two percent "floor." First, concern about revenue loss arises, because many of the expenses in this category historically have been subject to abuse in the sense that taxpayers have claimed deductions to which they are arguably not entitled. These deductions are also claimed by millions of lower and middle income taxpayers so that widespread cheating entails a very substantial revenue loss. Second, the floor also simplifies the preparation of returns for many lower-income taxpayers whose deductions are likely to be less than the floor. On the other hand (and this illustrates that many simplifying changes may cause increased complexity in individual returns), in the case of a joint return, this 2 percent floor is calculated on the combined income of husband and wife; where both spouses have income but only one has expenses subject to the floor, the filing of separate returns may yield a lower tax because the 2 percent floor is then calculated only on the income of the spouse that has the expenses subject to the floor.

Finally, there are several miscellaneous expenses that may be deducted, including certain retirement plan contributions, penalties on early withdrawal of savings from retirement plans, and alimony. These last three deductions (and a very small number of other itemized deductions) are not subject to the two percent floor.

## §8.7  Deductions and Exemptions

In addition to business and income production expenses, the IRC permits the deduction of certain personal expenses. The most important of these are state and local income and property taxes, property and sales taxes, mortgage interest, medical expenses, charitable contributions, and casualty losses. The reasons underlying these deductions vary: encouraging charitable contributions, lessening the financial burden on the unfortunate family struck by a major casualty loss or catastrophic medical expenses, and so forth.

The policies underlying some of these deductions have often been viewed as suspect by tax theorists, because they involve personal rather than business expenditures. From a political standpoint, however, some of them are immensely popular. These personal expenses have also involved a fair amount of petty cheating by large numbers of taxpayers. In 1986, Congress took several steps to limit the widespread use and misuse of these deductions. The most important substantive changes were that it limited the deduction of state taxes to income and real estate taxes, excluding state sales taxes, and limited the deduction of interest on nonbusiness loans basically to those arising from the purchase of residential real estate or, to a limited extent, loans secured by liens on such real estate.

The IRC limits personal deductions in several ways. First, the most important device is the availability to all taxpayers of the **standard deduction** that may be used in lieu of the **itemization** of all **personal deductions.** The size of the standard deduction varies with the filing status of the taxpayer and is indexed for inflation.

As of 2001, standard deductions are as follows:

> Single persons: $5,650
> Heads of households: $7,750
> Married persons filing jointly: $8,500
> Married persons filing separately: $4,700

These amounts are increased for taxpayers aged 65 and older and for the blind. The standard deduction substitutes only for itemized personal deductions. It does not affect the deductibility of employee business expenses or expenses incurred in the production of income. It is an amount that may be claimed by every taxpayer as an alternative to itemization. If the standard deduction exceeds the itemized deductions one can take, it makes sense not to itemize but simply to take the standard deduction. This has multiple advantages from the standpoint of the system. It eliminates petty cheating, it simplifies the preparation of returns for many taxpayers, and it improves equity, because more taxpayers compute their taxes on precisely the same basis.

The second important device designed to limit personal deductions is the imposition of a floor on specific types of expenses similar to that imposed on employee business expenses. For example, medical expenses are deductible only to the extent that they exceed 7.5 percent of AGI, thereby eliminating deductions in all but extraordinary situations given the amount of available income. A similar floor is imposed on casualty losses. Again, the policy of limiting the deduction to extraordinary losses given the amount of available income is clear. In both instances, only the deductible portion of medical or casualty losses is taken into account to determine whether the standard deduction is advantageous.

A third approach is to require specific documentation about claimed deductions to be filed with the return. This is required, for example, for charitable deductions claimed for contributions of noncash property, where valuation is likely to be overly optimistic. Finally, personal deductions are reduced for taxpayers with AGI in excess of specified amounts. For example, for the 2001 tax year, personal deductions are phased out beginning at AGI of $132,950 for a joint return.

**Personal exemptions** are entirely different from personal deductions. Exemptions permit the subtraction of arbitrary amounts for the taxpayer and spouse (if a joint return is filed) and dependents. The personal exemption for the 2001 tax year is $2,900 for each allowable exemption. For taxpayers reporting more than $199,450 on a joint return, the exemption amount is phased out.

## §8.8  Calculation of Tax Due

Once taxable income is calculated, the next step is the calculation of the actual tax that is due. This is done either from a set of tables or by a mathematical calculation.

There are four different categories of individual taxpayers with different-sized brackets depending on marital or family status. The three basic categories of taxpayers are (1) a married couple filing jointly or a surviving spouse (defined as a person whose spouse has died within the previous two years), (2) a "head of household" (defined as an unmarried person who is not a surviving spouse and who maintains a home for a dependent child or relative), and (3) a single person. The fourth category, married taxpayers filing separately, is created by simply halving every entry in the joint return category. This ensures that married couples with two incomes cannot take advantage of the single person tax schedule but remain on a tax parity with families in which one spouse is the wage earner and the other is a homemaker.

In order to calculate the tax due on a given amount of taxable income, one finds the range in which the income number falls from the first two columns of the tax rate schedule, subtracts the lower number of the range from taxable income, calculates the marginal tax on the income in excess of the lower number, and adds to that the base amount of tax, which gives the total tax. Thus, for a single taxpayer with taxable income of $150,000, the taxpayer would subtract $136,750 from $150,000, which leaves $13,250. The tax on $13,250 at 35.5 percent is $4704, which when added to the base amount of tax of $36,361 indicates a total tax of $41,065. Therefore, one might say that the effective tax rate on $150,000 of income for a single taxpayer is about 27 percent even though the marginal tax rate (the rate on each next dollar of income) is 35.5 percent.

## §8.9 Passive Losses and Investment Interest

One of the primary goals of the 1986 Act was to deal with perceived abuses in tax shelters, that is, business arrangements and transactions designed primarily to generate losses that could be used to reduce taxable income from other sources. For example, a taxpayer might borrow funds to purchase a deferred income investment and then seek to deduct the interest in the current tax year as a way of reducing taxable salary income. A more aggressive tactic might be to buy a rental property for $100,000 with a useful life of say five years for $10,000 in cash and a $90,000 loan. Assuming that the rents just covered the interest payments and other cash expenses, the taxpayer would be left with a $20,000 depreciation deduction each year for five years (assuming straight-line depreciation). In other words, in exchange for a single $10,000 investment, an investor would get a total of $100,000 in deductions over five years and (assuming a 40 percent marginal tax rate) would save $40,000 in taxes over that period. To add insult to injury, from the viewpoint of the IRS, the taxpayer may have entered into this arrangement as a limited partner in a partnership that may have obtained a non-recourse loan. As a result, the transaction might involve little or no risk to the taxpayer.

In an effort to put a stop to transactions of this sort, the 1986 Act set up three sources of income and loss generating activities and provided that losses and expenses from one type of activity may not be used to offset income from another type of activity. Specifically, the IRC now provides for the segregation of income and losses from passive activities, portfolio activities, and an active trade or business.

A **passive activity** includes virtually all investments in real estate and a trade or business in which the taxpayer does not materially participate. **Material participation** means that the taxpayer must be involved in the operation of the venture on a regular, continuous, and substantial basis. Thus, a limited partner in a real estate venture would not qualify. Losses and expenses from passive activities may only be used to offset income and gains from other passive activities. There is an exception for hotels and for losses from rental properties up to $25,000 (but the latter exception is phased out for taxpayers with AGI of $100,000 and disappears altogether for taxpayers with AGI of $150,000 or more).

The second category, **portfolio activities**, includes investments in securities and other financial instruments. As with passive activities, losses and expenses from these activities may not be used to offset income from other sources.

Losses that cannot be used may be carried forward indefinitely and used in subsequent years when there is income of the same category. Losses may also be deducted when the taxpayer sells or otherwise disposes of the entire interest in the property. But the use of these losses is limited to offsetting other gains and no more than $3000 in losses may be used to offset ordinary income from active sources. The treatment of capital gains and losses is discussed more fully below.

Finally, expenses and losses generated by an **active trade or business** in which the taxpayer materially participates may be used to offset income from any other source.

Although it is easy to see why these rules were added to the IRC, it also should be apparent that they generate difficult questions of interpretation at the edges and add a significant additional level of complexity to an already complex regime.

## §8.10 The Alternative Minimum Tax (AMT)

The **alternative minimum tax (AMT)** attacks the proliferation of preferential provisions in the IRC and limits the ability of a taxpayer to avoid all taxes by using these provisions, either singly or in combination as of the 2001 tax year. It is applicable only to taxpayers with taxable incomes in excess of $49,000. The alternative minimum tax essentially requires a second tax calculation using an entirely different set of computational rules. If the alternative minimum tax is greater than the tax computed in the normal manner, then the taxpayer's tax liability is based on the alternative minimum tax rather than on the normal computation of tax.

The alternative minimum tax is figured on an amount computed as follows: One starts with the adjusted gross income of the taxpayer computed on the normal basis, and adds back in specific **tax preference items** claimed by the taxpayer in the calculation of adjusted gross income. From this amount, one subtracts (1) $49,000, and (2) allowable deductions for charitable contributions, interest on mortgages on the personal residence of the taxpayers, and investment interest. The alternative minimum tax is 26 percent of the amount so computed up to $175,000, and it is 28 percent thereafter.

The tax preference items that must be added back into income for the computation of the amount subject to the alternative minimum tax include accelerated depreciation on property, capital gains deductions, portions of incentive stock options excluded from income, and percentage depletion.

The alternative minimum tax provision is an effort to overcome the deficiencies of the normal income tax structure by overlaying a separate tax schedule on most loopholes. The alternative minimum tax obviously complicates the tax returns of all high-income taxpayers.

## §8.11 Sales and Exchanges of Property

A major area of tax law deals with gains and losses from the sale or exchange of property. At the most basic level, a sale or exchange of property gives rise to taxable income. Say that a farmer swaps a side of beef for a bolt of cloth from the local dry goods store. The exchange is a taxable transaction, and each participant should report gain or loss from the transaction on his or her federal income tax return. Obviously, in the barter economy that quietly exists in many communities, a lot of tax evading goes on, because it is likely that few, if any, transactions of this type are reported.

Of course, in the barter of the beef for the cloth, both parties are swapping goods that involve their trade or business. But that is not essential. If you sell your secondhand car at a profit, the gain should be reported to the IRS as income. Similarly, if you swap your car for a motorcycle or a used computer, the gain should be reported. (Losses from such personal transactions are not deductible at all, and hence need not be reported.)

The calculation of the amount of the gain from sales or exchanges involves the use of technical language that is fundamental to any understanding of the tax laws:

1. **Basis** is the investment the seller of the property has in the property. It is the cost or purchase price of the property that the seller pays or incurrs in acquiring the property. In the case of property acquired by gift, the basis in the hands of the donee is usually the same as the basis in the hands of the donor (a **substituted basis**); in the case of property acquired by inheritance, it is generally the fair market value of the assets on the death of decedent (a **stepped-up basis**).

2. **Adjusted basis** is the basis of the property (1) plus capital improvements made by the seller, commissions originally paid by the seller, legal costs for defending or perfecting title, and so forth, and (2) minus returns of capital, particularly **depreciation** claimed as tax deductions, **depletion**, deducted **casualty losses**, insurance reimbursements, and the like.

3. The **amount realized** includes the cash received for the property on a sale or the fair market value of the property received in exchange for the property. Selling expenses, including brokerage commissions that the seller pays,

reduce the amount realized. In the case of property subject to a mortgage, the amount realized also includes the amount of mortgage debt that the seller is relieved from paying as a result of the sale. For example, if an owner of real estate encumbered by a $50,000 mortgage sells the property for $10,000 cash over and above the mortgage, which the buyer agrees to assume and pay, the amount realized from the sale is $60,000, not $10,000. If the property is sold with the seller giving the buyer $5,000 for assuming the mortgage of $50,000, the amount realized is $45,000.

4. **Gain** on a transaction equals the amount realized minus the adjusted basis. If the adjusted basis is greater than the amount realized, the difference is the loss.

## §8.12 Recognition of Gain or Loss

In order to be taxable, a gain or loss must be **recognized** as well as **realized**. Realized means that the transaction is closed and the sale or exchange has occurred. Recognized means that the gain or loss is also to be taken into account as a taxable transaction. If a realized gain or loss is not recognized, it is deferred to a later year.

Generally, gain or loss is recognized whenever property is sold or exchanged, but there are significant exceptions: **like kind exchanges** of property, **involuntary conversions** of property, sales of residences followed by a **rollover** of the purchase price into a new residence, sales between related persons, and many transactions by a corporation involving its own stock.

A gain on the sale or exchange of the property may be recognized, although a loss on the sale of the same property is not deductible. This includes, for example, a sale of personal assets such as the family home. The loss is not recognized in the case of personal assets, because it is considered a result of the personal consumption involved in living in a home rather than an economic loss.

The recognition concept is particularly important in connection with transactions relating to the formation and reorganizations of corporations. Many corporate transactions would be economically impractical if gains or losses from the transaction were recognized. For example, consider the problem of investors in a new corporation planning to contribute not cash but property in exchange for its stock. Assume further that the property has a fair market value today of $25,000 and a basis in the hands of the investor of $16,000. The stock being received also has a fair market value of $25,000. In the absence of a nonrecognition provision, the exchange of the real estate for the stock would result in the realization of gain in the amount of $9,000 (the difference between the fair market value of the property being received in the exchange and the basis of the property being exchanged). The result would be that the investor would owe some $3,000 in tax as a result of making the investment. Fortunately, the IRC permits the transfer of assets to a corporation controlled by the transferor (or a group of which he or she is a member) without recognition of gain if the investors in the corporation are in **control** of the corporation after the transaction. In this context, control means ownership of at least 80 percent of the voting stock of the corporation and at least 80 percent of all other classes of stock. If this provision applies, the investor does not recognize any gain from the exchange of stock for property, and the basis of the stock received is $16,000, the basis of the property exchanged.

Gain may be recognized, however, if the transferor takes back cash or property other than stock, or his or her debt is assumed in the transfer. Such rebates are often called **boot**. For example, if in the above transaction, the investor is contributing real estate with a fair market value of $25,000 and a basis of $16,000 that is subject to a $19,000 lien that the corporation is to assume, the difference between the basis ($16,000) and the amount of the lien ($19,000) must be recognized as gain from the transaction. The basis of the stock received is then $19,000.

Another very important nonrecognition area in the law of corporations deals with different kinds of **reorganizations**—statutory mergers, acquisitions of all the assets of one corporation in exchange for stock of another corporation, and the like. These provisions are among the most complicated in the Code, and significantly different tax consequences may follow, depending on how the transaction is structured.

## §8.13 Capital Gains and Losses

For the individual taxpayer, most sales and exchanges of property involve capital assets. The IRC defines the term **capital asset** and provides special rules and limitations with respect to gains and losses from sales or exchanges of such assets. A capital asset is any property held by a taxpayer other than inventory, depreciable and real property used in a trade or business, copyrights, receivables and several other less important items. A taxpayer's personal residence is thus a capital asset, but if the same property were used in a trade or business it would not be a capital asset. Depreciable property used in a trade or business (such as a house) is often entitled, however, to special treatment that is even more favorable than if it were a capital asset. Stock in a corporation is a capital asset in the hands of the stockholder. On the other hand, an interest in a proprietorship is not a capital asset but a collection of individual assets.

A **capital gain** or **capital loss** arises from the **sale or exchange** of a capital asset. A distinction is also made between long-term and short-term capital gains and losses. A **long-term capital gain** (or loss) is a gain (or loss) from the sale or exchange of a capital asset held for more than one year. A **short-term capital gain** (or loss) is a gain (or loss) from the sale or exchange of a capital asset held for one year or less. (This holding period has varied over the years from six to eighteen months.)

Before the 1986 Act, long-term capital gains were taxed at the same rate as **ordinary income** (**OI**) but only after the exclusion of a substantial portion of the gain (50 to 60 percent), thus reducing the effective rate on such income. Under the 1986 Act, this system was eliminated, and capital gains were taxed at the same (relatively low) rates as ordinary income. By 1993, however, marginal tax rates on ordinary income had been increased to as high as 39.6 percent, but the maximum rate on capital gains was left at 28 percent. In 1997,

the maximum tax rate on most long-term capital gains was lowered to 20 percent for assets held more than one year, and 18 percent for assets held more
than five years (if acquired after the year 2000). Long-term capital gains from
the sale or exchange of collectibles (such as works of art and antiques) remain
taxed at the 28 percent rate. Short-term capital gains are generally taxed at the
same rate as ordinary income.

There is a special rule for gains by an individual from the sale or exchange
of qualified small business stock acquired directly from the issuing corporation
and held for more than five years. Fifty percent of this gain may be excluded.
Thus, the tax rate is 50 percent of the otherwise applicable rate. There is also
a special rule for gain from the sale of a personal residence. A taxpayer may
exclude up to $500,000 in gain from such a transaction (on a joint return) as
long as the taxpayers (or one of them) occupied the house as a principal residence for at least two of the preceding five years and as long as the taxpayers
have not used the exclusion in the past two years. The exclusion is $250,000
for a single taxpayer.

The treatment of capital losses is somewhat more complex. In general,
long-term capital losses must first be subtracted from long-term capital gains,
and short-term capital losses must first be subtracted from short-term capital
gains. The two resulting figures are then netted out against each other, and any
resulting gain is taxed according to its character. In other words, if net short-
term gains exceed net long-term losses, then the net gain is taxed as a short-
term gain and vice versa. If the result is an overall loss, then the taxpayer may
deduct up to $3,000 in any one tax year against ordinary income, regardless
of the character of the loss. Any excess loss may be carried forward indefinitely
and may be used to reduce gains in future tax years or deducted against ordinary
income to the extent of $3,000 per year. Short-term losses must be eliminated
first. There is a special rule for losses from small business stock and partnership
interests that allows a taxpayer to deduct up to $100,000 against ordinary
income on a joint return.

In general a capital loss on the sale or exchange of an asset held for personal
use is not recognized for tax purposes. Thus, a loss on the sale of a personal
residence may not be deducted or used to reduce other capital gains.

The tax treatment of gain or loss on depreciable property (which includes
most property other than land that is used in a trade or business) is complicated
by the fact that such property is depreciable. The essential idea behind depreciation (or **cost recovery** as it is now called under the IRC) is that an asset
declines in value as it is used. Thus, the IRC allows a business taxpayer to
deduct the decline in value as an expense, and this deduction has the effect of
reducing ordinary income. The basis of the asset must be correspondingly reduced by the amount of the deduction. In theory, the **adjusted basis** of the
property should be equal to its fair market value. But it hardly ever works out
that way. The **accelerated cost recovery system** (**ACRS**) tax law generally
allows generous deductions (in part in order to encourage investment). The
effect is that the cost of many assets is written off faster than is economically
justified. (Few taxpayers complain about ACRS, because the effect of the system
is to reduce taxable income and thus the tax to be paid.) As a result, however,
the fair market value of an asset is often higher than its adjusted basis. (The

value of the asset may also have increased because of inflation or other economic factors.) If the property is then sold at a price that exceeds the adjusted basis the taxpayer must usually recognize gain. The problem is that the gain has been taxed at a lower rate, whereas the periodic deductions have been used to reduce ordinary income. Again, few taxpayers would complain, but the potential for abuse is evident. As a result, the IRC contains elaborate rules requiring the **recapture** of cost recovery deductions in situations in which gain is the result of overly aggressive cost recovery accounting (rather than some other factor such as inflation). When the deduction is recaptured, the gain or a portion of it is usually treated as ordinary income and taxed in the year of recapture.

## §8.14  The Collection Process

The IRS has the responsibility for collection of federal income, gift, estate, and excise taxes. The discussion here is limited to the process of collection of income taxes.

Income taxes are collected on a highly efficient "pay as you go" basis. For most Americans, the "pay as you go" system means simply that employers must withhold from each paycheck an amount that approximately covers the employee's tax liability by the end of the year. Probably every reader has had some contact with this **withholding** system, involving the filing of a Form W-4 with one's employer declaring the number of exemptions claimed, and the receipt from the employer each January of a W-2 Form that shows the amounts actually withheld during the previous calendar year. The withholding schedules and tax rates are structured so that if a person accurately declares the number of exemptions and uses the standard deduction, he or she ends up having more deducted from paychecks than the amount of tax actually due. Most taxpayers therefore receive refunds every year. Of course, these refunds are paid in effect from funds painlessly collected from the taxpayer by his or her employer over the course of the preceding year without interest. The fact that most people are entitled to refunds each year materially increases the political acceptability of the system. The arrangement is attractive to the federal government as well: The collection process is painless and does not give rise to large amounts of resentment, the government has the interest-free use of funds for nearly a year, and tax collections are spread around the year and not bunched in a single month.

The employer is required to pay over to the IRS the amount withheld from employees at the end of each calendar quarter. Although the IRC requires that these withheld funds be placed in a separate account, most employers do not segregate the funds but simply use them as part of general working capital until the check is written to the IRS. Of course, from time to time a business may become insolvent without having forwarded the money withheld from employees to the IRS. There is a 100 percent penalty against an individual with the responsibility for these funds who fails to pay them over to the IRS. In other words, the corporate treasurer or individual with analogous responsibilities is personally liable for the amount withheld if it is not in fact paid over. Like other claims arising under the IRC, this liability is not discharged in bankruptcy. Whether or not the Service successfully collects the withheld taxes from the employer, however, the employee is entitled to credit against his or her taxes of the amounts shown as withheld on statements reported to the IRS.

If persons have income or gains not subject to withholding, they may be required to file quarterly declarations of **estimated tax**, which are intended to provide a "pay as you go" system to taxpayers with substantial amounts of self-employment activity, personal investments, and other sources of nonwithheld income, such as gambling or stock market trading. Quarterly declarations are due April 15, June 15, September 15, and January 15, and must be accompanied by a proportional amount of the estimated tax that is shown to be due on the estimate. A person subject to withholding is theoretically required to file a quarterly declaration whenever taxes withheld are less than 90 percent of taxes due, but such persons may avoid this filing if they increase the amount of withholding so that the estimated tax for that quarter is shown to be zero. The obligation to file quarterly declarations of estimated tax, and to pay the proportional amount of tax due, is enforced by penalties applied when the final return is filed for the year showing substantial underpayment of tax. What is substantial in this context is very specifically defined in the IRC: if the amount paid by withholding and quarterly estimates is less than 90 percent of the actual tax shown to be due on the return. The 1986 Act imposes a stiff penalty if the total "pay as you go" payments fail to equal 90 percent of the actual tax; in earlier years, a smaller penalty was due only if the payments were less than 80 percent of the actual tax due. There are also other bases on which this penalty may be avoided.

## §8.15 Tax Accounting

The IRC obviously requires the use of accounting concepts for determining in which years items of income and deduction should be reported. Tax accounting differs materially from traditional income accounting in numerous specific respects. Tax returns are not prepared on generally accepted accounting practices (GAAP) principles, so income for tax purposes and income for accounting purposes may vary substantially.

Most individual taxpayers are on the **cash basis**, that is, they report income when it is received rather than when it is earned and take advantage of deductions when they are paid rather than when they are incurred or when they are due. This permits some income and deduction shifting from one year to another. For example, a doctor who does not bill for November or December services until January takes the income arising from these services into his or her tax return for the second year, not the first. It is almost always advantageous to defer taxes even if tax rates are identical, because of the time value of a deferred payment. Sometimes, year-end planning may also permit a taxpayer to shift income from a high-income year to a lower-income year so that it is taxed at lower marginal rates. Similarly, a taxpayer may be able to shift two years' real estate property taxes into a single year by paying one year's taxes in January and prepaying the next year's taxes in December of the same year. Combining two years' taxes into a single year may be advantageous if the standard deduction is claimed for the year in which no payments of real estate tax are made. Strategies of this type do offer some modest degree of tax saving and tax avoidance for individuals.

There are some exceptions to the straight cash basis of individual taxpayer accounting. The doctrine of **constructive receipt** does not permit a taxpayer to defer reporting income items that are within his or her immediate control. An income item, for example, cannot be deferred merely by not depositing a check until the following year. There are also special rules relating to receipt of interest. Interest on financial instruments such as zero coupon bonds purchased at a discount from face value (**original issue discount** or **OID**) must be reported as it is earned rather than being deferred until the instrument is paid. (Zero coupon bonds and other similar instruments are discussed in the chapters on trading markets and investment strategies.) Similarly, interest that a taxpayer pays in a lump sum to cover several accounting periods cannot be deducted in the year of payment but must be deducted ratably over the relevant periods, although it is paid in a single year. Restrictions are also imposed on the deductibility of prepaid amounts. These various qualifications to the general cash method of accounting reflect pragmatic judgments designed to limit revenue loss from tax-minimizing transactions.

It has long been a fact of corporate life that many publicly held corporations reflect substantial earnings in their financial statements and reports to shareholders but pay little or no federal income tax. Undoubtedly, much of this difference is due to tax benefits intentionally given to business, such as the accelerated cost recovery system (ACRS) for calculating depreciation deductions. However, the difference is partly due to differences in accounting principles.

Financial accounting for publicly held corporations must comply with GAAP, which does not permit the use of cash accounting for most businesses. The IRC similarly prohibits corporations and specified other types of businesses from adopting a cash basis of accounting for tax purposes. However, tax accounting and GAAP are designed for different purposes, and as a result there are many differences in detail and the way specific transactions are handled. The primary goal of financial accounting is to provide useful information to management, shareholders, creditors, and others who are properly interested in the business. The primary goal of the income tax system, on the other hand, is to protect the public **fisc**. The general principle of tax accounting is that the method used must clearly reflect income. The tax system, for example, may require that receipts of cash be included in income immediately, while GAAP requires that they be taken into income only when the services have been performed or the goods delivered. Similarly, GAAP may call for the creation of reserves for losses and the treatment of amounts allocated to them as expenses reducing earnings. Such expenses are often not recognized as deductions for income tax purposes.

The differences between tax accounting and financial accounting is a specialized area of interest primarily to accountants and attorneys who represent businesses in tax matters. They are the outgrowth of basic differences in the purposes of the two accounting systems. Because the systems are different, businesses must usually keep tax books and financial books separately.

In 1986, a controversial and novel accounting-related concept was introduced into the tax accounting system. It requires corporations to include a fraction of the difference between their taxable income and their net book income as reported to shareholders in the calculation of the alternative minimum tax for corporations. The purpose of this provision is to ensure that corporations that show substantial book earnings in reports to shareholders also pay a reasonable amount of tax. However, it is uncertain how important this provision is in practice, because the manner of calculating a corporation's alternative minimum taxable income already takes into account the impact of some of the most important corporate tax preferences, such as ACRS.

## §8.16 Corporations and Other Business Forms

Corporations are generally treated as separate taxable entities under the IRC with their own sets of rules and their own tax schedules. Unincorporated business entities, including partnerships, limited partnerships, and limited liability companies, on the other hand, are not treated as separate taxable entities. Rather, unincorporated businesses file an **information return** showing the results of operations and allocating the profit or loss among the owners, who then must include the income or loss in their own personal returns, whether or not any monies are in fact distributed to them. This method of taxation is usually called **pass through** or **conduit taxation**. (The limitations on deductions of passive losses and investment interest discussed earlier are applicable to losses incurred through an unincorporated business.) Because corporation income is taxed at the corporate level and again at the individual level if there is a distribution to the shareholders, it is sometimes said that corporations are subject to **double taxation**. It is possible, however, for smaller corporations (with 75 or fewer shareholders and meeting certain other requirements) to elect to be treated as an **S Corporation**, which status allows many but not all of the benefits of pass through taxation. The differences between these ways of taxing business income (as well as various planning strategies designed to minimize the differences) are discussed more fully in the chapter on forms of business organizations.

The accompanying table shows corporate tax rates as of 2001.

### 2001 Corporate Tax Rate Schedule

| If taxable income is: | | | |
|---|---|---|---|
| Over— | But not over— | Tax is: | Of the amount over— |
| $0 | 50,000 | 15% | -0- |
| $50,000 | 75,000 | $7,500 + 25% | $50,000 |
| 75,000 | 100,000 | 13,750 + 34% | 75,000 |
| 100,000 | 335,000 | 22,250 + 39% | 100,000 |
| 335,000 | 10,000,000 | 113,900 + 34% | 335,000 |
| 10,000,000 | 15,000,000 | 3,400,000 + 35% | 10,000,000 |
| 15,000,000 | 18,333,333 | 5,150,000 + 38% | 15,000,000 |
| 18,333,333 | — | 35% | -0- |

In addition, there is an alternative minimum tax for corporations that taxes a corporation's alternative minimum taxable income at a flat 20 percent. This income is computed by taking the corporation's regular taxable income and increasing it by specified tax preferences.

## §8.17 Taxation of Trusts and Estates

Trusts and estates are also separate taxpayers for purposes of the federal income tax law. They must file income tax returns and must often pay income taxes. This responsibility is independent of the possible responsibility of such entities for gift and estate taxes. Both estates and trusts, however, may largely avoid the payment of income tax by making distributions of income to beneficiaries. The beneficiaries must then include those distributions in their tax returns as income.

When a person dies, his or her representative must file a final return in the decedent's name for the period ending with death. The estate must then file an estate income tax return for the period beginning the day after the date of death and ending on a date selected by the fiduciary for the estate. Annual returns from the estate may be necessary thereafter until the estate is completely distributed. The income items included in the return of the estate may include investment income from assets that the estate owns, gains from the sale or exchange of estate property, and post-death income items attributable to services of the decedent, such as fees for services provided by the decedent before death if payment is received after death. These latter items are called **income in respect of a decedent**.

An important rule affecting the income tax consequences of the death of a person is the **step-up** in basis of property that automatically occurs upon the death of the owner. The basis of all property that the decedent owned automatically becomes its fair market value on the date of death. This principle often results in elderly or ill individuals refraining from selling or disposing of appreciated properties during the remainder of their lifetimes. The appreciation in value during the lifetime of the decedent escapes taxation entirely except to the extent that it is taxed as part of the estate.

The federal **estate tax** is a separate tax on the value of decedents' estates. As a tax on value, the estate tax is a **wealth tax** rather than an **income tax**, although as noted above an estate may also have income and be subject to income tax. As of 2001, the maximum tax rate for an estate is 55 percent. But there is an exemption for the first $675,000 in value. Only estates in excess of that value are taxed at the federal level. Moreover, in the case of a married couple, the estate tax is paid only when the second person dies. Formally, federal law allows for an unlimited **marital deduction**. In other words, one spouse may inherit the entire estate without the payment of estate tax. Thus, in operation the exemption is twice the specified amount. (Additional exemption amounts are allowed for small business interests including farms.)

Given the relatively high exemption, most estates do not owe tax. Most states, however, also impose estate taxes at lower rates but without the relatively high exemptions afforded by federal law. For those estates that do pay federal estate tax, it is not entirely accurate to say that appreciated assets escape taxation because of the stepped-up basis at which they are taken by the heirs. Indeed, because the estate tax is assessed on the value of the assets at the date of death and without any regard for the tax basis of the assets, the tax paid may in some cases be far in excess of the income tax that would have been paid if the asset had been sold. Of course, the proceeds if still held by the estate would then be taxed at the estate tax rate to the extent assets exceed $675,000. Thus, it still makes sense, from an estate planning viewpoint, to hold appreciated assets until death.

One fairly straightforward way to avoid paying estate tax would seem to be simply giving away the taxable portion of one's estate during one's lifetime. As one might guess, this simple loophole has been blocked. Federal law also imposes a **gift tax** under which any gift in excess of $10,000 per individual recipient in a single year must be deducted from the estate tax exemption. Once the exemption is used up, gifts in excess of $10,000 are taxable at the same rate as an estate and are aggregated from year to year so as to track the progressivity of the estate tax. The estate is then ultimately taxed as if it includes the aggregate of the lifetime gifts with a credit for gift taxes previously paid.

The estate and gift tax rate is scheduled to decline gradually to 45 percent in 2009. And the exemption amount is scheduled to increase to $3,500,000 over the same period. The estate tax is then repealed for the year 2010. But unless Congress acts in the meantime to make this repeal permanent, the estate tax is restored to 55 percent on amounts over $1,000,000. In addition, in 2010 the step-up in basis is replaced with a carry-over basis for assets in excess of $3,000,000 passing to a surviving spouse and $1,300,000 passing to other beneficiaries.

The taxation of trusts is considerably more complicated than the taxation of estates and cannot be adequately summarized in a brief comment. A taxpayer may create numerous trusts, and each will be a separate taxpayer unless the IRS determines that tax avoidance was a principal factor in their creation and the beneficiaries are substantially identical. In addition, trusts may be created in which the trustee has authority to distribute income or accumulate it for long periods. Further, a grantor of a trust may reserve substantial powers of management and control, and may also retain a reversionary interest in the trust. These **grantor trusts** and **revocable trusts** are usually not recognized as separate taxpayers. The income from such trusts is taxed directly to the creator.

# INSOLVENCY AND BANKRUPTCY

## §9.1  Introduction

This brief chapter deals with issues that arise when a business or an individual is in financial difficulty. The two most basic lessons of this chapter are (1) it is not a crime or a sin to be unable to pay one's debts and (2) a lot of people successfully avoid paying their debts even though they have the assets to do so. In large part, this is a result of federal bankruptcy law, which provides for a fresh start for most individual debtors and which may even enable them to preserve a portion of their assets and continue living without being hounded or threatened by unpaid creditors.

A corporation that is unable to pay its obligations is also eligible for bankruptcy law protection, but more often is simply liquidated, abandoned, or merged when it is in serious financial difficulty. In the absence of misconduct of some kind, shareholders are not liable for unpaid corporate debts in these situations. Shareholders lose whatever they have invested in the corporation but no more, and creditors receive whatever assets the corporation has and no more.

Thus creditors of insolvent individuals or corporations often end up **writing off** substantial amounts of claims as being uncollectible.

Businesses that are not hopelessly insolvent but are in stressful situations with respect to creditors may file for **reorganization** under Chapter 11 of the federal Bankruptcy Code. Chapter 11 reorganization is basically a time-buying process during which a debtor devises a plan to pay off some or all of its liabilities. The plan must be approved by certain categories or percentages of creditors and by the federal Bankruptcy Court. The debtor typically remains in control of the business or assets while the plan is being devised, considered, and approved; he is a **debtor-in-possession (DIP)**. In the process of reorganization, creditors may be compelled to accept partial or deferred payments in lieu of previous obligations. Many corporations and individuals that file for reorganization ultimately emerge owning successful and profitable businesses.

A somewhat similar alternative is available to individuals with a regular income and potentially manageable amounts of debt. They may take advantage of the reorganization procedure set forth in Chapter 13 of the federal Bankruptcy Code. Chapter 13 reorganization requires court confirmation but does not require creditor approval.

This chapter concentrates on the rights of **unsecured creditors** and the rights and duties of debtors. It does not deal with the rights that secured creditors possess with respect to the collateral securing their debts. It also does not consider claims that a creditor may have to proceed against **sureties**, persons who have committed themselves to pay certain obligations if the debtor is unable or unwilling to do so.

## §9.2 Creditors' Rights Generally

As described in the first chapter, debt is widely used to finance many purchases or investments. While undoubtedly most debt is paid off when due, it is not uncommon for a person to discover that she has incurred unexpected expenses or was overly optimistic and is unable to continue to make payments that are required or to pay off the entire obligation when it falls due. Creditors usually have some patience with honest debtors in these situations and will give them an opportunity to work matters out. This may involve a negotiated arrangement between creditor and debtor to pay the debt off over time. However, at some point if creditors are not paid they will usually take steps to enforce the obligation. This may involve self-help, classically in the form of **repossession** of a vehicle or commencing a proceeding to **foreclose on a mortgage** or **lien**, or the filing of a law suit to enforce the obligation.

Of course, one cannot squeeze blood from a turnip. If the debtor is truly insolvent and without substantial assets, the debt will probably be written off by the creditor either as uncollectible or because the cost of collection makes pursuit of the claim uneconomic.

Although most debt is created voluntarily, it is also possible for a debt to arise involuntarily, for example, from a tort judgment. It is important to distinguish mentally between these two types of debt, because **voluntary creditors** can (and should) protect themselves through negotiation or obtaining security as a condition for making the loan. In contrast, **involuntary creditors** (e.g., the plaintiff who has a tort claim against the defendant) generally do not have this option; they usually must look to actual or threatened litigation to collect on their claims.

When a debt is not paid when due and negotiation fails to work out an acceptable compromise, the creditor will usually sue to enforce the claim. If the debtor has no defense, the creditor will probably be able to obtain a **default judgment** in his favor. However, it is important to recognize that obtaining a judgment is only the beginning of the collection process.

The fact that a plaintiff has been awarded a dollar judgment against a defendant does not mean that money flies automatically out of the defendant's bank account and into the plaintiff's account. Indeed, after a judgment is entered, not very much happens at all. The plaintiff simply has a judicial determination that she should recover a specified amount from the defendant. There is no promise or obligation on the part of the judgment defendant to cooperate by voluntarily making the demanded payment. A judgment defendant who does not want to pay a judgment can simply sit tight. The next move is up to the plaintiff.

Each state provides procedures for collecting upon a judgment. While procedures vary somewhat from state to state, the traditional remedy is for the plaintiff to obtain a writ of execution from the court directed to the local sheriff, directing the sheriff to seize **nonexempt property** owned by the defendant and to sell it at public sale, i.e., at a public auction. If the value of the defendant's property that is seized is equal to or greater than the amount of the judgment, the plaintiff will appear at the auction and bid the amount of his judgment. He has little incentive to bid more because if he does the excess proceeds will be paid over to the defendant. On the other hand, the defendant may—and often does—appear at the auction to bid to assure that his property will not be sold to someone at a bargain price.

The collection process is complicated because certain types of property are exempt from execution and sale. The property that is exempt varies widely from state to state. It may be specified by item (for example, one automobile or horse or certain household furniture) or may be specified as an amount (for example, $5,000 of personal property). In many states, a person's primary residence (or **homestead**) is exempt from execution, either in whole or up to a specified value.

In addition to execution and sale, a judgment creditor has the right to **garnish** amounts owed by third parties to the judgment debtor. A **writ of garnishment** is served on a person who owes the judgment debtor money; that writ commands the creditor to pay the amount of the debt to the plaintiff rather than to the judgment debtor. Bank accounts are the most commonly garnished property. Many states limit the kinds of accounts that may be garnished; many, for example, limit or prohibit the garnishment of wages due to the judgment debtor. Federal law also prohibits wage garnishments in excess of 25 percent of disposable earnings of an employee in any work week.

A third course of action available to judgement creditors in many states is **abstracting a judgment**. "Abstracting" a judgment simply means recording the judgment (or an abstract, transcript, or certificate of its existence) in the land records of the county in which the judgment debtor owns property. Abstracting a judgment in conformity with statute impresses a lien on the real (and in some states) personal property owned by the debtor that is located within the state or within the county. States often require that the abstract also be indexed so that it will be routinely discovered in a title search. The advantage of this process is that the judgment debtor is thereafter unable to dispose of his property without paying off the **judgment lien**. While this avoids the cost of having the sheriff seize the property, the creditor may have to be patient, since the judgment debtor may decide not to sell the property for a long time. On the other hand, abstracted judgments also usually cover subsequently acquired property as well as statutory interest that accrues on the original judgment so there may be some incentive on the part of the debtor to obtain a release of the lien.

These collection procedures (other than abstracting a judgment) are relatively expensive. Property must be located and care must be taken that the sheriff seizes and sells the right property. The sheriff typically requires a bond or an indemnification agreement to protect him in the event the property he is directed to seize and sell turns out not to be owned by the judgment debtor or to be exempt from execution.

Because of the uncertainties and costs of the collection process, it is not uncommon for a judgment creditor to offer to accept a partial payment in full settlement of the judgment and for the judgment debtor to accept the offer.

## §9.3 Assignments for the Benefit of Creditors

State law authorizes persons who are hopelessly insolvent to make an **assignment for the benefit of creditors**. The debtor assigns all his nonexempt property to a third person trustee who is charged with the duty of liquidating the assets and distributing the proceeds to creditors as expeditiously as possible.

Voluntary assignments for the benefit of creditors were recognized at common law, though in this context, the word "voluntary" must be taken with a grain of salt. Debtors are naturally reluctant to throw in the towel and usually make a voluntary assignment only following considerable pressure from major creditors who may argue that otherwise expensive involuntary bankruptcy proceedings will be filed in federal court.

Many states have statutes that regulate the voluntary assignment process. They require recording of the assignment, filing of schedules of assets and liabilities, and giving notice to creditors. These statutes also describe the obligations of the assignee who is generally required to liquidate the assets of the estate and distribute the proceeds to creditors as expeditiously as possible. In the unlikely event that the assets exceed the liabilities, the assignee must return the balance to the assignor. In the more likely event that some liabilities remain unsatisfied in whole or in part following the distribution of assets by the assignee, the debtor remains liable for those liabilities. For this reason, an individual debtor usually prefers to go through the federal bankruptcy process that may lead to discharge from unsatisfied liabilities. As a result, most voluntary assignments for the benefit of creditors involve corporate debtors, not individual debtors.

An assignment for the benefit of creditors is itself an act of bankruptcy that permits any creditor to commence an involuntary bankruptcy proceeding in federal court. However, during the pendency of the assignment process, creditors may not attach or seize the assigned property or bring direct suits to collect upon unpaid obligations of the debtor.

If an insolvent debtor favors certain creditors before entering into a voluntary assignment for the benefit of creditors, the assignee may be able to set aside the earlier transfers as fraudulent conveyances, discussed in §9.7 below. However, an assignee does not possess a general power to set aside preferential payments to creditors before the assignment; those transactions may be set aside only by the institution of involuntary bankruptcy proceedings in a federal court.

## §9.4 Compositions and Extensions

A **composition** is an agreement between an insolvent or embarrassed debtor and two or more of his creditors by which the creditors agree to accept a partial satisfaction of their claims and forgive the balance. Consideration for the forgiveness consists of the mutual agreement by the two or more creditors to forgo their legal rights and to accept what is offered for their common benefit, i.e. the partial payment by the debtor.

A composition differs from an assignment for the benefit of creditors primarily because the composition is a contract between the debtor and the specific creditors settling their claims. An assignment for the benefit of creditors, in contrast, is a liquidating arrangement that is not dependent on the assent of creditors and does not involve any release of claims by creditors. It is possible, however, for a composition and assignment for the benefit of creditors to occur simultaneously, as where a debtor agrees to make an assignment for the benefit of creditors and each creditor agrees to forgive any claim for the amount by which its claims exceed the amount payable to the creditor pursuant to the assignment.

A composition does not affect the rights of creditors who are not parties to the agreement; they may continue to seek to enforce their claims against the debtor by legal or extralegal means. Creditors who are induced to enter into a composition agreement by the fraud or misrepresentation of the debtor may rescind the composition agreement or sue for damages for fraud. On the other hand, creditors who understate the amount of their claims in an effort to induce the debtor to enter into a composition, may be bound to the terms of the composition.

An **extension agreement** is an agreement between one or more creditors and a debtor that gives the debtor additional time to discharge its obligations, but does not affect the obligation except to extend the period of the statute of limitations.

## §9.5 Workouts

A **workout** is a process by which one or more creditors of a troubled debtor in effect take over a portion or all of the operation of the debtor's business in order to develop the cash flow necessary to pay the debtor's obligations. Many banks and commercial lenders maintain workout departments that specialize in this process, an indication that workouts are a common phenomenon. These arrangements are called workouts because the goal of the creditors is to change the debtor's operations so that it can pay off (or work out) the debtor's indebtedness. A workout may take a few months or a year or more to complete.

Because the goal of a workout is to pay off the obligations of the debtor, managers of the workout concentrate on control over cash flow, and may direct cash to be used for the payment of outstanding indebtedness to the maximum extent consistent with continuing obligations of the business. Workout managers have the sole power to disburse funds of the debtor and to veto proposed disbursements of funds. They may cause the debtor to enter into transactions such as the sale of components or parts of the business for the primary purpose of raising cash to off debts.

A workout is not a pleasant process for the debtor and its prior managers. A workout may lead to a partial or complete liquidation of the business. On the other hand, the workout managers also assume certain risks. They may be held to be the principal in an agency relationship and to have assumed control of the business subject to the duties implicit in that relationship. If this relationship is found to exist, the claims of the lender who controls the workout process may be subordinated to other claims in the event of insolvency, and it is conceivable that the workout managers or their firm may be held liable for the unsatisfied claims of other creditors, either as insiders under federal bankruptcy law or as having aided and abetted one or more fraudulent transfers (both of which are discussed below).

Undoubtedly many workouts are successful in the sense that many businesses survive and come out of the process smaller, more efficient, and more profitable. However, the identity of the owners may have changed in the process. And in some instances, the workout is not successful and the business disappears into insolvency and bankruptcy.

## §9.6  Bankruptcy and Insolvency

The words **bankrupt** and **insolvent** are often used loosely and interchangeably, but they have more precise definitions depending on the circumstances. From a legal standpoint, the words **insolvent** or **insolvency** have two different common meanings. They may refer to situations where the debtor is unable to meet its obligations as they come due. This is referred to as **equity insolvency** or **insolvency in the equity sense**. A different meaning of these terms appears in §101(26) of the federal Bankruptcy Code. A debtor is "insolvent" under §101(26) if "the sum of such entity's debts is greater than all of such entity's property, at a fair valuation," excluding exempt property and certain other items. This definition of "insolvency" is usually referred to as **balance sheet insolvency** or **insolvency in the bankruptcy sense**. Balance sheet insolvency requires the use of some kind of accounting principles (though the phrase "at a fair evaluation" obviously assumes that realistic asset values should be used rather than unrealistic book values).

The difference between equity insolvency and balance sheet insolvency can be significant. These concepts focus on different aspects of the financial position of the business. Equity insolvency focuses on the *liquidity* of a continuing entity while balance sheet insolvency focuses on the *liquidation* of a terminating entity. A person or entity may easily be insolvent in the bankruptcy sense but highly solvent in the equity sense. A first-year law student may have liabilities greatly in excess of his current assets and thus be insolvent in the bankruptcy sense (assuming he died today), but highly solvent in the equity sense if one considers his nighttime job and the contract he has to work for a law firm over the summer. That student may well be insolvent in the bankruptcy sense and yet able to deal with her bills month and after month indefinitely. A person also may be insolvent in the equity sense but solvent in the bankruptcy sense if, for example, he has substantial illiquid assets and resources but no cash to meet current bills.

The word **bankrupt** also has several varied and loose meanings. It may be used loosely, either to identify any person whose liabilities exceed his assets, or more technically, as the person who is the debtor in a bankruptcy proceeding, but most modern statutes, including the federal Bankruptcy Code, use the term **debtor**. Formerly, federal bankruptcy law referred to specific **acts of bankruptcy** and the word "bankrupt" was sometimes used to refer to a person who had committed one or more of those acts. The federal Bankruptcy Code eliminated all references to the concept of acts of bankruptcy in 1978, but persons who are insolvent in either the equity or insolvency sense may be sometimes colloquially referred to as being bankrupt.

Many state statutes use the single word "insolvent" in the equity sense as a legal standard. For example, state law uniformly prohibits corporations from making distributions to shareholders if to do so would render the corporation insolvent. Usage is not uniform, however, and some statutory references to "insolvent" may refer to insolvency in the bankruptcy sense. One may have to examine carefully the precise language of a specific statute to determine which type of insolvency is intended. The accounting profession generally uses the word "insolvent" in the bankruptcy or balance sheet sense and not in the equity sense.

## §9.7 Fraudulent Conveyances and Fraudulent Transfers

The law of **fraudulent conveyances** or **fraud on creditors** is a common law doctrine designed to protect creditors from transactions entered into by debtors that have the purpose or effect of hindering or defeating the creditor's power to collect on the debt. The doctrine has a long history, with its roots in the statute of 13 Elizabeth enacted in 1570, and is part of the English common law inheritance in all states.

The doctrine has been codified in many states. The **Uniform Fraudulent Conveyance Act (UFCA)**, approved by the Commissioners on Uniform State Laws in 1919, and adopted by 25 states. A revision and modernization of this statute was approved in 1984 as the **Uniform Fraudulent Transfers Act (UFTA)** and has been adopted by 40 states. Four states continue to follow the

UFCA. The two laws are quite similar, but the focus here is on the particular language of the UFTA.

UFTA provides that two broad classes of transactions may be invalidated: (1) transfers made with an actual intent to defraud or made under circumstances in which intent may be inferred, and (2) transfers made when the debtor is insolvent. As for transfers with actual or constructive intent to defraud, §4(a) of UFTA provides that:

> (a) A transfer made or obligation incurred by a debtor is fraudulent as to a creditor, whether the creditor's claim arose before or after the transfer was made or the obligation was incurred, if the debtor made the transfer or incurred the obligation: (1) with actual intent to hinder, delay, or defraud any creditor of the debtor; or (2) without receiving a reasonably equivalent value in exchange for the transfer or obligation, and the debtor: (i) was engaged or was about to engage in a business or a transaction for which the remaining assets of the debtor were unreasonably small in relation to the business or transaction; or (ii) intended to incur, or believed or reasonably should have believed that he [or she] would incur, debts beyond his [or her] ability to pay as they became due.

Section 4(b) lists eleven specific factors that may be considered in determining whether actual intent existed:

> (b) In determining actual intent under subsection (a)(1), consideration may be given, among other factors, to whether: (1) the transfer or obligation was to an insider; (2) the debtor retained possession or control of the property transferred after the transfer; (3) the transfer or obligation was disclosed or concealed; (4) before the transfer was made or obligation was incurred, the debtor had been sued or threatened with suit; (5) the transfer was of substantially all the debtor's assets; (6) the debtor absconded; (7) the debtor removed or concealed assets; (8) the value of the consideration received by the debtor was reasonably equivalent to the value of the asset transferred or the amount of the obligation incurred; (9) the debtor was insolvent or became insolvent shortly after the transfer was made or the obligation was incurred; (10) the transfer occurred shortly before or shortly after a substantial debt was incurred; and (11) the debtor transferred the essential assets of the business to a lienor who transferred the assets to an insider of the debtor.

These factors are often referred to as **badges of fraud**. Section 5 of UFTA provides that transactions that occur when the debtor is insolvent or is rendered insolvent by the transaction are **voidable**. There are two basic types of transactions described in sections 5(a) and 5(b): (a) a transfer made without receiving a reasonably equivalent value in exchange and the debtor was insolvent at that time or becomes insolvent as a result of the transfer; and (b) a transfer made (i) to an insider for an antecedent debt, (ii) when the debtor was insolvent at that time, and (iii) the insider had reasonable cause to believe that the debtor was insolvent.

Section 7 of UFTA provides remedies for fraudulent transfers. Generally, a fraudulent transfer is voidable to the extent necessary to satisfy the creditor's claim upon suit by the creditor, an assignee for the benefit of creditors, or a bankruptcy trustee. Alternatively, the creditor may ignore the transfer and simply proceed against the property by **attachment** or other private remedy. A creditor may also in an appropriate case enjoin a transfer or obtain the appointment of a receiver to take charge of the asset.

Section 8 grants basic protection to good faith transferees. A transfer is not voidable under section 4(a)(1) against a person who took the property in good faith and for a reasonably equivalent value. Further, a **good faith transferee** is protected from loss to the extent of the value of any improvements he may have made in good faith to the property. Subsequent transferees are completely protected, but creditors may recover the proceeds of a subsequent sale by the initial transferee if the initial transferee paid less than reasonably equivalent value.

Fraudulent transfer statutes have sometimes been applied to management buyouts and other going private transactions. In such a transaction, management of a publicly held company may offer to repurchase the shares owned by the general public at a price significantly above the current market price. The offer is financed by loans to the corporation by banks and other third parties. Following the elimination of public shareholders, the liabilities of the business are likely to exceed its assets, but it may reasonably be expected that the future cash flow of the business will be sufficient to pay off the corporation's debts (old and new) in due course. The lenders typically condition their loans on receipt of a **solvency letter**, that is, written assurance from an outside expert (typically an accounting firm or an investment bank) that despite the additional debt the firm will continue to be solvent in the equity sense. If the letter turns out to be incorrect and the business fails, trade creditors may seek to set aside liens and subordinate claims of the lenders on the theory that the transaction that eliminated the public shareholders was a fraudulent transfer, rendering the company insolvent. (The repurchase may also constitute an illegal dividend as a matter of corporation law.)

## §9.8 An Overview of the Federal Bankruptcy Code

The United States Constitution expressly grants power to Congress to enact "uniform laws" on the subject of bankruptcy. The first general bankruptcy statute was enacted in 1898; the current statute was enacted in 1978. Substantial amendments to the administrative provisions of this statute were made in 1984 and important substantive changes were made in 1994.

Major features of the federal Bankruptcy Code that distinguish it from state law are (1) a power to avoid **prefiling transfers** of property to ensure equality of treatment among creditors of the same class; (2) the application of an **automatic stay** against all collection efforts by creditors immediately upon filing a bankruptcy petition; and (3) the availability of a **discharge** from prefiling debts so as to give "honest" debtors a fresh start.

Three chapters of the Bankruptcy Code deal with individual and corporate bankruptcies.

Chapter 7 deals with "straight" bankruptcy proceedings for both individuals and businesses. In Chapter 7 bankruptcy proceedings, the nonexempt assets of the bankrupt are liquidated under the supervision of a trustee, and distributed to creditors. Usually the bankrupt will receive a discharge from obligations not fully satisfied by the distribution of assets.

Chapter 11 deals with reorganizations of the assets of businesses (and sometimes individuals) that are troubled but may avoid liquidation. Examples of Chapter 11 reorganizations include Johns Mansville obtaining protection from asbestos claimants, A.H. Robins obtaining protections from Dalkon shield claimants, and Texaco, Inc. obtaining protection against efforts by Pennzoil to collect upon its famous multibillion dollar judgment.

Chapter 13 deals with reorganizations by debtors that have a regular income, unsecured debts of less than $250,000 (as adjusted for inflation) and secured debts of less than $750,000 (as adjusted for inflation). Although many individuals qualify for Chapter 13, most nonetheless use Chapter 7.

Bankruptcy proceedings are generally administered in **federal bankruptcy courts** by **bankruptcy judges**. Bankruptcy judges are not Article III judges; they serve fourteen-year terms and are not immune from salary reduction. Procedures followed in bankruptcy proceedings depend on the type of case. Chapter 7 cases involve the appointment of a **trustee** to administer the **estate of the bankrupt**, that is, his assets that are subject to administration. A trustee is an individual appointed by the **United States Trustee**, an administrative official, and not by the Bankruptcy Judge. Chapter 11 cases have trustees only in cases of serious misconduct. The decision whether to have a trustee is made by the Bankruptcy Judge, and the selection of the trustee is by election conducted by the United States Trustee. In most districts, there is a standing trustee for Chapter 13 cases.

Bankruptcy proceedings are usually initiated by a **voluntary filing** by the debtor. Any person with debts may make a voluntary filing. It is not a requirement that the debtor be insolvent in either the equity or the balance sheet sense.

Bankruptcy proceedings in Chapters 7 or 11 may also be instituted by creditors seeking the involuntary institution of bankruptcy or reorganization proceedings against the debtor. Three creditors with unsecured claims totaling at least $10,000 (as adjusted for inflation) must join in the petition for **involuntary bankruptcy** or a single creditor with a claim exceeding $10,000 (as adjusted) may file the petition if the debtor has fewer than twelve creditors. Involuntary bankruptcy petitions must allege either (1) that the debtor is not paying debts as they mature, (2) that the debtor has made an assignment for the benefit of creditors within the previous 120 days, or (3) that a receiver or liquidator has been appointed for the debtor by a court within the previous 120 days. Chapter 13 proceedings are voluntary only.

The filing of an involuntary bankruptcy proceeding almost always severely disrupts the debtor's activities and injures its reputation. As a result, severe sanctions may be imposed on a creditor who files an involuntary petition in bad faith.

Chapter 11 may be used defensively by a business to protect itself from litigation and to effect a recapitalization or takeover. In some instances, debtors and creditors have agreed on the terms of a reorganization in advance of the filing, and go to bankruptcy court simply to obtain approval of the **prepackaged bankruptcy**. Creditors who were not part of the prior negotiation may vigorously object to the proposed reorganization. However, under federal bankruptcy law, approval by a majority of the creditors of a given class holding at least two-thirds of the claims of that class (by value) makes that plan effective with respect to that class. The bankruptcy judge may thereafter decide to **cram down** the plan with respect to members of other classes.

Creditors also may be quite aggressive in their use of bankruptcy rules against preferential payments. Trade creditors have increasingly been called on to return apparently routine payments made many years earlier by debtors contemplating going into bankruptcy. Whether these trends will continue or will lead to new legislation remains to be seen.

## §9.9  Unexpected Consequences of Bankruptcy

One important aspect of bankruptcy from the viewpoint of lawyers is that the filing of a bankruptcy petition has substantial consequences to both creditors and the debtor, and some of these consequences are unpleasant.

For example, upon the filing of a petition, an automatic stay goes into effect that requires the immediate cessation of all collection efforts, including efforts to foreclose upon liens or security interests in property. The rights of creditors will be determined in the bankruptcy proceeding and that may entail a significant delay in realization of even admittedly-due obligations.

Because liens and other security interests are generally respected in bankruptcy, ultimate recovery is likely unless the court determines that the grant was a **voidable preference**.

The bankruptcy trustee has the power to **disaffirm** executory contracts. A person with an executory contract may find that the contract is no longer enforceable and that it gives rise only to an **unsecured claim** that must be established in the bankruptcy proceeding. In the opposite direction, if the contract is advantageous to the debtor, the bankruptcy trustee may elect to enforce the contract for the benefit of the bankrupt estate.

If a creditor has been successful in obtaining payment of an antecedent debt within 90 days before the filing of the bankruptcy petition, the bankruptcy court may view the payment as a **voidable preference**, and compel the creditor to return the payment to the bankrupt estate. If the preferential payment is made to an officer, director, insider, or relative of the debtor, the period to determine whether a preference is preferential is extended to one year. A creditor who has assumed control of a debtor (as may be possible in a workout context) is generally considered an insider.

## §9.10  Limitations on a Bankruptcy Discharge

Voluntary bankruptcy petitions are filed by individuals usually with the goal of obtaining a bankruptcy discharge and a fresh start free of old obligations. However, some debtors are not entitled to a discharge at all, and a discharge does not cover all obligations.

A debtor in Chapter 7 bankruptcy is not entitled to a discharge at all if it is determined that he engaged in acts of dishonesty or refused to cooperate with the bankruptcy proceeding in specified ways: (1) making a fraudulent conveyance within one year of filing the bankruptcy petition; (2) failing to keep or preserve financial records; (3) refusing to testify after immunity is granted following the invocation of the privilege against self-incrimination; (4) failing to explain satisfactorily the loss of assets in connection with the bankruptcy proceedings, or (5) making a false claim against the estate.

These grounds are only applicable to Chapter 7 proceedings. They do not preclude discharge under Chapter 11.

A bankruptcy discharge also does not cover certain classes or types of claims involving individuals in Chapters 7 or 11: (1) most federal tax claims, (2) debts for money, property, or services obtained through fraud, false representations, or false financial statements relied upon by the specific creditor, (3) debts that are not scheduled in the bankruptcy proceeding, (4) child support and alimony, (5) tort liabilities arising from willful and malicious conduct, (6) fines, penalties or forfeitures payable to governmental entities, (7) educational loans, and (8) claims arising from driving while intoxicated.

These exceptions and exclusions are obviously based on policy and social grounds. Depending on the nature of the exception, a creditor of the bankrupt may have the duty to establish that certain of his claims against the debtor should be excluded from the discharge. Typically, however, when an objection to a proposed discharge is made, the debtor has the obligation to establish that he is entitled to the discharge.

# CHAPTER 10

# BUSINESS ORGANIZATIONS

# §10.1  Publicly Held and Closely Held Businesses

This chapter is an introduction to business forms in the United States. There have been important, almost revolutionary changes in this area since 1990.

The phrase "business forms" refers to the legal relationship between a business and its owners. A traditional form of classification is between **unincorporated business forms** (e.g., proprietorships, partnerships, and limited partnerships) on the one hand and **corporations** on the other. This is a useful classification if one is to study the legal principles that apply to various business forms, but it is not a particularly useful economic classification, because the corporate form is suitable for businesses of all sizes.

A second approach is to classify businesses by size (e.g., small businesses and large businesses). Businesses in the United States, however, range from the very small start-up business, perhaps as small as a lemonade stand on a front lawn in the summer, to immense corporations such as General Motors Corporation, with sales in the billions of dollars each year. There is a continuum of business sizes: For any specific business, it is always possible to find another that is either slightly bigger or slightly smaller. Lines drawn based solely on size are therefore necessarily arbitrary.

A third approach, and the one adopted here, is to classify businesses on the basis of whether they are closely held or publicly held. A **closely held business** is one for which there is no established public market for the ownership interests in the business. Usually closely held businesses are small and owned by a few persons. However, some closely held businesses are very large. For example, Brown & Root, Inc., a major construction company, was a publicly held company until 1962 when all of its stock was acquired by Halliburton Company. Brown & Root is still a Delaware corporation; its current name is Kellogg Brown & Root, Inc., and it is an *indirect* subsidiary of Halliburton. All of the Kellogg Brown & Root stock is owned by Dresser Industries, Inc., itself a Delaware corporation all the stock of which is wholly owned by Halliburton. Dresser Industries is a *direct* subsidiary of Halliburton. Halliburton itself is a publicly held corporation with stock traded on the **New York Stock Exchange** (**NYSE**). Its revenue from continuing operations in the third quarter of 2001 was $3.4 billion. What all closely held businesses have in common is that there is no established way for an outside investor to invest in the business and no assurance that current owners can sell their ownership interests and exit from the business. Of course, negotiated purchases or sales of interests in closely held businesses are always possible and occur all the time, but there is no established trading market.

**Publicly held** businesses are those in which a public market exists for ownership interests. The **New York Stock Exchange** (**NYSE**) is the best-known market for shares of stock; the second major market today is the over the counter market known as the **National Association of Securities Dealers Automated Quotation** (**NASDAQ**) system. In addition to these two national markets and the **American Stock Exchange (AMEX)**, several regional markets exist as well as several privately owned trading systems that only very large investors use.

In some other contexts, public businesses may refer to government-owned businesses, which are quite different from the meaning of publicly held business used here. There are several corporations that were formed by the Government of the United States: Two well-known governmental corporations are the Federal Deposit Insurance Corporation (FDIC) that insures bank deposits and the Home Owners Loan Corporation (HOLC) that provides indirect financing for home purchases. As used here, public businesses means private businesses owned in whole or in part by members of the general public. Virtually all publicly held businesses are corporations (though a few have adopted other business forms), and many of them are huge enterprises, with billions of dollars in assets and sales. Because almost all publicly held businesses are corporations, it is customary to refer to them also as publicly held corporations.

## §10.2  Availability of Information About Businesses

Closely held and publicly held businesses differ dramatically in the availability of information about their businesses and affairs. Closely held businesses are essentially private operations. There is usually little publicly available information about them. The only real sources of information are collected by credit reporting agencies and to a lesser extent by compilations of information done by Dunn & Bradstreet and similar organizations that rely on voluntary disclosures. In contrast, publicly held corporations operate in a virtual goldfish bowl: Each publicly held corporation must periodically file information with the Securities and Exchange Commission (SEC) and that information is immediately made available to the public through electronic and other means. If the corporation's shares are traded on a national or regional securities exchange, the corporation must also make public announcements about its affairs. Should someone want to know the compensation of the chief executive officer of Halliburton Corporation the previous year, that is public information available for the asking. However, if someone wants to know the compensation of the president of a closely held corporation, there is usually no way to find out if the business does not want that information known.

It may be noted in passing that the availability of information with respect to publicly held corporations is not directly tied to the presence of an active public market for shares. If a business has made a **public offering** of its ownership interests, it becomes subject to the disclosure requirements outlined above, whether or not a public market for those ownership interests develops. It is quite possible that a relatively small public offering of ownership interests may not lead to the development of an active trading market for shares. Although a market of sorts usually arises following a public offering for shares, that is not necessarily the case, and if a market does develop, it may involve relatively few transactions. The shares are said to be **illiquid**. (A **liquid market** is one in which there is a large amount of trading interest and prices are set by numerous transactions.) An example of an illiquid or nonexistent market that arose following a public offering was the sale of interests in limited partnerships investing in real estate in the 1980s.

## §10.3  The Significance of a Public Market

The absence of a public market for ownership interests in closely held businesses creates problems that do not exist in publicly held corporations. For one thing, there is no easy way to determine how much such an ownership interest is worth. A public market is marked by the presence of buyers and sellers ready, willing, and able to buy and sell. The prices struck in a market are the best guide for what an interest is worth. In a closely held business, one may infer or estimate the value based on techniques described elsewhere in this book, but these values are estimates of what an interest would be worth if there were an active trading market.

For a similar reason it may be difficult or impossible to sell an ownership interest in a closely held business. First one needs to find someone who is interested in making an investment in the business. And, if the present owner is having difficulty finding somebody who is interested in buying, any potential purchasers should realize that they may also have a problem of disposing of the interest if they buy and then later decide to sell. In many situations, the only persons interested in buying will be those who already own an interest in the business, and these buyers may not be willing to offer very much for the interest. This lack of power to exit is to some extent a function of the business form chosen for the closely held business; in some instances, a participant in a closely held business may have the power to compel the business to purchase his or her interest or to liquidate the business. Also, the lack of power to exit may be a function of lack of advance planning. Because of the absence of an established market, it is only prudent for a potential purchaser to obtain a contractual commitment from the business or other owners of the business that they will buy the interest when the purchaser desires to exit.

Yet another facet of the closely held business is that if there is more than one owner, it is possible that one or more persons owning minority interests in the business may be locked in to the business and yet be excluded from any financial participation in the benefits of the business. Minority owners of a closely held business may find that whatever financial rights they have can be granted or withheld by the controlling owner. Where a controlling owner possesses this power, the other owners may be **frozen out** or **squeezed out**. One recurring issue in the law of closely held businesses is the extent to which the legal system should protect minority owners in this situation when there is no contractual obligation by someone to buy that minority interest.

In contrast, investors in a publicly held corporation usually have the power to exit at any time: They can eliminate their investment simply by calling their broker and directing the broker to sell the interest at whatever the current market price is. On the other hand, there are some instances (1) in which very large shareholders of publicly held corporations may find it difficult to sell their interests because of the size of the holdings, and (2) in which SEC regulations prohibit certain owners of shares from reselling them during certain periods.

The balance of this chapter is devoted to a consideration of the various types of business forms that are currently in general use in the United States. Much of this discussion relates to closely held business forms. In the chapters that follow on securities, dividends, and markets, the emphasis is on publicly held corporations.

The radical changes that have occurred since 1990 all involve closely held businesses. They include the development of novel business forms that provide limited liability for owners, specifically, limited liability companies (LLCs) and limited liability partnerships (LLPs), and the promulgation by the Internal Revenue Service (IRS) of regulations, called **check-the-box regulations**, that greatly simplify the system of taxation to which a closely held business will be subject.

## §10.4 Proprietorships

Consider first a business that is to be operated by a single person. Perhaps it is a service business, (e.g., an accountant going into business on her own, an attorney hanging out a shingle, or a person good with his hands putting up a sign offering to do odd repair jobs). In these simple situations, it is almost always convenient to conduct the business as a proprietorship. A proprietorship is simply a business individually owned by a single person.

A business that a single person owns may also be conducted as a corporation. In many states, such a business may also be conducted as a one-person LLC. However, this section is limited to the proprietorship in which no alternative business form is elected.

A proprietor can simply go into business without any concern about business forms. In the very simplest cases, there may be little or no distinction between the affairs of the business and the affairs of the individual owner. However, most proprietors find it necessary or desirable to keep a fair degree of separation between the business and the owner for accounting and record-keeping purposes. At the very least, a set of books should be maintained independent of the personal accounts of the individual owner. This simplifies the preparation of tax returns and permits the owner to identify the profitability of his or her endeavors. It also permits ready identification of property that is formally devoted to the business. Today, a proprietorship also normally has its own bank account, stationery, and other distinguishing characteristics that indicate the separation of business transactions from personal ones.

Whether the degree of separation between the owner's personal and business affairs is large or small, it is useful to discuss the owner (the proprietor) and the business (the proprietorship) as though they were separate entities.

Proprietors may conduct business either in their own name or in a trade or assumed name. Many states have **assumed name statutes** that require a public disclosure of the identity of persons conducting business in a name other than their own, but that is a simple and straightforward process. Proprietorships often do business and enter into contracts in the form Joan Jones dba Jones Construction Company. The **dba** (or **d/b/a**) stands for "doing business as." In this way, both the proprietor and the trade name under which the proprietor is conducting business appear on most business transactions. There are few restrictions on the use of trade or assumed names: As long as the name is not misleadingly similar to the name of a competing business or otherwise used in a fraudulent or deceptive manner, a person may conduct business in any name he or she wishes. However, a few words, such as **Corporation, Incorporated**, or **Inc.** may not be used because they falsely imply that the business is incorporated. The word **company** does not carry this implication.

The owner of a proprietorship may act individually or employ one or more agents, employees, or managers to act on his or her behalf. As a result, the proprietor can delegate business-related activity and decisions freely to subordinates or employees. Thus, the benefits of efficiency and flexibility that arise from specialization and separation of functions are as readily available in a proprietorship as they are in other forms of business enterprise.

A proprietorship's owner is entitled to the fruits of the business, that is, its income and cash flow (after making due provision for its debts), without any formality or difficulty. For example, a proprietor may simply empty the cash drawer of the business to pay for his or her personal vacation if that does not disrupt business operations and if appropriate records are maintained.

For legal purposes, a proprietorship is not a separate entity. For example, the owner of a proprietorship is liable for all business debts. A proprietor of a business may borrow money on his or her personal credit either for personal use (e.g., a family vacation) or for use in the business. If such a loan is unsecured, the creditor may levy upon either personal or business assets if there is a default without regard to whether the loan was originally used for business or personal purposes. Loans may also be obtained solely in the name of, and on the credit of, the proprietorship, but proprietors are individually liable on such loans whether or not their name appears on the note or whether they actually negotiated the loan and signed the note. Often a proprietorship purchases inventory, supplies, or machinery in its assumed name on credit secured by a lien or security interest in the property being purchased. The owner of the business is personally liable on these obligations as well, though the creditor in these situations may as a practical matter look only to the property securing the loan or to the assets of the business itself in determining whether to extend credit.

Similarly, if the business becomes involved in litigation, the proprietor is the appropriate plaintiff; if the business is sued, the proprietor is the proper defendant. In litigation involving a proprietorship, it is customary in many jurisdictions to use the dba designation when describing the party suing or being sued.

A proprietorship is not a separate taxable entity and no separate federal income tax return is filed, though proprietors must file a **Schedule C** with their personal return showing revenues and expenses of the business. Proprietors must also obtain an employer's identification number from the IRS. The business may also need to obtain local permits to engage in specific businesses or occupy space for commercial purposes. Again, these permits are usually issued in the dba form. If it is a law, medical, or accounting practice, of course, the owner must be a licensed professional.

If the proprietorship opens an office in a different state, there are no additional formalities or consents required other than those applicable to anyone engaging in that business in the new state.

## §10.5  General Partnerships

General partnerships have a long history. Enterprises in Babylonian times had many characteristics of a modern partnership, and partnerships were well known in England in medieval times.

A partnership is a logical extension of a proprietorship when there is more than one owner. A partnership (sometimes called a **general partnership** to distinguish it from the **limited partnership**, discussed below) is the operation of a business by co-owners. It can be formed simply by a handshake. There is generally no need for a written agreement and no public filing of any document other than an assumed name certificate that may be required if the business is conducted under a trade name and not the names of the partners. With respect to local permits and qualifications, interstate operations and the like, generally the same rules apply to partnerships as to proprietorships.

Some additional complexity is created, of course, simply because there is more than one owner. In a proprietorship, the owner calls all the shots. In a partnership, there is more than one owner, and ground rules are needed for determining how decisions are to be made and how the rights of individual partners are to be ascertained.

## §10.6  Sources of Partnership Law

The law of partnership was largely codified in the **Uniform Partnership Act (UPA)**, approved in 1914, that was adopted by virtually every state without significant change. In the 1980s, interest in partnership law increased dramatically as a result of changes in federal income tax law, and some states adopted significant revisions to their uniform acts. These changes, in turn, led to a revision of the UPA in 1994. However, although some smaller states have adopted the **Revised Uniform Partnership Act (RUPA)** without change, many states have not. Further, some states made significant revisions to the 1994 version, with the result that statutory partnership law in the United States is now not at all uniform. In addition, some areas of partnership law are still governed by common law principles. Although significant variations in partnership law exist, there is, as in many areas of law, a common core of principles and understanding.

The primary source of law relating to a specific partnership is the partnership agreement. Partnership agreements may be written or oral, but there is a strong trend toward written agreements, at least for larger partnerships. Partners are able to structure their relationships by appropriate provisions in the partnership agreement to a considerably greater extent than participants in other forms of business enterprise. The partnership agreement is called the law of that particular partnership. The RUPA departs from this consensual model in two important respects:

1. RUPA includes a variety of **default provisions** that govern aspects of the partnership relation in the absence of express agreement. These default provisions are most likely to be applicable to handshake partnerships without formal written partnership agreements and partnership arrangements entered into by nonlawyers without legal assistance. However, even carefully drafted partnership agreements sometimes do not cover all matters. These default provisions may not always be the provisions that would have been selected by the partners for the specific situation if the possibility of that situation arising had been brought to their attention at the time the partnership agreement was being negotiated. It is generally desirable to agree explicitly on basic rights, powers, and duties rather than to rely on these default provisions.

2. The RUPA contains a list of provisions governing the relationships among partners that cannot be varied by the agreement among partners except to the extent specifically authorized by the statute. These mandatory provisions include the power of every partner to dissolve the partnership by his or her express will at any time, the unlimited liability of every partner for partnership obligations, and the apparent authority of partners to bind the partnership to obligations within the apparent scope of the corporate business. These mandatory provisions largely codify fundamental common law partnership principles.

## §10.7  Control and Management

In the absence of an agreement to the contrary, the partners in a partnership have equal rights to participate in the management of the business, which can be conducted with whatever degree of informality the partners desire. The default rule is that if a vote is taken on specific matters, each partner has one vote and the majority decision controls in the absence of an agreement to the contrary. There is no specification, however, of the required quorum. When financial contributions are unequal, the normal assumption is that votes should be weighted in accordance with relative financial interests rather than being on a per capita basis, but this is not the case unless the partners so agree.

The partnership agreement may create classes of partners with different voting and financial rights. For example, classes of junior or senior partners may be created, or a managing partner or management committee with designated rights and responsibilities may be established. Many law firms use classes of partners to ensure that senior partners have power to govern the affairs of the partnership and share in the returns of the partnership in a manner different from more junior partners. Some law firms distinguish between income partners and equity partners. Depending upon the terms of the specific partnership agreement, an income partner may be virtually indistinguishable from an associate in the law firm.

Partners also have apparent and actual authority to bind the partnership to obligations relating to the business of the partnership. Thus, a partner may bind the partnership on obligations that the partner was not authorized to create. The partner so acting is presumably in breach of the partner's obligations under the partnership agreement, but the partnership is nevertheless bound by the commitment entered into by the partner.

## §10.8  Financial Provisions

Partners may share profits and losses in any way they agree, and they may agree to share losses in a different way than they share profits. Profits may be shared on a flat percentage basis, in proportion to the relative financial investments in the partnership, on a sliding scale based on receipts attributable to each partner's efforts, or on some other basis. One or more partners may be paid a fixed salary that the agreement requires to be viewed as an expense of the business (i.e., deducted from revenues before calculating distributable income). Alternatively, the agreement may provide that the salary is to be charged against the partner's distributive share with the proviso that no refund is required in any year in which the salary exceeds that partner's distributive share for the year. This arrangement is called a **guaranteed payment**. In the absence of an agreement about how profits are to be shared, the default rule under both the UPA and the RUPA is that partners share profits equally, and that losses are shared in the same proportion as profits are shared.

Because profits are determined on an annual basis, **drawing accounts** or advances may be authorized so that each partner may draw specified amounts monthly or weekly against the ultimate distribution of profits. Many partnership agreements provide for different ownership accounts for each partner: a **capital account**, reflecting amounts invested by each partner in the business, an **income account** to which is credited income as it is ascertained and allocated among the partners, and the drawing account described above. The drawing account is usually closed out against the income account on an annual basis. Income earned in excess of distributions may be paid to each partner in a lump sum shortly after the close of the accounting period, or may be added to the capital account in whole or in part to be retained by the partnership or withdrawn by the partner at a later time.

Partnerships must retain a separate set of tax books to reflect the tax obligations of each partner. The central account in the tax records is the capital account of each partner. The capital account is the amount each partner has invested in the partnership; it is increased by earnings and decreased by distributions or losses. In partnership practice, a distinction is drawn between allocations of **income** and allocations of **cash available for distribution**. Allocations of income determine tax liability, while allocations of cash determine how much a partner can withdraw and is based on the cash flow within the partnership.

Each partner is unlimitedly liable for the debts of the partnership. This unlimited liability is ultimately independent of whatever agreement exists among the partners as to how losses should be shared. In other words, any partner may be called on by a creditor at any time to pay a specific partnership debt. But there are significant procedural hurdles in many states that effectively require the plaintiff to pursue the partnership first. Moreover, under the RUPA, the plaintiff must do so. If a partner pays a debt on behalf of the partnership, that partner then has a right to reimbursement from the partnership or from the other partners in accordance with the agreed-on loss-sharing ratio. If one or more partners is insolvent or unable to pay the agreed share of partnership losses, the solvent partners must do so. In the 1990s, a major variation of the general partnership, an LLP, described below, has been created that dramatically modifies these rules of unlimited personal liability for each partner.

A distinction is made in partnership law between **partnership obligations** and **nonpartnership obligations** of individual partners. The distinction is basically between business debts of the partnership and personal or individual debts of a partner. A personal creditor of a partner cannot attach or seize partnership assets: Such a creditor must proceed against the interest of the partner in the partnership through the device of a **charging order**. The protection of partnership assets against seizure by individual creditors reflects the fact that all partners have interests in partnership assets and that a partnership business should not be disrupted because of the financial problems of an individual partner.

## §10.9  Contributions of Property or Services

The contributions of one partner to a partnership may differ from the contributions of other partners either in amount or in kind. For example, it is very common for one partner to contribute his or her services, primarily or exclusively, while one or more other partners contribute capital or property, primarily or exclusively. Both service and capital partners may therefore participate in the management of the business financed by the capital-contributing partners.

In negotiating a partnership agreement that involves dissimilar contributions, interests may conflict; a single lawyer should be very cautious about agreeing to represent different interests simultaneously in such a situation. Each partner should be encouraged to have individual legal representation.

When one partner is contributing services over a period of time for a partnership interest, and another partner is contributing capital immediately, difficult issues may arise as to when the service partner should be deemed to have earned his or her interest, what the value of the contributed services is, and what the responsibilities of the respective partners are if the partnership incurs losses. The default provisions of the UPA and the RUPA are unhelpful in this regard because they simply provide that in the absence of agreement, (a) partners are not entitled to compensation for services rendered on behalf of the partnership and (b) as among themselves, each partner must contribute toward losses in accordance with the partner's share of the profits.

In law partnerships, when an associate is made a partner, provision may be made for the new partner to make a capital contribution to the partnership; as a practical matter this contribution is often in the form of reduced cash distributions for a limited period of time.

## §10.10 Dissolution, Winding Up, and Continuation of the Business

A partnership is dissolved in a variety of circumstances set forth in the UPA, including, for example, the death or bankruptcy of a partner, but the unique feature of partnership law that distinguishes it from corporation law is that each partner has the power to dissolve the relationship at any time. The word "**dissolution**" is used in an unusual way in the UPA; it refers to the termination of the legal relationship among the partners, not to the **winding up** and disposition of the partnership business. In the RUPA, the term "**dissociation**" is used to refer to the termination of the legal relationship; dissolution refers to the winding up of the business. In this section, dissolution is used in the UPA sense to refer to the legal relationship.

Exercise of the power to dissolve a partnership at any time may lead to adverse consequences, because any partner may exercise this power to advance his or her own personal interests. These problems may be avoided somewhat if the partnership agreement provides that the partnership is to continue for a specified term or until the occurrence of a specified event. If so, early dissolution by a partner is a breach of the partnership agreement and opens the dissolving party to liability for breach of contract. On the other hand, if the partnership agreement is silent and does not set forth a specified term, a **partnership at will** has been created that may be dissolved at any time without liability. Informal partnerships are almost always partnerships at will. A partnership that is to continue for a specified term or until the occurrence of a specified event is called a **partnership for a term**.

Partnership agreements often provide that upon the death or withdrawal of a partner, the partnership continues and the withdrawing partner is entitled to receive the value of the partnership interest as specified in the agreement. The agreement often specifies how the value is to be calculated and the period over which it is to be paid. Provisions of this nature are binding on the withdrawing partner in accordance with the general principle that the partnership agreement is the law of that partnership. In the absence of an agreement, the statutory default provisions of the original UPA provide that upon the dissolution of a partnership, the withdrawing partner may compel the partnership business to be wound up and liquidated or may permit the partnership business to continue and instead to receive the value of the partnership interest at the time of dissolution plus, at the election of the withdrawing partner, either interest or a continuing share of the profits until payment is made. The RUPA changes this pattern by giving the remaining partners an option to continue the partnership, if they wish, by paying the withdrawing partner the value of his or her partnership share plus interest. The option to receive either interest or profits was eliminated at the same time.

When the partnership continues, a question sometimes arises as to whether a new partnership has been created following the dissolution of the old, or whether the old partnership continues, at least with respect to the partners who remain in the business. This appears to be purely a conceptual question on which no substantive issue turns.

## §10.11 Fiduciary Duties

The relation among partners is one of trust and confidence. This follows necessarily from the agency powers of each partner to bind the partnership to obligations as well as the concept of cooperative enterprise inherent in a partnership. The relation of trust and confidence is enforced judicially through the recognition of a broad fiduciary duty each partner owes to the other in connection with all matters relating to the partnership. This duty may require voluntary disclosure of relevant information. It continues to exist even though the partners are antagonistic to each other and are in the process of dissolving their relationship; it also covers all activities relating to the use and distribution of partnership property. In many states, this fiduciary duty is vigorously enforced.

## §10.12 The Partnership as an Entity

A long and rather sterile debate exists as to whether a partnership should be viewed as a separate legal entity or whether it is, like a proprietorship, simply an extension of the individual partners without separate legal status. The distinction is usually phrased in terms of whether a partnership is an **entity** or an **aggregate** of the partners. The UPA contains internal evidence of both theories: Much of the early case law adopts the aggregate theory, but the RUPA and modern case law almost uniformly view the partnership as a separate legal entity. The characterization may be important when analyzing issues not specifically addressed in the UPA.

A partnership is not an entity for purposes of most state statutes requiring foreign entities to register if they transact business in the state. It is usually viewed as an entity for purposes of litigation (though rules differ from state to state). In many states, for example, it is possible to sue a partnership without suing any of the partners individually, and partners may be held individually liable only if the complaint or other process expressly states that recovery is being sought from their individual assets. These rules about procedure and civil process, of course, do not affect the basic responsibility of each partner for the debts of the partnership if they are made defendants in the litigation.

## §10.13 Federal Income Taxation of a Partnership

A partnership is not a separate taxable entity under the Internal Revenue Code (IRC). Under the IRC, a partnership must prepare an **information**

**return** each year that shows partnership income and expenses, and allocates the income or loss of the partnership to the individual partners in accordance with the partnership agreement. Each individual partner must then include in his or her personal income tax return the amount of the income or loss so allocated. A positive allocation of income to a specific partner for tax purposes may occur even though the partnership may not in fact make any distributions of cash or property to that partner with respect to the year in question. Similarly, a partnership may have a loss for tax purposes in one or more years even though it makes substantial capital distributions during those years to the partners.

The provisions of the IRC and the regulations issued thereunder are exceptionally complex. This complexity is doubtless a deterrent to the use of partnership forms in some instances, even though under the tax rules in effect in 1997, the partnership form of taxation usually minimizes the aggregate tax obligations of the business and owners. Partnership taxation and how it differs from the taxation of corporations is discussed in more detail later in this chapter.

## §10.14 Miscellaneous

A general partnership, unlike many other forms of business, does not make a public filing in order to be legally formed. When a partnership has offices in more than one state (as many law firms do), which state law governs that partnership? When the UPA (1914) was in effect in virtually all states, this question was not as important as it is today with the numerous differences in the state law of partnership that have developed. The RUPA refers to the home office of a partnership, but does not define it. Presumably, each partnership is free to designate which office is its home office.

It is highly desirable not only to have an agreement dealing with the various rights of partners but also to have it reduced to writing so that rights and duties are explicitly defined and known not only to the partners themselves but also to their heirs and assignees. The preparation of such an agreement usually requires the services of a lawyer and thus increases the costs of formation. Even in situations in which cost is no problem, a surprisingly large number of partnerships, including some law partnerships, operate successfully for many years without a written agreement. Of course, the partners may have verbal or implicit understandings as to how the business should be conducted. Major problems are likely to arise, however, if there is a falling out between partners and upon a partner's death or retirement.

Whether or not there is a formal written agreement, a partnership is inherently a more complex and expensive manner of conducting business than a single person running a proprietorship. Nevertheless, it is usually less expensive than alternative forms of business operation involving several owners, and is often the most convenient form of operation for many small businesses if the unlimited liability of each partner for partnership obligations is not a matter of serious concern to any partner.

## §10.15 Joint Ventures

Many cases involving partnership-like relations describe the relationship as a **joint venture** rather than a partnership. If there is any difference, it is that a joint venture involves a more limited business purpose than a partnership—perhaps a partnership for a single transaction. Most partnership rules are applicable to joint ventures; the major difference is the scope of the actual and apparent authority that each joint venturer possesses to bind the venture.

There is some tendency for courts to accept the categorization of the agreement itself. However, there appear to be relatively few practical differences in the legal principles applicable to a partnership and to a joint venture.

The phrase "joint venture" may also be used in a broader sense to refer to any cooperative enterprise, no matter what form of business the enterprise takes. For example, in 1943, when Dow Chemical Company and Corning Glass Works, Inc. decided to form a joint venture to develop the commercial and military use of silicones, the two companies actually formed a third corporation, Dow Corning, Inc., with each company owning 50 percent of the stock of Dow Corning. A more appropriate phrase for this type of enterprise might be a joint venture corporation.

Joint venture arrangements today may also take the form of an LLC.

## §10.16 Limited Partnerships

A limited partnership differs from a general partnership in that there are two classes of partners, one or more **general partners**, and one or more **limited partners**, who are not personally liable for the debts of the partnership and who are not expected to participate in the partnership's day-to-day affairs. In effect, limited partners are passive investors who stand to lose what they have invested in the enterprise but no more. Partners who are not specifically identified as limited partners are general partners and are unlimitedly liable for the debts of the business.

Limited partnerships were attractive in the 1970s and 1980s, because they provided a combination of factors that were not then obtainable in any other business form at the time: partnership type taxation for federal income tax purposes and limited liability for investors. The 1970s were the heyday of the **tax shelter** and most of these shelters were created as limited partnerships in real estate, race horses, railway freight cars, cable television companies, and a variety of other investments that promised to generate tax deductions in excess of the amount contributed. Many had hundreds or thousands of limited partners. Even after the Tax Reform Act of 1986 closed off the most egregious tax shelters, the limited partnership continued to be widely used for many types of real estate ventures in which this combination of income tax treatment and limited liability was attractive. Many of these limited partnerships continue to exist today. Unfortunately, most of them have turned out very badly for investors, and special legislation was enacted in 1990 in an effort to give these investors greater protection.

The development of the LLC in the early 1990s, discussed below, has greatly reduced the popularity of the limited partnership form of business. The LLC not only combines limited liability for all investors with federal partnership-type taxation but also avoids technical problems associated with the management roles of limited partners in a limited partnership. The limited partnership continues to be used in master limited partnerships described in §10.18 and in family limited partnerships described in §10.19. LLCs appear to have largely supplanted limited partnerships in all other areas.

## §10.17  Corporate General Partners

The tax shelter era shaped another development that continues to affect all unincorporated business forms—the use of a corporate general partner or corporate manager to manage the business and affairs of the unincorporated business. Until the middle of the 20th century, doubt existed whether a corporation could be a general partner in a partnership. But the modern view, accepted today apparently in all states, is that corporations may act as general partners to the same extent as individuals can.

Tax shelter limited partnerships created during the 1970s and 1980s typically had only one general partner, a corporation. There might be hundreds or thousands of limited partners whose sole function was to provide the capital needed for the enterprise, and who hoped to obtain tax benefits in the form of deductible losses exceeding the capital invested. Later, in the 1980s, investors in limited partnerships hoped to obtain tax-sheltered income rather than tax losses.

The use of a corporate general partner results in a partnership in which no individual may be personally liable for the partnership obligations. The IRS recognized these organizations as eligible for partnership taxation as long as the corporate general partner had substantial assets invested in the partnership. Today, under the check-the-box regulations, a limited partnership with a nominally financed corporate general partner may simply elect partnership taxation.

A major disadvantage of the limited partnership as a tax-oriented investment vehicle is that the provisions relating to distributions and allocations of income, loss, and excess cash flow in partnerships are extremely complex. This was particularly true of tax shelter limited partnership agreements, which usually provided for the allocation of income or loss on one basis and the allocation of excess cash on a different basis. These ratios might shift after the limited partners received the return of their cash investments in order to increase the shares allocable to the corporate general partner that was owned by the original promoters.

## §10.18  Master Limited Partnerships

In 1986, Congress amended the IRC to discourage tax shelters and to reduce marginal tax rates applicable to individuals and to corporations. One inadvertent consequence of these tax rate changes was to make partnership-type taxation much more attractive than corporate-type taxation for profitable businesses.

It did not take long for entrepreneurs to recognize that there was a tax advantage of creating publicly traded limited partnerships. These organizations created limited partnership interests that were readily marketable and traded either over-the-counter or on securities exchanges much as though they were shares of stock. This public trading was technically trading in the form of depository receipts for limited partnership interests rather than in the interests themselves. These organizations were known as **master limited partnerships**.

Most master limited partnerships were concentrated in certain types of businesses (e.g., extraction of natural resources), but the tax benefits were potentially available in many areas. As the use of master limited partnerships spread to new kinds of business, Congress was faced with the threatened disincorporation of publicly held businesses. A statute hurriedly enacted in 1987 closed off this approach by requiring that entities with publicly traded ownership interests must be taxed as corporations without regard to the business form adopted. However, master limited partnerships created prior to the effective date of this legislation were not phased out, and some of these organizations were permitted to continue indefinitely. With these exceptions, all business entities that have or develop a public market for ownership interests must be taxed as corporations.

## §10.19  Family Limited Partnerships

One area where limited partnerships continue to thrive are in **family limited partnerships** (**FLPs**). FLPs are family arrangements created by affluent parents and grandparents primarily to minimize gift and estate taxes upon the distributions of wealth to children and grandchildren. An FLP also facilitates the management and distribution of family assets, simplifies the annual gifting of assets to younger generations, and assures that unrestricted funds are not transferred to younger adults before they are capable of handling them.

FLPs provide tax savings essentially because gift and estate taxes are calculated on the value of the interest received by the donee and not on the cost of the interest to the donor. The way it works is as follows: Assume that Elderly Parent has liquid securities with a current market value of $3,000,000 that she wishes to give to her three adult children. At the gift tax rates applicable in 2001, if she simply gave each $1,000,000, her gift tax liability could be as much as $345,800 for each gift.

It would be much more sensible for Elderly Parent to create a limited partnership. With the assistance of her attorney she can create a limited partnership agreement that names himself (or a trusted relative) as the sole general partner, and also authorizes the creation of 300 limited partnership units each entitled to an equal share of the assets of the limited partnership. The limited partnership agreement provides that it will be irrevocable for ten years and thereafter may be terminated either by the general partner or by a majority vote of the holders of limited partnership interests, with voting weighted according to economic interests in the limited partnership. She then transfers the $3,000,000 to the limited partnership. As the sole general partner Elderly Parent then adopts a strategy of giving limited partnership interests each year to her three adult children (or their children). Assume that she gives a child ten limited partnership units. How is the value of that gift to be determined? The "cost" of those ten units is $100,000 when looked at from Elderly Parent's perspective. However, Elderly Parent is making a gift of limited partnership interests, not a gift of cash. The issue for gift and estate tax purposes is not the "cost" of the gift, but the value of the gift to the recipient. What are ten units worth today? The units are a minority interest in a limited partnership. They carry no power to participate in the management of the limited partnership for at least ten years, and the termination date of the limited partnership is not known. How much would a third person pay for an interest that is so uncertain? Certainly a purchaser would discount the value of the limited partnership units dramatically. And the value of the gift for gift tax purposes is that discounted value, whatever it is. Presumably a discount of 50 percent or even more from the $100,000 "cost" could be justified.

Gift tax liability is established by the value of the gift at the time it is made. Presumably Elderly Parent or her trusted relative will make similar gifts each year in the future; the number of units gifted in a particular year is at the discretion of the general partner; there is no requirement that equal distributions be made each year to each child, so that special needs may be taken into account if desirable.

In effect Elderly Parent has distributed a portion of her personal wealth while incurring a minimal gift tax. That is the beauty of FLPs (from the standpoint of wealthy parents): The FLP minimizes gift and estate taxes while preserving freedom of distribution in the future.

## §10.20  Corporations

A corporation is a relatively complex form of business that plays a vital role in American society. Aspects of financial concepts relating to corporations and trading in securities of corporations are discussed at length in subsequent chapters. This introductory discussion presents the most fundamental aspects of corporateness, primarily in the context of closely held businesses.

## §10.21  What Is a Corporation?

A corporation is usually viewed as a fictitious legal entity separate from its owners, the shareholders. The fictitious entity is created by a public filing with the secretary of state (or other designated public official in the state) and the payment of a filing fee. In comparison to proprietorships and general partnerships, this is a relatively expensive form of business organization, because legal assistance is usually involved not only in its creation but also in its continued operation. Operational costs at the state level are relatively high because all states impose annual franchise or stock taxes on corporations. Further, a corporation engaged in business in several states may need to qualify to transact business in each state and thereby become subject to taxation in each state.

The nature of the corporation has never been precisely defined. A corporation can be envisioned as an artificial person having most of the same powers, rights, and duties of an individual. This artificial person has no flesh, no blood, no eyes, or mouth, but it may nevertheless do many things that real people do: it may sue and be sued, enter into contracts, purchase property, run a business, and so forth. There is a particularly lively controversy over how publicly held corporations should be viewed. The oldest view is that the shareholders are the ultimate owners of the enterprise, and the officers, directors, and employees are agents whom the shareholders hire to manage the business on their behalf. Many legal theorists have rejected this approach because it does not accurately describe the role actually played by shareholders. Many prefer to view the corporation as a "nexus of contracts," an aggregate of various inputs being provided by contract to achieve the common goal of producing goods and services. Shareholders are simply one of the contract participants in this enterprise, providing equity capital and bearing the principal risk of loss. A majority of modern legal theorists adopt this view. A third approach, the team production model, views the corporation as a nexus or combination of team-specific assets created by shareholders, managers, employees, and others; the role of the board of directors is to allocate these gains from joint efforts among the firm participants in an acceptable way. In some of these modern views, the corporation may be analogized to a process or a form of management organization, and not viewed as a thing at all.

In considering what it really means to conduct business in the corporate form, it is useful to consider the one-person corporation, (i.e., a corporation in which one single individual owns all the outstanding shares of the corporation). In effect, the business is an incorporated proprietorship. One should understand precisely what the notion of a fictitious entity means in this situation. In practical and economic effect, the shareholder runs the business much as though it were a proprietorship. The shareholder decides what business the corporation should be in, whether it should enter into specific contracts, what price to charge for its products, and so forth. The shareholder in a sense also owns the entire corporation, because she owns all the outstanding shares. Indeed, the combination of total ownership and total control in this situation often leads the shareholder to believe that the shareholder owns the corporation's business and property much as though the business were conducted in the form of an unincorporated proprietorship. I own this business, the shareholder may proudly say. Although this is true in an economic sense, in the legal sense it is not at all true. If a business is incorporated, the business's assets are owned by the corporation, not by the person who owns the shares in the corporation. The shares are property, but they are not the corporate assets.

Further, the shareholder exercises control over corporation activities not through ownership of business assets but by serving the corporation basically as its sole agent. Then again, a fictitious entity can only act through agents. Assume that a sole shareholder decides she wants to be employed by the corporation and receive a salary. Acting as agent on behalf of the corporation, she offers herself employment with the corporation at a salary in a specified amount, and acting as an individual she may then accept the corporation's offer. This is not a sham transaction for most purposes: the IRS, for example, unhesitatingly recognizes the validity of such transactions if the compensation is reasonable in amount, giving the corporation a deduction for salaries paid, requiring the corporation to withhold for federal income taxes, FICA, and the like, and requiring the shareholder to include as wages the amount paid to her under this arrangement.

Where does the sole shareholder in this example obtain the authority from the fictitious entity to act as its agent and offer herself the employment contract? That is the subject of corporation law: The corporation's affairs are managed by a board of directors elected by the shareholders; the sole shareholder thus elects the board of directors (which may consist of only herself in most states), and the board of directors then appoints a president or other officer (who again may be the sole shareholder) to negotiate the employment contract on behalf of the corporation. It is all a bit incestuous.

The corporation provides limited liability for the shareholders, because all obligations are entered into in the name of the corporation rather than in the names of the individual owners, and the corporation is a separate legal entity. Further, an agent (who may or may not be a shareholder) who commits the corporation to a transaction giving rise to liability is not personally liable on obligations negotiated on the principal's—the corporation's—behalf under accepted agency principles. The result is that a corporation, unlike a general partnership, provides (at least in theory) limited liability for its owners, and, unlike the limited partnership, the persons with limited liability in a corporation may participate freely in its management and control as long as they stay in their proper role as agents of the fictitious entity. Of course, sophisticated creditors are unlikely to be willing to deal with a small corporation with limited assets unless the shareholders agree to give personal guarantees to pay the corporate debt. Thus, as a practical matter, in the very small corporation, the protection against unlimited liability provided by the corporate form is not as important as might first appear.

There is obviously an element of play-acting in closely held corporations, because the formalities that must be followed do not reflect the reality that the business is actually owned and operated by individuals; the theory assumes that the same individuals assume different roles as shareholders, directors, or agents, and act according to the appropriate role. But there is a serious aspect to these formalities. A failure to follow them may result in the court **piercing the corporate veil**—and holding shareholders personally liable on corporation debts.

Because a corporation can have only one shareholder, a sole proprietor may decide to incorporate his or her business without losing control and without having to cut other people in on the action.

## §10.22  Sources of Corporation Law

The major source of corporation law is state corporation statutes, the provisions of which vary from state to state. The variation is considerably wider than the statutes relating to partnerships or limited partnerships, although there is a surprising core of uniformity in these statutes. Part of this uniformity may be traced to the Model Business Corporation Act drafted by a committee of the American Bar Association, and part may be traced to the leadership of the state of Delaware in developing significant principles of corporation law. Part may be traced to the natural tendency of one state to copy statutes that embody good ideas that other states develop.

State corporation statutes deal with issues of formation, corporate purposes and powers, internal organization (the roles of shareholders, directors, and officers), permissible securities that corporations may issue in order to raise capital, mergers and consolidations of corporations, foreign corporations, and dissolution. In addition, states may require annual reports as well as franchise tax returns and other reporting requirements. These state statutes thus largely deal with the internal relationships within a corporation, but they also may affect other important aspects of corporation behavior. State corporation statutes are largely technical in nature and generally not the subject of extensive debate in state legislatures. Committees of the state bar association develop many proposed changes in corporation statutes, although these provisions must run the same legislative gauntlet as any other proposed legislation.

In the United States, there is no federal or national corporation statute. Every domestic corporation, no matter how large, is incorporated under the statute of some state—usually Delaware in the case of the largest corporations. Two New Deal federal statutes—the Securities Act of 1933 and the Securities Exchange Act of 1934—provide a substantial degree of federal regulation, particularly for large corporations with more than 500 shareholders.

In addition to state corporation statutes, all states have adopted blue sky laws that regulate the public sale of corporate securities within the state.

## §10.23  The Internal Structure of a Corporation

The internal organization of a corporation consists of three levels or tiers: shareholders, directors, and officers.

Shareholders are persons who own shares in a corporation. Shares represent the ultimate ownership interests in the corporation. Shares may be divided into two or more different classes with different financial and voting rights. As described above, one individual may own all the shares of a corporation; at the other extreme, there is no limit on the number of shareholders or the number of shares that a corporation may issue, so that a corporation may have thousands or even millions of shareholders. Despite the wide gulf between a corporation that one person owns and a corporation with hundreds of thousands of shareholders, the two corporations are largely governed by the same theoretical organizational structure.

The board of directors has the responsibility of managing, or overseeing the management of, the corporation's business. Historically, the traditional statute required a board of directors to consist of at least three directors; today, in most states, a board of directors may consist of a single director, though in some states the privilege of having a board of one or two members is limited to corporations with one or two shareholders. In a few states, three directors are still required; in these states, sole proprietors planning to incorporate their business must find two loyal persons to serve as directors with them.

The board of directors selects corporate officers to execute the decisions of the board and conduct the business on a day-to-day basis. Traditional officers are a president, one or more vice presidents, a secretary, and a treasurer, though many modern statutes do not require designated offices. Most modern statutes also permit a single person to hold more than one office simultaneously, though a fair number of statutes require the corporate president and secretary to be different persons. Corporate officers may also have discretion to appoint additional assistant officers and employees. In large, publicly held corporations, the corporate officers—often collectively referred to as management—may have the broadest discretion in fact on both routine and extraordinary matters. The theory, however, is that the ultimate power of management and control rests in the board of directors, not the officers of the corporation.

There is no requirement that officers or directors also be shareholders, though such a requirement may be imposed voluntarily by appropriate provisions in the corporation's governing documents. In some states, special close corporation statutes give small corporations the option of adopting management principles much as though they were general partnerships.

## §10.24 Documents Governing Corporate Internal Affairs

The two basic documents within every corporation are the **articles of incorporation** and the **bylaws**. The articles of incorporation are filed with the appropriate state agency to form the corporation and are the basic constitution of that particular corporation. Terminology in this respect is not uniform from one state to another: In some states this basic constitutional document is known as the **charter** or the **certificate of incorporation** or by other names. In many states, the filing authority issues a certificate of incorporation to reflect that articles of incorporation have been filed and approved. Amendment of articles of incorporation generally requires approval by a specified vote of the shareholders as well as approval by the board of directors.

The bylaws constitute an internal set of rules for the governance of a corporation. They deal with such matters as elections, notices, size of board of directors, restrictions on the transfer of shares, and similar matters. The bylaws may usually be amended by the board of directors acting alone, or by the shareholders.

Many provisions relating to the corporation's internal affairs may be placed either in the articles of incorporation or the bylaws, at the option of the management of the corporation. Provisions placed in the articles of incorporation become a matter of public record: Where the number of shareholders is large, they may be more difficult to amend. Many lawyers prefer that important and unusual governance provisions appear in the articles of incorporation rather than the bylaws, because the provisions are then a matter of public record.

## §10.25 The Population of Corporations

It is sometimes not fully appreciated that even though closely held and publicly held corporations differ widely in form and structure, they are all cast from the single mold of the state corporation statutes. Thus, both have the same internal tripartite structure described above: shareholders, a board of directors, and corporate officers. As a result, they share a common core of legal principles despite the very different—indeed, radically different—economic and social environments in which they operate.

Nearly half of all publicly held corporations are incorporated in the state of Delaware. The General Corporation Law of that state is therefore virtually a national code for publicly held corporations. Many corporations change their state of incorporation to Delaware when they plan to become publicly held.

Many publicly held companies are quite large. The so-called Fortune 500—the 500 largest corporations as determined by *Fortune* magazine—is comprised almost entirely of publicly held companies. These companies each have billions of dollars of assets and annual sales, thousands of employees, and usually tens or hundreds of thousands of shareholders. These corporations possess tremendous economic and political power merely from their size and their importance to the economy of communities, cities, and indeed, whole states.

Most corporations in the United States, however, are very small and closely held. In 1993, the IRS received about 3,965,000 corporate federal income tax returns. Of these returns, 3,278,000 reflected receipts of less than $1,000,000. It is unlikely that very many, if any, of these corporations had more than a handful of shareholders.

There were 687,000 corporations in 1993 that had annual receipts of more than $1,000,000. They constituted about 17 percent of all corporations filing tax returns in 1993. However, the economic importance of these 687,000 corporations dwarfs the other 3,278,000. The receipts of these 687,000 corporations constituted 94 percent of all business receipts reported by the 3,965,000 filing corporations.

The American Law Institute's Corporate Governance Project in 1984 estimated that there were between 1,500 and 2,000 corporations with more than 2,000 shareholders and $100,000,000 of assets, and that there were between 5,500 and 6,000 corporations with more than 500 shareholders and $3,000,000 of assets. These figures, which are unlikely to have changed materially since 1984, indicate that most corporations with more than $1,000,000 of business receipts are themselves relatively small when compared, for example, with the 30 corporations that compose the Dow Jones Industrial Average.

## §10.26  The Registration of Public Offerings of Securities

Corporations with more than $10 million of assets and an outstanding class of securities held by more than 500 shareholders of record are subject to special regulation under the federal **Securities Exchange Act of 1934** (the **1934 Act**), including requirements that the corporation register with the SEC and make public periodic financial information. Corporations with securities registered under the 1934 Act (often called, not surprisingly, **registered corporations**) are all publicly held corporations.

Corporations usually do not gradually grow in size and the number of shareholders until they become subject to the disclosure requirements of the 1934 Act. They instead first become subject to SEC regulation when they make an **initial public offering** (**IPO**) of their shares. The important point here is that a different federal statute, the federal **Securities Act of 1933** (**the 1933 Act**) requires that a corporation planning to make an initial public offering must have in effect a 1933 Act registration statement before it may sell securities to the public. The 1933 Act registration is an important and often difficult step for an unregistered corporation that is planning to make its IPO. Full disclosure of a wide variety of matters is required; sophisticated assistance is required to meet these disclosure requirements. In addition, it is often advisable to amend articles of incorporation and bylaws to make sure the corporation can operate effectively as a publicly held corporation. Usually, an unregistered corporation that makes its first public offering files a 1934 Act registration shortly after the public distribution is completed.

An offering to a very small number of unsophisticated potential investors may be a public offering under the 1933 Act, and as a result it is important that closely held corporations raising capital through the sale of securities make sure that an exemption from registration under the 1933 Act is available. As a result, the 1933 Act (and similar registration requirements under state **blue sky laws**) affect even small, closely held enterprises.

Corporations that have registered a class of securities under the 1934 Act may thereafter raise additional capital by a public offering under the 1933 Act. Registration of the new public offering under the 1933 Act is technically required, but that is usually relatively simple to do, because under the SEC's **integrated disclosure system**, most corporations may incorporate by reference their 1934 Act filings in a 1933 Act registration.

Although the vast majority of businesses affected by federal securities law are corporations, these statutes apply to any business, no matter what the form, that makes a public offering or that meets the $10 million in assets and 500 investor standard.

## §10.27  Closely Held Corporations

Typically a closely held corporation is one in which (1) the number of shareholders is small, (2) there is no outside market for its shares, (3) all or most of the principal shareholders participate in its management, and (4) the free transferability of shares is restricted by agreement. A closely held corporation is almost always one that has never made a successful IPO of securities and is not registered with the SEC under the 1934 Act. A publicly held corporation that is reducing its number of shareholders may withdraw from registration under the 1934 Act when it has fewer than 300 shareholders.

Because there is no market for shares of a closely held corporation, there is a substantial risk that minority shareholders may be locked in with no avenue to sell their shares if they become alienated from the majority shareholders. As a result, outside investors are usually reluctant to make equity investments in closely held corporations, and do so only if contractual commitments are entered into under which the shares of minority shareholders will be purchased by the corporation, or more rarely, by other shareholders under specified circumstances. Where a closely held corporation is involved, one should never assume that a market for the shares exists or that a dissatisfied minority shareholder has the option of selling his or her shares at a fair price.

## §10.28  Management of Corporations

The corporate model that appears in state incorporation statutes assumes that shareholders are the ultimate owners of the enterprise and that they elect directors to manage the affairs of the corporation. The directors in turn select officers to implement the board's policies. This is an idealized model that is not tailored specifically either for the closely held corporation or for the publicly held corporation. It is a model that is sufficiently broad and generalized that large portions of it are appropriate for both the very large and the very small. Despite this common core of legal principles, managements of publicly held and closely held corporations usually have little in common.

In a closely held corporation, the principal shareholders in the corporation are usually actively involved in management. Decisions are apt to be made without formal meetings or votes. If there is a single person who owns a majority of the shares, that person will effectively make business decisions for the corporation. In closely held corporations that are taxed as C corporations, it is unusual for the corporation to pay dividends. Rather, most of the earnings will be distributed in the form of salaries, interest, or rent to specific shareholders rather than distributed to the shareholders, generally in the form of dividends. A minority shareholder may easily be frozen out from financial participation merely by the controlling shareholders' refusing to allow the shareholder to participate in management decisions or to receive salary or other payments from the corporation. About 18 states have supplemented their general corporation statutes with optional special statutes designed to provide relaxed rules of management for closely held corporations.

In a publicly held corporation, the management structure is usually entirely different. There are many disorganized and diffuse shareholders; usually no individual or group owns a majority of the voting shares. Management usually comprises professional managers who own relatively small interests in the corporation, often less than one percent. Shareholders usually have little role in deciding who should be the managers of the corporation. Consider, for example, the role of the small shareholder in selecting directors in a publicly held corporation. He is presented with a list of candidates selected and recommended by the corporation's current managers. The shareholder may vote for them or withhold his vote; rarely does he have a choice among competing directorial candidates. Further, because the overwhelming majority of the shareholders are going to vote in favor of the persons proposed by management, it really does not make much difference whether the small shareholder casts his votes or pitches the proxy form into the nearest trash basket.

For purposes of locating the real source of selection of directors, one must usually look not to the election process, but to some earlier point where a decision was made as to which names should be presented to the shareholders as the management's candidates. For many years, this decision was made by the chief executive officer (CEO) individually; today, it is increasingly made by a committee composed of members of the board of directors. The extent to which this critical committee is influenced by the CEO's wishes varies from corporation to corporation. The important point, however, is that the actual selection of directors occurs not at the level of the shareholders but at the level of the chief executive officer or the board of directors. The role of shareholders in publicly held corporations is merely to ratify this selection.

Another reason for the seeming passivity of shareholders is that there tends to be self-selection by shareholders. The presence of an active market in shares means that shareholders dissatisfied with the management of a corporation may exercise the Wall Street option (i.e., sell their shares and invest the proceeds elsewhere) rather than fight incumbent management. Thus, by a process of self-elimination, shareholders who are unhappy with management tend to disappear, and the remaining shareholders tend to be pro-management, or at least not anti-management. Of course, the exercise of the Wall Street option is, in a sense, a vote. A poor operating performance by management results in depressed share prices and may lead indirectly to the ouster of management.

Another factor that limits the power of management is that the nature of shareholdings has changed dramatically in the last 50 years. Before World War II, the predominant view was that share ownership of publicly held corporations was almost atomistic, and that as a result management had virtually a free hand. Ownership had become separated from control. This was the position put forth by A. Berle and G. Means in their influential 1932 book, *The Modern Corporation and Private Property*, and was not seriously questioned until relatively recently.

Although it is doubtful that the Berle and Means view was ever entirely correct, more recent developments have created quite different share ownership patterns. A new type of public investor has grown tremendously in importance —the institutional investor. Institutional investors mainly collect and invest other people's money. They include life insurance companies, retirement funds, investment companies (mutual funds), bank trust departments, university endowments, and similar organizations. These institutional investors invest only in publicly held corporations, and often only in the largest and most widely traded companies. Overall, they invest huge amounts of capital in a large variety of securities traded on the major securities exchanges. As a group, they are now the largest single owner of publicly held corporations; their holdings in the aggregate are in excess of 40 percent of all the outstanding shares of listed publicly held corporations, and, in specific corporations, the percentage is well over 50 percent.

Funds invested by institutional investors ultimately belong to members of the general public in the form of pensions, life insurance proceeds, savings, or financial investments. In a sense, therefore, their growth has increased the broad base of ownership of the means of production. However, in terms of power and potential control, the growth of institutional investors represents a concentration of the base. Now only a relatively few persons—the managers of and investment advisers for the institutional investors—determine where huge investments are to be placed and how large blocks of shares are to be voted.

Institutional investors often have the power, if they band together, to dominate and control many large publicly held corporations. Until relatively recently, however, they have not done so. Most institutional investors have viewed their role as passive investors and have eschewed any interest in managing or exercising control over the business and affairs of corporations. In part, this view was based on perceived problems with respect to cooperative efforts by institutional investors. The SEC has long had rules that require persons soliciting proxies to disclose basic information and that make solicitations not conforming to these rules unlawful. There was concern that cooperative effort by institutional investors might violate these rules. This problem was resolved in 1992, when the SEC changed its regulations expressly allowing for communications among institutional investors as long as the communication does not solicit proxy votes or urge recipients to vote in a specific way.

It is difficult to evaluate the overall impact of institutional investors on corporate governance. There is anecdotal evidence about situations in which institutional investors have sought to replace ineffective managers. This is often done by communication with nonmanagement directors on the corporation's board of directors. However, there has been no systematic evaluation of the effectiveness of this development.

Even though institutional investors view themselves as predominantly ordinary investors, their sheer size raises unique market problems. For example, if an institutional investor decides to exercise its Wall Street option and sell its shares, the block may be so large that only other institutional investors have the capacity to absorb the shares. Large institutional holdings may therefore increase the volatility of share prices, because an independent decision by several large institutional investors to dispose of their shares might markedly depress short-run prices because there is not enough demand to absorb the shares being dumped on the market.

Institutional investors usually owe fiduciary duties to pension beneficiaries or beneficial owners of investment company shares. These duties may be construed as requiring that the institutional investor maximize its short-run market gains. It has been feared that this concern for short-run return by the largest and most important shareholders may in turn compel corporate management to concentrate on maximizing its short-term earnings to the possible detriment of longer-range profitability. Whether this fear is justified is uncertain.

## §10.29 Limited Liability Companies

The most astonishing development in the area of business forms in the 1990s was the growth and spread of a novel business form, the **limited liability company (LLC)**. The attractiveness of this hybrid business form basically arises from its combination of desirable tax and business features: (1) limited liability for all of its owners, (2) the pass-through tax treatment and capital structure of a partnership, and (3) almost complete internal flexibility in terms of management and control. This internal flexibility leaves the parties free to develop their own organizational and management structure, and, at least to some extent, their own governing rules and principles. The default rules for LLCs are drawn in part from corporation law, from general partnership law, and from limited partnership law. In short, the LLC is an eclectic mixture of features drawn from several different traditional business forms that create an attractive package for many enterprises.

LLCs bear a close resemblance to corporations in many aspects, because they have many corporate characteristics. However, they lack the fundamental corporate characteristic that determines the federal tax classification of the entity —they do not receive a "franchise" or "charter" from the state of incorporation. An LLC may also be analogized either to a limited partnership that comprises only limited partners or to a general partnership in which there is no personal liability to creditors. Neither of these analogies is entirely apt; an LLC is a limited liability business form that is neither a corporation nor a limited partnership.

Because LLCs have been in existence for only a brief period and the rules have evolved from varied sources, considerable diversity exists among the state LLC statutes. However, the **National Conference of Commissioners on Uniform State Laws (NCCUSL)** approved a **Uniform Limited Liability Company Act (ULLCA)** in 1995. A couple of years earlier, the ABA developed a prototype statute that differs in many respects from the ULLCA. Because virtually all states had adopted LLC statutes prior to the promulgation of ULLCA, that uniform statute has had relatively few adoptions. As of November 2001, it has been adopted by only eight states and the Virgin Islands. Consequently, variations in LLC statutes are greater than those that exist in traditional corporation, general partnership, and limited partnership statutes. These variations may create problems when an LLC formed in one state decides to conduct business in other states.

LLCs are used primarily for closely held enterprises. There is no inherent reason why an LLC could not have hundreds or thousands of members and be publicly held. However, once ownership interests become publicly traded, the entity becomes subject to C corporation tax treatment under the master limited partnership provisions of the IRC and the major advantage of the LLC is therefore lost.

## §10.30  The Development of LLCs in the United States

Business entities similar to LLCs exist in many foreign countries. Examples include the German **GmbH**, the **limitadas** that exist in Latin American countries (including the **sociedad de responsabilidad limitada (S.de R.L.)** of Mexico), and the Portuguese **sociedate por quotas responsibilitidade limitada**. Similar entities also exist in countries in the common law tradition. Perhaps the closest ancestor in the English tradition is the unincorporated **joint stock company** that developed in England as a commercial substitute for the royal corporate charters that created the City of London and the universities of Oxford and Cambridge. The American colonies were well acquainted with these joint stock companies and by and large detested them, because they had been given monopolies to trade with major portions of the New World.

The LLC also bears resemblance to partnership associations or **limited partnership associations** created in Pennsylvania, Michigan, New Jersey, Ohio, and Virginia in the late 1870s. These variant partnership forms, however, are apparently only of historic interest because there is no record of their being used during the 20th century.

Whatever its origins, the LLC is a distinctly modern creation in the United States. It can be traced to the attempt by the Hamilton Brothers Oil Company of Denver in the 1970s to form an entity in the United States similar to the limitada with which it was familiar in Central America. It chose Wyoming as the focus of its legislative effort. The Wyoming legislature adopted an LLC statute apparently on the belief if that was what a major business wanted, they should have it. The Hamilton Brothers company eventually did obtain a tax ruling that it should be classified as a partnership for tax purposes. However, in 1980 the IRS proposed new regulations that took the uncompromising position that an entity must be classified as a corporation for tax purposes if no investor is personally liable for its obligations. These proposed regulations were highly controversial and were ultimately withdrawn without ever having been promulgated, but they did delay the recognition of the LLC for nearly a decade.

The IRS recognized that an LLC was entitled to partnership-type tax treatment in 1988. This ruling opened the flood gates. Within six years, 47 states had adopted LLC statutes, and the remaining handful of states followed shortly thereafter.

Statistics on the number of business formations are maintained in many states by filing authorities. In many states, the number of LLC formations has risen dramatically so that it rivals the number of new incorporations. In these states, the number of limited partnership formations has declined precipitously, and it seems clear that the LLC is largely responsible for this decline. In 1997, one commentator estimated that by the end of 1995, more than 210,000 LLCs had been created in the United States.

## §10.31  Comparison with Other Business Forms

An LLC has organizational features that are part limited partnership and part corporation.

*Comparison with a Corporation.* An LLC is superficially similar to a corporation. It is a separate legal entity that is formed by filing articles of organization with the secretary of state (or other designated state official) and paying a filing fee. It may be formed for any lawful purpose, subject to exceptions for certain kinds of business such as banking and insurance. However, most state statutes do not require that an LLC be formed as a business for profit and there seems to be no inherent reason why an LLC should not be used in lieu of a not-for-profit corporation.

The relationship between the corporate statutes and LLC statutes is made vivid by contrasting statutory language. One speaks of articles of incorporation in a corporation and articles of organization in an LLC. Rather than having bylaws, an LLC has regulations or an operating agreement. The owners are called members rather than shareholders. Rather than having directors, LLCs may have managers. The managers may be chosen by the members in a manner similar to the way shareholders choose directors in a corporation. An LLC may have officers selected by the board of managers. Managers and officers need not be members unless the operative documents provide otherwise. LLC statutory provisions relating to purposes and powers are also closely modeled after similar provisions in state corporation statutes. LLC statutes authorize the merger or consolidation of LLCs with other LLCs or with other forms of business in language modeled directly on the language of corporation statutes. Some state LLC statutes provide expressly that a piercing the corporate veil principle applies to LLCs. The duties of managers of an LLC may be described by language directly taken from the corporation statutes relating to the duties of directors. Some states provide for dissenters rights in LLCs analogous to such rights in corporations.

In some respects, of course, the LLC does not resemble a corporation. An LLC may be member managed, in which event management principles are drawn from the general partnership model. The LLC statutes of most states provide flexibility with respect to the internal organization of an LLC; there are few mandatory statutory requirements, and internal relationships are largely governed by contract rather than by mandatory statutory provision. In contrast, corporation statutes are notoriously specific. They provide detailed rules for the financing and management of corporations that may be binding on all corporations. Most state corporation statutes have complex provisions regarding the issuance of securities and maintenance of capital; although LLCs may adopt similar provisions, they are free to construct simpler financial structures, such as those that typically appear in partnerships.

One important theoretical difference is that in a corporation the articles of incorporation control over bylaws or contractual obligations in case of a conflict; an LLC is based on the theory that it is a contract among the members, and thus the terms of the operating agreement control over the articles of organization in case of conflict.

As LLCs have proliferated, courts have been compelled to consider whether corporation or partnership principles should be applied when the LLC statute is silent. The limited number of reported cases indicates that courts will turn to corporation law for guidance. A lower court opinion in Delaware, for example, involved the question whether an LLC, like a corporation, may only appear in court through an attorney, or whether an officer or manager of the LLC who is not a lawyer may appear on behalf of the entity (much the way a partner may appear and represent a partnership in court). Without finding any governing or even relevant authority one way or the other, the court concluded that the corporate analogy should be applied, because the underlying purpose of the rule prohibiting the appearance of a corporation by anyone other than a member of the Delaware Bar also applied to the representation of LLCs.

Even though an LLC is not a corporation, some states subject it to corporate franchise tax treatment. This is true, for example, in Florida, Pennsylvania, and Texas. The reasons that states insist that LLCs be taxed as corporations is apparently based not so much on the corporate characteristics of an LLC as on the fear that otherwise state revenues will decline as firms change their business form to LLCs, and as new businesses elect to be LLCs from the outset. One consequence of this treatment is that the LLCs are less attractive than partnerships in these states.

*Comparison with a Partnership.* LLCs also have strong antecedents in the law of partnership. This is particularly true in the ULLCA, which draws from the partnership model in many respects. An LLC may elect to assume a management structure that is virtually identical to that of a general partnership except that members do not have personal liability for firm obligations. The operating agreement in many LLCs more closely approximates a partnership agreement than corporate bylaws. Some states permit LLC operating agreements to be oral rather than written, an option not available for corporate bylaws. Membership interests in an LLC also may have significant partnership characteristics. Agreements may provide that transferees of membership interests may be admitted only with the unanimous consent of the members. The death, bankruptcy, or retirement of a member may constitute a dissolution (or dissociation) of the LLC unless a majority in interest of the remaining members votes to continue the LLC. Under LLC statutes, partnership rules may be applicable unless the operating agreement provides to the contrary. Voting in an LLC may be on a per capita basis (though the default rule for voting in LLCs is usually the corporate default rule of voting by percentage of interest). An LLC, in short, is, or may elect to become, quite partnership-like without sacrificing the benefit of limited liability.

Statutes defining member-managed limited liability companies follow the partnership model. They provide that each member is an agent of the LLC for the purpose of its business, that each member has the right to possess LLC property for business purposes, and so forth. These statutes may also provide for partnership-type duties of care and loyalty.

Some state statutes provide that the default rule for an LLC is member-management rather than manager-management. Other statutes adopt the opposite default rule, presuming that all LLCs will be manager-managed unless specific provision to the contrary is made in the controlling documents. Pennsylvania adopts yet another approach, applying the management provisions of its limited partnership statute to manager-managed limited liability companies.

*Comparison with a Limited Partnership.* The LLC differs from a limited partnership in that all participants may actively take part in control of the business without restriction and without personal liability for business obligations. A member-managed LLC is similar to a general partnership, minus the personal liability of partners for partnership obligations.

The source of limited liability provided by an LLC is analogous to that provided by limited partnership statutes for limited partners. A limited partnership files a certificate with the designated state official, and the limited partners thereby obtain the shield of limited liability. Similarly, an LLC files articles of organization with a designated state official, and the members of the LLC thereby obtain the shield of limited liability. In this respect, an LLC resembles a limited partnership more than a corporation, which obtains limited liability through the fiction that a charter has been issued so that a separate legal entity has been created. A formal difference of this nature should make no practical difference. The fact that obtaining limited liability by incorporating leads immediately to classification as a corporation for income tax purposes (while obtaining limited liability by forming an LLC does not) illustrates the IRC's formalistic character in this respect.

## §10.32 Default Rules for LLCs

As a result of the unique historical development of limited liability companies, default rules vary significantly from state to state. Some states adopt default rules based on the corporate model while other states, particularly those enacting the Uniform Limited Liability Company Act, adopt default rules more similar to those applicable to partnerships. As a practical matter, careful examination of the LLC statute of the jurisdiction involved is necessary.

There are also some issues that may not be specifically addressed at all by the applicable statutes. In these situations there may be significant uncertainty as to what rule is applicable and, if foreseeable, specific provision should be made in the operating agreement. Two possible examples follow:

First, assume that A, a member of an LLC, assigns his entire interest to X. What does X have? In the absence of specific provision dealing with assignments, either the partnership or the corporate analogy may apply. If the partnership analogy is applied, X has all of A's financial interest but no right to participate in management. In the absence of specific provision to the contrary, A retains his management rights even though he has no financial interest in the enterprise. On the other hand, if the corporate analogy is followed, X has all of A's rights, financial and managerial, and is entitled to participate in management to the same extent as the provisions of the operating agreement permit all members to participate.

Second, to complicate the example somewhat, assume that the LLC has three members: A with 30 percent, B with 30 percent, and C with 40 percent financial interests. The agreement is silent with respect to assignments and whether management participation rights are per capita or in proportion to financial interests. C purchases B's 30 percent interest, thereby owning a 70 percent financial interest. Does C now have a 70 percent interest in the entire LLC or a 40 percent original interest and a 30 percent assignee's interest? Does C have a 70 percent voting interest (the corporate default rule), a one-out-of-two per capita voting power (the partnership default rule), or a right to cast two votes per capita, one for the original interest and one for the assigned interest? The choice of which rule should be applicable in these instances is perhaps not as important as that the rules be readily ascertainable by members or managers who may themselves not be lawyers.

## §10.33  Limited Liability Partnerships

The **limited liability partnership** (**LLP**) is essentially a new form of business enterprise. For most purposes, an LLP is a general partnership. It differs from a general partnership only because certain partners are by statute relieved of personal responsibility for certain liabilities. The earliest LLP statutes limited this immunity to liabilities created by errors, omissions, negligence, incompetence, or malpractice committed by other partners or by employees that other partners supervise. Partners involved in the wrongful or negligent acts remained personally liable; innocent partners were protected from this liability, but all partners remained personally liable for all contract liabilities. These early statutes were clearly peace of mind statutes for partners in large partnerships. Later statutes have created **full shields** for general partners and protect them from personal responsibility for all partnership obligations other than those created by their own personal misconduct. In 1996, amendments to the RUPA were promulgated recommending amendments of the full shield variety for all states, and it appears likely that most states will ultimately follow this approach.

The LLP is a new and potentially useful business form that is particularly attractive for professionals such as lawyers and accountants doing business in partnership form. However, there is no inherent reason why the LLP should be limited to professional partnerships, and under most LLP statutes, partnerships engaged in ordinary business activities may become registered LLPs. However, New York, and possibly other states as well, limits the LLP form of business to professional partnerships, broadly defined.

## §10.34  LLPs Contrasted with Other Business Forms

*Comparison with a Limited Partnership.* Even though an LLP sounds like it is similar to or a variant of a limited partnership, it is in fact quite a different animal. A limited partnership has two classes of partners—general partners and limited partners—with quite different management responsibilities and liability for partnership obligations. In a limited partnership, the limited partners are usually passive investors with virtually no powers of management and no personal liability at all for partnership obligations; a limited partner's risk of loss may not exceed his contributions of capital to the firm. In an LLP, on the other hand, all partners have the management responsibilities of partners in a general partnership and all have the benefit of whatever shield of limited liability the particular statute provides—either a protection against malpractice claims or a full shield of protection against all liabilities except those for which they are responsible because of their own misconduct or negligence. In contrast, limited partners in a limited partnership have no personal responsibility for any liabilities of any nature unless they voluntarily elect to become liable.

*Comparison with an LLC.* There is substantial confusion between LLCs on the one hand and LLPs on the other. This confusion arises because of the similarity of the names, not any similarity of the two forms of business. The statutes under which an LLC is created are quite different from the statutes under which LLPs are created. LLC statutes embody numerous corporate concepts and provide numerous options and default regulations that give great flexibility to the LLC form of business. For example, LLC statutes permit an LLC to elect between management by the members and management by managers who have roles analogous to directors in a corporation. If management by managers is authorized, the members have only limited rights to participate in management. In contrast, LLP statutes are part of the partnership law, and management rules for partnerships govern. Although some centralization of management in a general partnership may be created by provisions in the partnership agreement itself, the flexibility in management of an LLC is not available to an LLP. LLPs are partnerships with a special rule for personal liability.

## §10.35  Election of LLP Status

To become an LLP, a general partnership must file a registration statement with the secretary of state and adopt a name that includes a reference to being an LLP. Registration is usually on an annual basis and must be renewed each year if the shield of limited liability is to be maintained. Renewal may involve the payment of an annual fee for each partner protected by the LLP election. In addition, in some states the partnership must also keep a specified amount of liquid assets on hand or maintain malpractice insurance in a specified amount to assure possible claimants that the firm will be reasonably able to respond to claims that the statute covers. The requirement of annual registration is a revenue-raising device for some states.

## §10.36  Conflicts of Interest Within an LLP

At first blush, the LLP concept does not appear to involve serious internal conflicts of interest within partnerships. This is largely true under full shield LLP statutes but is not always the case if the general partnership operates under a "partial shield" statute. "Full shield" statutes typically provide for partner immunity from personal liability for all firm obligations except those that arise from the partner's personal misconduct. "Partial shield" statutes, in contrast, provide considerably less protection: They generally provide protection for innocent partners from claims based on misconduct of other partners but do not protect against general business liabilities of the partnership that arise from ordinary commercial operations.

Under partial shield statutes it is possible that (1) aggregate partnership liabilities will exceed the partnership assets and (2) at the same time some but not all partners will be required to contribute to the discharge of specific partnership liabilities because of their misconduct. Under partial shield statutes, the innocent partners will desire to have available assets first be applied against ordinary liabilities of the firm but the guilty partners will prefer that assets be first applied to reduce the liabilities for which they have personal liability. To the extent available assets are first applied to reduce the liability of the guilty parties, the liability of the innocent party for ordinary losses is increased. The result is a direct conflict of interest between two classes of partners.

The same conflict does not arise under full shield statutes, because innocent partners have no obligation with respect to the firm's ordinary business liabilities if they exceed the assets of the firm.

## §10.37　Limited Liability Limited Partnerships

Several states authorize a combination of limited partnerships and the LLP. A **limited liability limited partnership** (**LLLP**) is a limited partnership in which the general partners have elected to become an LLP. In such an organization, the limited partners have no liability for the firm's obligations under the limited partnership statute, and the general partners, among themselves, have personal liability only to the extent provided by the LLP statute.

Although the LLLP is a logical extension of the limited partnership and registered limited liability partnership statutes, it is not clear what benefits this form of business has over a simple LLC.

## §10.38　Professional Corporations

Certain professions—primarily law, medicine, and dentistry—have long been prohibited by ethical considerations from conducting business in the traditional corporation form. A **professional corporation** is a specially designed business form that enables professionals to obtain the benefits of incorporation while meeting ethical requirements. The professional corporation was originally developed to take advantage of special tax rules applicable to corporations, particularly the right to create more attractive pension and profit-sharing plans than sole proprietors could provide for themselves or partnerships could create for partners. These tax advantages were eliminated in 1982, but modest fringe benefits that cannot be claimed by proprietors or provided by a partnership to its partners are still available on a before-tax basis. The continuing popularity of the professional corporation now rests primarily on the advantage of limited liability that professional corporations provide in many (but not all) states.

In many states today, a law firm may conduct business as a general partnership, an LLC, an LLP, or a professional corporation.

## §10.39　Selection of Business Form

In the 1950s, there were three types of business forms for closely held businesses, each combining fairly precise rules about control and governance in their own unique ways: the partnership (or proprietorship), the limited partnership, and the corporation. These traditional businesses forms have now been supplemented by novel business forms, LLCs and LLPs, and variations thereof, that mix and match characteristics in new and challenging ways. These new business forms are so attractive and so flexible that it is quite possible that they will eventually become the dominant business forms for closely held enterprises. As far as publicly held businesses are concerned, virtually all are corporations, and, given the present tax rules, there is no incentive to use any of the newly developed business forms for publicly held enterprises.

The most significant factors in the selection of a business form are:

(1) considerations of internal efficiency, operational cost, and organizational convenience;
(2) considerations of limited liability and the responsibility of the owners of a business for its debts;
(3) the minimization of federal income taxation;
(4) the minimization of state income and franchise tax obligations;
(5) legal restrictions on the ability of certain businesses (e.g., law firms) to select specific business forms; and
(6) considerations relating to the ease of raising capital in the future.

Traditional legal texts often analyze the differences among the forms of business organization in terms of legal differences: continuity of life, centralization of management, and free transferability of interest. These factors are also discussed below; they are not truly unique characteristics of a specific form of business enterprise. By suitable advance planning, a considerable degree of continuity of life, centralization of management, and free transferability of interest may be granted to, or withheld from, any form of business organization. At one time, these factors were of central importance in determining the federal income tax regime applicable to a specific business. However, because these factors were manipulable, the selection of applicable tax regime also became manipulable. Ultimately, the IRS recognized this fact, and made selection of tax regime completely elective in late 1996 when it adopted its check-the-box regulations.

## §10.40 Limited Liability

As one reflects on the importance of limited liability, the first reaction of law students is usually that protection against unlimited liability is of great significance, and that in terms of selecting an appropriate business form, one should always opt for this protection. Of course, there is clearly some value in protection against unexpected liability, but one should not overstate its significance.

Sophisticated creditors often decline to deal with small limited liability enterprises unless the owners (or some of them) voluntarily agree to guarantee the payment of the obligations by the enterprise. These creditors understand that limited liability means that the creditor can only look to the assets of the business: They may (and usually do) decline to do business with a limited liability enterprise without substantial assets unless the owners voluntarily guarantee repayment of the debt. When owners are called on to make personal guarantees, the value of limited liability is obviously significantly diminished.

There are, however, some significant kinds of contract claims in which it is not customary or practical for the creditor to require the owners to give personal guarantees of the payment of the debt. An obvious example is employee wage and salary claims. Usually, the economic bargaining power of employees is such that they are in no position to ask for or obtain personal guarantees of their salaries. Small creditors also may not request guarantees, simply because the cost of requesting and obtaining them exceeds the amount of the credit they expect to extend. Other creditors may be satisfied with a purchase money security interest or other type of lien, and may not request personal guarantees. Thus, the protection of limited liability in these areas may have some favorable practical consequences from the standpoint of owners.

As for tort liabilities, in very small businesses the owner or owners will often be personally involved in the activities giving rise to the claim and thus will be individually liable irrespective of limited liability. In somewhat larger businesses, the owners usually have more wealth at stake and have a strong incentive to make sure that employees take due care in doing the work of the business. Thus limited liability is of limited value even on the tort side. Moreover, even limited liability enterprises purchase liability insurance to protect their assets from being consumed by a tort judgment. This insurance normally protects the owners of the business as well as the business's assets from tort claims. It is possible, of course, for a tort judgment to exceed the amount of liability insurance available, but that is at best a remote risk. One can also purchase insurance against excess liability—so-called umbrella policies—which is relatively inexpensive. The difference in annual cost between $100,000 of coverage and $10,000,000 of coverage, for example, is usually not very great.

There are some tort claims for which insurance protection is simply not available. Intentional torts fall into this category. However, the probability of such liability actually arising in a commercial context is quite small for most businesses. Further, where true intentional torts are involved, there is a fairly high possibility of liability being imposed through direct participation by the owners, by agency principles, or by piercing the veil of limited liability by a court.

There are other types of claims not falling clearly into either the contract or tort category that also may be affected by limited liability. Some tax claims, for example, may only be the responsibility of the limited liability entity; presumably owners of the business are not personally liable for such claims.

If one weighs the advantages and costs of limited liability from a realistic perspective, a fair conclusion is that limited liability is a definite but limited benefit from the standpoint of the owners. Its advantages are not so overwhelming that it should be insisted on in every case. For this reason, many law firms continue to conduct their business as general partnerships despite the availability of the LLP business form. Obviously, some individuals are more risk-averse than others: The more risk-averse, the more important limited liability is apt to appear.

## §10.41 Federal Income Taxation of Businesses in General

Federal income taxation is a major—if not a determining—factor in many business decisions. A basic understanding of the alternative tax regimes for businesses with more than a single owner is essential for every lawyer who deals with business matters.

On May 26, 2001, Congress enacted a major tax statute, the Economic Growth and Tax Relief Reconciliation Act of 2001, that provided significant income tax reductions for individuals. The precise scope of these changes is masked by numerous phase-ins and deferred effective dates, plus a provision that in 2011 "sunsets" the tax structure back to the rules prior to the enactment of the Reconciliation Act. Congress obviously contemplates that the tax structure for individuals will be revisited before this "sunset" occurs. While the goal of this 2001 legislation was entirely tax relief for individuals, Congress also clearly plans to enact tax relief for businesses in the near future. However, the plan to provide business tax relief may be affected by the consequences of the terrorist acts of September 11, 2001. Assuming that business tax legislation is enacted, it may simply affect tax rates or it may combine tax rate changes with structural changes in the manner in which various types of business forms are taxed.

The discussion in this and the following sections is directed exclusively to the tax structure applicable to businesses as of 2001. Because of the probability that business-oriented taxation will be modified in unpredictable ways in the future, this discussion is only a brief outline of the current rules relating to this exceptionally complex subject.

There are three separate tax regimes that are potentially applicable to businesses. These regimes are identified by reference to the subchapters of the Internal Revenue Code creating these specific tax regime. Corporate income taxation is described in Subchapters C and S of the Internal Revenue Code, while income taxation of unincorporated businesses is described in Subchapter K. The substantial differences between these tax regimes have long driven the selection of business forms in the past. In 1996, the Internal Revenue Service adopted regulations that simplify the selection of tax regimes for general and limited partnerships, limited liability companies, and other unincorporated business forms. These regulations, know as "check the box," give considerable discretion to these unincorporated business forms to elect to be taxed under Subchapters C or S as well as under Subchapter K. Businesses eligible for "check the box" obviously elect the tax regime that minimizes their overall tax obligation. Once made, however, the election is not easily changed.

Corporations are not eligible to elect Subchapter K taxation. They are taxed under Subchapter C as described in the following section unless they meet the requirements of Subchapter S, in which case they may elect to be taxed under that chapter, as described in §10.43. All publicly held corporations are taxed under Subchapter C.

## §10.42 Subchapter C Taxation

The starting point for corporate taxation under Subchapter C is the concept that the corporation is a separate taxable entity in its own right, independent of its shareholders. Subchapter C of the Internal Revenue Code imposes a tax on the income of corporations (without regard to dividends or distributions), and if dividends are paid to shareholders, they must be fully included as taxable income in the shareholders' tax returns without affecting the corporation's tax. The central concept of Subchapter C is that the corporation and its shareholders are different taxpayers, and dividends are simply additional taxable income to shareholders. In a fundamental sense, Subchapter C involves double taxation of the same income. This double taxation may not be particularly noticeable in large publicly held corporations with thousands of shareholders, but it is very evident in closely held corporations. Particularly in connection with family corporations, this double taxation has long been viewed as unfair, as a needless penalty on the use of the corporate form of business, and as the imposition of an unreasonably high tax on corporate earnings.

In 2001, the tax rate at the corporate level under Subchapter C begins at 15 percent on the first $50,000 of income and goes up to a maximum tax rate of 45 percent on income in excess of $10 million.

An illustration of the double taxation inherent in C corporation taxation using 2001 rates is helpful. If the corporation has $100,000 of taxable income, it must pay a tax of $22,250, reducing the income available to distribution to shareholders to $77,750. Assuming this amount is then distributed as a dividend to a single shareholder who is married, files a joint return, and is in the top individual tax bracket, the distribution of $77,750 increases the shareholder's tax bill by $27,990. Of the $100,000 of corporate income, the shareholder therefore receives $49,760 ($77,750 minus $27,990). On the other hand if there had been no corporation, and the same shareholder received the $100,000 directly as income, it would have been taxed at 36 percent, the highest individual tax bracket. Using a C corporation, in other words, cost the shareholder $14,240, the difference between $64,000 and $49,760.

C corporation taxation leads inevitably to tax minimization devices. For example, the double tax is avoided if the distribution to the shareholder is deductible by the corporation as salary, rent, interest, or other similar payment to the shareholder. An alternative is to allow earnings to accumulate in the corporation and then arrange for the gain to be taxable in some way at lower long-term capital gain rates; after World War II this strategy was so widely used by family corporations that it had a name of its own: the accumulate and bail out strategy. A reduction in the effective tax rate may be obtained by the shareholder selling some shares to lower-income family members, or making periodic gifts of shares to children or grandchildren. This double tax problem is primarily of concern to shareholders who are individuals; shareholders which are corporations are entitled to a **dividends received deduction** which largely eliminates the possibility of double taxation of intra-corporate dividends.

In some instances, individuals may use Subchapter C corporations to reduce federal income taxes. The initial tax rates applicable to C corporations are so low that it may be advantageous for individuals to place businesses in C corporations so long as they do not take taxable distributions from those corporations. When the assets of the corporation have increased sufficiently, the stock of the corporation may be sold and the gain taxed as long-term capital gain. Alternatively, the corporation may be merged in a tax-free reorganization with another entity under the control of the individual, though at some point a taxable event will occur.

The United States is apparently unique among industrialized nations in imposing a double tax burden on corporate distributions.

## §10.43  Subchapter S Taxation

Complaints about the double taxation in distributions by closely held corporations led to the enactment in 1957 of an alternative tax structure for certain close corporations. Subchapter S taxation eliminates the corporate tax and shifts the impact of the taxation to the shareholders. To be eligible for Subchapter S treatment, the corporation (1) must have no more than 75 shareholders; (2) all shareholders must be individuals, estates of decedents, certain trusts or charitable organizations; (3) no shareholder may be a nonresident alien; and (4) the corporation must have only one class of stock. While there is no size limitation on S corporations, most eligible businesses that elect Subchapter S are relatively small. A corporation that qualifies under Subchapter S is referred to as a "Sub-S" corporation.

An eligible corporation makes the S corporation election by filing a relatively simple form with the Internal Revenue Service, together with written consents by all persons who are shareholders on the day the election is made. Once made, the election continues indefinitely. It can be revoked voluntarily by a vote of a majority of the shareholders and is revoked automatically if the corporation fails to satisfy the requirements for qualification. An S corporation may convert to a C corporation, but it cannot return to being an S corporation for five years thereafter without the consent of the Internal Revenue Service.

S corporation tax treatment is a modified pass-through tax treatment that is similar to, but not identical with, the taxation of partnerships and limited liability companies under Subchapter K discussed in the following section. The technical differences between Subchapters K and S generally make Subchapter K more attractive than Subchapter S. To take one example, the contribution of appreciated property to a Sub-S corporation is treated differently from the treatment of the same contribution to a partnership. Under Subchapter S the gain would be allocated among the shareholders strictly in accordance with their ownership interests. Under Subchapter K the gain would be allocated entirely to the person making the contribution. Such a gain is called **built-in gain**, and from an economic standpoint, should be taxed entirely to the contributor and not partially to his co-shareholders. This and other technical differences in tax treatment are major reasons why businesses eligible for Subchapter S today often prefer to do business as limited liability companies under Subchapter K.

Another undesirable feature of the S corporation election is that technical rules about eligibility for that election make it relatively easy for a single share-holder to break the election. For example, a shareholder might destroy the S corporation election by selling shares from his own holdings to a corporation or to enough outsiders that the number of shareholders becomes greater than 75. Either action destroys the Sub-S election. In a situation where there is significant internal controversy within the corporation, the threat to destroy the Sub-S election may have considerable force. While a share transfer restriction may protect against some tactics, the S corporation election itself often becomes a bargaining chit in resolving intracorporate conflict.

## §10.44  Subchapter K Taxation and "Check the Box"

A partnership has always been taxed in a different way than a corporation. A corporation is viewed as an entity subject to taxation in its own capacity while a partnership is not viewed as being a separate taxable entity. Rather, each partner includes in her personal tax return the allocable portion of the partnership's profit or loss. The manner in which this allocation is made is quite simple. Each partnership must prepare and file an information return each year that shows partnership income and expense and their allocation to individual partners. The partnership itself does not pay any tax. Rather, each partner in-cludes in her personal income tax return the amount of each item allocated to the partner by the partnership, and then calculates her tax obligation based on the combined partnership and personal income or loss. A critical aspect of this tax treatment is that business income or loss is allocated by the **distributive share** allocated to each partner by the partnership and not by the actual cash distributions from the partnership to the individual partner. This method of taxation is called **pass-through** tax treatment.

Thus, the double taxation burden of a corporation can be avoided if the parties are willing to conduct business as a partnership. Historically, the "cost" of avoiding the double tax in this fashion was the personal liability of individual partners for all partnership obligations, certainly a cause of concern for relatively affluent partners. The Internal Revenue Service long took the position that these two principles were invariably linked together and that pass-through tax treatment was dependent on the existence of personal liability for firm obliga-tions.

As described in §10.30, the creation of the limited liability company di-rectly attacked this link. The LLC provides limited liability for all members within a business structure that is manifestly not corporate in character. After extensive review and reconsideration, in 1996 the IRS threw in the towel and in regulations universally known as "Check the Box" agreed that most noncor-porate business entities could elect among Subchapter C, Subchapter S, and Subchapter K tax treatment. While these regulations are relatively complex, the basic principles can be simply stated:

(1) An entity is classified as a corporation for tax purposes if it is formed under a statute that describes or refers to the entity "as incorporated as a corporation, body corporate, or body politic" or as a joint stock company or joint stock association. Such entities must be taxed under either Subchapter C or Subchapter S (if eligible).

(2) An entity that has two members and is not classified as a corporation may elect to be taxed under Subchapter K.

(3) An entity that has only one member may be taxed as a corporation or as a "nothing," i.e. as though it has no separate existence from its owner.

(4) After making an election, an entity may not change its classification within five years without permission of the IRS. An entity that is currently taxed as a corporation and changes its classification so that it will be taxed under Subchapter K, is viewed for tax purposes as having dissolved and reconstituted itself. Dissolution results in a presumed distribution of all unrealized appreciation of business assets to members and a tax therefore being imposed on them for that appreciation.

There is one major exception to the check-the-box regulations. It does not apply to unincorporated organizations that have publicly traded ownership interests without regard to the business form adopted by those organizations. As described in §10.16, in the 1980s a significant number of limited partnerships were formed with hundreds or thousands of limited partners and a single corporate general partner. These businesses were called **master limited partnerships**, and were essentially **tax shelters** designed to avoid the double taxation inherent in a corporation. In the Tax Reform Act of 1986, Congress directed that all entities with publicly traded ownership interests, no matter what business form chosen, must be taxed under Subchapter C. This statute also prevents the creation of publicly traded limited liability companies as way of avoiding Subchapter C corporation taxation.

# CORPORATE SECURITIES

## §11.1  Introduction

Perhaps no other area of corporation law is more confusing to persons without prior business backgrounds than corporate securities such as stock, bonds, and debentures. The language is new and unfamiliar, the concepts seem mysterious and sometimes illogical, and everything seems to build on historical concepts that today are of dubious relevance. This chapter should help to dispel the mystery.

This chapter focuses on publicly traded securities that large, publicly held corporations issue. It therefore provides important background for the following chapters of this book dealing with dividend policies, takeovers, securities markets, and investment strategies.

## §11.2  Common Shares

Shares of **common stock** are the fundamental units into which the proprietary interest of the corporation is divided. If a corporation issues only one class of shares, they may be referred to by a variety of similar names: common shares, common stock, capital stock, or possibly simply shares or stock. Whatever the name, they are the basic proprietary units of ownership and are referred to here as common shares or common stock.

The two fundamental characteristics of common shares are (1) they are entitled to vote for the election of directors and on other matters coming before the shareholders and (2) they are entitled to the net assets of the corporation (after making allowance for debts and senior securities) when distributions are to be made, either during the life of the corporation or upon its dissolution.

The fundamental incorporating document of every corporation must state the number of shares of common stock the corporation is authorized to issue. This number is known as the corporation's **authorized shares**. In states with older statutes, that document must also set forth the **par value** of the authorized shares or a statement that the shares are without par value. Par value is an arbitrary number without economic significance that, in older statutes, determines the amount of permanent capital and capital surplus in the original capitalization of the corporation.

Corporations usually authorize more common shares than they currently plan to issue. Additional authorized shares may be useful if it is decided, for example, to raise capital in the future by selling additional shares, to provide economic incentives to executives or key employees by granting them options to purchase shares at favorable prices, to create an **employee stock ownership plan** (**ESOP**) for all employees, or to issue debt or senior classes of securities that may be converted into common shares.

The capitalization of a corporation is based on the number of shares actually issued and the consideration received for them, not on the number of authorized shares. Capital received in exchange for shares is usually referred to as the corporation's invested capital (or sometimes its contributed capital), and from an accounting standpoint it is viewed as being invested in the corporation permanently or indefinitely.

Common shareholders receive **dividends** from the corporation as and when declared by the board of directors. Most publicly held corporations adopt a policy of paying a fixed dividend each year (a **regular** dividend) and, if the corporation has done well for the year or has excess funds, it may also declare an **extra** or **special dividend** for that year only.

## §11.3  Reporting of Earnings per Share

Publicly held corporations report publicly their earnings each year on an aggregate basis and on a per-share basis. **Earnings per share** equal net earnings divided by the number of shares outstanding. Publicly held corporations almost always have outstanding commitments to issue, or have granted rights in third persons to acquire additional shares either by purchase, option exercise, or conversion of convertible securities. These are potential shares, because the privilege of acquiring the shares has not yet been exercised. The number of potential shares may be large in comparison with the number of actually issued and outstanding shares. The question then arises, what should be done about potential shares when reporting earnings? Should earnings per share be calculated on shares actually outstanding or on shares potentially outstanding? The solution that the Securities and Exchange Commission (the SEC) adopted is very sensible. When the number of potential shares is material, earnings per share must be reported on both an actual share basis and a **fully diluted** basis, that is on the assumption that all options and rights to acquire additional shares have been exercised. Table 11-1 is an example of such reporting for the quarterly earnings of several publicly traded corporations.

## §11.4 Preferred Shares

**Preferred shares** differ from common shares in that (1) they usually are non-voting and have limited rights and (2) one or more of those rights has a preference over the rights of common shares. Preferential rights are almost always financial in character. Most preferred shares have preferential rights over common shares both in connection with the payment of dividends and in connection with distributions of assets in voluntary or involuntary dissolution of the corporation. A **dividend preference** means that the preferred shares are entitled to receive a specified dividend before any dividend may be paid on the common shares; a **liquidation preference** means that the preferred shares are entitled to receive a specified distribution from corporate assets in liquidation (after provision has been made for corporate debts) before the common shares are entitled to receive anything. However, some preferred shares may have only a dividend preference and no liquidation preference, or vice versa.

The rights of preferred shareholders are defined in the corporation's articles of incorporation (or other incorporating document), bylaws, or directors' resolutions filed with the articles of incorporation (in the case of series of preferred shares). If an existing corporation wishes to create a new class of preferred shares, it must usually formally amend its articles of incorporation. Collectively the provisions in these basic corporate documents describing and defining the terms and rights of preferred shareholders constitute the **preferred shareholders' contract** with the corporation. Preferred shareholders are generally limited to the rights set forth in these documents and have relatively few rights outside of those expressly set forth.

A single corporation may have outstanding several different classes of preferred shares with varying rights and preferences. Although a specific class of preferred may have rights subordinate to another class of preferred, both are still preferred shares, because both have preferences over the common shares. The dividend preference may be described either in terms of dollars per share ("$3.20 preferred") or as a percentage of par or stated value (the "5 percent preferred"). A dividend preference does not mean that the preferred is entitled to payment in the same way that a creditor is entitled to payment. A preferred dividend is still a dividend and may be paid only if the corporation has available

Table 11-1

# DIGEST OF CORPORATE EARNINGS REPORTS

## - A -

| COMPANY | PERIOD | REV (mill) | % CHG | INC CT OP (mill) | NET (mill) | % CHG | PER SHARE CURR | PREV | % CHG |
|---|---|---|---|---|---|---|---|---|---|
| AMX Corp | Q9/30 | 23.0 | −11 | ... | a(8.13) | ... | (.74) | .02 | ... |
| AMXC (Nq) L | 6 mo | 44.7 | −5.0 | ... | a(7.93) | ... | (.72) | (.05) | ... |
| a-Includes nonrecurring charges of $8,200,000. | | | | | | | | | |
| AXS-One Inc | Q9/30 | 9.49 | −29 | ... | a0.49 | −45 | .02 | .03 | −33 |
| AXO (A) ▼ | 9 mo | 30.7 | −18 | ... | a(5.55) | ... | (.22) | .03 | ... |
| a-Includes a restructuring gain of $166,000 in the quarter and a charge of $937,000 in the nine months. | | | | | | | | | |
| Abatix Corp | Q9/30 | 14.6 | 18 | ... | 0.38 | 71 | .22 | .13 | 69 |
| ABIX (Sc) ▲ | 9 mo | 41.5 | 12 | ... | 0.95 | 64 | .55 | .34 | 62 |
| Advance Finl Bnc | Q9/30 | ... | ... | ... | 0.30 | 40 | .34 | .25 | 36 |
| AFBC (Sc) ▲ | | | | | | | | | |
| Includes the results of Ohio State Financial Services Inc., acquired on September 7, 2001. | | | | | | | | | |
| Amer Fin'l Group | Q9/30 | ... | ... | ... | a(55.7) | ... | (.81) | (.38) | ... |
| AFG (N) | 9 mo | ... | ... | a(36.3) | (46.3) | ... | (.67) | .66 | ... |
| a-Includes one-time after-tax charges of $81,300,000, or $1.19 a diluted share. | | | | | | | | | |
| Amer States Water | Q9/30 | 59.4 | 7.5 | ... | 9.45 | 15 | .93 | .86 | 8.1 |
| AWR (N) | 12 mo | 194.1 | 6.1 | ... | 20.7 | 21 | 2.03 | 1.86 | 9.1 |
| Amerigon Inc | Q9/30 | 1.51 | −15 | ... | (1.79) | ... | (.38) | (.54) | ... |
| ARGN (Sc) | 9 mo | 4.96 | 35 | (5.35) | (5.35) | ... | (1.16) | (2.88) | ... |
| Annapolis Bancorp | Q9/30 | ... | ... | ... | 0.12 | −61 | .05 | .14 | −64 |
| ANNB (Sc) ▼ | 9 mo | ... | ... | ... | 0.32 | −52 | .14 | .30 | −53 |
| Arlington Hospital | Q9/30 | 22.6 | −5.5 | ... | 1.86 | −60 | .35 | .87 | −60 |
| HOST (Nq) ▼ | 9 mo | 59.0 | −4.2 | ... | 1.39 | −72 | .25 | .92 | −73 |
| Atlas Air Worldwide | Q9/30 | 150.7 | −28 | ... | a(4.20) | ... | (.11) | .60 | ... |
| CGO (N) L | 9 mo | 480.1 | −15 | a(53.2) | (54.8) | ... | (1.44) | 1.49 | ... |
| a-Includes a nonrecurring charge of $101,000,000 in the nine months related to settlement and restructuring. Also in the quarter and nine months are gains of $10,100,000 related to a federal grant. | | | | | | | | | |
| Audible Inc | Q9/30 | 2.16 | 94 | ... | (5.94) | ... | (.23) | (.29) | ... |
| ADBL (Nq) | 9 mo | 6.39 | 138 | ... | (21.5) | ... | (.83) | (.95) | ... |

## - B -

| COMPANY | PERIOD | REV (mill) | % CHG | INC CT OP (mill) | NET (mill) | % CHG | PER SHARE CURR | PREV | % CHG |
|---|---|---|---|---|---|---|---|---|---|
| Bluefly Inc | Q9/30 | 5.11 | 48 | ... | (2.43) | ... | (.33) | (1.01) | ... |
| BFLY (Sc) | 9 mo | 15.0 | 28 | ... | (23.6) | ... | (3.31) | (3.32) | ... |
| Boron LePore | Q9/30 | 46.0 | 16 | ... | 1.33 | 5.1 | .11 | .10 | 10 |
| BLPG (Nq) | 9 mo | 145.4 | 23 | ... | 4.63 | 27 | .38 | .30 | 27 |
| BriteSmile Inc | 13wk9/29 | 12.7 | 145 | ... | (4.79) | ... | (.13) | (.42) | ... |
| BSML (Nq) | 39 wk | 34.7 | 170 | ... | (14.1) | ... | (.43) | (1.06) | ... |

## - C -

| COMPANY | PERIOD | REV (mill) | % CHG | INC CT OP (mill) | NET (mill) | % CHG | PER SHARE CURR | PREV | % CHG |
|---|---|---|---|---|---|---|---|---|---|
| CIGNA Corp | Q9/30 | ... | ... | ... | a270.0 | −2.9 | 1.81 | 1.74 | 4.0 |
| CI (N) | 9 mo | ... | ... | ... | a798.0 | 12 | 5.26 | 4.33 | 21 |
| a-Includes net gains of $33,000,000 in the quarter and $63,000,000 in the nine months from the sale of certain assets. Also, the quarter and nine months includes a net charge of $25,000,000 related to the September 11, 2001 terrorist attacks. | | | | | | | | | |
| CarrAmerica Realty | Q9/30 | ... | ... | ... | a28.9 | −42 | .32 | .60 | −47 |
| CRE (N) ▼ | 9 mo | ... | ... | a91.8 | 91.8 | −37 | 1.03 | 1.76 | −41 |
| a-Includes one-time gains of $28,000 in the quarter and $1,082,000 in the nine months. | | | | | | | | | |
| Carver Bancorp | Q9/30 | ... | ... | ... | 0.49 | 74 | .19 | .10 | 90 |
| CNY (A) ▲ | 6 mo | ... | ... | ... | 1.65 | 285 | .66 | .15 | 340 |
| CCL Industries | Q9/30 | 392.6 | 0.9 | ... | a6.20 | −30 | .17 | .23 | −26 |
| TCCQ.B (T) ▼ | 9 mo | 1,227 | 2.0 | ... | a21.9 | −35 | .60 | .88 | −32 |
| Amounts in Canadian dollars. a-Includes nonrecurring charges of 2,700,000 in the quarter and 4,600,000 in the nine months. | | | | | | | | | |
| Chesapeake Util | Q9/30 | 55.6 | −6.2 | ... | (0.67) | ... | (.13) | (.20) | ... |
| CPK (N) | 12 mo | 372.4 | 26 | ... | 7.90 | −4.3 | 1.45 | 1.55 | −6.5 |
| Chippac Inc | Quar Sep: | 74.7 | −52 | (16.4) | (16.4) | ... | (.24) | (.03) | ... |
| CHPC (Nq) L | 9 mo | 251.9 | −30 | (33.6) | (33.6) | ... | (.49) | ... | ... |
| Citizens First Bcp | Q9/30 | ... | ... | ... | 2.35 | 15 | .27 | ... | ... |
| CTZN (Nq) | 6 mo | ... | ... | ... | 5.07 | 23 | .58 | ... | ... |
| Share earnings not shown: company went public in March 2001. | | | | | | | | | |

## - D -

| COMPANY | PERIOD | REV (mill) | % CHG | INC CT OP (mill) | NET (mill) | % CHG | PER SHARE CURR | PREV | % CHG |
|---|---|---|---|---|---|---|---|---|---|
| DSET Corp | Q9/30 | 2.02 | −85 | ... | a(7.56) | ... | (2.61) | (1.13) | ... |
| DSET (Nq) | 9 mo | 8.05 | −81 | ... | a(31.6) | ... | (10.90) | (.06) | ... |
| a-Includes nonrecurring charges of $4,580,000 in the quarter and $14,789,000 in the nine months. | | | | | | | | | |
| DuPont Photomasks | Q9/30 | 77.5 | −23 | (2.98) | (2.98) | ... | (.17) | .55 | ... |
| DPMI (Nq) L | | | | | | | | | |
| Dofasco Inc | Q9/30 | 719.2 | −9.4 | ... | 21.9 | −56 | .29 | .66 | −56 |
| TDFS (T) ▼ | 9 mo | 2,240 | −8.3 | ... | 27.4 | −85 | .36 | 2.38 | −85 |
| Amounts in Canadian dollars. | | | | | | | | | |

## Table 11-1 (*cont.*)

### - E F -

| COMPANY | PERIOD | REV (mill) | % CHG | INC CT OP (mill) | NET (mill) | % CHG | PER SHARE CURR | PREV | % CHG |
|---|---|---|---|---|---|---|---|---|---|
| Echo Bay Mines..........Q9/30 | | 58.5 | -23 | ... | (0.19) | ... | (.03) | .04 | ... |
| ECO (A) L | 9 mo | 186.7 | -12 | ... | 3.20 | -81 | (.07) | .04 | ... |
| Elamex SA De CV......13wk9/28 | | 31.5 | -14 | ... | a(1.06) | ... | (.15) | (.14) | ... |
| ELAM (Nq) | 39 wk | 103.4 | -23 | ... | a(9.65) | ... | (1.41) | 2.56 | ... |

a-Includes restructuring charges of $205,000 in the 13 weeks and $9,319,000 in the 39 weeks.

| COMPANY | PERIOD | REV (mill) | % CHG | INC CT OP (mill) | NET (mill) | % CHG | PER SHARE CURR | PREV | % CHG |
|---|---|---|---|---|---|---|---|---|---|
| EnergySouth Inc........Q9/30 | | 14.9 | 4.7 | ... | 0.70 | -23 | .14 | .18 | -22 |
| ENSI (Nq) | Yr | 107.8 | 45 | 7.56 | 6.14 | -30 | 1.23 | 1.78 | -31 |
| Family Steak House .. 13wk10/3 | | 10.2 | 9.3 | ... | (0.40) | ... | (.16) | (.14) | ... |
| RYFL (Sc) | 39 wk | 32.4 | 7.5 | ... | (0.71) | ... | (.29) | .19 | ... |
| Featherlite Inc...........Q9/30 | | 51.6 | 0.4 | ... | 0.11 | ... | .01 | (.10) | ... |
| FTHR (Sc) P | 9 mo | 173.7 | -6.8 | ... | a(3.97) | ... | (.61) | .17 | ... |

a-Includes restructuring charges of $1,150,000.

| COMPANY | PERIOD | REV (mill) | % CHG | INC CT OP (mill) | NET (mill) | % CHG | PER SHARE CURR | PREV | % CHG |
|---|---|---|---|---|---|---|---|---|---|
| First Indust Rlty........Q9/30 | | ... | ... | ... | 39.5 | 28 | .81 | .58 | 40 |
| FR (N) ▲ | 9 mo | ... | ... | 113.3 | 103.0 | 15 | 2.03 | 1.68 | 21 |
| FloridaFirst Bncp......Q9/30 | | ... | ... | ... | 1.45 | 43 | .27 | .19 | 42 |
| FFBK (Nq) ▲ | Yr | ... | ... | ... | 5.03 | 31 | .93 | .70 | 33 |
| Founders Food...........13wk9/30 | | 2.22 | 107 | ... | (0.07) | ... | (.02) | .01 | ... |
| GCFBU (Sc) L | 39 wk | 6.35 | 117 | ... | (0.10) | ... | (.03) | (.01) | ... |
| Frontier Airlines ........Q9/30 | | 116.0 | -12 | ... | a7.28 | -64 | .24 | .69 | -65 |
| FRNT (Nq) ▼ | 6 mo | 239.3 | -1.9 | ... | a15.0 | -59 | .50 | 1.27 | -61 |

a-Includes a net gain of $5,500,000 from a federal grant.

| COMPANY | PERIOD | REV (mill) | % CHG | INC CT OP (mill) | NET (mill) | % CHG | PER SHARE CURR | PREV | % CHG |
|---|---|---|---|---|---|---|---|---|---|
| Finning Int'l.............Q9/30 | | 799.7 | 50 | ... | 29.9 | 60 | .39 | .25 | 56 |
| TFTT (T) ▲ | 9 mo | 2,378 | 34 | ... | 76.1 | 47 | .99 | .66 | 50 |

Amounts in Canadian dollars

### - G -

| COMPANY | PERIOD | REV (mill) | % CHG | INC CT OP (mill) | NET (mill) | % CHG | PER SHARE CURR | PREV | % CHG |
|---|---|---|---|---|---|---|---|---|---|
| Genta Inc...................Q9/30 | | 0.02 | 35 | ... | (10.4) | ... | (.19) | (.05) | ... |
| GNTA (Nq) | 9 mo | 0.11 | 518 | ... | (28.8) | ... | (.54) | (.50) | ... |
| Great Amer Finl........Q9/30 | | ... | ... | ... | 18.4 | -40 | .42 | .72 | -42 |
| GFR (N) ▼ | 9 mo | ... | ... | 41.9 | 36.4 | -21 | .84 | 1.08 | -22 |
| Great Lakes REIT......Q9/30 | | ... | ... | ... | 5.39 | -7.6 | .27 | .29 | -6.9 |
| GL (N) | 9 mo | ... | ... | ... | 17.1 | -15 | .86 | 1.05 | -18 |
| Green Mountain Pwr ...Q9/30 | | 76.1 | -2.7 | ... | 3.62 | 65 | .58 | .36 | 61 |
| GMP (N) ▲ | 12 mo | 287.9 | 3.8 | 7.85 | 2.68 | ... | .48 | (1.26) | ... |
| Gumtech Int'l.............Q9/30 | | 2.72 | 122 | (0.10) | 17.3 | ... | 1.85 | (.14) | ... |
| GUMM (Nq) P | 9 mo | 10.6 | 72 | (1.93) | 15.4 | ... | 1.66 | (.55) | ... |

### - H -

| COMPANY | PERIOD | REV (mill) | % CHG | INC CT OP (mill) | NET (mill) | % CHG | PER SHARE CURR | PREV | % CHG |
|---|---|---|---|---|---|---|---|---|---|
| Hector Communicat ..Q9/30 | | 10.4 | 6.4 | ... | a1.97 | 92 | .52 | .27 | 93 |
| HCT (A) ▲ | 9 mo | 30.5 | 11 | ... | a3.80 | 23 | 1.01 | .80 | 26 |

a-Includes gains from the sale of securities of $2,335,909 in the quarter and $3,659,054 in the nine months.

| COMPANY | PERIOD | REV (mill) | % CHG | INC CT OP (mill) | NET (mill) | % CHG | PER SHARE CURR | PREV | % CHG |
|---|---|---|---|---|---|---|---|---|---|
| Home Properties-NY ..Q9/30 | | ... | ... | ... | 19.3 | 56 | .66 | .40 | 65 |
| HME (N) ▲ | 9 mo | ... | ... | ... | 48.7 | 58 | 1.61 | 1.10 | 46 |
| Hunt (JB) Trans........Q9/30 | | 537.2 | 5.4 | ... | 4.55 | -50 | .12 | .26 | -54 |
| JBHT (Nq) ▼ | 9 mo | 1,554 | -4.5 | ... | 14.8 | -41 | .41 | .71 | -42 |

### - I J -

| COMPANY | PERIOD | REV (mill) | % CHG | INC CT OP (mill) | NET (mill) | % CHG | PER SHARE CURR | PREV | % CHG |
|---|---|---|---|---|---|---|---|---|---|
| ITLA Capital Corp......Q9/30 | | ... | ... | ... | 4.04 | -13 | .62 | .65 | -4.6 |
| ITLA (Nq) | 9 mo | ... | ... | ... | 13.5 | 0.1 | 1.99 | 1.86 | 7.0 |
| Image Sensing Sys ...Q9/30 | | 1.64 | 9.4 | ... | (0.04) | ... | (.01) | (.03) | ... |
| ISNS (Sc) | 9 mo | 4.61 | 12 | ... | (0.34) | ... | (.11) | | ... |
| Insur Auto Auctions..Q9/30 | | 71.0 | -11 | ... | (0.21) | ... | (.02) | .20 | ... |
| IAAI (Nq) L | 9 mo | 224.3 | -11 | ... | a0.32 | -97 | .03 | .99 | -97 |

a-Includes a nonrecurring charge of $6,047,000.

| COMPANY | PERIOD | REV (mill) | % CHG | INC CT OP (mill) | NET (mill) | % CHG | PER SHARE CURR | PREV | % CHG |
|---|---|---|---|---|---|---|---|---|---|
| Interleukin Genetics .Q9/30 | | 0.02 | -35 | ... | (1.14) | ... | (.05) | (.06) | ... |
| ILGN (Sc) | 9 mo | 0.18 | -11 | ... | (3.42) | ... | (.16) | (.20) | ... |
| Iomed Inc...................Q9/30 | | 2.91 | 3.0 | ... | (0.57) | ... | (.09) | (.07) | ... |
| IOX (A) | | | | | | | | | |

surplus. Further, even if there are funds legally available from which a preferred dividend may be paid, the directors may decide to omit dividends. The incentive to pay a preferred dividend is that if it is omitted all dividends on the common shares must also be omitted. Articles of incorporation also sometimes provide that if a preferred dividend is omitted for a specified period, the preferred shareholders obtain a right to vote.

## §11.5  Cumulative and Noncumulative Dividends

Preferred stock may be **cumulative, noncumulative**, or **partially cumulative**. If **cumulative dividends** are not paid in some years, they are carried forward and both they and the current year's preferred dividends must be paid in full before any common dividends may be declared. Noncumulative dividends disappear each year if they are not paid. Partially cumulative dividends are usually cumulative to the extent of earnings (i.e., the dividend is cumulative in any year only to the extent of actual earnings during that year). Unpaid cumulative dividends are not debts of the corporation, but a continued right to priority in future distributions.

An example may help to illustrate the concept of cumulative, noncumulative, and partially cumulative dividends. Assume that a preferred stock has a preferential right to a dividend of $5 per share per year, but the directors, as is their right, decide to omit all dividends for two consecutive years. In the third year, the directors conclude that the corporation is able to resume the payment of dividends. If the preferred shares' preferential right is cumulative, the board of directors must pay $15 on each preferred share ($5 per share for each of the two years missed plus $5 per share for the current year) before any dividend may be paid on the common shares in the third year. If the preferred shares' preferential right is noncumulative, the preferences for the two omitted years disappear entirely, and a dividend on the common shares may be paid after the $5 preferred dividend for the third year is paid. If the dividend is cumulative to the extent earned, the earnings of the corporation in each of the two years in which dividends were omitted must be examined, and the dividend is cumulative each year only to the extent the earnings cover the $5 preferred dividend: If the corporation had a loss in one of those years, the preferred dividend for that year would be lost much as though the dividend were entirely noncumulative.

In evaluating dividend policies with respect to preferred shares, one should normally start with the assumption that the board of directors, which is elected by the common shareholders, will maximize the dividends payable on common shares at the expense of preferred shareholders to the extent they lawfully may do so. A noncumulative preferential dividend right therefore leaves the preferred shareholders quite exposed, because the common shareholders' position is improved in the future whenever a preferred dividend is omitted. Indeed, a policy of paying dividends erratically once every few years materially improves the position of the common shares with respect to the noncumulative preferred. Such a policy, however, may be subject to legal attack as a breach of the directors' fiduciary duty to treat all classes of outstanding shares fairly.

Cumulative dividends provide preferred shareholders considerably greater protection than noncumulative or partially cumulative dividends. But cumulative dividends are not a complete answer either, because the board of directors may defer the payment of all dividends indefinitely in an effort to depress the price of the preferred (if it is publicly traded), which may then be acquired on the open market. On the other hand, it is customary to provide that preferred shares may elect a specified number of directors if preferred dividends have been omitted for a specified period, and the presence of one or more directors elected by the preferred shareholders may minimize the possibility of such overtly unfair strategies.

## §11.6  Convertible Shares

Preferred shares may be made convertible at the option of the preferred shareholder into common shares at a specified price or a specified ratio. When **convertible** shares are converted, the original preferred shares are turned in and canceled, and new common shares are issued. The **conversion price** or **conversion ratio** is fixed and defined in the preferred shareholders' contract. The conversion ratio is usually made adjustable for share dividends, share splits, the issuance of additional common shares, and similar transactions affecting the underlying common shares. The provisions requiring such adjustments are called **anti-dilution provisions**.

The determination of the conversion ratio (i.e., how many shares of common stock a preferred shareholder receives upon the exercise of the conversion privilege) may involve negotiation between the corporation and a potential investor before the shares are issued. Convertible preferred stock may be issued to a venture capital fund or other investor in a closely held corporation to reflect a limited equity investment in the enterprise. Publicly held corporations may also issue convertible preferred stock, which may be publicly traded. Typically, when both the common and the convertible preferred are publicly traded, the original conversion ratio is established so that the common must appreciate substantially in price before it becomes attractive to convert the preferred into common. A similar combination of risk and reward can be achieved by the sale of a preferred stock with a warrant to purchase common shares attached. Convertible preferred shares are quite common. There has been an extended and rather inconclusive theoretical discussion about why this particular security is so popular.

The conversions discussed in this section are **downstream conversions** (or downhill conversions). An **upstream conversion** (or uphill conversion) is from common shares into preferred shares (or from preferred shares to debt). Securities with upstream conversion rights are extremely rare, and may not be permitted at all under the statutes of some states.

## §11.7  Redeemability of Preferred Shares

Preferred shares are usually made **redeemable** at the option of the corporation upon the payment of a fixed amount for each share. These shares may also be called **callable shares**. The **redemption price** is set in the articles of incorporation or the document creating the preferred shares and may be a matter of preissue negotiation between the corporation and an investor. Redemption prices are usually established at a level somewhat higher than the consideration that the investor originally paid for the preferred shares.

The power to redeem preferred shares usually applies only to the entire class or series of preferred as a unit. However, the preferred shareholders' contract sometimes provides that redemptions of a portion of a class or series are permitted; such provisions may also include rules for determining which shares are to be redeemed. If a convertible preferred is called for redemption, the conversion privilege typically continues after the announcement that the shares will be called for redemption until the shares are actually redeemed. In some cases, conversion rights are triggered by a call for redemption.

## §11.8 Series and Classes of Preferred Shares

Articles of incorporation may authorize preferred shares to be issued in **series**. The articles of incorporation in effect create a class of shares without any substantive terms (sometimes also called **blank check stock**) and authorize the board of directors to create series from within that class from time to time and to vary any of the substantive terms of each series. When preferred shares are to be sold by a corporation from time to time, allowing the board of directors to set financial terms simplifies financing, because the price, dividend, liquidation preference, sinking fund provision, voting rights, and other terms of each series may be tailored to then-current market conditions without incurring the expense of a proxy solicitation and the holding of a special shareholders' meeting to approve an amendment to the articles of incorporation setting forth the terms of the class. Shares of different series have identical rights except for the specified terms, which may be varied.

The power to create series of preferred shares may also be used by boards of directors of publicly held corporations to create poison pills without shareholder approval, as a defense against hostile takeovers. Poison pills are discussed more fully in the chapter on mergers and acquisitions.

There is little or no difference between a series or a class of shares except their manner of creation—by amendment to the articles of incorporation in the case of a class and by action of the board of directors, acting alone, in the case of a series. Indeed, the issuance of a new series of preferred usually requires that the corporation file an amendment to the articles of incorporation although no vote of the shareholders is required.

## §11.9 Novel Types of Preferred Shares

The high interest rates of the early 1980s led to the development of novel financing devices, many of which involved preferred shares. For example, many corporations issued preferred shares that were redeemable at the holder's option, or that became redeemable upon the occurrence of some external event, such as a change in interest rates or the lapse of a specified period of time. Still other corporations issued preferred shares with floating or adjustable dividend rates that depended on interest rates or some similar measure. These novel preferred were designed to give corporate holders of the preferred the tax benefits of the exclusion for intercorporate dividends, while at the same time giving the holders most of the benefits of traditional debt.

## §11.10 Market Price of Simple Preferred Shares

Many preferred shares are publicly traded on the major securities exchanges. Many are listed on the New York Stock Exchange. Most publicly traded preferred shares have fixed and fully cumulative dividend rights. As a practical matter, in the case of most of these preferred shares, there is virtually no chance that a dividend will ever be omitted. In effect, these securities, like publicly traded bonds, provide a permanent cash flow in a fixed amount. The value placed on these shares in the market represents little more than the present value of this discounted future cash flow. The yields on high-quality preferred shares (the return per dollar invested in the shares) was about 8 percent in the fall of 2001. At the same time, the yield on investment quality bonds was about 7 percent. Market prices and yields of both bonds and preferred stock vary widely, however, depending on the economic strength of the issuing corporation and the terms of the security. The volatility of these yields appear to have increased since the terrorist events of September 11, 2001.

## §11.11 Market Price of Convertible Preferred Shares and Arbitrage

The pricing of a **convertible** preferred is considerably more complex than the pricing of a nonconvertible preferred. Assume that a publicly held corporation has outstanding several million shares of common stock traded on the New York Stock Exchange. The current market price of the common is $20 per share, and management believes that it is likely to trade in the $20-$30 range for the indefinite future. A regular dividend of $1 per share has been paid on the common shares for the last three years, and management anticipates that this regular dividend will be continued at that rate for the indefinite future. In order to raise additional working capital, the corporation decides to make a public offering of a new class of convertible preferred shares with the following rights: It is to be entitled to a cumulative dividend of $6 per share per year and will be offered initially to the public at $54 per share in order to yield an initial investor an 11 percent return, the approximate yield of similar convertible preferred shares. There is no appreciable risk that the $6 dividend will be omitted in any year in the foreseeable future. Each preferred share is convertible into two shares of common stock at any time at the option of the holder and is callable by the corporation at any time for $65 per share. It is anticipated that the preferred will also be publicly traded on the New York Stock Exchange.

The basic financial characteristics described in this paragraph may be summarized:

|                            | Preferred shares | Common shares |
|----------------------------|:----------------:|:-------------:|
| Market price               | $54              | $20           |
| Dividend                   | $ 6              | $ 1           |
| Convertibility into common | 2:1              | N/A           |
| Callability                | $65              | N/A           |

When the preferred is issued, it begins to trade between $52 and $60 per share. At that price, no one exercises the conversion privilege: After all, why give up something worth $52 to $60 in order to acquire two shares of stock that can be bought for $40? Similarly, the corporation probably will not give serious consideration to calling the preferred at $65. If the corporation wishes to retire some preferred shares, it may buy them for $52 to $60. Why pay $65?

Now consider what happens to the price of the preferred when the price of the common begins to creep up. When it reaches $27.50 per share, the value of two shares of common has risen to $55, and the preferred must remain at or above $55 per share. If it drops to $53, traders can buy the preferred at $53 and convert it into common shares that can be immediately sold for $55, making an instant $2 profit. This type of transaction is known as **arbitrage**, a fancy term for the process of profiting on small differences in market prices of two different but equivalent securities or in the market prices of the same security in two different markets.

Assume now that the price of the common rises further to $32 per share. The floor under the preferred is now $64, and every purchaser of the initial preferred at $54 has made a tidy paper profit of at least $10 per share. (It is only a paper profit, because it has not been realized either by the sale of the preferred or by its conversion into common and the sale of the common.) More important, when the common is at $32, the preferred is no longer priced in the market as a straight preferred. Rather, its price is now directly tied to the price of the common in accordance with the conversion ratio. If the common declines in price by $1 per share, the preferred will decline by about $2 per share; if the common goes up by $3 per share to $35, the preferred will go up by about $6 per share. If the price of the common falls, the preferred will follow the common down (at a $2 decline per preferred share for each $1 decline in value of the common) until the preferred reaches a price that reflects its market value as a preferred stock (plus the value of an option to buy two shares of common at $27.50 per share); at that point, it will again trade much as a straight preferred.

Assuming that the common is trading for $32 per share, what price will the market place on the preferred? Will it be $64 or will it be even higher? At first it may seem that it must be higher than $64: if two shares of common with an aggregate $2 dividend sell for $64, a stock with the same market characteristics but with a $6 dividend is going to be worth more. How much more? One might expect it would be the present value of the stream of the $4 difference between the two dividends. It will, however, be much less than that, because it is unlikely that the difference in dividend rates will continue indefinitely. The corporation may call the preferred at some time in the future, and the $32 price may itself reflect the market anticipating an increase in the common dividend rate. It is not possible to calculate the values to be assigned to these variables mathematically and thus what the price of the preferred should be, except to conclude that it must be higher than $64—perhaps $67 or $68.

Another interesting question is this: Should a holder of the preferred convert when the common is at $32 if he believes that the price of the common will go even higher? A moment's thought should reveal that would be an unwise decision. Why give up a $6 cumulative dividend in order to obtain two common shares with a combined dividend of $2 per share? There is no risk that the expected increase in price of the common will escape the owner of the preferred, because the price of the preferred is now directly tied to the price of the common. In short, there is nothing to be gained and much to be lost by converting immediately.

## §11.12 Redemption of Convertible Preferred Shares

Consider the factors relating to the corporation's power to call the preferred shares for redemption at $65 per share. A critical point is that the corporation must announce an impending redemption in advance. The privilege to convert continues after the announcement and until the redemption becomes effective.

What happens after a call for redemption is issued depends essentially on the price of the underlying common shares at the time the redemption actually occurs. If the market price of two shares of common stock is less than $65 per share, shareholders should not convert their preferred shares into common stock, but rather should permit the shares to be called at $65 per share. Thus, if the corporation calls the shares for redemption when the price of the underlying common is $32.50 or less, it should end up redeeming the entire issue for cash. On the other hand, if the market price of the common is above $32.50 per share at the time of redemption, the shareholders should exercise the conversion privilege shortly before the call becomes effective and convert the preferred into the more valuable common. For example, if the common is at $35 per share, the choice is between permitting the shares to be called for a payment of $65 or converting them into shares of common stock worth $70. Such a conversion is sometimes called a **forced conversion**, because the economics are such that a rational investor has no choice but to exercise the power to convert (or to sell the preferred, in which case the purchaser will convert).

In the real world, things do not work perfectly. Preferred shareholders are scattered around the country and may not be able to select the best option at the very last minute. Some must decide several days in advance of the final date, and a last-minute price movement of the common may mean that some make the wrong decision. Also, a few may simply act too late, and find that their shares were redeemed when they intended to exercise the conversion privilege. Still others may be ill, out of the country, or unaware of the pending redemption or indeed of the fact that they own the shares of preferred stock, and make no decision at all. But the great bulk of shares will be handled rationally.

Why do corporations try to compel conversions? One reason is that the substitution of two shares of common for every share of preferred causes a reduction in dividend payments from $6 to $2 for every share of preferred. This reduction in dividend payments is pure gravy, because there is no capital outflow to eliminate the more expensive preferred shares. A forced conversion may also appeal to notions of equity as between holders of common and preferred, because the preferred receives the full benefit of runups in the price of the common but enjoys three times the dividend and has some protection against price declines on the downside. Finally, the elimination of the preferred shares simplifies the capital structure of the corporation and improves the appearance of the corporation's balance sheet.

If the directors call a convertible preferred for redemption, they are required to give the holders of the preferred accurate information about the reasons for the redemption. The corporation may not withhold from the preferred shareholders information regarding developments that would affect the decision of whether to convert the shares.

## §11.13 Protection of Conversion Privilege Against Dilution

In the example discussed in the last section, each share of the preferred stock is entitled to be converted into two shares of common stock. What happens if the board of directors decides to split the common shares, which are trading for $30, three-for-one—that is, the board decides to issue each shareholder two additional shares for each outstanding share so that each shareholder would have three shares instead of one? Let us further assume that the dividend rate on the new shares is one-third the rate on the old shares so that each new share sells for one-third of the price of each old share—about $10 per share if the old shares sold for approximately $30 per share before the split. What does this do to the conversion privilege of the preferred?

The black letter rule is very simple: If the drafters of the preferred shareholders' contract did not take this possibility into account, the conversion privilege is not adjusted for the share split. Each preferred share continues to be convertible into only two shares of common stock and the conversion privilege has lost two-thirds of its potential value. Provisions guarding the conversion privilege against changes of this type are called **anti-dilution provisions** and should always be included in preferred shareholders' contracts when there is a conversion privilege. Drafting an anti-dilution clause is tricky, because the courts are not going to help the draftsman out if he or she overlooks some possibility. Significant dilution may occur because of a variety of transactions, such as mergers, share dividends, executive compensation plans, and the like, and it is not always clear which issuances of new common shares the anti-dilution clause should cover. Nevertheless, the basic principle seems clear and straightforward, at least so far as shares splits are concerned: The drafters of the preferred shareholders contract should insert a clause providing that if the common stock is split, the conversion privilege should be adjusted so that each share of preferred is convertible into the number of new common shares that two shares of the old common stock became upon the split.

## §11.14 Classified Common Stock

State statutes give corporations broad power to create classes of common shares with different rights or privileges. For example, the rights of two classes of shares may be identical except that one class is entitled to twice the dividend per share of the second class. Or, shares of each class may have identical financial rights per share but each class of common shares, regardless of the number of shares, is entitled to elect one director (thereby assuring equal class representation on the board of directors even though the number of shares in the two classes are unequal). Classes of shares are widely used in closely held corporations.

Publicly held corporations also use classified common shares, although their use is not widespread. The New York Stock Exchange has historically refused to list shares of a corporation if the corporation also has a class of nonvoting shares or one or more classes with fractional or multiple votes per share.

Since the 1980s, several publicly held corporations have created **dual class voting structures**. This device is often used in corporations in which a given family has long been in control but is now concerned that a takeover attempt may be in the offing. With dual class voting, special classes of shares with "super" voting rights may be issued solely to family members. The terms of these special classes may provide, for example, that family-owed shares have 10 votes per share, but their voting power declines to 1 vote per share if they are sold or conveyed to a person who is not a family member. Dual class voting permits the controlling family to retain voting control over the corporation while at the same time permitting the corporation to raise capital through the sale of common shares. In 1988, the SEC adopted Rule 19c-4, which in effect outlawed new classes of such shares for publicly traded corporations, but the courts invalidated this rule as exceeding the powers of the SEC, which basically are limited to enforcing disclosure rules.

A similar gimmick is the creation of **tenure voting** common stock, permitting shareholders who have held their shares for a specified period (e.g., for 36 months to have 5 votes per share). If shares are transferred, the new holder has 1 vote per share until his holding period exceeds 36 months, when the shareholder regains the right to 5 votes per share. Tenure voting discourages takeover attempts, because a bidder who acquires shares finds his or her voting power significantly reduced.

Both dual class and tenure voting shares have generally been upheld under state law, at least in Delaware. However, the SEC has consistently attacked these devices as being discriminatory and unfair to public shareholders. Despite the invalidation of Rule 19c-4, the SEC has persuaded the securities exchanges to keep rules that require the **delisting** of corporations that issue dual class or tenure voting shares. Delisting means that the shares of that corporation cannot thereafter be traded on that exchange.

## §11.15 Transferable Warrants and Rights to Purchase Shares

Corporations may issue **warrants** or **rights** to purchase common shares. Warrants and rights are options to purchase shares at a fixed price during some defined time period. If the common shares are publicly traded, the warrants or rights may also be publicly traded.

Warrants are transferable long-term options to acquire shares from the corporation at a specified price. Warrants have many of the qualities of an equity security, because their price is a function of the market price of the underlying shares and the specified issuance price. Warrants have no voting or dividend rights. Warrants are often issued as a sweetener in connection with the distribution of a debt or preferred stock issue. They may also be issued in connection with a public exchange offer, or as compensation for handling the public distribution of other shares. Sometimes they are issued in a reorganization to holders of a class of security not otherwise recognized in the reorganization.

**Rights** are short-term warrants, expiring within one year. They may also be publicly traded and listed on securities exchanges. Rights are often issued in lieu of a dividend, or in an effort to raise capital from existing shareholders.

The price relationship between a warrant or right and the underlying security is a complex one. The value of any option has two components: **intrinsic value** and **time value**. For example, if the underlying security is selling at $15 per share, and the warrant can be exercised for $12 per share, the warrant has an intrinsic value of $3; one can exercise the option and immediately sell the shares for a $3 gain. If, on the other hand, the value of the underlying security is $10 per share, one might expect that the warrant would have no value. After all, who wants a right to purchase for $12 per share something that can be bought for $10? In fact, such a warrant has some value because of the possibility that the underlying security may rise in price above $12 during the life of the warrant. This value is called the time value of the option. If the time period before expiration is relatively short, or if the exercise price is much higher than the value of the underlying security, the time value of the option is very low, perhaps only a few cents per warrant. But all options have some time value.

If the underlying security does rise above $12 per share in the above example, the market price of the warrant will also rise in value almost dollar-for-dollar. Whether it would be sensible to exercise such a warrant before its expiration depends on the income forgone on the amount paid to exercise the warrant compared with the dividends likely to be declared on the underlying security.

## §11.16  Bonds and Debentures

The two types of debt instruments most commonly classed as securities are **bonds** and **debentures**. These types of securities may be publicly traded and have close economic similarities to publicly traded preferred stock.

Technically, a debenture is an unsecured corporate obligation, while a bond is secured by a lien or mortgage on specific corporate property. However, the word "bond" is often used to mean both bonds and debentures; this chapter will use it this way hereafter. The presence or absence of security in the form of a lien or mortgage for marketable debt interests is not as important as might be supposed, because if bondholders attempt to foreclose on corporate property, the corporation will obtain protection from the federal bankruptcy court and the attempt to levy upon the property will be stayed.

Debt securities are unconditional obligations to pay specific sums at a date in the future and usually to pay interest in specified amounts at specified times in the interim. They are long-term debt securities with maturities of 50 years or more in some cases, though 30 years is more common, and many bonds mature in 10 years or less.

Historically, bonds were **bearer securities**, negotiable by delivery, with interest payments represented by coupons that were periodically clipped and submitted to the issuer for payment. The Internal Revenue Code now requires virtually all new bonds to be **registered securities**, transferable only by endorsement, and as a result, bearer bonds have largely disappeared or have been made into registered securities. Registered securities are made payable to a specific payee and interest is paid to the registered owner by check or wire transfer in much the same way as dividends are paid to the registered owner of shares of stock. A bearer instrument can be transformed into a registered security at any time. Transfer of a registered bond is effected by endorsement rather than by mere physical delivery of the piece of paper. Article 8 of the Uniform Commercial Code makes registered bonds negotiable just like any other security.

Interest payments on debt securities are usually fixed obligations expressed as a percentage of the face amount of the bond and payable irrespective of the financial performance of the issuing company. However, so-called income bonds, in which the obligation to pay interest is conditioned on adequate earnings, also exist. Somewhat rarer are so-called **participating bonds**, where the amount of interest payable on the bonds increases with earnings. These securities are known as hybrid securities because they have some characteristics of an equity security. In recent years, debt securities with variable or floating interest rates—based on market interest rates—have also been created.

Debt securities are usually subject to redemption, often at a slight premium over face value. Unlike redemption of preferred shares, individual bonds may usually be redeemed without redeeming the entire issue. Bonds selected for redemption may be chosen by lot or by some other system. Many debt securities require the corporation to create sinking funds to redeem a part of the issue each year or to accumulate to pay off the entire issue when it matures. Similar provisions are also common in connection with issues of preferred stock.

Debt securities, like preferred stock, may also be made convertible into equity securities—almost always common shares—on some predetermined ratio. The conversion privilege for bonds operates in a very similar manner to the conversion privilege for preferred shares discussed above, except that with bonds the bond indenture (the instrument that sets forth the terms of the bonds) specifies some dollar amount of bonds per share of stock, because bonds are not issued in any share-like units. Like convertible preferred, the conversion ratio is usually protected against dilution by adjustments for share splits and share dividends. When convertible bonds are converted, they and the debt they represent disappear and new equity securities are issued in their place. Convertible bonds are treated as equity securities for some purposes; in calculating fully diluted earnings per share, for example, the common shares that would be issued upon conversion are taken into account in the calculation.

The interaction between the power of the corporation to call convertible debentures and the power of the holder to exercise the conversion privilege is similar to that of preferred shares. If a convertible debenture is called for redemption, the conversion privilege continues until the debentures are actually redeemed. If the value of the stock exceeds the redemption price, the conversion is forced, because it is obviously to the holders' advantage to convert following an announcement that the debentures will be called for redemption on a specified date. A conversion of bonds cleans up the balance sheet by substituting equity for debt, reducing the debt/equity ratio, and otherwise appearing to improve the financial health of the business.

When debt securities mature, the issuer may borrow funds (perhaps by creating a new debt issue maturing far in the future) to pay off the maturing obligations. This process is known as **rolling over** the debt.

Although debt securities are similar in many respects to preferred stock, there are some important legal differences that may affect the value of these securities. Table 11-2 sets forth the most important similarities and differences between these two types of securities.

## §11.17  Private Placements

**Private placement** refers to the raising of capital by the sale of securities directly to large investors. The advantages of private placement over the public sale of securities include cost savings, because registration of the issue with the SEC is unnecessary and no selling efforts are required. In addition, restrictions on the issuer's future actions are directly negotiated with the suppliers of credit and the possibility of future litigation is reduced. A significant fraction of all new issues each year—hundreds of billions of dollars of securities—are placed privately. In recent years, pension funds have become major purchasers of privately placed securities.

## §11.18  Record and Nominee Ownership of Securities

Historically, equity securities were registered in the name of the owner on the books of the issuing corporation, while debt instruments were issued in the

## Table 11-2

| Characteristic | Preferred stock | Bonds |
| --- | --- | --- |
| Manner of creation of new classes or issues | Amendment to articles of incorporation | Action by directors alone without shareholder approval |
| Maturity date | No | Yes |
| Voting | Usually only if dividend omitted | Rarely (prohibited in most states) |
| Treatment on balance sheet | Equity | Debt |
| Interim payments | Dividend | Interest |
| Amount | Fixed (usually) | Fixed (usually) |
| Omission of | No default; carries over if cumulative | Default |
| Tax effect on issuer | Not deductible | Deductible |
| Tax effect on recipient | Taxable, but dividend credit if receipient is corporation | Taxable |
| Callable | Usually | Usually |
| Convertible | Optional | Optional |
| Effect of conversion into common | Does not affect capital or debt/equity ratio; reduces dividend rates by difference between common and preferred rates; increases number of common shares | Reduces debt and increases equity; affects debt/equity ratio; eliminates interest payments; increases number of shares |

form of bearer securities. As a consequence, the issuer knew fairly precisely who the owners of its equity securities were and could communicate with them, but it knew nothing about who owned its debt securities. The corporation could pay a dividend by check to each registered owner of shares but could make interest payments on its debt securities only when it received the interest coupons with instructions as to where to make the payment. Numerous other practical differences existed between these two forms of ownership.

In the early 1900s, practices developed that blurred the distinction between registered and bearer securities, at least in the case of stock. One practice developed by institutional investors involved using **nominees** as **record owners** of equity securities rather than registering the securities directly in their own names. This practice originally developed apparently in order to avoid onerous legal requirements that existed in many states that required fiduciaries who were designated as record owners of certificates to exhibit evidence of their authority to transfer the securities. Using a nominee (such as a shell company called Abell & Company) avoided these legal requirements, because there was no evidence of fiduciary responsibility on the certificates themselves.

The second practice that blurred the distinction between registered and bearer securities was the growth of the practice of registering shares in **street name**. If a trader purchased shares of stock planning to resell them in the near

future when the price rose, it was often not convenient to register the ownership in the name of the trader for the few days that the trader might hold them.
Instead, shares were registered in the name of the brokerage firm handling the
trade and the obligation of traders to receive or deliver securities was met simply
by physical delivery of these certificates. These certificates became in effect
bearer securities.

In the 1960s and 1970s, trading volume increased dramatically, and the
street name system broke down in what became known as the back office crisis.
The physical delivery of street name certificates simply could not keep up with
the volume of trading. An entirely new system of securities ownership was
created, which has become the standard for both equity and debt securities.
This new system is called the **book entry** system and is quite different from
the historical nominee and street name practices outlined above. Because the
system has elements of nominee and street name practices, however, one sometimes sees references to securities held in book entry form as involving street
name or nominee ownership.

To see how this new system works, assume that you decide to purchase
100 shares of General Motors. This transaction will be handled by a securities
broker; after he purchases the shares on your behalf, you will need to provide
the funds necessary to pay for the shares within three days of the transaction.
You will not, however, receive a certificate for those shares (unless you make
special arrangements to do so, which may include a separate fee for providing
a certificate). Rather, you will simply receive a confirmation of the transaction,
and thereafter a monthly statement from your broker that shows that you own
100 shares of General Motors. When General Motors pays a dividend, the
correct dividend will be added to your account (or you may arrange for the
broker to send a check to you for the amount of each dividend). You will
receive periodic reports, proxy statement, annual reports, and the like, all prepared by General Motors, but they will come through your broker or through
a company that has a contract with your broker to forward these documents
to individual shareholders. When you decide to sell your shares of General
Motors, you simply call your broker and the proceeds will be added to your
account three days after the sale.

This is obviously much more convenient than the old system, but to the
user, it is not obvious how it works. What happens to the certificates? Today,
the registered owner of the great bulk of all publicly traded securities is Cede
& Company, the nominee for the **Depository Trust Company** (**DTC**). The
DTC is the principal clearing house for securities transactions in the United
States. Banks, institutional investors, and securities are members of the DTC
(or have affiliations with members of the DTC). Basically, certificates are im-
mobilized in the DTC and transactions are recorded by a netting process and
book entry. When you purchased the 100 shares of General Motors described
above, your broker may have sold shares of General Motors owned by other
customers the same day. At the end of the day, your broker reports to the DTC
its net change in General Motors shares in transactions with all other members
of the DTC. If it turns out that your broker had only one other customer who
sold 100 shares of General Motors and you were the sole purchaser of shares

of General Motors on the day of your purchase, your broker will adjust its records simply to show that the seller no longer owned the 100 shares and that you now owned them. The movement of share ownership was reflected solely by book entry. The DTC handles net changes in ownership interests of its members in exactly the same way. If it turns out that your broker had no sales of General Motors stock on the day of your purchase, it would report to the DTC that its holdings of General Motors increased by 100 shares, while the records of some other firm would be adjusted to reflect that someone sold 100 shares of General Motors to your broker. Again the transfer would be recorded by book entries and there would be no physical movement of stock certificates. Today, transfers of securities are arguably reflected by book entries, not by movements of certificates.

So where is the certificate for the 100 shares of General Motors that you bought? It is most likely to be part of a jumbo certificate for millions of shares issued by General Motors in the name of Cede & Company in the vaults of the DTC. Money and shares move around from investor to investor, but the certificates remain in the DTC's vault.

If you decide you want a certificate for your shares of General Motors, your broker will contact the DTC, which in turn will arrange for General Motors to issue a certificate in your name. But that is a nuisance and many investors do not bother. If you do obtain a share certificate, you may take possession of it yourself or leave it with the brokerage firm for safekeeping. If you later decide to sell these shares, you must arrange to endorse the certificate so that the shares may be transferred.

The book entry system is popular with brokers not only because of its simplicity, but also because it tends to tie the customer closely to the brokerage firm. A holder of shares held in book entry can sell the shares only through the broker who has a record of the ownership. Although it is possible to transfer shares from one brokerage firm to another, an investor may be reluctant to do so and it is certainly not encouraged by brokerage firms.

The book entry system is used for both debt and equity securities. Private placements of debt securities are routinely handled in book entry form. Interest and dividend payments are made by wire transfer to brokerage firms or institutional investors. Old habits, however, sometimes die hard. Some individual investors do not trust the new system of book entry and continue to request certificates. Today, these people are a small minority.

As one reflects on this system, it is clear that the solvency and honesty of brokerage firms is an essential element of the system. It is also a potential source of weakness. A brokerage firm may own shares of General Motors in its own proprietary account as well as holding shares for its customers. SEC regulations (and the revised Article 8 of the Uniform Commercial Code) require such a firm to separate its proprietary ownership on its own records and not to sell or **hypothecate** (borrow against) its customers' securities without their consent. However, a firm that is in financial difficulty may violate these rules or simply convert customer securities to its own use. A federally chartered corporation, the **Securities Investor Protection Corporation** (the **SIPC**), protects customers against loss caused by brokerage firm failure (up to specific limits). However, it is possible that a customer may own securities that exceed the coverage that the SIPC provides, and to that extent investors are at risk of loss because of the book entry system.

The book entry system is undoubtedly an ingenious solution to the problems created by the current volume of securities transactions. The SEC has, however, long considered it to be an interim solution. Not only is there a possibility that customers may lose valuable assets through the defalcation of brokers, but also there are problems of brokerage control over securities transactions of customers and of communication between the issuers and shareholders. Communication problems arise because of the presence of at least two intermediaries between issuer and shareholder—the DTC and the customer's broker.

The long-term solution that the SEC envisions is the elimination of all share certificates and the substitution of certificate-less shares with ownership records being kept by the issuer or its transfer agent. Transfers of shares would be recorded in the books of the issuer and not of the broker. This solution would require sophisticated computer technology. Moreover, the current intermediaries are not in favor of the idea for obvious reasons. Still, the SEC has begun implementing such a direct registration scheme.

## §11.19 Lost or Missing Certificates

An investor who permits his or her securities to be held in book entry form by a broker need not be concerned about the whereabouts of certificates for securities or bearer bonds. If, however, the investor personally wishes to maintain the tangible evidence of ownership and take delivery of certificates (perhaps because it affords freedom to shift among brokerage firms in order to pay the lowest commissions on trades), he or she usually rents a safe deposit box at a local bank as a secure place to keep the certificates. A safe deposit box, however, requires inconvenient and time-consuming trips to the bank whenever securities are purchased or sold. Another alternative is to leave the certificates with the broker for safekeeping. Some investors, however, use desk drawers, files in filing cabinets, and even the sock drawer as the storage place for securities. It is therefore not surprising that certificates are sometimes lost, stolen, mislaid, or inadvertently destroyed.

There is a well-established process by which certificates may be replaced. The process is time-consuming, taking from a minimum of about two weeks for share certificates to as long as four months for some bonds. During this time, the investor is "locked in" and unable to sell the securities. It is also expensive. It costs $200 to $400 to replace a certificate worth about $10,000.

When securities are lost, stolen, or misplaced, the investor's first step is to notify the issuer of the securities in writing. The investor will probably be referred to the transfer agent (for stock) or to a trustee (for a debt instrument). The agent or trustee places a "stop" on the certificate and notifies a central data base that it is missing. Brokerage firms and banks must contact this data base before buying shares or bonds from an unknown customer if the transaction involves $10,000 or more.

The investor is sent an affidavit of loss, which must be filled out and notarized. The investor must also purchase a "surety" or "indemnity" bond to protect the issuer and potential buyers in case the lost security has been negotiated. Some brokers assist customers with this paperwork, either for free or for a nominal charge, usually less than $20. The premium for the bond is usually from 2 to 4 percent of the market value of the securities. If the certificates show up within a year, some insurance companies may refund 50 percent of this premium, but others do not. Because bearer bonds are particularly susceptible to theft without discovery, some issuers require investors who lose them to buy a surety bond equal to twice the value of the lost securities.

# CHAPTER 12

# DIVIDENDS AND DISTRIBUTIONS

## §12.1   Introduction

This chapter deals with dividends and distributions in connection with common stock. The following discussion is primarily directed to issues in publicly held corporations but considers the legality of distributions and dividends in closely held enterprises in order to give a picture of statutory regulation of distributions. The material in this chapter requires knowledge of financial statements as discussed in earlier chapters.

The word "**distribution**" in corporation law is a general term referring to any kind of payment (in cash, property, or obligations of indebtedness) by the corporation to one or more shareholders on account of the ownership of shares. The word "**dividend**" is usually understood to be a narrower term referring to a pro rata distribution to one or more classes of shareholders by the corporation usually out of its current or retained earnings. An example of a distribution that is not a dividend is a partial payment to shareholders by a solvent corporation in the process of liquidation.

Payments to a shareholder in the form of salary, interest, or rent are not normally viewed as distributions because they are on account of services rendered or property supplied to the corporation by its shareholders rather than on account of the ownership of shares. In the case of a closely held corporation, however, if the payments are so large as to bear no reasonable relationship to the value of the services or property, all or part of the payment may be viewed as a disguised or informal dividend or distribution.

Several different and superficially unrelated transactions have the effect of making distributions to shareholders. In some states with older statutes, different legal rules may apply in determining the lawfulness of a distribution depending on the type of transaction involved, but modern statutes seek to apply a single legal standard to all distributions without regard to their form.

## §12.2  Distributions of Money or Property

The most common and best-known kind of distribution is a simple payment of money by the corporation to each shareholder, the amount of which is proportional to the number of shares that each shareholder owns. A corporation may also make a distribution of property other than cash, though such distributions create practical problems if the corporation has more than a handful of shareholders. Property, unlike money, is usually not readily divisible. A distribution of undivided interests in a piece of improved real estate, for example, is likely to create problems of management and control thereafter. Further, undivided interests in property may be difficult to sell except to other owners of undivided interests in the property who may be interested in reassembling the property for sale. Distributions of undivided interests in property are nevertheless sufficiently common for the corporate literature to distinguish between cash dividends and property dividends, and while most property dividends are made by closely held corporations, one sometimes encounters proposed distributions of property by publicly held corporations.

## §12.3  Share Repurchases

A very important type of distributive transaction is the purchase by a corporation of its own shares. This type of transaction is often called a **share repurchase** or **share buyback.** Superficially, a purchase of shares by the corporation may not be thought of as involving a distribution at all. It appears to be the purchase of an asset rather than the making of a distribution. That analysis, however, confuses transactions in which the corporation repurchases its own shares and transactions in which it purchases shares that another corporation issues. The former is a distribution, the latter is an investment.

When a corporation buys back its own shares, it does not receive anything of value. The remaining shareholders continue to own 100 percent of the corporate assets (now reduced by the amount of the payment used to reacquire the shares). A corporation cannot treat stock in itself that it has purchased as an asset any more than it can treat its authorized but unissued shares as an asset. One cannot own 10 percent of oneself and have one's total worth be 110 percent of the value of one's assets. Shares that another corporation issues are entirely different. Shares of Corporation B have value based on the assets that Corporation B owns; if shares of Corporation B are purchased by Corporation A, they are an asset in the hands of Corporation A.

The fact that a repurchase of shares constitutes a distribution can be most easily appreciated by considering a proportionate repurchase of stock in a closely held corporation. Assume that three persons each own 100 shares of stock in a corporation. The shareholders decide that each of them will sell 10 shares back to the corporation for $100 per share, or a total of $1,000 each. When the transaction is completed, each shareholder continues to own one-third of the corporation (now represented by 90 shares rather than 100 shares), the corporation has $3,000 less, and the shareholders each have $1,000 in cash. Clearly there has been a distribution even though the transaction was cast in the form of a repurchase of stock rather than as a dividend.

Under many state statutes, the 300 shares reacquired by the corporation in the previous example are called **treasury shares** and may be held by the corporation in a sort of twilight zone until they are either retired permanently or resold to someone else in the future. Treasury shares are not an asset, even though they may be sold at some later time. After all, exactly the same thing can be said of every share of authorized but unissued stock.

The difference between treasury shares and shares that other corporations issue is reflected in the accounting treatment of transactions in shares. When Corporation A buys shares in Corporation B, the transaction is reflected solely on the left-hand side of the balance sheet: The journal entry shows a reduction of cash and an increase in an asset account "investments in other corporations." However, when a corporation buys its own shares, the reduction of cash on the left-hand side of the balance sheet is offset by a reduction in one or more right-hand shareholders' equity accounts. A straight cash dividend is treated for accounting purposes in the same way: A reduction of the cash account on the left-hand side of the balance sheet is offset by a reduction in retained earnings or similar account on the right-hand side of the balance sheet.

A repurchase of shares by the corporation is a distribution even if the corporation purchases only shares that one shareholder owns rather than proportionately from each shareholder. Such a transaction is merely a disproportionate distribution. The corporation has made a distribution to a single shareholder equal to the purchase price it paid for the shares. This transaction is not all bad from the standpoint of the other shareholders, however, because it simultaneously increases their percentage interest in the corporation. For example, if the corporation with three shareholders in the above example repurchased all 100 shares owned by Shareholder A for $10,000, the interests of Shareholders B and C in the corporation are each increased from 33.3 percent to 50 percent. The assets of the corporation are reduced by the $10,000 purchase price paid to Shareholder A to eliminate his or her interest in the corporation.

Distributions in the form of repurchases of shares are very common in real life. In closely held corporations, the elimination of one shareholder's interest in a corporation is almost always effected by a repurchase of shares by the corporation. Such a transaction permits the use of corporate rather than personal assets, has favorable tax consequences, and does not affect the relative interests of the remaining shareholders.

## §12.4  Share Repurchases by Publicly Held Corporations

Publicly held corporations routinely repurchase their own shares in open market transactions. The announcement of a share repurchase usually has a favorable, upward effect on share price. Indeed, it is not at all uncommon for a corporation to announce a very large possible buyback and thereafter repurchase far fewer than the maximum number of shares. In extreme cases, share buyback offers may approach manipulation. One reason that is sometimes offered as to why buybacks increase the price of shares is that after the buyback, the number of outstanding shares will be reduced but the earnings of the corporation will not be significantly affected, so that earnings per share are likely to increase. There may be some truth in this explanation, but it assumes that the cash used to repurchase the shares did not generate income for the corporation.

Another reason for a share repurchase is that a publicly held corporation that has a large amount of excess liquid assets may become a target for takeover. Indeed, the liquid assets may be used by the bidder to pay back loans to finance part of the purchase of target shares. The alternative of paying a huge dividend may be less attractive because of federal income tax considerations: A dividend is taxable as ordinary income, while a buyback may give rise to capital gains treatment for those who sell shares back to the corporation. For those who do not sell shares, their reward is an increased value for the remaining shares.

A publicly held corporation may announce that it is buying back its own shares in order to have treasury shares available for a variety of possible uses (e.g., in compensation plans for executives or employees, or for acquisitions or other corporate purposes). It is sometimes difficult to accept these justifications at face value. More likely reasons are improvement of the market price for shares or a desire to reduce the attractiveness of the corporation as a takeover target. Nevertheless, a corporation that seeks to purchase another corporation with the purchase price being paid in shares rather than in cash may repurchase some of its own shares and offer them to the target, or it may simply issue new shares. A corporation may prefer to use repurchased shares because there is no dilutive effect on its own shareholders and because a market repurchase tends to increase the market price of its own shares. In contrast, the issuance of new shares to purchase a target company may place downward pressure on the market price of the bidder's shares. Many of the same considerations apply to using new shares to provide incentive compensation for senior executive officers.

For the target of an unwanted takeover attempt, a common defensive tactic is to announce a major buyback in order to sop up extra cash that the corporation may have and to drive up the price of its shares to make the outside offer unattractive. Such a defense is generally tolerated by the courts because the repurchase also increases the percentage of shares that the bidder owns. Thus, a repurchase may backfire as a defensive tactic, because it increases the control value of shares that the bidder has already obtained.

## §12.5  Distributions of Indebtedness

A corporation may also distribute obligations to make payments at some time in the future. The simplest way to do this is for the corporation to create instruments of indebtedness and distribute them directly to its shareholders. In closely held corporations, debt may be used to repurchase shares, because the corporation lacks ready assets to pay the full purchase price or does not want to borrow funds for this purpose or because the selling shareholder does not want to recognize all of the gain immediately for tax purposes. In any event, the use of debt obligations means that, in effect, a portion of the agreed-on purchase price of shares is to be paid out of future cash flow.

Distributions of indebtedness are sometimes used by publicly held corporations to make the corporation unattractive as a possible takeover candidate. Often such debt states explicitly that it will become payable in full upon any change in control. Such instruments are sometimes called **poison puts**.

## §12.6  Legal Restrictions on Distributions

All state statutes contain provisions governing and restricting the power of corporations to make distributions. These statutory provisions are primarily of importance to closely held corporations, but they also apply to publicly held corporations.

These statutes are confusing, sometimes internally inconsistent or self-contradictory, and often incomplete in that they do not address some recurring issues relating to distributions. Dividend statutes contain two different types of prohibitions: (1) a capital protection provision that prohibits distributions that in some sense invade or reduce the permanent capital of the corporation, and (2) a fraudulent conveyance provision prohibiting distributions that have the effect of rendering the corporation unable to meet its obligations as they mature. The first test is usually referred to as the **balance sheet test** and the second as the **equity insolvency test**.

## §12.7  The Balance Sheet Test

Statutes regulate and limit distributions by imposing restrictions on the right-hand balance sheet entries that may be debited for the payments. An oversimplified balance sheet should make this relationship clear:

| Assets | | Liabilities | |
|---|---|---|---|
| Cash | $20,000 | Bank Loans | $30,000 |
| Other | 40,000 | Owner's Equity | |
| | | Common Stock | 20,000 |
| | | Earnings | |
| | | Current | 3,000 |
| | | Retained | 7,000 |
| Total | $60,000 | Total | $60,000 |

In the owners equity portion of the balance sheet, current earnings represent earnings of the present year, while retained earnings represent earnings from previous years not distributed in the form of dividends. The common stock entry represents what the shareholders paid for the stock when it was originally issued. Now let us assume that the corporation decides to distribute $6,000 to its shareholders. The payment of $6,000 will reduce cash by $6,000; the offsetting entry must be a reduction of some right-hand entry. The only real choices are current earnings or accumulated earnings. The legality of the distribution depends on what the state's distribution statute says about which right-hand accounts may be charged with the distribution and which may not. Because all state statutes permit the payment of dividends out of either current or retained earnings, the $6,000 payment is consistent with the balance sheet test in all states. This payment is still a dividend even though it is made in part out of earnings of prior years. The Internal Revenue Code follows the same pattern: The distribution of retained earnings is taxable as an ordinary dividend in the same manner as the distribution of current earnings. Following the payment of a dividend of $6,000, retained earnings available for the payment of dividends in future years would be reduced to $4,000 ($7,000 − $3,000, where $3,000 is the portion of the distribution that exceeds earnings for the year in question).

Now let us assume that the corporation wishes to distribute $15,000 (rather than $6000) to its shareholders. Can it do so? It probably can afford to in the sense that even after paying out $15,000, the corporation will have assets of $45,000 and liabilities of only $30,000. That, however, is not relevant under the balance sheet test. What is important under that test is which right-hand account or accounts are to reflect the $15,000 payment. The earnings accounts can be reduced by $10,000 to $0 but the remaining $5,000 must be reflected as a reduction or invasion of capital. Another way of looking at this transaction is that the $15,000 payment represents a distribution of (a) $3,000 of this year's earnings, (b) $7,000 of retained earnings from previous years, and (c) $5,000 of capital. As to whether a corporation may invade or distribute capital in this manner, state statutes vary widely, with the most modern statutes permitting distributions of capital down to zero, and older statutes establishing a variety of different standards or tests on whether the distribution is permissible.

This simple example makes two critical points. First, in order to control distributions, the balance sheet test places restraints on which right-hand entries may be reduced when a distribution is made. The right-hand entries in the balance sheet serve as a kind of valve or control on distributions of assets that appear on the left-hand side of the balance sheet. Second, the balance sheet test is not directly concerned with solvency in the equity sense (i.e., the ability of the corporation to pay its bills as they become due), but rather with the preservation of capital. The balance sheet test is concerned with appearances: A corporation that says it has capital of a specified amount on its balance sheet may not make a distribution of all or a portion of that capital to shareholders. This test harks back to an early era of corporation law where the corporation's capital was viewed as a cushion or trust fund for the benefit of creditors who may be induced to extend credit in reliance on the corporation's balance sheet.

State corporation statutes have gone through at least three distinct phases in developing balance sheet tests regulating distributions. In the earliest statutes enacted in the 19th century, provisions addressing distribution policies were primitive. Apparently proceeding on the assumption that all capital contributed to a corporation was a permanent fund for the protection of creditors, these statutes provide either that dividends can only be paid from income or, alternatively, that all distributions from capital accounts are prohibited.

In the second phase, developed during the first half of the 20th century, statutes draw a distinction between permanent capital and surplus capital (with the permanent capital usually being defined as the aggregate sum of the par values of all shares issued by the corporation). Many state dividend statutes are currently of this type. Unfortunately, these statutes can easily be evaded by the manipulation of par value principles, for example, by amending the articles of incorporation to reduce par value. As a result, they are largely ineffective in requiring minimum amounts of capital to be retained as a cushion. Indeed, these statutes give a deceptive picture of how much capital the corporation is required to maintain. Rather than providing protection to creditors, these statutes in fact become primarily rites of initiation for new corporation lawyers: When one learns how to avoid all meaningful restrictions on corporate distributions under the balance sheet test, one has proved one is a corporation lawyer.

Modern statutes, largely developed in the last decade, recognize the impracticability of defining minimum amounts of capital, and freely allow the distribution of capital as long as, after the distribution, assets exceed liabilities plus amounts payable in liquidation to holders of preferred shares. In these statutes, greater reliance is placed on the equity insolvency test described below than on the balance sheet test in order to protect creditors.

No matter what specific tests are established in these balance sheet statutes, they all suffer from one major, indeed fundamental, flaw. If you have read Chapter 6, which discusses accounting principles, it should be apparent that the distinction between capital and income is most slippery in practice. Income and capital are not self-defining but are dependent on accounting principles adequate to handle a variety of complex and subtle issues such as the allocation of income and expense items to specific periods, the principles on which assets are to be valued, depreciation schedules, the time of recognition of asset appreciation and contingent liabilities, and the like. Different accounting principles may give widely varying answers as to the corporation's income. The creation of accounting principles by legislative fiat for all corporations, large and small, is a daunting task, and no state legislature has attempted to do this. It is basically up to the courts to decide what accounting principles must be followed. The issues usually arise, furthermore, in suits to surcharge directors for approving improper dividends. That is a particularly brutal kind of litigation from the standpoint of the defendants, who are asked to restore to the corporation the amount of the distribution out of their own personal pockets, even though they may have acted in good faith in reliance on expert legal and accounting advice, and did not receive any more than the portion of the distribution their shareholdings entitled them to. It is not surprising that courts tended to find reasons to uphold the legality of distributions out of sympathy with the defendants—often people of substance in the community—who are faced with substantial liability.

At one time, most state statutes imposed a minimum absolute amount of capital that every corporation was required to have upon incorporation— usually $1,000. These provisions were also ineffective and have been repealed in most states. An arbitrary minimum ($1,000 or some other amount) suffers from the problem that it must be nominal and will afford no protection once the corporation begins business and incurs its first operating loss (if any).

The almost total failure of elaborate balance sheet statutes in their basic purpose is also evident from the behavior of creditors, who pay no attention to the elaborate statutory provisions ostensibly designed for their protection. Instead, creditors protect themselves in different ways: (1) they rely on credit reporting agencies and similar private organizations before extending unsecured credit to businesses; (2) they obtain security interests when they sell goods on credit; and (3) in the case of larger transactions, they negotiate elaborate loan agreements with debtors by which they obtain contractual protection against unwise or improvident distributions to shareholders.

## §12.8  Equity Insolvency Test

All state statutes relating to distributions impose an equity insolvency test for distributions in addition to the largely ineffective balance sheet prohibitions described above. The traditional equity insolvency test is that a distribution to shareholders is unlawful if it makes the corporation insolvent (i.e., unable to pay its obligations as they become due in the future). At first blush, the equity insolvency test may sound like a variant of the balance sheet test for distributions. In fact, it is based on a totally different approach. The balance sheet test is based on financial statements and accounting principles. The equity insolvency test is based on an examination of estimated future cash flows after the distribution. It requires the board of directors to determine whether the corporation has or will have available funds to discharge its future obligations as they come due. This test is easily stated but requires difficult estimates and projections in practice. The board of directors must make an examination of anticipated cash flows and future cash needs arising from the maturation of debts and liabilities to determine whether, after the contemplated distribution, the corporation will be able to meet its obligations.

## §12.9 Protection of Preferred Shareholders

State statutes impose restrictions on distributions to common shareholders in order to protect the liquidation preferences of preferred shareholders. Preferred shareholders are in an anomalous position with respect to dividend restrictions. On the one hand they are viewed as contributors of equity capital rather than as creditors. On the other hand, their financial interest in the corporation is usually limited, and once their dividend preference is honored in any one year, common shareholders are entitled to all future dividends and distributions during that year. From an economic standpoint, the position of the preferred shareholders' liquidation preference is closely akin to a creditor's claim, because substantial distributions to common shareholders may effectively disable the corporation from honoring that liquidation preference. Many modern statutes require that liquidation preferences of preferred shareholders be treated as a liability for purposes of applying the restrictions on dividends.

## §12.10 Suits to Compel Distributions

Deciding whether to make a distribution involves business judgment by the board of directors as to whether it is prudent to preserve earnings for future needs or whether a distribution should be made and in what amount. Courts have long recognized that this decision involves business judgments about the future cash needs both in terms of satisfying liabilities and in terms of making necessary investments in existing or new productive facilities. As a result, courts are loath to second-guess directors in connection with such decisions, and they tend to accept the decision of the board on such matters.

Directors also owe fiduciary duties to shareholders in connection with their stewardship of the corporation, and the decision to pay (or more commonly, to omit) dividends or distributions may be evaluated within these broad duties. These duties may be phrased in terms of fair treatment of minority shareholders or of all classes of shares, or in terms of not favoring a class in which members of the board of directors have substantial personal interests. There is obvious tension between these fiduciary duties and the business judgment rule described in the previous paragraph. There are, however, a large number of cases in which courts have ordered that a dividend be paid, thus illustrating that often the fiduciary duty dominates.

A compulsory dividend is most likely to be ordered when the minority shareholder can demonstrate (1) actions by the majority shareholder that may be construed as constituting antagonism or bad faith against the minority; (2) liquid assets within the corporation in excess of the apparent needs of the business and apparently available for the payment of dividends; and (3) a policy of informal distributions to favored shareholders through salaries, loans, cash advances, and the like. Still, suits to compel the payment of dividends should be viewed as a long shot even in egregious circumstances.

## §12.11 Distribution Policies in Closely Held Corporations

In closely held corporations that are taxed as C corporations, distribution policies strongly tend in the direction of informal distributions in the form of tax deductible salary, rent, or interest payments rather than formally declared dividends. The principal motivation is federal income taxation: The payment of a reasonable salary to a shareholder, for example, is deductible by the corporation and to that extent avoids the double tax on income that otherwise increases the tax cost of operating as a C corporation. Such deductions are allowed only to the extent that they are "reasonable," but that standard permits considerable flexibility in distribution policy, often allowing the entire income of the corporation to be zeroed out to avoid all taxes at the corporate level.

Informal distributions of this type open the possibility of unfair treatment of minority shareholders, because they may not receive a proportionate part of the informal distribution. Even where the motive of the majority shareholder is not exclusionary, however, strict proportionality is dangerous, because it may suggest to the auditor in a subsequent tax audit that all or a portion of the corporate salary deductions should be disallowed as informal dividends.

The Internal Revenue Code contains a penalty tax against unreasonable accumulations of surplus which, if applicable, provides a strong tax incentive to pay dividends. Given current tax rates, it is unlikely that any corporation now finds it advantageous to accumulate unreasonable amounts of surplus so as to trigger the imposition of this tax.

If a corporation has elected S corporation tax treatment, corporate income is passed through to the shareholders for inclusion in their individual tax returns. There is no tax advantage in salary or other payments as a substitute for dividends. On the other hand, if the corporation fails to pay cash dividends when it has substantial taxable income, minority shareholders may find it difficult or impossible to pay their personal tax bills swollen by the inclusion of corporate income. In extreme cases, it may be necessary for minority shareholders to seek to revoke the S corporation election, if that is practical, or if it is not, to bring suit to compel the payment of dividends based on breach by the board of directors of its fiduciary duties to act in good faith and treat all shareholders fairly.

## §12.12 Distribution Policies in Publicly Held Corporations

Distribution policies within a publicly held corporation are quite different from the policies within a closely held corporation. In a closely held corporation, the distribution policy is likely to be viewed as primarily a tax issue: How to get corporate funds into the hands of the shareholders at the lowest tax cost.

In a publicly held company, on the other hand, the standard operating procedure is to establish an announced or regular dividend and maintain it indefinitely, or at least over several years. A regular dividend may be paid even though the corporation has suffered a loss in that year; the dividend is paid out of earnings accumulated from prior years. Most shareholders in a publicly held corporation, of course, are passive investors who come to rely on the regular dividend as part of their regular cash flow. However, the reluctance to change an announced dividend—particularly the reluctance to reduce the dividend in periods of adversity—is not based on concern about shareholders' cash flow. Rather, a change in dividend policy is widely viewed in the securities markets as a signal of management's future expectations with respect to the company. An increase in the announced dividend is viewed as signaling improved prospects. It is a strong signal, because it means that the corporate prospects have improved to the point that management thinks an increased dividend rate can be maintained indefinitely. On the other hand, a reduction in the dividend rate is a warning of rough seas ahead. The communication of bad news has a potential for serious adverse market repercussions and is not to be made prematurely or before management is reasonably certain that it is imprudent to continue the present dividend. Certainly, such a signal should not be given because of a temporary dip in earnings.

If a corporation has an unusually good year, or has the good fortune to receive a nonrecurring windfall, management may be reluctant to announce an increase in the regular dividend, because it may be unsure that the rate can be maintained in the future. In this circumstance, management usually declares a special or nonrecurring dividend that is paid on a one-time basis and does not create an expectation that a similar payment will be forthcoming in future years. Some corporations have adopted a policy of declaring "extras" above the announced rate almost every year, but that is not the customary practice.

Rather paradoxically, some corporations as a matter of policy pay no cash dividends at all. One of the most successful enterprises of all time, Berkshire Hathaway, managed by the financier Warren Buffett, has not declared a dividend in recent times. A corporation that reinvests its cash flow productively rather than paying it out to shareholders will see a steady increase in the market price of the corporation's shares. And so it has been with Berkshire Hathaway. Similarly, a corporation that has recently gone public may have positive (and growing) earnings, but may need all available cash for internal growth purposes. In these situations a shareholder receives no immediate cash return, but the shareholder is rewarded by the steady increase in the market price of the stock. In effect, the market accepts and approves of the policy of deferring cash dividends to foster growth.

An extended theoretical discussion has transpired about why corporations adopt a particular dividend policy. Miller and Modigliani proved that with certain simplifying assumptions shareholders should theoretically be indifferent to the dividend policy that a corporation adopts. If the corporation fails to pay out earnings in the form of dividends, the value of the corporation's shares should rise so as to equal the amount of the dividend not paid. This irrelevance theorem suggests that shareholders in a non-dividend-paying corporation who wish current cash flow may simply sell a portion of their holdings in order to keep the value of their shares constant, and they will be as well off as if the corporation had made a distribution of current earnings. Given the present tax laws (under which dividends are taxed as ordinary income and gains on the sale of shares are taxed at lower capital gains rates), it should follow that paying dividends reduces the value of the corporation, and that no corporation should ever pay dividends. This logically correct theorem has only one problem: It does not reflect reality, because most publicly held corporations do in fact pay dividends.

A number of possible explanations have been offered to explain this dividend puzzle. The signaling idea discussed earlier may explain why dividends are paid. Another theory suggests that lower income investors are drawn to dividend-paying stocks because the tax difference is not relevant. Yet another theory is that paying dividends reduces agency costs by limiting the authority of managers in handling free cash flow. There are difficulties with each of these explanations, and it may be that securities markets and investors simply do not, on the average, have the transparency that economic theory presupposes. It is not at all clear, for example, that the market price of non-dividend-paying stocks increases rapidly enough to equal the value of the dividends not paid.

## §12.13  Share Dividends

Publicly held corporations often pay share dividends or announce **share splits**. These two transactions are very similar in principle and effect, and their basic equivalence is sometimes not fully understood by investors. The following section deals specifically with splits.

A **share dividend** (or **stock dividend**) is a distribution of shares of common stock by a corporation to its shareholders in proportion to their shareholdings. Thus, a 10 percent share dividend means that the corporation issues one new share to each shareholder for every 10 shares held; a holder of 100 shares will receive 10 new shares when the distribution is made, and will then own 110 shares in all. From a purely economic or logical point of view, this is not a dividend at all, because the number of shares that each shareholder owns has been increased by exactly the same percentage, and each shareholder's proportional interest in the corporation has not been changed. In other words, a shareholder owning one percent of the outstanding shares before the share dividend is paid will own precisely one percent of the outstanding shares after it is paid. The percentage ownership has not changed even though the number of shares has increased. Despite this inescapable logic, many small shareholders welcome share dividends and many sell them shortly after they are received, perhaps not realizing (or not caring) that by doing so they have slightly reduced their (already infinitesimal) interest in the corporation. In some cases, the corporation will pay cash in lieu of fractional shares as authorized by many state statutes.

A share dividend does have one favorable consequence if the corporation also pays a regular cash dividend. It is customary to leave the regular dividend unaffected after a share dividend so that following the dividend the corporation's total dividend payout is increased (because the same rate is applied to a somewhat larger number of shares).

Why do corporations pay share dividends at all? The usual reason offered is that a share dividend is a tangible signal to shareholders that the corporation is profitable (despite the absence of a cash dividend) and is investing all available funds into the growth of the business. Although unsophisticated shareholders may view such a dividend as a little something that can be sold without reducing one's investment in the corporation, in fact it is nothing but a signal. On the other hand, a share dividend may constitute a vouch by management that even with more shares outstanding and a larger distribution of cash, things are going well enough that the stock price is likely to be maintained. In this sense, a share dividend may in fact have positive information content, particularly if management is not free to discuss publicly why prospects are rosy.

## §12.14  Share Splits

A **share split** is essentially a large share dividend. In a two-for-one split, for example, a corporation with 1,000,000 shares outstanding to begin with ends up with 2,000,000 shares outstanding after the split, and a shareholder with 100 shares before the split ends up with 200 shares after the split. True share splits are quite rare, because if the shares have par value, as most still do, the par value per share must be formally changed by amendment to the articles of incorporation so as to reflect that each outstanding share after the split represents only half as much in stated capital as before the split. Technically, in a two-for-one share split, the corporation issues two new shares for each old share that each shareholder holds. The old share is cancelled so that each shareholder now owns two shares, whereas before each owned only one share. Because this process is cumbersome, and because there will inevitably be some old shares that are never turned in for new shares, true share splits are very rare. Instead, in order to effect a two-for-one share split, for example, a corporation usually issues a dividend of one new share for each old share and simply calls it a two-for-one split.

It is customary to reduce the regular or stated dividend rate when a share split (true or otherwise) is completed; if the regular dividend is halved in connection with a two-for-one split, one would expect the market price of each new share to be approximately one-half of the market price of the pre-split shares. Often, however, the effective dividend rate is increased in connection with a share split: Thus, in a three-for-one split where the old dividend rate was 90 cents per share, the dividend rate on the split shares may be set, for example, at 35 cents, equal to a rate of $1.05 on the pre-split shares. It is difficult to square this practice with the dividend irrelevance theorem of Miller and Modigliani.

Many corporation finance officers think that there is an appropriate trading range for the company's common shares. For example, the common stock of a corporation may have historically traded in the $20 to $30 range. If the price gradually rises to $40, the corporation may split the stock two-for-one to return the price to the lower range. One advantage of maintaining a lower trading range is that if the price of a stock rises significantly to a new plateau but the stock is not split, trading volume may decline from previous levels because most investors trade in round lots and may feel they cannot afford to invest in higher priced stocks. (Trading in round lots is discussed more fully in Chapter 14, which discusses markets.)

A split differs from a share dividend in certain minor respects relating to how the transaction is recorded for accounting purposes. These differences, however, rarely affect the shareholder.

A corporation may also "split" its stock to reduce the number of shares outstanding. This is called a **reverse stock split** and is not really a split at all. Rather, the corporation amends its articles of incorporation to reduce the number of authorized shares, and the amendment provides that each 10 (or 100 or 1,000) old shares are to be exchanged for 1 new share. Reverse stock splits often create fractional shares, and may be used to liquidate the interests of small shareholders by establishing a procedure (authorized in many state statutes) to eliminate all fractional shares for cash. Some corporations have used reverse stock splits to eliminate public shareholders by establishing the split ratio at a level sufficiently high that all nonmanagement shareholders become owners of fractional interests, which are then eliminated through a cash payment.

## §12.15  Determining Who Is Entitled to a Distribution

Whenever a dividend or cash or stock distribution is contemplated, the question may arise as to who is entitled to the distribution if the shares have been sold or transferred around the time of the declaration or payment. This problem is particularly acute in publicly held corporations where many thousands of shares are traded each day among anonymous persons. The New York Stock Exchange has adopted an **ex-dividend policy** to establish whether the buyer or seller of publicly traded shares is entitled to a distribution.

Table 12-1 is taken from *The Wall Street Journal*. It is the standard chart showing dividend announcements made on the previous business day. An examination of this table reveals much about the dividend practices of publicly held corporations and the law relating to dividend declarations. First of all, the table distinguishes between various types of dividends, including regular dividends (pursuant to an announced dividend policy); irregular dividends (occasional or special payments not pursuant to an announced policy); funds, REITs, investment companies, and limited partnerships (all essentially pass through entities that distribute more or less all income); and stock dividends (as discussed above).

There are four important dates to note with respect to each dividend or distribution: (1) the date of announcement; (2) the **record date**; (3) the **payable date**; and (4) the **ex-dividend date**. The announcement date is the date of the press release that a cash or stock dividend is to be paid or a distribution is to be made. Typically, the announcement is made on the same day that the board declares the dividend. The record date determines to whom the dividend is to be paid, namely, the shareholder of record on the books of the corporation

Table 12-1

# CORPORATE DIVIDEND NEWS

## DIVIDENDS REPORTED NOV. 2

| COMPANY | PERIOD | AMT. | PAYABLE DATE | RECORD DATE |
|---|---|---|---|---|
| **REGULAR** | | | | |
| AVX Corp | Q | .0375 | 11-16-01 | 11-09 |
| ArchDanielsMidland | Q | .05 | 12-04-01 | 11-12 |
| Avon Products | Q | .19 | 12-03-01 | 11-15 |
| Centex Corp | Q | .04 | 1-09-02 | 12-11 |
| City National Corp | Q | .185 | 11-19-01 | 11-09 |
| CommunityBkshrsVA | Q | .20 | 11-30-01 | 11-16 |
| Dover Corp | Q | .135 | 12-14-01 | 11-30 |
| EMC Insurance Grp | Q | .15 | 11-19-01 | 11-12 |
| Grtr Community Bcp | Q | .085 | 10-31-01 | 10-15 |
| Intel Corp | Q | .02 | 12-01-01 | 11-07 |
| LexingtonB&L Finl | S | .15 | 1-18-02 | 1-02 |
| Manpower Inc | S | .10 | 12-14-01 | 12-03 |
| MineSafety Applncs | Q | .14 | 12-10-01 | 11-23 |
| Pittston Brink's | Q | .025 | 12-03-01 | 11-15 |
| Pointe Finl Corp | Q | .05 | 12-03-01 | 11-15 |
| SCANA Corp | Q | .30 | 1-01-02 | 12-10 |
| Sealed Air pf A | Q | .50 | 1-02-02 | 12-12 |
| Span-Amer Med Sys | Q | .03 | 12-04-01 | 11-16 |
| Superior Uniform | Q | .135 | 11-23-01 | 11-12 |
| TXU Inco PRIDES | Q | .578125 | 11-16-01 | 11-15 |
| TXUCrpl grthPRIDES | Q | .207187 | 11-16-01 | 11-15 |
| Temple-Inland Inc | Q | .32 | 12-14-01 | 11-30 |
| UniSource Energy | Q | .10 | 12-10-01 | 11-15 |
| Wisconsin Energy | Q | .20 | 12-01-01 | 11-14 |
| **IRREGULAR** | | | | |
| Global Payments | Q | .04 | 11-30-01 | 11-16 |
| Pwr CorpCan subvtg | – | b.175 | 12-31-01 | 12-14 |
| Rockwell Collins | Q | .09 | 12-03-01 | 11-12 |
| **FUNDS, REITS, INVESTMENT COS, LPS** | | | | |
| Cohen&StrsAdvInRty | M | .105 | 11-30-01 | 11-15 |
| Cohen&StrsTotRtn | M | .08 | 11-30-01 | 11-15 |
| DelawareGrpDivInco | M | .125 | 11-30-01 | 11-16 |
| Duke Realty Corp | Q | .45 | 11-30-01 | 11-14 |
| Duke Rlty pfD | Q | .46094 | 12-31-01 | 12-17 |
| Duke Rlty pfE | Q | .51563 | 12-31-01 | 12-17 |
| Duke Rlty pfF | Q | .50 | 1-31-02 | 1-17 |
| Duke Rlty1 | Q | .52813 | 12-31-01 | 12-17 |
| Eaton Vance Sr Inc | M | .056 | 11-19-01 | 11-12 |
| Retail HOLDRs | – | .003552 | 12-28-01 | 12-07 |
| MFS Charter Inco | M | .05 | 11-30-01 | 11-15 |
| MFS Govt Mkts Inco | M | .032 | 11-30-01 | 11-15 |
| MFS Intermd Inco | M | .036 | 11-30-01 | 11-15 |
| MFS Multimkt Inco | M | .038 | 11-30-01 | 11-15 |
| MFS Muni Inco Tr | M | .044 | 11-30-01 | 11-15 |
| MFS Special Value | M | .1375 | 11-30-01 | 11-15 |
| Pilgrim Prime Rate | M | .047 | 11-23-01 | 11-12 |
| ProLogis Trust | Q | .345 | 11-23-01 | 11-12 |
| Regency Centers | Q | .50 | 11-26-01 | 11-12 |
| Sabine Royalty Tr | M | .23238 | 11-29-01 | 11-15 |
| Seligman Qlty Muni | M | .0562 | 11-21-01 | 11-14 |
| Seligman Selt Muni | M | .0511 | 11-21-01 | 11-14 |
| VK IncoTr | M | .0435 | 11-30-01 | 11-15 |
| VK AdvMunInc | M | .076 | 11-30-01 | 11-15 |
| VK AdvMunII | M | .071 | 11-30-01 | 11-15 |
| VK AdvPA Mun | M | .082 | 11-30-01 | 11-15 |
| VK CAMun | M | .0445 | 11-30-01 | 11-15 |
| VK CAQltyMuni | M | .083 | 11-30-01 | 11-15 |
| VK CAValMun | M | .0785 | 11-30-01 | 11-15 |
| VK FLQltyM | M | .0745 | 11-30-01 | 11-15 |
| VK HiIncoTr | M | .047 | 11-30-01 | 11-15 |
| VK HiIncoTrII | M | .0615 | 11-30-01 | 11-15 |
| VK InvGdMun | M | .041 | 11-30-01 | 11-15 |
| VK MAValMun | M | .0725 | 11-30-01 | 11-15 |

## DIVIDENDS REPORTED NOV. 2

| COMPANY | PERIOD | AMT. | PAYABLE DATE | RECORD DATE |
|---|---|---|---|---|
| **FUNDS, REITS, INVESTMENT COS, LPS** | | | | |
| VK MuniInco | M | .044 | 11-30-01 | 11-15 |
| VK MuniOpp | M | .083 | 11-30-01 | 11-15 |
| VK MuniOpII | M | .07 | 11-30-01 | 11-15 |
| VK Municipal Tr | M | .0685 | 11-30-01 | 11-15 |
| VK NYValMun | M | .0755 | 11-30-01 | 11-15 |
| VK NYQltyMuni | M | .076 | 11-30-01 | 11-15 |
| VK OHQlty | M | .08 | 11-30-01 | 11-15 |
| VK OHValMun | M | .064 | 11-30-01 | 11-15 |
| VK PAQlty | M | .081 | 11-30-01 | 11-15 |
| VK PAValMun | M | .076 | 11-30-01 | 11-15 |
| VK SelSectMuni | M | .068 | 11-30-01 | 11-15 |
| VK SeniorInco | M | .0439 | 11-30-01 | 11-15 |
| VK Strat Sect Mun | M | .0715 | 11-30-01 | 11-15 |
| VK TrInsMun | M | .079 | 11-30-01 | 11-15 |
| VK InvGrdNJ | M | .082 | 11-30-01 | 11-15 |
| VK InvGrdFL | M | .0775 | 11-30-01 | 11-15 |
| VK InvGrdCA | M | .0765 | 11-30-01 | 11-15 |
| VK TrInvGrd | M | .078 | 11-30-01 | 11-15 |
| VK InvGrdNY | M | .084 | 11-30-01 | 11-15 |
| VK InvGrdPA | M | .086 | 11-30-01 | 11-15 |
| VK ValMuni | M | .073 | 11-30-01 | 11-15 |
| Voyageur AZ Muni | M | .0675 | 11-30-01 | 11-16 |
| Voyageur CO Muni | M | .0675 | 11-30-01 | 11-16 |
| Voyageur FL Muni | M | .066 | 11-30-01 | 11-16 |
| VoyMinnMuniII | M | .07 | 11-30-01 | 11-16 |
| VoyMinnMuniIII | M | .063125 | 11-30-01 | 11-16 |
| VoyMinnMuni | M | .07 | 11-30-01 | 11-16 |

### FOREIGN

| COMPANY | PERIOD | AMT. | PAYABLE DATE | RECORD DATE |
|---|---|---|---|---|
| Dr. Reddy's Labs | – | t.10 | – | 11-23 |

### INCREASED AMOUNTS

| COMPANY | PERIOD | NEW | OLD | PAYABLE DATE | RECORD DATE |
|---|---|---|---|---|---|
| Masco Corp | Q | .135 | .13 | 11-19-01 | 11-09 |
| Stepan Co | Q | .1825 | .175 | 12-14-01 | 11-30 |

### REDUCED AMOUNTS

| COMPANY | PERIOD | NEW | OLD | PAYABLE DATE | RECORD DATE |
|---|---|---|---|---|---|
| RFS Hotel Investrs | Q | .10 | .385 | 11-26-01 | 11-12 |
| Timken Co | Q | .13 | .18 | 12-03-01 | 11-16 |

### INITIAL

| COMPANY | PERIOD | AMT. | PAYABLE DATE | RECORD DATE |
|---|---|---|---|---|
| Credit&Asset Repck | – | .1489 | 12-03-01 | 11-15 |
| SureWest Comms | – | .25 | 12-14-01 | 11-30 |

### SPECIAL

| COMPANY | PERIOD | AMT. | PAYABLE DATE | RECORD DATE |
|---|---|---|---|---|
| Russ Berrie & Co | Q | .50 | 12-14-01 | 11-29 |

A-Annual. M-Monthly. Q-Quarterly. S-Semi-annual.
b-Payable in Canadian funds. c-Corrected. h-From Income. k-From capital gains. r-Revised. t-Approximate U.S. dollar amount per American Depositary Receipt/Share before adjustment for foreign taxes.

## STOCKS EX-DIVIDEND NOV. 6

| COMPANY | AMOUNT | COMPANY | AMOUNT |
|---|---|---|---|
| Arch Chemicals | .20 | Providence&Worc RR | .04 |
| Autoliv Inc | t.11 | Stifel Financial | .03 |
| Dole Food Co | .10 | TJX Companies | .045 |
| GreatPlains 4.5%pf | 1.125 | | |
| GreatPlains3.8%pf | .95 | t-Approximate U.S. dollar amount |
| GreatPlains4.35%pf | 1.0875 | per American Depositary Re- |
| Retail HOLDRs | .00225 | ceipt/Share before adjustment for |
| Libbey Inc | .075 | foreign taxes. |

at the close of business on the record date. The payable date is the date the checks or certificates are actually mailed; a delay of one to four weeks is customary and may be necessary for the corporation to go through the mechanical process of making the distribution in the proper amounts to thousands or millions of record holders. The ex-dividend date is three business days before the record date. Ex-dividend means without the dividend. The ex-dividend date convention assigns the dividend to the buyer or seller as follows: A buyer in a transaction that occurs before the ex-dividend date is entitled to receive the dividend and the seller is not; a seller in a transaction that occurs on or after the ex-dividend date is entitled to keep the dividend. The reason for the three-day gap between the ex-dividend date and the record date is that the standard practice is settlement three business days after the transaction. On the settlement date, the buyer must pay the purchase price and the seller must deliver the shares. The ex-dividend date is a carryover from a much earlier period when securities transactions were settled by a delivery of certificates issued in the name of the seller, and endorsed to permit new certificates to be issued to the buyer. A buyer who is entitled to the certificates on or before the ex-dividend date is theoretically able to register the transfer with the corporation and become the record owner before the close of business on the record date for the dividend or distribution. The ex-dividend date is established as the last day on which that is possible. In the age of book entry registration, this may sound rather formalistic, but one must have a clear rule as to who is entitled to the dividend or distribution, and the rule so established seems as reasonable as any.

The day a stock goes ex-dividend, its market price should decline by approximately the amount of the dividend, other things being equal, because the day before, every buyer of the stock was entitled to the dividend but on and after the ex-dividend date, buyers of the stock do not receive the dividend. Of course, this relationship may not be precise, because market conditions can change overnight.

The ex-dividend date is a convention that is not at all dependent on whether a buyer actually arranges for certificates to be issued. The ex-dividend convention does not apply to shares sold directly by one person to another not using the facilities of an exchange or the over-the-counter market. In a face-to-face transaction, the parties may make any agreement they wish regarding entitlement to declared but unpaid dividends or distributions.

# MERGERS AND ACQUISITIONS

## §13.1 Introduction

Beginning in the late 1960s and continuing through the late 1980s, the business world was roiled by a wave of **hostile takeovers** in which one huge business acquired another. The target of a hostile takeover attempt usually fiercely resisted by using all legal, economic, and political resources at its disposal. Stories of these battles filled the newspapers and business journals, providing grist for endless discussion and speculation and leading to the development of a colorful vocabulary. For a variety of reasons, hostile takeovers had largely disappeared as of about 1990, and for a few years there were relatively few large mergers and acquisitions of any kind. By the mid 1990s, however, the **market for corporate control** had heated up again, and the number of such transactions was probably as large as ever. The difference was that in the 1990s the great majority of mergers and acquisitions were consensual or **friendly deals** in which the board of directors of the target company negotiated on behalf of the company and its shareholders. It was by no means uncommon, however, for hostile bids to be launched even in the 1990s, and indeed although the number and size of friendly deals had increased, there were roughly the same number of hostile bids per year as there were in the mid 1980s. In the early 2000s, the merger pace has slowed somewhat, owing primarily to the downtown in the high technology sector, but big deals remain quite common.

This chapter outlines the various methods by which whole companies are bought and sold and describes the economic and financial forces that lead to such transactions. In the following discussion, the company that is the object of a takeover attempt is usually called the **target** company and the company seeking to take over the target the **bidder**. Individuals as well as corporations may act as bidders, but for simplicity it is assumed throughout this chapter that the bidder is a corporation.

## §13.2 Historical Context

Before discussing the mechanics of mergers and acquisitions, it may be useful to put them into historical perspective. There have been several well-documented periods of merger movements in American history. In the late 19th century a series of acquisitions and mergers created monopolies in several basic American industries, and gave rise to the Sherman Antitrust Act. A period of similar activity before World War I led to Teddy Roosevelt's famous trust-busting activities and ultimately to the second major antitrust statute, the Clayton Act. A somewhat similar period of merger activity occurred during the 1950s, usually involving conglomeration (i.e., the assembling of a number of unrelated industries within a single corporate enterprise). The takeover movement that culminated in the 1980s was different in several significant respects from merger waves of earlier periods. Many of these takeovers involved breaking up mergers from earlier periods.

Merger movements prior to the 1960s usually involved consensual or "friendly" transactions. Management of a target corporation could have usually blocked a takeover simply by refusing to cooperate. Only when both sides agreed on the terms could one company acquire another. Thus, takeovers became a matter of negotiation over price, continuity of management, and other factors. That was not the case in the 1980s. Bidders quite regularly went over the heads of management and pitched their takeover proposals directly to shareholders of the target corporation. The pitch to shareholders, furthermore, usually involved offers of cash for stock that individual target shareholders found attractive. If the target stock was held for the benefit of others (as was very often the case, given that about half of all stock was held by large institutional investors such as mutual funds, pension plans, and insurance companies), the shareholder institution might even have felt compelled to accept the offer to avoid claims of breach of fiduciary duty owed to beneficiaries. (Indeed, as a matter of federal laws governing retirement plans, pension plans set up by the target company itself were sometimes more or less required to sell target company stock to a hostile bidder offering an attractive price.) The success or failure of a hostile takeover thus depended on the sum total of a large number of individual decisions by shareholders rather than on a single yes-or-no decision by the managers of the target entity.

Prior to the 1960s, typical takeover transactions involved large corporations becoming larger by taking over smaller ones. In the 1980s, smaller corporations (or even individuals) successfully acquired control of publicly held corporations that sometimes had assets much larger than those of the acquirer. Rather paradoxically, many acquisitions in the 1980s involved **bust-up** transactions in which many or most portions of the acquired business were put up for sale shortly after the acquisition. Because the bidder typically borrowed funds to pay cash for target shares, the successful bidder often ended up with both the target and huge amounts of debt. Thus, the bidder was often compelled to break up and sell off components of the acquired business to raise additional cash in order to reduce the debt to manageable levels.

Local and state political forces usually viewed the threatened hostile takeover of a large local enterprise as an unmitigated disaster. They saw jobs and major industrial plants disappearing or being moved to other areas of the country if the takeover occurred. Therefore, local communities and even entire states often joined together with threatened target management to try to defeat takeover attempts.

Unlike state and local governments, the federal government has been essentially neutral with respect to takeovers. In part, this is a result of the fact that the Securities and Exchange Commission (the SEC) has been receptive to arguments based on economic analysis. The federal government does, however, have an important role in the regulation of takeover attempts. The **Williams Act** was enacted by Congress in 1968 in response to the first wave of tender offers. Technically it consists of several amendments to Sections 13 and 14 of the Securities Exchange Act of 1934 (the 1934 Act).

The purposes of the Williams Act are to create a level playing field between bidder and target and to protect shareholders from unfair or deceptive tactics. The important substantive provisions of this legislation impose disclosure requirements on bidders and targets and establish basic ground rules for the conduct of a **tender offer**. In addition, Section 14(e) of the Williams Act contains an anti-fraud provision relating to tender offers. There have been many attempts to use this provision to obtain judicial review of the tactics used by both targets and bidders. The United States Supreme Court has held, however, that an unsuccessful contestant for control does not have standing to attack the other party's actions, because the statute was intended solely to protect independent shareholders (*Piper v. Chris-Craft Industries, Inc.,* 430 U.S. 1 (1977)). Following this decision, federal courts have generally refused to consider the validity of specific tactics under federal law (although increasingly state courts do so under state law relating to duties of directors). It now appears to be accepted, at least as a matter of federal law, that the ultimate success or failure of a takeover attempt should be determined on the economic playing field rather than on the federal judicial one. Some economists argue that even the minimal degree of existing federal regulation of takeovers is too much; other persons strongly advocate greater participation by the federal government in regulating the takeover movement.

The high point of the 1980s-style leveraged transactions came in 1989, with the $25 billion buyout of RJR Nabisco by the leading takeover firm of the era, Kohlberg, Kravis, Roberts (KKR). Thereafter, the "go-go" days of takeovers abruptly ended, and the number of leveraged transactions declined to virtually zero. Although one reason for this development was a variety of legal restrictions placed on the use of junk bonds, the principal reason appears to have been financial and political rather than legal. Drexel Burnham Lambert was criminally prosecuted along with Michael Milken, its most powerful partner and the leading market-maker for junk bonds. Publicity surrounding the savings and loan crisis (which was exacerbated by a number of savings and loan associations that had made disastrous investments in junk bonds), and concern over the financial stability of the banking and insurance industries (which in many cases had made similar investments) did not help. Loan and investment policies tightened dramatically. The failure of several large leveraged buyout transactions also contributed, as the surviving entities found it impossible to make debt payments and filed for bankruptcy reorganization. To make matters even worse, suits have been filed in these bankruptcy proceedings against banks, investment firms and advisers, controlling shareholders, and others, on the theory that the leveraged buyout itself constituted a fraudulent conveyance. These suits also doubtlessly dampened any interest in financing leveraged buyout transactions.

The market for junk bonds improved in the early 1990s, as yields on investment-grade securities declined, but little of the cash so raised was earmarked for takeover purposes. A few large transactions occurred in 1994 and 1995, and the pace quickened thereafter. But most of these transactions were either stock-for-stock transactions or based on internally generated rather than borrowed funds. Although it is always possible that speculative, leveraged transactions may return, the frenzied activity of the 1980s appears unlikely to recur.

Aside from a lack of easy money, there were other factors that caused hostile takeovers to decline in number. First, most publicly traded companies adopted almost impermeable defenses, in particular "poison pills." These defenses effectively require any prospective bidder to gain the consent of management in connection with any takeover. However, these defensive tactics are limited by a judicially created rule that once a company is for sale it must be sold to the highest bidder after a fair auction unimpeded by the target board's favoring any particular bidder. Defensive tactics and poison pills, and the judicial limits on their use, are discussed in detail in later sections of this chapter.

In addition to target company defensive tactics, most states have adopted takeover statutes that limit the ways in which takeovers may be effected or the ability of a successful bidder to dispose of target assets after control is achieved. Undoubtedly, the most important of these statutes is the Delaware statute, which provides that unless a bidder obtains the consent of target management before acquiring 15 percent or more of target company stock (or acquires 85 percent or more of target company stock), the bidder may not buy, sell, merge, or otherwise dispose of any portion of the target company for a period of three years. The intent and effect of this statute is to make a bidder either negotiate with management or make an offer so attractive that it garners virtually all of the target shares.

Yet another possible cause for the decline of hostile takeovers may be that extraordinarily high prices in the stock market up to early 2000 made it impractical to buy target company stock. Indeed, takeovers in the 1980s may have been motivated by the undervaluation of target companies by the stock market, while takeovers in the 1990s appear to have been motivated by economic considerations such as gaining access to an ensured source of supply, acquiring a new product line, or securing developed expertise in a given area of business in which the bidder is weak. Intuitively, these motivations for mergers are more likely to lead to a negotiated transaction than to a hostile one.

Finally, it may be that management styles have changed as a result of the takeover wars of the 1980s. It may be that managers are now willing to take steps voluntarily that hostile bidders threatened in the 1980s. Indeed, hardly a day goes that a publicly held company does not announce that it is selling off or downsizing a division or line of business in an effort to increase efficiency and presumably its stock price. Successful bidders commonly used these tactics during the 1980s.

## §13.3 Methods by Which One Corporation Can Acquire Another

There are several ways in which one corporation can combine with another either in whole or in part. The simplest method is by **merger**. In what is often called a **plain vanilla merger**, two (or more) corporations become one, and by operation of law the **surviving corporation** acquires all of the assets and liabilities of the corporations that cease to exist. In a **consolidation**, the surviving corporation is a new corporation that acquires the assets and liabilities of all of the constituent corporations. In order for a merger or consolidation to be effected, the boards of directors of the constituent corporations must agree to a plan of merger that is then submitted to a vote of the shareholders of each corporation. In most jurisdictions, the merger must be approved by the shareholders of each corporation by a majority of all the shareholders eligible to vote, although the required number may be increased in the articles of incorporation or bylaws of a corporation. (Often only a single set of proxy materials will be prepared in order to reduce the expenses of holding the vote and to minimize the possibility of discrepancies.) The shareholders of the corporation that ceases to exist may receive stock of the surviving corporation, cash, notes, or any other property that the plan of merger specifies. If the shareholders of the disappearing corporation receive stock, the merger is called a **stock-for-stock merger**; if they receive cash, it is called a **cash merger**. A shareholder who objects to a merger usually has a statutory **right of dissent and appraisal** and may demand payment in cash of the value of his or her shares as of the day before the merger.

A corporation may sell all or substantially all of its assets, with or without assignment of its liabilities, to another corporation. When a corporation seeks to sell all or substantially all of its assets, the approval process is generally the same as for a merger. The board must adopt a plan, and the shareholders must approve the proposed transaction by majority vote. It is not, however, necessary for the shareholders of the acquiring corporation to approve the transaction. In most jurisdictions, shareholders of the selling corporation also have the right of dissent and appraisal in sale of asset transactions, although in Delaware they do not. One of the recurring issues in connections with sales of assets is what constitutes **all or substantially all** of the selling corporation's assets. Although the phrase seems clear enough, courts have ruled that the sale of the largest division or line of business (sometimes constituting less than half of the earning power of the selling corporation) may be significant enough to require a shareholder vote.

The primary advantage of a sale of assets, aside from a somewhat simpler approval process, is that the purchasing corporation may decide which liabilities it does not wish to assume. The primary disadvantage is that each individual asset and liability must be separately identified and valued in a sale of assets. Moreover, there may be complicated filing or recordation requirements for some assets (e.g., real estate) so transferred. There is also a danger that a court will deem additional liabilities to have been assumed by the purchasing corporation even though they are not expressly assumed. For example, management of a corporation facing potential products liability or environmental claims may figure that the assets can be sold for an attractive price and the corporation dissolved and the proceeds distributed to the shareholders before the claims arise. (The law generally requires a corporation that is dissolving to set aside enough to pay known claims, but that does not necessarily prevent unscrupulous managers from trying to avoid them.) Although former management of the dissolved corporation and shareholders who receive distributions in dissolution may be held liable to a limited extent, the courts often also hold the purchasing corporation liable on vague theories (e.g., that the sale of assets constituted a "de facto merger" or that the acquiring corporation was a "mere continuation" of the selling corporation). Despite this danger of **successor liability**, there is an old adage in doing deals: "Buy assets, sell stock."

In addition to mergers and sales of assets, many states also allow for a **share exchange**. In a share exchange, the purchasing corporation issues its shares directly to the target corporation shareholders. The exchange, however, is mandatory, not voluntary. The effect of the transaction is that the target becomes a wholly owned subsidiary of the purchasing company but does not go out of existence (as it would in a merger) or remain as an independent company (as it would in a sale of assets). A share exchange is generally subject to the same approval process as a merger.

There are several special forms of mergers. A **short-form merger** allows a parent company that owns 90 percent or more of the stock of a subsidiary company to effect a merger of the subsidiary into the parent without advance notice to the subsidiary company and without the need to gain the approval of the subsidiary board or hold a vote of either subsidiary or parent shareholders. Subsidiary shareholders do, however, have a right of appraisal in a short-form merger.

The words "parent" and "subsidiary" have no precise meaning. Generally speaking, a **parent company** controls a **subsidiary company** (or **sub**) by virtue of owning at least a majority of the voting stock in the subsidiary. If the parent company owns all of the subsidiary's stock, it is called a **wholly owned subsidiary**. A parent-subsidiary merger in which the subsidiary is not wholly owned presents special problems of fiduciary duty, because the parent may theoretically dictate the terms of a merger possibly to the detriment of minority shareholders in the subsidiary. The parent company naturally desires to acquire the stock of the subsidiary it does not already own at as low a price as possible. These mergers are sometimes called **cash out mergers**, and they are subject to a heightened scrutiny by the courts under an **entire fairness** test.

Another specialized merger form is the **triangular merger**. In a triangular merger, the acquiring corporation forms a new wholly owned subsidiary corporation and causes it to merge with the target corporation; the subsidiary is the surviving corporation. A triangular merger avoids a vote by the parent company shareholders and thereby the possibility that some of those shareholders may exercise their right of dissent and appraisal to force the company to buy their shares. In a **reverse triangular merger**, the subsidiary is merged into the target corporation, which survives, but the parent company ends up owning all the target company shares. A short-form merger may then be used to combine the target with the parent without any further shareholder vote.

Mergers are often used for purposes of simply reorganizing an existing enterprise. When a parent corporation merges into a subsidiary, the merger is said to be a **downstream merger**. When the subsidiary merges into the parent, the merger is said to be an **upstream merger**. For example, every state permits mergers with corporations from other states, so-called **foreign corporations**. Indeed, if a corporation wants to change its state of incorporation, the change is usually effected by setting up a **shell corporation** in the desired state and merging the existing corporation into the new corporation; the new corporation survives and simultaneously changes its name to the name of the old corporation. In many jurisdictions it is possible for noncorporations (for example, limited partnerships and limited liability companies) also to engage in mergers either with similar or different entities. The discussion here, however, is limited to mergers in the context of corporations. A downstream merger may also be used to eliminate dividend arrearages on preferred stock by specifying in the plan of merger that the preferred stockholders receive, for example, common stock in the surviving company. As a general rule, however, if a class of shareholders will have different rights under the surviving corporation's articles of incorporation, that class may vote as a class on the merger and thus may often exact a premium price in exchange for their approval.

Most states have adopted statutory provisions that dispense with the requirement of a shareholder vote (and the right of dissent and appraisal) for the surviving corporation if the number of outstanding shares of the acquiring corporation will be no more than 120 percent of the number outstanding before the merger (both in terms of voting power and in terms of financial participation). The idea is that such a merger has relatively little effect on the control or financial interests of the acquiring company shareholders. Therefore, the decision to acquire the target corporation is in the nature of an ordinary business decision that the board should be able to make without a shareholder vote.

A single corporation may also split itself into two or more successor corporations. Although at least one state has a statute allowing for the division of a corporation, it is always possible for a corporation simply to form a new wholly owned subsidiary and to contribute (or **drop down**) specified assets into the new corporation. The original corporation may then distribute the shares in the subsidiary to its own shareholders with the result that the new corporation becomes effectively independent from the old. The original corporation may also elect to sell the shares to some third party buyer. One issue that arises in split-ups is whether both successor corporations are liable for all the obligations of the original corporation.

## §13.4 Planning, Tax, and Accounting Considerations

It is important to understand that the form of a transaction is almost wholly a matter of choice. A sale of assets can be structured in such a way as to accomplish precisely the same outcome as a merger. For example, a target company may agree to accept survivor company stock in exchange for its assets and thereafter dissolve, distributing the stock to its shareholders. The net effect of this transaction is that the target shareholders become shareholders of the surviving company just as they would in a stock-for-stock merger. But there may be significant differences in the way the two transactions are taxed. Whereas a merger is usually tax-free to both the target corporation and its shareholders, a sale of assets is generally taxable unless at least 80 percent of the consideration is stock. In many cases, the parties of course will want the transaction to be tax-free, but in some cases they may prefer it to be taxable, because the surviving corporation can then take a higher basis (a **stepped-up basis**) in the assets acquired and claim larger depreciation deductions in subsequent years. (Depreciation and basis are discussed in detail in the chapter on accounting and tax.) Reverse triangular mergers are popular, because they leave the target intact and often avoid the triggering of tax on the gain from what might be deemed to be a sale of the target's assets. A reverse triangular merger may also preserve any carryover losses that the target may have for tax purposes.

Similar considerations may arise in connection with accounting for a merger or sale of assets. Prior to 2001, a plain vanilla stock-for-stock merger was treated as a **pooling of interests** for accounting purposes. That is, the assets and liabilities of the target were simply added to the surviving company's balance sheet at the same values at which they were carried on the target's balance sheet irrespective of the fact that the stock used to "buy" the target may have been worth much more than the net book value of the target. A sale of assets, on the other hand, was usually treated as a **purchase**, which, among other things, required the purchasing company to create a goodwill asset reflecting the difference between the price paid for the target and the aggregate values assigned to individual assets and liabilities. The goodwill asset was then amortized and the yearly amortization expense had the effect of reducing earnings in later years under generally accepted accounting principles (GAAP). If stock was used as consideration in both cases, there was no economic difference between the two transactions, but subsequent reported earnings were higher if the transaction was a pooling than if the transaction was a purchase. Studies indicate that the stock market pays no attention to these differences in reported income and values the stock of surviving companies according to underlying fundamentals. But many corporate managers apparently believed that stock price would be higher if the transaction was treated as a pooling transaction and per share earnings thereafter were higher than if the transaction was treated as a purchase. In 2000, the FASB eliminated pooling accounting by adopting a rule requiring purchase accounting in all deals. At the same time, however, the FASB eliminated the requirement that goodwill be amortized and thus the primary objection to purchase accounting.

A corporation may contribute appreciated assets to a new corporation and spin off the shares as a dividend to existing shareholders who then may keep or sell the shares as they see fit. The contribution of the assets to the new corporation is a tax-free incorporation. The **spin-off** of the shares as a dividend will also be tax-free if there is a business purpose for the transaction and certain other tests are met. Although, in a sense, the recipient shareholders do not receive anything they did not have before, they do end up with more choice and therefore possibly more liquidity. In addition, the two corporations may perform better separately than they did together. In any event, tax-free spin-offs have become a major part of the deal landscape. One of the largest such deals involved the spin-off of Lucent Technologies (the former Bell Labs) from AT&T.

A spin-off or **divisive reorganization** is one of the few remaining ways to extract assets from corporate solution without triggering a tax at the corporate level because of the transaction being deemed a sale of assets by the corporation. Prior to 1986, it was possible to disincorporate tax-free under the so-called *General Utilities* doctrine. The doctrine was, however, abolished by Congress in the Tax Reform Act of 1986, although it is unclear why *incorporation* should be tax free as a mere change of the form of doing business and *disincorporation* should not be, except of course that it is a way of maximizing tax receipts because of the dual tax structure that applies to corporations.

The accounting and tax treatment of corporate groups can be quite complex even in the absence of a formal merger or other transaction. Under both GAAP and the Internal Revenue Code (IRC), a corporation that exceeds a certain percentage ownership level is required to report earnings and pay taxes on a consolidated basis as if the legally separate entities were one.

## §13.5 Anatomy of a Hostile Takeover

Although most mergers and acquisitions today are friendly deals, it is impossible to understand the array of laws, rules, and contractual devices governing mergers without understanding the hostile takeovers that prompted the adoption or invention of these laws, rules, and devices.

Assume that a potential bidder has found what it believes to be a suitable target. The target is a medium-sized publicly owned corporation. From the target's SEC filings and other publicly available information, it is known that the target has 20,000,000 shares of common stock trading outstanding at about $30 per share. The market therefore currently values the target at $600,000,000. Of the 20,000,000 shares outstanding, it is estimated that 40 percent are held by some 20 or 25 institutional investors. The extent of institutional ownership is significant, because the more concentrated the stock ownership, the easier it is to make direct approaches to the holders of blocks of stock that may be decisive in a struggle for control. Like many other publicly held corporations of approximately this size, management owns an insignificant fraction of the outstanding stock: less than 100,000 shares. The target is apparently well managed and has been consistently profitable, with earnings per share of about $3 in the latest year. At a market price of $30 per share, the target's stock is selling for 10 times earnings, a rather low price/earnings (P/E) ratio for the industry. According to its latest financial statements it has about $50,000,000 of cash (or cash equivalents) on its balance sheet that appears to be in excess of its current operating requirements. The most recent annual report states that funds have been accumulated to finance needed plant expansion and acquisitions of smaller companies that complement the operations of the target corporation. The relatively low price of the target stock may be the result of the market's judgment that such expansion is unwarranted and perhaps that the available cash should be distributed as a dividend instead. In any event, the fact that the company seems to be undervalued and that it has available cash makes it an attractive takeover target.

The potential bidder is also a publicly held corporation. It has built up a "war chest" of over $300,000,000 in cash for acquisitions, and it has arranged lines of credit (usable only for takeovers) that enable it to borrow up to an additional $2,200,000,000 to finance one or more takeovers.

At the outset, the bidder knows relatively little about the target, because it does not have access to internal corporate information. Because the target is publicly held, the bidder does have available the basic data and financial information that is publicly filed with the New York Stock Exchange (the NYSE) and the SEC. It also has available private credit reports and industry and trade information about the operations of the target. It may also have the benefit of some information through hearsay, rumor, and even espionage. Although everything the bidder learns tends to confirm that it is desirable for it to attempt a takeover, this conclusion is necessarily based on incomplete and partial information, and a substantial misjudgment as to value is possible.

At this point, the bidder must decide whether to go ahead and obtain a **toehold** in the target corporation's stock. At the same time, it must make a tentative decision as to how to proceed thereafter: either by a direct appeal to the shareholders through a cash tender offer or by a negotiated transaction with target management. Both alternatives have positive and negative features. A negotiated takeover usually has the advantage of making additional information about the target's affairs available to the bidder before an irrevocable commitment is made. This additional information should permit a more accurate estimate of the value of the target's business and minimize the danger of paying too much for the business. On the other hand, a proposal for a consensual takeover alerts the target to the threat of a direct tender offer to the shareholders and gives it an opportunity to adopt defensive tactics that might make a takeover much more difficult or even impossible. An immediate tender offer has the advantage of surprise and is more likely to succeed, even though it suffers from the disadvantage of having to proceed on less reliable information.

## §13.6 Toehold Acquisitions

Once the decision to go ahead is made, the first step in practically every takeover attempt is for the bidder to purchase a substantial number of target company shares on the open market. These purchases are made at current market prices on the New York Stock Exchange or other market where the target stock is traded but are disguised. Orders may be placed with different brokers in different cities in a variety of different names. The buy orders may be executed at different times as the brokers try to acquire shares at the most favorable prices while hiding the fact that an accumulation of shares for the benefit of one entity is underway.

Under federal law, a bidder may purchase up to 5 percent of the outstanding shares of the target without disclosure. For this reason, one often reads stories about bidders acquiring 4.9 percent of the target's outstanding shares. These announcements are made because the bidder has the independent responsibility of disclosing to its own shareholders that it has made a material investment in another corporation. When ownership exceeds 5 percent, the Williams Act requires the bidder to file a statement with the SEC and to notify the target company within 10 days; but during that 10-day "window," the bidder may continue to purchase the stock. Thus, a bidder may accumulate a significant holding above 5 percent before being required to show its hand.

Assembling a block of 4.9 percent or more of the target's stock undoubtedly will drive up the price of that stock, perhaps from $30 per share to $33 or even $35 per share. If the target is at all sophisticated, it will have detected the surge of buying interest underlying this price run-up. It should suspect that a potential bidder is accumulating shares, because target management should know whether there are pending internal developments to justify the increased interest in the shares. (If there are any such developments, of course, the problem becomes one of insider trading.) Although the target may surmise that someone is accumulating its shares, it probably does not know who it is. If it has not previously adopted takeover defenses, it may hurriedly do so at this time.

The statement that must be filed with the SEC at the expiration of the 10-day window is known as a **13D statement**. The reason for this name is that the statement is required by Section 13(d) of the Securities and Exchange Act. This statement must include information about the identity of the acquirer and the reason for the accumulation of shares. If an immediate takeover attempt is planned, that must be disclosed. If the bidder wishes to keep its options open, it may state that its purpose is to make an investment and that it has no plans to seek control at this time. If a takeover offer is made shortly thereafter, however, a legal attack may be made on the adequacy of the disclosure in the original 13D filing, and the bidder may be prohibited from voting the shares already acquired.

Assume that at the expiration of the 10-day window the bidder has accumulated 8 percent of the target's stock and has moved the price of target shares to $35 per share. Thus, at the time the bidder goes public by filing its 13D statement, it has purchased 1,600,000 shares of target stock at prices ranging between $30 and $35 per share. If the average price per share was $34, the total investment of the bidder in obtaining a toehold is $54,400,000. Let us also assume that its 13D statement straightforwardly states that it has purchased these shares with a view toward obtaining control of the target.

## §13.7  The Dynamics of a Cash Tender Offer

Now that the bidder has resolved to seek control of the target without negotiating with management, one way to do so is to announce a cash tender offer for 42.1 percent of the stock (42.1 percent plus 8 percent already acquired in the open market equals 50.1 percent) of the target at or about the time the 13D statement is filed. (Although such **partial offers** for a bare controlling interest in the target are perfectly legal in the United States—but not in the United Kingdom—and were quite common until the early 1980s, it became standard practice by the late 1980s to offer to purchase all of the remaining shares for cash, largely because of the ready availability of financing and because of potential competition from other bidders.) Target management may receive informal notification of the offer before it is announced, or it may receive no notification at all.

Basically, a cash tender offer is an open invitation for shareholders to submit (**tender**) shares for purchase by the bidder at a specified price. Persons desiring to accept the bidder's offer must submit their shares to a specified depository by a specified date. If enough shareholders tender their shares for purchase, the bidder has achieved its goal. If not enough do, the bidder may return all the tendered shares and not buy any of them. In this event, its investment in the target is limited to the cost of the toehold shares plus the expenses of the unsuccessful offer. If a higher bid then comes in from a third party, the bidder may tender its toehold for purchase by the new bidder, making a substantial profit.

To make a cash tender offer, the offeror must set a price, decide how many additional shares to seek, file a **14D statement** (required, not surprisingly, by section 14(d) of the 1934 Act), and publicly announce the offer. For example, in the above example, the bidder could decide to make a public offer to purchase 42.1 percent of the shares at $50 per share, with the offer to expire in 20 business days (the minimum period permitted under SEC regulation). The 14D statement must disclose, among other things, the source of financing of the purchase price and the plans the bidder has for the target if the offer is successful, as well as the precise terms of the offer.

A cash tender offer is most likely to be effective in corporations in which management owns or controls only a small percentage or proportion of the shares. In the publicly held corporation, nonmanagement shares are held by institutional investors, brokerage firms, speculators, long-term investors, and others. Many of these shareholders may be willing to sell their shares outright at a price above the current market price (e.g., at $50 per share when the current market price is $35), even though they might hesitate to vote to oust incumbent management if they are to remain as shareholders. By offering an attractive price, the bidder appeals to the target shareholders over the head of management. The appeal is not "I can do a better job" but rather "do you want to sell at $50 per share?" If enough holders accept the offer, the offer succeeds and the bidder becomes the majority shareholder.

If the bidder acquires exactly 42.1 percent of the target stock, it will then own 50.1 percent of the target's voting stock. That is certainly sufficient to elect a majority of the target's board of directors, and is sufficient to elect the entire board of directors if the corporation does not have cumulative voting (which is likely to be the case in a publicly held corporation) or has not staggered the election of the board as a takeover defense tactic. If the bidder is able to replace a majority of the board of directors with its own people, it may thereafter replace the old target management with its own people, or it may permit that management to continue to operate the target as a subsidiary of the bidder, if the incumbent management is willing.

It is important to recognize that even if the bidder acquires over 50 percent of the outstanding shares and replaces the target's board of directors and management, it does not have a free hand with respect to the target's assets. The target is still a publicly owned company with the public owning 49.9 percent; the presence of this minority interest sharply circumscribes and limits what the bidder can do with the target's assets. For example, the bidder may not simply distribute the $50,000,000 in excess cash to itself or combine a manufacturing division owned by the target with a similar division owned by the bidder. Transactions of these types would almost certainly be viewed as in breach of the fiduciary duty new management has assumed to the former target company and would likely give rise to immediate shareholder derivative suits. Transactions between the bidder and its new partially owned subsidiary must be made at arm's length and, even then, there is a substantial opportunity for distracting litigation brought by minority shareholders of the target. Hence, there is a strong incentive for the bidder ultimately to eliminate all minority shareholders and obtain 100 percent of the stock. Once it obtains all the shares, there are no outside shareholders to complain if the bidder, for example, uses the target's $50,000,000 to defray a portion of the cost of purchasing the 8,420,000 shares (although creditors may be able to complain if the target later becomes insolvent).

Corporation law effectively allows minority shareholders to be "cashed out" involuntarily, as is discussed more fully below. The transaction to eliminate the minority shareholders is often called a **back-end merger** or **mop-up merger**. The terms of a back-end merger may be significantly less attractive than the terms of the original offer.

Say the bidder decides to make a partial offer for 42.1 percent of the target's stock: 8,420,000 shares. What price should the bidder offer? It must be high enough above the current market price of $35 per share to attract a sufficient number of tenders to yield 8,420,000 shares of stock. It should also be high enough to discourage other possible bidders who may also be looking at the target. On the other hand, one does not want to throw money away with abandon. The bidder is offering to purchase for cash 8,420,000 shares, and the decision whether to offer $45 per share or $50 per share involves a cool $43,000,000. Average takeover premiums during the 1980s were about 50 percent over the pre-offer market price. Thus, $50 per share seems a reasonable price to offer. If this offer is successful, the bidder is committing itself to invest another $431,000,000 in addition to the $54,000,000 invested in the original toehold, in order to obtain control (50.1 percent) of the target. In terms of similar transactions during the 1980s, this nearly half-billion dollar transaction is a relatively small transaction.

Very large offers may be contingent on obtaining financing. That is not necessary in our hypothetical, because the bidder has already lined up $2,200,000,000 of cash or commitments, which is more than ample to pay for the target stock. It is common, however, to include other conditions, such as the absence of objections from the antitrust authorities. Some of these conditions may be fairly general (e.g., an absence of material changes in market conditions) so that a tender offer has some of the attributes of an option rather than of a firm offer to be accepted by individual shareholders tendering their shares. It is rare, however, for a bidder to attempt to invoke these "out" clauses to back out of a successful offer.

In a partial offer, as here, the offer is said to be over-subscribed if the total shares tendered for purchase by the deadline exceed 8,420,000 shares. In this event, the offeror (bidder) may either purchase only 8,420,000 shares or, at its option, purchase all the shares that have been tendered. Under the Williams Act and SEC rules adopted to implement it, if the bidder elects to limit its purchases to 8,420,000 shares, it must purchase shares pro rata from each tenderer; it may not purchase shares on a first-come, first-served basis. Pro rata means that if 12,000,000 shares are tendered, the bidder must purchase 8,420,000/12,000,000 of each individual tender. The federal prohibition against a first-come, first-served offer stems from the worry that it might cause shareholders to tender hastily without opportunity for reflection (in order to make sure that tendered shares are actually purchased) and that it tends to favor centrally located shareholders (principally in New York) at the expense of shareholders who live in more remote locations.

SEC rules under the Williams Act also provide that tendered shares may be withdrawn during the offer and after 60 days if they have not been purchased. As previously noted, the offer must remain open for at least 20 business days, and the bidder may extend it for a longer period or increase the price (e.g., in response to a competing bid at a higher price). If the bidder does increase the price, however, it must buy all shares at the higher price including shares tendered at the lower price. It is arguable, however, that **proration** discourages shareholders from tendering, and indeed it may have been a factor in the trend away from partial offers. That is, to the extent that shareholders are averse to the prospect of a partial purchase of tendered shares, a bidder who offers to buy any and all shares tendered makes a more attractive offer, other things equal, and will presumably attract more tenders. In any event, market professionals figured out, that by tendering borrowed shares they could avoid the risk of proration, prompting the SEC to adopt a rule against **short tendering**. On the other hand, a bidder may let one offer expire and then immediately make a new offer at a higher price, thereby achieving the same result without paying everyone the increased price. SEC rules under the Williams Act also require that tender offers be made to all shareholders. That is, specific groups of shareholders may not be excluded. As long as the tender offer is open, the bidder may purchase shares only through the tender offer. The bidder may not negotiate separately with large institutional shareholders. On the other hand, immediately after the offer expires, the bidder may negotiate with shareholders and purchase their shares in private transactions. This tactic is called a street sweep and is discussed more fully below.

SEC rules also effectively prohibit lowering the price to be paid during the course of a tender offer, although theoretically a lower price may be paid if earlier tendering shareholders agree to the reduction. The **highest price rule** is apparently prompted by notions of fairness—that if some shares are worth the high price, all shares are worth the high price—though quite clearly the rule does not extend back to shares purchased in the open market on the sly to gain a toehold and, as a matter of federal law at least, does not extend forward to any cash out merger of nontendering shareholders. The highest price rule may have the effect of discouraging tender offers, because it effectively increases the price that must be paid by bidders. If bidders could make stair-step offers and were not required to pay all tendering shareholders the highest price paid to any, it would probably be cheaper to acquire control and more offers might be made. And given that many shareholders sell their shares in the open market during a tender offer (at prices affected by the pendency of the offer) rather than take the risk that the offer may fail or be over-subscribed and result in proration, many shareholders effectively opt into a stair-step bid anyway.

## §13.8   Open Market Purchases as an Alternative to a Tender Offer

A few instances have occurred in which a bidder sought to obtain a majority of the outstanding shares of the target by a series of open market purchases without ever making a public tender offer. A 13D statement must be filed when the purchaser breaks the 5 percent level, but no 14D filing is required, because no public tender offer is being made. Moreover, the bidding rules do not apply. Or so the argument goes. There are problems with this approach, however. For one thing, a stream of purchases of this magnitude may drive the market price of the target stock significantly above the price that would bring forth the same number of shares if a tender offer were made. In other words, a tender offer at $50 per share—a one-shot, limited-time offer— may draw more stock out for purchase at $50 per share than could be obtained on the open market at an average price of $50 per share even if the price began at $35 per share. Second, if the bidder communicates directly with large investors while actively purchasing shares in the open market, it may be argued that the communications constituted a tender offer (even though made only to selected persons). This is illegal under the Williams Act when it is not made to all shareholders and not made pursuant to a filed 14D statement. Curiously, the Williams Act contains no definition of what constitutes a tender offer.

## §13.9  Role of Arbitrageurs in Takeovers

When a cash tender offer is made for target shares, the subsequent market activity in the stock strongly influences the offer's outcome. A major run-up in price usually occurs at or shortly before the announcement of the tender offer. Major run-ups in price before the offer probably are caused by information leaks about the contemplated offer. Until recently, a large amount of trading in advance of an offer transpired. Many individuals involved in such trading have been prosecuted, and it is likely that this type of insider trading is a thing of the past. Indeed, the courts have held that information about a planned tender offer is presumed to be improperly obtained.

Leaving aside the possibility of insider trading, when a tender offer is publicly announced the market price for the target shares typically jumps almost instantly to a price nearly as high as the offer price. (The price of the bidder's shares may well decline, but that is another story as discussed more fully below.) Post-offer market activity is largely a result of trading by sophisticated speculators, known as **arbitrageurs**, who accumulate shares and plan to tender them to the bidder (or to the highest competing bidder). On the day the bidder announces its $50 bid, arbitrageurs immediately enter the market, buying target shares at whatever prices they are offered below $50 (and in some cases above $50 if they have reason to believe the bid will be increased or competing offers will be made). These transactions are not classic arbitrage, because the success of the offer is not guaranteed and therefore a degree of risk is involved. For a discussion of the traditional meaning of that term, see Chapter 11, which discusses corporate securities. One should not overstate the degree of risk. Market wisdom is that once a company is "put into play" by a tender offer, its chances of remaining an independent entity are small. In other words, arbitrageurs typically have been able to liquidate their positions in target stock at a profit. Indeed, arbitrage was so profitable in the 1980s that the financial resources of arbitrageurs increased to the point that they were a major force in takeover battles and were able to absorb billions of dollars worth of target shares as they were offered on the market.

The result of arbitrage is that upon the announcement of a bid the price of target stock is quickly driven up from the pre-offer price to a price in the neighborhood of the offered price. The precise relationship of the market price of the target's shares following the announcement to the announced tender offer price is a complex one that depends on the answers to several questions:

1. What is the probability that the offer will succeed?
2. If it does succeed (and the offer is a partial one), to what extent will it be oversubscribed?

3. If it is oversubscribed, will the offeror acquire all shares or will the offer be prorated?
4. If the offer is prorated, what are the terms of the proposed back-end or mop-up merger, if any, likely to be?
5. What are the chances that a higher offer may be forthcoming from a different source?
6. What are the chances that management will attempt a leveraged buyout or a reorganization that provides shareholders with more value than the offer?

Depending on these variables, the market price may be substantially below, slightly below, slightly above, or substantially above, the tender offer price.

Consider the position of shareholders in the target corporation when the offer is made. Upon the announcement of the offer, the shareholders see the market price of their shares advance significantly. The shareholders can choose to (1) hold their shares, hoping that the offer fails and that incumbent management remains in control or that the offer succeeds and that they will get the benefit of new and revitalized management; (2) tender their shares to the bidder pursuant to the offer, hoping that the offer succeeds and is not oversubscribed, but with the risk that they may get back some or all of their shares if the offer is prorated; or (3) sell their shares on the open market and be out of the situation entirely.

The first choice is usually unattractive, because, if the offer fails, history shows the market price of the target shares declines to levels that may be even below the pre-offer price; on the other hand, if the offer succeeds, the nontendering shareholder may be at a serious disadvantage by being remitted to whatever rights he or she may have in the subsequent back-end or mop-up transaction that is likely to occur. The second choice carries the risk that the offer may be oversubscribed and some of the shares returned with the result that the shareholder may again be remitted in part to the back-end offer. Further, tendering involves a mechanical process of complying with the terms of the tender offer and delivery of shares in advance of payment that many shareholders find complex and uncertain. The simplest thing to do is to sell the shares. One thereby obtains the benefit of most of the run-up in price with none of the problems or risks of actually making a tender. The cost of this strategy is that the selling shareholder loses any benefit of subsequent offers by third persons or the benefit of any increase in the offer price by the bidder. And, of course, the selling shareholder must pay a commission to his or her broker.

One thing is virtually certain: If shareholders of the target sell their shares during the pendency of the offer, they will be acquired by arbitrageurs and will be tendered to somebody. Open market sales are thus virtually a vote for the bidder. Put another way, arbitrageurs and bidders are natural allies in the takeover wars.

Institutional investors are under pressure to tender their shares or sell for a different reason. Many of them hold and invest funds as fiduciaries for other groups—employees, insurance policy holders, small investors, and so forth. They have fiduciary responsibilities to obtain the maximum financial return for the current beneficiaries. They may conclude that these fiduciary duties require them to maximize short-run profit by taking advantage of the run-up in price resulting from a tender offer either by tendering shares to the bidder or by selling them during the offer.

## §13.10  Street Sweeps

As described in the previous section, when a corporation is put into play, very large market accumulations of stock are made by arbitrageurs and other speculators in anticipation of the target being taken over by another entity. Occasionally, the bidder is unexpectedly stymied by defensive techniques and thereby compelled to withdraw its offer. At that point, there is a risk that there will be no takeover at all and arbitrageurs face massive losses, because they have paid high prices for shares that will now decline dramatically in price when the takeover threat disappears.

Even in this situation, arbitrageurs have usually avoided substantial losses. Despite the withdrawal of the tender offer, the target remains in a very precarious situation because of the concentration of share ownership in the hands of arbitrageurs and other speculators who are anxious to sell. The percentage ownership of target shares by this relatively small group may approach or exceed 50 percent of the outstanding shares. The target is even more ripe for a takeover than it was before the offer was originally made because of this concentration of ownership in the hands of persons who have no loyalty to the target and who are interested only in an immediate financial return. It is easy for either the bidder that withdrew its recent offer or an opportunistic third person to contact the arbitrageurs directly and offer to buy their holdings of target shares. The price offered for the shares may be somewhat below the price previously offered in the withdrawn tender offer but certainly above the pre-offer price, because the shares being purchased may determine who has working control of the target enterprise. This practice of purchasing shares directly from arbitrageurs and speculators immediately after an unsuccessful tender offer has come to be known as a **street sweep** (the street being Wall Street).

The SEC unsuccessfully challenged street sweeps as violations of the Williams Act and as being unfair to smaller shareholders who are not offered the opportunity to sell their shares in the sweep. The SEC proposed a rule that would make all street sweeps within 10 days after an offer is withdrawn subject to the Williams Act, but the rule was never adopted.

## §13.11  Back-End Transactions

As described above, most bidders ultimately desire to acquire 100 percent of the outstanding shares of the target. However, it is not possible as a practical matter to acquire 100 percent of the shares of a publicly held corporation by a tender offer. Even in an irresistibly attractive tender offer for all shares, a few shareholders always fail to tender by reason of inadvertence or inattention, and there always are a few small shareholders who hold out and refuse to accept an offer at any price. A follow-up transaction to eliminate the remaining public shareholders is an essential step when 100 percent ownership is desired. These follow-up transactions, often called back-end or mop-up transactions, are statutory mergers. A back-end transaction is not necessary if the bidder is willing to accept the status of a majority shareholder in a publicly held corporation with minority shareholders.

In a public cash tender offer, the bidder may make the back-end transaction an affirmative weapon. The bidder may make a partial tender offer, seeking to acquire a controlling interest but less than all of the target's outstanding shares, and at the same time announce, as part of its takeover strategy, the terms of the back-end merger that will eliminate all of the remaining outstanding shares if the original partial offer is successful. Such an offer is known as a **two-step offer** or **two-tier offer**. The terms of the back-end part of the two-step offer, moreover, may be less attractive than the terms of the original cash tender offer, thereby encouraging (or coercing) all shareholders to tender promptly to avoid the less attractive terms of the follow-up transaction. Such an offer is known as a **front-end loaded offer** and is sometimes referred to as a **coercive offer** (although coercion comes in many forms). Many states have enacted statutes restricting back-end transactions.

Assume (as in the foregoing hypothetical) that the bidder has acquired 50.1 percent of the outstanding shares of the target for a total consideration of $485 million. It has decided to force out the remaining 49.1 percent of the shares at $50 per share. The bidder creates a wholly owned subsidiary and transfers to that subsidiary cash and notes to enable the subsidiary to pay the holders of the 49.1 percent of the target shares the bidder does not own. The bidder then proposes a merger of the target corporation into the subsidiary (i.e., a merger in which the surviving corporation is the subsidiary) under the terms of which the holders of the 49.1 percent minority shares are to receive a consideration of $50 in cash and notes for each of their shares in the target. Although the bidder as the majority shareholder of the target is technically entitled to receive the same consideration as the minority shareholders, as the sole shareholder of the surviving subsidiary, the bidder need not bother to pay itself. Approval of this transaction is no problem: The bidder already owns all the stock of one party to the transaction (its subsidiary) and 50.1 percent of the stock of the other (the target), and because a simple majority of the outstanding shares of each constituent corporation is all that is required to approve the merger, the result of the vote is a foregone conclusion. When the transaction is closed, each minority shareholder receives $50 per share. All shares of the target are cancelled; because the wholly owned subsidiary is the surviving corporation in the merger, it ends up with the property and business of the target and the bidder is the owner of 100 percent of the outstanding shares of that corporation. The net effect of this merger is that the remaining shareholders of the target are forced to accept cash and notes for their shares, while the bidder keeps the business as the sole shareholder of the surviving company.

Seemingly, the minority shareholders of the target must be satisfied with whatever pittance the bidder—the new majority shareholder—decides to give them. There are, however, several important protections for minority share-holder interests. The first is the statutory right of **dissent and appraisal** that permits any minority shareholder dissatisfied with the proffered terms (1) to reject them; (2) to obtain an independent judicial appraisal of the value of his or her shares; and (3) to receive that value in cash in lieu of the consideration offered in the cash merger transaction. This alternative is not really as attractive as it might first appear. There are major practical problems with appraisal rights from the standpoint of small shareholders: the cost of maintaining any judicial proceeding, delays (during which the shareholder loses the use of money), and the uncertainty in outcome inherent in any judicial proceeding. Moreover, the courts of some states adhere to the view that if the stock in question is publicly traded, the market price is presumed to be fair, despite the fact that bidders invariably must offer a substantial premium over the market price in order to induce sufficient tenders to gain control. Indeed, in certain circumstances, some states deny dissenters rights for certain types of transactions involving publicly traded companies. Delaware even denies dissenters' rights in connection with transactions structured as sales of assets rather than mergers. Nevertheless, if the new majority shareholder is too stingy with the minority, it will find itself involved in litigation with unhappy minority shareholders over the value of the minority shares, with a contingent obligation to pay the dissenting shareholders immediately in cash whatever amount the court ultimately determines to be the fair value of the minority shares. Thus, bidders have a strong incentive to offer back-end consideration that will minimize the number of dissenters.

A second major safety valve is the recognition by the Delaware Supreme Court that the majority shareholder, when it decides to vote its 50.1 percent of the target's stock to approve the transaction, is engaged in a self-dealing transaction that must meet a standard of **entire fairness**. (*Weinberger v. UOP, Inc.*, 457 A.2d 701 (1983)). Entire fairness requires fair dealing (including full disclosure of all relevant facts as well as a fair opportunity for some type of negotiation on behalf of the minority) and fair price, with the bidder having the burden of proof in any lawsuit brought by the minority that the standard of fairness has been met. This burden may be shifted to the plaintiff sharehold-ers, however, if the transaction is approved after full disclosure by the minority shareholders voting separately—a majority of the minority vote in Delaware. Although such a minority vote is not required under the Delaware merger statute, approval by the minority may, as a practical matter, be necessary if the merger is to withstand judicial scrutiny. Although the majority of the minority vote is a court-created protection under Delaware law, the Model Business Corporation Act and several of the states that follow it closely have adopted the device as a matter of statute.

A third safety valve is that Delaware case law permits more powerful de-fensive tactics by a target against a proposed takeover bid if the target reason-ably believes that the proposed back-end transaction makes the entire transaction inadequate or coercive to minority shareholders.

If a bidder announces a two-tier offer in which the amount offered for the back end of the offer is openly stated to be less than the amount offered in the front-end offer, the offer is called a "front-end loaded" tender offer. In one famous case involving the takeover of Marathon Oil by United States Steel in 1981, the bidder, United States Steel, announced a tender offer at $125 per share for 51 percent of the shares and also announced that if the first offer were successful a back-end transaction would be proposed eliminating the unpurchased shares for a consideration to be paid in the form of bonds worth approximately $76 per share. (The eventually successful offer was arranged in cooperation with the target, because of an earlier unwelcome offer by Mobil Oil.) Such an offer places economic pressure on all shareholders to tender into the original offer in order to take advantage of the front-end price and avoid the lower back-end price. As a result, a transaction structured in this way is generally viewed as highly coercive, though its use has been defended on abstract grounds by some economists. Their argument is that the true price being offered for the target company is the **blended price** obtained by averaging the front-end and back-end prices. If this blended price is above the pre-offer market price, the transaction still creates value for the target shareholders as a whole. This argument assumes implicitly that all shareholders will tender into the front-end offer, as they rationally should do. The shareholders then sustain no harm, because they all will effectively obtain the blended price (because all will share proportionately in both the front-end and back-end prices when the over-subscribed offer is prorated). However, these arguments mask a considerable potential for unfairness to individual shareholders, not all of whom may be aware that a rational decision is required or be able to act on a timely basis to accept the front-end offer. Devices such as short tendering also exist; these devices allow sophisticated shareholders to obtain the purchase of a larger percentage of their shares at the front-end price than other shareholders.

A second approach toward front-end loaded offers is illustrated by the offer of Mesa Petroleum for Unocal Corporation. Mesa offered $54 per share in a tender offer for enough shares (an additional 37 percent) to raise its holdings to just over 50 percent of Unocal, and in the back-end offer, proposed a consideration of "highly subordinated" Unocal debt securities "with a market value of $54." Presumably the "subordination" referred to new bank loans to be obtained by Unocal to assist Mesa in financing the original purchase of the 37 percent of Unocal. Unocal vigorously opposed this transaction, pejoratively describing the debt securities that Mesa proposed as junk bonds, and proposing an exchange offer to all of its remaining shareholders—except Mesa—that would have provided each shareholder with a substantial amount of senior Unocal debt. This discriminatory offer was upheld by the Delaware Supreme Court in *Unocal v. Mesa Petroleum Co.*, 493 A.2d 946 (Del. 1985), and ultimately Mesa's offer was defeated. Following the Unocal opinion, the Securities and Exchange Commission adopted an **all holders rule** to prohibit the kind of discriminatory offer that Unocal made in this case.

As a general proposition, it is difficult to quarrel with the Delaware Supreme Court's categorization of Mesa's offer for Unocal. An all-cash $54 offer is more attractive than an offer of debt and securities "with a market value of" $54, because of the uncertainties of valuation and the possibility that the market may value the debt securities at a lower price than what the offeror optimistically estimates. Further, the ready marketability of the debt may be doubtful, particularly for large holders. Hence, this type of offer appears also to be a type of front-end loaded offer, though perhaps not as blatant as a dual-price cash offer.

Front-end loaded offers declined dramatically after 1985. The most common pattern became to announce that in the back-end offer the same amount of cash would be paid as in the front-end offer (or to state that no plans for a back-end offer existed). Several factors caused the apparent abandonment of the front-end loaded offer. A number of corporations adopted **fair price amendments** to their articles of incorporation requiring back-end transactions to be made at prices at least as favorable as the front-end offer price. Several states imposed similar fair price requirements for such mergers by statute: Maryland was the first state to adopt this type of statute. (But neither fair price amendments nor fair price statutes dealt with the possibility that the bidder might simply decline to do a back-end merger and leave the minority shareholders frozen into their investment in a controlled corporation.) Judicial antagonism to front-end loaded offers, epitomized by the Delaware Supreme Court's categorization of Mesa's offer for Unocal as an "inadequate and coercive two-tier tender offer," indicated a willingness by courts to permit extreme defensive measures to defeat such offers. Finally, because a noncoercive all cash offer is more attractive to target shareholders, competition from other bidders tended to force serious initial bidders to make all cash **any-or-all offers** in the first place, in part because it became quite easy to raise larger amounts of cash through junk bonds. Nevertheless, a two-tier offer prevailed in the 1994 Viacom bid for Paramount, suggesting either that target shareholders had forgotten what they learned earlier or that the terms of offers may change over time much as fashions do.

## §13.12 The Proxy Fight

The oldest type of nonconsensual takeover technique, long antedating the development of the cash tender offer, is the proxy fight. In a **proxy fight**, the bidder solicits the target's shareholders with a proposal that they vote for an alternative slate of directors. If holders of a majority of the shares vote for the alternative slate, the bidder obtains control of the board of directors of the target. Thereafter, a cash-out merger with the bidder may be negotiated or the target may remain in business as a separate entity indefinitely under the new management. The proxy fight is much more akin to a traditional political campaign than a tender offer; shareholders who vote in favor of the bidder generally remain shareholders after the change in management occurs. Proxy fights are subject to significant regulation under the proxy rules adopted by the SEC. These rules basically require full and open disclosure of objectives and plans.

The proxy fight has not been a popular device in the recent past primarily because the probability of its success is relatively low and because cash is usually available to buy control directly through a cash tender offer. The reason for the low probability of success is that it is difficult to persuade shareholders to vote out incumbent management when they will remain as shareholders in the target corporation after the change in management occurs. Nevertheless, a handful of attempts have taken place during the recent takeover movement to use the proxy fight as an auxiliary device to place additional pressure on the target short of making an outright offer to purchase control. This usually occurs when it appears the target is so large, or its defenses seem so impregnable, that it is impractical for the bidder to mount a cash tender offer.

With the development of powerful takeover defenses by corporations and the enactment of statutes by Delaware and other states that make takeovers more difficult, it is possible that proxy fights may be more widely used in the future than in the past.

## §13.13  Exchange Offers

A few takeover offers have been based not on offers of cash for target securities but on offers of exchanges of bidder debt for shares of the target. Ted Turner once unsuccessfully attempted to acquire a controlling interest in rival CBS, Inc. by an offer to swap a variety of debt instruments, including several zero coupon notes, for CBS stock. The offer did not succeed, in part because CBS installed substantial takeover defenses that probably would have made it impractical for Turner to use CBS assets or cash flow to service any of the additional debt.

Transactions are cast in the form of exchange offers when the bidder finds it impractical to raise sufficient cash to mount a straight tender offer. Exchange offers suffer from problems of uncertainty over the market value of the proffered debt securities and concerns over the potential lack of marketability of large blocks of those securities. In addition, a substantial risk of default may take place: The bidder may be unable to satisfy the obligations set forth in the debt securities it is offering, and the market may discount the securities accordingly. These securities are sometimes called "funny money," a phrase that reflects the skepticism of the market about this type of transaction.

An offer of bidder-issued debt for stock in the target in a sense proposes that the shareholders of the target themselves finance the takeover of their own company. Rather than the bidder borrowing money from third parties by issuing debt and using the money to purchase shares, the bidder offers the debt directly to the target shareholders. On the other hand, one could think of such an offer as a firm commitment to cause the target company to make generous distributions, and indeed many offers have been prompted by the target company's stinginess in making distributions and its decision to invest extra cash in questionable ways. Nevertheless, it is not surprising that offers of funny money have not proved to be attractive.

## §13.14  Defensive Tactics in General

When the first cash tender offers were made, the targets were virtually defenseless. They were often unprepared for the offer, and a successful purchase of the majority of the outstanding shares often occurred before the simplest defensive measures could be taken. The Williams Act sharply cut down the advantage of surprise by its disclosure requirements and the provision that all tender offers must remain open for at least 20 business days, thereby eliminating pressure on shareholders to tender immediately or lose out.

Today, **defensive tactics** are well understood and practically every publicly held corporation has erected a shield consisting of a number of different types of defenses. Defenses may be classified into two basic types: (1) those put into place before any tender offer is made and designed to discourage the approach in the first place and (2) those instituted after a cash tender offer has been launched in an effort to defeat that particular offer.

The simplest types of pre-offer defenses involve the use of devices long provided for in corporation statutes that make it difficult to obtain working control of the target even if the bidder obtains a majority of its outstanding voting shares. These provisions, known as **shark repellants** or **porcupine provisions**, may either make the process by which the board of directors is replaced by a new majority shareholder more difficult or impose additional costs on the corporation in the event of a successful takeover.

A popular defense is to stagger the election of directors so that directors have three-year terms and only one-third of the board is elected each year. At the same time, it is necessary to provide that directors may only be removed for cause in order to prevent a new majority shareholder from calling a meeting of shareholders and simply removing all the directors without cause, as is permitted under most state corporation statutes. The theory of these provisions is that it may take the bidder two years after obtaining a majority of the shares before it is able to replace a majority of the board of directors with its own designees.

Another popular provision limits the power of shareholders to call special meetings on the theory that the new majority shareholder may be unable to act except at a meeting. In states that permit the shareholders to act by majority consent informally without a meeting (an option that is available in Delaware and a limited number of other states), bylaw or charter provisions may also be adopted defining and circumscribing that power, again making it difficult for a new majority shareholder to translate its shareholdings into operating control of the target.

Pre-offer defensive tactics may also involve economic changes designed to make the corporation less attractive as a target. This is a second line of defense independent of the internal corporate changes described above. For example, corporations may grant officers and mid-level employees **golden parachutes** or **tin parachutes** triggered by a takeover of the management of the corporation over the objection of incumbent management. Golden parachutes are lucrative severance contracts for top management whose employment with the corporation may be terminated upon a successful takeover. Tin parachutes are smaller severance contracts for middle-level management. The total payments required under individual contracts may run into the tens of millions of dollars for high-level individual officers. Aggregate payments may be several times larger. Even with large payments, however, it is unlikely that they will seriously deter a bidder who is already contemplating a transaction running into the hundreds of millions or billions of dollars. Moreover, it is arguable that golden parachutes allow management to serve the corporation during the pendency of a takeover bid without concern about their personal economic futures and encourage management to consider the interests of the target shareholders seriously.

Another type of economic defense against unwanted takeover attempts involves restructuring the corporation to reduce its attractiveness as a takeover target. Many corporations, for example, have distributed excess cash to shareholders either in the form of an extraordinary dividend, or, more commonly, in the form of open market share repurchases. A major share repurchase plan (1) reduces the number of outstanding shares; (2) leaves total earnings per share virtually unchanged or may indeed increase earnings per share (because the cash used is excess and not essential for the operation of the target's business and because of the reduced number of shares); and (3) increases the market price of the target shares through simple reduction in supply.

The business may also be recapitalized by the sale of nonessential lines of business and distribution of the proceeds to the shareholders in the form of extraordinary distributions or a share repurchase program. Large amounts may also be borrowed in order to leverage up the target and increase its debt/equity ratio; the cash is again distributed to shareholders. Such a transaction is often called a **leveraged recapitalization**. This makes the target "leaner and meaner" and basically does what a successful bidder would be likely to do if it obtained working control of the target. Whether these transactions are desirable from the standpoint of the economic well-being of the target may be questionable.

Yet another popular defensive tactic is to make it difficult for a successful bidder to obtain approval of back-end merger transactions. These provisions may no longer be necessary in Delaware corporations (and corporations formed in states with statutes similar to Delaware's), because a statute now limits such transactions. Corporations formed in other states may adopt super-majority provisions that require approval by more than a majority vote of the shareholders: a two-thirds or even higher percentage vote of the shareholders may be required for approval of transactions between the target corporation and the bidder or a corporation that the bidder controls. To avoid imposing impossible restraints on desired transactions with major shareholders, the super-majority provision may be made waivable by the board of directors or applicable only to transactions with a person who recently acquired a substantial interest in the target's stock. A more radical type of provision grants rights of redemption to minority shareholders at the same price paid by a bidder who acquires a majority of the outstanding shares. Another provision limits the power of a bidder to impose a back-end transaction on terms less favorable than the terms on which the bidder obtained its controlling interest. Other pre-offer defenses are poison pills and control share acquisition plans, both of which are discussed below.

Once an offer is made, the nature of defensive tactics changes materially. The object is to defeat the offer by any fair (or not so fair) means. The following are typical (though the list is not exhaustive):

1. Acquiring another corporation that creates antitrust problems for the bidder if it completes the purchase of the target company.
2. Attacking the funding of the offer, usually by direct approaches to the financial institutions named in the bidder's 14D statement.

3.  Driving up the price of target stock so that it is above the tender offer price. This may be accomplished by making a major distribution (a type of restructuring or recapitalizing), or by a large share repurchase plan that may reduce the number of outstanding shares by 20 percent or more.

4.  Disposing of desirable assets — **crown jewels** — to friendly entities on terms that are less than favorable to the target. The object of these transactions is to make the target less attractive as a target. At the most extreme, the target may destroy itself as a viable economic entity to avoid capture. This is a **scorched earth** tactic.

5.  Granting **lock up** options or rights to friendly interests to purchase additional shares of target stock at bargain prices. Such transactions increase the number of shares needed to be purchased by the bidder.

6.  Making a competing tender offer for the bidder's stock. Often referred to as the **pac man defense**, this strategy may lead to the bizarre situation in which each corporation has acquired a majority of the outstanding shares of the other corporation. This strategy has only rarely been attempted.

7.  Finding a more congenial suitor — a **white knight** — and arranging a consensual transaction.

8.  Arranging a **leveraged buyout** with a new entity in which incumbent management participates.

9.  Adopting poison pill or control share acquisition provisions (discussed in the two following sections).

10. Changing the state of incorporation to take advantage of more favorable state laws or seeking changes in home-state corporation laws, which in some cases may be easier, cheaper, and quicker than amending the corporation's articles or bylaws.

Some of these defensive tactics may lead to the defeat of the takeover attempt outright, while others tend to encourage bidding contests by introducing new contestants for control of the target.

## §13.15  Poison Pills

A **poison pill** is a special type of stock or debt issued by a potential target corporation with rights that are designed to make a hostile takeover attempt difficult, impractical, or impossible. Poison pills were invented in the early 1980s and have become one of the most popular takeover defenses. Hundreds of publicly held corporations have adopted them.

The board of directors usually creates a poison pill without a shareholder vote pursuant to its power to specify the rights of preferred shares to be issued (if authorized to do so in the articles of incorporation). Although a poison pill theoretically could be created by shareholder action, boards of directors usually prefer not to submit such a controversial issue to the shareholders. Because shareholder approval is not obtained, it has been argued that poison pills are intended primarily to entrench incumbent management and that their adoption is in violation of duties owed to the corporation and its shareholders. The Delaware Supreme Court has held, however, that a poison pill is legal if the pill is fashioned so as to prevent only coercive takeovers. (*Moran v. Household International, Inc.*, 500 A.2d 1346 (1985)).

The unique characteristic of a poison pill is that additional rights are granted to shareholders when a bidder makes a public tender offer for target shares or acquires a specified percentage of the target shares. Typical triggering events are either a tender offer for 30 percent of the target's shares or the acquisition of 20 percent or more of target shares. The additional rights may consist of increased voting rights for shareholders other than the bidder. For example, shareholders other than the bidder or potential bidder may become entitled to 10 votes per share when the pill is triggered, while the voting rights of the bidder are unchanged. A poison pill may also grant additional financial rights in the target such as the right to acquire additional shares or indebtedness issued by the target corporation at a bargain price if the poison pill is triggered (a **flip-in plan**), or rights to purchase bidder shares at bargain prices in the event of a back-end merger, such as the right to purchase $200 worth of the common shares of the tender offeror for $100 in the merger (a **flip-over plan**). Typically, management may disarm these potent devices by redeeming the poison pill preferred at a nominal price.

Voting rights poison pills have been invalidated in two cases (arising under New Jersey law) on the ground that the corporation statute of that state does not contemplate that differential voting rights may be created for some common shares while being withheld from others. Because these decisions do not appear to be based on unique New Jersey law, many companies avoid voting rights poison pills.

In practice, poison pills turn out to be negotiating devices more than deterrents. They tend to compel potential bidders to negotiate with incumbent management for a takeover and are rarely actually triggered by a tender offer. Poison pills are not foolproof defenses. They may be neutralized in the context of an unwanted tender offer in several ways. For example, the bidder may make a tender offer on condition that the board redeems the poison pill, or the bidder may tender for both shares and rights under the poison pill, or it may tender and simultaneously solicit consents to replace the board and redeem the rights, or it may acquire over 50 percent of the target shares and then cause the target to self-tender for the rights.

Litigation may also be possible on the premise that the target board of directors may not arbitrarily reject a tender offer or refuse to redeem rights in order to preserve their positions within the corporation. And indeed the Delaware courts have required redemption in cases in which there is no threat of coercion. Some companies have attempted to avoid this by specifying that the pill may not be redeemed except by the same board or one with common members (a **dead hand pill**) or after a specified waiting period such as 90 days or six months (a **slow hand pill**). The Delaware courts have generally struck down these pills as impermissible restrictions on the authority of the board of directors.

Section 203 of the Delaware General Corporation Law, which requires in effect 85 percent ownership of target stock before any back-end merger may be effected, may largely duplicate the protection that poison pills provide, but as a practical matter it is likely that corporations with poison pill defenses already in place will simply retain them. Section 203 is discussed in more detail below.

A closely related preemptive defensive tactic is a **dual class recapitalization**. Hostile takeovers depend on the bidder's ability to amass voting stock. One way for a potential target to avoid takeover is to eliminate voting stock in the hands of the public. A dual class recapitalization is a transaction in which the potential target firm offers shares of nonvoting common stock in exchange for shares of voting stock. Assuming that two shares of nonvoting stock are issued for each share of voting stock and both classes have equal financial rights, the trade appears to be attractive from the point of view of the shareholder whose vote likely counts for little anyway. Assume, however, that management owns 10,000,000 shares before the exchange and that 90,000,000 shares are owned by scattered public shareholders. If all of the shareholders other than management accept the exchange, there will be 190,000,000 shares outstanding and the public shareholders will have 180,000,000 nonvoting shares. In other words, their aggregate ownership interest will have increased from 90 percent to just 94.7 percent, but because management now has all the voting shares the company can never be taken over in a hostile transaction. Although any increase in the relative financial rights of the shareholders is no doubt welcome, the voting rights recapitalization in effect gives the public shareholders only about a 5 percent premium for their shares compared to an average of about 50 percent in third-party transactions. Moreover, the offer itself is arguably highly coercive. A shareholder who declines the offer and keeps voting shares will see the financial value of his or her shares diluted by almost half. Clearly, if a shareholder cannot mount an organized campaign to oppose the trade, he or she cannot afford to refuse to take the deal.

One problem with voting rights recapitalizations was that the New York Stock Exchange prohibited the listing of companies with nonvoting or lesser voting stock. Moreover, several courts have held that takeover defenses that entail violation of stock exchange rules and that cause the company to be delisted constitute irreparable harm to the shareholders and may be enjoined. The credible threat of takeovers being launched against even very large companies, however, led several such companies, among them General Motors, to oppose (and even violate) the rule. With the extraordinary growth of NASDAQ in the 1980s, it was at least possible that the NYSE might lose many listings because of its rule. The SEC eventually proposed that all stock exchanges be required to adopt a uniform listing standard prohibiting voting rights recapitalizations but allowing differential voting rights in newly offered stock. The rule was struck down as being beyond the power of the SEC (*Business Roundtable v. SEC*, 905 F.2d 406 (D.C. Cir. 1990)), but the major exchanges, with some prodding from the SEC, have continued to adhere to it anyway. As a result it is now quite common for companies to offer only lesser voting stock in their IPOs.

## §13.16 State Takeover Statutes

States often oppose takeovers of corporations with significant local connections. The first attempts by states to slow down takeover activity led to the enactment by virtually all states of registration requirements for cash tender offers. These registration requirements applied to publicly held corporations with significant local contacts (usually defined in terms of having property with a specified value in the state, having its principal executive offices in the state, being organized under the laws of the state, or having a specified number of shareholders in the state). In *Edgar v. Mite Corporation*, 457 U.S. 624 (1982), the United States Supreme Court effectively invalidated most of these **first-generation state takeover laws** as an unreasonable burden on interstate commerce. Based on this decision, some commentators concluded that the national market for control of publicly held corporations was beyond the scope of state regulation. This, however, did not prove to be the case.

In 1987, the United States Supreme Court upheld the Indiana **control share acquisition statute** (*CTS Corporation v. General Dynamics Corp. of America*, 481 U.S. 69 (1987)). This statute defines a control share acquisition as any acquisition that causes the shareholder to break through the 20 percent, the 33.3 percent, or 50 percent levels of share ownership. A person making an acquisition of control shares of an Indiana corporation does not obtain the right to vote the newly acquired shares unless a majority of disinterested shareholders (excluding both the shares that the acquirer of the control shares owns and the shares that incumbent management owns) vote to grant voting rights to the acquirer. A proposed acquirer may compel a vote by disinterested shareholders on whether voting rights should be granted upon the acquisition if the acquirer agrees to pay for the cost of the shareholders' meeting. The Supreme Court upheld this statute largely under the traditional power of states to regulate internal affairs of domestically created corporations. Following this decision, states rushed to enact similar statutes, amid dire predictions by law and economics scholars that the result would be inefficiency and less competent management.

The precise impact of the Indiana control share acquisition statute and similar statutes is difficult to assess in the abstract. These statutes were clearly enacted with the intention of making takeovers more difficult, but it is not clear that they will have that result. Certainly, the possibility of losing the right to vote newly acquired shares despite a major financial investment may be a serious deterrent to takeover attempts. On the other hand, it may be possible to obtain a vote of the shareholders before the decision to purchase is final. Bidders may prefer to have a vote in advance on their proposed takeover attempt so they can gauge in advance the degree of support they have from the shareholders. It was partly for this reason that Delaware decided to adopt a different type of statute.

Many states have adopted statutes that deter takeovers by regulating the back-end transaction. Many of these statutes are **fair price statutes** that require the price paid to minority shareholders to be not less than the price paid by the interested shareholder. If this price condition is not met, the transaction requires the approval of (1) the board of directors in office before the interested shareholder acquired its shares; (2) a supermajority (e.g., 80 percent) of all voting shares; or (3) a majority of the disinterested shares, that is, those owned by shareholders other than the interested shareholder. These statutes, the terms of which vary from state to state, are generally patterned on the Maryland statute.

A second type of statute prohibits all back-end mergers with an interested shareholder for a specified period of time following the acquisition of shares by the interested shareholder, unless the transaction is approved in one of the ways described in the previous paragraph. Most of these **business combination statutes** are modeled on the New York statute, which prohibits back-end transactions for a period of five years.

Section 203 of The Delaware General Corporation Law, enacted in 1988, is a statute of the New York type. It generally prohibits a wide variety of transactions between the corporation and a shareholder owning more than 15 percent of the corporation's shares within a period of three years after the transaction in which the shareholder acquired the shares. Approval by the board of directors (in office before the acquisition) or by two-thirds of the remaining shareholders permits a transaction to proceed immediately. The transaction may also proceed immediately if the interested shareholder acquires over 85 percent of the corporation's stock. A similar though much more restrictive Wisconsin statute was upheld in *Amanda Acquisition Corp. v. Universal Foods Corp.*, 877 F.2d 496 (7th Cir.), *cert. denied*, 493 U.S. 955 (1989), and based on that decision, it is generally believed that such statutes are constitutional.

## §13.17  State Regulation of Defensive Tactics

An unusual mosaic of state and federal law governs takeovers and defensive tactics. The Williams Act, a federal statute, largely controls the mechanics of tender offers. Attempts by states to interfere are largely foreclosed by the **Mite** decision. Curiously, however, state law largely rules defensive tactics. In this regard, decisions by the Delaware Supreme Court have been particularly influential.

Directors of a target corporation have a potential conflict of interest: On the one hand, their personal positions of profit and honor within a large public entity may evaporate if the bidder is successful. (For this reason, basic decisions as to whether to oppose an offer may be delegated to the directors who are not also officers or employees of the corporation.) The accepted state law principles on defensive tactics are that the adoption of such tactics in the good faith belief that the offer is not in the best interests of the target is a matter of judgment subject to review under the common law "business judgment rule" but that defenses designed to entrench incumbent management are judged by the rigorous fiduciary duties relating to self-dealing. The business judgment rule provides a very lenient standard of review, while the standard of review for self-dealing transactions is considerably more onerous. The line between these two principles is hardly a clear one, because most defensive tactics can be viewed as either legitimate defense or as motivated primarily by a desire on the part of management to stay in power, usually called **management entrenchment**.

The Delaware Supreme Court has held that the decision to impose a poison pill takeover defense in advance of an actual takeover is evaluated under the business judgment rule with the important qualification that the defense must be reasonable in light of the potential threat (*Moran v. Household International, Inc.*, 500 A.2d 1346 (1985)). Thus, offers that involve unfair or coercive partial tender offers may be opposed by virtually any available means (*Unocal Corp. v. Mesa Petroleum Co.*, 493 A.2d 946 (1985)). Although the SEC prohibited the specific tactic used in the *Unocal* case when it adopted its all holders rule, that rule does not affect the scope of the Delaware holding as to permissible defensive tactics against inadequate or coercive offers.

In a third important decision, the Delaware Supreme Court held that quite a different set of principles applies once the board has resolved to sell the company. At that point, the duty of the directors shifts to obtaining the best possible price for the shareholders: The board may not favor one contender for control over another except on the basis of maximizing the price that the target shareholders obtain (*Revlon v. MacAndrews & Forbes Holdings, Inc.*, 506 A.2d 173 (1986)). The Delaware Supreme Court has since reaffirmed that this principle applies only after the board of directors has decided to sell the company (*Ivanhoe Partners v. Newmont Mining Corp.*, 555 A.2d 1334 (Del. 1987); *Mills Acquisition Co. v. MacMillan, Inc.*, 559 A.2d 1261 (Del. 1989)).

The central issue in determining whether the Revlon rule applies is determining whether the target company is in fact for sale. In *Paramount Communications, Inc. v. Time, Inc.*, 571 A.2d 1140 (Del. 1989), Time and Warner Brothers had agreed to a "strategic combination" of the two companies involving a stock-for-stock merger in which Warner Brothers would be the surviving corporation under the name Time-Warner. Paramount interceded with a hostile tender offer for Time at a substantial premium. Time and Warner then abandoned the merger plan, and Time made a tender offer for Warner and adopted a number of defenses designed to thwart the Paramount bid. Paramount then sued on the theory that the Revlon rule required a fair and open auction for Time. The Delaware Supreme Court disagreed on the grounds that Time had never been for sale and its breakup had never been contemplated. And the various tactics undertaken to preserve the combination of Time and Warner were not enough when viewed in context to trigger a Revlon duty to seek the highest bidder. The case spawned yet another defensive tactic known as the **just say no** defense. Many thought that one way for a target company to avoid an auction under the Revlon rule was simply to deny that the company was for sale and to structure any desired deal as a strategic combination. When that defense was asserted, however, in connection with a proposed combination of Paramount and Viacom in which QVC made an unwelcome competing bid for Paramount, the Delaware Supreme Court noted that in the originally proposed deal, which had been publicly described as a sale, Viacom management would assume complete control over Paramount, and held that the transaction triggered a Revlon duty to maximize the price of the sale thus requiring that QVC be given a fair opportunity to compete for the target Paramount (*Paramount*

*Communications v. QVC Network, Inc.*, 637 A.2d 34 (Del. 1994)). Viacom eventually prevailed. As a result, the focus of Delaware law relating to takeover defenses appears to have shifted to an inquiry into whether the transaction involves a shift of control at the shareholder level.

Although the principles relating to defensive tactics have been largely created under Delaware law, federal courts are often called on to resolve issues relating to defensive tactics in litigation involving federal law issues or diversity of citizenship. Other state courts also have resolved litigation relating to defensive tactics in ways generally consistent with Delaware law. In practice, however, courts have sometimes invalidated takeover defenses on the grounds that they involve entrenchment or they fail to meet the lenient standards of the business judgment rule. For example, the Second Circuit invalidated options on crown jewel assets given to one contender for control when it appeared that the options were granted at a price significantly below the market value of the assets involved (*Hanson Trust PLC v. ML. SCM Acquisition, Inc.*, 781 F.2d 264 (1986)). This decision appears to be based solely on state law. Other decisions involving similar transactions have upheld the tactic. There appears to be no overarching principle in this complex area except evaluation of the motives of the directors and the court's view of the overall fairness of the transaction from the standpoint of target shareholders.

## §13.18 Leveraged Buyouts and Going Private

In many takeover battles, one contender is a group of investors that includes incumbent management and that plans, if successful, to continue the enterprise as a privately held, unregistered corporation. These transactions were first described as **going private**, and more recently have come to be known as **leveraged buyouts**. In these deals, a new entity is created in which both individual members of management and outside investors are represented. The new entity obtains unsecured loans required to finance the tender offer. Incumbent management may be required to invest relatively small amounts in the new enterprise but their investments are almost trivial—perhaps a few million dollars in a transaction involving hundreds of millions of dollars. Almost all of the purchase price is borrowed. Once the new entity acquires the publicly held shares and a second step, mop-up merger has been effected, the target corporation is merged with the new entity, which obtains a new loan secured by a lien on the target assets and uses the proceeds to pay off the unsecured loan. The unsecured loan is thus often called **bridge financing** or **mezzanine financing**. The target ends up with the obligation to pay off the loan used to acquire its assets out of its own income or cash flow. These transactions are thus sometimes called **bootstrap acquisitions**. They are also highly leveraged because virtually the entire purchase price is borrowed.

Following a leveraged buyout, the target may sell off portions of its business in order to pay down the new indebtedness. Improvements in earnings and cash flow may arise from savings inherent in not being a reporting corporation (including elimination of various expenses that go with being publicly held), from freedom to focus on longer-term projects, from elimination of potential shareholder suits, and from the discipline of massive debt. The ideal scenario, from the standpoint of management and its partners in the leveraged buyout, is (1) to reduce the burden of the indebtedness created by the buyout by selling off nonessential portions of the target's business; (2) to improve the profitability of the core businesses that remain; and (3) to arrange a new public offering of shares in the restructured target at a significantly higher price than was paid to take the corporation private. In a few instances, this pattern of public to private and then back to public resulted in profits of hundreds of millions of dollars to individuals who originally invested only a small fraction of that amount.

By the mid 1980s, leveraged buyouts (LBOs) had become as common as cash tender offers from third-party bidders. Outside offers from third parties were regularly met with a proposed leveraged buyout in which management participated actively. Issues of fiduciary duty in competitive takeover situations are quite obvious in these situations, where one of the competitors is a management-organized bidder. Needless to say, the board of directors may well be tempted to favor the leveraged buyout offer, thereby increasing both the reality and the appearance of conflict of interest, although the law is quite clear that the board must be neutral and seek only to maximize the price paid to the shareholders.

In determining whether a corporation is a plausible candidate for an LBO, an analysis is typically made of operating cash flow. Indeed, many LBOs involve the taking on of so much debt that the company will show a negative net worth on its balance sheet. In such a case, the deal will depend on obtaining a so-called solvency letter from an investment bank or accounting firm. If the buyout in fact renders the firm insolvent, payments to the shareholders for their stock may be challenged as fraudulent conveyances or as contrary to corporation law standards governing distributions to shareholders. Indeed, in one failed buyout, it was reported that the shareholders might be required to return the payments they had received more than three years earlier, although as a matter of bankruptcy law such payments have in some cases been held to be exempt settlement payments. That is, some courts have ruled that such payments have the same status as any run-of-the-mill payment for stock as a brokerage firm might credit to an investor who has sold some shares.

## §13.19  Where Does All the Money Come From?

One factor that sharply distinguished takeover activity in the 1980s from earlier periods can be stated in one word: cash. Most acquisitions in the 1980s were fueled by the ready availability of cash to enable bidders to buy out target shareholders in transactions that in the aggregate often ran into the billions of dollars. Transactions involving amounts so large as to be almost unimaginable in a private transaction even in the 1970s became routine in the 1980s and 1990s. It is reasonable to ask this question: Where does all the cash come from?

Funds that large corporations raise to finance takeover attempts are easier to explain than those raised by single individuals or small groups with limited personal resources. Many large corporations have accumulated substantial funds from internal operations. The favorable tax rules adopted in the early years of the Reagan administration (rules that were largely repealed by 1986) permitted the growth of internally generated war chests of billions of dollars that were often used to fuel takeover bids. A second important source of internal funds is the sale of unprofitable or nonessential lines of businesses. Over the years, most large corporations acquire a variety of tangential businesses, usually as a byproduct of other transactions. Historically, companies stuck with these small components try to make them profitable rather than disposing of them on the theory that growth in aggregate sales is a mark of successful business operation. In a world of leveraged buyouts, cash flow is paramount. Marginal businesses should be sold, not retained. These transactions may also generate funds available for takeover attempts. A few individuals have also assembled personal fortunes that are sufficient to enable them to launch takeover bids. Many of these fortunes are the product of modest takeovers followed by increasingly large transactions. Some are based on the success of privately owned businesses.

Most of the money used in takeovers in the 1980s was borrowed money, not internally generated money. This was true of most third-party offers as well as virtually all leveraged buyouts. Who is willing to lend this kind of money to finance the apparently risky takeovers? Financing commitments running into billions of dollars may come from a variety of sources. Commercial banks, pension funds, insurance companies, investment bankers, brokerage firms, and the like traditionally have not made speculative loans, but this policy began to change in the 1970s. By the 1980s, these entities often made substantial amounts available to fund takeover attempts in the form of short-term bridge loans that permitted transactions to proceed with the understanding that longer-term loans—perhaps junk bonds or secured loans in leveraged buyouts—would be obtained to pay off these interim loans. (Some of these sources may also commit large amounts to long-term loans.) A second important source of loan money includes speculators who pool large amounts of funds into trading partnerships in contemplation of engaging in takeover activity. (Perhaps the best known such firm is Kohlberg, Kravis, Roberts (KKR).) This pool of capital grew steadily as one successful transaction followed another during the 1980s. A third major source of loan funds are foreign lending sources with large dollar accounts arising from the imbalance of foreign trade with the United States. Indeed, foreign corporations have often launched takeover attempts, relying largely on foreign loan sources for their capital.

One brokerage firm (Drexel Burnham Lambert) developed the ability to raise billions of dollars through the placement of less-than-investment-grade debentures—junk bonds, as they are called. Before its collapse, this firm developed a large network of financing sources who were willing to advance millions of dollars in funds to finance takeover attempts.

Junk bonds were popular investments because of the high rates of return—perhaps 13 or 14 percent, while investment grade securities had a return of perhaps 9 or 10 percent. The use of junk bonds was severely curtailed by changes to the IRC that limited the amount of interest that could be deducted in connection with acquisition loans. In addition, the Federal Reserve Board (the Fed) ruled that unsecured junk bonds were in effect loans for the purpose of buying stock and thus constituted margin borrowing which by Fed rule is limited to 50 percent of the purchase price of the stock.

The growth of financing sources for takeovers is based in part on the realization that investments in takeover transactions may not be as risky as they first appear. For one thing, financing is based on loan commitments that command substantial commitment fees. If the takeover attempt fails, the potential financier simply pockets the fee and advances no funds. It is thus profitable for the lending sources to make commitments without honoring them. If the proposed takeover is successful, the commitment is called in and funds must be provided, but at that point the assets and cash flow of the target are available to service the loans.

In the late 1990s and early 2000s, most deals have involved the use of stock as consideration. But with falling stock prices on NASDAQ and very low interest rates, cash and hostile deals may again become more common.

## §13.20 Profitable Unsuccessful Takeover Attempts

One paradoxical fact about many takeover attempts in the 1980s was that it was often profitable from the standpoint of a bidder for its takeover bid to fail. Indeed, some of the best-known corporate raiders were widely believed to be more interested in failing than succeeding.

When a target is put into play by a cash tender offer, the probability is high that the target will be taken over by someone. Some bidders may thus make a tender offer with the hope that a bidding contest may develop. If someone else ultimately acquires the target, the unsuccessful bidder simply sells its investment in the target to the successful bidder, usually at a profit. The unsuccessful bidder may also receive additional consideration for discontinuing its offer.

Another possible source of profit from unsuccessful offers involves **greenmail**. After a hostile takeover attempt is launched, negotiations may occur between the bidder and the target. One possible outcome of this negotiation is that the target agrees to buy out the bidder's investment at a profitable price (usually above the now-inflated market price) and the bidder agrees to make no further investments in the target for an extended period. In effect, the target buys peace from the bidder; such payments are usually called greenmail. Greenmail is not illegal, but many observers view it as questionable. Some states have enacted statutes allowing the corporation to recover greenmail payments, and in 1987 Congress imposed a nondeductible excise tax on the receipt of greenmail in an attempt to discourage the practice.

Agreements between a target and a bidder may also take the form of a **standstill agreement** under which the bidder agrees not to increase its holding in the target beyond a specified size for a specified period of time, perhaps 10 years. Some kind of consideration to the bidder typically accompanies a standstill agreement. A standstill agreement often does not prevent the former bidder from profitably selling its shares to another bidder who seeks to obtain control of the target.

## §13.21  Are Takeovers Economically or Socially Desirable?

Unlike earlier periods of merger activity where concerns of increased monopoly power were dominant, most economists argued that the 1980s takeover movement was socially desirable and that takeovers should not be prohibited or regulated in any significant way. Indeed, there is an impressive degree of unanimity in the academy that shareholders in the aggregate benefit from takeovers.

Whether the degree of concentration is increased or decreased in specific industries as a result of takeover transactions is difficult to evaluate. In other periods of merger activity, it was generally agreed that economic concentration in many industries was increasing as a result of the transactions taking place. It is not clear that this was true in the 1980s or that it is true today. Indeed, increased monopoly power does not appear to be the goal of most recent takeovers at all. Rather, in the 1980s, the process appeared to have been driven by the relationship between the value of the business and the market prices of the securities issued by the corporation. In the 1990s and 2000s, the urge to merge seems to be generated by strategic considerations such as gaining access to an ensured source of supply, acquiring a new product line, or securing developed expertise in a given area of business in which the bidder is weak.

There are also many deals in which an established company divests itself of a subsidiary or division perhaps because the unit is performing poorly compared with other operations or simply to generate shareholder gains from the spin off of shares in the newly independent company. Another reason for voluntary "deconglomeration" is that a business may fear potential takeover attempts. Potential targets thus attempt to make themselves less attractive targets by voluntarily disposing of nonessential assets that a successful bidder might be expected to sell. In short, just as business combinations have become consensual, so have bust-up transactions. These transactions clearly reduce the degree of concentration in American industry.

Numerous attempts to explain the takeover phenomenon in economic terms have arisen, but there is no consensus as to a single best explanation for why bidders in hostile takeovers are willing to pay premiums that average 50 percent over market price.

There is one point on which there is broad consensus. If the proper measure of social welfare in corporation law is the maximization of economic returns to shareholders as a group, takeovers improve social welfare. Virtually every empirical study of price movements in connection with takeovers reveals that on the average, shareholders of the target corporation enjoy substantial increases in value. Although shareholders of the bidder usually lose a bit, the gains of the target shareholders significantly exceed any losses suffered by the bidder's shareholders.

The loss suffered by the bidder's shareholders on the average suggests that bidders sometimes pay too much for their targets. This is a phenomenon that is sometimes called the **winner's curse**. This should come as no surprise: If a bidding war arises for a target, the winner will usually be the most optimistic bidder.

The reason why takeovers at substantial premiums over market price arise in the first place is less clear. One plausible explanation is that target corporations are relatively poorly managed, and that the net gain to target shareholders reflects the improvement in target profitability resulting from the change in management. In other words, before the takeover the securities that the target issues are depressed, because of the relatively poor financial outlook of the target. The outlook improves dramatically with the prospect of fresh management, and the price of target shares increases to reflect this improvement in outlook. This theory is strongly endorsed by members of the "Chicago School," an influential group of conservative economists and law professors whose opinions (on takeovers and mergers particularly) today constitute a distinct school of thought. The theory seems both neat and consistent with the efficient capital market hypothesis. The major problem with the theory is that it explains only a relatively small number of takeovers that occurred during the 1980s. Rather, many target corporations appeared to be well-managed companies; indeed, the bidder often announced in advance that it did not plan to make major changes in target management if the takeover was successful.

A somewhat different theory suggests that the ability of bidders to borrow money through junk bonds in order to buy the stock of target shareholders indicates that target companies are overcapitalized with equity. Another suggestion is that shareholders developed a distinct preference for generous dividends, because they were afraid that management would invest available cash in projects with unattractive rates of return. In any event, the substitution of debt for equity, which on balance is what happened in junk bond financed takeovers, has the effect of increasing leverage and forcing the distribution of cash. Although it is not fair to say that under-leveraged companies with excess cash are mismanaged, it is fair to say that investors may have a different opinion as to how such companies should be managed. As for the extra risk of insolvency created by additional junk bond debt, it is not clear that this risk is of serious concern to investors in junk bonds who are receiving stock-like returns. If the company cannot pay, the junk bond investors will in all likelihood be forced to take stock in a reorganization (which is essentially what their cash bought in the first place). Moreover, in many cases a reorganization may be accomplished privately through a pre-packaged bankruptcy proceeding in which the votes to approve the plan are solicited in advance of filing. Viewed in this way, junk bonds look very much like stock with a promise to pay dividends.

It may be too that investor tastes changed significantly during the 1970s and 1980s. During that period, many investors began to invest in diversified mutual funds and through other institutional vehicles. A diversified investor is more or less indifferent to risk as long as the prospective gain from a transaction is high enough. It matters little that a few companies end up insolvent if other companies make enough more to generate an acceptable net gain. Management, however, tends to view things differently: They have much of their own personal wealth tied up in the company and are naturally reluctant to enter into risky transactions. Thus, the diversification of investors through institutional investing may have created a conflict between investor and management preferences that did not previously exist.

Another possible explanation is that the takeover movement was motivated by empire building on the part of a few entrepreneurs who believe that bigger is better. In the long run, a strategy of growth for growth's sake would seem doomed to fail unless size in some way reflects greater efficiency. Economists argue that an empire building explanation is not consistent with the empirical evidence of real shareholders' gains from the takeover movement.

Another explanation is based on the concept of **synergy**. Two separate businesses may fit together so that the combined value of two together is greater than the sum of the values of the two separately. Although it is possible that synergy may explain a few successful combinations, it does not begin to explain most of the transactions that occurred during the 1980s. Indeed, the argument about synergy was most strongly put forward in the late 1960s and early 1970s during the period when many conglomerates were created; the combination of unrelated business was generally so unsuccessful that much of the takeover activity after that period was prompted by the prospect of gains from buying the combined companies and selling the pieces for amounts in the aggregate that exceeded the value of the whole. Such deals came to be known as bust-up takeovers.

Another possible explanation is that takeovers are caused by failure of the securities markets to reflect accurately the break-up value of targets. This explanation may be inconsistent with the efficient capital market hypothesis, but cannot be dismissed out of hand for that reason. After all, many companies are sold off in pieces for more than they cost to acquire. On the other hand, one would naturally expect the market to ignore break-up value if there were no prospect that break-up would occur.

In addition to the foregoing, some have suggested that takeovers are motivated primarily by tax considerations (particularly the fact that interest on takeover debt may be deductible), peculiarities in financial accounting standards, and the transfer of wealth from other constituencies (such as bondholders) to shareholders.

The most likely explanation of the takeover phenomenon is that several factors were at work and that no single factor explains all transactions.

# TRADING IN STOCKS AND BONDS

## §14.1  Introduction

This chapter describes the public markets for stocks and bonds, beginning with the New York Stock Exchange (NYSE) and other stock exchanges. This is followed by a discussion of the over-the-counter (OTC) market, focusing primarily on the National Association of Securities Dealers Automated Quotation (NASDAQ) system. In recent years, these markets have been supplemented by the development of financial futures and options, primarily through innovative securities introduced by the commodities exchanges. Commodities trading and futures and these new financial instruments are described in the chapter on options, futures, and derivatives.

The markets discussed in this chapter are **secondary markets** in which persons who already own outstanding shares and wish to sell them deal with persons wanting to buy them. These markets are not the place where a corporation goes to raise new capital through the sale of new securities to the public (although it is common for companies planning a public offering to arrange in advance for listing on an exchange so that trading facilities will be immediately available to investors). Rather, the markets discussed in this chapter provide basic liquidity so that persons who invest in publicly traded securities can be confident that they can dispose of them if and when they wish.

## §14.2 The Efficient Capital Market Hypothesis

One of the most important insights into how the markets work is the **efficient capital market hypothesis (ECMH)**, which is sometimes also called simply the **efficient market theory**, and which is also discussed in the chapter on mergers and acquisitions. The implications of this theory are both far-reaching and startling. In brief, the predominant version of the ECMH states that securities prices quickly reflect everything publicly known about individual companies and the economy as a whole. When new information becomes available, the market absorbs and discounts it instantaneously and efficiently. Furthermore, the market accurately assesses the known information and is not misled, for example, by announced changes in accounting principles that affect book earnings but not the real worth of a business. The market's efficiency is explained by the efforts of large numbers of analysts and speculators who follow the market closely and exploit any opportunity to profit from temporary deviations of market prices from the prices that reflect all known information. These temporary deviations provide an incentive for analysts and speculators to continue to search for them, but the deviations are small and their existence is fleeting. In short, the independent efforts of hundreds or thousands of persons to make profits in the market is the driving force toward market efficiency.

There are several different versions of the ECMH. The version described above is called the **semi-strong form** and has the widest degree of acceptance. Under the semi-strong version, market prices do not encapsulate information that is not publicly available (e.g., inside information about the issuer, or the unexpected possibility that a specific takeover offer may be made in the future). The hypothesis therefore does not deny that profits may be made on inside information about the issuer or about planned takeover moves, as long as the information is acted on before it becomes public.

Two other versions of the ECMH are the **weak form** and the **strong form**. The weak form states that past price movements are no indication of future price movements. Economists largely regard the weak form as proven by statistical analysis. The strong form states that market prices reflect nonpublic information as well as public information. Although few (if any) subscribe to the whole of the strong form, there is evidence, for example, that target company prices tend to rise well before a takeover is announced. To be sure, the increase in price may be due to leaks and illegal insider trading, but that suggests that even nonpublic information is partially reflected in market prices.

The ECMH in its semi-strong form has significant implications for securities trading and securities prices. First of all, if the theory is correct, one cannot predict the future movement of stock prices based on presently available information; because all current information is already embedded in a security's price, the price will change only because of events or information that cannot now be foreseen. (If the event could be foreseen it would have been already embedded in the current price.) Second, at any instant in time, the next price movement of a stock is as likely to be down as to be up, irrespective of the direction of the previous price movement. Stock prices move randomly, showing no historical pattern. Thus, historical analysis of previous stock price movements (a version of **technical analysis**) is useless for the prediction of future prices. It is true that many persons successfully charge substantial fees for technical analysis, but they are either charlatans or just plain lucky. Third, extensive reading and study of historical information about a company is also a waste of time: That information is already embedded in the price. Fourth, in-and-out trading is a losing strategy, because one cannot beat the market in the long run, and active trading simply runs up brokerage costs. Finally, and perhaps most important, the goal of money managers and institutional investors to beat the averages in the long run is impossible: An investor can only do as well as the market as a whole.

There is no doubt that many market professionals do not agree with the ECMH in all of its implications. To be sure, one often hears about mutual fund managers or large investors who have beaten the market 5 or 10 years in a row. Economic theorists tend to reject such anecdotal evidence on the ground that it merely reflects the laws of chance. After all, someone may be able to guess the outcome of 10 coin flips once in a while. There are, however, some anomalies that theory alone cannot explain. For example, the market tends to go up in January. Moreover, initial public offerings tend to increase in price in the aftermarket. Another example was the sharp market break that occurred in October 1987: There appears to have been nothing during the period of that decline that can account for a decline of nearly one-third in the value of many stocks. Nevertheless, the evidence supporting the ECMH at least during periods of normal market activity is great, and it is clear that the theory provides a valuable insight as to how the market operates. The ECMH is accepted as a reasonably accurate description of securities markets by many market professionals and investors. For example, as described in the chapter on investment companies and investment advice, many institutional investors now try only to equal the performance of the market, not to beat it.

On the other hand, the theory seems paradoxical. If the market were truly efficient and everyone believed it to be so, then no one would bother to do research and the market would become inefficient. The answer to this **efficiency paradox** is that it is really no paradox at all. At the very least, it makes sense for investors to do research as a hedge against the possibility that others will stop doing research. Moreover, in the real world investors have no very reliable way of knowing exactly how much time, effort, and money to invest in research. At best, an investor will rely on intuition and hunch in deciding when to stop digging for more information. In other words, investors are likely to compete with each other not only in doing research but in deciding when to stop doing research.

It is also arguable that the ECMH is trivial. After all, the market is the traders who compose it. No officially correct price is ever announced. Thus it is hardly surprising that on the average investors do on the average.

One important point about the ECMH that is not always appreciated is that the studies tending to show the efficiency of the securities markets are largely based on examination of securities that are widely traded on the largest markets, particularly trading in shares of the largest companies registered on the NYSE. Some parts of the OTC market also attract a large amount of interest and probably rival the NYSE markets in efficiency. When one moves into other parts of the NYSE or the over-the-counter market or into local securities traded on regional exchanges, however, there are many fewer analysts following specific stocks, and one would expect the market to be less efficient than it is for the most widely traded stocks. Many publicly held securities are traded in a **thin market**, with trades occurring infrequently and with only one or two brokers regularly quoting prices.

It is also important to understand that the ECMH does not necessarily apply to investments for purposes of gaining control (or even voice) in a publicly traded company. Tender offers are routinely made for public companies at prices well in excess of the market price of target company shares.

Several theories have been advanced to explain "anomalies" in market pricing. They look to **noise** or **chaos** inherent in active trading markets. In other words, although the interaction of many traders has the effect of ultimately driving market prices to a close to proper level, market prices by their very nature tend to fluctuate as certain theories, opinions, and even fads gain favor among investors. The theory has intuitive appeal given that anecdotal evidence suggests that investors often copy each other's trades. Moreover, it may even be that managers at mutual funds and other large institutional investors are inclined to follow the crowd because it is safer (as a matter of job security) to match the performance of other large traders than it is to strike out on an independent course and possibly underperform compared to other funds. This has led to the proposal of the **arbitrage pricing theory** (**APT**), or the idea that market prices are the result of competition among traders focusing on constantly changing theories of value, and indeed some recent academic work suggests that over the long haul all stocks revert back to a more or less equal rate of return.

In any event, the essential idea behind alternative theories of how the market works is that although a trader may not be able consistently to beat the market, it does not necessarily follow that the market consistently establishes, say, the highest price that a bidder for control would be willing to pay. Indeed, one would not expect the market to do so unless it were reasonable to assume that every company that might be better managed is or will be promptly taken over. Rather, one might expect that some portion of the current trading price of a company represents its value as a takeover target discounted for the probability that such a bid will occur.

In addition to market anomalies and the takeover phenomenon, there are several large investors, perhaps most notably Warren Buffett, the CEO of Berkshire Hathaway, who have consistently made large gains as a result of large investments in publicly traded companies. In the case of Buffett, such investments have been made for the long term and in some instances have involved Buffett's active participation or at least consultation in the management of the firms in which investments are made. Although such examples are not explainable by a simplistic view of market efficiency, they are consistent with a limited view of what efficiency means, namely, that it is very difficult for passive investors to beat the market through a strategy of active trading.

## §14.3  The New York Stock Exchange

The NYSE is a place—a building located at the corner of Wall Street and Broad Street in New York City. All transactions in shares occurring on the NYSE take place (at least formally) in a series of large rooms in this building known collectively as the **floor**. On the floor, there are numerous **posts** at which specific securities are traded and around which members interested in specific stocks congregate.

Only stocks that are listed on the NYSE are traded there. To be listed, a company must meet specific size and share ownership requirements. Among other things, a company must have aggregate pre-tax earnings over the previous three years of $6.6 million, must have an aggregate market value of publicly traded stock of at least $100,000,000, must have at least 1,100,000 publicly held shares, and must ordinarily have at least 2,200 stockholders. In addition, each company must enter into a standard listing agreement with the NYSE that imposes certain obligations on the listing company. Among these obligations is a commitment to make information about developments affecting the company publicly available on a timely basis. Moreover, NYSE **listing standards** require more extensive shareholder voting rights than required by state law. The listing requirements ensure that only the largest and most successful of the publicly held corporations are traded on the NYSE. This is the market for the blue chip stocks that are household names: General Motors, IBM, and so forth. However, among the 3000 or so companies (and 3,300 or so stocks) currently listed on the NYSE, there are many that are not widely known.

Only members of the NYSE have the privilege of trading on the floor. Most members are brokerage firms that deal with the general public; transactions are executed on behalf of members of the general public on the floor of the NYSE by representatives of those brokerage firms. Some individuals (called floor traders) also are members of the NYSE and handle trades for other brokers. To be entitled to membership, an individual or firm must buy a seat on the NYSE that entitles the member (or a broker employed by a member firm) to go onto the floor of the NYSE during trading hours and execute transactions. The number of seats is limited, and a limited market of sorts exists for seats. Because most NYSE members trade on behalf of the public, the value of a seat depends in part on market activity in securities. Since 1990, seats have sold for as much as $2,000,000 and as little as $250,000.

The NYSE retains a hefty share of the volume of stock trading. Its success is based on several factors: (1) it is the most prestigious exchange and many companies desire to be listed there; (2) the NYSE has historically provided a highly successful continuous and orderly market; and (3) the NYSE prohibits members from executing transactions in many listed securities other than on the NYSE floor. Today, the NYSE is a highly computerized operation capable of handling trades of hundreds of millions of shares per day. The following sections describe more fully how this institution operates.

## §14.4  A Prototypical NYSE Transaction

Assume that you decide to buy 100 shares of IBM at the currently reported market price of $115 per share. To buy 100 shares of IBM requires $11,500 in cash plus commissions, but you have that amount on deposit with your broker. You therefore call up your broker and instruct him to buy 100 shares of IBM "at the market." This last phrase means that your order will be executed at the market price in effect at the time your order arrives on the trading floor. (You may also give a limit order, that is, an order that will be executed only at a price you specify, if the market reaches that price, as discussed further below.)

An order for 100 shares is known as a **round lot** and is the standard trading unit for shares on the NYSE. One can sell blocks of less than 100 shares; a unit of less than 100 shares is known as an **odd lot** and is handled in a different way than round lots. Market orders for up to 30,099 shares may be handled by computer. In order to describe the mechanics of the NYSE, however, we will assume that your order will be filled in the traditional manner for all trades before 1976 and that continues today for larger orders.

Before the computerization of the NYSE in 1976, your broker would receive your order and telephone it to its New York office (or, if your broker was not a member of the NYSE, to the New York offices of a broker regularly used by your broker to fill orders). The order would then be conveyed by telephone to the NYSE where an employee of your brokerage firm or a floor broker would receive your order. He or she would walk to the post where IBM is traded. At this post is the **specialist** who handles IBM. There are also a number of other brokers surrounding this post who are interested in IBM. Many have orders of their own to fill. Today, the latest price at which IBM traded and the current bid-and-asked prices are on computer screens for all to see. These quotations might be "115 bid 115.10 asked." At this point, one of two things might happen:

1. The broker with your order may signify that he wants to buy 100 IBM at the market. Another broker in the trading crowd at the post may have an order to sell 100 IBM, also at the market. A deal may be struck then and there at a price negotiated on the spot. This price would either

be the last price, the bid price, the asked price, or in between, whatever is agreed on. The identities of the buying and selling brokers and the amount and price of the trade are noted by a floor reporter who sends information electronically about the transaction to the tape, where the transaction will appear in a few seconds, as well as to the involved brokerage firms.

2. The broker with your order may not find another broker with an order to sell that matches your order to buy. At this point, the specialist may step in and complete the transaction, normally at the **asked** (or **offered**) price. (If your order is to sell, it would typically be executed at the **bid** price.) The stock that the specialist supplies may come from either of two sources. The specialist keeps a list of **limit orders**—orders to buy or sell IBM stock at various prices other than the market price at the time the limit order was entered. Your buy order may be used to fill one of the sell orders from this book. Indeed, if your order can be filled from this source, it must be so filled. Alternatively, if the order cannot be filled from this source, the specialist sells the shares needed to complete your order from its own inventory. In other words, public and limit orders have priority over specialist participation. Again, the transaction is noted to a reporter, is confirmed to your brokerage firm, and appears on the tape within seconds of completion.

It is the responsibility of the selling broker to report trades. Thus, reported trades appearing on the tape are sales and not purchases, although there of course is a purchase for every sale. The significance of sale reporting, however, is that the tape does not reflect the fact that in a sale of, say, 20,000 shares there may have been 5 different purchasers. By the same token, the tape does not reflect the fact that several sales by different sellers may have been to the same purchaser. Such information is very difficult to come by unless one is on the floor, which is one of the reasons that being on the floor is an advantage.

Having completed the purchase, your broker will **clear** the trade that night through a **clearing firm**. That is, the clearing firm will net out purchases and sales for numerous firms. Your broker will usually send you a **confirmation**. The **settlement** actually takes place three days later. At or before that time, you must have sufficient cash or other consideration on deposit with your broker to cover the trade, and your broker must likewise have covered the trade with its clearing firm. As of settlement, you become entitled to the certificate for the shares. You could direct the broker to obtain a certificate for the shares in your name if you plan to hold the shares for a while, or, if you do not give this instruction, the broker simply records on the next statement of your account that you own 100 shares of IBM. You may also arrange to obtain shares registered in your own name but leave them with your broker for safekeeping.

Most investors choose to leave their securities on deposit with their broker and registered in their broker's name (sometimes called **street name**) as a matter of convenience, as is discussed more fully in the chapter on securities. This practice is important to the securities industry, because it allows for much more efficient settlement of trades. Indeed, with the volume of trading as high as it now is, it is doubtful that the markets could function if most investors insisted on certificates. Moreover, uncertificated shares are the primary source of supply for shares that are lent to short sellers (discussed below). Thus, without the book entry system, it would be much more difficult and expensive to effect a short sale, and the market would be somewhat less efficient. The Uniform Commercial Code makes it clear that if a brokerage house mistakenly (or fraudulently) pledges securities held in its name, for example, in connection with a loan of working capital to the firm, the lender has priority over the true owners of the securities. Although losses from theft or misuse of securities left on deposit with a broker are insured against by the **Securities Investor Protection Corporation** (**SIPC**), a major scandal involving delays or even losses to numerous investors who left securities in street name with brokers could lead many investors to insist on certificated shares in the future and could severely hamper the markets.

Although settlement is three days after the transaction, you are the immediate owner of 100 shares of IBM for most purposes. If you become unhappy with your investment before the three-day period for closing lapsed—even later on the same day—your broker can "close out your position" by entering into a commitment to sell 100 shares of IBM. You would, of course, owe two commissions and if the market declined between the time you purchased and the time you sold, you would lose that amount also.

## §14.5 Limit Orders

The above example involved an order to purchase 100 shares of IBM at the market. When placing an order, one may specify the price at which it is to be executed, say a purchase of IBM "at 114 or lower" or a sale of IBM at "116 or higher." These are **limit orders**.

Limit orders are handled quite differently from market orders. Today they are largely entered through the SuperDOT system (described below), but the way they are handled can best be understood by first describing the process in the preelectronic era.

Assume you place a limit order to buy 100 shares of IBM at 114 when the market price is 115½. When the broker arrives at the IBM post with your order, he finds that the market price for IBM is about 1½ points (dollars) above your order price. Obviously no seller is going to sell for 114 under these circumstances. The broker is also not going to wait around at the IBM post for 30 minutes or so to see whether IBM will conveniently drop a point and one-half while he waits. Rather, the broker gives the limit order to the specialist who records it in the limit order book as an offer to buy at 114. (The book formerly was in fact a book, but is now maintained electronically.) If the price of IBM drops to 114, the purchase orders in the limit order book are filled in the order that they were received by the specialist. Because of this priority in execution, it is possible that IBM's price may drop briefly to $114 and yet your order might not be executed if the market then rises.

The limit order book records both offers to buy and to sell at various prices. An investor is normally interested in buying low and selling high. Thus, most limit orders are of the two types described above, that is, "buy at 114 or lower," or "sell at 116 or higher." Not all limit orders are of these types, however. Another type of limit order is a **day order**: for example, "buy at $114 or better but in any event buy at the close of trading at the market." Yet another type of limit order is a **stop order**, which is an order to sell when the price has *declined* to a particular point or to buy when the price has *increased* to a particular point. A stop order to sell may be placed by a person who wants to save a profit or cut a loss by selling when a stock falls in price. Similarly, a person may think that a stock will continue to go up if it breaks through a particular price; hence a stop order to buy may be placed.

Limit orders (other than day orders) are good until cancelled. Orders that remain open are called **good-til-cancelled** (**GTC**) and are stored on SuperDOT as described below. In other words, they remain on the specialist's book awaiting execution until they are cancelled by the person placing the order. Brokers usually recommend that limit orders that are unlikely to be executed promptly or that have lost their original justification be cancelled.

Before 1996, prices of most stocks were quoted on the NYSE in eighths of a dollar; a few were quoted in sixteenths ("teenies"). In 1997, the NYSE began preparing for the conversion of stock quotations to decimals. The goals were to make prices more easily understood by investors, to reduce spreads, and to bring the United States into conformity with international securities practices. The SEC mandated a deadline of April 9, 2001, for this conversion. The conversion was actually completed by the NYSE on January 29, 2001.

One consequence of the move to decimal quotation has been a tightening of the bid-ask spread—the differential between the buyer's bidding price and seller's asking price. This tightening should be somewhat beneficial to small investors and those trading in the most active stocks.

## §14.6 The Role of the Specialist

Specialists have existed on the NYSE throughout most of its history. A **specialist** is charged with the responsibility of maintaining an orderly market for the stocks assigned to them. They are expected to maintain an inventory of assigned stocks and to buy when the market is declining or to sell when the market is rising in order to ensure a **deep and continuous market**. In the absence of specialists, the price of a stock—even a stock as widely traded as IBM—might have erratic fluctuations due to temporary blips in demand or supply arriving at the post. Indeed, there might even be brief periods when there might be only buyers and no sellers, or only sellers and no buyers. In the absence of a specialist, prices might fluctuate excessively in a manner unrelated to underlying value. Specialists are thus supposed to smooth out artificial fluctuations by trading against the market when necessary to ensure that the market remains orderly. Specialists are not expected to try to prevent market declines (and indeed usually could not do so even if they tried). Their objective is to let the market find its proper level in an orderly way. During the October 1987 crash, some specialists concluded that buying stock was futile and could only bankrupt the specialist without improving the orderly flow of the market. They therefore withdrew from the market for brief periods and requested halts in trading until an acceptable price to reopen trading could be established. A price is acceptable in this context when it clears the market, that is, when it leads to a balance between shares offered for purchase and shares offered for sale at that price without intervention by the specialist.

At first blush, it might seem that specialists are sure to lose money in their trading activities when they trade against the trend. In fact, this is not the case. Although specialists may need to purchase stock for their own account during a price decline, they may ultimately profit if the market recovers and they dispose of that stock at higher price levels. Indeed, studies indicate that market prices tend to be mean-reverting (i.e., prices tend to fall or rise back to some average that is appropriate for the riskiness of the stock in question). (Given that most investors these days are portfolio investors, mean-reversion is hardly surprising.) Thus, over the long haul, the specialist who buys on the way down and sells on the way up should make money. Moreover, most of the time the market is more or less stable (due in part to the activities of specialists) and during such times the specialist functions largely as a market maker buying at the bid and selling at the ask, while brokers in the crowd may trade with each other at or between the specialist's bid and asked quotes.

The second major source of income for specialists is commissions for acting as agent for brokers who place limit orders with them for execution. The specialist earns a commission on the execution of each such order. In January 1996, for example, approximately 63 percent of all executed SuperDOT orders (representing about 75 percent of shares so traded) were limit orders.

The NYSE designates over 50 firms as specialist firms, and about 400 individuals actually perform the functions of specialists on behalf of these firms. There is only one specialist per stock, but with 3,300 listed stocks, specialist firms obviously serve as specialist for many stocks. The largest firm acts as specialist for more than 100 stocks. The individuals who actually perform the specialist functions usually handle four or five stocks each, although an individual specialist may occasionally handle as many as 10 stocks at a time. Specialist firms must meet stringent capital requirements and their performance is closely monitored, particularly during times of market turmoil.

Specialists are **downstairs brokers**, because they deal only with members of the NYSE on the floor but not with members of the general public. The brokerage firms that deal with the public are known as **upstairs brokers**, because some of them have had offices physically located above the trading floor (although most big brokerage houses are no longer housed in the exchange building). Upstairs brokers are often many times larger than the downstairs specialist firms, and the question has arisen whether upstairs firms should be permitted to acquire specialists. The major concern is the fear of leakage of sensitive market information to the upstairs firm. Several upstairs firms, however, have acquired specialists on regional exchanges and on the New York and American stock exchanges without apparent leakage of information.

Specialists on the NYSE are assigned by the Exchange. In one incident in 1991, an issuer decided to withdraw its listing application when it was assigned a specialist that did not appear on a list of acceptable specialists it had previously submitted to the NYSE. The company continues to trade on the National

Market System of NASDAQ. In 1997, the NYSE changed its policies to permit listed companies to have a greater voice in the selection of their specialists.

Many observers question whether it is really necessary to have a specialist who is assigned the exclusive right on the floor to make a market in each NYSE stock. The specialist system is somewhat controversial, because NYSE Rule 390 prohibits members from trading most NYSE-listed stocks for their own account anywhere other than on the NYSE, a practice known as **off-board trading**. (Securities and Exchange Commission (SEC) rules provide that stocks listed after April 26, 1979, are exempt from the rule.) In effect, Rule 390 prohibits NYSE members from competing with specialists by making a market off the Exchange. On the other hand, it can be argued that Rule 390 makes the NYSE more efficient and fair by requiring that all trades cross on the floor, thus ensuring that there is substantial volume and that all investors will have an opportunity to participate in every trade (particularly with block trades discussed below).

Still, few other major stock exchanges use the specialist system. Some (e.g., the Toronto Stock Exchange) have done away with specialists altogether, while others (e.g., the Chicago Stock Exchange) allow for competing specialists. Some exchanges have no market makers of any kind. The International Stock Exchange (formerly the London Stock Exchange), for example, is totally electronic, as is the Cincinnati Stock Exchange. The Tokyo Stock Exchange and the Paris Bourse both have something like a specialist who monitors trading but who cannot trade for his or her own account.

## §14.7 Block Trades

A block trade is traditionally defined as a trade involving a minimum of 10,000 shares. These transactions are very common on the NYSE. In 2000 there were 5.5 million block transactions involving 10,000 shares or more; transactions involved 135.8 billion shares.

Block trades may also be defined somewhat differently as transactions involving the purchase or sale of a basket of 15 or more stocks that are valued at one million dollars or more. In 2000, block trades so defined accounted for approximately 22.0 percent of total NYSE volume in 2000, or 228.8 million shares daily.

Examples of program trading strategies include index arbitrage (the purchase or sale of a basket of stocks in conjunction with the sale or purchase of a derivative product, such as stock index futures, in order to profit from the price differences between the basket and the derivative product), liquidation of positions, and portfolio realignment or liquidation.

Most block trades, of course, involve institutional investors such as mutual funds, pension plans, insurance companies, and similar entities, which own about half of the outstanding stock among United States shareholders. As one might expect, institutional investors have a strong incentive to trade among themselves and avoid commissions as well as regulations that may require trades to be split up among many buyers or sellers on an exchange. Thus, most institutional investors use private trading systems when trading among themselves. These private trading systems are discussed more fully below.

Most of the work of putting a block trade together occurs "upstairs," in the institutional trading departments of the member firms. Some of these departments develop expertise in effecting transactions in stocks of certain types of companies (e.g., utilities or banks). Other departments tend to specialize in stocks of specific companies. Some firms act as **block positioners** and use their own capital to take part (a **stub end**) of a block trade that cannot be entirely placed with institutional investors. Block positioners must register with the NYSE and meet minimum capital requirements.

Salespeople and traders of institutional departments maintain constant communication with many institutional investors. Many maintain direct phone lines to the trading desks of the institutions. When a department receives an order to buy or sell a large block of stock, it contacts institutions to see whether they want to participate on the other side of the trade. An electronic network, **Instinet**, also exists; it connects trading desks of institutional investors that may be used for simultaneous inquiries about possible interest in the block. (Instinet is owned by Reuters, which carefully controls who can trade on the system. Instinet trades are included in the consolidated tape of the NYSE. There are several other electronic trading systems that are described more fully below.) The issuing company itself may be contacted if it has announced a share repurchase program. An inquiry may also be made of the specialist to determine how much of the block might be absorbed by public orders at the contemplated price. Inquiries sometimes generate additional interest on the same side of the transaction as the original block. The managing firm may thus put together an even larger transaction, involving several buyers and sellers on each side of the transaction.

When the transaction is put together "upstairs," it must ordinarily be **crossed** on the NYSE floor. (As discussed above, if a trade that a member firm handles involves a stock listed on or before April 26, 1979, the trade must be made on the NYSE.) Small numbers of shares not otherwise committed may be handled by the specialist or sold to customers of floor brokers present at the post. Crossing the trade on the floor also ensures that public orders for the same stock (held either as limit orders by the specialist or by floor brokers) may participate in the offering if it is favorable for them to do so. If the managing firm is a block positioner, SEC rules allow it to take some or all shares for its own account if the price is at or between the quotes, but the public must be allowed to participate if the block trade is to be executed at a price above the current offer or below the current bid.

## §14.8 NYSE Trading Practices in 2001

In the 1960s, when the NYSE began to computerize aspects of its operations, average trading volume was about 3,000,000 shares per day, and trading was recorded by hand on paper. Since then, trading volume has grown exponentially. By 1997, it was quite common for 600 million shares to be traded in a single day; on December 15, 2000, the largest single day's volume of trading to date, more than 1.56 billion shares were traded. The NYSE has been able to handle this massive explosion in trading volume by taking advantage of the dramatic improvements that have been made in computerization and electronic communication. Indeed, the tremendous growth in trading that has occurred over the last forty years would not be conceivable without these improvements.

The following description of NYSE operations in 2001 is drawn from NYSE publications available on the NYSE website.

The NYSE marketplace blends public pricing with assigned dealer responsibilities. Aided by advanced technology, public orders meet and interact on the trading floor with a minimum of dealer interference. The result is competitive price discovery at the point of sale. Liquidity in the NYSE market system is provided by individual and institutional investors, member firms trading for their own accounts, and assigned dealers.

NYSE-assigned dealers, also known as specialists are responsible for maintaining a fair and orderly market in the securities assigned to them. Most trading, however, is conducted by brokers acting on behalf of customers, rather than by dealers trading for their own account. For this reason, the NYSE is often described as an agency auction market. The interaction of natural buyers and sellers determines the price of a NYSE-listed stock.

Orders are sent to the NYSE from member firms through the Exchange's order delivery system SuperDot and through the Exchange's order management system BBSS (Broker Booth Support System). Orders can be routed to the specialist's Display Book or to brokers' BBSS terminals at the Booth. The vast majority of orders, representing about 57.7% of the volume, are routed directly to the Specialist. Larger sized orders are handled by BBSS and brokers. In addition, orders requiring special handling are phoned to the trading floor for broker handling.

Brokers now have access to a variety of technology tools to help in the communication and execution of orders on the trading floor, including: pagers, cell phones, broker-to-broker booth phones, and most recently, e-broker handheld computers. These e-broker handhelds provide a fast, efficient mechanism to receive orders, send reports and transmit messages to booths. Through automatic routing controls brokers can receive orders in the trading crowd directly from a member firm trading desk and immediately report back execution details. . . .

During 2000, SuperDot processed an average of 1,556,750 orders per day for a year-end total of 258 subscribers. . . . SuperDot volume of 261.1 billion shares in 2000 exceeded all prior activity records. The NYSE has doubled the capacity of the system to provide the order processing capability to now handle 2,000 messages per second, without system queuing. . . .

At the trading post, SuperDot orders that come in from member firms systems appear on the specialist's Display Book screen. The Display Book is an electronic workstation that keeps track of all limit orders and incoming market orders. Various window-like screen applications allow the specialist to view one or more issues at a time at various levels of detail. Incoming SuperDot limit orders automatically enter the Display Book. The Display Book sorts the limit orders and displays them in price/time priority. Similarly, when a floor broker gives the specialist a limit order, the specialist's clerk can enter the order into the Display Book using the keyboard. SuperDot market orders are displayed at the terminal for execution. The order execution may be against a market order, against another in the display book, against the specialist inventory, or against an order represented by a floor broker in the crowd.

The SuperDot system is designed to support orders destined to the Specialist or the BBSS system that are sized as high as 3 million shares. The Specialist Display Book is designed for rapid turnaround of market orders and in 2000 the average time for an execution and report back to a member firm was 15-16 seconds for eligible market orders. . . .

The BBSS system is a comprehensive order management tool for trading floor brokers and member firm trading desks. There are currently over 150 BBSS terminals at member firm locations and about 900 BBSS terminals at Booth locations on the trading floor. The System provides for order entry, delivery, routing, and reporting. BBSS provides routing to other BBSS terminals, Display Books, e-Broker Hand Held Devices, and the Crossing Session. Advanced order management features include customizable order display summaries; average price calculation and report recaps across multiple orders; quick order entry; report allocation; and report correction capability. The system also provides e-mail capability to facilitate communication between the broker, booth, and trading desk. . . .

The e-Broker System extends BBSS's advanced order management capabilities to the Broker at the point of sale. Using state-of-the-art wireless, handheld computers, the e-Broker System enables brokers in the trading crowd to receive orders and requests for market information electronically from the trading desk. Trade reports are entered by the broker at the point of sale and sent instantaneously back to the trading desk, eliminating errors and facilitating Straight Through Processing.

Used in conjunction with BBSS, e-Broker enables brokers to give their customers unparalleled access to the trading floor, fulfilling their need for real-time order status and market information throughout the trading day. . . .

## §14.9 Regional Exchanges Also Trade in NYSE-Listed Stocks

In addition to the NYSE, there are several **regional stock exchanges**: the Boston Stock Exchange, the Chicago Stock Exchange, the Cincinnati Stock Exchange, the Pacific Stock Exchange, and the Philadelphia Stock Exchange. Regional exchanges may list and freely trade in stocks listed on the Exchange. SEC approval is required for **unlisted trading privileges**, but it is routinely granted. The **Intermarket Trading System** (the **ITS**) is a computer system that provides automated price quotations on these stocks traded in multiple markets and an automated routing system that sends orders to the market providing the most favorable price. The ITS does not guarantee the best price, however, because trades sent from one market to another are not necessarily treated with the same priority as trades sent directly to that market.

The regional exchanges may also list stocks of companies with a regional following, but there are very few stocks so listed, possibly because listing standards on NASDAQ are so low that most small companies opt for national exposure there.

There were 4,664 issues eligible for trading on ITS as of the end of 2000 and the volume of trading for the year was 7.1 billion shares.

## §14.10  Newspaper Reports of NYSE Trading

The financial pages of a newspaper give considerable information about the trading activity each day on the NYSE, about the trading in specific stocks, and about the specific investment characteristics of each stock traded on the NYSE. This section, based on the *Wall Street Journal* reporting system, describes the information that is available.

Table 14-1 shows the breakdown of trading in NYSE-listed stocks by market, and on a half-hourly basis, for Wednesday, November 7, 2001 (a routine but relatively active trading day chosen more or less at random). Over 1.7 billion shares were traded. Trades executed on the regional exchanges are included in the composite figures and are broken down separately. Although the NYSE still accounts for the great bulk of trading, the regional exchanges' share of the market for trades involving less than 3,000 shares has gradually increased to about 65 percent of the trades of that size; of course, when trades of all sizes are concerned, the NYSE still predominates, executing more than 80 percent of trades on most days.

Table 14-1 also shows (in the section titled "Diaries") overall price movements for all stocks traded on Wednesday, November 7, 2001, as well as the previous day and a week earlier. Again, block trades, the last entry, are single trades of 10,000 shares or more; they are indicative of the degree of institutional investor activity.

Table 14-1 also gives information about the most active stocks traded on the NYSE on Wednesday, November 7, 2001, both in terms of total volume and in terms of the largest percentage gainers and losers. Note that there is little overlap between the two lists. This is to be expected, because almost all large percentage gainers or losers are relatively low-priced stocks.

Table 14-2 sets forth information about trading in some NYSE stocks for November 7, 2001. Most of the symbols and footnotes used in Table 14-2 are explained in Table 14-3, which also gives precise definitions for many of the figures that appear in the report of trading. For example, the table shows "composite transactions" of the various securities; Table 14-2 states that "composite quotations" include trades in the listed securities in regional exchanges and by NASD.

To take an example from Table 14-2 more or less at random, Delta Airlines (in the far right hand column under D-D-D) is referred to as "DeltaAir" with the symbols "DAL". All stocks in this table are common stocks. If one were to look at the tape reporting NYSE transactions, only the abbreviated symbol "DAL" followed by the price of the last transaction would appear on the tape. The entry itself is bold-faced; the reason for that is described in the Explanatory Notes in Table 14-3 — the stock price changed by 5 percent or more from the previous closing price. The "dd" notation under PE sets forth more bad news for Delta: It had a "loss in the most recent four quarters." (Thus, it is impossible to calculate a P/E ratio based on these trailing earnings.) The columns in the left part of the table continue the description of bad news: The year-to-date change (YTD%CHG) in the price of Delta common stock compares the price of Delta common on the first trading day of the year with the current price; the change was a negative 48.8%. The "52 WEEKS HI LO" column sets forth the highest and lowest prices for Delta common stock between November 7, 2000, and November 7, 2001. During this 52-week period, the high-low range was a high of $52.94 and a low of $20 per share. The closing price on November 7 was $25.69 per share, above the low for the year, but still very depressed. The column on the far right (NETCHG) shows the change between the closing price on November 7 and the closing price on the preceding trading day. The net change figure thus is unrelated to the high and low trading prices during the trading day (**intraday**).

The terrorists' attack on September 11, 2001, did not involve the hijacking of a Delta Airlines plane. However, the effect of the events of that date on airline travel and the airline industry generally was substantial; Delta's overall economic performance nearly two months later can be explained directly by those events.

On November 7, 2001, 23,157 "round lots" of 100 shares of Delta Airlines were traded. At a price of $25.69 per share (using the closing price, but still a good indicator) the total value of Delta shares traded on that day was in the range of $59,490,000. This data, for a single stock on a single day, gives some idea of the magnitude of trading on the NYSE, day after day. Clearly, billions of dollars of stocks are traded each day.

In the short run of day-to-day trading, November 7 was a relatively good day for Delta; its share price increased by $1.49 per share over the closing price the previous day. Does that mean that Delta would be a good investment? One way to make an assessment is to consider the yield that appears in the second column to the right. For Delta, the yield is 0.4. In other words, Delta's dividend of 10 cents per share represents a return of 0.4 percent on a $25 investment. That is certainly not very impressive. On the other hand, Delta pays a dividend despite the fact that it had a loss in the most recent quarter. Moreover, the market seems to think Delta has value, presumably because it will have positive earnings in the future. Thus, the $25 share price of Delta must be some multiple of the expected earnings.

If one looks through the stocks in Table 14-2, one sees that there are other companies that show a positive yield but have no P/E ratio. For example DPL, Inc. has a yield of $.94 but no P/E ratio. Another company, DST Systems has a P/E ratio of 22 but no yield. In the case of DPL, it appears that while the company had no earnings the previous year it nevertheless paid a dividend of $.94 per share. In the case of DST Systems the reverse is true. The company had earnings during the previous year (of approximately $1.90 per share) but paid no dividend. Its stock price was $42.44 per share, or approximately 22 times its earnings.

Finally, brief mention should be made about publicly traded preferred stocks. These stocks are traded on the New York Stock Exchange and other exchanges. The Wall Street Journal has a separate table that lists trading in many of these shares on the New York, the Amex, and Nasdaq. Table 14-4 is an excerpt from this table. Many utility companies have outstanding several issues of preferred shares carrying varying rates of dividends. Alabama Power, traded on the NYSE, is a good example. It lists three classes of preferreds and four classes of notes, with various dividend or interest rates, various yields, and various prices. No P/E ratio is set forth for preferreds, because they are limited participation securities with no claim to increased dividends based on increases in earnings. Their value is therefore determined largely by their distribution rights. The yields on the Alabama Power securities are in the 6 to 7 percent range. It may be noted that some companies, including Pacific Gas & Electric traded on the Amex, have suspended dividends, though they continue to have potential value and are actively traded. That is a reflection of the unusual current situation, since in general terms, preferred stocks listed on these exchanges are high-grade securities on which continued dividend payments are highly probable.

## §14.11 The American Stock Exchange

A second important trading market is the **American Stock Exchange** (**AMEX**). The AMEX is considerably smaller than the NYSE. The summaries for its operations on November 7, 2001 are also set forth in Table 14-1. It operates in essentially the same way as the NYSE, but there is no cross-listing of individual stocks between the AMEX and NYSE. Some AMEX stocks are also traded on regional exchanges and price quotations for these stocks are disseminated by ITS. Listing standards for the AMEX are lower than for the NYSE. Thus, most companies listed on the AMEX are smaller than companies on the NYSE. Moreover, most AMEX stocks are lower priced. This is well illustrated by Table 14-5, which reflects trading in stocks on this smaller exchange. Most NYSE stocks sell for more than $20 per share, while most AMEX stocks sell for less than $10 per share. These ranges are maintained over long periods by individual stocks through the device of splitting the stock if it rises in price beyond its traditional trading range.

## §14.12 The Over-the-Counter Market

The **over-the-counter (OTC) market** is quite unlike the organized exchanges described in the previous sections. There is no single place or location for the over-the-counter market. Rather, it consists of a large number of brokers and dealers who deal with each other by computer or telephone, buying and selling shares for customers or for their own account. A **dealer** is a securities firm that trades for its own account, while a **broker** executes orders for a customer. Large securities firms commonly act both as broker and as dealer in OTC securities, and may act as both a broker and a dealer in the same transaction as long as that fact is disclosed to customers. As a result, the term **broker-dealer** is typically used in statutes and rules dealing with the securities industry. Dealers involved in the OTC market are organized into a semi-public association called the **National Association of Securities Dealers** (**NASD**). By federal law, all broker-dealers must be members of the NASD.

The core of the OTC market is the **market maker**. A market maker is a dealer who stands ready to buy or sell a specific stock at quoted prices; the price at which a market maker is willing to sell (the **asked** or **offered** price) is, of course, somewhat higher than the price at which it is willing to buy (the

Table 14-1

## STOCK MARKET DATA BANK                    11/7/01

### MAJOR INDEXES

| †12-MO HIGH | LOW | | DAILY HIGH | LOW | CLOSE | NET CHG | | % CHG | †12-MO CHG | | % CHG | FROM 12/31 | | % CHG |
|---|---|---|---|---|---|---|---|---|---|---|---|---|---|---|
| **DOW JONES AVERAGES** | | | | | | | | | | | | | | |
| 11337.92 | 8235.81 | 30 Industrials | 9644.12 | 9522.41 | x9554.37 | − | 36.75 | − 0.38 | −1352.69 | − | 12.40 | −1232.48 | − | 11.43 |
| 3145.65 | 2033.86 | 20 Transportation | 2309.64 | 2275.94 | x2307.50 | + | 16.35 | + 0.71 | − 469.57 | − | 16.91 | − 639.10 | − | 21.69 |
| 416.11 | 289.42 | 15 Utilities | 296.94 | 292.66 | x294.21 | − | 3.02 | − 1.02 | − 95.99 | − | 24.60 | − 117.95 | − | 28.62 |
| 3392.23 | 2489.27 | 65 Composite | 2749.14 | 2722.92 | x2732.61 | − | 7.98 | − 0.29 | − 527.23 | − | 16.17 | − 584.80 | − | 17.63 |
| 330.17 | 222.35 | DJ US Total Mkt | 259.72 | 256.62 | 257.22 | − | 0.52 | − 0.20 | − 72.95 | − | 22.09 | − 49.66 | − | 16.18 |
| **STANDARD & POOR'S INDEXES** | | | | | | | | | | | | | | |
| 1409.28 | 965.80 | 500 Index | 1126.62 | 1112.98 | 1115.80 | − | 3.06 | − 0.27 | − 293.48 | − | 20.82 | − 204.48 | − | 15.49 |
| 1678.22 | 1113.25 | Industrials | 1305.82 | 1289.12 | 1292.48 | − | 5.29 | − 0.41 | − 385.74 | − | 22.99 | − 235.38 | − | 15.41 |
| 353.03 | 237.27 | Utilities | 247.08 | 242.39 | 243.27 | − | 3.81 | − 1.54 | − 82.17 | − | 25.25 | − 107.34 | − | 30.62 |
| 547.06 | 404.34 | 400 MidCap | 475.13 | 470.37 | 472.05 | + | 0.27 | + 0.06 | − 50.40 | − | 9.65 | − 44.71 | − | 8.65 |
| 236.76 | 181.09 | 600 SmallCap | 210.76 | 208.94 | 209.41 | − | 0.28 | − 0.13 | − 7.20 | − | 3.32 | − 10.18 | − | 4.64 |
| 301.50 | 209.52 | 1500 Index | 244.50 | 241.69 | 242.24 | − | 0.60 | − 0.25 | − 59.26 | − | 19.66 | − 41.86 | − | 14.73 |
| **NASDAQ STOCK MARKET** | | | | | | | | | | | | | | |
| 3231.70 | 1423.19 | Composite | 1868.31 | 1820.28 | 1837.53 | + | 2.45 | + 0.13 | −1394.17 | − | 43.14 | − 632.99 | − | 25.62 |
| 3076.70 | 1126.95 | Nasdaq 100 | 1559.04 | 1506.11 | 1524.67 | + | 1.58 | + 0.10 | −1534.42 | − | 50.16 | − 817.03 | − | 34.89 |
| 1759.43 | 1027.69 | Industrials | 1289.60 | 1270.20 | 1273.36 | − | 4.04 | − 0.32 | − 486.07 | − | 27.63 | − 209.63 | − | 14.14 |
| 2367.59 | 1882.75 | Insurance | 2633.60 | 2338.52 | 2338.75 | − | 26.55 | − 1.12 | + 442.18 | + | 23.31 | + 145.38 | + | 6.63 |
| 2240.86 | 1673.11 | Banks | 2058.02 | 2036.79 | 2037.11 | − | 12.90 | − 0.63 | + 289.03 | + | 16.53 | + 97.66 | + | 5.04 |
| 1897.54 | 653.13 | Computer | 946.57 | 912.60 | 927.30 | + | 5.06 | + 0.55 | − 970.24 | − | 51.13 | − 367.67 | − | 28.39 |
| 584.07 | 192.87 | Telecommunications | 228.56 | 219.50 | 224.11 | + | 0.62 | + 0.28 | − 356.09 | − | 61.37 | − 239.33 | − | 51.64 |
| **NEW YORK STOCK EXCHANGE** | | | | | | | | | | | | | | |
| 666.57 | 504.21 | Composite | 572.52 | 567.54 | 568.48 | − | 1.81 | − 0.32 | − 93.32 | − | 14.10 | − 88.39 | − | 13.46 |
| 826.70 | 620.11 | Industrials | 711.24 | 704.75 | 705.91 | − | 3.07 | − 0.43 | − 113.94 | − | 13.90 | − 97.38 | − | 12.12 |
| 465.97 | 322.62 | Utilities | 331.05 | 326.58 | 327.18 | − | 3.80 | − 1.15 | − 138.79 | − | 29.79 | − 113.36 | − | 25.73 |
| 494.71 | 332.91 | Transportation | 398.71 | 393.91 | 398.62 | + | 1.99 | + 0.50 | − 37.99 | − | 8.70 | − 64.14 | − | 13.86 |
| 657.52 | 494.41 | Finance | 579.13 | 570.92 | 575.23 | + | 2.05 | + 0.36 | − 39.76 | − | 6.47 | − 71.72 | − | 11.09 |
| **OTHERS** | | | | | | | | | | | | | | |
| 958.75 | 780.46 | Amex Composite | 822.61 | 815.02 | 821.98 | + | 4.55 | + 0.56 | − 98.65 | − | 10.72 | − 75.77 | − | 8.44 |
| 752.13 | 507.98 | Russell 1000 | 591.88 | 584.74 | 586.17 | − | 1.29 | − 0.22 | − 165.96 | − | 22.07 | − 113.92 | − | 16.27 |
| 517.23 | 378.90 | Russell 2000 | 444.66 | 440.64 | 440.80 | − | 1.98 | − 0.45 | − 59.88 | − | 11.96 | − 42.73 | − | 8.84 |
| 777.77 | 529.66 | Russell 3000 | 617.42 | 610.18 | 611.51 | − | 1.44 | − 0.23 | − 166.26 | − | 21.38 | − 114.24 | − | 15.74 |
| 422.43 | 294.60 | Value-Line | 342.56 | 338.97 | 339.95 | − | 0.05 | − 0.01 | − 71.33 | − | 17.34 | − 53.52 | − | 13.60 |
| 13152.56 | 8900.45 | Wilshire 5000 | 10374.92 | 10259.07 | 10279.22 | − | 25.17 | − 0.24 | −2873.34 | − | 21.85 | −1896.66 | − | 15.58 |

†-Based on comparable trading day in preceding year.

Table 14-1 (*cont.*)

## MOST ACTIVE ISSUES

| NYSE | VOLUME | CLOSE | CHANGE | |
|---|---|---|---|---|
| EnronCp | 111,471,200 | 9.05 | − | 0.62 |
| Compaq | 55,797,200 | 7.99 | − | 0.51 |
| AOL Time | 28,378,000 | 34.50 | − | 0.65 |
| LucentTch | 27,721,800 | 7.01 | − | 0.36 |
| EMC Cp | 27,137,800 | 15.02 | − | 0.28 |
| GlblCross | 21,872,900 | 0.82 | − | 0.16 |
| QwestComm | 21,614,700 | 11.51 | − | 0.28 |
| HewlettPk | 21,225,200 | 19.18 | − | 0.63 |
| AmTower A | 20,180,100 | 5.98 | − | 1.02 |
| NortelNtwks | 20,001,700 | 6.81 | + | 0.01 |
| Nokia | 16,322,900 | 22.20 | − | 0.86 |
| GenElec | 15,125,200 | 39.35 | − | 0.45 |
| TX Instr | 12,380,600 | 31.85 | + | 0.36 |
| Citigroup | 11,909,400 | 48.10 | + | 0.55 |
| ChespkeEngy | 11,730,400 | 6.17 | + | 0.06 |
| **NASDAQ** | | | | |
| CiscoSys | 116,907,300 | 18.93 | + | 0.46 |
| SunMicrsys | 65,439,100 | 12.59 | + | 0.20 |
| Intel | 58,700,900 | 28.29 | + | 0.04 |
| Qualcomm | 45,080,000 | 55.11 | + | 0.38 |
| OracleCp | 43,179,900 | 15.58 | + | 0.36 |
| Ciena | 38,525,900 | 17.40 | + | 1.16 |
| i2 Tch | 32,609,000 | 6.42 | + | 0.27 |
| JunprNtwk | 31,810,700 | 23.02 | + | 0.59 |
| Microsoft | 29,064,100 | 64.25 | − | 0.53 |
| Nextel | 26,876,600 | 9.04 | + | 0.14 |
| DellCptr | 26,457,700 | 26.25 | + | 0.01 |
| SiebelSys | 24,632,100 | 22.19 | + | 0.41 |
| MetrmdFibr | 23,665,900 | 0.72 | − | 0.07 |
| **AMEX** | | | | |
| NASDAQ100 | 90,095,700 | 38.14 | − | 0.05 |
| SPDR | 19,635,800 | 112.25 | − | 0.15 |
| IvaxCp | 8,927,300 | 18.95 | + | 1.95 |
| Semi HOLDRs | 4,276,300 | 41.50 | + | 0.06 |
| DJIA Diam | 2,936,200 | 95.75 | − | 0.40 |

## DIARIES

| NYSE | WED | TUE | WK AGO |
|---|---|---|---|
| Issues traded | 3,348 | 3,330 | 3,321 |
| Advances | 1,607 | 2,063 | 1,939 |
| Declines | 1,541 | 1,053 | 1,183 |
| Unchanged | 200 | 214 | 199 |
| New highs | 117 | 108 | 39 |
| New lows | 36 | 42 | 62 |
| zAdv vol (000) | 614,129 | 904,974 | 688,540 |
| zDecl vol (000) | 797,383 | 422,755 | 614,791 |
| zTotal vol (000) | 1,420,082 | 1,341,787 | 1,323,453 |
| Closing tick[1] | +148 | +970 | +437 |
| Closing Arms[2] (trin) | 1.35 | .92 | 1.46 |
| zBlock trades | 27,358 | 26,416 | 25,009 |
| **NASDAQ** | | | |
| Issues traded | 3,861 | 3,885 | 3,886 |
| Advances | 1,644 | 2,054 | 2,197 |
| Declines | 1,891 | 1,490 | 1,351 |
| Unchanged | 326 | 341 | 338 |
| New highs | 51 | 47 | 36 |
| New lows | 37 | 29 | 38 |
| Adv vol (000) | 1,358,023 | 1,496,091 | 1,346,721 |
| Decl vol (000) | 666,804 | 406,369 | 511,857 |
| Total vol (000) | 2,041,773 | 1,921,957 | 1,875,017 |
| Block trades | n.a. | 25,211 | 24,132 |
| **AMEX** | | | |
| Issues traded | 798 | 777 | 776 |
| Advances | 333 | 415 | 398 |
| Declines | 351 | 270 | 286 |
| Unchanged | 114 | 92 | 92 |
| New highs | 29 | 25 | 15 |
| New lows | 12 | 17 | 14 |
| zAdv vol (000) | 20,240 | 60,768 | 46,942 |
| zDecl vol (000) | 44,126 | 7,755 | 29,355 |
| zTotal vol (000) | 65,972 | 69,529 | 76,842 |
| Comp vol (000) | 151,047 | 163,058 | 169,568 |
| zBlock trades | n.a. | 1,404 | 1,517 |

Table 14-1 (*cont.*)

## PRICE PERCENTAGE GAINERS...

| NYSE | VOL | CLOSE | CHANGE | | % CHG | |
|---|---|---|---|---|---|---|
| FrnklnCovey | 40,200 | 4.75 | + | 1.16 | + | 32.3 |
| LandsEnd | 2,061,400 | 42.15 | + | 6.41 | + | 17.9 |
| PentonMedia | 434,200 | 8.15 | + | 1.18 | + | 16.9 |
| OmegaProtein | 42,300 | 2.65 | + | 0.37 | + | 16.2 |
| PrmrFarnl | 18,400 | 7.12 | + | 0.92 | + | 14.8 |
| AmeriCredit | 6,340,400 | 18.40 | + | 2.30 | + | 14.3 |
| Aquila A | 3,303,200 | 20.55 | + | 2.56 | + | 14.2 |
| CarltonXCAP | 40,600 | 21.51 | + | 2.52 | + | 13.3 |
| Conseco pfV | 78,000 | 12.66 | + | 1.44 | + | 12.8 |
| E Trade | 6,737,900 | 8.10 | + | 0.90 | + | 12.5 |
| Conseco pfT | 88,700 | 13.10 | + | 1.45 | + | 12.5 |
| Conseco pfH | 73,500 | 13.73 | + | 1.47 | + | 12.0 |
| BritAir | 92,700 | 25.20 | + | 2.67 | + | 11.9 |
| LamsonSes | 28,800 | 4.13 | + | 0.43 | + | 11.6 |
| IntgtElec | 66,300 | 3.90 | + | 0.40 | + | 11.4 |
| Fansteel | 3,800 | 3.25 | + | 0.32 | + | 10.9 |
| ChmpshpAuto | 684,100 | 14.49 | + | 1.39 | + | 10.6 |
| CompnhiaSidr | 66,500 | 12.80 | + | 1.19 | + | 10.3 |
| Holingrint A | 292,900 | 10.02 | + | 0.93 | + | 10.2 |
| Conseco pfG | 44,500 | 13.10 | + | 1.21 | + | 10.2 |
| **NASDAQ** | | | | | | |
| NaProBioTh | 553,200 | 8.22 | + | 2.11 | + | 34.5 |
| AmOnlnLtn A | 929,600 | 6.00 | + | 1.20 | + | 25.0 |
| Enrgs ADS | 4,000 | 6.25 | + | 1.25 | + | 25.0 |
| AkamaiTch | 5,233,200 | 4.25 | + | 0.75 | + | 21.4 |
| RaindncCom | 1,860,000 | 6.85 | + | 1.19 | + | 21.0 |
| SIPEX Cp | 1,707,000 | 10.05 | + | 1.68 | + | 20.1 |
| RstrlnHrdwr | 356,900 | 4.74 | + | 0.78 | + | 19.7 |
| DgtlThnk | 234,300 | 9.50 | + | 1.51 | + | 18.9 |
| IstaPharma | 46,000 | 3.62 | + | 0.57 | + | 18.7 |
| MultilinkTch | 1,247,000 | 7.17 | + | 1.12 | + | 18.5 |
| I-Many | 1,193,000 | 6.80 | + | 1.06 | + | 18.5 |
| MexicnRestr | 22,100 | 2.62 | + | 0.40 | + | 18.0 |
| Genencorintl | 491,500 | 14.30 | + | 2.18 | + | 18.0 |
| EP MedSys | 14,000 | 2.75 | + | 0.40 | + | 17.0 |
| **AMEX** | | | | | | |
| TrnsntlFnl | 35,500 | 2.56 | + | 0.36 | + | 16.4 |
| UniMart | 5,900 | 2.29 | + | 0.29 | + | 14.5 |
| IvaxCp | 8,927,300 | 18.95 | + | 1.95 | + | 11.5 |
| TitanPharm | 1,335,200 | 8.60 | + | 0.87 | + | 11.3 |
| FreqElec | 48,300 | 13.35 | + | 1.20 | + | 9.9 |

## AND LOSERS

| NYSE | VOL | CLOSE | CHANGE | | % CHG | |
|---|---|---|---|---|---|---|
| Vestalns | 1,145,800 | 6.67 | – | 5.83 | – | 46.6 |
| Alpharma A | 5,568,000 | 20.90 | – | 6.80 | – | 24.6 |
| IT Gp | 462,900 | 1.90 | – | 0.40 | – | 17.4 |
| AmTower A | 20,180,100 | 5.98 | – | 1.02 | – | 14.6 |
| OrbitalScl | 1,259,400 | 2.45 | – | 0.38 | – | 13.4 |
| Alstom ADS | 39,900 | 11.10 | – | 1.65 | – | 12.9 |
| CollnsAikman | 47,500 | 6.21 | – | 0.79 | – | 11.3 |
| SLI Inc | 37,800 | 2.13 | – | 0.27 | – | 11.3 |
| AON Cp | 6,062,800 | 35.95 | – | 4.21 | – | 10.5 |
| Turkcell ADS | 130,800 | 13.50 | – | 1.50 | – | 10.0 |
| RoperInd | 428,700 | 37.50 | – | 3.90 | – | 9.4 |
| ResortQuest | 32,900 | 4.50 | – | 0.45 | – | 9.1 |
| Elan ADS wt | 8,800 | 31.50 | – | 3.00 | – | 8.7 |
| FL ECstInd A | 110,800 | 18.97 | – | 1.77 | – | 8.5 |
| Dynegy A | 6,820,500 | 33.00 | – | 3.00 | – | 8.3 |
| EngyPrtnrs | 48,800 | 6.66 | – | 0.59 | – | 8.1 |
| GerbScnfc | 121,600 | 10.03 | – | 0.87 | – | 8.0 |
| ACM IncFd | 1,337,200 | 8.30 | – | 0.70 | – | 7.8 |
| NTL Inc | 2,537,100 | 4.20 | – | 0.35 | – | 7.7 |
| APW | 97,700 | 1.86 | – | 0.14 | – | 7.0 |
| **NASDAQ** | | | | | | |
| Medialink | 177,700 | 2.20 | – | 0.80 | – | 26.7 |
| OpticalComm | 640,400 | 2.91 | – | 0.80 | – | 21.6 |
| Duratek | 93,800 | 5.56 | – | 1.46 | – | 20.8 |
| SBA Comm | 2,302,900 | 6.25 | – | 1.55 | – | 19.9 |
| AeroGen | 12,100 | 2.61 | – | 0.63 | – | 19.4 |
| AspenTch | 1,452,400 | 13.35 | – | 3.14 | – | 19.0 |
| NatusMed | 1,214,400 | 4.00 | – | 0.85 | – | 17.5 |
| Nanogen | 789,800 | 6.86 | – | 1.34 | – | 16.3 |
| TanningTch | 64,400 | 1.76 | – | 0.34 | – | 16.2 |
| GTSI | 226,800 | 6.06 | – | 1.12 | – | 15.6 |
| EdgePete | 131,400 | 4.65 | – | 0.85 | – | 15.5 |
| Netopia | 327,400 | 3.98 | – | 0.72 | – | 15.3 |
| DIGI Intl | 562,100 | 4.10 | – | 0.69 | – | 14.4 |
| SkillSoft | 730,200 | 21.20 | – | 3.51 | – | 14.2 |
| **AMEX** | | | | | | |
| Cognitron | 22,000 | 4.40 | – | 0.75 | – | 14.6 |
| Rheometric | 25,800 | 1.90 | – | 0.30 | – | 13.6 |
| SitcoInd | 33,300 | 4.93 | – | 0.72 | – | 12.7 |
| IRIS | 30,800 | 2.73 | – | 0.27 | – | 9.0 |
| SunlinkHlth | 5,400 | 2.45 | – | 0.24 | – | 8.9 |

Table 14-1 (*cont.*)

## VOLUME PERCENTAGE LEADERS

| NYSE | VOL % DIF* | CLOSE | CHANGE | | NASDAQ | VOL % DIF* | CLOSE | CHANGE | |
|---|---|---|---|---|---|---|---|---|---|
| Crawfrd A | 163,100 1712.6 | x9 | + | 0.07 | SilganHldgs | 3,235,900 11650.7 | 19.00 | – | 0.10 |
| Alpharma A | 5,568,000 1642.1 | 20.90 | – | 6.80 | ArtisnCmpnt | 497,000 1646.8 | 9.52 | + | 0.24 |
| LandsEnd | 2,061,400 1201.0 | 42.15 | + | 6.41 | FrontierFnl | 669,700 1608.0 | 26.55 | – | 0.93 |
| StorageUSA | 1,855,000 1157.2 | 42.89 | + | 0.09 | Stericycle | 2,927,600 1344.1 | 51.15 | – | 0.64 |
| ChespkeEngy | 11,730,400 1065.0 | 6.17 | + | 0.06 | BostnAc | 108,300 1304.7 | 9.42 | + | 0.01 |
| AmTower A | 20,180,100 903.9 | 5.98 | – | 1.02 | PocahntsBcp | 110,700 1245.7 | 7.80 | – | 0.20 |
| Aquila A | 3,303,200 903.9 | 20.55 | + | 2.56 | ClosureMed | 300,100 1208.0 | 16.87 | + | 0.80 |
| Midas | 444,800 894.7 | 9.95 | – | 0.10 | VirageLogic | 1,032,400 1132.5 | 11.67 | + | 1.07 |
| DelMnteFood | 792,900 887.4 | 8.02 | – | 0.03 | Entrust | 4,191,900 1076.4 | 6.88 | – | 0.42 |
| EnronCp | 111,471,200 803.0 | 9.05 | – | 0.62 | SIPEX Cp | 1,707,000 999.8 | 10.05 | + | 1.68 |
| BcoSanti ADR | 136,700 738.6 | 21.00 | + | 0.40 | WitnessSys | 534,000 916.5 | 9.00 | + | 0.33 |
| Aetna | 6,751,100 730.2 | 31.24 | – | 0.77 | PediatricSvc | 152,700 a809.1 | 7.35 | + | 0.10 |
| Vestalns | 1,145,800 689.5 | 6.67 | – | 5.83 | GTSI | 226,800 790.7 | 6.06 | – | 1.12 |
| FL ECstInd A | 110,800 642.8 | 18.97 | – | 1.77 | ATMI Inc. | 3,289,900 765.6 | 18.21 | + | 0.46 |
| ChmpshpAuto | 684,100 606.3 | 14.49 | + | 1.39 | EPIQ Sys | 885,300 723.2 | 34.00 | + | 3.84 |
| AustriaFd | 47,500 430.4 | 6.25 | + | 0.05 | Genencorlntl | 491,500 638.7 | 14.30 | + | 2.18 |
| FraGrthFd | 107,400 429.6 | 7.48 | + | 0.18 | **AMEX** | | | | |
| CrdntComm | 137,100 422.7 | 7.42 | + | 0.42 | Vasogen | 219,700 1070.0 | 5.26 | – | 0.41 |
| TelLeste | 56,800 415.8 | 15.92 | + | 1.32 | iShrSP400G | 137,800 614.5 | 105.80 | + | 0.52 |
| Roperlnd | 428,700 410.3 | 37.50 | – | 3.90 | HollywdCno | 190,100 537.8 | 8.80 | + | 0.10 |
| | | | | | CrssMediaMktg | 115,200 420.4 | 7.80 | + | 0.35 |
| | | | | | IvaxCp | 8,927,300 364.9 | 18.95 | + | 1.95 |

*Common stocks of $5 a share or more with average volume over 65 trading days of at least 5,000 shares.
a-has traded fewer than 65 days. b-10,000% or greater.

## BREAKDOWN OF TRADING IN NYSE STOCKS (9:30 a.m. to 4 p.m. Eastern time)

| BY MARKET | WED | TUE | WK AGO | ½-HOURLY | WED | TUE | WK AGO |
|---|---|---|---|---|---|---|---|
| New York | 1,420,082,430 | 1,341,786,730 | 1,323,453,010 | 9:30-10 | 159,360,000 | 139,680,000 | 157,360,000 |
| Chicago | 76,227,440 | 66,872,910 | 70,065,400 | 10-10:30 | 135,827,690 | 101,095,090 | 131,110,970 |
| CBOE | .... | .... | 100 | 10:30-11 | 126,462,310 | 93,234,910 | 93,649,030 |
| Pacific | 2,813,800 | 2,694,900 | 2,428,800 | 11-11:30 | 92,385,190 | 79,656,210 | 85,063,990 |
| Nasdaq InterMkt | 160,002,350 | 160,957,160 | 131,834,460 | 11:30-12 | 86,874,810 | 67,523,790 | 71,766,010 |
| Phila | 9,051,600 | 9,416,800 | 7,353,600 | 12-12:30 | 70,056,110 | 64,788,100 | 66,851,920 |
| Boston | 35,861,200 | 31,464,800 | 26,617,500 | 12:30-1 | 82,313,890 | 60,321,900 | 77,218,080 |
| Cincinnati | 10,517,100 | 8,268,900 | 7,583,100 | 1-1:30 | 89,903,960 | 56,707,570 | 66,542,990 |
| Composite | 1,714,555,920 | 1,621,462,200 | 1,569,335,970 | 1:30-2 | 89,826,040 | 69,482,430 | 66,317,010 |
| | | | | 2-2:30 | 100,599,290 | 104,858,000 | 89,327,590 |
| | | | | 2:30-3 | 97,860,710 | 118,992,000 | 85,882,410 |
| | | | | 3-3:30 | 106,316,690 | 118,999,150 | 97,148,730 |
| | | | | 3:30-4 | 182,295,740 | 266,447,580 | 235,214,280 |

NYSE first crossing 2,992,100 shares, value n.a.
Second (basket) 15,521,008 shares, value $482,111,793
[1] The net difference of the number of stocks closing higher than their previous trade from those closing lower; NYSE trading only.
[2] A comparison of the number of advancing and declining issues with the volume of shares rising and falling. Generally, an Arms of less than 1.00 indicates buying demand; above 1.00 indicates selling pressure.

x-Ex-dividends of Exxon Mobil Corp $0.23 and IBM Corp. $0.14 lowered the Industrial Average by 2.56. Ex-dividend of Roadway Corp $0.05 lowered the Transportation Average by 0.24. Ex-dividend of American Electric Power $0.60 lowered the Utilities Average by 0.37 The above ex-dividends lowered the Composite Average by 1.20.
z-NYSE or AMEX only.

Table 14-2

# NEW YORK STOCK EXCHANGE COMPOSITE TRANSACTIONS

| YTD %CHG | 52 WEEKS HI | LO | STOCK (SYM) | DIV | YLD % | PE | VOL 100s | LAST | NET CHG |
|---|---|---|---|---|---|---|---|---|---|
| +165.5 | 8.15 | 1.94 | CKE Restr CKR | .08b | 1.1 | dd | 2884 | 7.30 | -0.12 |
| -28.2 | 32.25 | 19.49 | CMS Engy CMS | 1.46 | 6.4 | dd | 9618 | 22.75 | +0.62 |
| -12.5 | 37 | 28.81 | CMS EngyTr CMP | 3.63 | 11.9 | ... | 317 | 30.63 | -0.05 |
| -46.5 | 60.75 | 14.75 | C-MacInd EMS | ... | .33 | ... | 4286 | 23.75 | -0.15 |
| -31.6 | 40.24 | 23 | CNA Fnl CNA | ... | ... | dd | 936 | 26.49 | -0.11 |
| -0.4 | 14.70 | 11 | CNA Surety SUR | .60 | 4.2 | 13 | 36 | 14.20 | +0.02 |
| -29.0 | 39.88 | 21.05 | CNF CNF | .40 | 1.7 | dd | 3138 | 24 | +0.61 |
| -32.5 | 10.06 | 5 | ▲CNH Global CNH | .10m | 1.2 | dd | 519 | 5.82 | +0.16 |
| +18.8 | 22 | 15.70 | CNOOC ADS CEO n | .24p | ... | ... | 66 | 19.15 | -0.05 |
| -19.3 | 24.50 | 12.70 | CPI-Cp CPY | .56 | 3.5 | 20 | 27 | 16.15 | -0.30 |
| -10.6 | 11.38 | 6.21 | CP Ships n | ... | ... | 902 | 9.92 | +0.78 |
| +102.6 | 8.75 | 2.50 | CSK AutoCp CAO | ... | dd | 433 | 7.85 | -0.07 |
| +27.1 | 27.28 | 18.63 | CSS Ind CSS | ... | ... | 26 | 27.01 | -0.23 |
| +36.0 | 41.30 | 23.19 | CSX CSX | .40 | 1.1 | 26 | 6270 | 35.27 | +0.34 |
| -58.5 | 47.88 | 13.49 | CTS Cp CTS | .12 | .8 | cc | 1573 | 15.13 | -0.27 |
| -59.0 | 63.75 | 22.89 | CVS Cp CVS | .23 | .9 | 13 | 55582 | 24.55 | +0.82 |
| +3.6 | 24.80 | 20.94 | CabcoTr BFH | 1.69 | 7.1 | x | 62 | 23.95 | -0.20 |
| -63.7 | 45.63 | 11.01 | CablWirels CWP | .80e | 5.5 | ... | 2491 | 14.49 | -0.42 |
| -17.9 | 24.75 | 10.45 | CableDsgn CDT | ... | 27 | 1117 | 13.80 | +0.40 |
| -50.2 | 77.72 | 32.50 | CablevsnNY A CVC s | ... | 5 | 23177 | 35.95 | +1.00 |
| -5.4 | 28 | 18.20 | CablvisnRainbw A RMG n | ... | 1284 | 21.75 | -0.49 |
| +29.7 | 42.24 | 21.81 | ▲Cabot Cp CBT | .52 | 1.5 | 21 | 2145 | 34.22 | +0.16 |
| +24.3 | 23.88 | 18 | ▲CabotIndlTr CTR | 1.48 | 6.2 | 15 | 10439 | 23.85 | ... |
| -25.8 | 34.35 | 16.25 | CabotO&G COG x | .16 | .7 | 9 | 1139 | 23.15 | +0.24 |
| -13.4 | 30 | 24 | CadburySch CSG | .68e | 2.7 | ... | 819 | 25.10 | -0.57 |
| -10.9 | 32.69 | 14.10 | CadenceDsgn CDN | ... | 45 | 13940 | 24.50 | -0.15 |
| +57.2 | 9.50 | 4.75 | CalgonCarb CCC x | .20 | 2.2 | 33 | 2173 | 8.94 | +0.14 |
| -5.9 | 28.60 | 22.88 | CalWtrSvc CWT | 1.12 | 4.4 | 25 | 152 | 25.40 | -0.45 |
| -22.5 | 27.18 | 11.83 | CaltwyGlf ELY | .28 | 1.9 | 15 | 1290 | 14.43 | -0.27 |
| -61.6 | 17 | 5.90 | ▲CalnPete CPE | ... | 5 | 196 | 6.40 | -0.20 |
| -45.6 | 58.04 | 18.90 | Calpine CPN s | ... | 13 | 46893 | 24.52 | -0.18 |
| -14.2 | 58.30 | 30.40 | Cambrex CBM x | .12 | .3 | 21 | 777 | 38.81 | -0.13 |
| +5.4 | 39.50 | 28.13 | ▲CamdnProp CPT | 2.44 | 6.9 | 19 | 1531 | 35.32 | -0.41 |
| +41.3 | 28.43 | 14.25 | CamecoCp g CCJ | .50bg | ... | ... | 111 | 24.73 | -0.27 |
| -7.6 | 0.69 | 0.19 | CampbIRes CCH | ... | dd | 72 | 0.26 | +0.01 |
| -10.5 | 35.44 | 25.52 | CampblSoup CPB | .63m | 2.0 | 20 | 199729 | 31 | -0.25 |
| -5.1 | 31.26 | 23.06 | CanLifeFnl CLU | .52g | 2.0 | 10 | 22 | 26.46 | -0.27 |
| +5.3 | 36.95 | 28 | CIBC g BCM | 1.48g | ... | ... | 151 | 32.97 | -0.03 |
| +45.5 | 46.44 | 27.25 | CanNtlRlwy g CNI | .78g | ... | ... | 2051 | 43.21 | +0.49 |
| -8.2 | 34.51 | 23.96 | CndNatRes CED | .40g | 1.6 | 3 | 239 | 25.25 | -0.42 |
| -6.0 | 22.25 | 13.20 | CanPacRailwy n | ... | 1012 | 17.95 | -0.27 |
| -9.9 | 43.10 | 25 | Canon ADS CAJ | .19e | .6 | ... | 941 | 30.36 | -0.43 |
| -22.3 | 12.44 | 5.70 | CanwestGlbl g CWG | .30g | ... | ... | 12 | 6.12 | +0.06 |
| -24.4 | 72.58 | 36.40 | CapOneFnl COF | .11 | .2 | 18 | 46515 | 49.76 | +2.53 |
| -22.1 | 2.85 | 1.39 | CapSrLvng CSU | ... | dd | 47 | 1.90 | +0.05 |
| +3.7 | 6.50 | 4 | CapTr A CT | ... | 15 | 24 | 5.12 | +0.13 |
| +96.1 | 29.50 | 10.99 | CapstdMtg CMO s | 19.06e | 75.8 | 5 | 271 | 25.16 | -0.03 |
| -4.2 | 44.90 | 25.50 | CarboCermcs CRR | .36 | 1.0 | 20 | 222 | 35.85 | +0.75 |
| -3.8 | 77.32 | 56.67 | CardnlHlth CAH s | .10 | .2 | 32 | 73863 | 63.90 | -1.60 |
| -2.6 | 18.50 | 10.06 | CaremarkRx CMX | ... | 36 | 41603 | 13.21 | -0.49 |
| -27.3 | 45.69 | 25.52 | Carlisle CSL | .84f | 2.7 | 34 | 513 | 31.20 | +0.36 |
| -22.5 | 34.94 | 16.95 | Carnival CCL | .42 | 1.8 | 14 | 12685 | 23.88 | -0.50 |
| +1.3 | 26.25 | 24.75 | CarolPwr QUICS | 2.14 | 8.5 | ... | 128 | 25.25 | +0.02 |
| -33.7 | 38.25 | 19.80 | CarpTch CRS | 1.32 | 5.7 | 21 | 684 | 23.20 | -0.18 |
| -7.9 | 33.29 | 27 | ▲CarrAmRlty CRE | 1.85 | 6.4 | 23 | 2739 | 28.85 | -0.18 |
| +306.4 | 8.74 | 1.06 | CarriagScv A CSV | ... | dd | 738 | 6.35 | -0.12 |
| -43.7 | 16.75 | 8.40 | CascadeCp CAE | .40 | 4.4 | 10 | 313 | 9.04 | -0.06 |
| +5.8 | 22.50 | 17.31 | CascadeNG CGC | .96 | 4.8 | 13 | 133 | 19.90 | -0.60 |
| +86.5 | 10.50 | 3.63 | CashAmInt PWN | .05 | .6 | dd | 465 | 8.16 | -0.09 |
| -26.7 | 41 | 24 | CatalinaMktg POS | ... | 31 | 919 | 28.54 | +0.11 |
| -2.3 | 19.63 | 15.50 | ▲CatellusDev CDX | ... | 21 | 2672 | 17.90 | +0.20 |
| +2.1 | 56.83 | 34.56 | Caterpillar CAT | 1.40 | 2.9 | 19 | 24066 | 48.30 | +0.51 |
| +20.9 | 3.50 | 0.75 | CavlrHomes CAV | j | ... | dd | 184 | 2.65 | +0.10 |
| +12.5 | 23.50 | 17.75 | CedarFair FUN | 1.64f | 7.9 | 17 | 414 | 20.65 | +0.15 |
| -15.9 | 23.76 | 13.91 | Celanese CZ | .35e | 2.3 | ... | 438 | 15.40 | +0.20 |
| -30.2 | 79.44 | 19.30 | CelGenApplera CRA | ... | dd | 5435 | 25.23 | +0.20 |
| -25.8 | 76.40 | 20.69 | ▲Celestica CLS | ... | 82 | 30378 | 40.28 | +0.30 |
| -9.5 | 45 | 14.80 | Celltech ADS CLL | ... | 44 | 29.40 | -0.40 |
| +30.1 | 28.30 | 17.13 | ▲Cemex ADS CX | .96e | 4.1 | ... | 3901 | 23.50 | +0.23 |
| +44.8 | 21.53 | 8.63 | Cendant CD | ... | 14 | 60397 | 13.94 | +0.09 |
| -21.5 | 49.75 | 33.80 | Cendant DECS JCD n | ... | ... | 1479 | 38.39 | +0.69 |
| -16.8 | 6.45 | 3.25 | ▲CenterTr CTA | .16 | 4.1 | 33 | 151 | 3.90 | +0.36 |
| +1.4 | 50.90 | 44.25 | CtrotProo CNT | 2.10 | 4.4 | 21 | 730 | 47.91 | -0.09 |
| -23.4 | 25.24 | 16.30 | ▲CrescentRE CEI | 1.50m | 8.8 | 9 | 2097 | 17.05 | +0.01 |
| +9.1 | 31.90 | 20.25 | CrsttnCap CLJ | ... | 3 | 91 | 28.10 | +0.03 |
| -62.9 | 16.51 | 2.50 | Crimi CMM s | ... | 3697 | 2.60 | -0.05 |
| +0.1 | 20.75 | 14.00 | Crls/Ckte ADR CGW | .65e | 3.9 | ... | 90 | 16.70 | +0.96 |
| -28.8 | 12.94 | 9.54 | Cromptpn CK | .20 | 2.7 | dd | 1478 | 7.48 | -0.12 |
| +5.8 | 23.20 | 13.63 | CrpsTimRlty CRT s | 2.45e | 14.4 | ... | 45 | 17 | -0.08 |
| +43.1 | 8.72 | 5.13 | ▲CrownAmRlty CWN | .84 | 11.1 | ... | 224 | 7.60 | -0.18 |
| -61.4 | 32.25 | 7.40 | CrownCastl CCI | ... | dd | 23103 | 10.44 | -0.56 |
| -79.0 | 9.75 | 1.23 | ▲CrownCork CCK | j | ... | dd | 9409 | 1.56 | -0.24 |
| -48.2 | 17.75 | 4.62 | ▲CrownPac CRO | j | ... | dd | 1458 | 4.63 | -0.11 |
| +5.6 | 44.82 | 20 | CryoLife CRY s | ... | 64 | 904 | 31.95 | -0.87 |
| -33.1 | 43.44 | 23.61 | ▲CullnFrst CFR | .86 | 3.1 | 16 | 1634 | 27.98 | +0.33 |
| +15.0 | 5.25 | 1.63 | Culp CFI | .14 | 6.1 | dd | 5 | 2.30 | +0.01 |
| -8.7 | 45.50 | 28 | Cummins CUM | 1.20 | 3.5 | dd | 2090 | 34.65 | +0.15 |
| -5.6 | 53.70 | 39.82 | ▲CurtWright CW | .52 | 1.2 | 12 | 903 | 43.90 | -0.65 |
| -2.1 | 45 | 44.75 | CurtWright wi CWB@ | ... | ... | 538 | 43.80 | -0.96 |
| +17.1 | 39.69 | 13.72 | CyprsSemi CY | ... | dd | 28110 | 23.06 | +1.09 |
| -37.5 | 41.31 | 19 | ▲CytecInd CYT | ... | 8 | 1771 | 24.95 | -0.37 |

## -D-D-D-

| YTD %CHG | 52 WEEKS HI | LO | STOCK (SYM) | DIV | YLD % | PE | VOL 100s | LAST | NET CHG |
|---|---|---|---|---|---|---|---|---|---|
| -28.5 | 33.81 | 22.05 | ▲DPL Inc DPL | .94 | 4.0 | ... | 2487 | 23.73 | -0.51 |
| -43.3 | 36.75 | 18.15 | ▲DQE DQE | 1.58 | 9.0 | 5 | 3047 | 18.57 | -0.27 |
| -36.7 | 74.94 | 36.25 | DST Sys DST | ... | 22 | 4349 | 42.44 | -1.06 |
| +6.8 | 47.13 | 33.13 | DTE Engy DTE | 2.06 | 5.0 | 24 | 5612 | 41.59 | -0.04 |
| -6.3 | 18 | 12.95 | ▲DVI Inc DVI | ... | 13 | 756 | 15.99 | -0.26 |
| -0.3 | 25.90 | 24.40 | LehCBTCS 2001-9 n | .78e | 3.1 | ... | 37 | 25.17 | +0.07 |
| -12.0 | 52.72 | 25.60 | OmIrChrylr DCX | 2.08e | 5.7 | ... | 4431 | 36.25 | +0.16 |
| +25.1 | 19.49 | 11.31 | ▲DalTile DTL | ... | 12 | 1820 | 17.75 | +0.01 |
| -71.2 | 3.25 | 0.65 | DanRivr A DRF | ... | dd | 670 | 0.64 | -0.03 |
| -28.3 | 26.90 | 10.25 | ▲Dana Cp DCN | .04m | .4 | dd | 11092 | 10.98 | -0.16 |
| -15.2 | 69.81 | 43.90 | Danaher DHR | .08 | .1 | 24 | 6348 | 57.97 | -0.53 |
| -23.6 | 31 | 22.70 | Danone ADS DA | .33e | 1.4 | ... | 128 | 23.47 | -0.32 |
| +39.9 | 32.50 | 19 | Darden DRI | .08 | .3 | 19 | 3662 | 32 | -0.07 |
| -37.7 | 12.25 | 5.19 | ▲DaveBusters DAB | ... | 7 | 151 | 6.85 | +0.02 |
| +13.9 | 22.73 | 10.38 | DaVita DVA | ... | 15 | 6382 | 19.50 | -0.30 |
| -15.9 | 9.10 | 4.75 | DeRigo ADR DER | .10e | 1.6 | ... | 7 | 6.20 | -0.01 |
| +47.0 | 46.95 | 26 | DeanFood DF | .90 | 2.0 | 26 | 2189 | 45.10 | -0.25 |
| -11.1 | 47.13 | 33.50 | Deere DE | .88 | 2.2 | 30 | 7130 | 40.74 | +0.28 |
| +10.6 | 11.50 | 5.97 | DelMnteFood DLM | ... | 7929 | 8.02 | -0.03 |
| +7.3 | 61.40 | 50 | DelhzeFrs ADS DEG n | 1.19p | ... | ... | 157 | 54.61 | -0.64 |
| +8.8 | 17.50 | 9.50 | ▲DelphiAuto DPH | .28 | 2.3 | dd | 10284 | 12.24 | -0.06 |
| -18.8 | 42.25 | 26.45 | ▲DelphiFnl DFG | .28 | .9 | dd | 230 | 31.25 | -0.73 |
| -46.8 | 52.94 | 20 | DeltaAir DAL | .10 | .4 | dd | 23157 | 25.69 | +1.49 |
| -17.2 | 26.30 | 19.75 | LehCBTCS 2001-6 CYA n | ... | 40 | 20.40 | -0.55 |
| -14.4 | 26.80 | 16.17 | Delta&Pine DLP | .16 | .9 | 23 | 278 | 17.93 | -0.15 |
| -24.4 | 1.56 | 0.75 | DeltaWdsde DLW | ... | dd | 32 | 0.85 | ... |
| +8.1 | 29.90 | 18.94 | DelticTimber DEL | .25 | 1.0 | 36 | 45 | 25.80 | +0.10 |
| ▲+8.0 | 36.35 | 17.31 | DeluxeCp DLX s | 1.48 | 4.0 | 18 | 3801 | 37.13 | +0.79 |
| -28.2 | 12.30 | 6.63 | ▲DnbryRes DNR | ... | 2 | 536 | 7.90 | +0.20 |
| -43.7 | 15.88 | 5.90 | Dept56 DFS | ... | 5 | 721 | 6.47 | -0.06 |
| ▲+13.4 | 61.60 | 51.90 | DtscheBK DB n | ... | 595 | 62.28 | +0.68 |
| -44.8 | 37.31 | 12.91 | ▲DtscheTel ADR DT | .56e | 3.5 | ... | 13901 | 16.16 | +0.51 |
| +39.6 | 19.22 | 11.63 | DevDivRlty DDR | 1.48 | 8.0 | 15 | 1113 | 18.53 | -0.39 |
| -24.8 | 41.50 | 26.75 | DeVry DV | ... | 33 | 3991 | 28.40 | -0.25 |
| -5.4 | 45.49 | 36.63 | Diageo ADS DEO | 1.44e | 3.4 | ... | 4501 | 41.99 | +0.02 |
| +78.5 | 53.25 | 20.38 | DiagnstPdt DP s | .24 | .5 | ... | 926 | 48.76 | -0.24 |
| +55.5 | 18.78 | 10 | DialCp DL | .16 | .9 | dd | 2633 | 17.10 | -0.16 |
| -32.2 | 45.65 | 22.83 | DmndOffshr DO | .50 | 1.8 | 22 | 10300 | 27.12 | +0.95 |
| +12.1 | 40.50 | 25.25 | Diebold DBD | .64 | 1.7 | 31 | 2967 | 37.40 | -0.44 |
| +52.0 | 21.50 | 11.50 | DillrdCapTr DDT | 1.88 | 9.4 | ... | 90 | 19.95 | -0.06 |
| +17.4 | 22.50 | 9.94 | Dillards DDS | .16 | 1.2 | 21 | 3247 | 13.87 | -0.03 |
| +18.0 | 43 | 22.43 | DimeBcp DME | .48 | 1.4 | 12 | 4315 | 34.59 | +0.29 |
| +17.5 | 11.61 | 2.88 | ▲Dimon DMN | .20 | 3.1 | 9 | 811 | 6.46 | ... |
| ▲+236.5 | 18.95 | 4.88 | DiscntAuto DAP | ... | 15 | 1155 | 16.51 | -0.44 |
| -36.2 | 38.25 | 15.50 | Disney DIS | .21 | 1.1 | 92 | 91691 | 18.46 | -0.29 |
| -34.2 | 18.38 | 10.10 | Dist&Srv ADR DYS | .14e | 1.2 | ... | 155 | 11.48 | +0.36 |
| +21.8 | 24.37 | 11.75 | DoleFood DOL | .40 | 2.0 | dd | 8472 | 19.94 | -0.06 |
| -22.0 | 24.05 | 10.50 | DlrGenl DG | .13 | .9 | 24 | 8722 | 14.73 | -0.37 |
| -41.2 | 25.78 | 8.40 | ▲DlrThrfty DTG | ... | 8 | 435 | 11.03 | -0.47 |
| +22.3 | 25.05 | 14.25 | DominResVA DOM | 3.23e | 17.1 | ... | 267 | 18.90 | +0.15 |
| -9.4 | 69.99 | 55.13 | ▲DominRes D | 2.58 | 4.3 | 19 | 6467 | 60.70 | -1.17 |
| -1.9 | 66.56 | 55.50 | ▲DominRes PIES | 5.19e | 8.5 | ... | 30 | 61.34 | -0.01 |
| -8.4 | 10.71 | 6.80 | ▲Domtar g DTC | .14g | ... | ... | 228 | 8.42 | +0.07 |

Table 14-3

# EXPLANATORY NOTES

The following explanations apply to New York exchange listed issues, the Nasdaq Stock Market and to some fields in the American exchange list. NYSE and Amex prices are composite quotations that include trades on the Chicago, Pacific, Philadelphia, Boston and Cincinnati exchanges and reported by the National Association of Securities Dealers. Stock quotations are expressed in decimal form.

**Boldfaced quotations** highlight those issues whose price changed by 5% or more if their previous closing price was $2 or higher.

**Underlined quotations** are those stocks with large changes in volume, per exchange, compared with the issue's average trading volume. The calculation includes common stocks of $5 a share or more with an average volume over 65 trading days of at least 5,000 shares. The underlined quotations are for the 40 largest volume percentage leaders on the NYSE and the Nasdaq National Market. It includes the 20 largest volume percentage gainers on the Amex.

**YTD percentage change** reflects the stock price percentage change for the calendar year to date, adjusted for stock splits and dividends over 10%.

**The 52-week high and low** columns show the highest and lowest price of the issue during the preceding 52 weeks plus the current week, but not the latest trading day. These ranges are adjusted to reflect stock payouts of 1% or more, and cash dividends or other distributions of 10% or more.

**Dividend/Distribution rates,** unless noted, are annual disbursements based on the last monthly, quarterly, semiannual, or annual declaration. Special or extra dividends or distributions, incuding return of capital, special situations or payments not designated as regular are identified by footnotes.

**Yield** is defiend as the dividends or other distributions paid by a company on its securities, expressed as a percentage of price.

**The P/E ratio** is determined by dividing the closing market price by the company's diluted per-share earnings, as available, for the most recent four quarters. Charges and other adjustments usually are excluded when they qualify as extraordinary items under generally accepted accounting rules.

**Sales figures** are the unofficial daily total of shares traded, quoted in hundreds (two zeros omitted; f-four zeros omitted.)

Exchange ticker symbols are shown for all New York and American exchange common stocks, and Dow Jones News/Retrieval symbols are listed for Class A and Class B shares listed on both markets. Nasdaq symbols are listed for all Nasdaq NMS issues. A more detailed explanation of Nasdaq ticker symbols appears with the NMS listings.

**Footnotes: ↑-**New 52-week high. **↓-**New 52-week low. **a-**Extra dividend or extras in addition to the regular dividend. **b-**indicates annual rate of the cash dividend and that a stock dividend was paid. **c-**Liquidating dividend. **cc-**P/E ratio is 100 or more. **dd-**Loss in the most recent four quarters. **e-**indicates a dividend was declared in the preceding 12 months, but that there isn't a regular dividend rate. Amount shown may have been adjusted to reflect stock split, spinoff or other distribution. **FD-**First day of trading. **f-**Annual rate, increased on latest declaration. **g-**indicates the dividend and earnings are expressed in Canadian money. The stock trades in U.S. dollars. No yield or P/E ratio is shown. **gg-**Special sales condition; no regular way trading. **h-**Temporary exemption from Nasdaq requirements. **i-**indicates amount declared or paid after a stock dividend or split. **j-**indicates dividend was paid this year, and that at the last dividend meeting a dividend was omitted or deferred. **k-**indicates dividend declared this year on cumulative issues with dividends in arrears. **m-**Annual rate, reduced on latest declaration. **n-**Newly issued in the past 52 weeks. The high-low range begins with the start of trading and doesn't cover the entire period. **p-**Initial dividend; no yield calculated. **pf-**Preferred. **pp-**Holder owes installment(s) of purchase price. **pr-**Preference. **r-**Indicates a cash dividend declared in the preceding 12 months, plus a stock dividend. **rt-**Rights. **s-**Stock split or stock dividend, or cash or cash equivalent distribution, amounting to 10% or more in the past 52 weeks. The high-low price is adjusted from the old stock. Dividend calculations begin with the date the split was paid or the stock dividend occured. **stk-**Paid in stock in the last 12 months. Company doesn't pay cash dividend. **un-**Units. **v-**Trading halted on primary market. **vj-**In bankruptcy or receivership or being reorganized under the Bankruptcy Code, or securties assumed by such companies. **wd-**When distributed. **wi-**When issued. **wt-**Warrants. **ww-**With warrants. **x-**Ex-dividend, ex-distribution, ex-rights or without warrants. **z-**Sales in full, not in 100s.

Table 14-4

# PREFERRED STOCK LISTINGS

Thursday, November 8, 2001

## AMEX

| STOCK | DIV | YLD | CLOSE | CHG |
|---|---|---|---|---|
| Alcoa pf | 3.75 | 5.6 | 66.75 | +0.25 |
| AmCoinTrl pf | 1.05 | 12.5 | 8.40 | −0.10 |
| Baylake TruPs | .62p | ... | 11.25 | ... |
| Bremer CapTr pf | ... | | 26.50 | +0.05 |
| CarolP&L pf | 5.00 | 6.9 | 72 | ... |
| CntlMEPwr pf | 3.50 | 7.2 | 48.50 | −0.50 |
| ClrdoBus pf | 1.00 | 9.7 | 10.35 | +0.05 |
| EBI CapTr pf | 2.13 | 10.0 | 21.40 | +1.40 |
| EBH pfA | .75 | 8.6 | 8.75 | +0.10 |
| FCB/NC CapTrll | ... | | 26.25 | −0.15 |
| GlcrWtrTr pf | 2.27 | 11.4 | 20 | +0.20 |
| IndepCap pf | .85 | 8.8 | 9.70 | −0.30 |
| IntrustCap pf | 2.06 | 8.0 | 25.75 | +0.30 |
| KBK Cap pf | .95 | 12.3 | 7.75 | ... |
| KinamGold pfB | j | ... | 10 | ... |
| MBHI Cap pf | 2.50 | 9.4 | 26.50 | ... |
| MrLy Sellnx2006 | ... | | 8.85 | +0.19 |
| MerLyStratNts 04 | ... | | 8.51 | +0.06 |
| MerLyStrat | ... | | 10 | ... |
| MerLyInstitHol | ... | | 9.10 | ... |
| MerLySelTen | ... | | 8.44 | −0.06 |
| Metromedia pf | j | ... | 7.25 | +0.13 |
| MongPwr pfA | 4.40 | 6.4 | 68.50 | −4.50 |
| MongPwr pfC | 4.50 | 6.5 | 69 | −4.75 |
| MSDW QCOM | 2.12e | 8.1 | 26.10 | −0.14 |
| NewSoTr pfA | .85 | 8.9 | 9.50 | +0.27 |
| NolN PS pf | 4.25 | 6.9 | 61.55 | +1.00 |
| PG&E Cap pfA | j | ... | 19.36 | −0.14 |
| PS BusParks pfA | 2.31 | 9.1 | 25.51 | +0.01 |
| PS BusParks pfD | '94e | 3.6 | 26.20 | −0.04 |
| PacEnt pfC | 4.50 | 8.1 | 55.50 | −5.25 |
| PacGE pfA | j | | 16.03 | +0.01 |
| PacGE pfC | j | | 13.50 | −0.25 |
| PacGE pfD | j | | 13.45 | −0.50 |
| PacGE pfE | j | | 13.51 | −0.24 |
| PacGE pfG | j | | 12.85 | −0.15 |
| PacGE pfI | j | | 11.56 | −0.26 |
| PacGE pfU | j | | 19 | −0.25 |
| QuadCityCap | .92 | 9.2 | 10 | −0.25 |
| SY Bcp | ... | | 11.65 | −0.15 |
| SlmnSmBr nts | ... | | 15.45 | +0.20 |
| SlmnSmBr nts06 | ... | | 7.58 | +0.18 |
| SanDgoGE pfB | .90 | 7.5 | 12 | −0.80 |
| SoCA Ed GUIDS | ... | | 19.05 | −0.05 |
| SoCA Ed pfC | j | | 11.60 | −0.20 |
| SoCA Ed pfD | j | | 11.60 | −0.30 |
| SoCA Ed pfE | j | | 12.92 | −0.18 |
| SoCapTr pfA | .83 | 8.1 | 10.25 | +0.15 |
| SpktrmCap pf | 1.00 | 9.6 | 10.40 | +0.34 |

| STOCK | DIV | YLD | CLOSE | CHG |
|---|---|---|---|---|
| StmhavnRlty pfA | .95 | 18.3 | 5.20 | −0.05 |
| SumSource pf | 2.90 | 11.6 | 25 | −0.01 |
| TDS Cap pfA | 2.13 | 8.5 | 25 10 | ... |
| TDS Cap pfB | 2.01 | 8.1 | 24.94 | −0.01 |
| ToledoEd pfD | 10.00 | 9.3 | 107.10 | +0.10 |
| ToledoEd pfA | 8.32 | 8.1 | 102.50 | +1.00 |
| US HomGrdn pfA | 2.35 | 18.5 | 12.70 | +0.10 |

## NASDAQ

| STOCK | DIV | YLD | CLOSE | CHG |
|---|---|---|---|---|
| ABI Cap pf | .85 | 8.8 | 9.65 | ... |
| BBC Cap pf | 2.38 | 9.6 | 24.75 | −0.10 |
| BNB Cap pf | .95 | 9.4 | 10.15 | +0.05 |
| BkUtdCap pfB | 2.40 | 9.5 | 25.32 | +0.17 |
| CapCross pf | 1.03 | 9.9 | 10.45 | −0.10 |
| CityHldg pf | j | ... | 18.45 | +0.10 |
| CstlBcp cum pfA | 2.28 | 9.1 | 25 | +0.10 |
| CstlBcp pfA | 2.25 | 9.0 | 25.01 | −0.14 |
| DuraAuto pf | 1.88 | 11.1 | 17 | +0.15 |
| Dynex pfA | .29e | 1.7 | 16.73 | +0.08 |
| Dynex pfB | .29e | 1.7 | 17 | −0.05 |
| Dynex pfC | .36e | 1.7 | 21 | +0.15 |
| EmmComm pfA | 3.13 | 11.9 | 26.20 | −0.20 |
| FB Cap pf | .98 | 9.8 | 10.01 | ... |
| FstBks pf | 2.31 | 9.0 | 25.75 | −0.25 |
| FstCtyFnl pf | j | ... | 7.12 | +0.12 |
| GBCI Cap pf | 2.19e | 9.0 | 24.20 | +0.44 |
| GBB Capi pf | 2.44 | 9.5 | 25.69 | −0.07 |
| GrSoCapTr pf | .90 | 8.5 | 10.55 | ... |
| GtrCmtyBcp pf | 2.50 | 9.9 | 25.20 | −0.35 |
| HanckHldg pfA | .40p | ... | 24.50 | +0.25 |
| IndCapl pf | 2.32 | 9.1 | 25.40 | +0.29 |
| Integra Cap pf | 2.06 | 8.3 | 24.90 | −0.05 |
| Jamesnlnn pfA | 2.31 | 14.7 | 15.74 | +0.49 |
| Jamesnlnn pfS | 1.70 | 14.3 | 11.85 | −0.60 |
| Lakeland pf | .90 | 8.9 | 10.16 | ... |
| LtchfldCap pf | ... | | 10.50 | ... |
| MCI QUIPS | 2.00 | 8.2 | 24.49 | ... |
| Mariner pf | .83 | 8.4 | 9.85 | +0.15 |
| MasDix pf | 2.52 | 8.6 | 29.22 | +0.10 |
| MasDixll pf | 1.68 | 8.4 | 20 | +0.35 |
| MatrixBcp pf | 2.50 | 10.0 | 24.92 | +0.32 |
| McLeodUSA pf stk | ... | | 22 | ... |
| Middltn pfA | 2.13 | 11.5 | 18.50 | −0.75 |
| MpowerHldg pfD | j | ... | 0.80 | +0.20 |
| NPB Cap pf | 2.25e | 8.7 | 25.75 | +0.25 |
| NHTB Cap | e | ... | 10.50 | +0.40 |
| PCC Cap pf | .94 | 9.4 | 10 | +0.15 |
| PFBI CapTr | 2.44 | 9.9 | 24.70 | +0.50 |
| PeopBcsh pf | .98 | 9.5 | 10.35 | +0.37 |
| PeopPfd pfA | 2.44 | 9.9 | 24.55 | −0.06 |
| Popular pfA | 2.09 | 7.8 | 26.95 | +0.40 |
| PriceLegacy pf | 1.40 | 9.4 | 14.95 | +0.01 |

| STOCK | DIV | YLD | CLOSE | CHG |
|---|---|---|---|---|
| ProFac A pf | 1.72 | 10.2 | 16.90 | +0.10 |
| SndySprgCap | 2.34 | 8.7 | 27 | ... |
| SlmnFrst pf | 1.14 | 8.8 | 13 | ... |
| SmurfitStn A | 1.75e | 9.1 | 19.25 | +0.25 |
| SterBcsh pf | 2.32 | 9.1 | 25.50 | −0.45 |
| SuccesCap pf | .90 | 9.5 | 9.45 | −0.15 |
| SunCap pf | 2.46 | 9.8 | 25 | −0.10 |
| W Hldg pfC | ... | | 25.45 | −0.18 |
| WstBk pf | .96 | 9.0 | 10.66 | +0.21 |
| WintrstCap pf | 2.25 | 8.7 | 25.90 | +0.40 |

## NYSE

| STOCK | DIV | YLD | CLOSE | CHG |
|---|---|---|---|---|
| ABN Am pfA | 1.88 | 7.4 | 25.50 | +0.01 |
| ABN Am pfB | 1.78 | 7.1 | 25.10 | +0.10 |
| ACE CapTr | 2.22 | 8.3 | 26.70 | −0.06 |
| ACE LtdPRIDES | 4.13 | 5.1 | 81.50 | −0.35 |
| AGL Cap TruPs | .97e | 3.8 | 25.59 | −0.10 |
| AICI CapTr pf | 2.25 | 13.5 | 16.65 | −0.07 |
| AK Steel pfB | 3.63 | 9.3 | 39 | +2.00 |
| AMB Prop pfA | 2.13 | 8.4 | 25.35 | −0.10 |
| AMR PINES | 1.97 | 9.9 | 20 | −0.15 |
| ANZ pf | 2.00 | 7.8 | 25.59 | −0.19 |
| ANZ II pf | 2.02 | 7.8 | 25.79 | −0.06 |
| AT&T 8 1/4 PNS | 2.06 | 7.9 | 26.03 | +0.07 |
| AT&T 8 1/8 PNS | 2.03 | 7.9 | 25.70 | −0.10 |
| AbbeyNtl pfA | 2.19 | 8.3 | 26.24 | +0.06 |
| Aetna nts | .96e | 3.8 | 25.41 | −0.19 |
| Agrium COPrS | 2.00 | 8.7 | 23.11 | +0.01 |
| AL PwrCap pfA | 1.90 | 7.6 | 25 | −0.05 |
| AL PwrCap pfB | 1.84 | 7.3 | 25.05 | −0.25 |
| AL Pwr pfD | 1.46 | 6.3 | 23.15 | +0.10 |
| AL Pwr ntsA | 1.78 | 7.1 | 25.16 | −0.09 |
| AL Pwr ntsB | 1.75 | 7.0 | 25 | −0.05 |
| AL Pwr ntsC | 1.75 | 7.0 | 25 | +0.10 |
| AL Pwr ntsJ | 1.69 | 6.6 | 25.77 | +0.17 |
| AlbEngy pfA g | 2.38 | ... | 27.40 | +0.30 |
| AlexRlEstEq pfA | 2.38 | 9.0 | 26.35 | +0.35 |
| ALLETE QUIPS | 2.01 | 8.0 | 25.20 | ... |
| Allstate QUIBS | 1.78 | 7.1 | 25.10 | +0.06 |
| AllstFng QUIPS | 1.99 | 7.9 | 25.30 | ... |
| AllstFng CorTS | ... | | 26.90 | +0.15 |
| Amerco pfA | 2.13 | 8.6 | 24.80 | +0.05 |
| AmAnnuity TOPrS | 2.32 | 9.4 | 24.70 | ... |
| AmExpress pfA | 1.75 | 7.0 | 25.06 | −0.04 |
| AmFnlCap TOPrS | 2.28 | 9.2 | 24.65 | +0.02 |
| AmGenl TOPRS A | 1.97 | 7.4 | 26.65 | −0.10 |
| AmGenCap TruPs | 1.64e | 6.1 | 27.09 | −0.01 |
| AmReCap QUIPS | 2.13 | 8.3 | 25.55 | +0.15 |
| AmWtrWks pfB | 1.25 | 5.4 | 23 | ... |
| ApacheCp pfC | 2.02 | 4.7 | 42.79 | −1.01 |
| Apartmtlnv pfC | 2.25 | 9.3 | 24.09 | +0.09 |
| Apartmtlnv pfD | 2.19 | 9.2 | 23.70 | −0.03 |

| STOCK | DIV | YLD | CLOSE | CHG |
|---|---|---|---|---|
| Apartmtlnv pfG | 2.34 | 9.5 | 24.72 | +0.22 |
| Apartmtlnv pfH | 2.38 | 9.7 | 24.60 | +0.06 |
| Aptlnv CIQ Pfd. | 2.25 | 9.6 | 23.35 | −0.14 |
| Aptlnv CIQ Pfd | 1.23e | 4.9 | 25.32 | +0.07 |
| Apartmtlnv pf | .38e | 1.5 | 25.05 | −0.10 |
| AppalchPwr ntsA | 1.80 | 7.3 | 24.69 | ... |
| AppalchPwr pfA | 2.06 | 8.2 | 25.25 | −0.10 |
| AppalchPwr ntsB | 1.83 | 7.4 | 24.80 | +0.16 |
| AppalchPwr pfB | 2.00 | 7.8 | 25.50 | +0.15 |
| Archstone pfC | 2.16 | 8.5 | 25.30 | +0.10 |
| ArchstoneSmith pfA | 2.21 | 6.6 | 33.65 | +0.15 |
| ArchstoneSmith pfD | 2.19 | 8.4 | 26 | −0.05 |
| ArmWldInd QUIBS | 1.86 | 18.8 | 9.90 | −0.14 |
| AssocEstate pf | 2.44 | 9.8 | 25 | ... |
| Aus&NZ Bk pf | 2.28 | 8.5 | 26.75 | −0.15 |
| AvalnBay pfC | 2.13 | 8.4 | 25.40 | −0.16 |
| AvalnBay pfD | 2.00 | 7.9 | 25.37 | −0.01 |
| AvalnBay pfH | 2.17 | 8.1 | 26.86 | −0.05 |
| Avista pfA | 1.97 | 8.9 | 22.26 | +1.21 |
| BBVA pfA | 1.96 | 7.8 | 25 | −0.18 |
| BCH Cap pfA | 2.63 | 10.0 | 26.20 | −0.15 |
| BCH Cap pfB | 2.36 | 8.5 | 27.75 | −0.05 |
| BCH Int pfA | 2.47 | 9.5 | 26.09 | ... |
| BGE Cap pfA | 1.79 | 7.1 | 25.16 | ... |
| BNYCapTr pfE | 1.72 | 6.8 | 25.15 | +0.12 |
| BRE Prop pfA | 2.13 | 8.2 | 25.90 | ... |
| BSCH Fin pfC | 2.03 | 8.1 | 25.05 | −0.11 |
| BSCH Fin pfD | 2.19 | 8.5 | 25.70 | −0.15 |
| BSCH Fin pfE | 2.13 | 8.4 | 25.50 | +0.24 |
| BSCH Fin pfF | 2.03 | 8.0 | 25.47 | +0.15 |
| BSCH Fin pfG | 2.03 | 7.9 | 25.60 | ... |
| BSCH Fin pfH | 1.95 | 7.9 | 24.60 | +0.05 |
| BSCH Fin pfJ | 1.84 | 7.5 | 24.45 | +0.20 |
| BSCH Fin pfQ | 2.16 | 8.4 | 25.77 | +0.20 |
| BcoBilV pfA | 2.44 | 9.6 | 25.30 | ... |
| BcoBilV pfB | 2.25 | 8.5 | 26.40 | −0.10 |
| BcoBilV pfC | 2.00 | 7.9 | 25.35 | +0.05 |
| BcoBilV pfE | 2.00 | 7.9 | 25.38 | +0.03 |
| BancwestCap pf | 1.74e | 6.4 | 27.30 | +0.01 |
| BkAmCap TOPrS | 1.94 | 7.7 | 25.35 | +0.07 |
| BankAm TOPrS | 1.75 | 6.9 | 25.25 | −0.08 |
| BNY CapII pfC | 1.95 | 7.6 | 25.74 | ... |
| BNY CapIII pfD | 1.76 | 6.9 | 25.34 | +0.13 |
| BankOneCap pf | 1.50e | 5.7 | 26.31 | −0.01 |
| BkOneCap | 2.00 | 7.6 | 26.19 | −0.11 |
| BnkOne pf II | 2.13 | 7.6 | 28 | +0.30 |
| BnkOne pf VI | ... | | 24.96 | −0.09 |
| BT Cap pfA | 2.03 | 8.0 | 25.35 | −0.02 |
| BkUtdCap pfC | 2.25 | 9.1 | 24.85 | ... |
| Barclays pf | 2.00 | 7.5 | 26.60 | +0.25 |
| BBVA Pfd. | .49p | ... | 25.40 | −0.06 |
| BearStearn Trll | 1.88 | 7.5 | 25.15 | +0.05 |

Table 14-5

# AMERICAN STOCK EXCHANGE COMPOSITE TRANSACTIONS

Composite Regular Trading
Wednesday, November 7, 2001

| STOCK | SYM | VOL 100s | LAST | CHG | STOCK | SYM | VOL 100s | LAST | CHG | STOCK | SYM | VOL 100s | LAST | CHG | STOCK | SYM | VOL 100s | LAST | CHG |
|---|---|---|---|---|---|---|---|---|---|---|---|---|---|---|---|---|---|---|---|
| **-A-B-C-** | | | | | AmpexCp A | AXC | 540 | 0.18 | +0.01 | BowlAm A | BWLA | 15 | 11.10 | +0.05 | Computrac | LLB | 80 | 0.31 | −0.04 |
| | | | | | AndreaElec | AND | 99 | 0.82 | −0.03 | BridgeVwBcp | BVB | 5 | 15.75 | −0.20 | Congoleum A | CGM | 2722 | 1.94 | −0.01 |
| | | | | | AntexBio | ANX | 208 | 1.70 | −0.10 | BrillntDgtl | BDE | 105 | 0.40 | +0.01 | ♣ConTomka | CTO | 54 | 18.42 | +0.02 |
| AMC Entn | AEN | 764 | 13.01 | +0.01 | AnworthMtg | ANH | 105 | 8.24 | +0.12 | ♣BritAmTob ADS | BTI | 2191 | 16.96 | +0.13 | ContangoO&G | MCF | 126 | 2.90 | ... |
| AMCON | DIT | 10 | 4.60 | ... | ApexMtg | AXM | 837 | 10.50 | −0.06 | ♣CE Frkln | CFK | 11 | 2.25 | ... | ♣ContlMatrl | CUO | 2 | 19.10 | +0.20 |
| ARV AsstLvg | SRS | 163 | 1.80 | +0.26 | ApexSilvr | SIL | 370 | 9.44 | +0.24 | CET Envr | ENV | 61 | 0.65 | +0.15 | Cntnucare | CNU | 140 | 0.45 | ... |
| AT Cross A | ATX | 180 | 4.85 | −0.18 | AppldGrphcs | AGD | 170 | 0.40 | ... | CPI Aero | CVU | 53 | 1.60 | +0.10 | CoreMatls | CME | 127 | 1.10 | −0.15 |
| ATEC Gp | TEC | 342 | 0.44 | ... | AquaCellTch | AQA | 10 | 4.70 | −0.19 | CabltelComm | TTV | 75 | 0.80 | ... | CortexPharm | COR | 86 | 2.81 | +0.01 |
| AT Plastics g | ATJ | 2 | 1.21 | +0.03 | ♣ArrhythRsch | HRT | 2 | 2.85 | ... | Calton Inc | CN | 67 | 0.51 | ... | CreatvCp | CAP | 11 | 0.45 | +0.10 |
| ATSI Comm | AI | 1923 | 0.30 | −0.01 | AtlTeleNtwk | ANK | 46 | 13.50 | ... | ♣Cambior | CBJ | 55 | 0.44 | −0.03 | CreditStr | CDS | 5 | 1 | ... |
| AXS One | AXO | 10 | 0.41 | +0.01 | AtlasPipeln | | 138 | 27.25 | −0.97 | Cdn88Engy | EEE | 612 | 1.31 | +0.06 | CrssMediaMktg | XVM | 1152 | 7.80 | +0.35 |
| ABC TRuPs | BHC+ | 72 | 10.30 | +0.20 | ♣AvinHldg A | AWX | 50 | 2.25 | ... | CannonExp A | A8 | 24 | 1.25 | +0.18 | ♣Crystllbxtnt | KRY | 1724 | 1.42 | +0.01 |
| ♣AblAuctions | AAC | 77 | 1.13 | −0.02 | **AvanirPhrm** | **AVN** | **463** | **3.25** | **−0.24** | ♣CanynRes | CAU | 27 | 1.13 | ... | ♣CubicCp | CUB | 49 | 36.88 | −0.12 |
| AbraxasPete | ABP | 1092 | 1.52 | −0.06 | Avitar | AVR | 219 | 1.08 | −0.03 | ♣CapAIIncInc | CAA | 8 | 12.50 | −0.10 | Cybexintl | CYB | 31 | 1.20 | +0.19 |
| AccessPharm | AKC | 431 | 4.47 | +0.07 | AzcoMng | AZC | 1070 | 0.55 | −0.01 | ♣CapPacHldg | CPH | 44 | 3.99 | −0.01 | **-D-E-F-** | | | | |
| AcmeUtd | ACU | 2 | 3.06 | −0.09 | B&H Ocean | BHO | 4 | 5.39 | +0.14 | CapitalPrpty | CPI | 11 | 9.39 | +0.14 | | | | | |
| AdvMagnet | AVM | 8 | 3.35 | −0.15 | ♣BNP ResProp | BNP | 16 | 10.28 | +0.13 | CarbonEngy | CRB | 1 | 9.39 | ... | ♣DCH Tch | DCH | 486 | 0.67 | −0.01 |
| ♣AdvPhotonix | API | 462 | 0.70 | −0.02 | ♣BadgerMeter | BMI | 42 | 20.05 | −0.15 | **Cardietech** | **CTE** | **736** | **2.20** | **−0.12** | ♣DRS Tch | DRS | 2231 | 37.95 | −0.95 |
| AdvtgMktg | AMM | 27 | 2.65 | ... | ♣BakerMichl | BKR | 42 | 13.50 | +0.15 | CareerEngine | CNE | 226 | 1.60 | +0.10 | DanlsnHldg | DHC | 67 | 3.50 | −0.05 |
| AegisRlty | AER | 78 | 11.19 | +0.04 | BalancCare | BAL | 9800 | 0.18 | +0.07 | Careside | CSA | 2 | 2.01 | +0.01 | ♣Darlingint | DAR | 3 | 0.75 | ... |
| ♣Aerocent | ACY | 42 | 5.23 | −0.02 | Balchem | BCP | 5 | 20.90 | ... | CarverBcp | CNY | 10 | 8.64 | −0.01 | DaxorCp | DXR | 5 | 16.80 | −0.18 |
| Aerosonic | AIM | 40 | 20.75 | +0.25 | ♣BaldwinTch | BLD | 205 | 0.90 | +0.05 | CashTch | TQ | 95 | 0.95 | −0.04 | DaytonMng | DAY | 84 | 0.29 | ... |
| AirnGlobalTch | AGT | 65 | 0.45 | ... | BarHrbr8ksh | BHB | 38 | 16.50 | +0.75 | CastleAM | CAS | 97 | 7.75 | −0.06 | Decoratrlnd | DII | 20 | 3.40 | +0.07 |
| **AlarisMed** | **AMI** | **882** | **2.75** | **−0.20** | ♣Barnwell | BRN | 10 | 18.10 | −0.20 | ♣CelSci | CVM | 871 | 1.12 | ... | DelLabs | DLI | 8 | 15.95 | +0.15 |
| AllncBcpNE | ANE | 3 | 10.70 | +0.10 | BaristrGlbl | BIS | 1 | 0.43 | ... | Celsion | CLN | 660 | 0.60 | ... | DeltaApprl | DLA | 2 | 18.70 | −0.15 |
| AlldRsch | ALR | 498 | 13.89 | −0.46 | ♣BaycpHldgs | MWH | 38 | 9.35 | −0.45 | ChadThraput | CTU | 383 | 3.10 | ... | `DepoMed | DMI | 80 | 5.50 | ... |
| ♣AllouHlth | ALU | 225 | 3.50 | −0.10 | BayouStl A | BYX | 1392 | 0.49 | −0.06 | ChartrMuni | CHC | 973 | 15.74 | +0.02 | DevonEngy | DVN | 7113 | 37.99 | +0.68 |
| ♣AlphaPro | APT | 103 | 1.18 | +0.02 | ♣BellIndus | BI | 295 | 2.01 | +0.07 | ChaseCp | CCF | 69 | 11.70 | +0.70 | ♣DeWolfe | DWL | 161 | 9.50 | +0.55 |
| Alteon | ALT | 103 | 3.04 | +0.04 | ♣BemaGold | BGO | 3550 | 0.40 | −0.01 | CheniereEngy | CXY | 68 | 1.05 | −0.07 | DiaSysCp | DYX | 66 | 0.47 | −0.03 |
| AlterraHlth | ALI | 470 | 0.18 | +0.02 | BennettEnvr | BEL | 121 | 4.20 | +0.25 | Chqemtelnt | DDD | 587 | 0.16 | −0.01 | DgtlPwr | DPW | 15 | 0.82 | +0.03 |
| AmBkCT | BKC | 66 | 31.70 | +0.20 | BntlyPharm | BNT | 125 | 8 | +0.03 | ChilesOffshr | COD | 7 | 18.91 | −0.09 | DixonTi | DXT | 20 | 1.70 | +0.10 |
| AmBiltrite | ABL | 8 | 10.59 | +0.14 | BrkshreHlls | BHL | 10 | 18.90 | −0.01 | Citadel A | CDLA | 2 | 1.75 | ... | ♣Drewlnd | DIW | 8 | 9.60 | −0.10 |
| ♣AmCmnlyProp | APO | 1 | 4.91 | −0.08 | BigCtyRad A | YFM | 2 | 1.50 | +0.05 | ♣Ctznslnc A | CIA | 96 | 9.30 | −0.05 | DriverHar | DRH | 10 | 1.10 | +0.05 |
| AmMtg 85 | AII | 119 | 7.60 | ... | BioAqua A | SEA | 178 | 2.55 | +0.06 | ClassicVacGp | CLV | 118 | 0.17 | ... | EFC Bcp | EFC | 2 | 12.60 | −0.15 |
| AmMtg | AIA | 21 | 2.55 | ... | BioAqua wt | | 20 | 0.24 | +0.14 | CoastDistr | CRV | 23 | 0.42 | ... | E-Medsoft | MED | 7875 | 1.20 | +0.03 |
| AmMtg 86 | AIJ | 52 | 3.61 | +0.01 | Bionova | BVA | 66 | 0.15 | −0.10 | **Cognitron** | **CGN** | **226** | **4.40** | **−0.75** | eResource | RCG | 563 | 0.27 | −0.01 |
| AmMtg88 | AIK | 26 | 5.60 | +0.11 | BioRadLab A | BIOA | 543 | 61 | −2.25 | ColdMetal | CLQ | 22 | 0.41 | −0.11 | EtzLavud | ETZ | 10 | 2.90 | −0.10 |
| AmIsrlPapr | AIP | 6 | 34.40 | +0.40 | Biotime | BTX | 202 | 5.05 | +0.10 | CoilgtPac | BOO | 4 | 5.35 | −0.06 | EXX inc A | EXXA | 13 | 0.67 | ... |
| AmMrtgage | AMC | 84 | 14.44 | −0.11 | BrmghmUt | BIW | 12 | 15.50 | −0.50 | ClmbiaLabs | COB | 440 | 4.40 | −0.20 | ♣EZEM A | EZMA | 50 | 6.85 | −0.38 |
| ♣AmSciEngrg | ASE | 741 | 19 | −0.80 | ♣BlairCp | BL | 313 | 15.75 | −0.50 | Comforce | CFS | 170 | 1.40 | −0.06 | ♣EZEM B | EZMB | 39 | 6 | ... |
| AmShrdHosp | AMS | 33 | 3.05 | ... | Blimpielnt | BLM | 271 | 2.64 | +0.02 | Commodore | CXI | 20 | 0.12 | ... | EglWrlsintl | EAG | 1367 | 0.79 | −0.06 |
| AmTchCeram | AMK | 126 | 10.20 | −0.45 | ♣BlndrTng | BDR | 144 | 3.74 | +0.09 | CmntyBkshSC | SCB | 4 | 11.65 | +0.20 | ♣EasternCo | EML | 1 | 12.20 | −0.10 |
| AT&T Fund | ATF | 73 | 115.45 | −1.95 | booktech.com | BTC | 246 | 0.06 | −0.01 | CmntyBk | CTY | 10 | 25.11 | −0.15 | EchoBayMn | ECO | 1028 | 0.64 | −0.02 |
| AmVngrd | AVD | 70 | 16.80 | −0.25 | BootsCoots | WEL | 409 | 0.54 | ... | CmntyCap | CYL | 56 | 10.40 | ... | ♣EcolgyEnvr | EEI | 67 | 11.12 | −0.03 |
| ♣AmeriVest | AMV | 86 | 5.65 | +0.10 | ♣BstnfdBcp | BFD | 10 | 22.80 | −0.20 | CompTch | CTT | 34 | 2.97 | −0.03 | EDT Lrng | EDT | 119 | 0.55 | +0.04 |
| | | | | | Boundless | BND | 47 | 1.04 | −0.01 | **CmptrThermal** | **C1O** | **972** | **2.05** | **−0.14** | ♣ElPasoElec | EE | 1137 | 13.49 | +0.04 |

bid price). The difference between the two quotes is called the **spread** and is the source of the market maker's profit. The bigger the spread, the bigger the profit on a purchase and sale. Spreads are directly related to the risk inherent in the quoted stock.

The OTC market was originally completely unregulated and unorganized. Dealers would make a market in specific stocks simply by announcing price quotations in that stock. The accepted method of communication was through the insertion of representative **bid-and-asked quotations** in a daily publication called the **pink sheets**. A broker with an order to fill would check the pink sheets to see which dealers were making a market and would then telephone one or more of them seeking the best price. For many years, this market functioned quietly, with virtually no information available as to actual prices at which trades occurred or to actual volumes of transactions in specific shares.

Today, most bid-and-asked quotations for OTC stocks appear in the **National Association of Securities Dealers Automated Quotation (NASDAQ)** system, a computerized quotation system. However, many quotations for less heavily traded stocks appear on a computerized bulletin board system that the NASD maintains and some that are even less actively traded continue to appear in the pink sheets. Today, pink sheet stocks trade quite infrequently (if at all). Indeed, many are not "publicly traded" in the usual sense. For example, there may be bid prices but no ask prices and vice versa. In any event, a broker with an order to buy or sell an OTC stock finds the best price quotation from a market maker, either from the NASDAQ screen or by using the telephone, and then places the order with the one with the best price. There may be more than one price in the OTC market, because for most stocks there are several market makers. The OTC market thus consists of a web of brokers and dealers dealing with each other by telephone or by computer.

The NASD was originally organized as a **self regulatory organization (SRO)** under authority granted in the federal securities laws. Over the years, however, the NASD came to promote NASDAQ as an alternative trading model, and as a result of controversy over trading practices, the regulatory and disciplinary functions of the NASD are formally split into two separate organizations, **NASD Regulation (NASDR)** and NASDAQ.

Because the OTC market is a dealer market in which the dealer acts as principal for its own account, dealer compensation was traditionally in the form of **markups** or **markdowns** rather than in the form of **commissions** as charged by brokers. If the dealer is a market maker, it profits on the spread between the bid and ask price, but if the firm that receives an order is not a market maker, the traditional practice was for the firm to contact a market maker, arrange for the purchase or sale of the stock in question, and then resell the stock (in the case of purchase) to the customer at a markup. To be sure, a non-market maker could handle such a trade as a broker, but competitive pressures generally limited the amount of commission that could be charged to about the same as charged by NYSE firms. These days, most OTC trades are brokered and a commission is charged. Indeed, a customer will often be charged a commission even if his or her firm is a market maker in the security.

## §14.13 The NASDAQ National Market

As a result of 1975 legislation aimed at deregulating the stock markets, the NASD developed the **NASDAQ National Market** for widely traded securities. The principal market makers for these securities now report actual trades and prices, and the reporting of such transactions is superficially indistinguishable from that of the exchanges. There are nearly 5,000 stocks in the National Market. The average National Market stock has 11 market makers, and over 200 heavily traded stocks have 26 or more. To be eligible for listing on the National Market, a company must have at least 400 holders of round lots, and meet one of three alternative sets of standards. Standard 1 requires $15 million of stockholders' equity, $1 million of pretax in latest fiscal year or 2 of last 3 years, a public float of 1.1 million shares with a market value of $8 million, and 400 or more holders of round lots. Standard 2 requires $30 million of shareholders' equity, a public float of 1.1 million shares with a market value of $18 million and an operating history of two years. Standard 2 does not require any specific level of pretax income. Standard 3 requires a market capitalization of $75 million and a public float valued at $20 million or more but no requirement of minimum shareholders' equity, pretax income, or operating history. As might be expected the standards for continued listing are somewhat relaxed (as they are on the NYSE). To continue to be listed, a company must have either (1) $10 million of stockholders' equity and a public float of 750,000 shares with a market value of $5 million, or (2) $50 million of market capitalization, and a public float of 1.1 million shares with a market value of $15 million.

The National Market has eclipsed the NYSE in size and number of listings. As of 2001, there are 4734 companies listed on the National Market as compared with 2,862 on the NYSE, and 765 listed on Amex. There are 2002 companies in the National Market with a capitalization above $100 million, 497 of which have capitalizations in excess of $1 billion.

The large national securities firms are major market makers in OTC securities. Some may make markets in more than 1,000 different securities at any one time, ranging from securities traded in the National Market System to securities primarily of regional or local interest. As of the end of 2001, there were more than 1000 market participants including 425 active market makers.

Table 14-1 reflects the November 7, 2001 activity in the NASDAQ National Market, and Table 14-6 shows the price quotations for numerous stocks in that market.

NASDAQ maintains a computerized order system known as the **Small Order Execution System (SOES),** which was developed in response to the 1987 crash when numerous NASDAQ market makers simply refused to accept orders. SOES differs from the NYSE DOT system in that the market maker who receives an SOES order is required to execute the order (up to a specified quantity depending on the stock). Thus, SOES is a limited automatic execution system.

In 1995, the Justice Department began an investigation of NASDAQ to determine whether market makers had colluded to fix prices. The investigation was prompted by an academic study that found "missing eighths" in the quotes

Table 14-6

# NASDAQ NATIONAL MARKET ISSUES

Composite Regular Trading
Wednesday, November 7, 2001

| YTD %CHG | 52 WEEKS HI | LO | STOCK (SYM) | DIV | YLD % | PE | VOL 100S | LAST | NET CHG |
|---|---|---|---|---|---|---|---|---|---|
| | | | **-A-A-A-** | | | | | | |
| + 89.7 | 23.22 | 6.50 | aaiPharma AAII | | ... | cc | 168 | 19.33 | − 0.61 |
| + 57.7 | 22.56 | 10.33 | AAON Inc AAON s | | ... | 12 | 273 | 16.80 | + 1.40 |
| + 33.9 | 13.50 | 8 | ABC Bcp ABCB | .48 | 3.8 | 11 | 481 | 12.55 | − 0.26 |
| − 55.2 | 15.13 | 2.65 | A B Wtly ABWG | | ... | dd | 152 | 3.05 | + 0.07 |
| − 48.5 | 4.75 | 0.69 | ACE COMM ACEC | | ... | dd | 118 | 1.19 | + 0.04 |
| + 171.5 | 23.50 | 5.75 ▲ AC MooreArt ACMR | | | ... | 26 | 169 | 22.23 | ± 0.27 |
| − 91.0 | 33.13 | 1.61 | ACT Mfg ACTM | | ... | dd | 18991 | 1.42 | − 0.22 |
| + 59.3 | 11.35 | 3.89 | ACT Telcnf ACTT | | ... | 47 | 2403 | 11.35 | + 0.35 |
| − 65.4 | 5.69 | 0.22 ▲ A CnsltgTm TACX | | | ... | dd | 105 | 0.40 | + 0.05 |
| + 38.5 | 3.63 | 1 | Adam ADAM | | ... | 14 | 150 | 2.25 | − 0.19 |
| − 79.3 | 27.06 | 2.63 | ADC Tel ADCT | | ... | dd | 81566 | 3.76 | − 0.29 |
| − 45.4 | 22.88 | 8.40 | ADE Cp ADEX | | ... | 42 | 39 | 9.63 | − 0.19 |
| + 15.8 | 46.94 | 16.56 | ADTRAN Inc ADTN | | ... | 43 | 1898 | 24.60 | + 0.30 |
| − 50.5 | 68.05 | 19.44 | AEP Ind AEPI | | ... | dd | 29 | 22.10 | − 0.05 |
| + 24.4 | 26.29 | 16.13 | AFC Ent AFCE n | | ... | | 291 | 25.34 | − 0.16 |
| − 80.0 | 12.88 | 1.21 ◆ AHL Svcs AHLS | | | ... | dd | 2812 | 2.01 | + 0.56 |
| + 15.3 | 14.59 | 10.25 | AMCOR g AMCR | .84e | ... | | 143 | 13.26 | − 0.22 |
| − 49.6 | 7.63 | 1.86 ◆ AMX AMXC | | | ... | dd | 273 | 2.90 | + 0.02 |
| + 97.6 | 22.50 | 8.75 | ANSYS Inc ANSS | | ... | 27 | 2154 | 22.23 | + 0.97 |
| − 29.5 | 6 | 1.42 | APAC CstSvc APAC | | ... | dd | 1417 | 2.60 | + 0.11 |
| − 56.5 | 11.81 | 1.90 | APA Optics APAT | | ... | dd | 118 | 2.83 | − 0.02 |
| − 25.8 | 33.50 | 8.39 ▲ ARM ADS ARMHY | | | ... | | 3796 | 16.75 | − 0.26 |
| + 4.4 | 19 | 6.80 | ASE Tst ASTSF | | ... | | 3188 | 8.88 | + 0.03 |
| + 82.0 | 27.29 | 9.25 | ASM Int ASMI | | ... | 8 | 2489 | 16.95 | − 0.40 |
| + 46.0 | 15.50 | 6.38 ▲ ASV Inc ASVI | | | ... | cc | 54 | 11.68 | + 0.18 |
| + 0.8 | 31.06 | 27.01 | AT&T Canada B ATTC | | ... | dd | 1542 | 29.43 | − 0.13 |
| − 4.1 | 1.94 | 0.41 | ATG Inc ATGC | | ... | dd | 43 | 0.75 | + 0.05 |
| + 42.4 | 11.23 | 3.63 | ATI Tch ATYT | | ... | dd | 2842 | 8.19 | − 0.39 |
| − 6.6 | 32.73 | 14.38 ◆ ATMI Inc. ATMI | | | ... | cc | 32899 | 18.21 | + 0.46 |
| − 75.0 | 18.13 | 2.69 | ATS Med ATSI | | ... | dd | 523 | 3.55 | − 0.20 |
| − 76.5 | 6.50 | 0.61 | AVAX Tch AVXT | | ... | dd | 305 | 0.88 | − 0.03 |
| + 98.1 | 11 | 2.91 | AVI BioPhrm AVII | | ... | dd | 2372 | 9.41 | + 0.11 |
| + 79.4 | 4.81 | 1 | AVI BioPhrm wts | | ... | | 315 | 3.59 | − 0.10 |
| + 33.3 | 4.22 | 1.06 | AVI BioPhrm wt | | ... | | 163 | 2.50 | + 0.20 |
| − 63.3 | 46.44 | 9.90 | AXT AXTI | | ... | 12 | 845 | 12.12 | − 0.20 |
| + 17.7 | 2.60 | 0.75 | AastrmBio ASTM | | ... | dd | 1503 | 1.03 | − 0.04 |
| − 29.3 | 7.25 | 2.31 | Abaxis ABAX | | ... | dd | 379 | 4.20 | ... |
| − 48.6 | 94.88 | 15.31 | Abgenix ABGX | | ... | dd | 14041 | 30.37 | + 0.37 |
| + 33.3 | 17 | 8.75 | AbingtnBcp ABBK | .40 | 2.7 | 10 | 20 | 14.75 | + 0.64 |
| − 8.5 | 32.36 | 10.50 ◆ Abiomed ABMD | | | ... | dd | 562 | 22.18 | + 0.26 |
| − 32.6 | 33 | 5.16 ◆ AcaciaResrch ACRI | | stk | ... | | 424 | 12 | − 0.38 |
| + 79.3 | 43.25 | 15.51 ◆ Acambis ADS ACAM n | | | ... | | 1695 | 32.50 | + 2.29 |
| − 88.5 | 13.94 | 0.12 | AcclrtdNtwk ACCL | | ... | | 888 | 0.32 | + 0.04 |
| − 58.6 | 4.38 | 1.25 | Accelio ACLO | | ... | dd | 7 | 1.32 | − 0.03 |
| + 7.7 | 39.95 | 23.50 | AccredoHlth ACDO s | | ... | 49 | 3983 | 36.03 | − 0.97 |
| − 83.6 | 5.11 | 0.13 | AccrueSftwr ACRU | | ... | dd | 712 | 0.41 | + 0.03 |
| − 12.6 | 14 | 7.25 | AceCashExp AACE | | ... | 73 | 40 | 9.45 | − 0.25 |
| + 12.6 | 10.59 | 7.63 | Aceto ACET | .321 | 3.2 | 14 | 51 | 10.13 | + 0.03 |
| − 54.6 | 19.50 | 4.31 | ACLARA ACLA | | ... | dd | 1494 | 4.94 | − 0.26 |
| + 40.8 | 12.75 | 4 | ACME Comm ACME | | ... | dd | 353 | 5.40 | − 0.05 |
| − 19.0 | 35.50 | 15.27 ▲ Actel ACTL | | | ... | cc | 1176 | 19.60 | − 0.34 |
| − 77.8 | 21.75 | 2.40 | Acterna ACTR n | | ... | dd | 1733 | 3 | − 0.10 |
| + 966.9 | 29.25 | 2.25 | ActionPerf ACTN | | ... | dd | 1469 | 25.34 | − 1.17 |
| − 23.4 | 6.75 | 1.11 | ActionPoint ACTP | | ... | dd | 65 | 1.58 | ... |
| − 30.9 | 27 | 6 | ActivCrd ADS ACTI | | ... | dd | 737 | 9.20 | − 0.45 |
| − 73.3 | 37.69 | 3.56 | ActivePwr ACPW | | ... | dd | 4093 | 5.85 | + 0.64 |
| + 155.1 | 41.15 | 10.31 | Activision ATVI | | ... | | 9076 | 38.59 | − 1.68 |
| + 20.3 | 44.30 | 15.25 | ActradeFnl ACRT | | ... | 12 | 478 | 26.55 | − 0.43 |
| − 69.5 | 36.31 | 2.80 | Actuate ACTU | | ... | dd | 6395 | 5.84 | + 0.31 |
| − 59.8 | 12.75 | 1.35 | ACTV IATV | | ... | dd | 847 | 1.71 | − 0.09 |
| − 67.2 | 45.75 | 7.06 | Acxiom ACXM | | ... | dd | 8118 | 12.76 | + 0.56 |
| + 64.2 | 15.10 | 8.13 | AbglAdmBcp AANB | .48 | 3.5 | 10 | 17 | 13.55 | − 0.04 |
| + 3.4 | 1.91 | 0.25 | AdamsGolf ADGO | | ... | dd | 42 | 0.42 | − 0.01 |
| ▲ + 78.4 | 14.23 | 5.76 | Adaptec ADPT s | | ... | dd | 18878 | 14.23 | + 0.05 |
| − 79.4 | 3.88 | 0.22 | ADB Systems ADBI s | | ... | dd | 311 | 0.27 | ... |
| − 81.2 | 10.13 | 0.68 | Adelphia ABIZ | | ... | | 729 | 0.80 | + 0.04 |
| − 56.5 | 52.25 | 18.76 | AdlphComm A ADLAC | | ... | dd | 16444 | 22.44 | − 0.11 |
| − 72.8 | 39.50 | 2.85 ▲ AdeptTch ADTK | | | ... | dd | 1665 | 3.94 | + 0.11 |
| + 124.6 | 21.95 | 7.62 | AdmrltyBcp B AAAB x | stk | | 88 | 41 | 19.25 | + 0.92 |
| − 48.3 | 87.31 | 22.20 | AdobeSys ADBE | .05 | .2 | 30 | 51062 | 30.06 | + 1.48 |
| − 33.6 | 29.32 | 9.85 | Adoior ADLR n | | ... | | 1278 | 14.60 | − 0.25 |
| + 29.4 | 40.15 | 14.50 | AdvancePCS ADVP s | | ... | 58 | 38561 | 29.44 | − 1.29 |

| YTD %CHG | 52 WEEKS HI | LO | STOCK (SYM) | DIV | YLD % | PE | VOL 100S | LAST | NET CHG |
|---|---|---|---|---|---|---|---|---|---|
| + 70.8 | 26.25 | 9.50 ▲ AmBcp AMBC | | .60 | 2.9 | 15 | 7 | 20.50 | + 0.05 |
| + 218.1 | 23.72 | 4.38 ▲ AmBusFnl ABFI s | | .32b | 1.9 | 7 | 783 | 16.81 | − 1.84 |
| + 6.0 | 29.50 | 20.69 ◆ AmerCapStrg ACAS | 2.28f | 8.5 | ... | 3503 | 26.70 | + 0.47 |
| + 8.4 | 43 | 16.95 | AmEagleOut AEOS s | | ... | 20 | 30740 | 30.53 | + 0.25 |
| − 20.0 | 3.25 | 1.47 | AmEcology ECOL | | ... | 24 | 139 | 1.70 | − 0.05 |
| + 23.7 | 27.33 | 17.69 ◆ AmFnHldg AMFH | .66 | 2.6 | 20 | 412 | 25.51 | − 0.13 |
| + 265.9 | 44.12 | 7 | AmHlthways AMHC | | ... | cc | 1436 | 41.98 | − 0.77 |
| + 67.4 | 22.20 | 3.75 | AmHmMrtg AHMH | .09e | .5 | 11 | 2314 | 17.45 | + 0.57 |
| + 59.1 | 13.50 | 4.50 | AmLocker ALGI | | ... | | 6 | 15 | 8.60 | − 0.74 |
| − 29.6 | 25.04 | 10.25 | AmMgtSys AMSY | | ... | 21 | 1991 | 13.94 | − 0.34 |
| + 15.3 | 22.38 | 7.10 | AmMedSysHldg AMMD | | ... | | 96 | 1114 | 18.30 | + 1.00 |
| + 23.4 | 25 | 12.63 | AmNtlBcsh AMNB | .68 | 3.8 | 12 | 10 | 17.90 | ... |
| + 188.9 | 9.60 | 1.82 | AmerNtFnl ANFI s | .50t | 6.0 | 7 | 67 | 8.40 | + 0.45 |
| + 12.5 | 83.74 | 81 | AmNatIns ANAT | 2.96f | 3.6 | 30 | 45 | 82.10 | − 0.90 |
| + 27.3 | 8.94 | 4 | AmerCorp APFC | | ... | 5 | 13 | 7 | − 0.00 |
| + 1.0 | 23.60 | 13.44 | AmPhysCap ACAP n | | ... | | 947 | 16.73 | − 0.34 |
| + 15.7 | 19.39 | 9.50 ▲ AmPwrConv APCC | | | ... | 23 | 5798 | 14.22 | + 0.20 |
| + 18.4 | 18.57 | 11.79 | AmRvrHldgs AMRB s | .27b | 1.7 | 10 | 400 | 15.65 | + 0.20 |
| − 1.1 | 3.63 | 1.05 ▲ AmSftwr A AMSWA | | | ... | dd | 189 | 1.36 | − 0.07 |
| − 61.1 | 49.56 | 8.35 | AmSuprcnd AMSC | | ... | dd | 515 | 11.12 | + 0.20 |
| + 10.5 | 12 | 9.55 | AmWstBcp AWBC s | | stk | ... | 11 | 316 | 11.30 | + 0.10 |
| + 141.5 | 52 | 14.50 | AmWoodmk AMWD | .20 | .5 | 15 | 531 | 38 | + 0.50 |
| + 1.7 | 22.55 | 17 | AmeriGp AMGP n | | ... | | 8952 | 21.25 | + 0.35 |
| + 13.8 | 37.16 | 14.69 | Ameripath PATH | | ... | 42 | 3975 | 28.45 | − 0.65 |
| + 4.7 | 5.99 | 3.88 ▲ AmeriServFncl ASRV | .36 | 8.1 | dd | 599 | 4.45 | − 0.05 |
| + 267.4 | 21.90 | 4.50 ▲ AmeristarCno ASCA | | | ... | 17 | 362 | 18.83 | + 0.54 |
| − 8.3 | 16.19 | 3.33 | AmeriTrade A AMTD | | ... | | 10551 | 6.42 | + 0.47 |
| − 6.3 | 75.06 | 45.44 | Amgen AMGN | | ... | 56 | 79062 | 59.94 | + 0.68 |
| − 8.2 | 27 | 9 | AmkorTch AMKR | | ... | dd | 10155 | 14.24 | − 0.08 |
| − 17.5 | 10.25 | 3.51 ◆ Ampl-Am AMPL | | | ... | dd | 212 | 5 | + 0.15 |
| + 8.9 | 1.50 | 0.65 | AMRESCO Cap AMCT s | 9.95e | 737.0 | 1 | 41 | 1.35 | + 0.02 |
| − 5.8 | 31.13 | 13.88 | AmSurg AMSG | | ... | 34 | 6877 | 22.95 | + 0.61 |
| − 1.9 | 14.50 | 4.06 | AmtchSys ASYS | | ... | 9 | 358 | 7.85 | + 0.50 |
| − 59.8 | 22.75 | 5.50 | Amtran AMTR | | ... | dd | 99 | 5.83 | − 0.16 |
| + 4.1 | 15.01 | 4.94 ▲ AmylinPharm AMLN | | | ... | dd | 3470 | 8.20 | + 0.10 |
| + 13.0 | 25.75 | 10.22 | ANADIGICS ANAD | | ... | dd | 13964 | 18.50 | − 0.51 |
| − 21.5 | 50 | 33.50 ◆ Analogic ALOG | .28 | .8 | 30 | 181 | 34.96 | − 0.04 |
| − 18.9 | 7.88 | 2.43 | AnalyInf ANLY | .04m | 1.3 | ... | 255 | 3.09 | − 0.21 |
| + 44.0 | 2.44 | 0.28 | AnlySurvy ANLT | | ... | dd | 236 | 0.54 | + 0.04 |
| − 38.4 | 5.30 | 2 | Anangel ASIPY s | 3.00e | 148.5 | 1 | 205 | 2.02 | ... |
| − 76.5 | 77 | 10 | Anaren ANEN s | | ... | 39 | 811 | 15.82 | − 0.18 |
| − 82.6 | 7 | 0.45 | ANCRntl ANCX | | ... | dd | 3139 | 0.61 | + 0.01 |
| − 1.6 | 18.51 | 12.88 | AnchrBcpWI ABCW | .33 | 2.1 | 12 | 108 | 15.75 | − 0.02 |
| + 50.0 | 66.75 | 31.13 | AnchorGamg SLOT s | | ... | dd | 4220 | 58.50 | + 3.47 |
| + 30.0 | 11.26 | 6.50 | AndersnGp ANDR | | ... | dd | 2 | 9.67 | + 0.02 |
| + 12.9 | 10 | 7.50 | Andersons ANDE | .26 | 2.7 | ... | 76 | 9.74 | + 0.24 |
| − 3.0 | 27.50 | 13.19 ◆ AndrewCp ANDW | | | ... | 28 | 4988 | 21.09 | − 0.38 |
| + 11.3 | 94.88 | 38.50 ◆ AndrxGp ADRX | | | ... | | 14834 | 64.41 | − 0.57 |
| + 5.4 | 65.50 | 31.06 | AngiotchPhrm ANPI | | ... | | 122 | 48.50 | − 0.67 |
| − 29.3 | 1.81 | 0.69 | AnikaThrptcs ANIK | | ... | dd | 41 | 1.01 | + 0.01 |
| + 138.5 | 19.61 | 5.75 ◆ AnsoftCp ANST | | | ... | dd | 755 | 16.10 | − 0.29 |
| + 24.1 | 18.13 | 2.53 | answerthink ANSR | | ... | | 745 | 4.50 | + 0.32 |
| − 79.0 | 22.75 | 3.50 | AntennaTV ANTV | | ... | | 281 | 4 | + 0.15 |
| + 40.1 | 21.38 | 10.25 | Antigenics AGEN | | ... | dd | 655 | 15.50 | − 0.50 |
| − 22.1 | 3.56 | 1.40 ◆ AP Pharma APPA | | | ... | dd | 231 | 1.85 | − 0.05 |
| − 10.8 | 30 | 6.95 | Aphton APHT | | ... | | 579 | 16.05 | + 0.35 |
| + 174.4 | 15.70 | 4.63 | ApogeeEnt APOG | .22f | 1.5 | 17 | 622 | 14.75 | + 0.05 |
| + 16.3 | 40.13 | 13.92 ◆ ApolloUnvPhnx UOPX s | | | ... | | 923 | 25 | − 0.46 |
| + 30.5 | 46.89 | 21.63 ◆ ApolloGp A APOL s | | | ... | | 5224 | 42.79 | − 0.11 |
| + 31.7 | 27.12 | 13.63 | AppleCptr AAPL | | ... | dd | 62733 | 19.59 | + 0.02 |
| + 51.7 | 33.08 | 18 | Applebee APPB s | .07 | .2 | 18 | 3717 | 31.80 | − 0.46 |
| − 31.6 | 3.44 | 0.11 | AppldDgtlSI ADSX | | ... | | 101442 | 0.47 | + 0.06 |
| + 148.2 | 8.99 | 1.06 | AppldExtr AETC | | ... | dd | 413 | 7.68 | + 0.38 |
| − 1.4 | 37.94 | 7.69 ▲ AppldInfo AFCO | | | ... | dd | 356 | 20.16 | + 0.51 |
| − 34.6 | 4.50 | 1.01 | AppldImagng AICX | | ... | dd | 346 | 2.37 | + 0.12 |
| − 7.5 | 16.88 | 5.35 | AppldInnovt AINN | | ... | 16 | 127 | 7.92 | − 0.18 |
| + 3.0 | 59.10 | 26.59 | AppldMatl AMAT | | ... | 23 | 161014 | 39.34 | − 0.58 |

of market makers. That is, a statistical survey of quotes determined that market makers appeared to avoid quotes ending in odd eighths (that is, $\frac{1}{8}$, $\frac{3}{8}$, $\frac{5}{8}$, or $\frac{7}{8}$). More precisely, such quotes showed up less often than they should have as a matter of statistical distribution. In addition, the Department of Justice (with the cooperation of some of the same brokerage firms that had come to be known as the SOES Bandits) listened in on trading sessions in which market makers lambasted other market makers for breaking ranks and not maintaining spreads.

One explanation for the "missing eighths" could be an implicit agreement to keep spreads wider than they would otherwise be, thus increasing market maker profit from each trade. On the other hand, it could be that OTC market makers tend to play follow the leader in the same way that commercial banks do in setting the prime rate, and that changes are undertaken very carefully, because no one wants to initiate a change that no one else will follow. Indeed, the presence of the SOES Bandits would itself counsel caution in changing quotes. Both the Justice Department and the SEC brought civil actions against NASDAQ and 24 market making firms. The actions were settled, with the defendants agreeing to monitoring of trading practices. Related private actions were also settled with the payment of nearly $1 billion by the offending broker-dealers.

Although the combination of commercial and enforcement activities in one organization was one of the primary criticisms leveled at NASDAQ during these investigations, federal law has long mandated such a structure and that organizations such as the NYSE, the AMEX, and the various regional exchanges all combine such activities under one roof. Indeed, in the commodities markets, the exchanges are responsible for even more of the enforcement activities, including many that are left to the SEC in the securities area. Moreover, and perhaps more important, the combination of commercial and enforcement activities may make more sense than at first appears. The various stock markets compete vigorously with each other, and one of the few ways in which one market can attract more listed companies or more investors is to offer a more trustworthy trading environment. In other words, it is always in the interest of a market to enforce just and equitable principles of trade, and it is unclear that separating traders from enforcement officers is the best way to do that.

## §14.14 Other Levels of the OTC Market

There are four levels of the OTC market. The first level is the National Market described above, for which the NASD provides daily information on actual trades and volumes.

The second level is the **NASDAQ SmallCap Market**. The general standards for listing on the small cap market are a stockholders' equity of $5 million, a public float of at least 1,000,000 shares owned in round lots by at least 300 shareholders, at least three market makers, and one year's operating history. However, listing may be obtained if the company has a market capitalization of $50 million or net income over $750,000 in the last fiscal year or two of the last 3 fiscal years.

The third level, introduced in 1990, is the NASDAQ Bulletin Board, which provides members with electronic quotations for many stocks previously listed only in the pink sheets. The Bulletin Board displays real-time bid and asked quotations, and, if entered by market makers, they must be firm for a minimum size based on the price of the security quoted. These quotations may be continuously updated. As of November 2001, 1,872 companies had quotations listed on the Bulletin Board.

The fourth and lowest level of the OTC market is the quotations in the daily pink sheets of inactively traded OTC securities as maintained and disseminated by an organization formerly known as the National Quotations Bureau and now called Pink Sheets LLC. Beginning in 1904 and continuing until 1999, the Bureau distributed long skinny lists on pink (or yellow) paper of bid and asked quotations for hundreds or thousands of inactively traded securities of small companies. They ranged from insolvent shells to solid, old-line companies that have barely enough outside holdings of shares to justify a listing in the sheets. Many of them have so few shares publicly held that they are not registered with the SEC.

Computerization has caught up with this last remnant of the old days of the free-wheeling and unregulated OTC market. In 1999, the National Quotations Bureau changed its name to "Pink Sheets LLC" and introduced an Internet-based Electronic Quotation Service. In June 2000 it created www.pinksheets.com, "the premier financial web portal for information about OTC securities." As of November 2001, 3,911 companies securities have daily quotations reported to the world only from this website.

## §14.15  The Third Market and the Fourth Market

Despite NYSE Rule 390, a substantial off-board market for NYSE traded stocks has evolved. This market is called the **third market**. (The NASDAQ presumably is the second market.) The third market is in essence an OTC market in NYSE listed stocks. Although NYSE members are prohibited from making a market in NYSE stocks listed on or before April 26, 1979, numerous nonmember firms do make markets in such stocks, and NYSE member firms may direct trades to these off-board market makers if they choose to do so. Although third market firms will often guarantee immediate execution at the current bid or offer quoted by the NYSE specialist, they generally do not offer price improvement. (They argue that waiting for price improvement takes time and that prices may change adversely in the meantime, though NYSE specialists often will stop a market order, thus guaranteeing that the investor will get the **national best bid or offer** (**NBBO**) at the time of the stop.) Moreover, many third market firms pay rebates to brokers who send them trades. Such **payment for order flow** is itself controversial, because it suggests that third market firms keep the profits from potential price improvement for themselves and referring brokers. The NYSE has responded to these practices by developing a system that allows investors to designate orders on SuperDOT for execution on the NYSE rather than in the third market. In addition to payment for order flow, several NASDAQ market makers were targeted in investigations by the Justice

Department and the SEC in connection with allegations that they maintained wider-than-necessary spreads in OTC stocks as discussed above. Although it is impossible to manipulate spreads in connection with third market trading (where quotes necessarily track those of the NYSE specialist), the scandal gave NASDAQ and the OTC model of trading a black eye and by implication suggests that the specialist system may be more open and honest and better for the investor.

Third market trades in NYSE listed stocks are reported as part of NYSE volume on the **consolidated tape**. The consolidated tape, which was inaugurated on June 16, 1975, as a result of a legislative mandate by Congress, includes all trading in NYSE stocks on the NYSE itself as well as on regional exchanges and in the third market.

There are several **proprietary trading systems** (**PTSs**) used primarily by institutional investors as an alternative to block trading on the NYSE. These systems include Instinet and the **Crossing Network** (also owned by Reuters), **POSIT** (for portfolio system for institutional trading), and the **Arizona Stock Exchange** (**AZX**). These PTSs account for a small fraction of total NYSE volume during regular trading hours. Such private trading among institutions is sometimes called the **fourth market**.

With POSIT, potential buyers and sellers use computers to list their orders. At 11:00 A.M. and 1:30 P.M., the orders, almost all involving 5,000 shares or more, are automatically matched for trades, in most cases at the midpoint between the bid and asked quote at some randomly selected moment. The cost is about 2 cents per share, half the normal commission paid by institutional investors for trades over the NYSE, and about one-tenth what a small investor is charged for trades on the NYSE.

The growth of private computer-driven electronic trading systems could have a major impact on NYSE specialists. Many floor traders, however, express little fear of these systems, because they regularly get better prices for their customers than electronic systems provide, perhaps in part because trading on the floor allows for a higher level of anonymity for the customer and for the size of the order placed.

In addition, NYSE-listed stocks are traded in foreign markets such as those in London, Paris, Frankfurt, and Tokyo. Indeed, there are only a few hours during the day when a major market is not open for business.

In an effort to recapture some of this business, the NYSE in 1991 instituted two **crossing sessions** after regular trading hours, which allow trades of individual stocks and portfolios of stocks to be traded at the closing NYSE price. Crossing Session I operates from 4:15 to 5:00 p.m. and handles orders for individual stocks over the SuperDOT system. Crossing Session II operates from 4:00 to 5:15 p.m., handles orders for **baskets** of at least 15 different NYSE stocks valued at a total of $1,000,000 or more.

## §14.16 Market Indexes

Stock market indexes or averages attempt to measure the general level of stock prices over time. The best known indexes are the Dow Jones Averages,

Table 14-7

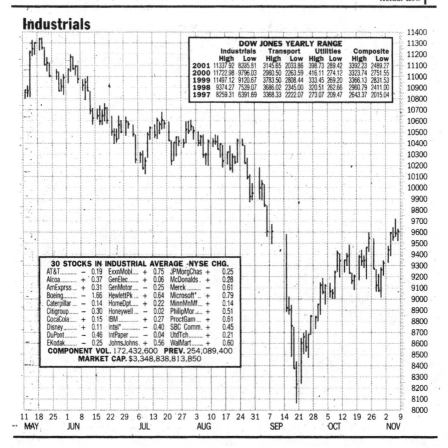

# THE DOW JONES AVERAGES

© 2001 Dow Jones & Company, Inc. All Rights Reserved.

Actual High
Close
Actual Low

## Industrials

**DOW JONES YEARLY RANGE**

|  | Industrials | | Transport | | Utilities | | Composite | |
|---|---|---|---|---|---|---|---|---|
|  | High | Low | High | Low | High | Low | High | Low |
| 2001 | 11337.92 | 8235.81 | 3145.65 | 2033.86 | 398.73 | 289.42 | 3392.23 | 2489.27 |
| 2000 | 11722.98 | 9796.03 | 2980.50 | 2263.59 | 416.11 | 274.12 | 3323.74 | 2751.55 |
| 1999 | 11497.12 | 9120.67 | 3783.50 | 2808.44 | 333.45 | 269.20 | 3366.13 | 2831.53 |
| 1998 | 9374.27 | 7539.07 | 3686.02 | 2345.00 | 320.51 | 262.66 | 2960.79 | 2411.00 |
| 1997 | 8259.31 | 6391.69 | 3368.33 | 2222.07 | 273.07 | 209.47 | 2643.37 | 2015.04 |

**30 STOCKS IN INDUSTRIAL AVERAGE -NYSE CHG.**

| AT&T | − 0.19 | ExxnMobl | + 0.75 | JPMorgChas | + 0.25 |
| Alcoa | + 0.37 | GenElec | + 0.06 | McDonalds | + 0.28 |
| AmExprss | + 0.31 | GenMotor | − 0.25 | Merck | − 0.61 |
| Boeing | − 1.66 | HewlettPk | + 0.64 | Microsoft* | + 0.79 |
| Caterpillar | − 0.14 | HomeDpt | + 0.22 | MinnMnMf | + 0.14 |
| Citigroup | − 0.30 | Honeywell | − 0.02 | PhilipMor | + 0.51 |
| CocaCola | + 0.15 | IBM | + 0.27 | ProctGam | + 0.61 |
| Disney | + 0.11 | Intel* | − 0.40 | SBC Comm. | + 0.45 |
| DuPont | + 0.46 | IntPaper | − 0.04 | UtdTch | + 0.21 |
| EKodak | − 0.25 | JohnsJohns | + 0.56 | WalMart | + 0.60 |

**COMPONENT VOL.** 172,432,600 **PREV.** 254,089,400
**MARKET CAP.** $3,348,838,813,850

11 18 25  1  8  15 22 29  6  13 20 27  3  10 17 24 31  7  14 21 28  5  12 19 26  2  9
MAY        JUN            JUL            AUG            SEP           OCT          NOV

Table 14-7 (*cont.*)

## DOW JONES AVERAGES HOUR BY HOUR

| DATE | OPEN | 10 AM | 11 AM | 12 NOON | 1 PM | 2 PM | 3 PM | CLOSE | CHG | % CHG | HIGH (THEORETICAL) | LOW (THEORETICAL) | HIGH (ACTUAL) | LOW (ACTUAL) |
|---|---|---|---|---|---|---|---|---|---|---|---|---|---|---|
| **30 STOCKS INDUSTRIAL AVERAGE:** (divisor: 0.14452124) | | | | | | | | | | | | | | |
| Nov 9 | 9586.96 | 9544.81 | 9590.00 | 9575.34 | 9594.71 | 9606.06 | 9599.00 | 9608.00 | + 20.48 | + 0.21 | 9692.35 | 9478.74 | 9630.41 | 9519.77 |
| Nov 8 | 9558.39 | 9621.22 | 9716.22 | 9691.93 | 9667.23 | 9662.04 | 9608.35 | 9587.52 | + 33.15 | + 0.35 | 9765.00 | 9506.91 | 9721.75 | 9558.39 |
| Nov 7 | 9584.68 | 9562.61 | 9603.77 | 9577.48 | 9620.18 | 9600.73 | 9589.18 | 9554.37 | − 36.75 | − 0.38 | 9695.67 | 9457.99 | 9644.12 | 9522.41 |
| Nov 6 | 9437.09 | 9420.48 | 9424.36 | 9422.97 | 9397.86 | 9394.47 | 9441.03 | 9591.12 | + 150.09 | + 1.59 | 9627.44 | 9315.79 | 9600.60 | 9386.51 |
| Nov 5 | 9326.59 | 9441.45 | 9438.35 | 9425.95 | 9413.01 | 9444.56 | 9460.69 | 9441.03 | + 117.49 | + 1.26 | 9534.58 | 9329.01 | 9476.45 | a9326.17 |
| **20 STOCKS TRANSPORTATION AVERAGE:** (divisor: 0.20545179) | | | | | | | | | | | | | | |
| Nov 9 | 2320.45 | 2304.53 | 2307.40 | 2305.87 | 2306.38 | 2308.33 | 2311.78 | 2320.69 | − 0.29 | − 0.01 | 2339.56 | 2281.51 | 2320.74 | 2296.36 |
| Nov 8 | 2307.45 | 2320.79 | 2332.96 | 2326.82 | 2326.53 | 2331.35 | 2326.29 | 2320.98 | + 13.48 | + 0.58 | 2355.25 | 2290.46 | 2335.20 | 2304.04 |
| Nov 7 | 2290.22 | 2287.30 | 2288.52 | 2281.46 | 2292.27 | 2304.48 | 2304.09 | 2307.50 | + 16.35 | + 0.71 | 2323.71 | 2261.75 | 2309.64 | 2275.94 |
| Nov 6 | 2284.72 | 2264.86 | 2265.45 | 2264.81 | 2260.29 | 2259.31 | 2265.49 | 2291.15 | + 6.43 | + 0.28 | 2310.91 | 2237.17 | 2292.36 | 2257.71 |
| Nov 5 | 2246.73 | 2279.42 | 2279.56 | 2275.72 | 2271.87 | 2275.72 | 2283.55 | 2284.72 | + 38.06 | + 1.69 | 2309.93 | 2240.04 | 2291.78 | 2245.49 |
| **15 STOCKS UTILITY AVERAGE:** (divisor: 1.60419800) | | | | | | | | | | | | | | |
| Nov 9 | 297.87 | 296.78 | 299.10 | 300.54 | 300.45 | 300.87 | 300.07 | 299.76 | + 1.48 | + 0.50 | 303.24 | 294.92 | 301.04 | 296.35 |
| Nov 8 | 294.22 | 296.74 | 298.85 | 298.62 | 296.94 | 298.34 | 298.93 | 298.28 | + 4.07 | + 1.38 | 301.73 | 292.43 | 299.44 | 294.22 |
| Nov 7 | 296.75 | 294.10 | 293.80 | 293.52 | 293.14 | 293.72 | 294.85 | 294.21 | − 3.02 | − 1.02 | 298.50 | 290.54 | 296.94 | 292.66 |
| Nov 6 | 297.20 | 294.78 | 294.07 | 294.15 | 293.78 | 293.81 | 294.53 | 297.23 | − 0.18 | − 0.06 | 299.27 | 291.69 | 297.27 | 293.39 |
| Nov 5 | 289.40 | 296.54 | 297.16 | 295.59 | 295.34 | 296.75 | 296.14 | 297.41 | + 7.99 | + 2.76 | 299.63 | 290.92 | 298.14 | a289.4 |
| **65 STOCKS COMPOSITE AVERAGE:** (divisor: 0.85151491) | | | | | | | | | | | | | | |
| Nov 9 | 2748.38 | 2735.25 | 2748.04 | 2747.73 | 2750.92 | 2754.20 | 2752.10 | 2755.35 | + 6.19 | + 0.23 | 2780.77 | 2714.84 | 2759.95 | 2729.60 |
| Nov 8 | 2733.29 | 2751.77 | 2774.98 | 2769.03 | 2761.64 | 2764.33 | 2755.20 | 2749.16 | + 16.55 | + 0.61 | 2794.04 | 2717.09 | 2776.36 | 2733.29 |
| Nov 7 | 2738.73 | 2728.88 | 2735.59 | 2728.96 | 2738.14 | 2738.84 | 2738.73 | 2732.61 | − 7.98 | − 0.29 | 2768.60 | 2698.31 | 2749.14 | 2722.92 |
| Nov 6 | 2713.25 | 2700.69 | 2700.19 | 2699.98 | 2693.95 | 2693.09 | 2703.77 | 2740.59 | + 26.67 | + 0.98 | 2755.37 | 2670.41 | 2742.02 | 2691.81 |
| Nov 5 | 2670.21 | 2711.04 | 2711.74 | 2705.78 | 2702.08 | 2711.05 | 2714.53 | 2713.92 | + 44.20 | + 1.66 | 2740.06 | 2671.90 | 2722.45 | a2670.14 |

a-Actual high or low exceeds theoretical value due to computational method. c-Corrected. r-Revised

which are actually four different averages: of 30 industrial companies, 20 transportation stocks, 15 utilities, and a composite average of the 65 stocks. The Dow Jones Averages have been calculated since 1896.

The Dow Jones Averages for November 7, 2001, are shown in Table 14-1 as they appear in the *Wall Street Journal*, which is itself published by Dow Jones & Co., Inc. This company also owns the **broad tape**, which is a major news service covering financial, business, and national news, and which is relied on heavily by market professionals during the trading day.

The 30 stocks that make up the **Dow Jones Industrial Average (DJIA)** are set forth in Table 14-7. In one sense, the DJIA is narrowly based, reflecting the price movements of only 30 stocks; it is a **blue chip** average, because the 30 companies are among the largest and most influential in the country. Because of this emphasis on the largest companies, it is not uncommon for the DJIA to move in one direction while the broader-based indexes described in the following section move in the opposite direction.

## §14.17 The DJIA and Circuit Breakers

It is not entirely clear why the DJIA has achieved the prominence that it has. It is predominantly an average of large industrial companies. As such, it has not always reflected important parts of the market such as growth stocks. It tends to overrepresent the capital goods and energy sectors of the market and gives too little weight to financial and service companies. Despite its critics, it is still a venerable and widely watched stock market barometer. A major advantage, certainly, is its antiquity, providing over 100 years of data. Moreover, despite its limitations, its movements are very similar to the movements in the more scientific indexes described in the following section.

When dramatic price movements in stocks occur, the headlines in national and local newspapers usually describe them by reference to the DJIA. The most famous market crash occurred in October 1987. The DJIA had reached a then historic high of 2722 on August 25 of that year. There followed a period of increasingly volatile trading, with increases in volume accompanied by moderate decreases in the DJIA. On Monday, October 19, however, the NYSE unexpectedly suffered its largest one-day loss up to that time: a decline of 508 points in a single day. It closed at 1738, down one-third from its August high. The dollar loss to investors on that single day was over one trillion dollars.

A smaller crash followed two years later. Following those events, the NYSE in cooperation with the futures exchanges, instituted a series of so-called **circuit breakers** to be triggered when the market rose or fell by 50, 100, 250, and 400 points (when compared with the previous day's close). At this time the market was around 2200, so that a 250 point change represented a 12 percent decline in the market. By late 1996, the DJI had risen to the 8,000 range and these circuit breakers had become less meaningful. At that time the higher circuit breakers were increased to 350 and 550, and an additional 700 point circuit breaker was added.

If the 50 or 100 point circuit breakers are triggered, the SuperDOT trading system is closed for program trading for a brief period, while triggering the higher circuit breakers entirely closes the market for trading for one or two hours, respectively.

The 50 and 100 point circuit breakers have been triggered numerous times. The higher circuit breakers have been triggered only one time. On October 27, 1997, the DJIA fell 554 points and triggered first the 350 and then the 550 circuit breaker, closing the NYSE about an hour early. On the following day the DJIA regained 337 points on a record volume of more than 1.2 billion shares, indicating that the previous day did not portend a major price decline and that the circuit breakers were not performing their desired function.

In April 1998, the circuit breakers were revised so as to be triggered by percentage drops of 10, 20, and 30 percent rather than fixed drops in the DJIA. Technically, the trigger points are still fixed, but they are periodically reset to the specific percentages. As of April, 1998 the circuit breaker trigger points were set at 850, 1750, and 2600.

The DJIA can easily be criticized as a market measure. It has traditionally been an average of large industrial companies. As such, it has not always reflected important parts of the market such as growth stocks, has overrepresented the capital goods and energy sectors of the market, and has given too little weight to financial and service companies. The mix of stocks was changed somewhat in 1997, however, in an effort to include more growth stocks, thus increasing the likelihood of increases in the average. Despite its critics, the DJIA remains a venerable and widely watched stock market barometer. Moreover, despite its shortcomings, there is usually very little difference between day-today percentage changes in the Dow and changes in the more scientific indexes, thus demonstrating that a little diversification goes a long way.

There are other widely followed indexes besides the DJIA. Table 14-1 sets forth several other indexes as presented by the *Wall Street Journal*. Several of these are broad-based indexes covering hundreds or thousands of stocks. None of them, however, have achieved the wide following of the DJIA. All of them reflected the crashes that occurred in 1987 and 1997, indicating that the decline was marketwide and not limited to the blue chip stocks that compose the DJIA.

The two most widely followed alternative indexes are the **New York Stock Exchange Composite Index** (**the NYSE Composite**) and the **Standard & Poor's 500 Index** (**S&P 500**). These indexes differ conceptually from the DJIA. In the DJIA, a dollar change in the price of a single stock in the average has the same effect as a change of one dollar in the price of any other stock in the average. There is no weighting of the individual stocks by the size of the company or the number of shares outstanding. Both the S&P 500 and NYSE Composite are true indexes in that they measure changes in total market value of the stocks that make up the index, and the index number is the percentage change compared with a base period. The NYSE Composite is indexed to December 31, 1965 (when the base was 50), while the S&P 500 is indexed to the period from 1941 to 1943 (when the base was 10). The NYSE Composite is based on all of the stocks traded on the NYSE; the S&P 500 is based on the 500 largest domestic stocks, which with a few important exceptions are traded on the NYSE.

The **Value Line Composite Index** is based on 1,650 stocks, 300 of which are traded OTC and 100 of which are AMEX stocks. The **Wilshire 5000** is even broader, covering 5,000 stocks traded on all the principal securities markets. The **Russell 1000, Russell 2000**, and **Russell 3000** are also widely used particularly as a comparison for the performance of various mutual funds.

An important function of these alternative indexes is to serve as the basis for options and futures trading on indexes. This subject is described in the chapter on options and commodities. Trading strategies based on indexes have become so important that the addition of a stock to an index (or its removal) can significantly affect the stock's price. In other words, stock market indexes are not merely statistics. This is not particularly surprising, however, given the importance of diversification in investing. Although it may sound curious, because of diversification, investors (in the aggregate) appear to care much more about how the market as a whole performs than about the prices of individual stocks, which explains why index funds (i.e., funds that try to match the market) have become so popular in recent years.

## §14.18 Margin

Buying on **margin** involves borrowing money from your broker to enable you to buy stock or other securities. By obtaining such a loan, an investor may make a larger investment than he or she could have without the loan. Buying on margin creates leverage. Because the loan is secured by a lien on the readily marketable securities purchased, it is a very safe loan from the point of view of the broker and the bank that lends to the broker. (Indeed, the sometimes publicized **broker-loan rate** or **call-money rate**, the rate at which banks lend to brokers with securities as security, tends to be less than the prime rate.)

Margin trading is subject to federal regulation, because it was believed that excessive margin trading before the collapse of the securities markets in 1929 contributed significantly to the magnitude and severity of that collapse. An analysis of the way margin trading may have contributed to the dramatic collapse of securities prices in 1929 is instructive because it both reflects the dangers of leverage and explains how margined securities transactions work.

The late 1920s was a period of unparalleled optimism in the securities markets. Securities prices were going up and seemed to have no way to go but up even further. Many brokers provided purchasers of shares with 90 percent or even higher margin privileges. A person buying 1,000 shares of $10 stock could therefore buy $10,000 worth of stock simply by putting up $1,000 in cash and borrowing $9,000 from the broker. When the price of the stock went from $10 to $12, the investor more than doubled his money: He sold for $12,000 the stock he had purchased for $10,000, returned the $9,000 to the broker and kept $3,000 (minus brokerage commissions and interest) for himself. These transactions occurred time and time again during the 1920s: Buying stock on margin was like finding money. Furthermore, many people pyramided: They would take the potential gain from the run-up in price (without actually selling the stock and liquidating the position) and use that equity to borrow additional margin to buy additional stocks on the 90 percent debt/10 percent equity ratio. To make matters even more dangerous, many persons of very modest means were speculating on margined stocks and pyramiding. This is, of course, classic leverage that is also involved in buying commercial real estate or many businesses. When prices are going up, profits roll in at a fast clip; when prices decline, disaster strikes.

When the first breaks in price occurred in the summer of 1929, many margin purchasers found themselves facing margin calls, that is, requests from the broker to put up more collateral, because the price of the stock had declined and the stock did not fully secure the broker's loan. In the example above, if the price declined to $9 per share, the broker would be seriously at risk: The collateral is worth only $9,000 and declining, while the loan is $9,000 plus accrued interest and increasing steadily (from additional interest charges). Most margin purchasers had no additional capital to deposit with the broker (even if they wished to do so). To cut the potential losses, brokers began selling margined shares to recoup as much as they could. Positive feedback (and panic) resulted, driving down prices even further as more margin calls were triggered, increasing the sharpness of the crash. In the process, many brokerage firms were wiped out along with their customers, because the customers were insolvent and the firms were unable to cover their customer commitments. Brokerage firm failures wiped out the assets of solvent customers, because all accounts were uninsured. Customers became unsecured creditors in the broker's bankruptcy proceeding. The bottom of the market collapse did not occur until 1931 and 1932, when many securities prices had declined by over 70 percent. It was not uncommon for the $10 stock sold in 1929 to be selling for $2 per share or less in 1931.

One lesson learned from the 1929 market debacle was that limits should be placed on the amount of margin customers can borrow on the security of marketable securities of fluctuating value. This regulatory power is vested in the Federal Reserve Board (the Fed). Over the years, the required margin has varied; but the requirement has been stable at 50 percent for over 30 years. This means that today an investor may borrow no more than 50 percent of the purchase price. Lower margin requirements apply to some safer securities such as treasury securities, which require only a 10 percent down payment. Margin requirements are also lower for commodities, although margin has a different function in the commodities markets (as explained in the next chapter).

If one has $10,000, and wants to buy a $100 stock, one can borrow an additional $10,000 from a broker, and buy 200 shares — $20,000 worth of the stock. From the broker's standpoint, the risk is not very great, because the $10,000 loan is secured by stock worth $20,000. Because the stock is collateral for the loan, the broker will retain possession of the certificate if the stock is certificated or, if not, will simply note in its records that the stock is subject to a security interest. (Needless to say, it is much easier for the investor to borrow against uncertificated stock, which does not need to be delivered to the broker and does not even need to be endorsed by the investor.) Moreover, interest charges on the margin loan create an incentive for investors to close out margined positions if the stock does not move upward promptly.

The effect of 50 percent margin is to double the consequence of each dollar of increase or decline in the stock over what the consequence would have been in an unmargined investment. As was true in 1929, at some point decline may be large enough that the broker will feel compelled to make a margin call. NYSE rules require additional margin when the value of the collateral has declined to the point that the equity in the account is less than 25 percent of the value of the shares. In other words, if one bought 200 shares of a $100 stock on margin (putting up $10,000 in cash and borrowing the remaining $10,000), a **margin call** would be issued when the stock declined to a value of $13,333 or $66.66 per share. Many brokerage firms, however, make margin calls before this level is reached; several leading brokerage firms require additional margin at 30 or 35 percent rather than at the 25 percent minimum required by the NYSE.

Technically, **initial margin** is the amount that must be put up on the original purchase (50 percent currently), while **maintenance margin** is the point at which a margin call is made to preserve an outstanding position. Both, however, are usually referred to as "margin."

Margin calls are made on the basis of the value of the entire portfolio of securities that the customer maintains with the broker, not on each individual stock. When the value of the portfolio has dropped so that a margin call is necessary, the broker is expected to telephone the customer no later than the next day; depending on the brokerage firm's policies (and the perceived creditworthiness of the customer), the customer may be allowed a day or two, or as long as a week, to supply the additional capital in the form of either cash or additional marginable securities. If the additional capital is not received, the securities in the account are sold and the proceeds used to repay the outstanding margin loan.

Margin regulations apply to all borrowing to buy securities, including borrowing from banks and other sources—even a friend or family member. When a person borrows money from a bank secured by a lien on shares of stock, for example, he or she must sign a statement that the purpose of the loan itself is not to invest in marketable securities.

Not all stocks may be purchased on margin. The Fed maintains a list of stocks that qualify as security for margin loans. Generally speaking, stocks that trade for less than $5 per share may not be counted toward account equity for margin purposes. And until the late 1960s, OTC stocks could not be bought on margin at all.

Although margin increases risk by enhancing moves both up and down, it can also be used to reduce risk by increasing diversification. That is, an investor with, say, $10,000 to invest could buy 5 round lots of $20 stocks (ignoring commissions) ($20 × 100 shares × 5 stocks = $10,000), but with margin the investor could buy 10 round lots ($20 × 100 shares × 10 stocks = $10,000 cash + $10,000 margin loan). (Although the investor could buy odd lots of many more securities, commission rates on such purchases are significantly higher.) As discussed in more detail in following sections, diversification reduces risk significantly with no sacrifice in return. Thus, margin may make sense for a smallish investor who wishes to manage his or her own account, but who cannot buy enough different stocks to achieve adequate diversification. With thousands of mutual funds available to small investors with as little as $2,500 to invest, diversification is readily available, though in a mutual fund one gives up control over the exact composition of the portfolio.

Aside from allowing the investor to achieve more diversification, margin is a way of increasing leverage at the investor level. Increased leverage should be recognized for what it is: increased risk. The desire to take more risk may be rational: more risk means more return. Thus, an investor who is willing to take more risk than may be available with plain vanilla stocks may leverage a portfolio with margin. It is now also possible to buy no-load mutual funds on margin. In any event, the decision to invest on margin should be carefully considered. Margin makes sense only if the expected rate of return on the portfolio exceeds the interest rate on the margin loan. Moreover, interest on the margin loan must be paid in cash, while the stocks in the portfolio may only generate paper gains.

It is possible with publicly traded options to achieve much more leverage than with margin. Options are discussed in more detail in the next chapter.

## §14.19  Short Selling

A **short sale** enables an investor to speculate on a price decline to the same extent as the purchase of shares constitutes speculation on a price increase. The idea is simple: A short seller borrows shares from a broker and sells them. When the price declines (if the price declines), the short seller buys shares to replace the shares borrowed and sold. The short seller's profit is the difference between the higher sales price and lower purchase price, less commissions, interest, and any dividends paid on the borrowed stock (all of which are the short seller's obligation). At first blush, it may seem unethical to profit on a decline in prices or to sell something one does not actually own. Yet as long as the person from whom the shares are borrowed consents to the transaction and gets the shares back, no one is hurt. It is no more unethical than borrowing money to finance a profitable business venture. Would anyone suggest that the lender of money should in fairness be entitled to the borrower's profit?

Between 1929 and 1932, many fortunes were made by systematic short selling (or "shorting") of stocks. In these campaigns, known as **bear raids**, traders borrowed shares and sold them, further driving down prices in an already soft market. Profits from successful short sales were used as collateral to short more stock, driving prices down further. This may appear to be predatory behavior. From another perspective, the "shorts" were simply more accurate in predicting the future than were the "longs," who bought shares during this period believing that the worst was over and that prices would be going up. Moreover, it is unclear that short selling in fact permanently drives the price of a stock down. After all, the short seller must eventually buy back the shares, and the price should rise as a result by just as much as the price fell in the first place. Thus, many traders regard open short interest as supportive of the current price of a stock and would be positively inclined to buy stocks that have been sold short to an unusual extent.

The mechanics of short selling require some explanation. First of all, how and from whom does one borrow stock? The answer is that there is a large supply of securities held at brokerage houses that is available for borrowing. These are typically shares held for investors by brokerage firms under the book entry system. If the owner of stock that has been lent decides to sell, the broker must deliver the shares either by getting them back from the short seller, or more commonly by using other shares in the floating supply until the short seller closes out the short position and returns the shares. Large stockholders, including pension funds and mutual funds, also routinely lend shares. The incentive for lending (aside from fees charged) is that these loans are collateralized with cash from the borrower on which no interest is customarily paid but on which the lender earns interest. For example, an institutional investor may lend shares in its portfolio simply to earn interest on the collateral. (A savvy short seller will use securities as collateral, because interest or appreciation remains the property of the owner or will negotiate with the lender for interest on a cash deposit. In the commodities markets, traders who borrow physical commodities to cover delivery are said to "rent" the commodity.) There is no downside for the lender, because the short seller—the person borrowing the stock and selling it—is also responsible for any dividends that may be declared on the stock while it is borrowed.

From the standpoint of the short seller, the borrowing of stock is similar to a margin transaction. The borrower must provide collateral equal to 50 percent of the value of the stock being borrowed. Upon receiving the borrowed stock and selling it, the proceeds are retained in the customer's account and cannot be drawn down.

If the short seller guesses wrong, and the price of the stock goes up, the investor may face a margin call much as a margin buyer faces a margin call when the stock price goes down. Theoretically, the liability of a short seller is infinite, because there is no maximum limit on the rise of a stock price, while the most a margin buyer can lose is twice the amount of capital invested if the stock drops to zero (assuming a 50 percent margin requirement). These are theoretical maximum losses, however, not realistic ones.

A more serious risk in short selling is that someone buying the same stock will **corner the market**, that is, buy enough of the outstanding stock that it becomes increasingly difficult for short sellers to find shares to buy back to cover their short positions. A **corner** requires a very large amount of capital to buy a large proportion of the stock available for public trading (the **float**) and to absorb the short sales made by persons expecting the price to go down further. There have been no attempted corners in recent years in the securities markets, although there have been attempts in the commodities markets. An attempt to corner a stock or a demand for the return of shares at a time when substitute shares are not available (perhaps because they are thinly traded) is sometimes called a **short squeeze** or **squeezing the shorts**.

Financial newspapers publish regular reports of short positions for many widely traded stocks. These reports show uncovered short positions for the week and previous week, thus allowing for easy calculation of changes; they also show the number of days worth of trading volume that would be required to cover outstanding positions, thus giving some indication of how readily available the stock is to cover an open position and how likely it is that a corner will arise. Table 14-8 shows information about short selling as published periodically in the *Wall Street Journal*.

Assuming that uncovered short sales for a given stock have increased in the most recent period, is that a "bullish" or "bearish" sign? (A **bull market** is a rising market, whereas a **bear market** is a falling market.) An increase in uncovered short positions obviously means that many investors thought prices were going down; that should be bearish. However, most analysts put an opposite spin on the data. All the uncovered short sales reported for the month have been made and absorbed by the market; they will need to be covered in the future. Thus, an increase in uncovered short sales represents a potential increase in demand, and is a bullish sign.

In some instances, an investor may enter into a short sale by borrowing the stock and selling it although the investor already owns the stock. This is called a **short sale against the box**. (The "box" is a theoretical safe deposit box.) This is primarily a tax maneuver or one designed to hedge against the possibility of a drop in price when for some reason an investor cannot sell his own stock.

Among securities traders, selling shares short while planning to cover in the near future by purchasing shares is as common a market stratagem as purchasing shares while planning to resell them in the near future. Indeed, the terminology of traders suggests equivalence: A trader who owns shares is said to be long, while one who owes shares to the market is said to be short. SEC regulations distinguish between regular security sales from a long position and true short sales in one respect. Aggressive short selling has the capacity to

Table 14-8

# NYSE AND AMEX SHORT-SELLING HIGHLIGHTS

## LARGEST SHORT POSITIONS

| RANK | Dec. 15 | Nov. 15 | CHANGE |
|---|---|---|---|
| NYSE | | | |
| 1 Sprint-PCS Group | 152,045,892 | 153,369,604 | -1,323,712 |
| 2 Global Crossing | 120,013,085 | 116,531,183 | 3,481,902 |
| 3 Lucent Technolog | 108,395,174 | 114,617,460 | -6,222,286 |
| 4 AT&T Wireless Svcs | 90,940,148 | 52,490,243 | 38,449,905 |
| 5 Enron Corp | 88,629,900 | 31,095,796 | 57,534,104 |
| 6 Cendant Corp | 87,357,091 | 67,777,088 | 19,580,003 |
| 7 Motorola Inc | 79,669,987 | 88,995,279 | -9,325,292 |
| 8 Nortel Networks | 76,159,102 | 76,883,413 | -724,311 |
| 9 AOL Time Warner | 66,864,418 | 70,225,765 | -3,361,347 |
| 10 Tyco Int'l | 66,065,906 | 62,321,818 | 3,744,088 |
| 11 Rite Aid Corp | 61,905,440 | 56,141,772 | 5,763,668 |
| 12 Xerox Corp | 56,210,995 | 25,621,145 | 30,589,850 |
| 13 Disney (Walt) Co | 54,846,232 | 56,454,576 | -1,608,344 |
| 14 Corning Inc | 53,004,710 | 46,076,906 | 6,927,804 |
| 15 AT&T Corp | 52,290,299 | 61,861,866 | -9,571,567 |
| 16 Conseco Inc | 48,735,949 | 47,824,805 | 911,144 |
| 17 Kmart Corp | 46,478,968 | 33,940,235 | 12,538,733 |
| 18 Wal-Mart Stores | 42,967,749 | 51,463,659 | -8,495,910 |
| 19 Micron Technology | 37,519,798 | 39,387,390 | -1,867,592 |
| 20 Johnson & Johnson | 36,270,106 | 41,581,240 | -5,311,134 |
| AMEX | | | |
| 1 Nasdaq-100 Trust r | 186,467,864 | 171,793,620 | 14,674,244 |
| 2 SPDR 500 | 41,244,060 | 39,759,610 | 1,484,450 |
| 3 DJIA Diamonds Trust | 14,668,551 | 13,291,806 | 1,376,945 |
| 4 Devon Energy | 12,486,398 | 10,995,400 | 1,490,998 |
| 5 iShrs Russell3000 | 9,969,747 | 15,144,389 | -5,174,642 |

## LARGEST CHANGES

| RANK | Dec. 15 | Nov. 15 | CHANGE |
|---|---|---|---|
| NYSE | | | |
| INCREASES (in shares) | | | |
| 1 Enron Corp | 88,629,900 | 31,095,796 | 57,534,104 |
| 2 AT&T Wireless Svcs | 90,940,148 | 52,490,243 | 38,449,905 |
| 3 Xerox Corp | 56,210,995 | 25,621,145 | 30,589,850 |
| 4 Cendant Corp | 87,357,091 | 67,777,088 | 19,580,003 |
| 5 Kmart Corp | 46,478,968 | 33,940,235 | 12,538,733 |
| 6 Agilent Technolog | 15,078,255 | 5,788,882 | 9,289,373 |
| 7 Duke Energy Corp | 15,894,053 | 8,893,810 | 7,000,243 |
| 8 Newmont Mining | 15,484,037 | 8,541,048 | 6,942,989 |
| 9 Corning Inc | 53,004,710 | 46,076,906 | 6,927,804 |
| DECREASES (in shares) | | | |
| 1 Solectron Corp | 26,500,839 | 54,411,136 | -27,910,297 |
| 2 Hewlett-Packard | 31,200,620 | 56,329,359 | -25,128,739 |
| 3 FirstEnergy Corp | 3,499,936 | 14,903,364 | -11,403,428 |
| 4 AT&T Corp | 52,290,299 | 61,861,866 | -9,571,567 |
| 5 Motorola Inc | 79,669,987 | 88,995,279 | -9,325,292 |
| 6 Wal-Mart Stores | 42,967,749 | 51,463,659 | -8,495,910 |
| 7 Lucent Technolog | 108,395,174 | 114,617,460 | -6,222,286 |
| 8 Pharmacia Corp | 10,349,584 | 15,933,075 | -5,583,491 |
| AMEX | | | |
| INCREASES (in shares) | | | |
| 1 Nasdaq-100 Trust r | 186,467,864 | 171,793,620 | 14,674,244 |
| 2 iShrs TrRus1000Indx | 3,224,810 | 1,121,451 | 2,103,359 |
| 3 iShrs Russll1000V | 7,732,300 | 6,097,386 | 1,634,914 |
| 4 Devon Energy | 12,486,398 | 10,995,400 | 1,490,998 |
| 5 SPDR 500 | 41,244,060 | 39,759,610 | 1,484,450 |
| DECREASES (in shares) | | | |
| 1 iShrs Russell3000 | 9,969,747 | 15,144,389 | -5,174,642 |
| 2 Oil ServiceHOLDRS | 4,863,389 | 7,109,750 | -2,246,361 |
| 3 SPDR Fin Select XLF | 4,222,062 | 5,943,484 | -1,721,422 |
| 4 Nabor Industries | 8,996,871 | 10,589,704 | -1,592,833 |
| 5 Internet HOLDRs HHH | 1,507,592 | 2,573,108 | -1,065,516 |

### NYSE Short Interest
In billions of shares

D J F M A M J J A S O N D
2001

### Short Interest Ratio: 5.0

D J F M A M J J A S O N D
2001

Short-interest ratio is the number of trading days at average daily volume required to convert total short-interest position.

## LARGEST SHORT INTEREST RATIOS

The short interest ratio is the number of days it would take to cover the short interest if trading continued at the average daily volume for the month.

| RANK | Dec. 15 SHORT INT. | AVG DLY VOL-a | DAYS TO COVER |
|---|---|---|---|
| NYSE | | | |
| 1 PhilippnLD pf | 2,144,200 | 2,460 | 872 |
| 2 AFP Prov ADR | 1,801,501 | 11,720 | 154 |
| 3 Telecom NZ | 4,092,436 | 46,585 | 88 |
| 4 WHX Corp | 3,460,336 | 45,810 | 76 |
| 5 Revlon Inc | 2,644,927 | 42,675 | 62 |
| 6 Trex Co | 2,104,798 | 35,125 | 60 |
| 7 USG Corp | 11,850,463 | 205,320 | 58 |
| 8 Canadian Imperial | 1,604,770 | 29,705 | 54 |
| 9 Toronto-Dominion Bk | 2,522,048 | 46,535 | 54 |
| 10 Westpoint Stevens | 4,514,981 | 98,435 | 46 |
| 11 Armstrong Hldgs | 3,469,517 | 76,555 | 45 |
| 12 SWS Group Inc | 5,650,857 | 127,071 | 44 |
| 13 Salton Inc | 3,669,942 | 87,865 | 42 |
| 14 Yankee Candle Co | 2,286,778 | 55,975 | 41 |
| 15 Alberto-Culver | 3,823,055 | 92,400 | 41 |
| 16 Hellenic Telecomm | 5,238,183 | 126,705 | 41 |
| 17 Station Casinos | 8,075,648 | 208,115 | 39 |
| 18 Natl Australia Bk | 1,327,552 | 34,360 | 39 |
| AMEX | | | |
| 1 MerLyn notes15index | 1,933,897 | 23,215 | 83 |
| 2 iShrs Trust 500 Ivw | 4,862,899 | 65,080 | 75 |
| 3 iShrs SP500 | 4,367,099 | 78,110 | 56 |
| 4 iShrsMidCap400 | 2,238,363 | 43,395 | 52 |
| 5 iShrs S&P Smallcp | 1,901,793 | 39,020 | 49 |

a-Includes securities with average daily volume of 20,000 shares or more. n-New. r-Revised.
Issues that split in the latest month are excluded.
The largest percentage increase and decrease sections are limited to issues with previously established short provisions in both months.

## LARGEST % INCREASES

| RANK | Dec. 15 | Nov. 15 | % |
|---|---|---|---|
| NYSE | | | |
| 1 Boise Cascade | 2,221,413 | 245,425 | 805.1 |
| 2 Satyam Computer | 637,147 | 73,265 | 769.6 |
| 3 Teppco Partners | 923,596 | 109,196 | 745.8 |
| 4 Abercrombie Fitch | 5,185,044 | 1,187,866 | 336.5 |
| 5 Petroleum Geo-Svcs | 3,787,380 | 1,031,915 | 267.0 |
| 6 Reinsurance Group | 892,833 | 246,387 | 262.4 |
| 7 ACM Inco Fd Inc | 3,338,143 | 959,063 | 248.1 |
| 8 Peoples Energy | 1,872,134 | 595,661 | 214.3 |
| 9 Enron Corp | 88,629,900 | 31,095,796 | 185.0 |
| 10 Ultramar Diamond | 1,370,129 | 484,259 | 182.9 |
| 11 Veritas DGC Inc | 4,834,658 | 1,732,047 | 179.1 |
| 12 Tri-Continental Corp | 2,177,523 | 808,401 | 169.4 |
| 13 Stillwater Mining | 1,067,855 | 407,056 | 162.3 |
| 14 Agilent Technolog | 15,078,255 | 5,788,882 | 160.5 |
| 15 Rockwell Int'l | 1,970,509 | 767,288 | 156.8 |
| 16 Diageo PLC | 1,545,578 | 610,928 | 153.0 |
| 17 Rockwell Collins | 997,163 | 402,251 | 147.9 |
| 18 Cablevision-Rainbow | 4,233,330 | 1,813,860 | 133.4 |
| 19 Copel ADS | 1,033,101 | 454,249 | 127.4 |
| 20 USX Marathon Grp | 3,660,307 | 1,654,164 | 121.3 |
| 21 Unisys Corp | 4,059,449 | 1,841,680 | 120.4 |
| 22 IMS Health Inc | 2,969,773 | 1,348,698 | 120.2 |
| AMEX | | | |
| 1 iShrs Gldmn Networking | 1,083,900 | 103,952 | 942.7 |
| 2 streetTRK MSHiTech | 870,950 | 278,502 | 212.7 |
| 3 iShrs TrRus100Indx | 3,224,810 | 1,121,451 | 187.6 |
| 4 SPDR Cyclical/Trans XLY | 1,116,125 | 546,888 | 104.1 |
| 5 iShrs NASDAQ Biotch | 2,600,074 | 1,657,208 | 56.9 |

## LARGEST % DECREASES

| RANK | Dec. 15 | Nov. 15 | % |
|---|---|---|---|
| NYSE | | | |
| 1 UrstadtBiddlePr A | 1,000 | 715,222 | -99.9 |
| 2 Co Anon Nac Tele | 301,497 | 3,259,769 | -90.8 |
| 3 Home Properties-NY | 165,450 | 1,629,816 | -89.8 |
| 4 FirstEnergy Corp | 3,499,936 | 14,903,364 | -76.5 |
| 5 Allegheny Technol | 492,691 | 1,853,119 | -73.4 |
| 6 Trizec Hahn Corp | 421,967 | 1,503,679 | -71.9 |
| 7 Charter One Fin'l | 876,894 | 2,579,890 | -66.0 |
| 8 Steris Corp | 369,675 | 894,708 | -58.7 |
| 9 Noble Affiliates | 752,861 | 1,585,625 | -52.5 |
| 10 Gucci Group N.V. | 822,063 | 1,702,602 | -51.7 |
| 11 Solectron Corp | 26,500,839 | 54,411,136 | -51.3 |
| 12 Genuine Parts Co | 726,104 | 1,444,090 | -49.7 |
| 13 Black & Decker | 1,111,166 | 2,028,257 | -45.2 |
| 14 Hewlett-Packard | 31,200,620 | 56,329,359 | -44.6 |
| 15 Rohm & Haas Co | 1,797,492 | 3,202,014 | -43.9 |
| 16 Kinder Morgan Inc | 4,697,725 | 8,364,345 | -43.8 |
| 17 Westwood One Inc | 788,770 | 1,371,086 | -42.5 |
| 18 Energy East Corp | 1,847,547 | 3,184,913 | -42.0 |
| 19 VF Corp | 1,643,806 | 2,815,037 | -41.6 |
| 20 Humana Inc | 1,723,531 | 2,896,019 | -40.5 |
| AMEX | | | |
| 1 SPDR Cons Staple XLP | 260,019 | 1,270,080 | -79.5 |
| 2 iShrs MSCI EAFE | 253,289 | 859,841 | -70.5 |
| 3 Telecom HOLDRs TTH | 525,793 | 1,398,593 | -62.4 |
| 4 Internet HOLDRs HHH | 1,507,592 | 2,573,108 | -41.4 |
| 5 iShrs Russell3000 | 9,969,747 | 15,144,389 | -34.2 |

depress a security's price to unrealistically low levels in the short term, particularly in an already declining market. Federal securities law requires that short sales be made only on an **uptick** (i.e., only following a market transaction that was at a higher price than the preceding transaction) or on a **zero uptick** (i.e., only after one or more transactions at a level price if the last previous price movement was an uptick). This provision (dating from the 1930s) is designed to prevent the supposedly depressing effect of sequential short sales.

A similar rule was adopted in 1994 for NASDAQ-listed stocks. This marks a major change in regulatory philosophy from the early 1980s; at that time, there was a movement to repeal the uptick rule in its entirety on the grounds that it restricted the freedom of market forces and was ineffective because the same trading strategy could be achieved by trading in put options (which are discussed in detail in a later chapter).

In 1991, the SEC proposed that short holdings of major investors be disclosed when they exceed 5 percent of the outstanding issue. This proposal, which was not adopted, was in response to an increase in the volume of short selling. In its proposal to require disclosure of large short positions, the SEC described the following advantages of permitting short selling:

> Short selling provides the market with two important benefits: market liquidity and pricing efficiency. Substantial market liquidity is provided through short selling by market professionals, such as market makers, block positioners, and specialists, who facilitate the operation of the markets by offsetting temporary imbalances in the supply and demand for securities. To the extent that short sales are effected in the market by securities professionals, such short sale activities in effect add to the trading supply of stock available to purchasers and reduce the risk that the price paid by investors is artificially high because of a temporary contraction of supply. An exchange specialist, for example, is required to maintain price continuity and to minimize the effects of temporary disparities between supply and demand, i.e. to maintain a fair and orderly market. Thus, the specialist may sell short in order to supply stock to satisfy purchase orders. While an over-the-counter ("OTC") market maker is not under the same affirmative obligation to maintain a fair and orderly market, OTC market makers frequently sell short in order to supply stock to fill customers' purchase orders. Similarly, block positioners may provide liquidity in the market through short sales to satisfy large customer purchase orders.
>
> Arbitrageurs contribute to pricing efficiency by utilizing short sales to profit from price disparities between a stock and a derivative security, such as a convertible security or an option on that stock. For example, an arbitrageur may purchase a convertible security and sell the underlying stock short to profit from a current price differential between two economically similar positions. In addition, where an issuer proposes to issue securities (of a class already outstanding) in exchange for the securities of another issuer, pursuant to a merger or exchange offer, arbitrageurs may sell short the security proposed to be issued to hedge their purchases of the security proposed to be acquired.
>
> Short selling also contributes to the pricing efficiency of the equities markets. Efficient markets require that prices fully reflect all buy and sell interest. When a short seller speculates on a downward movement in a security, his transaction is a mirror image of the person who purchases the security based upon speculation

that the security's price will rise. Both the purchaser and the short seller hope to profit by buying the security at one price and selling at a higher price—the primary difference being that the sequence of transactions is reversed. Market participants who believe a stock is "overvalued" may engage in short sales in an attempt to profit from the perceived divergence of prices from true economic values. Such short sellers add to stock pricing efficiency because their transactions assure that their perception of future stock price performance (and, inferentially, issuer performance) is reflected in the market price.

Some short selling may be effected for manipulative purposes. (The Commission notes that such manipulative trading practices are prohibited by the general antifraud provisions of the Exchange Act and the rules thereunder.) It appears, however, that historically downward price manipulations have been less frequent than upward manipulations. (Stock market manipulations may involve efforts to achieve an illegal profit by depressing the price of securities through (i) selling activity, including short sales, made for the purpose of inducing the sale of the security by others; or (ii) establishing a short position coupled with publicizing negative, materially misleading statements concerning the issuer.)

## §14.20  The Bond Market

Many corporations have outstanding interest-bearing debt that is not due for many years. These publicly held, negotiable securities are technically called **bonds** if the debt is secured or **debentures** if it is unsecured. The term "bond" is typically used, however, to describe both secured and unsecured instruments.

The federal government, state governments, political subdivisions, and governmental agencies such as the Federal National Mortgage Association also issue huge amounts of bonds to finance their activities. The United States Treasury issues a variety of debt instruments over a range of maturities. **Treasury bills** have maturities of up to 26 weeks. **Treasury notes** have maturities of up to 10 years. And **treasury bonds** have maturities of more than 10 years. One of the most popular United States bonds was a bond with a 30-year maturity. Unexpectedly in late 2001 the United States Treasury announced that it would issue no further 30-year bonds, and that new issues would have a maturity date of twenty years or less. This development created some consternation among bond traders, who viewed the 30-year bond as creating the benchmark interest rate for United States bonds with shorter maturity dates.

Treasury securities are usually sold by competitive bid at auctions based on yield or interest rate rather than on price. Long-term commercial loans may also be privately negotiated and evidenced by promissory notes rather than negotiable certificates. Most long-term bank loans are of this character. This section, however, deals only with negotiable bonds.

Corporate bonds are issued subject to an **indenture**, which in essence is a loan agreement setting forth the terms of debt securities. Each indenture must comply with strict requirements set forth in the federal securities laws under the jurisdiction of the SEC, and compliance with the indenture is monitored by an **indenture trustee**—usually a bank or trust company—for the benefit of the scattered bondholders.

Before turning to pricing, it is necessary to describe the characteristics of publicly traded debt instruments. Bonds are issued in $1,000 denominations or in multiples of $1,000. Each bond carries with it a right to receive a stated amount of interest every half year (or every full year in some cases). The ratio between this fixed amount and the $1,000 face value is called the **coupon rate**. Historically, bonds were **bearer bonds** (i.e., interest and ultimately principal was payable to whomever possessed the bonds) and the right to receive each semiannual payment was reflected by a coupon attached to the bond; every six months or year the holder would clip off the maturing coupon and submit it for payment. Today, new bonds are issued in **registered** form (i.e., they are **registered bonds**), which means they are issued in the name of a person rather than in bearer form and the interest payments are not represented by negotiable coupons. The issuer simply sends a check to the registered owner periodically for the interest. The Internal Revenue Code (the IRC) now denies an interest deduction to the issuing corporation in connection with bearer bonds, with the result that all bonds are now issued in registered form.

The coupon rate is set when the bond is created and is an integral part of the bond's description. For example, a $1,000 bond that commits the issuer to pay $45 every six months has a coupon rate of 9 percent: $90 per year is 9 percent of the face value of $1,000. This coupon rate is constant for the life of the bond and the bond is usually described as a 9 percent bond.

When bonds are originally issued, the coupon rate is usually fixed at or very close to the then going market interest rate so that the bond initially sells for approximately $1,000. Sales at the **face amount** of the bond are said to be at **par** or at face value. Once the bonds are issued and sold to the public, a market in them develops. As interest rates and risk of nonpayment change, the bonds will fluctuate in price as determined by the market for debt instruments. The market price is unrelated to par or face value. For example, if interest rates are higher than the coupon rate, the bond sells at a discount from par, that is, for less than $1,000. The market price is the price that makes the return that a purchaser of the bond obtains equal the higher market rate of interest. If market interest rates are lower than the coupon rate, the bond sells at a premium, that is, at a price higher than the par value of $1,000.

An illustration may be useful. A small volume of bonds are traded each day on the NYSE and other exchanges. Table 14-9 is an excerpt from the *Wall Street Journal*. The entry "ATT 6½29" means that these are bonds issued by AT&T maturing in the year 2029. The coupon rate is 6.5 percent per year. In other words, the holder of each $1,000 bond receives $65 every year. Trading prices for bonds are quoted without one zero for reasons of space. (The quote may be thought of as a percent of par.) The AT&T bond closed at 84⅝ or $846.25 for each $1,000 face value bond. How could it be that a bond sells for so much less than its face value? That is the market compensating for the fact that the current market interest rate for a bond with this bond's financial return and risk characteristics is slightly higher than the coupon rate.

What is the actual market interest rate for this bond? The column headed CUR YLD (current yield) gives a clue: For the ATT, this column shows an entry of 7.7 percent. It turns out that the 7.7 percent figure is only an approximation. All interest-bearing bonds have two features. The purchaser who buys

Table 14-9

# U.S. EXCHANGE BONDS

Tuesday, December 11, 2001
Quotations as of 4 p.m. Eastern Time

## DOW JONES BOND AVERAGES

| | 2000 | | 2001 | | | 2001 | | | 2000 | |
|---|---|---|---|---|---|---|---|---|---|---|
| | HIGH | LOW | HIGH | LOW | | CLOSE | CHG. | %YLD | CLOSE | CHG. |
| | 97.41 | 93.23 | 104.66 | 97.85 | 20 Bonds | 103.20 | + 0.14 | 7.22 | 96.60 | − 0.16 |
| | 96.99 | 90.69 | 102.87 | 96.85 | 10 Utilities | 101.75 | + 0.57 | 6.95 | 95.37 | − 0.12 |
| | 98.86 | 95.53 | 106.89 | 98.86 | 10 Industrials | 104.65 | − 0.29 | 7.49 | 97.83 | − 0.21 |

### VOLUME

| | |
|---|---|
| Total New York | $11,054,000 |
| Corporation Bonds | $10,393,000 |
| Foreign Bonds | $657,000 |
| Amex Bonds | $631,000 |

### SALES SINCE JAN. 1

**New York**

| | |
|---|---|
| 2001 | $2,589,349,000 |
| 2000 | $2,230,709,000 |
| 1999 | $3,084,453,000 |

**AMEX**

| | |
|---|---|
| 2001 | $204,653,000 |
| 2000 | $110,778,000 |
| 1999 | $176,387,000 |

### DIARIES

| | DOMESTIC | | ALL ISSUES | |
|---|---|---|---|---|
| New York | TUE. | MON. | TUE. | MON. |
| Issues Traded | 124 | 132 | 132 | 139 |
| Advances | 49 | 37 | 52 | 42 |
| Declines | 47 | 64 | 51 | 66 |
| Unchanged | 28 | 31 | 29 | 31 |
| New highs | 3 | 4 | 3 | 4 |
| New lows | 2 | 0 | 3 | 0 |

| | ALL ISSUES | | | |
|---|---|---|---|---|
| AMEX | TUE. | MON. | FRI. | THU. |
| Issues Traded | 17 | 17 | 13 | 16 |
| Advances | 7 | 2 | 8 | 9 |
| Declines | 5 | 9 | 4 | 3 |
| Unchanged | 5 | 6 | 1 | 4 |
| New highs | 3 | 1 | 2 | 2 |
| New lows | 3 | 0 | 0 | 0 |

### NEW YORK BONDS

**Corporation Bonds**

| BONDS | CUR YLD. | VOL. | CLOSE | NET CHG. |
|---|---|---|---|---|
| AES-Cp 4½s05 | cv | 93 | 85 | − 2½ |
| AES Cp 8s8 | 9.4 | 460 | 85½ | − ½ |
| AMR 9s16 | 9.5 | 45 | 95 | − 2 |
| ATT 7⅛s02 | 7.1 | 45 | 100½ | − 3/32 |
| ATT 6¾s04 | 6.5 | 36 | 103¼ | + ⅛ |
| ATT 5⅝s04 | 5.5 | 55 | 101½ | + ¾ |
| ATT 7½s06 | 7.2 | 20 | 104 | − ½ |
| ATT 7¾s07 | 7.4 | 1 | 105¼ | − ⅛ |
| ATT 6s09 | 6.3 | 360 | 94⅝ | + ½ |
| ATT 8½s22 | 8.0 | 106 | 101⅜ | ... |
| ATT 8⅛s22 | 8.0 | 10 | 101 | + ⅛ |
| ATT 6½s29 | 7.7 | 61 | 84⅝ | + 1 |
| ATT 8⅜s31 | 8.4 | 110 | 102⅝ | ... |
| Aames 10½s02 | 11.0 | 6 | 95 | ... |
| ARetire 5¾s02 | cv | 17 | 61³¹/32 | − 3½2 |
| BauschL 7⅛s28 | 8.8 | 193 | 81 | − 4½ |
| BellPa 7⅛s12 | 7.0 | 3 | 101⅞ | + ⅜ |
| Bellso 6⅜s28 | 6.8 | 16 | 94⅛ | + 1¾ |
| BellsoT 6¼s03 | 6.0 | 12 | 103⅝ | − ⅜ |
| BellsoT 5⅞s09 | 5.8 | 53 | 100⅝ | ... |
| BellsoT 7⅞s32 | 7.7 | 28 | 102⅝ | − 1⅛ |
| BellsoT 7½s33 | 7.3 | 8 | 102⅛ | ... |
| BellsoT 6¾s33 | 7.0 | 20 | 96½ | − ¼ |
| BellsoT 7⅞s35 | 7.4 | 3 | 103⅞ | + ⅝ |
| vjBethS8.45s05f | ... | 144 | 19¼ | + ⅛ |
| Bordn 8⅜s16 | 10.5 | 40 | 79½ | − 1⅜ |
| BoydGm 9¼s03 | 9.1 | 5 | 102 | ... |
| CallonP 10¼s04 | 10.7 | 1 | 95½ | ... |
| Capstar 4¾s04 | cv | 5 | 81 | ... |
| vjChiq 10s09f | ... | 15 | 80 | − ½ |

| BONDS | CUR YLD. | VOL. | CLOSE | NET CHG. |
|---|---|---|---|---|
| ClrkOil 9½s04 | 9.7 | 77 | 97¾ | − ¼ |
| Coeur 13¾s03 | cv | 12 | 62 | − 3 |
| Coeur 6⅞s04 | cv | 96 | 32 | + 1⅞ |
| CmclFd 7.95s06 | 8.0 | 19 | 99 | + ⅜ |
| Consec 8⅛s03 | 10.9 | 136 | 74½ | − 1½ |
| Conseco 10½s04 | 12.6 | 9 | 83 | + 1 |
| Conseco 10¼s02 | 11.5 | 102 | 89¾ | + ⅛ |
| CrownC 7⅛s02 | 11.9 | 511 | 60 | ... |
| CrwnCk 7⅜s26 | 19.4 | 20 | 38⅛ | − 1⅞ |
| CrwnCF 6¾s03 | 13.8 | 20 | 49 | ... |
| CypSemi 4s05 | cv | 18 | 89 | − 2 |
| DR Hrtn 10s06 | 9.6 | 60 | 104 | ... |
| DelcoR 8⅝s07 | 8.6 | 20 | 100 | + 1 |
| Dole 7⅞s13 | 7.8 | 13 | 101⅜ | − ⅝ |
| DukeEn 6⅞s23 | 7.0 | 110 | 98 | − ⅝ |
| DukeEn 6⅞s25 | 6.9 | 2 | 97¾ | − 1⅛ |
| FnclFed 4½s05 | cv | 12 | 106 | ... |
| FstData 2s08 | cv | 24 | 112 | ... |
| FordCr 6⅝s08 | 6.5 | 20 | 97¾ | − ⅛ |
| GMA 6¾s02 | 6.7 | 25 | 100⅜ | − ⅝ |
| GMA 8½s03 | 8.2 | 5 | 104 | + ¼ |
| GMA 5⅞s03 | 5.8 | 25 | 101¼ | ... |
| GMA 6⅛s08 | 6.2 | 60 | 98⅞ | + 1⅜ |
| GMA zr12 | ... | 177 | 434¾ | − 3⅝ |
| GMA zr15 | ... | 43 | 360½ | + ½ |
| Hertz 7s03 | 6.9 | 5 | 102 | − ½ |
| Hilton 5s06 | cv | 71 | 88⅛ | − ¼ |
| Hollngr 9¼s06 | 9.1 | 30 | 101⅜ | + 1¾ |
| Honywll zr05 | ... | 25 | 79⅞ | + ⅜ |
| Honywll zr09 | ... | 20 | 61 | + ⅜ |
| HuntPly 11¾s04f | ... | 58 | 16½ | + 1½ |
| IllPwr 6¾s05 | 6.9 | 50 | 98¼ | − 3¾ |
| IBM 7½s02 | 7.0 | 16 | 103³/16 | ... |
| IBM 5⅜s09 | 5.4 | 40 | 98⅞ | + ½ |
| IPap dc5½s12 | 6.1 | 170 | 84½ | − 1½ |
| JPMChse 6½s08 | 6.1 | 45 | 100⅛ | − ½ |
| JPMChse 6¾s08 | 6.4 | 25 | 104¾ | + 2 |
| KCS En 8⅞s06f | ... | 85 | 81 | + 2 |
| K&B Hm 9⅜scld | ... | 13 | 99¹⁵/16 | ... |
| K&B Hm 7¾s04 | 7.5 | 10 | 103 | + ½ |
| K&B Hm 9⅝s06 | 9.1 | 52 | 106 | + ¾ |
| KerrM 5¼s10 | cv | 8 | 110 | − 2 |
| LehmnBr 8¾s02 | 8.6 | 10 | 102 | − 1⅞ |
| Leucadia 7¾s13 | 7.5 | 110 | 103⅝ | + ⅞ |
| Loews 3⅛s07 | cv | 7 | 87 | + ½ |

| BONDS | CUR YLD. | VOL. | CLOSE | NET CHG. |
|---|---|---|---|---|
| LglsLt 8.2s23 | 7.8 | 65 | 105¾ | + 1¾ |
| Lucent 7¼s06 | 8.0 | 707 | 90¼ | + ¼ |
| Lucent 6½s28 | 9.0 | 175 | 72⅝ | + 2⅝ |
| Lucent 6.45s29 | 9.0 | 560 | 71¾ | + 1¼ |
| MBNA 8.28s26 | 8.6 | 76 | 96 | − ½ |
| MailWell 5s02 | cv | 15 | 90½ | ... |
| MarO 7s02 | 6.9 | 5 | 101¾ | + ½2 |
| Masco zr31 | cv | 27 | 39 | − 1 |
| McDnl 7.05s25 | 7.1 | 10 | 99 | ... |
| MPac 4¼s05 | 4.5 | 20 | 95⅛ | − ⅛ |
| Motrla zr13 | ... | 4 | 75 | − 2 |
| NatData 5s03 | cv | 5 | 104 | ... |
| NStl 8¾s06 | 23.3 | 63 | 36 | − ¼ |
| NatwFS 8s27 | 8.1 | 8 | 99⅛ | ... |
| NETelTel 7⅞s22 | 7.6 | 18 | 103⅝ | + ½ |
| NYTel 7¼s24 | 7.1 | 25 | 101⅜ | + 1⅝ |
| NYTel 7s25 | 7.0 | 4 | 100 | + 1 |
| OffDep zr07 | ... | 14 | 80 | ... |
| OreStl 11s03 | 11.2 | 125 | 98⅛ | + ⅝ |
| PhilPt 7.2s23 | 7.1 | 27 | 102 | − 1 |
| PSEG 6¼s07 | 6.2 | 50 | 100⅞ | − ⅛ |
| PSvEG 7s24 | 7.1 | 50 | 99 | + 1⅛ |
| Quanx 6.88s07 | cv | 6 | 99 | − 3 |
| RalsP 8⅜s22 | 7.4 | 5 | 117⅛ | ... |
| ReynTob 7⅝s03 | 7.5 | 20 | 102 | − ⅛ |
| ReynTob 9¼s13 | 8.8 | 30 | 105⅛ | − 1⅜ |
| Ryder 9s16 | 8.6 | 20 | 105⅛ | − 1⅞ |
| SallM zr14 | ... | 5 | 36 | + ¾ |
| SalSB 03t | ... | 90 | 99 | − ⅜ |
| Sequa 9s09 | 9.3 | 55 | 97 | ... |
| SilicnGr 5¼s04 | cv | 55 | 57 | ... |
| Sizeler 8s03 | cv | 288 | 98⅝ | ... |
| StdCmcl 07 | cv | 15 | 92 | ... |
| TVA 6s13 | 5.9 | 20 | 101⅝ | − 2⅞ |
| TVA 8¼s42 | 7.0 | 25 | 117 | − 3½ |
| TerR 4s19 | 4.6 | 15 | 86⅞ | + ¾ |
| THilfig 6½s03 | 6.5 | 9 | 99½ | ... |
| US Timb 9⅝s07 | 14.6 | 380 | 66 | + 3 |
| vjUSG 8½s05f | ... | 50 | 76 | + 3½ |
| UtdAir 10.67s04 | 13.7 | 322 | 78⅛ | − 1⅛ |
| Webb 9s06 | 8.8 | 10 | 102⅜ | + 1¼ |
| Webb 10¼s10 | 9.3 | 5 | 110 | + 1 |
| WebbDel 9⅞s09 | 8.9 | 191 | 105⅝ | − ½ |
| Weirton 11⅜s04f | ... | 15 | 10 | − 1 |
| Weirton 10¾s05f | ... | 105 | 10 | ... |
| XeroxCr 7.2s12 | 8.7 | 18 | 82½ | + ½ |

**Foreign Bonds**

| BONDS | CUR YLD. | VOL. | CLOSE | NET CHG. |
|---|---|---|---|---|
| CrnCkFn 6¾s03 | 14.8 | 20 | 45½ | − 2½ |
| Inco cv04 | cv | 85 | 98½ | ... |
| Inco 7¾s16 | cv | 60 | 99 | − ¼ |
| SeaCnt 12½s04A | 15.3 | 257 | 81¾ | + ½ |
| SeaCnt 9½s03 | 11.5 | 40 | 82⅞ | + ⅝ |
| TelMex 4¼s04 | cv | 20 | 124 | + 2 |
| TelArg 11⅞s04 | 14.5 | 190 | 81⅞ | − 3⅛ |
| TrnMarMx 03 | ... | 110 | 80 | + 1 |
| TrnMarMx 06 | ... | 20 | 66 | − 2 |

### AMEX BONDS

| BONDS | CUR YLD. | VOL. | CLOSE | NET CHG. |
|---|---|---|---|---|
| ABN DIS12s02 | cv | 25 | 84½ | ... |
| ABN GE 12s02 | cv | 52 | 96 | − ¼ |
| ABN HD11½s03 | cv | 1 | 102 | + 3 |
| AdvMd 7¼s02 | cv | 45 | 99 | ... |
| AltLiv 5¼s02 | cv | 15 | 2 | ... |
| JoyGlbl 10¾s06 | 11.2 | 13 | 96 | + 1½ |
| LehNdq100 04 | ... | 50 | 98¾ | − ¾ |
| Leh Prudents04 | ... | 25 | 92 | − 1¼ |
| Leh Prudents06 | ... | 35 | 101½ | − 1½ |
| Simula 8s04 | cv | 25 | 76¼ | ... |
| ThmElec 4s05 | cv | 50 | 93 | + 1⅞ |
| TrnsLux 7½s06 | cv | 65 | 85⅞ | ... |
| Trump 11¾s03f | ... | 90 | 75¼ | + ¾ |
| UBS CSCO 02 | cv | 25 | 67¼ | + ¾ |
| UBS Gap 02 | ... | 20 | 54½ | − 2¼ |
| UBS HD02 | cv | 45 | 98½ | + ½ |
| UBS WCOM02 | cv | 50 | 76½ | + 2 |

### NASDAQ BONDS

| BONDS | CUR YLD. | VOL. | CLOSE | NET CHG. |
|---|---|---|---|---|
| Agnico 3½s04 | cv | 40 | 90 | + 1 |
| Jacobsn 6¾s11 | cv | 5 | 47 | − 8 |
| OHM 8s06 | cv | 74 | 5 | − 6 |

## EXPLANATORY NOTES

(For New York and American Bonds)

Yield is Current yield. Volume is in thousands.

**cv**-Convertible bond. **cf**-Certificates. **cld**-Called. **dc**-Deep discount. **ec**-European currency units. **f**-Dealt in flat. **ll**-Italian lire. **kd**-Danish kroner. **m**-Matured bonds, negotiability impaired by maturity. **na**-No accrual. **r**-Registered. **rp**-Reduced principal. **st, sd**-Stamped. **t**-Floating rate. **wd**-When distributed. **ww**-With warrants. **x**-Ex interest. **xw**-Without warrants. **zr**-Zero coupon.

**vj**-In bankruptcy or receivership or being reorganized under the Bankruptcy Act, or securities assumed by such companies.

the bond is entitled to receive two things: (1) $65 every year from now until the year 2029, and (2) on a specified day in the year 2029, $1,000 in cash. For this combination of two benefits, a purchaser today pays $46.25. The 7.7 percent current yield in the table reflects only the return on the current market price that the interest payments yield. No account is taken of the fact that in 2029 the holder will also receive $1,000.

The true measure of yield that takes into account both factors is called the **yield to maturity**. The yield to maturity is the interest rate that in a present value calculation would make all the cash payments over the remaining life of a bond—both interest payments and repayment of principal at maturity—equal to the bond's market value.

Calculations of yield to maturity are closely related to present value calculations. The current yield is widely used because (1) it is much easier to calculate than the yield to maturity and (2) when the payment date is far in the future, the difference between the current yield and the yield-to-maturity will rarely be significant. Recall how small the present values of payments due in the distant future are.

The method of calculation of current yield probably explains some apparent anomalies in the table. For example, why does the ATT 5⅝04 show a current yield of 5.5 percent and price of 101½ while the ATT 6½29 shows a current yield of 7.7 percent and a price of 84⅝? Why would the market charge the very same company such different interest rates? The answer is that the 04 bond matures about three years from the date of the quote, while the 29 bond matures in about 28 years. Clearly, the repayment of principal upon maturity is a significant component of value that is ignored by current yield.

Current yield is not shown for convertible bonds that may be exchanged for common stock (or other securities) at a ratio fixed in the bond indenture. Typically, a convertible bond carries a below-market interest rate, because the conversion feature constitutes an added element of return. Thus, it would be misleading to compare the yield, whether current or to maturity, of a convertible bond with that of a nonconvertible bond.

To facilitate price comparisons in active trading in debt securities, traders usually refer to basis points rather than price. A **basis point** is one hundredth of one percent in yield. A price movement of 25 basis points is a change in price equal to a change in the yield to maturity of one quarter of one percent.

When investment grade bonds are bought and sold, it is customary to apportion the interest due as of the date of closing. Bonds that are in default, or are significantly below investment grade, are **dealt in flat**, that is, there is no apportionment of interest and each holder is entitled to any payments received without regard to the period these payments represent.

Most bond trading occurs over-the-counter rather than on the NYSE. The NYSE has a "nine bond rule" that provides that transactions involving more than nine bonds may be executed off the NYSE floor. Thus, the published quotations in Table 14-9 do not reflect the prices at which the vast majority of bond trades actually occurred: Indeed most publicly traded bonds are not even listed on the NYSE, but rather are traded through dealers in an OTC market.

Investments in corporate bonds by individual investors may appear attractive because of their relatively high interest rate and relatively low risk of default.

There are, however, potential pitfalls for individual investors. There may be little liquidity where the number of bonds being purchased is small; over-the-counter traders may not be interested in purchasing bonds in units of less than $100,000 of face value (which is considered a round lot for corporate bonds) except at a discount. This risk can usually be avoided by investing in a bond fund. An investment in a bond fund, however, is not precisely equivalent to an investment in a bond, because a bond fund has no maturity date. This difference can be significant as a matter of tax treatment, because the repayment of bond principal at maturity is tax-free, whereas cashing out a bond fund may not be if there is a gain.

## §14.21  Junk Bonds

**Junk bonds** are bonds that are below investment grade as determined by one or more investment rating services. They have been widely used to raise very large amounts of capital—billions of dollars in many cases—for takeover bids by outsiders. In these situations, common in the 1980s, the cash flow of the target corporation was usually the anticipated source of funds to service the debt represented by the junk bonds.

The risk of default is significantly higher with junk bonds than with investment grade securities, ranging from a low of about 0.6 percent in 1994 to a high of 10.3 percent in 1991 after the secondary market for junk bonds collapsed. Nevertheless, junk bonds pay a higher rate of return than investment grade bonds and with lower risk than common stocks. Thus, as long as one invests in a diversified portfolio (as one always should), junk bonds may be an appropriate investment even for conservative investors. Indeed, there are many investment funds that specialize in junk bonds, thus allowing even the small investor access to this market.

## §14.22  Zero Coupon Bonds

The bonds issued by Motorola (Motrla) shown in Table 14-9 are examples of **zero coupon bonds**. These are bonds that are issued at deep discounts from par value and do not pay interest. A **zero** issued by Motorola and due in 2013 can be purchased for $750 for a $1,000 bond. The difference represents interest that is in effect paid in a lump sum in 2013 when the bond matures. Because zeros by definition do not pay current interest, there is no current yield.

An individual buying a zero must include in his or her tax return each year the amount of imputed interest payable on the investment although it is not received until maturity. As a result, zeros are attractive investments only for tax-exempt entities, particularly Keogh plans and individual retirement accounts (IRAs) owned by individuals.

Brokerage firms invented zeros by stripping interest-bearing coupons from long-term government bonds and selling the stripped bond and the interest coupons separately. Such securities are known by colorful feline acronyms: certificates of accrual on treasury securities are known as **CATS**, while treasury investment growth receipts are known as **TIGRs**. In response, the United States Treasury decided to issue its own zeros—Separate Trading of Registered Interest and Principal of Securities, or **STRIPS**. Zeros based on government securities are attractive, because there is virtually no risk of nonpayment at maturity. The same cannot be said for corporate zeros, such as those issued by Allied Chemical Corporation.

Zeros that are publicly traded fluctuate in price in response to changes in interest rates and are very volatile. For example, a 20-year bond selling at par might be stripped of its coupons and be sold at $146 per $1,000 bond to yield 9.55 percent to maturity. If the price of the unstripped bond rises from $1,000 to $1,010, the price of the stripped zero would rise about $28, or a price increase of nearly 20 percent over the original $146 price.

**Deep discount bonds** are similar to zeros except that they pay current interest rates well below effective market interest rates. The discount may arise either because the bond was issued with a coupon rate below the market rate (in which case the discount is called **original issue discount** (**OID**) and carries the adverse tax consequences described above) or because the market rate for a bond of comparable risk has risen since the bond was issued (in which case the discount is called **market discount** and income tax is payable only when the difference is received). When a bond trades at a discount because the default risk has increased since issuance, the bond is sometimes called a **fallen angel**.

## §14.23  Short-Term Debt

Some short-term debt obligations do not involve a separate payment of interest by the borrower. Rather, the borrower simply agrees to pay a specific amount—say, $10,000 in 30 days—and then sells this obligation at whatever price it can get at an auction or by a negotiated sale. A person may buy such an obligation for, say $9,930. The $70 difference in price is the interest. The effective interest rate for the 30-day period is a little less than 8 percent per year. That interest is computed by comparing the amount invested ($9,930) and the interest earned ($70). Rather confusingly, interest rates on transactions of this type are often quoted as the percentage the discount bears to the face amount—$70 as a fraction of $10,000 rather than as a fraction of $9,930. The difference is usually not great, but the latter quotation slightly understates the true rate of interest on the investment. Quoted interest rates on short-term discounted debt are usually annualized for convenience of making comparisons. This effective annual interest rate is sometimes called the **coupon-equivalent yield**, the **bond-equivalent yield**, or the **investment yield**. The calculation normally reported (that compares the interest received to the face amount of the bill) is the **discount rate**.

The United States government is a major issuer of debt instruments at a discount. The United States Treasury issues discount instruments—known as **Treasury bills** (also called **T-bills** or simply bills)—with maturities as short as three months. Large volumes of discounted bills due in six months or one year are also sold each month. The minimum purchase is $10,000 of face value and a round lot is $5,000,000 of face value. These instruments are viewed as entirely riskless and the price is established solely on the basis of market interest rates in the economy. The higher the interest rates, the greater the discount and, hence, the lower the price a $10,000 bill would command.

Secondary markets in discounted securities are made by securities dealers in all maturities of Treasury issues so that holders may sell securities before they mature. This secondary market also enables persons to make investments in these short-term interests at times when the Treasury is not making a direct offering in the primary market. New issues may be purchased directly from the United States Treasury without payment of any commissions or fees through the Treasury Direct program. The price and yields are established by auctions that the government conducts on a regular basis. Information about this program may be obtained from the nearest Federal Reserve Bank or directly from the Treasury's Bureau of the Public Debt.

Short-term discounted instruments are also sold by state and local governments, corporations, and other entities. Corporate short term debt is often called **commercial paper**.

## §14.24 Municipal Bonds

Bonds issued by states, municipalities, and state-created taxing authorities are called **municipal bonds**. They are attractive investments primarily because interest on them is exempt from federal income taxation. Because of this tax-exempt feature, municipals carry significantly lower interest rates than taxable bonds of the same risk.

Some municipals that a specific state issues may also be exempt from state income taxes as well as from municipal income taxes. These bonds are referred to as **double tax exempt** or **triple tax exempt** bonds. Such bonds should normally be purchased only by persons who can take full advantage of the multiple tax exemptions.

In the Tax Reform Act of 1986, Congress restricted the purposes for which municipal bonds that are entitled to federal tax exemption may be used. Because the tax exemption is an important part of the value of municipals, it is important to obtain reliable advice as to the tax status of specific municipals before any investment is made.

Tax-exempt municipal bonds are predominantly investments for the affluent taxpayer in high tax brackets. As with corporate bonds, the small investor should normally invest in municipals through a mutual fund. Many such funds are structured to offer double and triple tax exempt status to investors in particular states.

## §14.25 Risk in Fixed-Income Investments

There are four basic types of risks with fixed-income investments: interest rate risk, credit risk, prepayment risk, and currency risk.

*Interest Rate Risk.* If interest rates rise, the value of bonds and fixed-income investments go down. The worst thing to do is to buy long-term fixed-income investments at the low point in the interest rate cycle. One minimizes interest rate risk by purchasing short term and avoiding long term securities. For example, a bond with a 7 percent coupon purchased at par ($1,000) will decline by the following amounts with a one percent rise in interest rates:

A 3-year bond will decline to $973.80
A 5-year bond will decline to $959.40
A 7-year bond will decline to $947.20
A 10-year bond will decline to $932.00
A 30-year bond will decline to $886.90

In general, yields and interest rates are higher for bonds with longer maturities. For example, in December 2001 a 20-year Treasury bond yielded 5.83 percent, whereas a bond maturing in November 2003 yielded 2.95 percent. But the longer a bond's maturity, the greater its price volatility.

A stripped treasury—a treasury bond that has been converted into a zero coupon bond by selling off the stream of interest payments is sold at a substantial discount to reflect the yield. The yield to maturity of a regular treasury—a treasury bond that still carries the right to interest payments—is calculated on the assumption that future interest payments are invested at a constant rate. Of course, future interest rates are not stable. Variations in the differences between the yields to maturity of zero treasuries and regular treasuries may therefore reflect a market estimate of the future trends in interest rates. If it is believed that rates are likely to go down, the yield to maturity of the zero should be slightly above the yield to maturity of the interest-bearing treasury, and vice versa, if it is expected that interest rates are likely to rise.

In the early 1990s, there was a spectacular decline in the interest rates paid on all kinds of interest-bearing deposits, **certificates of deposit (CDs)**, and fixed-income investments. In the late 1980s, six-month CDs might have paid interest at the rate of 7 percent or even more in some instances. By 1991, rates had declined to 5 percent, and a year later had declined to between 2 and 3 percent. These very low rates made fixed-income investments unattractive and made equity investments more attractive. Billions of dollars of maturing CDs were not renewed, with money often placed temporarily in interest-bearing demand deposits and then moved to alternative uninsured investments—stocks, bonds, mutual funds, and annuities—that offer a higher yield. This trend out of CDs became so strong that many banks set up in-house brokerage services in an effort to capture the funds represented by maturing CDs. Although these brokerage firms may be closely affiliated with specific banks, the investments that they offer are traditional mutual funds and the like, which are both uninsured and more risky than the CDs in which the funds were previously invested. This trend has never completely reversed.

*Credit Risk.* There is a danger that issuers of fixed income securities will default and be unable to pay. Credit risk does not necessarily involve actual default however. Any change in the economic terms of a debt security that increases the risk of default causes a decline in the security's market price. This, too, is credit risk.

A good example involved a proposal by Marriott Corporation in 1992 to divide into two different corporations: Marriott International, Inc. which would manage Marriott's vast hotel chain, and Host Marriott Corporation, which would own Marriott real esate. Most of the Marriott long-term debt would be assumed by Host Marriott Corporation, while Marriott International, Inc., would receive a significant fraction of Marriott's current cash flow, but would assume virtually none of Marriott's outstanding long-term debt. On the day of the announcement, Marriott's 10 percent bonds maturing in 2012, which Marriott had sold to investors just six months earlier, declined in price from 110 to 80, a loss of $300 for each bond with a face amount of $1,000. Standard & Poor's Corporation announced that it would lower the credit rating of the Marriott bonds if the division occurred. Even though this transaction was not prohibited by any covenant in the bond indentures, the uproar and litigation that followed this proposal were so substantial that Marriott found it necessary to make significant changes in the proposed corporate split. Litigation was based on the argument that Marriott withheld relevant information when the bonds had been sold six months earlier. The indenture trustee for one bond issue resigned; Merrill Lynch withdrew as an adviser to Marriott, apparently because of concern that in the future, institutional investors would not purchase debt securities underwritten by Merrill Lynch if Merrill Lynch was associated with the Marriott plan. Even though Marriott's plan did not succeed as first formulated, it reveals the limited value of standard covenants designed to protect bondholders against credit risk. It also reveals, however, that bondholders are not without some political power of their own.

Credit risk also exists in the case of debt securities that foreign governments issue (e.g., Russian bonds issued before 1917) or by state or municipal governments. Although defaults on government obligations are relatively rare, the risk nevertheless exists.

Credit risk is usually measured through one or more rating companies that estimate the risk involved in investing in specific debt instruments and then "rate" the investment, using a code consisting of alphabetical (or alphabetical and numerical) ratings. The two principal rating systems and their codes for fixed-income investments are set forth in the following table:

|  | *Moody's* | *S&P* |
|---|---|---|
| Highest quality | Aaa | AAA |
| High grade | Aa | AA |
| Upper medium grade | A | A |
| Medium grade | Baa | BBB |
| Speculative | Ba | BB |
| Uncertain position | B | B |
| Poor | Caa | CCC |
| Speculative to a high degree | Ca | CC |
| Extremely poor prospects | C | C |
| In default | — | D |

Moody's applies numerical modifiers—1, 2, and 3—in the generic classifications Aa through B; 1 indicates that the security ranks at the higher end of the rating category, while 3 indicates that the issue ranks at the lower end. Standard and Poor's uses a plus (+) or minus (−) for ratings of AA through CCC to provide further gradations of quality within a specific grade. High-quality bonds are generally rated AAA through AA in Standard and Poor's, while medium quality bonds are ranked as A through BBB. Junk or high-yield bonds are assigned ratings of BB through C, if they are rated at all.

*Prepayment Risk.* The issuer may refinance high interest rate obligations for the same reason that a homeowner decides to refinance a mortgage. Hence, a security that does not have a significant credit risk but is paying attractive rates should be examined closely to make sure that the obliger cannot call or prepay the obligation.

The most common mistake unsophisticated bond buyers make is to buy a bond on the basis of yield but without regard to callability. In times of low interest rates (e.g., the early 1990s), the most reliable and conservative indication of value is **yield to call**, that is, the yield until the time before maturity that the bonds may be redeemed (if any), because high coupon bonds in a period of low interest rates will almost certainly be called as soon as legally possible. For example, in 1991, the prepayment rates on mortgage-backed securities issued by the Federal National Mortgage Association jumped to 17.36 percent from 7.67 percent in 1990. The yields of these funds, which in earlier years were well over 12 percent, declined rapidly as high rate mortgages were refinanced and replaced by lower rate mortgages.

The general rule of thumb is that if an older bond has a coupon rate 1.5 percent above a new bond, the odds are strong that the old bond will be called in a transaction financed by the issue of new bonds. The United States Treasury stopped issuing callable bonds in 1985. Municipal bonds typically have an optional call beginning 10 years after the issue date. They may also contain an extraordinary call provision if they were issued to finance a project such as housing, which may be paid off early. Municipals often pay $1,020 for each $1,000 of face value when called, except that extraordinary calls pay at par. Corporate bonds are usually callable.

*Currency Risk.* Investors who consider high returns available from investments in foreign countries should take into account the possibility that foreign currencies might be devalued, with the consequence that a portion of the investment may be lost. Mexico treasury bills may yield 15 percent, for example, but if the peso is devalued, as it has been in the past, there will be an automatic reduction in the value of the investment that may well eclipse any gain from the high yield. That is currency risk.

# CHAPTER 15

# OPTIONS, FUTURES, AND DERIVATIVES

## §15.1 Introduction

This chapter describes a variety of investment vehicles, including options, futures, and options on futures. Many of these vehicles are extremely high-risk investments: They are attractive from a speculative standpoint primarily because they combine relatively small initial investments with a substantial potential for gain or loss. As such they are suitable investments only for the sophisticated. These investment devices may also be used, however, to **hedge** established positions, that is, to protect existing investments from changes in value. In this context, they are conservative rather than speculative in character.

The instruments that this chapter discusses are called derivatives, because their value may be based on, or derived from, price movements in individual stocks or on changes in stock indexes that reflect a portfolio of publicly traded stocks. Elaborate computer-based trading strategies were developed during the 1980s to take advantage of these instruments by trading them in tandem with the underlying securities. These strategies link the markets for derivatives with the traditional markets for securities and have increased the volume of trading in traditional markets. Indeed, many observers believed that these strategies were contributing forces to the October 1987 market crash, although others have argued that market linkage in fact makes all markets more stable.

Some of the investments vehicles that this chapter describes are of comparatively recent origin. Others, such as trading in commodities futures, have existed for more than a century.

This chapter deals primarily with standardized options and futures that are traded on established markets. This is the tip of an iceberg. A vast, and largely unregulated, over-the-counter market for custom-made derivatives also exists. Some of these are so complicated that the risks involved may not be well understood even by the persons who create them.

## §15.2 Puts and Calls

The easiest way to describe how standardized securities options work is to use a real-life example. Table 15-1 shows trading in options for AOL (identified as AmOnline) for December 12, 2001.

There are two types of options: (1) **call options** are options to purchase at a fixed price for a limited period, and (2) **put options** are options to sell at a fixed price for a limited period. The left-hand column of Table 15-1 simply names the stock in question and the closing price for that stock. The second column, **Strike**, is the price at which a specific option in question is exercisable, sometimes called the exercise price. The **strike price** is fixed when the option is created and remains unchanged during the life of the option. The AOL options shown expire at the close of trading on the third Friday of the months of December and January.

The columns under "Call-Last" and "Put-Last" are closing market prices for the options at the listed strike prices expiring in the month in question. Thus, for AOL there are options potentially being traded at 6 different strike prices at intervals of $2.50 between $27.50 and $40.

Puts and calls are traded in blocks of options on 100 shares. The option unit on 100 shares is called a **contract**. The price quotations in Table 15.1, however, are on a per share rather than a per contract basis, although the volume is the number of contracts traded.

The price of the AOL January 40 call option was $.30 per share. The price of a contract for this option was therefore $30. Obviously, a purchase of several hundred contracts would be feasible for even a person with modest means. A person who purchased this call contract would have acquired, at a cost of $30 (plus commissions), the right to purchase 100 shares of AOL at $40 per share at any time until expiration on Friday, January 18, 2002 (the third Friday of the month).

Let us assume for the moment that the speculator has reason to believe that there will be a substantial run-up in AOL in the next week. Indeed, she expects that the price of AOL will rise 50 points in the next two weeks—from 32 to 82. This may sound unlikely, and indeed it is, but it is not impossible. Such increases in price commonly occur in takeover-candidate stocks in very short periods of time.

Assume also that our speculator has only about $10,000 to invest. If she were to buy stock, she can afford to purchase only about 300 shares at $32. If she can arrange a margin purchase, she can buy an extra 300 shares. If the price in fact rises to 82, our speculator will have made $15,000 less commissions on a straight purchase. If she makes a margin purchase, she will make about

Table 15-1

# LISTED OPTIONS QUOTATIONS

Tuesday, December 11, 2001

Composite volume and close for actively traded equity and LEAPS, or long-term options, with results for the corresponding put or call contract. Volume figures are unofficial. Open interest is total outstanding for all exchanges and reflects previous trading day. Close when possible is shown for the underlying stock or primary market. **XC**-Composite. **p**-Put. **o**-Strike price adjusted for split.

## MOST ACTIVE CONTRACTS

| OPTION/STRIKE | | | | VOL. | EXCH | LAST | NET CHG | a-CLOSE | OPEN INT |
|---|---|---|---|---|---|---|---|---|---|
| Microsft | Jan 03 | 70 | | 47,641 | XC | 9.90 | − 0.20 | 67.32 | 53,028 |
| Gucci | Jan | 80 | | 31,460 | XC | 12 | − 0.50 | 91.35 | 4,200 |
| Cisco | Dec | 20 | p | 29,521 | XC | 0.40 | − 0.10 | 20.78 | 58,129 |
| MerrLyn | Jan 03 | 50 | | 22,281 | XC | 10.50 | + 0.30 | 52.94 | 8,843 |
| Nasd100Tr | Jan | 39 | p | 20,561 | XC | 1.40 | − 0.15 | 41.23 | 15,430 |
| Gucci | Jan | 75 | | 20,550 | XC | 17 | − 0.50 | 91.35 | 3,380 |
| Nasd100Tr | Jan | 36 | p | 20,245 | XC | 0.70 | − 0.10 | 41.23 | 40,254 |
| Microsft | Dec | 70 | | 19,305 | XC | 0.40 | − 0.05 | 67.32 | 61,081 |
| Microsft | Jan 03 | 65 | p | 18,400 | XC | 8.40 | − 0.30 | 67.32 | 48,753 |
| Calpine | Jan | 20 | | 18,240 | XC | 1.10 | − 0.80 | 15.50 | 8,125 |
| Oracle | Jan | 16.25 | | 17,899 | XC | 0.90 | + 0.05 | 15.11 | 30,868 |
| DellCptr | Jan 04 | 35 | | 14,015 | XC | 6.80 | + 0.40 | 29.06 | 2,515 |
| PepsiCo | Apr | 47.50 | p | 14,000 | XC | 3.20 | + 0.90 | 46.60 | 6,158 |
| Nasd100Tr | Dec | 42 | | 13,931 | XC | 0.90 | − 0.05 | 41.23 | 75,161 |
| Nasd100Tr | Dec | 41 | p | 13,918 | XC | 1.15 | − 0.25 | 41.23 | 30,500 |
| Gucci | Jan | 85 | | 13,915 | XC | 6 | − 1.00 | 91.35 | 5,505 |
| Lucent | Jan | 10 | p | 13,017 | XC | 2.25 | + 0.15 | 7.81 | 44,553 |
| Microsft | Jan 03 | 70 | p | 12,275 | XC | 10.90 | − 0.30 | 67.32 | 79,937 |
| Baxter | Dec | 40 | | 12,133 | XC | 11.50 | + 0.60 | 51.38 | 2,703 |
| Microsft | Jan 03 | 85 | | 12,056 | XC | 4.50 | − 0.10 | 67.32 | 58,896 |

| OPTION/STRIKE | | | | VOL. | EXCH | LAST | NET CHG | a-CLOSE | OPEN INT |
|---|---|---|---|---|---|---|---|---|---|
| Merck | Dec | 65 | p | 12,034 | XC | 5.10 | + 4.45 | 60.70 | 11,903 |
| Microsft | Jan 03 | 85 | p | 12,000 | XC | 20.40 | + 0.10 | 67.32 | 1,327 |
| Nasd100Tr | Dec | 40 | p | 11,610 | XC | 0.75 | − 0.15 | 41.23 | 117,188 |
| TexasInst | Dec | 30 | p | 11,497 | XC | 0.80 | − 0.15 | 31.05 | 8,107 |
| Oracle | Dec | 15 | | 11,469 | XC | 0.85 | − 0.05 | 15.11 | 102,246 |
| Intel | Dec | 35 | | 11,175 | XC | 0.30 | ... | 33.19 | 60,997 |
| Pfizer | Dec | 75 | | 10,661 | XC | 0.30 | − 0.05 | 40.35 | 37,999 |
| Cooper | Jan | 30 | p | 9,890 | XC | 1.95 | + 0.10 | 37 | 11,058 |
| Nasd100Tr | Dec | 42 | p | 9,764 | XC | 1.65 | − 0.25 | 41.23 | 41,802 |
| DellCptr | Dec | 30 | p | 9,112 | XC | 1.40 | − 0.10 | 29.06 | 12,052 |
| DellCptr | Dec | 30 | | 8,955 | XC | 0.45 | ... | 29.06 | 19,610 |
| VeritasSf | Jan | 50 | | 8,759 | XC | 1.85 | + 0.30 | 42.65 | 2,085 |
| NextelCm | Jan | 12.50 | | 8,705 | XC | 0.80 | + 0.20 | 11.62 | 12,617 |
| Willamette | Jan | 45 | | 8,562 | XC | 2.90 | − 0.60 | 45.25 | 8,138 |
| Compaq | Jan | 10 | | 8,559 | XC | 0.80 | − 0.20 | 9.49 | 47,110 |
| Baxter | Dec | 45 | | 8,499 | XC | 6.50 | + 0.30 | 51.38 | 691 |
| DellCptr | May | 35 | | 8,415 | XC | 1.75 | + 0.25 | 29.06 | 13,621 |
| JDS Uni | Dec | 12.50 | p | 8,322 | XC | 2.40 | − 0.20 | 10.06 | 10,934 |
| Nasd100Tr | Mar | 38 | p | 8,222 | XC | 2.15 | − 0.15 | 41.23 | 15,929 |
| Nasd100Tr | Jun | 35 | p | 8,217 | XC | 2.10 | − 0.10 | 41.23 | 3,357 |

WSJ .com **Journal Link:** Complete equity option listings and data are available in the online Journal at **WSJ.com/JournalLinks**

| OPTION/STRIKE | | EXP. | -CALL- VOL. | -CALL- LAST | -PUT- VOL. | -PUT- LAST |
|---|---|---|---|---|---|---|
| ADC Tel | 5 | Dec | 5867 | 0.50 | 10 | 0.10 |
| AmOnline | 27.50 | Jan | 15 | 5.50 | 2586 | 0.85 |
| 32.00 | 30 | Dec | 432 | 2.50 | 1552 | 0.60 |
| 32.00 | 32.50 | Dec | 2562 | 0.95 | 1241 | 1.60 |
| 32.00 | 35 | Dec | 2662 | 0.25 | 1950 | 3.10 |
| 32.00 | 35 | Jan | 2834 | 1.10 | 442 | 3.80 |
| 32.00 | 37.50 | Jan | 2031 | 0.60 | 77 | 6 |
| 32.00 | 40 | Jan | 1486 | 0.30 | 14 | 7.90 |
| AT&T | 15 | Jan | 1849 | 2.25 | ... | ... |
| 16.65 | 17.50 | Dec | 5039 | 0.25 | 232 | 1.05 |
| AdobeS | 40 | Apr | 1157 | 3.40 | ... | ... |
| AdvDln | 17.50 | Dec | 1367 | 0.35 | 22 | 1.50 |
| AdvFibCm | 20 | Dec | 44 | 1 | 1477 | 1.15 |
| AffCmpS | 105 | Jan | 1231 | 1.70 | ... | ... |
| Agilent | 25 | Dec | 2001 | 4.70 | ... | ... |
| Alkerm | 25 | Dec | 4007 | 0.60 | 1550 | 1.70 |
| AlliantT | 65 | Jan | 1500 | 11 | ... | ... |
| 73.55 | 70 | Feb | 1516 | 8 | ... | ... |
| Altera | 27.50 | Dec | 2074 | 0.35 | ... | ... |
| 24.56 | 30 | Jan | 1662 | 0.85 | ... | ... |
| AmIntGp | 75 | Jan | 12 | 6 | 1362 | 1.25 |
| Amgen | 60 | Jul | ... | ... | 1166 | 5.20 |
| 64.30 | 65 | Dec | 2832 | 1.25 | 682 | 1.90 |
| 64.30 | 65 | Jan | 1766 | 2.75 | 22 | 2.95 |
| AppleC | 30 | Apr | 1209 | 0.60 | ... | ... |
| ApldMat | 17.50 | Dec | 1839 | 0.40 | 102 | 3.10 |
| 43.94 | 45 | Dec | 2085 | 1.15 | 1877 | 2.20 |
| BEA Sys | 17.50 | Dec | 3750 | 0.55 | 320 | 1.30 |
| BancOne | 20 | Jan | 2550 | 19 | ... | ... |
| 38.71 | 22.50 | Jan | 1750 | 16.50 | ... | ... |
| 38.71 | 25 | Jan | 7400 | 14 | ... | ... |
| 38.71 | 30 | Dec | 4950 | 9 | ... | ... |
| 38.71 | 30 | Jan | 3178 | 9 | ... | ... |
| 38.71 | 32.50 | Dec | 1270 | 6.50 | ... | ... |
| 38.71 | 35 | Dec | 2638 | 4 | ... | ... |
| Bk of Am | 65 | May | 1528 | 3.80 | 16 | 6.10 |
| Baxter | 40 | Dec | 12133 | 11.50 | ... | ... |
| 51.38 | 45 | Dec | 8499 | 6.50 | 200 | 0.10 |
| Biogen | 65 | Jan | 3875 | 0.50 | 1 | 9.30 |
| BiotechT | 125 | Jan | 3 | 10.80 | 1743 | 4.20 |
| 131.85 | 130 | Dec | 27 | 5 | 2568 | 3 |
| 131.85 | 135 | Dec | 1567 | 2.45 | 13 | 5.50 |
| BostSc | 25 | Dec | 1 | 1.60 | 2000 | 0.40 |
| BrMSq o | 55 | Dec | 1290 | 0.45 | 1078 | 1.80 |
| Broadcom | 45 | Dec | 1087 | 2.95 | 1570 | 2.25 |
| 45.81 | 50 | Dec | 3840 | 1 | 737 | 5.20 |
| Brocade | 35 | Dec | 1539 | 4.50 | 2097 | 0.60 |
| 38.80 | 40 | Dec | 1936 | 1.30 | 439 | 2.85 |
| Calpine | 10 | Apr | 16 | 7.10 | 1435 | 1.50 |
| 15.50 | 12.50 | Jan | 2520 | 4.50 | 162 | 1.25 |
| 15.50 | 12.50 | Apr | 71 | 5.30 | 1590 | 2.10 |
| 15.50 | 15 | Dec | 569 | 1.75 | 3941 | 1.20 |
| 15.50 | 15 | Jan | 488 | 2.85 | 4226 | 2.25 |
| 15.50 | 17.50 | Dec | 2696 | 0.75 | 1011 | 2.60 |
| 15.50 | 17.50 | Jan | 1104 | 1.75 | 1141 | 3.80 |
| 15.50 | 17.50 | Jul | 2778 | 3.60 | 2757 | 5.10 |
| 15.50 | 20 | Dec | 3928 | 0.25 | 1406 | 4.70 |
| 15.50 | 20 | Jan | 18240 | 1.10 | 6008 | 5.40 |
| 15.50 | 20 | Apr | 2868 | 2 | 501 | 6.20 |
| 15.50 | 22.50 | Jan | 1439 | 0.65 | 494 | 7.60 |
| 15.50 | 25 | Jan | 1349 | 0.45 | 52 | 9.60 |

| OPTION/STRIKE | | EXP. | -CALL- VOL. | -CALL- LAST | -PUT- VOL. | -PUT- LAST |
|---|---|---|---|---|---|---|
| CapOne | 40 | Mar | ... | ... | 1510 | 1.55 |
| 51.08 | 45 | Jun | ... | ... | 1510 | 4.30 |
| ChkPoint | 40 | Dec | 1216 | 2.35 | 475 | 1.45 |
| 40.90 | 45 | Dec | 3763 | 0.65 | 37 | 4.50 |
| ChkFree | 22.50 | Dec | 1150 | 0.40 | ... | ... |
| CienaCp | 17.50 | Jan | 16 | 3.10 | 2492 | 1.65 |
| 18.93 | 20 | Dec | 3103 | 1 | 167 | 2.10 |
| 18.93 | 22.50 | Jan | 2615 | 1.35 | 53 | 4.90 |
| CirCty | 22.50 | Jan | 2143 | 1.05 | ... | ... |
| Cisco | 15 | Apr | 28 | 6.40 | 1336 | 0.65 |
| 20.78 | 20 | Dec | 1286 | 1.20 | 29521 | 0.40 |
| 20.78 | 20 | Jan | 1235 | 2 | 900 | 1.15 |
| 20.78 | 20 | Apr | 269 | 3.10 | 3189 | 2.20 |
| 20.78 | 20 | Jul | 11 | 4.10 | 1226 | 2.80 |
| 20.78 | 22.50 | Dec | 2341 | 0.15 | 452 | 1.75 |
| 20.78 | 22.50 | Apr | 2787 | 2.10 | 183 | 3.50 |
| Citigrp | 42.50 | Mar | ... | ... | 1801 | 1.30 |
| 48.61 | 45 | Mar | 28 | 5.60 | 1876 | 2 |
| 48.61 | 50 | Dec | 2533 | 0.40 | 595 | 1.95 |
| Comeric | 45 | Dec | 1200 | 8.80 | ... | ... |
| 53.56 | 50 | Dec | 1300 | 3.80 | ... | ... |
| Compaq | 7.50 | Jan | 480 | 2.20 | 2245 | 0.35 |
| 9.49 | 7.50 | Apr | 2 | 2.80 | 1550 | 0.70 |
| 9.49 | 10 | Dec | 1288 | 0.30 | 6199 | 0.80 |
| 9.49 | 10 | Jan | 8559 | 0.80 | 1666 | 1.30 |
| Comvers | 20 | Dec | 56 | 3.20 | 1858 | 0.95 |
| Cnseco | 5 | Jan | 243 | 0.40 | 3100 | 1.50 |
| Cooper | 30 | Jan | ... | ... | 9890 | 1.95 |
| 37.00 | 35 | Dec | 2432 | 3.20 | 14 | 1.50 |
| 37.00 | 35 | Jan | 801 | 5.60 | 1515 | 3.40 |
| 37.00 | 40 | Jan | 1750 | 2.85 | ... | ... |
| 37.00 | 40 | Apr | 2505 | 4.40 | 5 | 7.50 |
| 37.00 | 50 | Apr | 2500 | 1.30 | ... | ... |
| Corning | 10 | Dec | 1197 | 0.50 | 159 | 0.40 |
| DellCptr | 30 | Dec | 8955 | 0.45 | 9112 | 1.40 |
| 29.06 | 35 | May | 8415 | 1.75 | 45 | 7.10 |
| DevonEn | 35 | Dec | 3205 | 1.60 | 241 | 1.05 |
| Disney | 20 | Jan | 2086 | 2.70 | 37 | 0.35 |
| Documnt | 22.50 | Dec | ... | ... | 1500 | 4.60 |
| DuPont | 45 | Dec | 162 | 0.50 | 2153 | 1.75 |
| 43.87 | 45 | Apr | 368 | 2.65 | 2060 | 3.80 |
| DukeEngy | 30 | Apr | 156 | 6.20 | 1435 | 1.75 |
| 33.92 | 35 | Apr | 500 | 2.85 | 5634 | 3.90 |
| Dynegy | 20 | Jan | 10 | 7.80 | 2540 | 1.25 |
| 25.95 | 22.50 | Mar | ... | ... | 4960 | 3.20 |
| 25.95 | 22.50 | Jun | 40 | 8.30 | 5570 | 3.90 |
| 25.95 | 25 | Dec | 231 | 2.30 | 4056 | 1.35 |
| 25.95 | 25 | Jan | 185 | 4 | 3613 | 2.60 |
| 25.95 | 30 | Dec | 3053 | 0.45 | 1355 | 4.60 |
| 25.95 | 30 | Mar | 2116 | 3.10 | 2045 | 7.20 |
| eBay | 65 | Dec | 203 | 6.10 | 5567 | 1 |
| 70.10 | 65 | Jan | 329 | 8.40 | 1742 | 3.40 |
| 70.10 | 70 | Dec | 2568 | 2.50 | 1640 | 2.50 |
| EMC | 17.50 | Dec | 7274 | 0.35 | 2405 | 1.50 |
| 16.20 | 17.50 | Jan | 4858 | 0.80 | 250 | 1.95 |
| EMC o | 30 | Jan | 3600 | 0.05 | 5 | 12.40 |
| EKodak | 30 | Jan | 83 | 2.20 | 3273 | 1.20 |
| 30.97 | 30 | Apr | 86 | 3.40 | 3157 | 2.30 |
| Eclipsys | 15 | Jan | ... | ... | 1500 | 2.40 |
| ElPasoCp | 30 | Jan | 630 | 9.90 | 1489 | 0.85 |
| 39.17 | 35 | Dec | 558 | 4.80 | 1172 | 0.80 |

| OPTION/STRIKE | | EXP. | -CALL- VOL. | -CALL- LAST | -PUT- VOL. | -PUT- LAST |
|---|---|---|---|---|---|---|
| 39.17 | 35 | Jan | 134 | 5.50 | 2300 | 1.75 |
| 39.17 | 35 | Apr | 90 | 7.70 | 2393 | 3.70 |
| 39.17 | 40 | Jan | 1833 | 2.70 | 304 | 3.60 |
| Emulex | 40 | Dec | 1141 | 2 | 1126 | 2.80 |
| Enron | 10 | Jan | 2822 | 0.05 | ... | ... |
| EqOffPT | 25 | Dec | 1322 | 5 | ... | ... |
| 29.98 | 25 | Jan | 1200 | 4.90 | ... | ... |
| ExxonMob | 37.50 | Dec | 337 | 0.35 | 1838 | 1.05 |
| 36.81 | 37.50 | Jan | 450 | 1 | 3440 | 1.50 |
| 36.81 | 37.50 | Apr | 295 | 2.05 | 2074 | 2.55 |
| 36.81 | 40 | Jan | 312 | 0.40 | 1274 | 3.40 |
| 36.81 | 40 | Apr | 152 | 1.10 | 1255 | 4 |
| FannieMae | 75 | Dec | ... | ... | 2673 | 0.30 |
| Finisar | 25 | Dec | ... | ... | 1279 | 12.20 |
| Fiserv | 35 | Jan | 1050 | 6.80 | 2250 | 0.30 |
| Flextrn | 27.50 | Dec | 506 | 1.20 | 2088 | 1.35 |
| Gap | 12.50 | Dec | ... | ... | 1731 | 0.25 |
| Genentc | 55 | Dec | 434 | 1.15 | 1234 | 2.40 |
| Gen El | 37.50 | Dec | 6405 | 0.65 | 7294 | 1.40 |
| 36.70 | 37.50 | Jan | 520 | 1.25 | 5182 | 2.20 |
| 36.70 | 40 | Dec | 1356 | 0.10 | 1267 | 3.40 |
| GenMotrs | 50 | Dec | 3183 | 0.45 | 2654 | 1.90 |
| 48.65 | 60 | Dec | ... | ... | 1500 | 11.40 |
| 48.65 | 65 | Jan | ... | ... | 1500 | 16.40 |
| GM H | 15 | Dec | 1670 | 0.10 | ... | ... |
| 14.01 | 15 | Jan | 1100 | 0.40 | 1600 | 1.30 |
| GnMicrochp | 70 | Jan | 1324 | 3.30 | ... | ... |
| GenzymGn | 60 | Dec | 2252 | 1.05 | 10 | 3.70 |
| GaPcGP | 30 | Dec | 1218 | 0.80 | 1070 | 1.20 |
| Gucci | 75 | Jan | 20550 | 17 | ... | ... |
| 91.35 | 80 | Jan | 31460 | 12 | ... | ... |
| 91.35 | 85 | Dec | 1165 | 6 | 5 | 1.65 |
| 91.35 | 85 | Jan | 13915 | 6 | 75 | 2.70 |
| 91.35 | 120 | Jan | ... | ... | 1650 | 35.70 |
| Halbtn | 15 | Dec | 2213 | 0.45 | 1138 | 1.50 |
| 14.00 | 15 | Jan | 1920 | 1.30 | 464 | 2.20 |
| 14.00 | 17.50 | Jan | 1211 | 0.70 | 38 | 3.90 |
| Hlthsth | 15 | Dec | 1835 | 0.30 | 69 | 0.95 |
| HewlettPk | 22.50 | Jan | 1484 | 1.35 | 946 | 1.80 |
| HomeDp | 45 | Dec | 257 | 3.40 | 2264 | 0.40 |
| Houshl | 65 | Jul | 1188 | 3.50 | ... | ... |
| ICN Phma | 35 | Mar | 6184 | 1.60 | 20 | 5.40 |
| IDEC | 70 | Jan | 3182 | 4 | 172 | 5.80 |
| Imclne | 70 | Dec | 1472 | 2.45 | 729 | 2.10 |
| Inktomi | 12.50 | Apr | 2508 | 0.40 | ... | ... |
| Instinet | 7.50 | Dec | ... | ... | 1392 | 0.20 |
| Intel | 27.50 | Jul | ... | ... | 4598 | 1.95 |
| 33.19 | 30 | Jul | 4706 | 6.70 | 79 | 2.75 |
| 33.19 | 32.50 | Dec | 2875 | 1.40 | 5978 | 0.65 |
| 33.19 | 32.50 | Jan | 5499 | 2.40 | 7555 | 1.60 |
| 33.19 | 35 | Dec | 11175 | 0.30 | 985 | 2.10 |
| 33.19 | 35 | Jan | 6840 | 1.15 | 218 | 2.95 |
| 33.19 | 35 | Apr | 1213 | 2.75 | 70 | 4.20 |
| 33.19 | 35 | Jul | 1218 | 3.80 | 1146 | 5.30 |
| I B M | 100 | Dec | 544 | 21.60 | 2205 | 0.10 |
| 121.50 | 100 | Jan | 47 | 23 | 2792 | 0.45 |
| 121.50 | 110 | Dec | 177 | 11.50 | 3309 | 0.20 |
| 121.50 | 110 | Jan | 752 | 13.20 | 1308 | 1.40 |
| 121.50 | 115 | Jan | 365 | 9.20 | 3710 | 2.20 |
| 121.50 | 120 | Dec | 7559 | 2.95 | 4754 | 1.55 |
| 121.50 | 125 | Dec | 2373 | 0.80 | 258 | 4.50 |

Table 15-1 (*cont.*)

| OPTION | STRIKE | EXP. | CALL VOL. | CALL LAST | PUT VOL. | PUT LAST |
|---|---|---|---|---|---|---|
| 121.50 | 125 | Jan | 1402 | 3 | 72 | 6.60 |
| 121.50 | 130 | Jan | 2271 | 1.40 | 43 | 9.10 |
| JDS Uni | 10 | Dec | 1417 | 0.55 | 706 | 0.50 |
| 10.06 | 12.50 | Dec | 513 | 0.10 | 8322 | 2.40 |
| JPMorgCh | 35 | Dec | 6 | 3.70 | 2501 | 0.30 |
| 38.50 | 40 | Dec | 1392 | 0.40 | 683 | 2 |
| JohnJn | 55 | Dec | 1272 | 1.80 | 646 | 0.60 |
| 56.14 | 60 | Jan | 1466 | 0.55 | 1010 | 4 |
| 56.14 | 60 | Apr | 2591 | 1.75 | 12 | 5 |
| JnprNtw | 25 | Dec | 5324 | 1.35 | 637 | 1.85 |
| 24.52 | 25 | Jan | 1164 | 3 | 83 | 3.40 |
| K mart | 5 | Jan | 80 | 1.40 | 1187 | 0.30 |
| KingPh | 45 | Apr | 1500 | 2 | 750 | 7.10 |
| KnghtTri | 12.50 | Dec | 2372 | 0.70 | 38 | 0.30 |
| LegatoSy | 12.50 | Dec | 3592 | 0.60 | 32 | 1 |
| Level3 | 5 | Mar | 20 | 2.60 | 3003 | 0.80 |
| Lilly | 80 | Dec | 2215 | 1.35 | 1505 | 1.20 |
| Lucent | 7.50 | Dec | 1983 | 0.50 | 54 | 0.20 |
| 7.81 | 7.50 | Jan | 325 | 0.85 | 1631 | 0.50 |
| 7.81 | 10 | Jan | 933 | 0.15 | 13017 | 2.25 |
| MarvellT | 32.50 | Dec | 1250 | 5.70 | 50 | 0.60 |
| Medtrn | 40 | Jan | ... | ... | 2631 | 0.30 |
| Merck | 50 | Apr | ... | ... | 1551 | 1 |
| 60.70 | 60 | Dec | 579 | 1.70 | 1939 | 1.15 |
| 60.70 | 60 | Jan | 1502 | 2.60 | 2557 | 2.15 |
| 60.70 | 65 | Dec | 4828 | 0.25 | 12034 | 5.10 |
| 60.70 | 65 | Jan | 1088 | 0.75 | 1226 | 5.50 |
| 60.70 | 70 | Dec | 683 | 0.20 | 3172 | 9.80 |
| 60.70 | 70 | Jan | 1816 | 0.30 | 63 | 9.50 |
| MerrLyn | 55 | Dec | 1539 | 0.55 | 230 | 2.30 |
| 52.94 | 55 | Apr | 1139 | 4.40 | 11 | 6.10 |
| MicrochTc | 45 | Dec | 1372 | 0.50 | ... | ... |
| Microsft | 50 | Jan | 100 | 18.40 | 5450 | 0.15 |
| 67.32 | 55 | Jan | 1557 | 12.80 | 7737 | 0.35 |
| 67.32 | 60 | Dec | 82 | 7.80 | 2460 | 0.15 |
| 67.32 | 65 | Dec | 2077 | 3 | 1452 | 0.65 |
| 67.32 | 65 | Jan | 578 | 4.50 | 7328 | 8.40 |
| 67.32 | 65 | Apr | 3 | 7.40 | 1601 | 4.40 |
| 67.32 | 70 | Dec | 19306 | 0.40 | 407 | 3.10 |
| 67.32 | 70 | Jan | 1932 | 1.85 | 3795 | 4.40 |
| 67.32 | 70 | Apr | 4337 | 4.50 | 2230 | 6.80 |
| 67.32 | 70 | Jul | 1282 | 6.60 | ... | ... |
| 67.32 | 90 | Apr | 2755 | 0.35 | ... | ... |
| MSDWDis | 60 | Dec | 5335 | 0.45 | 62 | 4.70 |
| Motorola | 20 | Jan | 1170 | 0.25 | 22 | 3.60 |
| 16.82 | 20 | Apr | 2799 | 1 | ... | ... |
| Nasd100Tr | 27 | Jan | ... | ... | 5000 | 0.05 |
| 41.23 | 35 | Mar | 139 | 8.10 | 4056 | 1.35 |
| 41.23 | 35 | Jun | 2 | 9.10 | 8217 | 2.10 |
| 41.23 | 36 | Jan | 6 | 6.80 | 20245 | 0.70 |
| 41.23 | 38 | Dec | 282 | 3.60 | 3254 | 0.35 |
| 41.23 | 38 | Jan | 7868 | 4.60 | 1249 | 1.15 |
| 41.23 | 38 | Mar | 7840 | 6 | 8222 | 2.15 |
| 41.23 | 39 | Dec | 1009 | 2.90 | 4803 | 0.50 |
| 41.23 | 39 | Jan | 127 | 3.80 | 20561 | 1.40 |
| 41.23 | 40 | Dec | 3907 | 2 | 11610 | 0.75 |
| 41.23 | 40 | Jan | 2550 | 3.10 | 4287 | 1.80 |
| 41.23 | 41 | Dec | 7898 | 1.40 | 13918 | 1.15 |
| 41.23 | 41 | Jan | 1088 | 2.45 | 1879 | 2.20 |
| 41.23 | 41 | Mar | 1268 | 3.80 | 86 | 3.30 |
| 41.23 | 41 | Jun | 1049 | 5.30 | 3016 | 4.50 |
| 41.23 | 42 | Dec | 13931 | 0.90 | 9764 | 1.65 |
| 41.23 | 42 | Jan | 3477 | 2 | 1911 | 2.75 |
| 41.23 | 43 | Dec | 4799 | 0.50 | 1121 | 2.30 |

| OPTION | STRIKE | EXP. | CALL VOL. | CALL LAST | PUT VOL. | PUT LAST |
|---|---|---|---|---|---|---|
| 41.23 | 43 | Jan | 1405 | 1.55 | 568 | 3.30 |
| 41.23 | 44 | Dec | 2278 | 0.30 | 358 | 3 |
| 41.23 | 44 | Jan | 1353 | 1.20 | 1006 | 3.80 |
| 41.23 | 45 | Jan | 2767 | 0.90 | 315 | 4.60 |
| 41.23 | 45 | Mar | 3088 | 2 | 14 | 5.40 |
| 41.23 | 45 | Jun | 4066 | 3.50 | 10 | 6.50 |
| 41.23 | 50 | Jun | 5277 | 1.95 | ... | ... |
| NetBank | 10 | Jul | 3708 | 1.20 | ... | ... |
| NetwkApp | 17.50 | Jan | 130 | 5.30 | 2434 | 0.80 |
| 21.37 | 20 | Dec | 1763 | 1.95 | 2123 | 0.60 |
| 21.37 | 25 | Jan | 1234 | 1.10 | 83 | 4.80 |
| NextelCm | 10 | Jan | 1422 | 2.20 | 321 | 0.45 |
| 11.62 | 12.50 | Jan | 8705 | 0.80 | 103 | 1.50 |
| NokiaA | 22.50 | Jul | 138 | 6.30 | 3032 | 2.90 |
| 25.50 | 25 | Dec | 2135 | 1.45 | 1372 | 0.70 |
| 25.50 | 25 | Jan | 2645 | 2.30 | 554 | 1.50 |
| 25.50 | 25 | Jul | 133 | 4.70 | 1728 | 3.90 |
| 25.50 | 27.50 | Jan | 1387 | 1.25 | 66 | 2.80 |
| 25.50 | 30 | Jan | 2364 | 0.50 | 84 | 4.40 |
| NortelNwk | 7.50 | Jan | 1746 | 1.30 | 3040 | 0.35 |
| NvidiaCp | 65 | Dec | 1272 | 1.60 | 112 | 3.70 |
| OpenwvSys | 12.50 | Dec | 4171 | 0.20 | 760 | 1.95 |
| 10.60 | 12.50 | Jan | 2718 | 0.85 | 8 | 2.40 |
| Oracle | 15 | Dec | 11469 | 0.85 | 951 | 0.50 |
| 15.11 | 16.25 | Jan | 17899 | 0.90 | 168 | 1.60 |
| 15.11 | 17.50 | Mar | 1492 | 0.95 | 33 | 2.90 |
| Penney | 22.50 | Jan | 320 | 1.70 | 2224 | 1.50 |
| Peoplesoft | 40 | Dec | 1879 | 1.55 | 278 | 2 |
| 39.36 | 42.50 | Jan | 3525 | 2.40 | ... | ... |
| PepsiCo | 45 | Jul | 1501 | 4.80 | ... | ... |
| 46.60 | 47.50 | Apr | 503 | 2.55 | 14000 | 3.20 |
| Pfizer | 35 | Mar | 24 | 6 | 1193 | 0.80 |
| 40.35 | 40 | Dec | 1571 | 1.20 | 2645 | 0.85 |
| 40.35 | 40 | Jan | 670 | 1.80 | 1843 | 1.30 |
| 40.35 | 40 | Mar | 397 | 2.75 | 2951 | 2.10 |
| 40.35 | 45 | Jan | 1775 | 0.25 | 238 | 4.70 |
| 40.35 | 75 | Dec | 10661 | 0.30 | 293 | 2.35 |
| 40.35 | 75 | Jan | 4950 | 0.80 | ... | ... |
| 40.35 | 75 | Mar | 2682 | 1.40 | 270 | 3.60 |
| 40.35 | 75 | Jun | 9 | 2.35 | 1335 | 4.40 |
| PharmRes | 30 | Feb | 1720 | 3,70 | ... | ... |
| Pharmacia | 45 | Dec | 5077 | 0.25 | 113 | 1.75 |
| Ph Mor | 42.50 | Dec | 10 | 3.10 | 1669 | 0.20 |
| ProcG | 65 | Dec | ... | ... | 1200 | 0.05 |
| 76.70 | 70 | Dec | 5 | 7.60 | 1871 | 0.10 |
| 76.70 | 70 | Jan | 43 | 7.30 | 1844 | 0.60 |
| 76.70 | 70 | Apr | 1 | 8.80 | 1703 | 1.90 |
| 76.70 | 75 | Jan | 590 | 3.40 | 1721 | 1.65 |
| Qualcom | 60 | Dec | 4632 | 1.20 | 346 | 3.50 |
| QwestCom | 12.50 | Dec | 3769 | 0.50 | 1767 | 0.75 |
| RF MicD | 25 | Dec | 3872 | 1.70 | 468 | 1.05 |
| 25.52 | 30 | May | 2002 | 3.60 | 1902 | 8 |
| SBC Cm | 40 | Dec | 2480 | 0.15 | 23 | 2.25 |
| 38.00 | 40 | Jan | 165 | 0.75 | 1547 | 2.65 |
| STMicroel | 35 | Jan | 35 | 1.50 | 1500 | 3.90 |
| Sanmina | 20 | Dec | 1246 | 4.80 | 28 | 0.10 |
| 25.60 | 25 | Dec | 1207 | 1.30 | 29 | 0.80 |
| Schering | 35 | Dec | 2783 | 3.60 | 1581 | 0.15 |
| 38.65 | 37.50 | Dec | 6641 | 1.55 | 1539 | 0.55 |
| 38.65 | 40 | Dec | 1466 | 0.55 | 162 | 2.10 |
| 38.65 | 40 | Jan | 1531 | 1.25 | 98 | 2.45 |
| Schlmb | 45 | Jan | ... | ... | 1630 | 0.95 |
| SiebelSys | 25 | Dec | 1871 | 1.20 | 1440 | 1.30 |
| 24.91 | 25 | Jan | 1902 | 2.50 | 62 | 2.70 |
| 24.91 | 27.50 | Dec | 3445 | 0.40 | 51 | 2.90 |

| OPTION | STRIKE | EXP. | CALL VOL. | CALL LAST | PUT VOL. | PUT LAST |
|---|---|---|---|---|---|---|
| Solectr | 5 | Jan | ... | ... | 5000 | 0.70 |
| SunMicro | 12.50 | Dec | 3884 | 1.10 | 446 | 0.30 |
| 13.39 | 15 | Dec | 2075 | 0.10 | 74 | 1.65 |
| 13.39 | 15 | Jan | 1596 | 0.65 | 473 | 2.20 |
| TexasInst | 30 | Dec | 1208 | 1.75 | 11497 | 0.80 |
| 31.05 | 32.50 | Jan | 1204 | 1.80 | 25 | 3.10 |
| TibcoSft | 12.50 | Jan | 11 | 2.60 | 1408 | 0.90 |
| 14.50 | 15 | Jan | 1309 | 1.25 | ... | ... |
| TycoIntl | 55 | Dec | 296 | 2.10 | 1200 | 0.55 |
| 56.49 | 60 | Dec | 1785 | 0.15 | 10 | 3.50 |
| 56.49 | 60 | Jan | 1375 | 1 | 88 | 4.50 |
| USA Netw | 25 | Jan | 8207 | 1.95 | ... | ... |
| UPS B | 55 | Dec | 1559 | 1.50 | 292 | 0.35 |
| Verisign | 45 | Dec | 1336 | 0.60 | 90 | 5 |
| VeritasSf | 40 | Dec | 1152 | 3.70 | 735 | 1.25 |
| 42.65 | 45 | Dec | 4232 | 1.20 | 32 | 3.50 |
| 42.65 | 50 | Jan | 8759 | 1.85 | 41 | 9 |
| VerizonCm | 50 | Dec | 3408 | 0.20 | 60 | 2.15 |
| 47.86 | 50 | Jan | 1694 | 0.70 | 24 | 3.20 |
| Vitesse | 15 | Dec | 1483 | 0.60 | 216 | 1 |
| Vodfne | 30 | Jan | 1515 | 0.35 | 500 | 4.10 |
| WDigit | 5 | Jul | 15 | 2 | 1550 | 1 |
| Willamette | 40 | Jan | 750 | 6.50 | 5477 | 1.30 |
| 45.25 | 40 | Apr | 4450 | 7.70 | 278 | 1.85 |
| 45.25 | 45 | Dec | 1489 | 1.45 | 1860 | 1 |
| 45.25 | 45 | Jan | 8562 | 2.90 | 4602 | 2.50 |
| 45.25 | 45 | Apr | 1575 | 4 | 570 | 3.50 |
| 45.25 | 50 | Jan | 4297 | 0.75 | 30 | 5.20 |
| 45.25 | 50 | Apr | 2440 | 1.75 | ... | ... |
| WilmsCos | 25 | Dec | 645 | 0.80 | 2363 | 1 |
| WorldCom | 15 | Dec | 2101 | 0.40 | 552 | 0.40 |
| 14.94 | 15 | Jan | 2672 | 0.90 | 23 | 0.85 |
| XTO Engy | 15 | Dec | 2400 | 1 | 530 | 0.55 |
| 15.45 | 20 | Dec | 2200 | 0.05 | ... | ... |
| Xerox | 7.50 | Jan | 1288 | 1.45 | 12 | 0.30 |
| 8.51 | 7.50 | Apr | 21 | 2 | 1650 | 0.80 |
| Xilinx | 25 | Dec | 2400 | 0.50 | ... | ... |
| Yahoo | 15 | Jan | 252 | 4 | 3606 | 0.80 |

**VOLUME & OPEN INTEREST SUMMARIES**

Includes all equity and index contracts

| | | | |
|---|---|---|---|
| **AMERICAN** | | | |
| Call Vol: | 438,576 | Open Int: | 22,203,874 |
| Put Vol: | 357,575 | Open Int: | 10,108,086 |
| **CHICAGO BOARD** | | | |
| Call Vol: | 567,045 | Open Int: | 58,147,119 |
| Put Vol: | 411,115 | Open Int: | 34,671,566 |
| **INTL SECURITIES** | | | |
| Call Vol: | 197,601 | Open Int: | 46,853,560 |
| Put Vol: | 148,097 | Open Int: | 27,103,896 |
| **PHILADELPHIA** | | | |
| Call Vol: | 200,961 | Open Int: | 37,769,667 |
| Put Vol: | 143,864 | Open Int: | 18,844,440 |
| **PACIFIC** | | | |
| Call Vol: | 166,882 | Open Int: | 60,764,384 |
| Put Vol: | 109,714 | Open Int: | 24,525,097 |
| **TOTAL** | | | |
| Call Vol: | 1,571,065 | Open Int: | 225,738,604 |
| Put Vol: | 1,170,365 | Open Int: | 115,253,085 |

# LEAPS – LONG TERM OPTIONS

| OPTION | STRIKE | EXP. | CALL VOL. | CALL LAST | PUT VOL. | PUT LAST |
|---|---|---|---|---|---|---|
| AOL TW | 55 | Jan 03 | 511 | 0.90 | 3 | 22.90 |
| 32.00 | 60 | Jan 04 | 1053 | 2.30 | ... | ... |
| 32.00 | 65 | Jan 03 | 720 | 0.55 | ... | ... |
| 32.00 | 70 | Jan 04 | 1018 | 1.30 | ... | ... |
| 32.00 | 80 | Jan 04 | 2250 | 1 | ... | ... |
| AMD | 10 | Jan 03 | ... | ... | 1005 | 1.10 |
| Biogen | 70 | Jan 03 | 701 | 6 | ... | ... |
| BrMySq | 55 | Jan 03 | 562 | 6.70 | ... | ... |
| CMGI | 5 | Jan 03 | 1335 | 0.60 | 20 | 3.10 |
| CNA Fn | 25 | Jan 03 | ... | ... | 5000 | 2.95 |
| Calpine | 20 | Jan 03 | 489 | 3.60 | 60 | 7.40 |
| 15.50 | 20 | Jan 04 | 2864 | 5.10 | 15 | 8.20 |
| Cisco | 10 | Jan 04 | 10 | 13 | 4115 | 1.15 |
| 20.78 | 20 | Jan 04 | 525 | 7.50 | ... | ... |
| 20.78 | 25 | Jan 03 | 871 | 3.50 | 28 | 6.80 |
| 20.78 | 25 | Jan 04 | 2930 | 5.70 | 112 | 8.20 |
| Comcst sp | 20 | Jan 03 | ... | ... | 7015 | 0.35 |
| Compaq | 7.50 | Jan 03 | 50 | 3.40 | 2525 | 1.25 |
| Corning | 40 | Jan 03 | 600 | 0.05 | ... | ... |
| DellCptr | 35 | Jan 03 | 1435 | 4 | ... | ... |
| 29.06 | 35 | Jan 04 | 14015 | 6.80 | ... | ... |
| EKodak | 45 | Jan 03 | 500 | 0.95 | ... | ... |
| Enron | 5 | Jan 04 | 453 | 0.40 | 226 | 4.60 |
| EricTel | 5 | Jan 03 | 84 | 2 | 5003 | 0.85 |
| FordM | 17.50 | Jan 03 | 2524 | 2.05 | ... | ... |
| GenMotrs | 55 | Jan 03 | 1030 | 3.50 | 1155 | 11.30 |
| 48.65 | 60 | Jan 04 | 511 | 4.40 | ... | ... |
| GMH | 12.50 | Jan 03 | ... | ... | 1920 | 2 |
| Gucci | 120 | Jan 03 | ... | ... | 1100 | 35.70 |

| OPTION | STRIKE | EXP. | CALL VOL. | CALL LAST | PUT VOL. | PUT LAST |
|---|---|---|---|---|---|---|
| Hallibtn | 17.50 | Jan 03 | 2030 | 3 | 10 | 6.20 |
| 14.00 | 20 | Jan 04 | 2022 | 3.40 | 5 | 8.70 |
| 14.00 | 30 | Jan 04 | 2195 | 1.80 | ... | ... |
| HomeDp | 70 | Jan 04 | 800 | 3.80 | 29 | 23.20 |
| Intel | 35 | Jan 04 | 1185 | 8.50 | 16 | 8.20 |
| 33.19 | 50 | Jan 04 | 250 | 4.20 | 3000 | 18.50 |
| IBM | 115 | Jan 03 | 6 | 20.50 | 1033 | 11.80 |
| 121.50 | 150 | Jan 03 | 1446 | 6.50 | ... | ... |
| LeapWre | 20 | Jan 04 | ... | ... | 1400 | 8.60 |
| Merck | 90 | Jan 04 | 1001 | 4 | 48 | 24.80 |
| MerrLyn | 50 | Jan 03 | 22281 | 10.50 | 2020 | 7 |
| Microsft | 65 | Jan 03 | 25 | 12.60 | 18400 | 8.40 |
| 67.32 | 65 | Jan 04 | 2 | 17.80 | 6652 | 11.30 |
| 67.32 | 70 | Jan 03 | 47641 | 9.90 | 12275 | 10.90 |
| 67.32 | 85 | Jan 03 | 12056 | 4.50 | 12000 | 20.40 |
| 67.32 | 100 | Jan 03 | 1050 | 1.80 | ... | ... |
| 67.32 | 115 | Jan 04 | 1314 | 3.30 | ... | ... |
| Nasd100Tr | 35 | Jan 03 | 61 | 10.80 | 2016 | 3.30 |
| 41.23 | 40 | Jan 03 | 638 | 7.70 | 61 | 5.30 |
| 41.23 | 45 | Jan 03 | 838 | 5.60 | 1000 | 7.90 |
| 41.23 | 50 | Jan 03 | 6322 | 3.70 | 9 | 11 |
| 41.23 | 50 | Jan 04 | 1227 | 6.70 | ... | ... |
| NobleDr | 30 | Jan 03 | ... | ... | 1000 | 5.90 |
| 30.91 | 30 | Jan 04 | ... | ... | 1000 | 7.50 |
| Nokia | 30 | Jan 03 | 1565 | 4.50 | 17 | 8.20 |
| 25.50 | 40 | Jan 03 | 653 | 2.05 | 5 | 15.80 |
| Oracle | 15 | Jan 03 | 2648 | 4 | 15 | 3.10 |
| 15.11 | 20 | Jan 03 | 270 | 2.30 | 2576 | 6.60 |
| 15.11 | 20 | Jan 04 | 136 | 3.80 | 2550 | 7.50 |

| OPTION | STRIKE | EXP. | CALL VOL. | CALL LAST | PUT VOL. | PUT LAST |
|---|---|---|---|---|---|---|
| PMC Srra | 70 | Jan 03 | 840 | 2.60 | ... | ... |
| PepsiCo | 50 | Jan 04 | 768 | 6.40 | ... | ... |
| 46.60 | 60 | Jan 04 | 1000 | 3.50 | 188 | 14.40 |
| Pfizer | 40 | Jan 03 | 155 | 5.40 | 469 | 4.40 |
| 40.35 | 45 | Jan 03 | 731 | 2.90 | 161 | 7.40 |
| 40.35 | 50 | Jan 04 | 78 | 3.80 | 1746 | 11.40 |
| ProvidF | 10 | Jan 03 | 1400 | 0.60 | ... | ... |
| Qualcom | 60 | Jan 03 | 6 | 14.20 | 7132 | 15 |
| 57.53 | 60 | Jan 04 | 38 | 20.10 | 6800 | 18.80 |
| RiteAid | 5 | Jan 04 | 525 | 1.75 | 320 | 1.95 |
| TycoIntl | 80 | Jan 04 | 1268 | 4.90 | ... | ... |
| UAL | 15 | Jan 03 | ... | ... | 500 | 3 |
| UPS | 40 | Jan 04 | ... | ... | 468 | 1.95 |
| 56.18 | 65 | Jan 04 | 760 | 4.60 | ... | ... |
| WillmsCo | 25 | Jan 03 | 6 | 4.20 | 502 | 4.40 |
| 25.14 | 25 | Jan 04 | 866 | 5.90 | 100 | 5.60 |
| WorldCm | 17.50 | Jan 03 | 76 | 2.10 | 500 | 4 |

**VOLUME & OPEN INTEREST SUMMARIES**

| | | | |
|---|---|---|---|
| **CHICAGO BOARD** | | | |
| Call Vol: | 39,631 | Open Int: | 13,998,626 |
| Put Vol: | 23,429 | Open Int: | 7,310,543 |
| **PACIFIC** | | | |
| Call Vol: | 13,635 | Open Int: | 13,874,105 |
| Put Vol: | 17,730 | Open Int: | 7,224,836 |

$30,000 less commissions and interest. These are certainly tidy profits for a two-week investment.

But consider what happens if the speculator takes $10,000 and buys January 40 call options. She can buy 333 contracts and thereby obtain the right to buy 33,300 shares. Now, when the price goes up 50 points, our speculator is able to exercise the call option and buy the shares at 40 per share and immediately sell them for 82. The net profit after deducting the $10,000 cost of the options is $1,055,600 (less commissions).

One can obviously get rich quickly on call options if one can correctly predict when a big run-up in price will occur. Indeed, some who made fantastic profits on inside information about takeovers used call options to maximize their gains. It should be added that such trading is illegal, and violators are subject to civil and criminal penalties.

It is not necessary for the speculator to exercise the options to purchase the shares and then immediately resell. The options themselves can be sold. Thus, the profit can be realized by the speculator whether or not she has the capital to exercise the options. Indeed, one would expect the AOL January 40 calls to rise in price to about $42 per share ($4,200 per contract) in the example. If the option had longer to run, the price would be even higher, because there is a chance that the stock will rise even higher before expiration. When the price of the underlying stock is greater than the strike price of a call option, the option is said to be **in the money**.

There is no danger that the option writer will renege. His performance is guaranteed by both the exchange on which the option is traded and the broker who arranged for the option to be written. Nor is there much danger that an investor will allow a valuable option to go unexercised before it expires. Indeed, brokerage firms regularly **sweep** option customers' accounts and sell all options that are in the money shortly before expiration.

There must be a downside to get-rich-quick trading in options. Indeed there is. What happens if the speculator is wrong and the price of AOL remains stable? If the speculator bought the stock itself, she is about even: AOL has remained stable in price and the investment can be recovered (less commissions) simply by selling the stock. Even if the speculator had bought more shares on margin, she still would lose only a little interest in addition to commissions. But if the speculator had bought call options, they would expire, and she would lose the entire investment.

The call option used in the last example is an **out of the money** option, because AOL would need to rise 8 points in price before the option has any value at expiration. The December 30 option, on the other hand, is in the money, because the stock is selling at 32 and the option has an intrinsic value of $2.00. This option sold for $2.50 on the quoted date. The difference between $2.00 and $2.50 represents a **premium** for the possibility that the stock may increase in price before the option expires. The difference is sometimes called the **time value** of the option to distinguish it from the option's **intrinsic value**. The time value of an option increases in proportion to the length of time to expiration. Thus the December 35 call option traded for $.25 on the same day that the January 35 call option traded for $1.10.

The person who commits to sell shares at the option of the purchaser is called the **writer** of the option. When a person writes an option and sells it, the writer receives the sales price of the option: The writer of the AOL calls described above pockets the $10,000 sales price for the options (less a broker-age commission). If the option expires valueless, the writer keeps the $10,000, thereby improving the yield on his portfolio. If AOL unexpectedly moves up in price and the option is exercised, the writer will be required to sell the shares. The writer still has a profit, but all profits above the strike price inure to the purchaser of the call option. Writing call options at above-market strike prices is generally profitable in stable or declining markets, because few will be exercised.

Some investors write call options without actually owning the shares. This is called **going naked** or writing **naked options**, and is considerably more risky than writing **covered options**—options for which the writer already owns the shares. Writing a naked call option is similar in terms of risk to a short sale. If the price moves up, both the short seller and the writer of the uncovered call are required to buy similar stock to close out the transaction. Because the broker selling the uncovered call option is responsible for delivery of the shares if the call is exercised, it is essential that the writer of an uncovered call post margin and that the margin be increased if the price of the underlying stock rises during the life of the option.

Call options may also be used to speculate on a variety of potential takeover candidates by persons with limited financial resources. A person having identified, say, 10 companies that are likely takeover candidates may purchase call options on all 10 stocks at a cost considerably less than directly investing in the stocks themselves. If one or two of the 10 actually become takeover candidates, the gain on these calls may well exceed the cost of all of the call options. Of course, if none of the 10 actually become takeover candidates during the period of the options, the speculator may easily lose the entire investment.

Probably the most common strategy among options traders is to buy near-to-the-money options to speculate on smaller moves in the price of a stock. Although it is almost inconceivable that AOL would rise by $50 per share, it would not be at all unusual for it to rise by $5 even on a single day. If a trader were to buy a $35 call and sell it after the stock had risen to $37, the trader could make a $2 per share profit (ignoring commissions) on this one-day investment. Assuming that the option does not expire at least for a few more days, the price of the option is likely to rise by just about the same amount as the price of the stock on any given day. Indeed, the trader who buys a $35 call option can even make a profit if the stock only moves up to $33 or $34 (again ignoring commissions), because the option itself may be sold for the premium.

Call options may be purchased in order to hedge short sale positions. Recall that a short seller borrows shares and sells them, hoping prices will decline so that he or she can replace the borrowed shares at a lower price. A short seller gets squeezed when prices move up rather than down. If the short seller is concerned about this prospect she can reduce or eliminate the risk by buying a call option on the same stock. If the price goes up, the loss on the short sale position will be offset by the gain on the call. Whether this is desirable depends on how expensive the call is, because that is the premium for this type of insurance.

A put option enables the purchaser of the put to profit on market declines. A put is the mirror image of a call option. The writer of a put option commits to buy the stock at the strike price for the specified period at the option of the buyer of the option. In a call, the writer commits to sell and the buyer of the call has the option whether buy. In a put, the writer commits to buy and the buyer of the put has the option whether to sell. For example, Table 15-1 shows that the AOL December 30 put option traded at $.60. If a person bought this put, and the price of AOL declined to 25, the holder of the put would show a profit equal to the difference between 30 and 25, minus the cost of the put option. In the vernacular, the holder of the put could buy AOL at 25 and put it to the writer at 30. That is why it is called a put. Table 15-1 shows the inverse relationship between puts and calls. When a call is in the money and has intrinsic value, the corresponding put is out of the money, and vice versa.

Because the writer of a put option only commits to purchase a stock at a specified price, there is no precisely analogous concept to writing naked call options on the put side. The writing of puts, however, can create devastating losses if there is a sudden strong downward movement in the stock's price. The risk involved in writing put options is not apparent in a generally rising market. Such a market existed from early 1982 through August 1987. Many brokers recommended to relatively unsophisticated clients during this period that the clients write put options to increase the investment yield of their portfolios. It seemed to be a relatively safe way of increasing investment return. In the abrupt market decline that occurred in October 1987, many of these investors' savings were wiped out as brokerage firms liquidated their accounts in order to meet obligations under put contracts, and some investors ended up owing their brokerage firms substantial amounts as well. The writer of a put option can limit future losses by buying an offsetting put option or by writing a call option. In a period of sharp market decline such as occurred in October 1987, the prices of puts advanced so rapidly (and the process of communicating securities orders was often so constricted) that these strategies were, as a practical matter, unavailable to at-risk put writers.

Puts may be purchased to shield portfolio positions from price declines; for example, a person with 100 shares of AOL who fears a short-term decline in the stock but who does not want to sell the shares, may purchase a put option for 100 shares. If the price does decline, the loss of value in the underlying stock will be offset to some extent by the rise in value of the put, although the precise amount of protection depends on the terms of the particular put purchased.

In 1990, the **Chicago Board Options Exchange (CBOE)** began trading in long-term put-and-call options, called **long-term equity anticipation securities (LEAPS)**. These options have expiration periods of as long as two years. The strike price for LEAPS is usually set quite far away from the stock's current price—for example, when a stock is trading at 50, LEAPS calls may be quoted at 60 and puts at 40. A one-year call option on a $95 stock with a strike price of $105 might be around $6. In order for the investor to break even, the stock would need to reach $111 by expiration, a 17 percent rise in price, although the value of the option itself might increase if the stock were to rise significantly in price. In any event, with LEAPs, the trade-off is that larger price swings are necessary rather than the quicker ones needed to make a profit with conventional short-term options, which are limited to a maximum duration of nine months (and which also explains why there is no indication of the expiration year in the tables for conventional options).

In general, the purchaser of a put or call option risks only the money he or she has invested in the option. If the price moves in the wrong direction, the holder of the option simply allows the option to expire unexercised. The writer of an option, on the other hand, is much more at the mercy of market forces.

In summary, there are many ways to speculate in stocks. If one thinks the price is going up, one should: buy the stock, or buy the stock on margin, or buy calls, or write puts. If one thinks the price is going down, one should: sell the stock, or sell the stock short, or write calls, or buy puts.

One can speculate simultaneously on upward and downward movements by the purchase of options (a strategy known as a straddle). One may buy, for example, an AOL December 30 put for $.60 and a December 35 call for $.25. The straddle thus costs $.85 per share plus commissions. One makes money on this straddle if the price of AOL drops below 30 or rises above 35. One loses only if AOL steadily trades in the range between 30 and 35 for the balance of the option period.

A **synthetic position** is a combination of options that roughly equals ownership of the underlying security. A speculator in a potential takeover stock, for example, may buy a call with a strike price near the current market price of the stock while simultaneously selling or writing a put option at the same price. This combination, which approximates ownership of the security itself, is usually considerably less expensive to create (even if the margin requirement for writing the put is taken into account) than purchasing the stock directly or on margin.

Another options strategy is a **covered strangle** or **covered write**: selling both a call option and put option on a stock the speculator already owns. On a $60 stock, the speculator might write a call option at $65 and a put option at $55. Because the stock is already owned, it serves as collateral for writing the put option. In effect, the speculator pockets two premiums at the risk of being compelled to sell her stock when the price approaches $65 or add to her holding if the price declines toward $55. In a broad sense, a covered strangle is the converse of going naked. An **uncovered strangle** is the sale of both a call option and a put option when the speculator does not already own the stock. Some investors may be concerned that an uncovered strangle does not provide protection against substantial losses if the stock were to explode or collapse in price. Such an investor may obtain considerable protection by adding "wings," purchasing out of the money puts and calls to cap the maximum exposure in either direction.

Another interesting strategy minimizes the cost of a planned investment of, say, 200 shares of a stock currently selling at $37 per share. The strategy consists of the purchase of 100 shares, while at the same time selling a long-term call at 45 and a long-term put at 25. There are three possible outcomes: If the stock remains between 45 and 25, the investor keeps the stock and the purchase price is reduced by the two premiums on the options. If the price goes above 45, the stock will be called away but the investor has realized a gain of $20 per share on 100 shares, plus the two premiums. If the price declines to 25, the investor will be compelled to buy another 100 shares, but the price of these shares is $25 minus the two premiums, and the average price of the 200 shares is below the $37 per share that the investor would have paid if he or she had bought the 200 shares as originally planned. Of course, if the stock does not thereafter go above $25, the original plan to buy 200 shares at $37 per share was a terrible idea anyway.

A **married put** permits a speculator to engage in a bear raid similar to that made famous in the 1930s. A married put involves the simultaneous purchase of the underlying shares and of deep-in-the-money puts. For example, a speculator might purchase 100,000 shares of a $75 stock and 1,000 put contracts (puts on 100,000 shares) at 90. The cost of this put might be $13.50 per share. The speculator then sells the 100,000 shares gradually, in a manner designed to create apprehension from other shareholders and encourage them to sell. Because no short sale is involved, the sales may occur sequentially without regard to the uptick rule that applies to short sales. The expectation is that the profits on the puts will exceed the loss incurred from selling the shares at gradually declining prices. Some brokerage firms decline to trade in married puts, and the strategy described above seems to be manipulative and in probable violation of the federal securities law.

Why does an options market exist if the efficient market theory is so well accepted? When considered as stand-alone investments, options are far riskier than stocks because they last for only a short period, because they depend for their value solely on increases or decreases in market price, and because one loses the entire premium paid if the option expires worthless. To be sure, buying call options is an inexpensive way to buy stock, in the sense that one need only pay a few dollars or even cents per share to buy a chance at market gains in excess of the exercise price. But this is a very expensive way to invest when one considers that if the stock does not increase to the exercise price, the option expires worthless and the premium is lost. If one buys the stock and it fails to increase in price or increase in price as much as expected, one still has the stock and will have lost nothing other than the interest that may have been earned on the money in the meantime. Studies of option trading continue to indicate that option buyers—both put and call buyers—lose money in more than 60 percent of all transactions. A speculator in options thus faces long odds in an efficient market.

A plausible answer to the question of why an options market exists is that options are ideal for hedging rather than direct investment. Of course, the fact that options may make sense for one purpose does not mean they cannot be used (or misused) for another purpose. A conservative investor may use options as a way of insuring against the possibility that a particular stock or a portfolio of stocks will rise or fall in price. In addition, an investor who wants to increase the return from a portfolio may sell (write) options allowing others to buy or sell. By doing so, the investor receives the premium from the buyer of the option and agrees to buy or sell the stock in question if the optionholder exercises. In a sense, the writer of the option is betting against price movements in the stock and getting paid to do so by those who are worried about price movements, a tactic that is perfectly consistent with the efficient market theory. Speculators (as opposed to hedgers) may also participate in the market, and although it may be very risky from their point of view, hedgers welcome their participation, because the more trading there is in options, the cheaper it is to use them to hedge.

## §15.3 Options on Indexes, Foreign Currencies, and Interest Rates

Options trading can be extended to any product that fluctuates in price. Rather than writing an option on a single stock, one can write an option on a portfolio of stocks, that is, on a stock index. One can write an option on foreign currencies (whose values fluctuate with respect to U.S. dollars and with respect to each other). One can write options on Treasury notes or Treasury bonds (whose values fluctuate in response to interest rate changes, because they are viewed as riskless investments). Indeed, options are traded on all of these. The only real difference in operation between traditional securities options described in the previous section and these nonstock options is that one cannot usually receive or deliver the underlying securities or commodities when the option is exercised; one simply settles up in cash.

Options on stock indexes were introduced in the 1980s and quickly became extremely popular. (Trading in stock indexes themselves is discussed below in connection with commodities and futures.) Table 15-2 shows index options traded on the CBOE and elsewhere. The original S&P 500 option was an **American Option** exercisable any time during the life of the option. In 1988, it was changed to a **European Option**, which may be exercised only on the expiration date. The advantage of the European Option is that institutional investors writing options as part of hedging transactions are assured that the option remains in existence until its expiration date.

The possibility of using puts and calls on individual stocks to hedge against price movements has previously been noted. Is there any social benefit to the trading of index options described in this section? Or do they amount to gambling on random movements in abstract numbers? These questions have evoked some controversy. Options isolate the risk of investments in units that can be traded separately. Index options permit investors with large and diversified portfolios to hedge against broad price movements. Thus, for those who invest in diversified portfolios, index options are arguably more important for hedging purposes than are options on individual stocks.

Table 15-2

# INDEX OPTIONS TRADING

Tuesday, December 11, 2001

Volume, last, net change and open interest for all contracts. Volume figures are unofficial. Open interest reflects previous trading day. p-Put c-Call

## CHICAGO

**DJ INDUS AVG(DJX)**

| STRIKE | | VOL. | LAST | NET CHG. | OPEN INT. |
|---|---|---|---|---|---|
| Feb | 64 p | 20 | 0.05 | - 0.05 | 1,754 |
| Jan | 72 p | 33 | 0.15 | - 0.25 | 488 |
| Mar | 72 c | 2 | 27.70 | - 2.20 | 2 |
| Feb | 76 p | 14 | 0.30 | - 0.10 | 7,441 |
| Jan | 80 p | 100 | 0.15 | ... | 6,066 |
| Feb | 80 p | 220 | 0.45 | - 0.10 | 17,123 |
| Dec | 84 p | 5 | 0.05 | ... | 8,458 |
| Mar | 84 p | 26 | 1.70 | ... | 14,759 |
| Dec | 86 p | 150 | 0.05 | ... | 11,526 |
| Dec | 88 p | 2 | 0.05 | ... | 40,647 |
| Jan | 88 p | 55 | 0.45 | ... | 3,136 |
| Dec | 90 c | 7 | 9.30 | - 0.60 | 8,690 |
| Dec | 90 p | 15 | 0.05 | - 0.05 | 47,617 |
| Jan | 90 p | 520 | 0.50 | - 0.10 | 12,480 |
| Feb | 90 p | 17 | 1.80 | + 0.15 | 6,665 |
| Dec | 92 c | 4 | 6.70 | - 1.80 | 23,031 |
| Dec | 92 p | 210 | 0.10 | - 0.05 | 26,507 |
| Jan | 92 c | 20 | 8.60 | ... | 562 |
| Feb | 92 p | 6 | 2.15 | + 0.20 | 7,232 |
| Dec | 93 p | 5 | 0.15 | - 0.05 | 4,689 |
| Dec | 94 p | 318 | 0.30 | + 0.05 | 18,786 |
| Jan | 94 p | 7 | 1.20 | + 0.05 | 5,326 |
| Feb | 94 p | 5 | 2.70 | + 0.55 | 6,879 |
| Dec | 95 c | 10 | 4.40 | - 0.50 | 168 |
| Dec | 95 p | 1 | 0.40 | ... | 2,153 |
| Dec | 96 c | 5 | 3.80 | - 1.00 | 5,675 |
| Dec | 96 p | 489 | 0.55 | - 0.05 | 20,534 |
| Jan | 96 c | 14 | 4.50 | - 0.30 | 1,066 |
| Jan | 96 p | 11 | 1.30 | - 0.40 | 2,149 |
| Feb | 96 c | 5 | 6.60 | - 0.80 | 1,323 |
| Feb | 96 p | 222 | 3.10 | + 0.10 | 9,664 |
| Mar | 96 p | 2 | 4.40 | - 0.20 | 1,861 |
| Dec | 97 c | 83 | 3.30 | - 0.10 | 5,030 |
| Dec | 97 p | 329 | 0.75 | ... | 12,173 |
| Dec | 98 c | 66 | 1.85 | - 1.15 | 25,661 |
| Dec | 98 p | 882 | 1.05 | ... | 18,091 |
| Jan | 98 c | 18 | 3.90 | + 0.20 | 2,093 |
| Jan | 98 p | 212 | 2.50 | + 0.15 | 3,756 |
| Dec | 99 c | 614 | 1.40 | - 0.55 | 2,337 |
| Dec | 99 p | 491 | 1.20 | - 0.30 | 7,243 |
| Dec | 100 c | 809 | 0.80 | - 0.30 | 14,358 |
| Dec | 100 p | 895 | 2.10 | + 0.15 | 25,880 |
| Jan | 100 c | 108 | 1.95 | - 0.45 | 5,084 |
| Jan | 100 p | 244 | 3.30 | + 0.20 | 10,085 |
| Feb | 100 c | 306 | 3.80 | - 0.20 | 3,487 |
| Feb | 100 p | 50 | 4.30 | - 0.40 | 8,918 |
| Mar | 100 c | 7 | 6.20 | - 0.30 | 3,216 |
| Mar | 100 p | 63 | 6.50 | + 0.30 | 5,283 |
| Dec | 101 c | 657 | 0.50 | - 0.25 | 2,526 |
| Dec | 101 p | 502 | 2.60 | + 0.10 | 977 |
| Dec | 102 c | 237 | 0.30 | - 0.15 | 4,409 |
| Dec | 102 p | 58 | 3.50 | + 0.50 | 3,998 |
| Jan | 102 c | 115 | 1.50 | ... | 655 |
| Jan | 102 p | 8 | 3.70 | - 0.40 | 338 |
| Feb | 102 p | 21 | 5.30 | + 0.40 | 80 |
| Dec | 103 c | 52 | 0.25 | - 0.05 | 1,783 |
| Dec | 103 p | 50 | 3.60 | ... | 1,070 |
| Dec | 104 c | 120 | 0.10 | - 0.05 | 10,667 |
| Jan | 104 p | 13 | 4.90 | - 0.70 | 701 |
| Feb | 104 c | 5 | 2 | - 0.55 | 11,620 |
| Feb | 104 p | 58 | 6.50 | + 0.50 | 2,549 |
| Dec | 105 c | 10 | 0.15 | ... | 468 |
| Dec | 106 c | 252 | 0.05 | - 0.05 | 4,436 |
| Jan | 108 p | 10 | 9.10 | + 1.60 | 30 |
| Feb | 108 c | 320 | 1.10 | + 0.05 | 6,785 |
| Feb | 112 c | 3 | 0.45 | - 0.35 | 4,041 |
| Mar | 124 p | 1 | 24 | - 2.20 | 81 |

Call Vol. 4,388 Open Int. 257,223
Put Vol. 6,945 Open Int. 583,154

**DJ TRANP AVG(DTX)**

| | | | | | |
|---|---|---|---|---|---|
| Dec | 250 c | 10 | 10.90 | - 4.10 | 10 |

Call Vol. 10 Open Int. 652
Put Vol. 0 Open Int. 739

**GC TECH COMPOSITE(GTC)**

| | | | | | |
|---|---|---|---|---|---|
| Dec | 220 c | 5 | 3.70 | - 0.20 | 29 |

Call Vol. 5 Open Int. 129
Put Vol. 0 Open Int. 85

**NASDAQ-100(NDX)**

| STRIKE | | VOL. | LAST | NET CHG. | OPEN INT. |
|---|---|---|---|---|---|
| Jan | 950 c | 6 | 713.50 | ... | ... |
| Dec | 1075 p | 20 | 0.10 | - 2.20 | 30 |
| Jan | 1100 p | 5 | 2 | - 0.85 | 318 |
| Dec | 1125 p | 25 | 0.20 | - 0.30 | 405 |
| Jan | 1200 p | 1 | 4.20 | - 1.80 | 210 |
| Jan | 1300 p | 22 | 8 | - 1.00 | 116 |
| Dec | 1375 p | 21 | 1 | - 0.90 | 681 |
| Dec | 1400 p | 285 | 2 | - 1.90 | 2,702 |
| Jan | 1400 p | 1 | 18 | - 5.00 | 882 |
| Dec | 1425 p | 82 | 1.75 | - 2.05 | 70 |
| Dec | 1450 p | 57 | 3 | - 4.00 | 2,767 |
| Dec | 1475 p | 72 | 3.50 | - 4.50 | 232 |
| Dec | 1500 p | 136 | 8.10 | - 3.10 | 1,161 |
| Jan | 1500 p | 12 | 35 | - 5.00 | 270 |
| Dec | 1525 p | 2 | 8.50 | - 7.50 | 183 |
| Dec | 1550 c | 1 | 130 | -32.00 | 91 |
| Dec | 1550 p | 1,062 | 13.40 | - 3.30 | 3,005 |
| Dec | 1575 p | 16 | 16 | - 5.00 | 2,072 |
| Dec | 1600 c | 1 | 95 | + 3.00 | 1,398 |
| Dec | 1600 p | 85 | 17.50 | -17.50 | 1,552 |
| Jan | 1600 c | 1 | 139 | -23.50 | 69 |
| Jan | 1600 p | 5 | 61 | - 5.00 | 1,704 |
| Dec | 1625 c | 2 | 80 | +13.00 | 1,233 |
| Dec | 1625 p | 4 | 26 | - 6.50 | 258 |
| Dec | 1650 c | 3 | 70 | +11.00 | 284 |
| Dec | 1650 p | 524 | 46.90 | - 3.10 | 633 |
| Dec | 1675 p | 1 | 48 | - 4.00 | 12 |
| Jan | 1675 c | 10 | 99.30 | + 1.30 | 61 |
| Dec | 1700 c | 113 | 40 | +12.50 | 1,913 |
| Dec | 1700 p | 34 | 53 | -24.50 | 1,734 |
| Dec | 1725 c | 2 | 27.50 | - 7.50 | 133 |
| Dec | 1750 c | 57 | 15.30 | - 0.20 | 842 |
| Dec | 1750 p | 3 | 105 | + 3.00 | 40 |
| Dec | 1775 c | 2 | 10.90 | -13.40 | 140 |
| Jan | 1775 c | 342 | 59.50 | +24.50 | 1 |
| Dec | 1800 c | 154 | 10.50 | + 4.00 | 2,186 |
| Jan | 1800 c | 1 | 48 | + 4.00 | 382 |
| Dec | 1825 c | 2 | 6.50 | - 1.50 | 48 |
| Dec | 1850 c | 11 | 4 | + 0.70 | 1,277 |
| Jan | 1875 c | 11 | 27 | + 6.40 | 3 |
| Dec | 1900 c | 15 | 1.85 | + 0.55 | 1,334 |
| Jan | 1900 c | 10 | 22 | + 3.40 | 507 |
| Dec | 1925 c | 2 | 1.25 | - 1.25 | 468 |
| Dec | 1950 c | 200 | 0.70 | - 0.60 | 1,155 |
| Dec | 1950 p | 4 | 287 | +43.00 | 10 |
| Jan | 1950 c | 3 | 10.10 | -10.00 | 66 |
| Dec | 2050 p | 1 | 355 | -120.00 | 24 |
| Mar | 2050 c | 15 | 27.50 | - 2.50 | 370 |
| Jan | 2100 p | 2 | 410 | +20.00 | 7 |
| Jan | 2150 c | 12 | 1.80 | - 1.30 | 20 |
| Jan | 2200 c | 4 | 1.25 | - 0.35 | 19 |
| Mar | 2200 c | 5 | 12 | + 3.20 | 514 |
| Mar | 2250 c | 50 | 9 | + 1.50 | 175 |

Call Vol. 872 Open Int. 34,097
Put Vol. 1,362 Open Int. 43,012

**RUSSELL 2000(RUT)**

| STRIKE | | VOL. | LAST | NET CHG. | OPEN INT. |
|---|---|---|---|---|---|
| Dec | 460 p | 4 | 2 | - 0.30 | 1,013 |
| Dec | 470 c | 15 | 12.10 | + 7.50 | 174 |
| Jan | 470 p | 50 | 10.20 | + 0.50 | 4 |
| Mar | 470 p | 25 | 18.40 | -61.50 | 10 |
| Dec | 480 c | 2 | 5.50 | - 1.80 | 395 |

Call Vol. 17 Open Int. 4,794
Put Vol. 79 Open Int. 6,147

**S & P 100(OEX)**

| STRIKE | | VOL. | LAST | NET CHG. | OPEN INT. |
|---|---|---|---|---|---|
| Dec | 450 p | 609 | 0.05 | - 0.05 | 1,294 |
| Dec | 460 p | 8 | 0.05 | - 0.05 | 2,595 |
| Jan | 460 p | 4 | 0.70 | - 0.20 | 1,822 |
| Feb | 460 p | 1,200 | 2 | - 0.55 | 186 |
| Dec | 470 p | 25 | 0.10 | - 0.05 | 1,476 |
| Dec | 480 p | 40 | 0.10 | - 0.05 | 2,650 |
| Jan | 480 p | 21 | 1.30 | + 0.05 | 1,816 |
| Dec | 490 p | 91 | 0.20 | ... | 3,349 |
| Jan | 490 p | 10 | 1.60 | + 0.30 | 61 |
| Dec | 500 p | 73 | 0.20 | - 0.05 | 7,846 |
| Jan | 500 p | 2 | 1.80 | - 0.45 | 2,257 |
| Feb | 500 p | 1 | 4.50 | + 0.50 | 366 |
| Mar | 500 p | 30 | 6.20 | + 0.90 | 830 |
| Dec | 510 p | 340 | 0.30 | - 0.10 | 2,747 |
| Jan | 510 p | 41 | 2.75 | + 0.15 | 165 |
| Dec | 520 p | 383 | 0.45 | ... | 7,617 |
| Jan | 520 p | 67 | 3.20 | - 0.20 | 2,643 |
| Feb | 520 p | 100 | 6.30 | + 0.90 | 310 |
| Mar | 520 p | 1 | 8.50 | + 0.50 | 1,029 |
| Dec | 530 p | 557 | 0.50 | - 0.40 | 4,111 |
| Jan | 530 p | 15 | 4.20 | - 0.50 | 3,746 |
| Dec | 535 p | 120 | 1 | - 0.10 | 1,360 |
| Dec | 540 c | 15 | 42 | - 9.00 | 767 |
| Dec | 540 p | 421 | 1.30 | - 0.10 | 2,726 |
| Jan | 540 c | 2 | 46.30 | - 6.80 | 38 |
| Jan | 540 p | 128 | 5.60 | - 0.40 | 1,273 |
| Feb | 540 c | 2 | 56 | - 4.00 | 14 |
| Feb | 540 p | 16 | 8 | - 3.30 | 147 |
| Mar | 540 p | 6 | 12 | ... | 888 |
| Dec | 545 p | 137 | 1.70 | + 0.20 | 1,068 |
| Dec | 550 c | 6 | 31 | -19.00 | 381 |
| Dec | 550 p | 365 | 2.25 | + 0.15 | 4,531 |
| Jan | 550 p | 28 | 7.90 | + 0.40 | 965 |
| Feb | 550 p | 1 | 12.10 | + 0.10 | 9 |
| Dec | 555 c | 6 | 26 | -18.00 | 101 |
| Dec | 555 p | 563 | 2.50 | - 0.20 | 539 |
| Dec | 560 c | 1 | 23 | - 2.00 | 1,842 |
| Dec | 560 p | 1,420 | 3.30 | - 0.10 | 3,186 |
| Jan | 560 p | 14 | 10.50 | + 1.00 | 1,350 |
| Feb | 560 c | 2 | 37.50 | ... | ... |

## RANGES FOR UNDERLYING INDEXES

Tuesday, December 11, 2001

| | High | Low | Close | Net Chg | From 12/31 | % Chg |
|---|---|---|---|---|---|---|
| DJ Indus (DJX) | 100.16 | 98.67 | 98.88 | - 0.33 | - 8.99 | - 8.3 |
| DJ Trans (DTX) | 260.27 | 257.38 | 258.66 | - 1.25 | - 36.00 | - 12.2 |
| DJ Util (DUX) | 281.80 | 274.46 | 275.10 | - 6.62 | - 137.06 | - 33.3 |
| S&P 100 (OEX) | 587.42 | 577.93 | 579.32 | - 1.92 | - 107.13 | - 15.6 |
| S&P 500 -A.M.(SPX) | 1150.89 | 1134.32 | 1136.76 | - 3.17 | - 183.52 | - 13.9 |
| CB-Tech (TXX) | 574.29 | 559.25 | 563.94 | + 4.69 | - 119.18 | - 17.4 |
| CB-Mexico (MEX) | 69.31 | 67.59 | 69.00 | + 1.40 | - 18.25 | - 20.9 |
| CB-Lps Mex (VEX) | 6.93 | 6.76 | 6.90 | + 0.14 | - 1.82 | - 20.9 |
| MS Multintl (NFT) | 691.63 | 678.99 | 680.57 | - 3.11 | - 93.62 | - 12.1 |
| GSTI Comp (GTC) | 217.08 | 211.73 | 213.52 | + 1.79 | - 70.05 | - 24.7 |
| Nasdaq 100 (NDX) | 1695.15 | 1654.72 | 1661.27 | + 15.91 | - 680.43 | - 29.1 |
| NYSE (NYA) | 582.02 | 575.15 | 576.11 | - 2.14 | - 80.76 | - 12.3 |
| Russell 2000 (RUT) | 478.19 | 473.43 | 474.77 | + 0.59 | - 8.76 | - 1.8 |
| Lps S&P 100 (OEX) | 117.48 | 115.59 | 115.86 | - 0.39 | - 21.43 | - 15.6 |
| Lps S&P 500 (SPX) | 115.09 | 113.43 | 113.68 | - 0.31 | - 18.35 | - 13.9 |
| Volatility (VIX) | 26.27 | 24.93 | 25.69 | - 0.31 | - 4.54 | - 15.0 |
| S&P Midcap (MID) | 500.92 | 495.72 | 496.73 | + 0.64 | - 20.03 | - 3.9 |
| Major Mkt (XMI) | 1025.71 | 1009.47 | 1010.74 | - 6.70 | - 66.82 | - 6.2 |
| Eurotop 100 (EUR) | 282.84 | 281.15 | 282.11 | - 0.28 | - 71.14 | - 20.1 |
| HK Fltg (HKO) | 230.22 | 230.22 | 230.22 | - 1.68 | - 65.30 | - 22.1 |
| IW Internet (IIX) | 156.96 | 150.33 | 153.31 | + 2.98 | - 126.29 | - 45.2 |
| AM-Mexico (MXY) | 94.56 | 92.57 | 94.11 | + 1.52 | + 3.18 | + 3.5 |
| Institut'l -A.M.(XII) | 624.59 | 614.41 | 615.71 | - 1.25 | - 120.60 | - 16.4 |
| Japan (JPN) | | | 111.47 | - 1.04 | - 32.95 | - 22.8 |
| MS Cyclical (CYC) | 533.37 | 526.65 | 530.09 | + 2.07 | + 18.91 | + 3.7 |
| MS Consumr (CMR) | 552.71 | 545.65 | 546.98 | - 5.57 | - 66.93 | - 10.9 |
| MS Hi Tech (MSH) | 541.73 | 527.88 | 532.83 | + 4.95 | - 135.39 | - 20.3 |
| MS Internet (MOX) | 15.18 | 14.51 | 14.85 | + 0.34 | - 13.94 | - 48.4 |
| Pharma (DRG) | 392.72 | 381.82 | 382.72 | - 7.84 | - 64.66 | - 14.5 |
| Biotech (BTK) | 583.78 | 565.00 | 572.04 | - 3.41 | - 62.28 | - 9.8 |
| Gold/Silver (XAU) | 52.41 | 51.75 | 52.33 | - 0.11 | + 0.92 | + 1.8 |
| Utility (UTY) | 313.95 | 305.37 | 306.01 | - 7.73 | - 87.25 | - 22.2 |
| Value Line (VLE) | 1223.03 | 1210.83 | 1213.30 | + 0.03 | + 88.53 | + 7.9 |
| Bank (BKX) | 857.64 | 840.43 | 848.41 | + 3.66 | - 53.01 | - 5.9 |
| Semicond (SOX) | 579.52 | 559.37 | 565.77 | + 6.40 | - 10.84 | - 1.9 |
| Street.com (DOT) | 205.05 | 198.73 | 199.74 | + 4.23 | - 100.89 | - 33.6 |
| Oil Service (OSX) | 79.53 | 77.85 | 79.08 | + 0.55 | - 45.70 | - 36.6 |
| PSE Tech (PSE) | 717.03 | 702.84 | 706.41 | + 3.57 | - 108.02 | - 13.3 |

# DOW JONES SPECIALTY INDEXES

Tuesday, December 11, 2001

| | CLOSE | NET CHG | %CHG | YTD %CHG | YLD |
|---|---|---|---|---|---|
| Equity REIT -a | 148.87 | + 0.68 | + 0.46 | - 6.63 | 6.67 |
| Equity REIT -tot ret | 353.59 | + 1.71 | + 0.49 | + 13.46 | ... |
| Composite REIT -a | 131.36 | + 0.60 | + 0.46 | + 7.05 | 6.72 |
| Composite REIT -tot ret | 323.86 | + 1.59 | + 0.49 | + 13.92 | ... |
| DJ Islamic Market -b | 1547.32 | - 2.63 | - 0.17 | - 18.19 | ... |
| DJIM Global Tech -b | 2586.97 | + 22.80 | + 0.89 | - 29.39 | ... |
| DJIM US Index | 1827.85 | - 7.68 | - 0.42 | - 16.18 | ... |
| DJ Composite Internet | 64.93 | + 1.47 | + 2.32 | - 52.43 | ... |
| DJ Internet Commerce | 52.10 | + 1.11 | + 2.18 | - 4.02 | ... |
| DJ Internet Services | 62.67 | + 1.38 | + 2.25 | - 66.95 | ... |
| DJ Canada 40 -c | 1135.99 | - 4.18 | - 0.37 | - 21.20 | ... |
| DJ Global Titans | 197.07 | - 0.06 | - 0.03 | - 15.03 | ... |
| DJ Asian Titans | 96.51 | - 0.11 | - 0.11 | - 25.66 | ... |
| DJ Sustainability | 859.86 | + 1.50 | + 0.17 | - 17.31 | ... |
| DJ US Large-Cap | 256.72 | - 0.98 | - 0.38 | - 17.11 | ... |
| DJ US Mid-Cap | 274.93 | + 0.58 | + 0.21 | - 6.34 | ... |
| DJ US Small-Cap | 293.90 | + 0.32 | + 0.11 | - 1.30 | ... |

a- Indexes of publicly traded Real Estate Investment Trusts, Jan.1990= 100. Yield based on indicated annualized dividend.

b- A global index of companies that meet Islamic investment guidelines, Dec. 31 1995 = 1000.

c- An index comprised of Canada's largest, most actively traded equities, Dec. 31, 1998 = 1000. Index in Canadian Dollars.

# Table 15-2 (*cont.*)

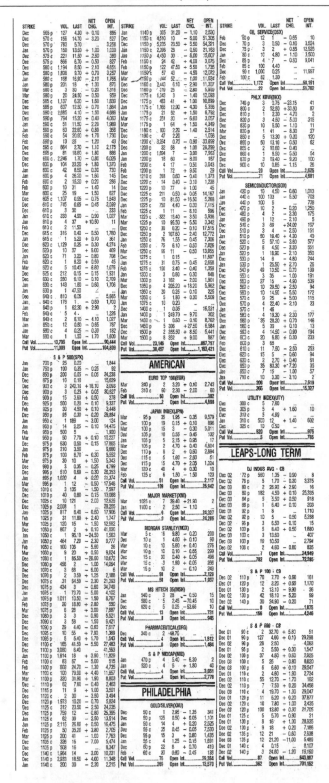

## §15.4 Commodities Markets

Commodities trading, primarily based in Chicago, and to a lesser extent in New York, has existed for more than a century. In recent years, these markets have been broadened to include trading in a variety of financial products. This section deals with traditional commodities trading; the following section briefly discusses financial products.

The traditional commodities market consists of two separate markets. The market for commodities available today—commodities located in warehouses or storage silos—is the **cash market** or **spot market**. Table 15-3 shows cash market prices for December 11, 2001. This market is used by suppliers, producers, and users of the various commodities that are traded. Most of the trading and speculative interest in commodities is not in the cash market, however, but in the futures market.

Table 15-4 shows the quotations for the futures markets for several agricultural commodities. Unlike the spot market, the **futures market** reflects trading in standard units for delivery at specific times in the future. The futures market for corn is a good example. Table 15-4 reflects trading in 5,000 bushel units of corn for future delivery. For example, one could buy or sell corn in 5,000-bushel units for delivery in December 2002 for $2.4275 per bushel or in December 2003 for $2.5575 per bushel. These transactions must be in the standard 5,000-bushel units. Assume that you decide to purchase 5,000 bushels of corn for December 2003 delivery. As a result of this transaction you have made a commitment to buy 5,000 bushels of corn. If the purchase were actually carried out, the transaction would involve $12,787.50 ($2.5575 × 5000). On the other hand, you have not actually bought any corn. You have simply committed yourself to buy corn in the future.

Both the Chicago Board of Trade (where your purchase was executed) and the **futures commission merchant** (**FCM**) (the equivalent of a broker) that placed your order are responsible for the performance of your obligation to buy the corn. (Commodities futures may also be traded through larger brokerage firms that typically have FCM units or relationships with FCMs who handle their orders.) Therefore, when you "buy the future," that is, when you enter into the contract to buy 5,000 bushels of corn, you must post some money to ensure that you will carry out your commitment. When you buy the future, you will be required to put up perhaps 10 percent of the total purchase price in cash, in this case $1,278.75. This up-front payment is called **margin**, but it differs in a fundamental way from a margin purchase of stock. In a purchase of stock on margin, the broker lends funds to purchase shares, and the margin required is a down payment on the purchase price. In a margin transaction for stock, interest is charged on the unpaid balance. In the case of margin in a commodities future transaction, no credit is extended to buy anything. Margin in this context is somewhat analogous to a performance bond. Further, no interest is charged on a commodities future transaction, because no funds have been advanced by the broker.

The futures market does not differentiate between buyers and sellers with respect to margin. If you believe that corn prices are going down, you can sell the future, that is, enter into a contract to sell 5,000 bushels of corn. The terms

Table 15-3

# CASH PRICES

Tuesday, December 11, 2001
(Closing Market Quotations)

## GRAINS AND FEEDS

| | Lo-Hi Range | | | Year |
|---|---|---|---|---|
| | Tue | Tue | Mon | Ago |
| Barley, top-quality Mpls., bu | u2.48 | sp | 2.48 | 2.45 |
| Bran, wheat middlings, KC ton | u69.00 | 73.00 | 71.00 | 76.50 |
| Corn, No. 2 yel. Cent. Ill. bu | bpu2.01 | sp | 2.02 | 1.945 |
| Corn Gluten Feed, Midwest, ton | 64.00 | 75.00 | 69.50 | 62.50 |
| Cottonseed Meal, Clksdle, Miss. ton | 127.50 | sp | 127.50 | 155.00 |
| Hominy Feed, Cent. Ill. ton | 43.00 | sp | 43.00 | 36.00 |
| Meat-Bonemeal, 50% pro Ill. ton | 169.00 | 172.50 | 169.75 | 197.50 |
| Oats, No. 2 milling, Mpls., bu | u2.225 | 2.285 | 2.2125 | 1.11 |
| Sorghum, (Milo) No. 2 Gulf cwt | u4.42 | 4.55 | 4.48 | 4.36 |
| Soybean Meal, Cent. Ill., rail, ton 44% | u140.00 | 148.00 | 145.00 | 190.00 |
| Soybean Meal, Cent. Ill., rail, ton 48% | u150.00 | 156.00 | 154.00 | 196.00 |
| Soybeans, No. 1 yel Cent. Ill., bu | bpu4.29 | sp | 4.345 | 4.92 |
| Wheat, Spring 14%-pro Mpls bu | u3.5175 | 3.6475 | 3.63 | 3.635 |
| Wheat, No. 2 sft red, St.Lou. bu | bpu2.955 | sp | 2.91 | 2.445 |
| Wheat, hard, KC, bu | 3.2325 | sp | 3.23 | 3.325 |
| Wheat, No. 1 sft wht, del Port Ore | u3.73 | sp | 3.73 | 2.98 |

## FOODS

| | | | | |
|---|---|---|---|---|
| Beef, Carcass Equiv. Index Value, choice 1-3,600-750 lbs | u106.26 | sp | 105.37 | 114.45 |
| Beef, Carcass Equiv. Index Value, select 1-3,600-750 lbs | u97.20 | sp | 98.03 | 105.76 |
| Broilers, Dressed "A" lb | ux.4987 | sp | .5077 | .4999 |
| Broilers, 12-Cty Comp Wtd Av | u.556 | sp | .556 | .5744 |
| Butter, AA, Chgo., lb | u1.225 | sp | 1.225 | 1.30 |
| Cheddar Cheese, barrels, Chgo lb | n121.50 | sp | 121.50 | 110.00 |
| Cheddar Cheese, blocks, Chgo lb | n122.00 | sp | 123.00 | 109.50 |
| Milk, Non-fat Dry, Chgo | 99.00 | sp | 99.00 | 103.00 |
| Cocoa, Ivory Coast, $metric ton | 1,545 | sp | 1,476 | 883 |
| Coffee, Brazilian, Comp | n.415 | sp | .415 | .66 |
| Coffee, Colombian, NY lb | n.625 | sp | .615 | .76 |
| Eggs, Lge white, Chgo doz | u.55 | .60 | .575 | .815 |
| Flour, hard winter KC cwt | 8.75 | sp | 8.75 | 8.95 |
| Hams, 17-20 lbs, Mid-US lb fob | u.45 | .47 | .52 | .73 |
| Hogs, Iowa-S.Minn. avg. cwt | u45.97 | sp | 48.97 | 43.33 |
| Hogs, Sioux Falls, SD avg cwt | u31.00 | sp | 32.50 | 43.00 |
| Pork Bellies, 12-14 lbs Mid-US lb | u.675 | .68 | .725 | .59 |
| Pork Loins, 13-19 lbs, Mid-US lb | u.88 | .91 | .915 | 1.1325 |
| Steers, Tex-Okla. ch avg cwt | z | sp | 64.17 | z |
| Steers, Feeder, Okl Cty, av cwt | u91.69 | sp | 93.69 | 95.00 |
| Sugar, cane, raw, world, lb. fob | 7.90 | sp | 8.12 | 10.12 |

## FATS AND OILS

| | | | | |
|---|---|---|---|---|
| Coconut Oil, crd, N. Orleans lb | xxn.16 | sp | .1575 | .17 |
| Corn Oil, crd wet/dry mill | u-s22.50 | 23.00 | 22.75 | 10.50 |
| Grease, choice white, Chgo lb | b.1175 | sp | .1175 | b.0975 |
| Lard, Chgo lb | .15 | sp | z | .12 |
| Palm Oil, ref. bl. deod. N. Orl. Lb | n.18 | sp | .1775 | .14 |
| Soybean Oil, crd, Central Ill. Lb | u.1498 | .1538 | .1555 | .12935 |
| Tallow, bleachable, Chgo lb | n.14 | sp | .13 | .10875 |
| Tallow, edible, Chgo lb | .15 | sp | .145 | .12 |

## FIBERS AND TEXTILES

| | Tue | Mon | Year Ago |
|---|---|---|---|
| Burlap, 10 oz 40-in NY yd | n.395 | .39 | .34 |
| Cotton, 1 1/16 str lw-md Mphs lb | .3186 | .3109 | .6159 |
| Wool, 64s Staple, Terr. Del. Lb | u1.10 | 1.10 | .93 |

## METALS

| | | | |
|---|---|---|---|
| Aluminum Comex lb | .644 | .6325 | .76 |
| Antimony, RN Spot, $/lb | d0.58-60 | .58-.60 | .69 |
| Copper, high gr lb., Cmx sp price | .6805 | .676 | .8835 |
| Copper Scrap, No 2 wire NY lb | h.56 | .56 | .64 |
| Lead, RN NA Solder, cts./lb | d40.445 | 40.006 | 39.994 |
| St. Steel Scrap, US, $/gross ton | d565.00 | 565.00 | 665.00 |
| Tin, RN NA Solder, cts./lb | d286.566 | 282.897 | 359.842 |
| Zinc, RN NA Dealer, cts./lb | d37.361 | 37.407 | 53.079 |

## MISCELLANEOUS

| | | | |
|---|---|---|---|
| Rubber, smoked sheets, NY lb | n.3025 | .3025 | .37 |
| Hides, hvy native steers lb., fob | u69.5-72 | 69.5-72 | 85.25 |

## PRECIOUS METALS

| | | | |
|---|---|---|---|
| Gold, troy oz | | | |
| Engelhard indus bullion | 273.31 | 273.76 | 271.86 |
| Engelhard fabric prods | 286.98 | 287.45 | 285.45 |
| Handy & Harman base price | 272.20 | 272.65 | 270.75 |
| Handy & Harman fabric price | 293.98 | 294.46 | 292.41 |
| London fixing AM 272.60 PM | 272.20 | 272.65 | 270.75 |
| Krugerrand, whol | a276.00 | 276.00 | 273.00 |
| Maple Leaf, troy oz | a283.00 | 283.00 | 280.00 |
| American Eagle, troy oz | a283.00 | 283.00 | 280.00 |
| Platinum, (Free Mkt.) | 458.00 | 468.00 | 620.00 |
| Platinum, indust (Engelhard) | 462.00 | 471.00 | 622.00 |
| Platinum, fabrc prd (Engelhard) | 562.00 | 571.00 | 722.00 |
| Palladium, indust (Engelhard) | 406.00 | 426.00 | 939.00 |
| Palladium, fabrc prd (Engelhard) | 506.00 | 526.00 | 954.00 |
| Silver, troy oz | | | |
| Engelhard indust bullion | 4.280 | 4.250 | 4.700 |
| Engelhard fabric prods | 4.922 | 4.888 | 5.405 |
| Handy & Harman base price | 4.275 | 4.250 | 4.705 |
| Handy & Harman fabric price | 4.916 | 4.888 | 5.411 |
| London Fixing (in pounds) | | | |
| Spot (U.S. equiv. $4.2450) | 2.9623 | 2.9594 | 3.2160 |
| Coins, whol $1,000 face val | a3,395 | 3,366 | 3,401 |

a-Asked. b-Bid. bp-Country elevator bids to producers. c-Corrected. d-Ryan's Notes. h-Reuters. n-Nominal. na-Not available. r-Rail bids. s-high price=asked, low price=bid u-U.S. Dept. of Agriculture. x-Less than truckloads. z-Not quoted. xx-f.o.b. tankcars. sp-Single price.

## Table 15-4

# FUTURES PRICES

Tuesday, December 11, 2001

**Open Interest Reflects Previous Trading Day.**

## GRAINS AND OILSEEDS

| | OPEN | HIGH | LOW | SETTLE | CHANGE | LIFETIME HIGH | LIFETIME LOW | OPEN INT. |
|---|---|---|---|---|---|---|---|---|
| **Corn (CBT) 5,000 bu.; cents per bu.** | | | | | | | | |
| Dec | 210 | 210½ | 208¼ | 209½ | + ½ | 275 | 198½ | 2,695 |
| Ja02 | 211½ | 212¼ | 211¼ | 211½ | − ½ | 243 | 202½ | 1,572 |
| Mar | 219¼ | 220½ | 218 | 219½ | .... | 270 | 205 | 257,343 |
| May | 225½ | 226¾ | 224½ | 225¾ | .... | 266½ | 217¾ | 59,587 |
| July | 231 | 232 | 230 | 231½ | + ¼ | 279½ | 210 | 47,389 |
| Sept | 236¼ | 236½ | 235 | 235¾ | .... | 262 | 231 | 12,018 |
| Dec | 242¾ | 243½ | 241¾ | 242¾ | .... | 272 | 239 | 33,925 |
| Mr03 | 250½ | 250¾ | 250 | 250¼ | .... | 258½ | 248 | 1,547 |
| July | 255 | 255¼ | 255 | 255¼ | − ¼ | 272 | 253 | 978 |
| Dec | 253 | 255¾ | 253 | 255¾ | − ¼ | 269 | 253 | 1,542 |
| Est vol 38,000; vol Mon 27,083; open int 418,596, −1,203. | | | | | | | | |
| **Oats (CBT) 5,000 bu.; cents per bu.** | | | | | | | | |
| Dec | 236¾ | 238 | 235 | 235¼ | − 2¾ | 238 | 108½ | 514 |
| Mr02 | 196½ | 200 | 193¼ | 198½ | + 3¾ | 216½ | 114½ | 6,716 |
| May | 180 | 186½ | 180 | 185¼ | + 4¼ | 202¾ | 118¾ | 2,626 |
| July | 169¾ | 170 | 167½ | 168 | + 2 | 179¾ | 135¼ | 1,310 |
| Est vol 1,600; vol Mon 2,281; open int 12,148, −464. | | | | | | | | |
| **Soybeans (CBT) 5,000 bu.; cents per bu.** | | | | | | | | |
| Jan | 443 | 444¾ | 435½ | 437½ | − 5½ | 540 | 426¼ | 66,845 |
| Mar | 446 | 447 | 439 | 440¾ | − 5½ | 546 | 432 | 42,570 |
| May | 449¼ | 451 | 442¾ | 444¼ | − 5 | 531 | 437 | 32,579 |
| July | 453 | 455½ | 447¾ | 449½ | − 4¼ | 533 | 441½ | 23,553 |
| Aug | 454 | 455 | 447¾ | 449½ | − 4½ | 529 | 443 | 1,717 |
| Sept | 454½ | 455½ | 449 | 450 | − 5 | 495 | 443 | 365 |
| Nov | 458 | 460½ | 452¾ | 454¼ | − 4¾ | 561 | 446½ | 8,162 |
| Est vol 56,000; vol Mon 30,210; open int 175,819, −2,592. | | | | | | | | |
| **Soybean Meal (CBT) 100 tons; $ per ton.** | | | | | | | | |
| Dec | 150.00 | 151.60 | 149.10 | 150.10 | − 1.00 | 180.00 | 139.00 | 3,865 |
| Ja02 | 149.10 | 150.00 | 147.60 | 148.70 | − .50 | 175.50 | 139.50 | 30,305 |
| Mar | 147.00 | 148.20 | 146.10 | 146.90 | − .70 | 174.00 | 141.00 | 36,443 |
| May | 146.80 | 147.00 | 145.40 | 146.10 | − .70 | 171.50 | 142.00 | 29,078 |
| July | 147.70 | 147.80 | 146.30 | 147.00 | − .90 | 170.50 | 143.00 | 26,890 |
| Aug | 147.00 | 148.00 | 146.80 | 146.90 | − .80 | 168.50 | 146.60 | 7,196 |
| Sept | 148.00 | 148.50 | 146.80 | 146.90 | − 1.50 | 168.00 | 146.60 | 5,453 |
| Oct | 148.00 | 148.00 | 147.00 | 147.30 | − .20 | 165.00 | 146.30 | 3,260 |
| Dec | 149.50 | 149.50 | 148.50 | 149.50 | − .80 | 160.20 | 147.10 | 7,623 |
| Est vol 27,000; vol Mon 17,972; open int 150,264, −827. | | | | | | | | |
| **Soybean Oil (CBT) 60,000 lbs.; cents per lb.** | | | | | | | | |
| Dec | 16.37 | 16.37 | 15.87 | 15.88 | − .42 | 21.25 | 14.78 | 2,775 |
| Ja02 | 16.46 | 16.54 | 16.01 | 16.03 | − .43 | 20.02 | 14.98 | 41,934 |
| Mar | 16.70 | 16.76 | 16.22 | 16.24 | − .47 | 20.15 | 15.28 | 42,879 |
| May | 16.92 | 16.96 | 16.43 | 16.44 | − .46 | 20.40 | 15.53 | 33,318 |
| July | 17.13 | 17.17 | 16.63 | 16.64 | − .48 | 20.55 | 15.80 | 21,519 |
| Aug | 17.07 | 17.15 | 16.73 | 16.73 | − .49 | 20.33 | 15.95 | 4,744 |
| Sept | 17.07 | 17.15 | 16.83 | 16.83 | − .48 | 18.00 | 16.05 | 3,272 |
| Dec | 17.60 | 17.61 | 17.20 | 17.20 | − .41 | 20.50 | 16.40 | 4,797 |
| Est vol 28,000; vol Mon 18,131; open int 158,669, −1,816. | | | | | | | | |
| **Wheat (CBT) 5,000 bu.; cents per bu.** | | | | | | | | |
| Dec | 276 | 278 | 271½ | 277¾ | + 4 | 343 | 260½ | 2,125 |
| Mr02 | 283¼ | 287 | 281 | 286¾ | + 3¼ | 346 | 273 | 76,379 |
| May | 287 | 289 | 284 | 288½ | + 2½ | 326 | 276½ | 9,461 |
| July | 286½ | 289 | 285½ | 288½ | + 1¾ | 365 | 272 | 14,602 |
| Sept | 290¼ | 292 | 290¼ | 291½ | + 1 | 315 | 287 | 968 |
| Dec | 300½ | 301 | 299½ | 300 | .... | 365 | 295¾ | 2,172 |
| Est vol 19,000; vol Mon 15,457; open int 105,783, −1,849. | | | | | | | | |
| **Wheat (KC) 5,000 bu.; cents per bu.** | | | | | | | | |
| Dec | 278 | 278 | 278 | 278 | − 1½ | 375 | 278 | 70 |
| Mr02 | 285½ | 288 | 285 | 287¾ | + ¼ | 383 | 284½ | 46,504 |
| May | 291½ | 294 | 291 | 293 | − ½ | 357 | 290½ | 9,730 |
| July | 299 | 300 | 296 | 299¾ | + ¼ | 384½ | 296 | 8,055 |
| Est vol 6,093; vol Mon 5,180; open int 68,104, −813. | | | | | | | | |
| **Wheat (MPLS) 5,000 bu.; cents per bu.** | | | | | | | | |
| Dec | 290 | 293 | 290 | 293 | − 5¾ | 389 | 290 | 4 |
| Mr02 | 306 | 306½ | 304½ | 304¾ | − 3¼ | 387 | 304½ | 19,029 |
| May | 313 | 313¼ | 311½ | 312 | − 2½ | 376 | 311½ | 2,676 |
| July | 320 | 320 | 318 | 319 | − 1½ | 381 | 318 | 1,538 |
| Est vol 2,266; vol Mon 1,879; open int 24,835, −286. | | | | | | | | |

## LIVESTOCK AND MEAT

| | OPEN | HIGH | LOW | SETTLE | CHANGE | LIFETIME HIGH | LIFETIME LOW | OPEN INT. |
|---|---|---|---|---|---|---|---|---|
| **Cattle-Feeder (CME) 50,000 lbs.; cents per lb.** | | | | | | | | |
| Jan | 83.12 | 83.50 | 82.70 | 83.27 | + .12 | 91.50 | 78.15 | 6,828 |
| Mar | 82.00 | 82.35 | 81.65 | 82.27 | + .20 | 90.80 | 77.15 | 4,095 |
| Apr | 82.00 | 82.35 | 81.67 | 82.20 | + .25 | 91.15 | 77.05 | 1,940 |
| May | 81.90 | 82.20 | 81.65 | 82.20 | + .27 | 90.30 | 76.85 | 1,592 |
| Aug | 83.50 | 83.60 | 83.45 | 83.60 | + .10 | 89.50 | 78.45 | 622 |
| Est vol 1,391; vol Mon 1,886; open int 15,221, +74. | | | | | | | | |
| **Cattle-Live (CME) 40,000 lbs.; cents per lb.** | | | | | | | | |
| Dec | 65.25 | 65.47 | 64.75 | 65.12 | .... | 77.20 | 61.75 | 12,602 |
| Fb02 | 68.20 | 68.70 | 68.15 | 68.50 | + .30 | 77.57 | 65.15 | 42,655 |
| Apr | 70.85 | 71.27 | 70.85 | 71.20 | + .37 | 78.72 | 67.25 | 18,974 |
| June | 68.10 | 68.27 | 67.85 | 68.10 | + .22 | 74.85 | 64.12 | 13,218 |
| Aug | 68.40 | 68.47 | 68.10 | 68.30 | + .07 | 75.20 | 64.25 | 5,803 |
| Oct | 70.65 | 70.65 | 70.30 | 70.45 | + .05 | 75.95 | 65.72 | 1,647 |
| Est vol 16,919; vol Mon 18,110; open int 95,482, +1,141. | | | | | | | | |
| **Hogs-Lean (CME) 40,000 lbs.; cents per lb.** | | | | | | | | |
| Dec | 45.60 | 45.60 | 44.87 | 45.15 | − .97 | 57.32 | 44.80 | 5,933 |
| Fb02 | 51.12 | 52.40 | 51.05 | 52.05 | + .45 | 57.90 | 47.75 | 15,280 |
| Apr | 55.10 | 56.55 | 55.10 | 56.17 | + .35 | 58.70 | 48.20 | 4,244 |
| May | 61.95 | 62.77 | 61.85 | 62.50 | .... | 64.25 | 58.80 | 1,078 |
| June | 63.10 | 63.80 | 63.00 | 63.60 | + .17 | 66.45 | 60.87 | 1,425 |
| July | 61.30 | 61.65 | 61.25 | 61.42 | + .15 | 63.70 | 59.05 | 514 |
| Aug | 60.05 | 60.40 | 60.00 | 60.05 | − .27 | 61.75 | 58.30 | 311 |
| Oct | 52.70 | 52.85 | 52.50 | 52.50 | − .15 | 55.80 | 52.50 | 385 |
| Est vol 10,705; vol Mon 8,144; open int 29,292, −1,529. | | | | | | | | |
| **Pork Bellies (CME) 40,000 lbs.; cents per lb.** | | | | | | | | |
| Feb | 72.80 | 74.20 | 72.30 | 74.00 | + .92 | 85.27 | 51.00 | 1,915 |
| Mar | 72.85 | 74.10 | 72.50 | 73.87 | + .85 | 85.00 | 52.00 | 279 |
| May | 74.75 | 75.60 | 74.25 | 75.60 | + .40 | 87.25 | 66.30 | 130 |
| Est vol 575; vol Mon 930; open int 2,375, −7. | | | | | | | | |

## FOOD AND FIBER

| | OPEN | HIGH | LOW | SETTLE | CHANGE | LIFETIME HIGH | LIFETIME LOW | OPEN INT. |
|---|---|---|---|---|---|---|---|---|
| **Cocoa (CSCE)-10 metric tons; $ per ton.** | | | | | | | | |
| Dec | 1,280 | 1,320 | 1,280 | 1,305 | + 58 | 1,380 | 805 | 277 |
| Mr02 | 1,241 | 1,295 | 1,241 | 1,290 | + 69 | 1,365 | 835 | 37,247 |
| May | 1,235 | 1,283 | 1,235 | 1,279 | + 69 | 1,354 | 850 | 14,718 |
| July | 1,233 | 1,270 | 1,233 | 1,268 | + 70 | 1,335 | 875 | 9,451 |
| Sept | 1,235 | 1,258 | 1,235 | 1,258 | + 72 | 1,323 | 907 | 5,561 |
| Dec | 1,190 | 1,219 | 1,190 | 1,218 | + 68 | 1,273 | 936 | 9,502 |
| Mr03 | 1,180 | 1,210 | 1,180 | 1,209 | + 71 | 1,287 | 986 | 8,144 |
| May | 1,174 | 1,205 | 1,174 | 1,204 | + 70 | 1,250 | 1,040 | 2,856 |
| Est vol 12,309; vol Mon 7,281; open int 93,021, −288. | | | | | | | | |
| **Coffee (CSCE)-37,500 lbs.; cents per lb.** | | | | | | | | |
| Dec | 44.40 | 44.40 | 43.50 | 43.90 | + .40 | 127.00 | 41.50 | 146 |
| Mr02 | 47.15 | 47.90 | 46.15 | 47.80 | + .95 | 107.00 | 44.75 | 33,624 |
| May | 49.00 | 49.80 | 48.15 | 49.60 | + .85 | 87.00 | 46.60 | 8,037 |
| July | 50.90 | 51.35 | 50.30 | 51.40 | + .80 | 84.00 | 48.10 | 4,322 |
| Sept | 52.50 | 52.95 | 51.90 | 53.00 | + .80 | 85.75 | 49.40 | 3,689 |
| Dec | 54.50 | 55.25 | 54.25 | 55.15 | + .90 | 72.25 | 51.25 | 2,820 |
| Mr03 | 56.60 | 56.95 | 56.60 | 57.50 | + .95 | 60.75 | 52.90 | 765 |
| Est vol 4,981; vol Mon 5,769; open int 53,405, −170. | | | | | | | | |
| **Sugar-World (CSCE)-112,000 lbs.; cents per lb.** | | | | | | | | |
| Mar | 7.53 | 7.56 | 7.31 | 7.35 | − .16 | 9.75 | 6.11 | 87,083 |
| May | 7.03 | 7.03 | 6.84 | 6.85 | − .15 | 9.64 | 6.01 | 26,413 |
| July | 6.56 | 6.57 | 6.40 | 6.42 | − .13 | 9.60 | 5.88 | 28,679 |
| Oct | 6.50 | 6.51 | 6.40 | 6.42 | − .08 | 8.50 | 6.12 | 17,092 |
| Mr03 | 6.60 | 6.60 | 6.50 | 6.52 | − .08 | 8.00 | 6.37 | 6,983 |
| May | 6.55 | 6.55 | 6.55 | 6.46 | − .08 | 7.65 | 6.39 | 2,118 |
| July | 6.46 | 6.49 | 6.45 | 6.41 | − .08 | 7.35 | 6.42 | 2,526 |
| Oct | 6.48 | 6.49 | 6.43 | 6.42 | − .06 | 6.60 | 6.43 | 1,465 |
| Est vol 30,458; vol Mon 18,280; open int 172,362, −2,085. | | | | | | | | |
| **Sugar-Domestic (CSCE)-112,000 lbs.; cents per lb.** | | | | | | | | |
| Mar | 21.47 | 21.47 | 21.47 | 21.47 | .... | 21.54 | 19.01 | 4,026 |
| May | 21.55 | 21.57 | 21.55 | 21.57 | .... | 21.70 | 20.75 | 3,763 |
| July | 21.66 | 21.66 | 21.66 | 21.66 | .... | 21.82 | 20.85 | 2,930 |
| Sept | 21.65 | 21.65 | 21.65 | 21.65 | .... | 21.82 | 21.04 | 1,888 |
| Est vol 83; vol Mon 206; open int 13,686, −213. | | | | | | | | |
| **Cotton (NYCE)-50,000 lbs.; cents per lb.** | | | | | | | | |
| Mar | 36.80 | 37.20 | 36.35 | 37.11 | + .77 | 67.10 | 29.86 | 30,133 |
| May | 38.00 | 38.48 | 37.75 | 38.48 | + .82 | 68.50 | 30.90 | 9,868 |
| July | 39.20 | 39.60 | 38.85 | 39.60 | + .79 | 68.50 | 31.90 | 9,575 |
| Oct | 41.20 | 41.25 | 41.20 | 41.65 | + .70 | 65.50 | 33.85 | 323 |
| Dec | 42.60 | 42.85 | 42.10 | 42.73 | + .73 | 64.75 | 34.65 | 5,481 |
| My03 | 46.00 | 46.50 | 46.00 | 46.50 | + 1.30 | 54.00 | 38.70 | 838 |
| July | 46.90 | 47.50 | 46.90 | 47.50 | + 1.30 | 50.50 | 39.50 | 424 |
| Est vol 5,907; vol Mon 7,285; open int 57,425, −838. | | | | | | | | |
| **Orange Juice (NYCE)-15,000 lbs.; cents per lb.** | | | | | | | | |
| Jan | 90.55 | 90.80 | 89.90 | 89.90 | − 1.55 | 97.25 | 80.20 | 10,818 |
| Mar | 93.30 | 93.40 | 92.50 | 92.50 | − 1.60 | 103.35 | 84.00 | 5,612 |
| May | 94.50 | 94.50 | 94.50 | 94.30 | − .70 | 99.60 | 86.25 | 1,196 |
| Est vol 1,985; vol Mon 1,899; open int 19,468, −483. | | | | | | | | |

## METALS AND PETROLEUM

| | OPEN | HIGH | LOW | SETTLE | CHANGE | LIFETIME HIGH | LIFETIME LOW | OPEN INT. |
|---|---|---|---|---|---|---|---|---|
| **Copper-High (Cmx.Div.NYM)-25,000 lbs.; cents per lb.** | | | | | | | | |
| Dec | 67.80 | 68.40 | 67.70 | 68.05 | + 0.45 | 92.00 | 60.35 | 3,954 |
| Ja02 | 68.15 | 68.70 | 68.15 | 68.30 | + 0.40 | 90.80 | 60.80 | 3,558 |
| Feb | 68.40 | 69.15 | 68.35 | 68.60 | + 0.40 | 90.00 | 61.20 | 1,519 |
| Mar | 68.40 | 69.45 | 68.40 | 68.90 | + 0.40 | 91.00 | 61.30 | 30,399 |
| Apr | 69.10 | 69.10 | 69.10 | 69.15 | + 0.40 | 89.70 | 61.50 | 1,226 |
| May | 69.45 | 69.90 | 69.30 | 69.45 | + 0.40 | 89.60 | 61.90 | 4,755 |
| June | 69.65 | 69.65 | 69.65 | 69.70 | + 0.40 | 89.50 | 62.35 | 1,127 |
| July | 69.90 | 70.25 | 69.70 | 70.00 | + 0.45 | 88.90 | 62.30 | 5,219 |
| Sept | 70.45 | 70.80 | 70.45 | 70.50 | + 0.45 | 88.00 | 62.95 | 2,988 |
| Dec | 70.95 | 71.45 | 70.95 | 71.15 | + 0.45 | 83.00 | 63.50 | 5,630 |
| Mr03 | 71.50 | 72.20 | 71.50 | 71.65 | + 0.45 | 80.40 | 65.30 | 357 |
| May | 72.80 | 72.80 | 72.80 | 72.05 | + 0.45 | 75.25 | 65.80 | 218 |
| July | 73.40 | 73.40 | 73.40 | 72.30 | + 0.45 | 75.60 | 66.80 | 120 |
| Sept | 73.15 | 73.15 | 73.15 | 72.55 | + 0.45 | 75.50 | 66.00 | 123 |
| Est vol 10,000; vol Mon 5,801; open int 65,119, −144. | | | | | | | | |
| **Gold (Cmx.Div.NYM)-100 troy oz.; $ per troy oz.** | | | | | | | | |
| Dec | 272.00 | 272.50 | 271.50 | 272.20 | .... | 429.50 | 260.00 | 639 |
| Fb02 | 272.80 | 273.40 | 272.10 | 272.90 | − 0.10 | 297.50 | 262.90 | 75,180 |
| Apr | 273.10 | 274.20 | 272.50 | 273.50 | − 0.10 | 297.50 | 267.50 | 6,254 |
| June | 274.30 | 274.70 | 273.00 | 273.90 | − 0.20 | 385.00 | 264.50 | 7,769 |
| Dec | 275.00 | 275.80 | 275.00 | 275.40 | − 0.70 | 358.00 | 268.10 | 8,097 |
| Dc04 | 293.00 | 293.00 | 293.00 | 292.70 | − 0.40 | 388.00 | 290.00 | 2,214 |
| Est vol 22,000; vol Mon 32,344; open int 115,712, +6,030. | | | | | | | | |
| **Platinum (NYM)-50 troy oz.; $ per troy oz.** | | | | | | | | |
| Jan | 473.00 | 473.00 | 456.00 | 460.70 | − 13.70 | 605.00 | 401.00 | 4,211 |
| Apr | 458.00 | 458.00 | 448.20 | 452.70 | − 12.70 | 468.00 | 407.00 | 1,892 |
| Est vol 1,344; vol Mon 1,343; open int 6,196, +138. | | | | | | | | |
| **Silver (Cmx.Div.NYM)-5,000 troy oz.; cnts per troy oz.** | | | | | | | | |
| Dec | 422.0 | 425.5 | 422.0 | 425.7 | + 3.2 | 680.0 | 401.5 | 121 |
| Mr02 | 424.0 | 429.5 | 423.0 | 427.5 | + 3.2 | 508.0 | 405.0 | 53,371 |
| May | 426.5 | 430.0 | 426.5 | 428.5 | + 3.2 | 525.0 | 407.0 | 2,406 |
| July | 428.0 | 429.0 | 427.0 | 429.3 | + 3.2 | 559.0 | 409.5 | 3,181 |
| Sept | 432.0 | 432.0 | 432.0 | 430.3 | + 3.2 | 480.5 | 412.5 | 1,598 |
| Dec | 430.0 | 434.0 | 430.0 | 431.5 | + 2.9 | 613.0 | 412.0 | 5,563 |
| Est vol 7,000; vol Mon 4,107; open int 68,669, −369. | | | | | | | | |
| **Crude Oil, Light Sweet (NYM) 1,000 bbls.; $ per bbl.** | | | | | | | | |
| Jan | 18.05 | 18.08 | 18.05 | 18.08 | − 0.29 | 29.40 | 17.12 | 100,251 |
| Feb | 18.79 | 18.83 | 18.32 | 18.46 | − 0.33 | 29.00 | 17.30 | 84,661 |
| Mar | 19.12 | 19.12 | 18.55 | 18.76 | − 0.32 | 28.00 | 17.55 | 42,639 |
| Apr | 19.25 | 19.25 | 18.85 | 18.99 | − 0.33 | 27.50 | 17.95 | 24,583 |
| May | 19.25 | 19.32 | 19.19 | 19.19 | − 0.33 | 27.35 | 18.20 | 15,973 |
| June | 19.62 | 19.62 | 19.34 | 19.34 | − 0.33 | 27.25 | 17.35 | 26,383 |
| July | 19.62 | 19.65 | 19.46 | 19.46 | − 0.33 | 26.30 | 18.75 | 13,573 |
| Sept | 19.80 | 19.80 | 19.65 | 19.65 | − 0.34 | 25.50 | 19.10 | 12,731 |
| Oct | 20.07 | 20.07 | 19.73 | 19.73 | − 0.35 | 26.36 | 19.50 | 9,648 |
| Nov | 19.75 | 19.90 | 19.75 | 19.79 | − 0.36 | 25.50 | 19.55 | 8,198 |
| Dec | 20.08 | 20.08 | 19.85 | 19.85 | − 0.36 | 26.95 | 15.50 | 20,799 |
| Mr03 | 20.30 | 20.30 | 20.03 | 20.03 | − 0.36 | 28.85 | 20.03 | 4,330 |
| Dc07 | 20.60 | 20.60 | 20.33 | 20.33 | − 0.27 | 21.50 | 19.50 | 842 |
| Est vol 149,042; vol Mon 118,942; open int 446,412, +4,719. | | | | | | | | |
| **Heating Oil No. 2 (NYM) 42,000 gal; $ per gal.** | | | | | | | | |
| Jan | .5070 | .5085 | .4960 | .4999 | − .0067 | .8680 | .3462 | 41,489 |
| Feb | .5190 | .5216 | .5090 | .5145 | − .0067 | .8543 | .5070 | 27,632 |
| Mar | .5190 | .5250 | .5180 | .5205 | − .0067 | .7950 | .5130 | 20,767 |
| Apr | .5250 | .5280 | .5235 | .5235 | − .0072 | .7700 | .5135 | 16,667 |
| May | .5250 | .5270 | .5225 | .5225 | − .0077 | .7350 | .5100 | 7,463 |
| June | .5275 | .5300 | .5250 | .5260 | − .0082 | .7190 | .5110 | 9,746 |
| July | .5370 | .5370 | .5350 | .5325 | − .0082 | .7125 | .5210 | 4,897 |
| Aug | .5430 | .5450 | .5400 | .5400 | − .0082 | .7140 | .5300 | 3,425 |
| Sept | .5510 | .5510 | .5490 | .5490 | − .0077 | .7030 | .5390 | 4,154 |
| Oct | .5630 | .5630 | .5580 | .5580 | − .0077 | .7230 | .5460 | 2,539 |
| Nov | .5665 | .5685 | .5660 | .5660 | − .0077 | .7280 | .5570 | 2,761 |
| Dec | .5765 | .5780 | .5735 | .5735 | − .0077 | .7350 | .5660 | 6,336 |
| Ja03 | .5830 | .5840 | .5795 | .5795 | − .0077 | .7185 | .5680 | 3,690 |
| Feb | .5830 | .5830 | .5795 | .5795 | − .0077 | .7145 | .5710 | 942 |
| Mar | .5725 | .5770 | .5715 | .5715 | − .0077 | .6965 | .5640 | 1,214 |
| Apr | .5700 | .5700 | .5615 | .5615 | − .0077 | .6340 | .5500 | 224 |
| Est vol 32,392; vol Mon 33,723; open int 154,252, +1,909. | | | | | | | | |
| **Gasoline-NY Unleaded (NYM) 42,000; $per gal.** | | | | | | | | |
| Jan | .5100 | .5140 | .4990 | .5061 | − .0048 | .7815 | .4895 | 35,346 |
| Feb | .5265 | .5280 | .5150 | .5220 | − .0040 | .7810 | .5000 | 18,945 |
| Mar | .5390 | .5390 | .5300 | .5365 | − .0040 | .7835 | .5190 | 14,132 |
| Apr | .5960 | .6030 | .5960 | .6025 | − .0040 | .8400 | .5830 | 14,116 |
| May | .6075 | .6087 | .6060 | .6087 | − .0038 | .8500 | .5850 | 14,492 |
| June | .6120 | .6120 | .6100 | .6110 | − .0035 | .8450 | .5900 | 9,809 |
| July | .6060 | .6100 | .6060 | .6100 | − .0035 | .7900 | .5925 | 6,679 |
| Aug | .6050 | .6050 | .6045 | .6045 | − .0035 | .7700 | .5800 | 5,645 |
| Sept | .5960 | .5960 | .5955 | .5955 | − .0035 | .7570 | .5788 | 6,178 |
| Nov | .5700 | .5700 | .5690 | .5690 | − .0035 | .5775 | .5523 | 155 |
| Dec | .5700 | .5700 | .5685 | .5685 | − .0035 | .5825 | .5685 | 368 |
| Est vol 28,158; vol Mon 26,515; open int 126,025, +2,488. | | | | | | | | |
| **Natural Gas, (NYM) 10,000 MMBtu.; $ per MMBtu's** | | | | | | | | |

## Table 15-4 (*cont.*)

| | OPEN | HIGH | LOW | SETTLE | CHANGE | LIFETIME HIGH | LIFETIME LOW | OPEN INT. |
|---|---|---|---|---|---|---|---|---|
| Jan | 2.795 | 2.820 | 2.670 | 2.803 | + .056 | 6.290 | 2.450 | 63,303 |
| Feb | 2.865 | 2.875 | 2.750 | 2.868 | + .041 | 6.030 | 2.440 | 34,883 |
| Mar | 2.865 | 2.865 | 2.750 | 2.861 | + .036 | 5.730 | 2.360 | 34,390 |
| Apr | 2.800 | 2.830 | 2.730 | 2.828 | + .031 | 4.920 | 2.290 | 39,067 |
| May | 2.870 | 2.879 | 2.810 | 2.879 | + .027 | 4.775 | 2.355 | 17,798 |
| June | 2.925 | 2.933 | 2.830 | 2.933 | + .023 | 4.770 | 2.345 | 17,493 |
| July | 2.970 | 2.980 | 2.890 | 2.978 | + .023 | 4.780 | 2.365 | 14,207 |
| Aug | 3.020 | 3.023 | 2.920 | 3.023 | + .023 | 4.790 | 2.412 | 12,356 |
| Sept | 3.000 | 3.011 | 2.925 | 3.011 | + .021 | 4.770 | 2.423 | 14,535 |
| Oct | 2.940 | 3.026 | 2.940 | 3.026 | + .021 | 4.785 | 2.465 | 24,397 |
| Nov | 3.180 | 3.206 | 3.120 | 3.206 | + .016 | 4.900 | 2.630 | 18,204 |
| Dec | 3.380 | 3.380 | 3.295 | 3.376 | + .011 | 5.010 | 2.720 | 10,643 |
| Ja03 | 3.445 | 3.456 | 3.405 | 3.456 | + .011 | 5.049 | 2.730 | 13,161 |
| Feb | 3.370 | 3.381 | 3.370 | 3.381 | + .011 | 4.874 | 2.695 | 10,873 |
| Mar | 3.280 | 3.291 | 3.280 | 3.291 | + .011 | 4.710 | 2.705 | 9,842 |
| Apr | 3.120 | 3.136 | 3.110 | 3.136 | + .011 | 4.520 | 2.610 | 9,660 |
| May | 3.130 | 3.146 | 3.130 | 3.146 | + .011 | 4.490 | 2.630 | 5,879 |
| June | 3.150 | 3.181 | 3.150 | 3.181 | + .011 | 4.400 | 2.610 | 7,290 |
| July | 3.230 | 3.230 | 3.190 | 3.226 | + .011 | 4.530 | 2.550 | 5,448 |
| Dec | 3.535 | 3.556 | 3.535 | 3.556 | + .006 | 4.820 | 3.350 | 6,452 |

Est vol 98,480; vol Mon 73,089; open int 417,617, +5,542.

**Brent Crude (IPE) 1,000 net bbls.; $ per bbl.**

| | OPEN | HIGH | LOW | SETTLE | CHANGE | LIFETIME HIGH | LIFETIME LOW | OPEN INT. |
|---|---|---|---|---|---|---|---|---|
| Ja02 | 18.20 | 18.21 | 17.80 | 17.91 | − 0.26 | 30.00 | 16.65 | 39,620 |
| Feb | 18.35 | 18.38 | 18.00 | 18.12 | − 0.24 | 27.77 | 16.82 | 59,400 |
| Mar | 18.38 | 18.44 | 18.12 | 18.19 | − 0.29 | 27.20 | 13.70 | 26,423 |
| Apr | 18.36 | 18.52 | 18.22 | 18.29 | − 0.29 | 26.85 | 17.40 | 10,278 |
| May | 18.49 | 18.48 | 18.37 | 18.42 | − 0.28 | 26.30 | 17.57 | 8,540 |
| Jun | 18.63 | 18.77 | 18.50 | 18.55 | − 0.28 | 28.76 | 17.70 | 20,641 |
| Jly | 18.74 | 18.81 | 18.71 | 18.67 | − 0.29 | 25.32 | 17.35 | 6,100 |
| Aug | 18.86 | 18.95 | 18.76 | 18.79 | − 0.30 | 25.18 | 17.95 | 5,759 |
| Sep | 19.09 | 19.09 | 19.03 | 18.89 | − 0.28 | 24.30 | 18.19 | 5,213 |
| Oct | 19.03 | 19.03 | 19.03 | 18.97 | − 0.28 | 24.25 | 18.30 | 4,152 |
| Nov | 19.13 | 19.13 | 19.13 | 19.04 | − 0.29 | 21.24 | 19.31 | 1,475 |
| Dec | 19.20 | 19.32 | 19.06 | 19.11 | − 0.30 | 25.41 | 17.35 | 24,357 |

Est vol 89,000; vol Mon 60,717; open int 220,160, +2,715.

### INTEREST RATE

**Treasury Bonds (CBT)-$100,000; pts 32nds of 100%**

| | OPEN | HIGH | LOW | SETTLE | CHANGE | LIFETIME HIGH | LIFETIME LOW | OPEN INT. |
|---|---|---|---|---|---|---|---|---|
| Dec | 101-13 | 102-08 | 101-10 | 101-18 | + 14 | 112-19 | 97-25 | 42,667 |
| Mr02 | 100-10 | 101-05 | 100-05 | 100-13 | + 14 | 111-16 | 97-11 | 427,858 |
| June | 99-08 | 99-29 | 99-04 | 99-08 | + 14 | 110-00 | 98-10 | 22,461 |

Est vol 200,000; vol Mon 242,436; open int 492,986, −17,452.

**Treasury Notes (CBT)-$100,000; pts 32nds of 100%**

| | OPEN | HIGH | LOW | SETTLE | CHANGE | LIFETIME HIGH | LIFETIME LOW | OPEN INT. |
|---|---|---|---|---|---|---|---|---|
| Dec | 05-315 | 106-15 | 105-23 | 106-00 | + 14.0 | 112-13 | 100-26 | 68,921 |
| Mr02 | 104-16 | 105-05 | 04-115 | 104-21 | + 14.0 | 11-085 | 101-23 | 508,240 |

Est vol 330,000; vol Mon 297,612; open int 579,956, −14,395.

**10 Yr Agency Notes (CBT)-$100,000; pts 32nds of 100%**

| | OPEN | HIGH | LOW | SETTLE | CHANGE | LIFETIME HIGH | LIFETIME LOW | OPEN INT. |
|---|---|---|---|---|---|---|---|---|
| Dec | 101-01 | 101-19 | 100-31 | 01-035 | + 13.0 | 101-25 | 100-10 | 2,307 |

Est vol 4,800; vol Mon 4,167; open int 35,228, +737.

**5 Yr Treasury Notes (CBT)-$100,000; pts 32nds of 100%**

| | OPEN | HIGH | LOW | SETTLE | CHANGE | LIFETIME HIGH | LIFETIME LOW | OPEN INT. |
|---|---|---|---|---|---|---|---|---|
| Dec | 106-23 | 07-025 | 106-21 | 06-275 | + 12.0 | 10-145 | 103-17 | 96,207 |
| Mr02 | 05-135 | 105-26 | 05-106 | 05-175 | + 11.5 | 109-08 | 104-20 | 406,238 |

Est vol 150,000; vol Mon 140,427; open int 501,645, −3,519.

**2 Yr Treasury Notes (CBT)-$200,000; pts 32nds of 100%**

| | OPEN | HIGH | LOW | SETTLE | CHANGE | LIFETIME HIGH | LIFETIME LOW | OPEN INT. |
|---|---|---|---|---|---|---|---|---|
| Dec | 105-09 | 105-13 | 105-08 | 105-11 | + 6.2 | 06-117 | 103-00 | 10,239 |

Est vol 12,000; vol Mon 7,595; open int 64,605, −610.

**30 Day Federal Funds (CBT)-$5 million; pts of 100%**

| | OPEN | HIGH | LOW | SETTLE | CHANGE | LIFETIME HIGH | LIFETIME LOW | OPEN INT. |
|---|---|---|---|---|---|---|---|---|
| Dec | 98.200 | 98.210 | 98.190 | 98.195 | .... | 98.295 | 96.350 | 39,794 |
| Ja02 | 98.28 | 98.28 | 98.25 | 98.26 | − .01 | 98.30 | 96.22 | 35,138 |
| Feb | 98.36 | 98.37 | 98.33 | 98.35 | .... | 98.37 | 96.05 | 47,866 |
| Mar | 98.33 | 98.35 | 98.29 | 98.33 | + .02 | 99.70 | 96.05 | 18,876 |
| Apr | 98.30 | 98.36 | 98.28 | 98.32 | + .05 | 98.36 | 96.53 | 21,724 |
| May | 98.18 | 98.27 | 98.16 | 98.21 | + .06 | 98.28 | 97.64 | 14,044 |

Est vol 52,000; vol Mon 29,612; open int 181,212, +4,380.

**Muni Bond Index (CBT)-$1,000; times Bond Buyer MBI**

| | OPEN | HIGH | LOW | SETTLE | CHANGE | LIFETIME HIGH | LIFETIME LOW | OPEN INT. |
|---|---|---|---|---|---|---|---|---|
| Dec | 103-10 | 103-11 | 103-00 | 103-01 | + 2 | 109-21 | 99-04 | 8,208 |
| Mr02 | 102-07 | 102-12 | 101-29 | 101-31 | + 2 | 107-23 | 101-17 | 5,682 |

Est vol 1,000; vol Mon 1,201; open int 13,890, +174.
Index: Close 102-24; Yield 5.73.

**Treasury Bills (CME)-$1 mil.; pts of 100%**

| | OPEN | HIGH | LOW | SETTLE | CHANGE | YIELD | CHANGE | OPEN INT. |
|---|---|---|---|---|---|---|---|---|
| Dec | 98.34 | 98.38 | 98.34 | 98.36 | + .04 | 1.64 | −.04 | 1,673 |

Est vol 110; vol Mon 1,010; open int 2,185, +383.

**Libor-1 Mo. (CME)-$3,000,000; pts of 100%**

| | OPEN | HIGH | LOW | SETTLE | CHANGE | YIELD | CHANGE | OPEN INT. |
|---|---|---|---|---|---|---|---|---|
| Dec | 98.12 | 98.12 | 98.09 | 98.10 | + .01 | 1.90 | −.01 | 20,454 |
| Ja02 | 98.18 | 98.22 | 98.18 | 98.21 | + .03 | 1.79 | −.03 | 8,955 |
| Feb | 98.20 | 98.23 | 98.20 | 98.21 | + .03 | 1.79 | −.03 | 7,180 |
| Mar | 98.18 | 98.21 | 98.17 | 98.20 | + .06 | 1.80 | −.06 | 293 |

Est vol 4,043; vol Mon 4,194; open int 37,505, −84.

**Eurodollar (CME)-$1 Million; pts of 100%**

| | OPEN | HIGH | LOW | SETTLE | CHANGE | YIELD | CHANGE | OPEN INT. |
|---|---|---|---|---|---|---|---|---|
| Dec | 98.11 | 98.16 | 98.11 | 98.14 | + .03 | 1.86 | −.03 | 823,773 |
| Ja02 | 98.15 | 98.18 | 98.13 | 98.15 | + .03 | 1.85 | −.03 | 23,193 |
| Feb | 98.13 | 98.17 | 98.10 | 98.14 | + .05 | 1.86 | −.05 | 16,376 |
| Mar | 98.01 | 98.09 | 97.99 | 98.05 | + .07 | 1.95 | −.07 | 670,438 |
| June | 97.53 | 97.67 | 97.52 | 97.58 | + .08 | 2.42 | −.08 | 644,903 |
| Sept | 96.84 | 97.03 | 96.84 | 96.96 | + .14 | 3.04 | −.14 | 533,854 |
| Dec | 96.14 | 96.33 | 96.13 | 96.26 | + .15 | 3.74 | −.15 | 523,960 |
| Mr03 | 95.57 | 95.70 | 95.56 | 95.64 | + .13 | 4.36 | −.13 | 292,876 |
| June | 95.05 | 95.16 | 95.04 | 95.11 | + .12 | 4.89 | −.12 | 202,318 |
| Sept | 94.71 | 94.78 | 94.67 | 94.71 | + .08 | 5.29 | −.08 | 173,766 |
| Dec | 94.36 | 94.46 | 94.33 | 94.37 | + .08 | 5.63 | −.08 | 133,833 |
| Mr04 | 94.18 | 94.29 | 94.18 | 94.22 | + .07 | 5.78 | −.07 | 117,613 |
| June | 94.04 | 94.12 | 94.01 | 94.04 | + .07 | 5.96 | −.07 | 94,737 |
| Sept | 93.87 | 93.98 | 93.87 | 93.89 | + .06 | 6.11 | −.06 | 94,427 |
| Dec | 93.71 | 93.80 | 93.69 | 93.72 | + .06 | 6.28 | −.06 | 62,126 |
| Mr05 | 96.69 | 93.78 | 93.66 | 93.69 | + .06 | 6.31 | −.06 | 66,139 |
| June | 93.61 | 93.69 | 93.57 | 93.60 | + .06 | 6.40 | −.06 | 60,612 |
| Sept | 93.53 | 93.61 | 93.49 | 93.52 | + .06 | 6.48 | −.06 | 63,510 |
| Dec | 93.40 | 93.50 | 93.38 | 93.41 | + .06 | 6.59 | −.06 | 48,288 |
| Mr06 | 93.40 | 93.51 | 93.39 | 93.42 | + .06 | 6.58 | −.06 | 42,437 |
| June | 93.35 | 93.45 | 93.32 | 93.36 | + .06 | 6.64 | −.06 | 29,133 |
| Sept | 93.28 | 93.40 | 93.28 | 93.31 | + .05 | 6.69 | −.05 | 33,729 |
| Dec | 93.16 | 93.30 | 93.16 | 93.20 | + .05 | 6.80 | −.05 | 25,295 |
| Mr07 | 93.18 | 93.32 | 93.18 | 93.22 | + .05 | 6.78 | −.05 | 18,890 |
| June | 93.13 | 93.27 | 93.13 | 93.17 | + .05 | 6.83 | −.05 | 18,939 |
| Sept | 93.09 | 93.23 | 93.09 | 93.12 | + .04 | 6.88 | −.04 | 15,198 |
| Dec | 92.98 | 93.12 | 92.98 | 93.02 | + .04 | 6.98 | −.04 | 12,952 |
| Mr08 | 93.01 | 93.15 | 93.01 | 93.04 | + .04 | 6.96 | −.04 | 11,804 |
| June | 92.96 | 93.10 | 92.96 | 92.99 | + .04 | 7.01 | −.04 | 10,937 |
| Sept | 92.92 | 93.06 | 92.92 | 92.94 | + .03 | 7.06 | −.03 | 8,778 |
| Dec | 92.81 | 92.95 | 92.81 | 92.84 | + .03 | 7.16 | −.03 | 5,084 |
| Mr09 | 92.84 | 92.98 | 92.84 | 92.86 | + .03 | 7.14 | −.03 | 2,328 |
| June | 92.85 | 92.93 | 92.80 | 92.82 | + .03 | 7.18 | −.03 | 2,345 |
| Sept | 92.82 | 92.90 | 92.77 | 92.78 | + .03 | 7.22 | −.03 | 2,689 |
| Dec | 92.68 | 92.80 | 92.66 | 92.68 | + .03 | 7.32 | −.03 | 2,419 |

Est vol 958,225; vol Mon 866,683; open int 4,907,760, −36,819.

**10 Yr. Canadian Govt. Bonds (ME)-C$100,000**

| | OPEN | HIGH | LOW | SETTLE | CHANGE | LIFETIME HIGH | LIFETIME LOW | OPEN INT. |
|---|---|---|---|---|---|---|---|---|
| Dec | .... | .... | .... | 103.85 | + 0.55 | 108.34 | 102.72 | 12,454 |
| Mr02 | 102.65 | 103.05 | 102.40 | 102.68 | + 0.48 | 105.13 | 101.81 | 67,197 |

Est vol 2,997; vol Mon 4,334; open int 79,651, −665.

**10 Yr. Euro Notional Bond (MATIF)-Euros 100,000**

| | OPEN | HIGH | LOW | SETTLE | CHANGE | LIFETIME HIGH | LIFETIME LOW | OPEN INT. |
|---|---|---|---|---|---|---|---|---|
| Dec | 89.65 | 90.00 | 89.65 | 89.80 | + 0.50 | 93.35 | 88.30 | 23,212 |
| Mr02 | 89.60 | 89.60 | 89.40 | 89.30 | .... | 89.64 | 89.12 | 1,207 |

Est vol 759; vol Mon 602; open int 24,419, −840.

**3 Yr. Commonwealth T-Bonds (SFE)-A$100,000**

| | OPEN | HIGH | LOW | SETTLE | CHANGE | LIFETIME HIGH | LIFETIME LOW | OPEN INT. |
|---|---|---|---|---|---|---|---|---|
| Dec | 94.98 | 95.04 | 94.94 | 95.03 | + 0.05 | 95.93 | 94.53 | 449,474 |
| Mr02 | 94.73 | 94.78 | 94.73 | 94.78 | + 0.05 | 95.04 | 94.67 | 11,131 |

Est vol 60,700; vol Mon 64,602; open int 460,605, −3,171.

**Euro-Yen (SGX)-Yen 100,000,000 pts Of 100%**

| | OPEN | HIGH | LOW | SETTLE | CHANGE | LIFETIME HIGH | LIFETIME LOW | OPEN INT. |
|---|---|---|---|---|---|---|---|---|
| Dec | 99.91 | 99.91 | 99.91 | 99.91 | .... | 99.93 | 97.84 | 89,570 |
| Mr02 | 99.85 | 99.85 | 99.85 | 99.85 | .... | 99.92 | 98.17 | 77,135 |
| June | 99.87 | 99.87 | 99.86 | 99.87 | + 0.01 | 99.93 | 98.11 | 83,260 |
| Sept | 99.85 | 99.85 | 99.85 | 99.85 | .... | 99.90 | 98.35 | 28,265 |
| Dec | 99.82 | 99.82 | 99.81 | 99.82 | + 0.01 | 99.86 | 98.28 | 12,359 |
| Mr03 | 99.78 | 99.78 | 99.78 | 99.78 | + 0.01 | 99.83 | 98.45 | 22,178 |
| June | 99.77 | 99.77 | 99.77 | 99.77 | + 0.01 | 99.80 | 98.40 | 19,764 |
| Sept | 99.72 | 99.72 | 99.71 | 99.72 | + 0.01 | 99.75 | 98.34 | 10,887 |
| Mr04 | 99.57 | 99.58 | 99.57 | 99.57 | .... | 99.58 | 98.19 | 10,858 |

Est vol 10,242; vol Mon 12,114; open int 360,466, +749.

**5 Yr. German Euro-Govt. Bond**
**(EURO-BOBL) (EUREX)-Euro 100,000; pts of 100%**

| | OPEN | HIGH | LOW | SETTLE | CHANGE | LIFETIME HIGH | LIFETIME LOW | OPEN INT. |
|---|---|---|---|---|---|---|---|---|
| Mar | 106.81 | 107.05 | 106.80 | 106.88 | + 0.20 | 110.21 | 105.01 | 338,204 |
| June | .... | .... | .... | 106.18 | + 0.20 | 107.96 | 106.55 | 2,471 |

vol Tue 345,003; open int 340,675, −13,275.

**10 Yr. German Euro-Govt. Bond**
**(EURO-BUND) (EUREX)-Euro 100,000; pts of 100%**

| | OPEN | HIGH | LOW | SETTLE | CHANGE | LIFETIME HIGH | LIFETIME LOW | OPEN INT. |
|---|---|---|---|---|---|---|---|---|
| Mar | 108.19 | 108.56 | 108.18 | 108.27 | + 0.27 | 113.00 | 107.49 | 480,858 |
| June | 107.61 | 107.70 | 107.61 | 107.51 | + 0.21 | 109.92 | 107.08 | 3,503 |

vol Tue 620,652; open int 484,361, −29,543.

**2 Yr. German Euro-Govt. Bond**
**(EURO-SCHATZ) (EUREX)-Euro 100,000; pts of 100%**

| | OPEN | HIGH | LOW | SETTLE | CHANGE | LIFETIME HIGH | LIFETIME LOW | OPEN INT. |
|---|---|---|---|---|---|---|---|---|
| Mar | 103.87 | 104.02 | 103.87 | 103.92 | + 0.10 | 105.38 | 103.37 | 474,831 |
| June | .... | .... | .... | 103.64 | + 0.10 | 104.98 | 104.25 | 9,212 |

vol Tue 387,506; open int 484,043, −16,846.

### CURRENCY

**Japan Yen (CME)-12.5 million yen; $ per yen (.00)**

| | OPEN | HIGH | LOW | SETTLE | CHANGE | LIFETIME HIGH | LIFETIME LOW | OPEN INT. |
|---|---|---|---|---|---|---|---|---|
| Dec | .7939 | .7957 | .7920 | .7927 | − .0002 | .9880 | .7914 | 80,235 |
| Mr02 | .7976 | .7994 | .7955 | .7962 | − .0003 | .8760 | .7950 | 65,136 |
| June | .7995 | .7995 | .7995 | .7999 | − .0004 | .8776 | .7995 | 624 |

Est vol 32,391; vol Mon 67,549; open int 146,350, +18,662.

**Deutschemark (CME)-125,000 marks; $ per mark**

| | OPEN | HIGH | LOW | SETTLE | CHANGE | LIFETIME HIGH | LIFETIME LOW | OPEN INT. |
|---|---|---|---|---|---|---|---|---|
| Dec | .... | .... | .... | .4557 | + .0010 | .4742 | .4400 | 194 |

Est vol 0; vol Mon 0; open int 194, unch.

**Canadian Dollar (CME)-100,000 dlrs.; $ per Can $**

| | OPEN | HIGH | LOW | SETTLE | CHANGE | LIFETIME HIGH | LIFETIME LOW | OPEN INT. |
|---|---|---|---|---|---|---|---|---|
| Dec | .6336 | .6354 | .6334 | .6346 | + .0011 | .6825 | .6230 | 49,515 |
| Mr02 | .6329 | .6360 | .6329 | .6342 | + .0011 | .6725 | .6230 | 25,270 |
| June | .6328 | .6345 | .6328 | .6343 | + .0011 | .6700 | .6230 | 2,111 |
| Sept | .6339 | .6345 | .6339 | .6345 | + .0011 | .6590 | .6234 | 708 |
| Dec | .6348 | .6350 | .6332 | .6348 | + .0011 | .6555 | .6236 | 495 |

Est vol 18,724; vol Mon 28,407; open int 78,101, +3,124.

**British Pound (CME)-62,500 pds.; $ per pound**

| | OPEN | HIGH | LOW | SETTLE | CHANGE | LIFETIME HIGH | LIFETIME LOW | OPEN INT. |
|---|---|---|---|---|---|---|---|---|
| Dec | 1.4330 | 1.4390 | 1.4308 | 1.4370 | + .0040 | 1.5600 | 1.3600 | 33,517 |
| Mr02 | 1.4276 | 1.4316 | 1.4234 | 1.4294 | + .0040 | 1.4700 | 1.3810 | 11,469 |

Est vol 11,696; vol Mon 20,015; open int 45,014, +3,540.

**Swiss Franc (CME)-125,000 francs; $ per franc**

| | OPEN | HIGH | LOW | SETTLE | CHANGE | LIFETIME HIGH | LIFETIME LOW | OPEN INT. |
|---|---|---|---|---|---|---|---|---|
| Dec | .6013 | .6046 | .6013 | .6044 | + .0033 | .6382 | .5506 | 43,165 |
| Mr02 | .6016 | .6047 | .6011 | .6044 | + .0033 | .6370 | .5540 | 12,982 |

Est vol 14,020; vol Mon 24,938; open int 56,181, +4,466.

**Australian Dollar (CME)-100,000 dlrs.; $ per A.$**

| | OPEN | HIGH | LOW | SETTLE | CHANGE | LIFETIME HIGH | LIFETIME LOW | OPEN INT. |
|---|---|---|---|---|---|---|---|---|
| Dec | .5140 | .5162 | .5134 | .5157 | + .0014 | .5641 | .4802 | 15,981 |
| Mr02 | .5118 | .5132 | .5102 | .5127 | + .0013 | .5300 | .4810 | 8,736 |
| June | .5105 | .5105 | .5105 | .5097 | + .0012 | .5145 | .4885 | 325 |

Est vol 7,118; vol Mon 13,120; open int 25,057, +587.

**Mexican Peso (CME)-500,000 new Mex. peso, $ per MP**

| | OPEN | HIGH | LOW | SETTLE | CHANGE | LIFETIME HIGH | LIFETIME LOW | OPEN INT. |
|---|---|---|---|---|---|---|---|---|
| Dec | .10878 | .10938 | .10855 | .10930 | + 00060 | .11100 | .09100 | 18,069 |
| Mr02 | .10670 | .10770 | .10630 | .10728 | + 00067 | .10770 | .09770 | 11,757 |

Est vol 12,928; vol Mon 10,668; open int 30,121, +3,110.

**Euro FX (CME)-Euro 125,000; $ per Euro**

| | OPEN | HIGH | LOW | SETTLE | CHANGE | LIFETIME HIGH | LIFETIME LOW | OPEN INT. |
|---|---|---|---|---|---|---|---|---|
| Dec | .8902 | .8921 | .8881 | .8913 | + .0019 | .9632 | .8337 | 87,591 |
| Mr02 | .8873 | .8891 | .8849 | .8881 | + .0019 | .9640 | .8336 | 22,296 |
| June | .8855 | .8855 | .8843 | .8857 | + .0018 | .9275 | .8365 | 331 |

Est vol 61,868; vol Mon 39,033; open int 110,285, +3,404.

### INDEX

**DJ Industrial Average (CBOT)-$10 times average**

| | OPEN | HIGH | LOW | SETTLE | CHANGE | LIFETIME HIGH | LIFETIME LOW | OPEN INT. |
|---|---|---|---|---|---|---|---|---|
| Dec | 9923 | 10025 | 9856 | 9890 | − 25 | 11535 | 7800 | 23,765 |
| Mr02 | 9927 | 10020 | 9865 | 9890 | − 26 | 11150 | 7900 | 3,806 |
| June | 9900 | 9900 | 9890 | 9897 | − 31 | 10951 | 9080 | 321 |

Est vol 18,000; vol Mon 17,312; open int 28,076, +650.
Idx prl: Hi 10015.90; Lo 9866.85; Close 9888.37, −33.08.

**S&P 500 Index (CME)-$250 times index**

| | OPEN | HIGH | LOW | SETTLE | CHANGE | LIFETIME HIGH | LIFETIME LOW | OPEN INT. |
|---|---|---|---|---|---|---|---|---|
| Dec | 113930 | 115200 | 113350 | 113650 | − 280 | 171460 | 93900 | 330,640 |
| Mr02 | 114550 | 115300 | 113500 | 113770 | − 300 | 134960 | 94100 | 216,567 |
| June | 114800 | 115370 | 113870 | 114020 | − 250 | 170550 | 95030 | 10,208 |

Est vol 117,540; vol Mon 105,444; open int 558.539, −392.
Idx prl: Hi 1150.89; Lo 1134.32; Close 1136.76, −3.17.

**Mini S&P 500 (CME)-$50 times index**

| | OPEN | HIGH | LOW | SETTLE | CHANGE | LIFETIME HIGH | LIFETIME LOW | OPEN INT. |
|---|---|---|---|---|---|---|---|---|
| Dec | 113925 | 115175 | 113350 | 113650 | − 275 | 125900 | 93850 | 243,860 |

Vol Mon 185,515; open int 245,434, +3,756.

**S&P Midcap 400 (CME)-$500 times index**

| | OPEN | HIGH | LOW | SETTLE | CHANGE | LIFETIME HIGH | LIFETIME LOW | OPEN INT. |
|---|---|---|---|---|---|---|---|---|
| Dec | 497.50 | 502.00 | 496.00 | 496.50 | + .50 | 556.60 | 392.00 | 13,159 |

Est vol 4,000; vol Mon 1,654; open int 14,978, +13.
Idx prl: Hi 500.92; Lo 495.73; Close 496.73, +.64.

**Nikkei 225 Stock Average (CME)-$5 times index**

| | OPEN | HIGH | LOW | SETTLE | CHANGE | LIFETIME HIGH | LIFETIME LOW | OPEN INT. |
|---|---|---|---|---|---|---|---|---|
| Dec | 10550. | 10585. | 10480. | 10545. | + 60 | 15220. | 9075. | 15,942 |
| Mr02 | 10525. | 10630. | 10525. | 10590. | + 60 | 14620. | 9245. | 2,784 |

Est vol 12,008; vol Mon 6,603; open int 18,749, +1,658.
Idx prl: Hi 10606.92; Lo 10467.61; Close 10473.91, −97.10.

**Nasdaq 100 (CME)-$100 times index**

| | OPEN | HIGH | LOW | SETTLE | CHANGE | LIFETIME HIGH | LIFETIME LOW | OPEN INT. |
|---|---|---|---|---|---|---|---|---|
| Dec | 164700 | 169700 | 164350 | 165550 | + 800 | 209900 | 109700 | 61,710 |

Est vol 26,316; vol Mon 19,914; open int 68,277, +624.
Idx prl: Hi 1695.15; Lo 1654.72; Close 1661.27, +15.91.

**Mini Nasdaq 100 (CME)-$20 times index**

| | OPEN | HIGH | LOW | SETTLE | CHANGE | LIFETIME HIGH | LIFETIME LOW | OPEN INT. |
|---|---|---|---|---|---|---|---|---|
| Dec | 1647.5 | 1697.0 | 1642.5 | 1655.5 | + 8.0 | 1901.0 | 1097.0 | 139,427 |

Vol Mon 173,429; open int 140,083, +497.

**GSCI (CME)-$250 times nearby index**

| | OPEN | HIGH | LOW | SETTLE | CHANGE | LIFETIME HIGH | LIFETIME LOW | OPEN INT. |
|---|---|---|---|---|---|---|---|---|
| Dec | 161.90 | 162.60 | 161.00 | 162.55 | .... | 201.90 | 159.90 | 11,889 |

Est vol 6,800; vol Mon 5,997; open int 18,105, +302.
Idx prl: Hi 162.66; Lo 160.54; Close 161.67, −.52.

**Russell 2000 (CME)-$500 times index**

| | OPEN | HIGH | LOW | SETTLE | CHANGE | LIFETIME HIGH | LIFETIME LOW | OPEN INT. |
|---|---|---|---|---|---|---|---|---|
| Dec | 473.50 | 479.00 | 473.00 | 475.00 | + 1.50 | 538.25 | 370.00 | 21,82[illegible] |
| Mr02 | 476.00 | 479.00 | 475.25 | 475.75 | + 1.50 | 537.00 | 387.35 | 5,48[illegible] |

Est vol 8,662; vol Mon 5,874; open int 27,310, +10.
Idx prl: Hi 478.19; Lo 473.43; Close 474.77, +.59

would be precisely the same as if you had purchased corn. You would need to post the same margin.

A speculator who expects the price of a commodity to go up buys a futures contract for that commodity. A person who expects the price to go down sells a futures contract. One can buy or sell commodities for future delivery in the futures market, speculating on the prices of commodities for years without ever acquiring, owning, or selling the commodities themselves. A speculator in corn, for example, never needs to own a single kernel of real corn despite a lifetime of trading in corn futures.

Virtually none of the delivery obligations that futures contracts create leads to delivery of the commodity. Assume that you buy a corn futures contract for $2.5575 per bushel. There is a drought, and the potential corn harvest declines, and the price of corn increases. By November 2003, the price of December 2003 corn has risen to $3.15 per bushel. Clearly, you have made a profit, but how do you realize upon it? In the world of commodities futures, you do not sell your contract to buy. Nor do you await delivery and then sell the corn itself on the spot market. Rather, you simply enter into another futures contract to sell December corn. When this transaction is executed, you have **closed out** your position. Because you now have commitments both to buy and to sell the standard trading unit of December corn, you do not owe the market any corn and the market does not owe you any corn. At that point, your account with your broker reflects the purchase of December corn for $12,787.50 and the sale of December corn for $15,750 ($3.15 × 5,000) for a profit of $2,962.50. You are neither **long** nor **short** in corn. Your cash account with the broker, available for future commodities speculation now contains the profit on the transaction in December corn plus the cash originally put up as margin.

This process of netting out works equally well if you originally sold a corn future. You simply buy a corn future with the same maturity, and your position is netted out. This process is so well established that it is reflected in the commission structure for commodities futures: Only a single commission is charged for the dual step of buying a future and then closing it out. Thus, if a position has not been closed out and the date of delivery is drawing near, one avoids the nuisance of accepting or tendering delivery by entering into an offsetting contract. This is not to say that deliveries under futures contracts never occur. If a user of corn (perhaps a producer of corn oil) decides it needs the corn in December, it simply keeps open its position. Then delivery of 5,000 bushels of real corn is required under the standardized futures contract. A speculator who fails to net out similarly would need to make or accept delivery. This transaction, however, would be in the form of a warehouse receipt. A speculator who is long in corn runs no risk of awakening one morning to see a truck pulling up with 5,000 bushels of corn to be dumped in the front yard.

For every futures transaction, there must be both a buyer and a seller. (The same is true with options.) The process, however, is as totally anonymous as on a securities exchange. The buyer has no idea of the identity of the seller and vice versa. Indeed, because the exchange guarantees each trade, it in effect becomes the buyer for each seller and the seller for each buyer, once the transaction has been verified. There is also no limit on the number of futures contracts that can be written. Theoretically, there may be more open contracts to deliver grain in the future than all the grain that actually exists in the world. Usually, however, the numbers are more modest. Table 15-4 provides information as to the number of open futures contracts, that is, the number of pairs of buy and sell commitments. As the table shows, there were 1542 December 2003 contracts, and a total of 418,596 contracts for all expiration dates, 1203 fewer than the day before, indicating that many contracts had been closed out by offsetting purchases or sales.

Futures trading may lead to huge speculative gains or losses on rather small investments. In the above example, there was a return of $2962.50 on a $1278.75 investment. That is a return of over 230 percent. Of course, the buyer assumed a considerable risk. If the price of corn had declined, the loss could easily have exceeded the initial investment. If the price of December corn had declined to $2.50, for example, the buyer would have incurred a loss of $287.50. If it had dropped to $2.30, the loss would have been $1278.50. Before losses of these magnitudes would occur, however, the FCM would make sure that the buyer had sufficient assets to cover the loss—either free capital or freshly posted additional margin made after a margin call—or the broker would close out the transaction on its own.

Speculation is possible in commodities futures, because (1) commodities often exhibit substantial price movements, and (2) a purchaser's or seller's net gain or loss on a futures transaction is measured by the price movement of a large amount of the commodity, but the actual capital invested is usually about 10 percent of the total value of the commodity. Again, it is a species of leverage, although in this case there is no actual use of borrowed capital.

Margin calls are common in the commodities futures business, because only a small deposit is required to carry a substantial position. In the foregoing example, a small deposit enables one to speculate on price movements on 5,000 bushels of corn worth 10 times the amount of the deposit. In this market, each person's account is **marked to market** on a daily basis. Marked to market simply means that the margin position of the account is recalculated each day. The price used is the price set forth in the "settle" column of Table 15-4. If the price moves in a favorable direction, the account, when marked to market, will show a surplus over the minimum needed to carry the position. That surplus may be withdrawn or used to buy additional futures contracts. In other words, one can pyramid a successful futures speculation very easily. If the price moves in an unfavorable direction, the margin in the account is marked down.

Trading in commodities futures is quite unlike trading on the NYSE and other securities exchanges. The CBOT and the other futures exchanges are places where traders come to trade, in many cases solely for their own account. Trading for each commodity takes place in a separate pit, with traders arranged within the pit according to the month of the contract they are trading. Trading is by **open outcry** and hand signals, with purchasers and sellers of the futures often trading on small price movements. You may have seen photographs of this hectic process—traders screaming and shouting in the pits. Repeated outcries of price are necessary, because prices remain valid only during the outcry. Because of price volatility and the small margins required to acquire futures positions, this trading is hectic and fortunes may be made or wiped out in very short periods of time. Traders (unlike speculators) do not ordinarily carry a net long or short position past the end of a trading session. In the jargon of the market, a trader rarely "goes to bed" with a position. Although proprietary trading is the rule on the commodities exchanges, it is illegal on the securities exchanges to hold a seat for purposes of trading primarily for your own account.

There are no specialists or market makers on the commodities exchanges, nor are there firm bid and ask quotations. Perhaps because of these differences, the commodities exchanges limit the maximum price movements that can occur in a single day in most contracts. Trading is suspended when the maximum change in a single day occurs. Prior to 1989, such limits were unknown in the securities markets, but so-called circuit breakers were instituted by the NYSE in response to the crashes of 1987 and 1989. Indeed, these circuit breakers, which are coordinated with trading in stock index futures on the commodities exchanges, were instituted largely because of the fear that trading in stock index futures tended to cause the stock market to move in tandem.

Commodities futures are widely used by producers and users of commodities to **hedge** against future price changes. A farmer growing corn, for example, may know that his corn will be harvested and ready to market in July 2003. The futures price for July corn is $2.5525. If that price is acceptable to the farmer for his crop, he can lock it in by purchasing July corn futures in the approximate amount of his expected harvest. He may even be required to do so by his bank if he has borrowed to finance the crop. If the price of corn declines, the farmer will sell his corn at a loss but recoup that loss on the profit on the futures contract. (It is almost always impractical, because of transportation costs to deliver the corn to the purchaser of the contract.) If the price goes up, the farmer has a loss on the futures contract, but is able to sell his harvested corn above $2.5525. Because the farmer does not know in advance what the size of his harvest will be, it is not possible to set up a perfect hedge, and banks do not usually require a complete hedge. Moreover, the hedge may be imperfect if the variety or quality of the corn that the farmer grows differs from the type of corn that is specified in the standard contract or if the price available to the farmer at his delivery location differs from that quoted at the standard delivery location (which for grains is usually on a barge on the Illinois side of the Mississippi River). Farmers may also get a better break if they buy crop insurance and hedge only a portion of the crop with futures.

A manufacturer that uses corn in its manufacturing process may similarly ensure itself of reliable raw material prices for an extended period in the future by buying futures contracts. Farmers or users of commodities may also hedge by buying or selling commodities "for forward delivery" at fixed prices without using the standardized futures market. But trading in standardized futures contracts, unlike trading in securities, is restricted by law to trading on a registered commodities exchange. In other words, there can be no legal third market in futures. Because hedgers own the commodity in which they are trading, they are not required to post as much margin as are speculators. Generally the required deposit is about half that required from speculators.

Futures trading resembles option trading, but there are important differences. An option does not commit the purchaser of the option to do anything. If the price moves in the wrong direction, the purchaser of the option simply lets it expire. A futures contract, on the other hand, commits the purchaser and seller to close out the position. If the price moves in the wrong direction, the purchaser or seller of the futures contract must take a loss that grows steadily as the price moves further in the wrong direction.

The margin required in a futures transaction is also superficially analogous to the purchase price of an option. Again, however, there is a difference. The price paid for an option is the cost of the right to enter into a transaction: The premium becomes the property of the writer of the option. The margin required in a futures contract is a guarantee of performance and remains the property of the person entering into the contract.

In a futures contract, both sides of every contract are subject to the risk of market forces. Moreover, commodities futures trading is "stacked" against the small outside speculator. About 90 percent of all individual commodity speculators lose money; the average lifetime of an individual futures account is less than a year. There are numerous trading systems or strategies that are commercially available for a fee, but the results of these systems or strategies are indifferent, despite advertising claims to the contrary. An article in the *Wall Street Journal* describes the situation faced by the small investor in this market: "In the best of times, an individual futures-market speculator, like a casino gambler, has a less than even chance of making money in the futures markets. The odds always favor the house, or the markets." Also, other participants in this market are sophisticated, powerful, and have superior access to information in the market. Huge grain-trading companies or banks actively participate in this market; they have nearly instant access to market-moving information, and their multi-million-dollar trades may themselves dramatically effect future prices in seconds, usually when it is advantageous to them. Further, professional futures-pit speculators are present on the trading floor and may make split-second trading decisions based on price changes before an individual speculator has time to pick up the phone and call a broker. Individual speculators must pay commissions on their transactions, while other participants in the market do not. Futures contracts expire every few months, and positions are bought and sold, often on a daily basis. Commissions are charged on each purchase and sale. Thus, it is not unusual for an individual's futures account to be eaten up by commissions in less than a year. The *Journal* article quotes an administrative law judge for the Commodity Futures Trading Commission as stating "You've got to be out of your gourd to trade futures."

## §15.5 Financial Futures and Options to Buy Futures

Today, most of the action in the futures business is in financial and index futures. Standardized contracts to buy or sell foreign currencies at stated times in the future—British pounds in 62,500 pound units, Canadian dollars in $100,000 units, Japanese yen in 12,500,000 yen units—are actively traded. Interest rate futures in Treasury bonds, and 5-year Treasury notes are traded in $100,000 units; Federal Funds are traded in $1,000,000 units. All of these financial futures can be bought or sold for approximately 10 percent down as a way of hedging against or speculating on interest rates or foreign exchange rates.

From a dollar standpoint, the most active trading is in stock index futures and government securities futures. Table 15-5 reflects trading in these contracts. A major difference between traditional commodities futures and these financial futures is that they settle in cash for the difference between the contract price and the price at expiration.

Because futures carry with them the risk of loss from adverse price movements in excess of the amount initially invested, a logical development is the creation of put and call options on futures. Table 15-5 is an example of price quotations for options on futures contracts.

## §15.6 Arbitrage and Program Trading

The development of index options and index futures opens up a variety of computerized trading strategies. **Arbitrage** is the process of taking advantage of small price differences in equivalent securities. Such differences may arise from different maturity dates on equivalent securities, trading in different geographical markets, or trading in securities with different forms but equivalent or interrelated values. Index options, index futures, and the underlying securities that compose the indexes all trade simultaneously in different markets. It would be impossible for an individual to determine whether the prices of the 500 stocks that make up the S&P 500 stock index are above or below what they should be given the price in the futures market for the index. Computers, however, allow for arbitrage transactions across markets of this type. Computerized trading programs may involve the simultaneous purchase of several hundred securities (in round lots via SuperDOT) that mimic the S&P 500 index with the simultaneous sales of S&P 500 index futures. This kind of trading is known as **program trading**. Because there are many arbitrageurs involved in program trading, and because many programs may dictate the simultaneous purchase or sale of large amounts of stock on the NYSE, program trading may have been a factor in the October 1987 market crash. On the other hand, it has also been argued that program trading has the effect of linking the stock and futures markets, causing gaps in prices between the two to narrow, making both markets more efficient, and ultimately reducing volatility in both. Thus, although there was also heavy program trading during the 1997 crash, there was little worry afterwards that it had somehow caused or worsened the fall in prices.

In essence, program trading involves buying stocks or futures, according to which is cheaper at the moment, and selling the other which is selling at a relatively high price. If futures are relatively cheap, one buys futures and sells stocks. The profit in the transaction is thus locked in because the trader can use the proceeds of the stock sale to close out the cheaper futures contracts, keeping the difference. Prior to 1987, most such trades were unwound only when the futures expired, causing huge increases in volume on so-called triple-witching days when many futures, options, and futures options expired simultaneously. These problems were addressed by changing the expiration of futures and other derivative instruments to the opening of trading on the expiration day rather than the closing, thus allowing the prices of stocks a full trading day to adjust to the massive volume. Moreover, it seems quite likely that specialists

Table 15-5

# FUTURES OPTIONS PRICES

Tuesday, December 11, 2001

## AGRICULTURAL

**Corn (CBT)**
**5,000 bu.; cents per bu.**

| STRIKE | CALLS-SETTLE | | | PUTS-SETTLE | | |
|---|---|---|---|---|---|---|
| PRICE | Jan | Feb | Mar | Jan | Feb | Mar |
| 190 | .... | .... | .... | ⅛ | .... | ¼ |
| 200 | 11½ | .... | 20 | ⅛ | .... | ¾ |
| 210 | 3¼ | .... | 12⅛ | 1½ | 1½ | 2⅞ |
| 220 | ½ | 4⅞ | 6⅝ | 9 | 5⅜ | 7¼ |
| 230 | ⅛ | 1¾ | 3⅜ | 18½ | .... | 13¾ |
| 240 | ⅛ | .... | 1⅝ | .... | .... | 21⅞ |

Est vol 8,300 Mn 5,554 calls 2,751 puts
Op int Mon 196,708 calls 124,732 puts

**Soybeans (CBT)**
**5,000 bu.; cents per bu.**

| STRIKE | CALLS-SETTLE | | | PUTS-SETTLE | | |
|---|---|---|---|---|---|---|
| PRICE | Jan | Mar | May | Jan | Mar | May |
| 400 | 37½ | 42 | .... | ⅛ | 1¼ | 3 |
| 420 | 17¾ | 25½ | 31¾ | ¼ | 5 | 7⅝ |
| 440 | 3⅜ | 13¾ | 20¾ | 5⅞ | 13 | 16½ |
| 460 | ⅛ | 7 | 12¾ | 22⅝ | 26¼ | 28½ |
| 480 | ⅛ | 3¼ | 8 | 42½ | 42½ | 43 |
| 500 | ⅛ | 1⅝ | 5 | 62½ | 60½ | 60 |

Est vol 14,000 Mn 5,514 calls 4,076 puts
Op int Mon 115,537 calls 63,436 puts

**Soybean Meal (CBT)**
**100 tons; $ per ton**

| STRIKE | CALLS-SETTLE | | | PUTS-SETTLE | | |
|---|---|---|---|---|---|---|
| PRICE | Jan | Mar | May | Jan | Mar | May |
| 140 | .... | .... | .... | .... | 1.60 | 3.00 |
| 145 | 4.10 | 5.25 | .... | 0.50 | 3.35 | 5.15 |
| 150 | 1.25 | 3.00 | 4.35 | 2.50 | 6.30 | 8.25 |
| 155 | 0.30 | 1.80 | 3.10 | 6.60 | 9.90 | 11.90 |
| 160 | 0.15 | 1.20 | 2.25 | 11.40 | 14.15 | 16.00 |
| 165 | 0.05 | 0.80 | 1.70 | 16.30 | 18.75 | 20.25 |

Est vol 1,700 Mn 516 calls 753 puts
*Op int Mon 16,558 calls 15,330 puts*

**Soybean Oil (CBT)**
**60,000 lbs.; cents per lb.**

| STRIKE | CALLS-SETTLE | | | PUTS-SETTLE | | |
|---|---|---|---|---|---|---|
| PRICE | Jan | Mar | May | Jan | Mar | May |
| 150 | 1.040 | .... | .... | .010 | .100 | .160 |
| 155 | .560 | .910 | .... | .030 | .180 | .260 |
| 160 | .200 | .600 | .880 | .160 | .350 | .450 |
| 165 | .080 | .380 | .680 | .550 | .600 | .740 |
| 170 | .030 | .270 | .530 | 1.000 | 1.030 | 1.080 |
| 175 | .010 | .200 | .410 | 1.480 | 1.460 | .... |

Est vol 4,800 Mn 1,158 calls 692 puts
Op int Mon 56,260 calls 27,374 puts

**Wheat (CBT)**
**5,000 bu.; cents per bu.**

| STRIKE | CALLS-SETTLE | | | PUTS-SETTLE | | |
|---|---|---|---|---|---|---|
| PRICE | Jan | Mar | May | Jan | Mar | May |
| 270 | 16⅞ | 19¾ | .... | ¼ | 3¼ | 6⅜ |
| 280 | 8 | 13⅝ | 18¾ | 1⅝ | 6⅞ | 10¾ |
| 290 | 2¾ | 9 | 14½ | 6 | 12¼ | 16 |
| 300 | ¾ | 6 | 11 | 13⅞ | 19¼ | 22¼ |
| 310 | ¼ | 4 | 8¼ | 23¼ | 27 | 29½ |
| 320 | .... | 2½ | 6⅜ | .... | 35½ | 37⅜ |

Est vol 7,500 Mn 676 calls 999 puts
Op int Mon 41,953 calls 28,969 puts

**Cotton (NYCE)**
**50,000 lbs.; cents per lb.**

| STRIKE | CALLS-SETTLE | | | PUTS-SETTLE | | |
|---|---|---|---|---|---|---|
| PRICE | Mar | May | Jly | Mar | May | Jly |
| 35 | 3.14 | 4.82 | 6.13 | 1.05 | 1.39 | 1.63 |
| 36 | 2.54 | 4.20 | 5.51 | 1.44 | 1.76 | 1.99 |
| 37 | 2.01 | 3.64 | 4.93 | 1.90 | 2.18 | 2.39 |
| 38 | 1.57 | 3.11 | 4.39 | 2.45 | 2.64 | 2.83 |
| 39 | 1.21 | 2.66 | 3.91 | 3.08 | 3.17 | 3.32 |
| 40 | 0.93 | 2.25 | 3.46 | 3.79 | 3.75 | 3.85 |

Est vol 3,044 Mn 3,203 calls 1,539 puts
Op int Mon 79,593 calls 37,252 puts

**Orange Juice (NYCE)**
**15,000 lbs.; cents per lb.**

| STRIKE | CALLS-SETTLE | | | PUTS-SETTLE | | |
|---|---|---|---|---|---|---|
| PRICE | Jan | Mar | May | Jan | Mar | May |
| 80 | 9.90 | 12.95 | 15.60 | 0.05 | 0.55 | 1.35 |
| 85 | 5.15 | 9.05 | 11.80 | 0.20 | 1.45 | 2.70 |
| 90 | 1.25 | 6.00 | 8.30 | 0.95 | 3.40 | 4.50 |
| 95 | 0.20 | 4.45 | 5.50 | 5.20 | 6.80 | 6.95 |
| 100 | 0.05 | 3.50 | 4.20 | 10.10 | 10.70 | 10.55 |
| 105 | 0.05 | 2.80 | 3.40 | 15.10 | 14.95 | 14.15 |

Est vol 1,060 Mn 65 calls 34 puts
Op int Mon 27,789 calls 15,782 puts

**Coffee (CSCE)**
**37,500 lbs.; cents per lb.**

| STRIKE | CALLS-SETTLE | | | PUTS-SETTLE | | |
|---|---|---|---|---|---|---|
| PRICE | Jan | Feb | Mar | Jan | Feb | Mar |
| 42.5 | 5.45 | 6.23 | 6.54 | 0.15 | 0.95 | 1.28 |
| 45 | 3.05 | 4.28 | 4.98 | 0.25 | 1.49 | 2.20 |
| 47.5 | 1.40 | 2.60 | 4.00 | 1.10 | 2.30 | 3.51 |
| 50 | 0.30 | 1.81 | 3.00 | 2.50 | 4.00 | 5.10 |
| 52.5 | 0.10 | 1.30 | 2.26 | 4.80 | 5.99 | 6.93 |
| 55 | 0.05 | 0.98 | 1.70 | 7.25 | 8.15 | 8.85 |

Est vol 2,230 Mn 1,291 calls 1,067 puts
Op int Mon 59,592 calls 18,214 puts

**Sugar-World (CSCE)**
**112,000 lbs.; cents per lb.**

| STRIKE | CALLS-SETTLE | | | PUTS-SETTLE | | |
|---|---|---|---|---|---|---|
| PRICE | Jan | Feb | Mar | Jan | Feb | Mar |
| 650 | 0.86 | 0.90 | 0.95 | 0.01 | 0.05 | 0.09 |
| 700 | 0.36 | 0.45 | 0.59 | 0.01 | 0.10 | 0.24 |
| 750 | 0.03 | 0.17 | 0.32 | 0.17 | 0.32 | 0.47 |
| 800 | 0.01 | 0.06 | 0.17 | 0.66 | 0.71 | 0.81 |
| 850 | 0.01 | 0.03 | 0.08 | 1.16 | 1.18 | 1.22 |
| 900 | 0.01 | 0.02 | 0.03 | 1.66 | 1.66 | 1.67 |

Est vol 4,941 Mn 1,966 calls 2,519 puts
Op int Mon 99,309 calls 59,931 puts

**Cocoa (CSCE)**
**10 metric tons; $ per ton**

| STRIKE | CALLS-SETTLE | | | PUTS-SETTLE | | |
|---|---|---|---|---|---|---|
| PRICE | Feb | Mar | Apr | Feb | Mar | Apr |
| 1200 | 107 | 126 | 129 | 17 | 37 | 51 |
| 1250 | 74 | 99 | 102 | 34 | 59 | 73 |
| 1300 | 49 | 76 | 82 | 59 | 86 | 103 |
| 1350 | 31 | 54 | 64 | 91 | 117 | 134 |
| 1400 | 19 | 44 | 50 | 129 | 153 | 170 |
| 1450 | 12 | 34 | 38 | 171 | 193 | 207 |

Est vol 3,745 Mn 1,713 calls 981 puts
Op int Mon 30,132 calls 24,604 puts

## OIL

**Crude Oil (NYM)**
**1,000 bbls.; $ per bbl.**

| STRIKE | CALLS-SETTLE | | | PUTS-SETTLE | | |
|---|---|---|---|---|---|---|
| PRICE | Jan | Feb | Mar | Jan | Feb | Mar |
| 1700 | 1.16 | .... | 2.84 | 0.08 | 0.77 | 1.09 |
| 1750 | 0.77 | 1.93 | .... | 0.19 | 0.97 | 1.29 |
| 1800 | 0.44 | 1.64 | 2.27 | 0.37 | 1.18 | 1.51 |
| 1850 | 0.22 | 1.40 | 2.02 | 0.64 | 1.45 | 1.76 |
| 1900 | 0.12 | 1.17 | 1.74 | 1.04 | 1.71 | 1.98 |
| 1950 | 0.07 | 1.00 | 1.53 | 1.49 | 2.04 | 2.27 |

Est vol 34,071 Mn 15,206 calls 10,967 puts
Op int Mon 374,735 calls 398,434 puts

**Heating Oil No.2 (NYM)**
**42,000 gal.; $ per gal.**

| STRIKE | CALLS-SETTLE | | | PUTS-SETTLE | | |
|---|---|---|---|---|---|---|
| PRICE | Jan | Feb | Mar | Jan | Feb | Mar |
| 48 | .0350 | .... | .... | .0151 | .0277 | .0346 |
| 49 | .0292 | .... | .... | .0193 | .0320 | .0390 |
| 50 | .0241 | .... | .... | .0242 | .0367 | .0437 |
| 51 | .0198 | .... | .... | .0299 | .0417 | .0487 |
| 52 | .0161 | .0419 | .0545 | .0362 | .0474 | .0540 |
| 53 | .0130 | .... | .0504 | .0430 | .0533 | .0599 |

Est vol 2,048 Mn 982 calls 727 puts
Op int Mon 51,606 calls 33,642 puts

**Gasoline-Unlead (NYM)**
**42,000 gal.; $ per gal.**

| STRIKE | CALLS-SETTLE | | | PUTS-SETTLE | | |
|---|---|---|---|---|---|---|
| PRICE | Jan | Feb | Mar | Jan | Feb | Mar |
| 49 | .... | .... | .... | .0182 | .0281 | .... |
| 50 | .0288 | .... | .... | .0227 | .0324 | .0342 |
| 51 | .0239 | .... | .0648 | .0278 | .0371 | .0385 |
| 52 | .0198 | .0441 | .... | .0337 | .0421 | .0432 |
| 53 | .0163 | .0398 | .0547 | .0402 | .0478 | .0482 |
| 54 | .0133 | .0358 | .0501 | .0471 | .0537 | .0536 |

Est vol 1,442 Mn 1,349 calls 502 puts
*Op int Mon 22,881 calls 23,753 puts*

**Natural Gas (NYM)**
**10,000 MMBtu.; $ per MMBtu.**

| STRIKE | CALLS-SETTLE | | | PUTS-SETTLE | | |
|---|---|---|---|---|---|---|
| PRICE | Jan | Feb | Mar | Jan | Feb | Mar |
| 270 | .252 | .436 | .491 | .149 | .269 | .331 |
| 275 | .226 | .412 | .471 | .173 | .294 | .360 |
| 280 | .202 | .388 | .446 | .199 | .320 | .385 |
| 285 | .181 | .366 | .425 | .228 | .348 | .414 |
| 290 | .161 | .345 | .405 | .258 | .377 | .444 |
| 295 | .143 | .326 | .386 | .290 | .408 | .475 |

Est vol 48,536 Mn 19,445 calls 24,993 puts
Op int Mon 418,218 calls 460,338 puts

Table 15-5 (*cont.*)

**Brent Crude (IPE)**
1,000 net bbls.; $ per bbl.

| STRIKE | CALLS-SETTLE | | | PUTS-SETTLE | | |
|---|---|---|---|---|---|---|
| PRICE | Feb | Mar | Apr | Feb | Mar | Apr |
| 1700 | 1.89 | 2.32 | 2.70 | 0.77 | 1.13 | 1.41 |
| 1750 | 1.61 | 2.02 | 2.41 | 0.99 | 1.33 | 1.62 |
| 1800 | 1.35 | 1.75 | 2.15 | 1.23 | 1.56 | 1.86 |
| 1850 | 1.13 | 1.50 | 1.90 | 1.51 | 1.81 | 2.11 |
| 1900 | 0.93 | 1.27 | 1.67 | 1.81 | 2.08 | 2.38 |
| 1950 | 0.76 | 1.07 | 1.46 | 2.14 | 2.38 | 2.67 |

Est vol 210 Mn 445 calls 376 puts
Op int Mon 18,529 calls 10,951 puts

## LIVESTOCK

**Cattle-Feeder (CME)**
50,000 lbs.; cents per lb.

| STRIKE | CALLS-SETTLE | | | PUTS-SETTLE | | |
|---|---|---|---|---|---|---|
| PRICE | Jan | Mar | Apr | Jan | Mar | Apr |
| 8250 | .... | .... | .... | .... | .... | .... |
| 8300 | 1.47 | .... | .... | 1.20 | .... | .... |
| 8350 | .... | .... | .... | .... | .... | .... |
| 8400 | 0.95 | 1.65 | 1.97 | 1.67 | 3.35 | 3.80 |
| 8500 | 0.60 | 1.10 | .... | .... | .... | .... |

Est vol 793 Mn 166 calls 302 puts
Op int Mon 4,493 calls 10,107 puts

**Cattle-Live (CME)**
40,000 lbs.; cents per lb.

| STRIKE | CALLS-SETTLE | | | PUTS-SETTLE | | |
|---|---|---|---|---|---|---|
| PRICE | Feb | Apr | Jun | Feb | Apr | Jun |
| 67 | 2.90 | .... | .... | 1.40 | .... | .... |
| 68 | 2.22 | .... | 3.00 | 1.72 | 1.60 | 2.90 |
| 69 | 1.70 | .... | .... | 2.20 | .... | .... |
| 70 | 1.25 | 3.45 | 2.07 | 2.75 | 2.30 | 3.95 |
| 71 | 0.90 | .... | .... | 3.40 | 2.75 | .... |
| 72 | 0.65 | 2.30 | 1.22 | 4.12 | 3.05 | 5.07 |

Est vol 1,063 Mn 277 calls 814 puts
Op int Mon 15,839 calls 31,587 puts

**Hogs-Lean (CME)**
40,000 lbs.; cents per lb.

| STRIKE | CALLS-SETTLE | | | PUTS-SETTLE | | |
|---|---|---|---|---|---|---|
| PRICE | Dec | Feb | Apr | Dec | Feb | Apr |
| 43 | .... | .... | .... | .... | .... | .... |
| 44 | .... | 8.27 | .... | 0.12 | 0.27 | 0.30 |
| 45 | 0.55 | .... | .... | 0.40 | 0.37 | .... |
| 46 | 0.17 | .... | .... | 1.02 | 0.47 | 0.42 |
| 47 | 0.05 | .... | .... | 1.90 | 0.65 | .... |
| 48 | 0.00 | .... | .... | 2.85 | 0.85 | 0.60 |

Est vol 1,271 Mn 849 calls 444 puts
Op int Mon 6,707 calls 5,660 puts

## METALS

**Copper (CMX)**
25,000 lbs.; cents per lb.

| STRIKE | CALLS-SETTLE | | | PUTS-SETTLE | | |
|---|---|---|---|---|---|---|
| PRICE | Jan | Feb | Mar | Jan | Feb | Mar |
| 64 | 4.40 | 5.10 | 5.65 | 0.10 | 0.50 | 0.80 |
| 66 | 2.65 | 3.60 | 4.25 | 0.35 | 1.00 | 1.40 |
| 68 | 1.35 | 2.40 | 3.10 | 1.05 | 1.80 | 2.20 |
| 70 | 0.55 | 1.50 | 2.25 | 2.25 | 2.90 | 3.35 |
| 72 | 0.15 | 0.85 | 1.70 | 3.85 | 4.25 | 4.75 |
| 74 | 0.05 | 0.55 | 1.25 | 5.75 | 5.90 | 6.30 |

Est vol 375 Mn 105 calls 15 puts
Op int Mon 8,343 calls 728 puts

**Gold (CMX)**
100 troy ounces; $ per troy ounce

| STRIKE | CALLS-SETTLE | | | PUTS-SETTLE | | |
|---|---|---|---|---|---|---|
| PRICE | Jan | Feb | Apr | Jan | Feb | Apr |
| 265 | 8.10 | 8.90 | 12.30 | 0.30 | 1.00 | 3.90 |
| 270 | 3.30 | 5.20 | 9.40 | 0.50 | 2.30 | 5.90 |
| 275 | 0.70 | 2.90 | 7.30 | 2.80 | 5.00 | 8.80 |
| 280 | 0.20 | 1.80 | 5.00 | 7.30 | 8.90 | 11.40 |
| 285 | 0.10 | 1.10 | 3.80 | 12.10 | 13.20 | 15.20 |
| 290 | 0.10 | 0.90 | 3.50 | 17.10 | 17.90 | 19.90 |

Est vol 4,000 Mn 1,662 calls 1,767 puts
Op int Mon 144,296 calls 58,559 puts

**Silver (CMX)**
5,000 troy ounces; cts per troy ounces

| STRIKE | CALLS-SETTLE | | | PUTS-SETTLE | | |
|---|---|---|---|---|---|---|
| PRICE | Jan | Feb | Mar | Jan | Feb | Mar |
| 375 | 52.5 | 52.9 | 53.8 | 0.1 | 0.5 | 1.4 |
| 400 | 27.6 | 29.2 | 31.3 | 0.1 | 1.7 | 3.8 |
| 425 | 5.3 | 11.9 | 15.0 | 2.8 | 9.4 | 12.6 |
| 450 | 0.8 | 5.1 | 7.4 | 23.3 | 27.6 | 29.9 |
| 475 | 0.1 | 2.6 | 4.5 | 47.6 | 50.0 | 51.8 |
| 500 | 0.1 | 1.5 | 3.0 | 72.5 | 74.0 | 75.3 |

Est vol 2,400 Mn 1,027 calls 244 puts
Op int Mon 56,391 calls 9,689 puts

## INTEREST RATE

**T-Bonds (CBT)**
$100,000; points – 64ths of 100%

| STRIKE | CALLS-SETTLE | | | PUTS-SETTLE | | |
|---|---|---|---|---|---|---|
| PRICE | Jan | Feb | Mar | Jan | Feb | Mar |
| 100 | 1-09 | 1-59 | 2-18 | 0-47 | 1-33 | 1-56 |
| 101 | 0-42 | 1-27 | 1-52 | 1-16 | 2-01 | 2-24 |
| 102 | 0-21 | 1-03 | 1-25 | 1-59 | 2-41 | 2-63 |
| 103 | 0-10 | 0-47 | 1-04 | 2-48 | 3-21 | 3-41 |
| 104 | 0-04 | 0-32 | 0-51 | 3-42 | 4-06 | 4-24 |
| 105 | 0-02 | 0-22 | 0-37 | 4-40 | 4-59 | 5-10 |

Est vol 60,000;
Mn vol 28,498 calls 43,913 puts
Op int Mon 362,526 calls 210,328 puts

**T-Notes (CBT)**
$100,000; points – 64ths of 100%

| STRIKE | CALLS-SETTLE | | | PUTS-SETTLE | | |
|---|---|---|---|---|---|---|
| PRICE | Jan | Feb | Mar | Jan | Feb | Mar |
| 104 | 1-10 | 1-51 | 2-04 | 0-32 | 1-09 | 1-26 |
| 105 | 0-39 | 1-17 | 1-35 | 0-61 | 1-39 | 1-57 |
| 106 | 0-18 | 0-55 | 1-08 | 1-40 | 2-13 | 2-30 |
| 107 | 0-08 | 0-36 | 0-51 | 2-30 | 2-57 | 3-08 |
| 108 | 0-03 | 0-23 | 0-35 | 3-25 | .... | 3-56 |
| 109 | 0-02 | 0-14 | 0-24 | 4-24 | .... | 4-45 |

Est vol 280,000 Mn 59,424 calls 47,651 puts
Op int Mon 703,253 calls 552,936 puts

**5 Yr Treas Notes (CBT)**
$100,000; points – 64ths of 100%

| STRIKE | CALLS-SETTLE | | | PUTS-SETTLE | | |
|---|---|---|---|---|---|---|
| PRICE | Jan | Feb | Mar | Jan | Feb | Mar |
| 10600 | 0-21 | 0-48 | 0-59 | 0-50 | 1-13 | 1-24 |
| 10650 | 0-12 | 0-36 | 0-46 | 1-09 | 1-33 | 1-43 |
| 10700 | 0-07 | 0-27 | 0-36 | 1-35 | 1-56 | 2-01 |
| 10750 | 0-03 | 0-21 | 0-28 | 2-00 | .... | 2-24 |
| 10800 | 0-02 | 0-15 | 0-22 | 2-31 | .... | 2-50 |
| 10850 | 0-01 | 0-11 | 0-17 | .... | .... | 3-12 |

Est vol 14,000 Mn 5,344 calls 8,389 puts
Jp int Mon 212,159 calls 98,038 puts

**Eurodollar (CME)**
$ million; pts of 100%

| STRIKE | CALLS-SETTLE | | | PUTS-SETTLE | | |
|---|---|---|---|---|---|---|
| PRICE | Dec | Jan | Feb | Dec | Jan | Feb |
| 9750 | 6.40 | 5.65 | .... | 0.00 | 0.10 | 0.20 |
| 9775 | 3.90 | 3.25 | 3.45 | 0.00 | 0.20 | 0.40 |
| 9800 | 1.45 | 1.30 | 1.70 | 0.05 | 0.75 | .... |
| 9825 | 0.10 | 0.35 | 0.60 | 1.20 | 2.30 | .... |
| 9850 | 0.00 | 0.12 | 0.25 | 3.60 | .... | .... |
| 9875 | 0.00 | .... | .... | 6.10 | .... | .... |

Est vol 500,613;
Mn vol 281,928 calls 96,128 puts
Op int Mon 5,015,723 calls 4,393,919 puts

**1 Yr. Mid-Curve Eurodlr (CME)**
$1 million contract units; pts of 100%

| STRIKE | CALLS-SETTLE | | | PUTS-SETTLE | | |
|---|---|---|---|---|---|---|
| PRICE | Dec | Jan | Feb | Dec | Jan | Feb |
| 9575 | 5.20 | 2.35 | .... | 0.10 | 3.40 | .... |
| 9600 | 2.80 | 1.45 | 1.85 | 0.20 | 5.00 | 5.40 |
| 9625 | 1.10 | 0.75 | 1.10 | 1.00 | 6.80 | .... |
| 9650 | 0.35 | 0.37 | .... | 2.75 | 8.92 | .... |
| 9675 | 0.15 | 0.15 | .... | 5.05 | 11.17 | .... |
| 9700 | 0.00 | 0.05 | .... | 7.40 | .... | .... |

Est vol 156,922 Mn 37,729 calls 23,466 puts
Op int Mon 1,330,312 calls 718,386 puts

**2 Yr. Mid-Curve Eurodlr (CME)**
$1 million contract units; pts of 100%

| STRIKE | CALLS-SETTLE | | PUTS-SETTLE | |
|---|---|---|---|---|
| PRICE | Dec | Mar | Dec | Mar |
| 9400 | 3.85 | .... | 0.10 | .... |
| 9425 | 1.75 | 3.00 | 0.50 | 3.30 |
| 9450 | 0.50 | 1.90 | 1.75 | 4.70 |
| 9475 | 0.10 | 1.10 | 3.85 | 6.37 |
| 9500 | 0.00 | 0.60 | 6.25 | 8.37 |
| 9525 | 0.00 | 0.35 | .... | 10.62 |

Est vol 250 Mn 1,350 calls 1,075 puts
Op int Mon 53,125 calls 24,955 puts

**Euribor (LIFFE)**
Euro 1,000,000

| STRIKE | CALLS-SETTLE | | | PUTS-SETTLE | | |
|---|---|---|---|---|---|---|
| PRICE | Dec | Jan | Feb | Dec | Jan | Feb |
| 96375 | 0.29 | 0.52 | 0.53 | .... | .... | 0.00 |
| 96500 | 0.17 | 0.40 | 0.41 | .... | 0.00 | 0.01 |
| 96625 | 0.05 | 0.29 | 0.31 | 0.00 | 0.01 | 0.03 |
| 96750 | 0.00 | 0.19 | 0.22 | 0.08 | 0.04 | 0.07 |
| 96875 | .... | 0.11 | 0.14 | 0.20 | 0.08 | 0.12 |
| 97000 | .... | 0.05 | 0.09 | 0.33 | 0.15 | 0.19 |

Vol Tu 82,925 calls 38,525 puts
Op int Mon 2,098,385 calls 1,254,718 puts

Table 15-5 (*cont.*)

**10 Yr. German Euro Gov't Bd (Eurobund) (Eurex)100,000;pts in 100%**

| STRIKE PRICE | CALLS-SETTLE | | | PUTS-SETTLE | | |
|---|---|---|---|---|---|---|
| | Jan | Feb | Mar | Jan | Feb | Mar |
| 10750 | 0.89 | 1.34 | 1.56 | 0.12 | 0.57 | 0.79 |
| 10800 | 0.54 | 1.05 | 1.28 | 0.27 | 0.78 | 1.01 |
| 10850 | 0.29 | 0.80 | 1.02 | 0.52 | 1.03 | 1.25 |
| 10900 | 0.13 | 0.59 | 0.81 | 0.86 | 1.32 | 1.54 |
| 10950 | 0.05 | 0.43 | 0.63 | 1.28 | 1.66 | 1.86 |
| 11000 | 0.02 | 0.31 | 0.49 | 1.75 | 2.04 | 2.22 |

Vol Tu 48,625 calls 36,462 puts
Op int Mon 638,288 calls 360,902 puts

# CURRENCY

**Japanese Yen (CME)**
**12,500,000 yen; cents per 100 yen**

| STRIKE PRICE | CALLS-SETTLE | | | PUTS-SETTLE | | |
|---|---|---|---|---|---|---|
| | Jan | Feb | Mar | Jan | Feb | Mar |
| 7850 | .... | .... | .... | .... | .... | .... |
| 7900 | 1.19 | .... | 2.05 | 0.57 | 1.14 | 1.43 |
| 7950 | 0.89 | .... | .... | 0.77 | 1.33 | .... |
| 8000 | 0.65 | 1.20 | 1.52 | 1.03 | 1.58 | 1.99 |
| 8050 | 0.45 | 0.98 | .... | 1.33 | 1.86 | .... |
| 8100 | 0.31 | 0.79 | 1.10 | 1.69 | 2.16 | 2.47 |

Est vol 2,085 Mn 529 calls 2,212 puts
Op int Mon 10,247 calls 18,006 puts

**Canadian Dollar (CME)**
**100,000 Can.$, cents per Can.$**

| STRIKE PRICE | CALLS-SETTLE | | | PUTS-SETTLE | | |
|---|---|---|---|---|---|---|
| | Jan | Feb | Mar | Jan | Feb | Mar |
| 6250 | 1.00 | .... | .... | 0.08 | .... | 0.35 |
| 6300 | 0.61 | .... | 0.94 | 0.19 | .... | 0.52 |
| 6350 | 0.32 | .... | 0.69 | 0.40 | .... | 0.77 |
| 6400 | 0.15 | 0.37 | 0.48 | .... | .... | 1.06 |
| | .06 | .... | 0.33 | .... | .... | 1.40 |
| 6500 | .... | 0.13 | 0.24 | .... | .... | 1.81 |

Est vol 171 Mn 56 calls 391 puts
Op int Mon 19,196 calls 3,877 puts

**British Pound (CME)**
**62,500 pounds; cents per pound**

| STRIKE PRICE | CALLS-SETTLE | | | PUTS-SETTLE | | |
|---|---|---|---|---|---|---|
| | Jan | Feb | Mar | Jan | Feb | Mar |
| 1410 | 2.34 | 3.04 | .... | 0.40 | .... | .... |
| 1420 | 1.68 | 2.36 | 2.88 | 0.74 | 1.42 | 1.94 |
| 1430 | 1.14 | .... | .... | 1.20 | 1.94 | .... |
| 1440 | 0.74 | .... | 1.94 | 1.80 | 2.48 | 3.00 |
| 1450 | 0.42 | .... | .... | 2.48 | .... | .... |
| 1460 | 0.22 | 0.72 | 1.26 | 3.28 | .... | 4.30 |

Est vol 367 Mn 59 calls 232 puts
Op int Mon 2,024 calls 5,002 puts

**Swiss Franc (CME)**
**125,000 francs; cents per franc**

| STRIKE PRICE | CALLS-SETTLE | | | PUTS-SETTLE | | |
|---|---|---|---|---|---|---|
| | Jan | Feb | Mar | Jan | Feb | Mar |
| 5650 | 1.16 | .... | .... | 0.22 | .... | .... |
| 6000 | .... | .... | 1.49 | 0.35 | .... | 1.05 |
| 6050 | 0.52 | .... | .... | 0.58 | .... | .... |
| 6100 | 0.36 | .... | 1.02 | 0.92 | .... | 1.58 |
| 6150 | .... | .... | .... | .... | .... | .... |
| 6200 | 0.14 | .... | 0.68 | 1.70 | .... | 2.23 |

Est vol 148 Mn 78 calls 229 puts
Op int Mon 2,841 calls 3,381 puts

**Euro Fx (CME)**
**125,000 euros; cents per euro**

| STRIKE PRICE | CALLS-SETTLE | | | PUTS-SETTLE | | |
|---|---|---|---|---|---|---|
| | Jan | Feb | Mar | Jan | Feb | Mar |
| 8800 | 1.27 | 1.84 | 2.22 | 0.46 | 1.03 | 1.42 |
| 8850 | 0.97 | 1.54 | .... | 0.66 | .... | .... |
| 8900 | 0.71 | .... | 1.69 | 0.90 | .... | 1.88 |
| 8950 | 0.50 | .... | .... | 1.19 | .... | .... |
| 9000 | 0.33 | 0.90 | 1.26 | 1.55 | .... | 2.44 |
| 9050 | 0.25 | 0.75 | .... | 1.94 | .... | .... |

Est vol 981 Mn 729 calls 374 puts
Op int Mon 20,339 calls 13,759 puts

# INDEX

**DJ Industrial Avg (CBOT)**
**$100 times premium**

| STRIKE PRICE | CALLS-SETTLE | | | PUTS-SETTLE | | |
|---|---|---|---|---|---|---|
| | Dec | Jan | Feb | Dec | Jan | Feb |
| 97 | 26.55 | .... | .... | 7.90 | 20.75 | .... |
| 98 | 19.65 | 32.25 | .... | 10.65 | 24.25 | .... |
| 99 | 13.70 | 26.25 | .... | 14.70 | 28.25 | .... |
| 100 | 8.90 | 21.30 | .... | 19.70 | 33.00 | 40.75 |
| 101 | 5.25 | 16.50 | .... | 26.25 | .... | 46.00 |
| 102 | 2.85 | 12.70 | .... | 33.80 | .... | 51.75 |

Est vol 300 Mn 123 calls 156 puts
Op int Mon 7,068 calls 14,983 puts

**S&P 500 Stock Index (CME)**
**$250 times premium**

| STRIKE PRICE | CALLS-SETTLE | | | PUTS-SETTLE | | |
|---|---|---|---|---|---|---|
| | Dec | Jan | Feb | Dec | Jan | Feb |
| 1125 | 23.10 | 38.50 | 43.70 | 11.60 | 25.80 | 36.10 |
| 1130 | 20.00 | 35.40 | .... | 13.50 | 27.70 | 38.00 |
| 1135 | 17.00 | 32.50 | .... | 15.50 | 29.80 | 40.20 |
| 1140 | 14.20 | 29.70 | .... | 17.70 | 32.00 | .... |
| 1145 | 11.80 | 27.10 | 37.50 | 20.30 | 34.40 | 44.80 |
| 1150 | 9.60 | 24.30 | 34.90 | 23.10 | 36.90 | 47.10 |

Est vol 5,497 Mn 4,795 calls 6,904 puts
Op int Mon 88,387 calls 179,129 puts

# OTHER OPTIONS

Final or settlement prices of selected contracts. Volume and open interest are totals in all contract months.

**10 Yr. Agency Note (CBT)**
**pts 64ths**

| STRIKE PRICE | CALLS-SETTLE | PUTS-SETTLE |
|---|---|---|
| | Dec | Dec |
| 101 | .... | .... |

Est vol 0 Mn 0 calls 0 puts
Op int Mon 2 calls 0 puts

**NASDAQ 100 (CME)**
**$100 times NASDAQ 100 Index**

| STRIKE PRICE | CALLS-SETTLE | | | PUTS-SETTLE | | |
|---|---|---|---|---|---|---|
| | Dec | Jan | Feb | Dec | Jan | Feb |
| 1650 | 51.40 | .... | .... | 45.90 | .... | .... |

Est vol 266 Mn 65 calls 31 puts
Op int Mon 2,978 calls 3,088 puts

**NYSE Composite (NYFE)**
**$500 times premium**

| STRIKE PRICE | CALLS-SETTLE | | | PUTS-SETTLE | | |
|---|---|---|---|---|---|---|
| | Dec | Jan | Feb | Dec | Jan | Feb |
| 576 | 6.55 | 13.35 | 17.85 | 6.80 | 13.30 | 17.80 |

Est vol 297 Mn 331 calls 62 puts
Op int Mon 1,496 calls 2,420 puts

**Wheat (KC)**
**5,000 bu.; cents per bu.**

| STRIKE PRICE | CALLS-SETTLE | | | PUTS-SETTLE | | |
|---|---|---|---|---|---|---|
| | Jan | Mar | May | Jan | Mar | May |
| 290 | 3 | 8¾ | 15 | .... | 11 | 11⅞ |

Est vol 474 Mn 186 calls 214 puts
Op int Mon 10,134 calls 11,260 puts

on the floor of the NYSE (and market makers in the over-the-counter (OTC) market to the extent that certain index stocks are traded there) quickly came to understand the dynamics of program trading and adjusted to it. Indeed, to the extent that program trading increases volume on the NYSE and in other stock markets, specialists and market makers benefit. Finally, traders also discovered that program trading itself tended to cause the gap to close between the prices of futures and the prices of stocks, so that the trade could be unwound shortly after it was made by simply entering into the opposite transaction.

## 15.7  Hedging, Portfolio Insurance, and Other Strategies

A second major source of futures trading is a variety of strategies known as **portfolio insurance**. It is widely believed that these strategies also contributed to the October 1987 crash and were largely unsuccessful in preventing substantial losses.

An institutional investor that holds a portfolio of securities similar to that reflected in the S&P 500 index may hedge that position by selling S&P 500 index futures in much the same way that a farmer with a long position in the form of a crop in the ground can hedge against a price decline. Portfolio insurance (sometimes called **dynamic hedging**) does not strive to produce a riskless portfolio. Rather, it attempts to offset the potential decline while not eliminating the possibility of gain (as a true hedge does) in the case of a market rise. This is accomplished by buying or selling with the movement of the market: selling index futures when prices are declining and buying futures when prices are rising. During the October 1987 market collapse, these strategies became impossible to execute, because they dictated sales of index futures in volumes that the market was unable or unwilling to absorb. When the market began to decline, portfolio insurance programs caused massive sell orders to be sent to the futures exchanges. The price of stock index futures thus began to decline, and because each sale of a stock index future represented a large sale of stock, the price of futures moved downward much more rapidly than the prices of the individual stocks in the index. When the gap between futures prices and the prices of the underlying stocks became sufficiently large, program trades (designed to lock in profits by simultaneously buying futures and selling stocks) were triggered, causing the price of stocks to fall further, and causing the entire process to repeat itself. These problems have been largely alleviated by the imposition of coordinated trading halts on the stock and futures exchanges, and, perhaps more important, by traders' having learned the limitations of such strategies and the markets themselves.

The creation of a variety of derivative securities has dramatically changed the securities markets for large investors. It is usually much cheaper in terms of commissions and other expenses to effect major changes in a large portfolio by transactions in the futures market or options market than by the sale and purchase of many different securities. For example, a debt portfolio can be converted rapidly to equity by simultaneously selling bond futures and buying stock index futures. Of course, commission costs will be incurred if the underlying debt portfolio is ultimately liquidated and the equity investment substituted. However, these transactions may be delayed indefinitely through the use of index futures.

**Tactical Asset Allocation (TAA)** is the name sometimes given to an investment strategy for large institutional investors that concentrates on classes of investments (e.g., equities, debt securities, and money market funds or cash equivalents) rather than on specific securities. These programs are computer-driven and rely on the purchase and sale of financial futures rather than on transactions in the underlying securities themselves.

The continued improvement in computer technology has led to increasingly sophisticated arbitrage trading strategies. The people who develop quantitative—mathematically based—investment strategies are often called **quants** or **rocket scientists**.

## §15.8 Swaps and Derivatives

A **swap** is a transaction in which two parties enter into an agreement providing for the exchange of defined streams of payments over a specified period of time. Typically, a fixed stream is swapped for a stream that varies with interest rate fluctuations, or vice versa. Through careful specification of payment streams, a customer of a bank may hedge against unprotected interest rate or currency exchange rate fluctuations and also arbitrage differences in world capital markets to obtain higher yields or lower borrowing costs.

The swap of a floating rate obligation for a fixed-rate obligation, or vice versa, permits companies to hedge against risks caused by fluctuations in interest rates. For example, Kohlberg Kravis Roberts (KKR), a takeover firm, issued large amounts of floating rate debt in connection with its acquisition of RJR Nabisco even though the cash flow from which these obligations were to be repaid was not interest rate sensitive. KKR hedged its variable rate obligations created in the RJR Nabisco acquisition by an interest rate cap. KKR paid a fee to a bank in return for the bank's agreement that if interest rates exceeded a certain level, the bank would pay the excess interest to KKR. The bank in turn took the fee it received from KKR and invested it in futures that increased in value with interest rate increases, thereby hedging its payment obligation to KKR. The global market for derivative securities—swaps, options, futures, and custom-made financial interests—has revolutionized how corporate and financial institutions handle risk.

Banks typically act in the capacity of principal in these transactions, though they promptly trade out their positions with other customers so as to minimize their exposure to fluctuations of interest or currency rates. In large transactions of this type, there is always some risk that one party may default; large and financially secure banks are necessary parties to these transactions, because they guarantee the parties against default by another party.

It is difficult for bank examiners and others even to gauge the risk that derivative contracts carry, because these transactions often do not fit the traditional definitions of assets and liabilities. Because the risk in these transactions is potentially great, the suggestion has been made that banks should be required to conduct these activities through an affiliate that is not insured by the Federal Deposit Insurance Corporation.

The concern about derivative securities and the risk inherent in them is in part generational. Banking officials who compose the senior management of most institutions generally are not familiar with the computer-driven markets for derivative securities and do not trust them; younger officials are more confident that serious problems will not arise. Only time will tell who is correct.

Although most swaps are arranged one-on-one in the vast OTC market for derivatives, the Chicago Board of Trade began trading futures swap contracts in June 1991. These contracts are for three-year and five-year interest rate swaps and are designed to permit hedging of long-term positions. In shorter-term swaps, a participant usually can hedge an exposed position through interest rate or Eurodollar futures.

Derivative instruments have been around for a long time in the form of options and futures contracts. The real change is that such instruments are increasingly traded privately and outside the confines of established exchanges. Until 1992, federal law prohibited the trading of futures contracts other than on a registered futures exchange. However, it has never been entirely clear just what a future is. A contract to sell wheat at a date in the future for a price set now or by reference to some benchmark price in the future is not necessarily a futures contract, though it may become one by virtue of being traded or tradeable. The current derivatives market was in effect created when bigger players found it desirable to arrange their own off-exchange or OTC trades and argued that the resulting instruments were not futures contracts. In 1992, the CFTC gained the authority to exempt private trades that were not equivalent to standardized contracts, and as of 2001 such trades are exempt by statute. (This most recent legislation also permits trading in single stock futures.) Generally speaking, whether a trade is exempt from regulation depends on the status of the parties to the transaction, whether the transaction is part of a class of fungible or standardized transactions, whether the transaction is entered into on a multilateral transaction facility, and whether the noncommodity portion of the transaction (if any) predominates over the commodity portion.

The reasons for avoiding exchange transactions are numerous and varied. Often, there is no exchange-traded contract that precisely matches the risks that one or the other of the parties wants to hedge. Further, there are practical limits on the variety of futures contracts that may be traded (particularly the need to have a ready pool of speculators to help provide liquidity), and many exchange-traded instruments are simply close substitutes for the commodity that a hedger really wants to hedge. (For example, a lemon grower might hedge some of his or her risk by buying or selling futures in frozen concentrated orange juice.)

No doubt cost is another reason for avoiding an exchange. As on any exchange, one must deal through a member broker, who charges a commission. Moreover, when one trades on an exchange, one must comply with exchange rules, such as those requiring margin, the good faith deposit that all traders must put down and maintain in order to keep a position open. This is not to say that the futures exchanges tend to over-regulate trading. Margin deposits make a good deal of sense in that they provide security that a trade will be honored. And the futures exchanges have no interest in dampening trading more than necessary. With OTC derivatives, there may be no margin requirement at all though participants in this market expend considerable time and money checking the credit of those with whom they trade and generally will not trade if there is any risk of a possible default. Nevertheless, OTC trading may carry higher levels of risk, particularly if a trader has entered into trades with a variety of partners or if the trader has failed to "get it right" in constructing an elaborate hedge.

Finally, the futures exchanges may be opposed to OTC derivatives transactions for competitive (or anticompetitive) reasons: The more business that is siphoned off by those who arrange their own trades elsewhere, the less business there will be on the exchanges. In all fairness, there may be a legitimate worry here. As bigger trades are accomplished away from the exchange, the market on the exchange becomes thinner and trading becomes riskier for those who trade on the exchanges, and smaller players may be left with a less-efficient market in which to hedge their smaller risks. In the end, however, most OTC trades are so specialized that they probably could not be accomplished very easily if at all by using the standardized contract traded on the exchanges. Ever since the advent of exchange-traded stock options (in 1973) and stock index futures (in 1982), the SEC and the CFTC have been more or less in competition over which agency will have control over new instruments that have some of the characteristics of both securities and futures. This struggle has been complicated by the fact that the CFTC has exclusive jurisdiction over futures, while the SEC has only jurisdiction over exchanges.

It is important to understand that the word "derivative" is used to refer to a wide variety of complex securities, some of which do not quite fit some of the simpler definitions of the word. Although it is usually said that a derivative is a security the price or return of which is derived from the price or return of one or more other securities, the word is often also used to describe securities that are created by breaking up other securities into smaller pieces. Thus, while virtually all commentators would agree that publicly traded stock index futures are derivatives (although they are among the least worrisome ones), many commentators would also classify a collateralized mortgage obligation (CMO) that pays a return based on the timely interest payments on a pool of residential mortgages as a derivative. In one sense, the latter security is not a derivative, because it makes no reference to any other security for purposes of determining the return to be paid. But in another sense, such a security is a derivative, because the return is based on the contractual obligation of the creator of the CMO to calculate current interest payments and pass them on to the holders of securities tied to that slice of the returns. By this definition, of course, even such familiar securities as Treasury strips would be seen as derivatives.

As a result of numerous scandals, the risks of derivatives are often overestimated and mischaracterized. It has been estimated that there is as much as $25 trillion in derivative instruments outstanding globally. This figure, assuming it is accurate, is the nominal (or notional) amount of derivatives. That is, it is the face amount on which the gain or loss from the derivative instrument will be calculated. For example, in the case of an exchange-traded stock index future on the S&P 500, the nominal amount is $500 times the value of the index. If the index stands at 800, then the nominal value of a contract is $400,000. Although it is theoretically possible that such an amount could be lost by the purchaser, such a result would only come to pass if all of the underlying stocks fell to zero. Although in some sense there is $400,000 at risk, there is virtually no chance that such an amount could be lost. Focusing on the nominal amount of derivatives outstanding is rather like estimating the size of the life insurance market by adding up the face amount of all the policies outstanding. One must keep in mind that a $100,000 policy may only involve the outlay of $300 per year by the insured.

Moreover, there is a tendency to think that derivatives losses somehow simply happen. In fact, derivatives are a **zero sum game**. For every loser there is a winner, though the losers make the headlines and the winners often prefer to remain in the shadows. To be sure, derivatives dealers make money by selling derivatives. That is, they do not sell such securities at cost. As with any other product, derivatives are sold at a markup (or markdown as the case may be). Thus, someone who buys a derivative instrument is getting something worth less than the purchase price. The real question is how much less? But whatever the markup, that amount is indeed gone forever as far as the buyer is concerned (short of litigation alleging some sort of fraud in the original purchase).

The scandals relating to derivatives have resulted from many different problems. The collapse of the Barings Bank involved unauthorized trading in stock index futures, which are actively traded on public futures exchanges and thus are subject to few doubts as to pricing. Ironically, some reports indicate that the Barings collapse may have been caused by slavish adherence to a market model at a time when the markets were not behaving as the model said they would. The same appears to have been the case with the collapse of Long Term Capital Management although there the trading involved mostly debt securities. Under any other circumstances, such discipline might be seen as quite conservative. Ironically, disciplined buying and selling of stock index futures according to market models is precisely the mechanism by which portfolio insurance was supposed to have worked prior to the 1987 crash.

The problems at Gibson Greetings, Procter & Gamble, and Orange County, California, involving derivatives sold by Bankers Trust and Merrill Lynch, appear to have arisen as a result of misrepresentations or misunderstandings about risk and price and do not involve questions of the propriety of such instruments for such buyers. Indeed, it has been reported that some companies have been hurt by their reluctance to become involved in the derivatives market. For example, Merck, which sells half of its products overseas, is said to have lost as much as $900,000,000 per year in revenues in the mid-1980s as a result of failing to hedge against currency risks.

Perhaps the most serious derivatives-induced problem is that of Orange County, which declared bankruptcy as a result of losses primarily in CMOs. Other local government entities (including several school boards) and small colleges have also suffered serious losses from investments in similar derivatives. Most of these cases appear to have been the result of overzealous sales efforts on the part of brokers. These incidents have prompted calls for more vigorous enforcement of suitability requirements in connection with institutional investors (particularly governments). The suitability rule is generally interpreted to protect only individual investors, although the various versions of the rule as adopted by the National Association of Securities Dealers (NASD) and the exchanges do not specifically limit the scope of the rule. It is possible that derivatives losses will lead to legal restrictions on the kinds of investments that various government entities may make. Such rules may have negative consequences, because local governments and similar agencies often face risks that may be hedged against by the use of derivatives.

The Orange County bankruptcy may have much broader implications for municipal finance than simply tighter regulation of investment practices. It appears that the affluent county's strategy was to attempt to avoid obligations rather than to raise taxes and pay up as has been the practice by other troubled municipalities. At the very least, such hardball tactics will raise interest rates that must be paid by other state and local governments, and may cause Congress to consider whether continuing tax exemption for these entities makes sense. Finally, it appears that the credit rating agencies maintained Orange County's top rating even though it was known that the county had undertaken risky investment strategies. This revelation may in itself have the effect of raising interest rates on state and local government obligations and prompting more scrutiny by rating agencies of investment strategies in the future.

Derivatives dealers have taken significant steps toward self-regulation in an effort to avoid government regulation. In 1994, major dealers agreed to a Wholesale Transactions Code of Conduct sponsored by New York Federal Reserve Bank. In 1995, six major derivatives firms and the SEC and CFTC entered into a more elaborate agreement touching on four areas: internal monitoring, enhanced reporting, capital adequacy, and informing customers. Under the agreement, dealers report their portfolio structure, their 20 largest positions by trading partner, and their internal estimates of risk. This information will not, however, be available to the public. Because capital adequacy is directly related to risk, one crucial issue in regulating derivatives is the system or model used to measure risk. But because risk measurement is the primary focus of competition among derivatives dealers, it was agreed that firms may use their own proprietary systems as long as they meet certain minimum requirements and the results are verifiable by an outside auditor.

The need for regulation aside, accounting for derivatives is another complicated issue. In the case of exchange-traded derivatives, there is little doubt as to what they are worth on any given day. But OTC derivatives are another matter. In October 1994, the Financial Accounting Standards Board (FASB) adopted a new rule (Statement of Financial Accounting Standard (SFAS) No. 117) requiring disclosure of derivatives holdings, how they are accounted for on the balance sheet, gains or losses therefrom, and the purpose for which they are held (i.e., hedging or speculation). With respect to derivatives held for speculation, the rule requires that the value of derivatives be disclosed as well. Although there is no requirement that the method of valuation be disclosed, the rule encourages risk disclosure that would allow users of financial statements to compare derivatives exposure firm to firm. The FASB rule is part of an increasing trend toward requiring current value accounting rather than historical cost accounting, at least in those areas where fluctuations in market prices are critical.

The collapse of Enron in late 2001 may result in further review of these rules. It appears that the problems of Enron may have resulted from bad bets on the future price of electricity that fell dramatically with other energy prices after the events of September 11, 2001. It has also been suggested that Enron's trading may have exacerbated the California energy crisis of 2001. In any event, it seems clear that the potential liabilities assumed by Enron in its private trading of energy contracts was not reflected in its financial statements and that its auditor, Arthur Andersen LLP, will pay dearly for those mistakes.

In the end, it should be remembered that most derivatives trading is undertaken for hedging purposes and thus is risk-reducing rather than risk-enhancing. But no hedge is perfect. For example, there is no futures market for lemons, but frozen concentrated orange juice is a close substitute. Still, even the best-intentioned hedge may sometimes backfire for reasons that are difficult to appreciate in advance. Moreover, it can be very difficult for an outsider to determine whether an elaborate position is in fact a hedge or a highly risky speculation. Ultimately, it is impossible to ensure that derivatives will not be used for speculation, and indeed, speculators serve the quite legitimate function of assuming risk for hedgers (presumably at a price). Thus, it is far from clear that one would want to ban speculation in derivatives.

# CHAPTER 16

# INVESTMENT COMPANIES AND INVESTMENT ADVICE

## §16.1  Introduction

This chapter focuses on investing. Investing must be distinguished from trading. To be sure, there are many traders who make a living (or try to) from buying and selling—but not holding—securities and other financial instruments. Moreover, trading is important to investors, because investors must use the trading markets to build a portfolio of investments and to adjust that portfolio from time to time as new money is invested, or as investments are cashed out, or simply to keep the portfolio in balance as some investments rise and others fall in value. Thus, an investor will care very much about getting the best price on any individual trade. But an investor cares mostly about longer-term risk and return.

This chapter first addresses the general topics of diversification and risk. It then describes a variety of investment companies and other investment vehicles that offer investors a prepackaged diversified portfolio of investments at various levels of risk. These include closed-end funds, open-end funds (known as mutual funds), unit investment trusts, real estate investment trusts, and hedge funds. The chapter then discusses various short-term funds and nonequity investments, including money market funds. Next, the chapter addresses a variety of issues that arise when one chooses to manage one's own investments rather than investing through professionally managed funds, including when one should consider such a strategy, dealings with brokerage houses, and the use of investment advisers.

## §16.2  Risk and Diversification

There are many different investment strategies for the small investor. It is assumed in this discussion that the typical small investor is relatively **risk averse**. That is, the investor is not willing to take large risks simply because the expected return is higher than with less risky investments. In most of the strategies described below, the investor's goal is to obtain a better return, either in the form of income or capital appreciation, than can be obtained from a riskless or virtually riskless investment. Obviously, one needs first to establish investment objectives and then make investments that are consistent with those objectives. Plausible investment goals include:

*Preservation of assets.* When safety is the most important concern, one may simply invest the entire amount in money market accounts, insured bank money market accounts or certificates of deposit, and short-term United States Treasury securities. The specific selection may depend on relative yields and the likelihood that the investor may require access to funds in the near future.

*Income.* When the primary goal is to earn investment income at minimal risk to principal, one might choose mutual funds concentrating in longer-term government securities, municipal bonds, quality corporate bonds, and high-income stocks such as utilities and blue chips (both domestic and foreign). One might also consider investing a portion of the principal in limited partnership interests investing in positive cash-flow-producing types of real estate investments.

*Growth.* When a person is willing to take a greater risk of loss of assets in exchange for the possibility of greater growth of principal assets, one might choose mutual funds that emphasize capital appreciation (although the performance of many of these funds historically has been disappointing) or direct investments in common stocks and real estate investments.

*Aggressive growth.* When a person is willing to assume a high risk of asset depreciation in exchange for higher growth or speculative increase in asset value, one might choose developmental projects such as real estate, investing either through stock or by direct purchases. One might also invest in stocks that are rumored to be candidates for takeover bids.

In general terms, the greater the risk of an investment, the higher its return must be. In investing, there is no such thing as a free lunch. Markets generally price investments efficiently; an investment that has a significantly higher yield than another must, somewhere, carry with it some additional element of risk. This is neatly illustrated by Table 16-1, which graphs the relationship between risk and return for the most common classes of investments.

Once an investor has determined the level of risk he or she desires, it is important to invest in a diversified portfolio of investments at that level of risk. That does not necessarily mean, however, that one must construct a portfolio of only investments that individually carry the desired risk and return combination. For example, if one puts half of one's portfolio in stocks (with a historical return of about 10 percent over the long haul) and half in government securities (with a historical return of zero percent after inflation), the blended return on the entire portfolio can be expected to be about 5 percent after inflation. Thus, while the investor has reduced the risk of the portfolio, it has been at the sacrifice of return. An investor who invests in an all-stock portfolio takes on more risk, but it is the level of risk that must be assumed to achieve (say) a 10 percent return.

Diversification largely eliminates the risk of massive losses from a single investment that performs poorly, but it does not provide protection against a marketwide decline in values. With a diversified portfolio of as few as 20 stocks, an investor can enjoy the same rate of return as with an investment in a single stock while avoiding as much as 90 percent of the risk that goes with an investment in a single stock portfolio. No investor should take more risk than necessary for a given level of return. Thus, it makes no sense to put all of one's

**Table 16-1**

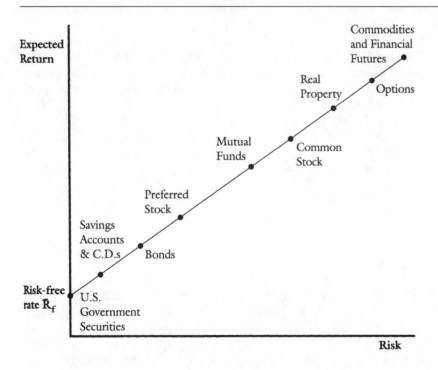

441

eggs in one basket. (The law of trusts has long recognized a similar principle that a trustee who fails to diversify may be held liable to the trust.)

Although such exotic-sounding ideas as the efficient capital market hypothesis (ECMH) and modern portfolio theory may seem to be more of academic interest than of practical value, they actually have profound implications for the small investor. Simply stated, the ECMH holds that it is impossible to beat the market consistently on the basis of publicly available information. The evidence supporting this proposition is overwhelming, although the theory does have limitations. It is important to understand that the ECMH does not mean that one cannot make money investing in stocks or other securities. Rather, it means that one can only expect to make a market rate of return.

Although an investor can reduce risk significantly by choosing 10 or 20 stocks or other securities at random, there has emerged a large body of learning, known as **modern portfolio theory** (**MPT**), about how diversification works and how portfolios should be structured for maximum risk-reduction effect. MPT implies that an investor can eliminate company-specific risk. In other words, a fully diversified investor takes only the risk that the market as a whole will rise or fall. One important insight that comes from MPT is that because it is possible to eliminate company-specific risk, securities are priced in the market as if such risk were not present. In other words, the market pays no additional return to investors who bet heavily on individual companies, that is, investors who engage in stock-picking strategies. This is not to say that one cannot win big with such a strategy. Rather, it is only to say that unless one has reliable inside information, the odds are longer than the prize is worth.

Taken together, these theories suggest that it makes no sense for the small investor to try to predict the performance of individual companies or the market as a whole. All that an investor should do is choose the level of risk or return desired and invest in a well-diversified portfolio of instruments bearing that risk. (One need only focus on one or the other measure, because the ECMH implies that instruments of comparable risk will be priced to yield comparable returns.) In other words, these theories taken together strongly suggest that an investor should buy and hold.

Risk is a slippery concept. The critical reader will have noticed that the idea that stocks return 10 percent over the long haul seems inconsistent with the idea that they are riskier. The answer to this seeming paradox is that risk is a time-sensitive concept. Even a diversified portfolio may have considerable risk over a period of 1 or 2 years, but much less risk over a period of 20 years. If the market on the average is focusing on a 5-year risk horizon, an investor who is willing to hold for a longer period assumes less risk, although that does not necessarily guarantee the historical rate of return.

Diversification has sometimes also been applied at the company level as a matter of business strategy. Some businesspeople figure that if it makes sense for an investor to diversify, then it also makes sense for a company to do the same thing in order to smooth out its earnings. That is not necessarily so. Investors can easily assemble a portfolio of companies making various products and thus hold precisely the constellation of businesses that they desire to hold. Similar acquisitions and divestitures by companies may be expensive. Moreover, they result in a company that offers prepackaged diversification that may appeal only to limited numbers of investors. (It is like a package in a supermarket containing a banana and an apple; a few may be interested in buying both, but many will prefer other combinations.) Finally, diversification may ultimately distract management from its task of doing the best possible job managing the company's operations. A CEO faced with running two or more unrelated operations will have less time to focus on each. All this is not to say that there is no such thing as synergy in business. Rather, it is only to say that synergy and diversification are two different things. Similar arguments can be made about many firm-level strategies involving the purchase and sale of derivative instruments. They may be designed to hedge against risks that diversified investors have already hedged against. Thus, reducing risk at the firm level may lead to a drop in a stock's market price rather than an increase.

A small investor may not be able to diversify effectively by purchasing small amounts of different publicly traded securities that different companies issue. The trading units for round lots may be too large for effective investment of small amounts of funds. And commissions charged on odd lot transactions make that alternative unattractive. In some cases, a small investor may be able to construct a sufficiently large portfolio by buying on margin, as explained in Chapter 14. There is, however, a very simple way to achieve diversification with an investment as small as $1,000: One simply invests in one or more mutual funds or other investment companies. They provide instant diversification for even the smallest investment.

## §16.3 Investment Companies

An **investment company** is a corporation or other entity that invests in securities of other corporations. An investment company therefore has at any given time a portfolio of securities and usually some cash or cash-equivalent assets awaiting investment. Investment companies are themselves entities that issue shares. (Many investment companies are organized as Massachusetts business trusts or as Maryland corporations.) Investors may purchase these shares and thereby obtain instant diversification, because the shares that an investment company issues in effect constitute investment in the portfolio owned by the investment company. Because the value of the investment company's portfolio is known, it is also relatively easy to determine the net asset value of each share of the investment company's stock. One simply values all the holdings in the investment company's portfolio and divides by the number of outstanding shares. A mutual fund is one type of investment company, but there are many others.

Not all companies that invest in securities are investment companies. If a company invests exclusively in controlling interests in several operating companies and itself has no other business, it is a **holding company**. A company that has business operations and also invests free cash in securities is not an investment company either, as long as its earnings are primarily attributable to its business orperations and not its investments. If an investment company is closely held by a few shareholders, it is a **personal holding company** for tax purposes. The investment companies described in the balance of this chapter are publicly held investment companies that are subject to a substantial degree of regulation by the Securities and Exchange Commission (the SEC) under the Investment Company Act of 1940. Investment companies that limit themselves to fewer than 100 investors or to only investors with a net worth of more than $3,000,000 and are exempt from SEC regulation. Such funds are called **hedge funds** and are discussed briefly below.

The investment goals of a publicly held investment company—the objective of its portfolio activities—are publicly stated. They may be to maximize long-term capital appreciation, to maximize current income, to invest in a diversified portfolio of public utility stocks, to invest in long-term investment grade bonds, or some combination of these goals. Investment companies generally do not seek controlling positions; most are diversified investors that limit their investments in portfolio companies to a small fraction (usually less than 5 percent) of the voting shares of each portfolio company.

Investment companies earn profits from two principal sources: trading profits from buying and selling portfolio securities and dividends or interest from investments. Investment companies that distribute substantially all of their earnings each year to shareholders are not themselves subject to tax. Rather, they are conduits whose income (e.g., capital gain, tax-exempt municipal bond interest) is passed through to the shareholders and retains its character in their hands. Thus, an investor who seeks only tax-exempt municipal bond income may invest in an investment company that invests only in such bonds, and the dividends that the shareholder receives are exempt from income tax to the extent they represent interest on tax-exempt municipal bonds. Management fees are subtracted from income prior to their distribution to shareholders and are not separately itemized in the distribution process.

An investment company itself has shareholders. It must hold shareholders' meetings, elect directors and officers, and so forth. Most investment companies contract with a brokerage firm or investment banker to obtain investment advice for a fee: The brokerage firm or investment banker may also handle share transfer and other related costs of the investment company operation. Of course, fees are also charged for these services.

Publicly held investment companies are broken down into two broad categories discussed in the following sections: closed-end companies and open-end companies. Open-end companies are called **mutual funds**.

## §16.4 Closed-End Investment Companies

**Closed-end companies** are the oldest type of investment companies. Their unique characteristic is that they have outstanding a fixed number of their own shares that are traded either on a securities exchange or over the counter. Closed-end funds lost their popularity as a result of the collapse of securities prices in the 1930s, but a number of new closed-end funds have been created since 1980. Many of these new closed-end funds concentrate in foreign securities of specific countries. Closed-end companies are also known as **publicly traded funds**, because their shares are listed on securities exchanges or traded in the over-the-counter (OTC) market like other securities.

An investor who decides to invest in a closed-end fund simply places an order with a broker to purchase the desired number of shares in the market in which the shares of the closed-end company are traded. A shareholder who decides to liquidate an interest in a closed-end company places an order to sell the shares in the appropriate market. In either event, investing in a closed-end fund or disposing of such an investment involves merely the payment of standard brokerage fees for executing the transactions. Table 16-2 taken from the *Wall Street Journal* shows prices for numerous closed-end funds.

The market price for shares issued by closed-end investment companies fluctuates according to market conditions, and may be either higher or lower than the net asset value of the shares. Shares of a closed-end fund are said to trade at a discount if the market price for its shares is less than the net asset value per share. Closed-end fund shares are said to trade at a premium if the market price of the fund shares is higher than the net asset value.

One attractive feature of closed-end funds is that they often trade at deep discounts from net asset value. If the discount narrows, an investor may have a substantial paper profit that is not based on a change in the net asset value of the fund shares. On the other hand, many closed-end companies trade at discounts over long periods, and a seemingly advantageous investment may turn out disadvantageous if the discount remains stable or increases.

Illustrative of the trading markets for closed-end funds are the tactics that professional traders typically follow. Basically, they play the discount, buying when the discounts widen and selling or short-selling when the discounts narrow or when prices creep up so that the shares are trading at a premium over net asset value. One experienced trader suggests the following trading strategy: One should buy when (1) the discount is 75 percent greater than the average discount over the previous six months and (2) the discount exceeds 3 percent for a balanced fund, 5 percent for a junk bond fund, and 10 percent for a country fund.

Experience demonstrates that it rarely pays to subscribe to a brand new issue of a closed-end fund offered at net asset value. After a period of price stabilization at or above the issue price while the issue is being marketed, the fund shares are permitted to seek their natural level in the market, which usually is significantly lower than net asset value. Investors that originally subscribed suffer the loss caused by the market's discounting of the shares. On the other hand, a number of new country-oriented or region-oriented closed-end funds have consistently traded at significant premiums over net asset value.

## §16.5 Open-End Investment Companies (Mutual Funds)

An **open-end investment company** is unlike a closed-end fund in two respects: First, an open-end company does not have a fixed number of shares outstanding. Rather, an open-end company stands ready at any time to issue new shares to persons desiring to invest in the fund. New shares are sold at **net asset value** (**NAV**), although in some cases a sales charge or **load** must also be paid at purchase. Second, an open-end company stands ready to redeem shares at net asset value at any time for investors who wish to liquidate their

## Table 16-2
## Mutual Fund Quotations

# CLOSED-END FUNDS

Closed-end funds sell a limited number of shares and invest the proceeds in securities. Unlike open-end funds, closed-ends generally do not buy their shares back from investors who wish to cash in their holdings. Instead, fund shares trade on a stock exchange.

### Friday, October 26, 2001

| STOCK (SYM) | EXCH | NAV | CLOSE | NET CHG | VOL 100s | PREM /DISC | DIV | 52 WK MKT RET |
|---|---|---|---|---|---|---|---|---|
| **General Equity Funds** | | | | | | | | |
| AdamsExp ADX | N | 17.25 | 15.35 | 0.10 | 583 | -11.0 | 1.85e | -32.8 |
| AllncAll AMO | N | 20.94 | 20.65 | 0.00 | 83 | -1.4 | 7.12e | -32.5 |
| Avalon Capital MIST | .0 | 15.70 | 15.00 | NA | NA | -4.5 | NA | 15.4 |
| BergstrmCap BEM | A | 162.67 | 152.50 | 1.00 | 3 | -6.3 | 11.25e | -31.2 |
| BlueChipVal BLU | N | 6.81 | 7.37 | 0.06 | 575 | 8.2 | .81e | 6.4 |
| BouldrTotR BTF | N | 17.16 | 15.95 | 0.02 | 27 | -7.1 | .20 | 47.1 |
| BrntlyCap BBDC | O | NA | 9.00 | 0.25 | 67 | NA | .62 | 16.1 |
| CntlSec CET | A | 27.68 | 24.40 | 0.00 | 87 | -11.8 | 4.20e | -17.9 |
| CmrstStratFd CRF | N | 9.51 | 7.85 | 0.00 | NA | -17.5 | .01 | -19.4 |
| CornstnStrat CLM | N | 8.82 | 7.36 | 0.04 | 52 | -16.6 | e | -30.7 |
| Engex EGX | A | 11.91 | 11.40 | 0.15 | 1 | -4.3 | | -58.9 |
| Equus II EQS | .N | 14.25 | 8.40 | 0.01 | 37 | -41.1 | .60e | -10.1 |
| GabelliTr GAB h | N | 8.46 | 10.21 | 0.13 | 1091 | 20.7 | 1.08a | 7.8 |
| GenAmInv GAM | N | 35.24 | 35.06 | 0.16 | 273 | -0.5 | 8.19e | 5.1 |
| LibtyASE ,USA | N | 10.29 | 11.25 | 0.11 | 1059 | 9.3 | 1.31e | -3.6 |
| LibtyASG ,ASG | N | 7.62 | 7.80 | 0.11 | 619 | 2.4 | 1.06e | -22.1 |
| MFS SpcVal MFV | N | 8.64 | 14.10 | -0.05 | 91 | 63.2 | 1.65a | 24.4 |
| MacrgFnshr MFUN c | O | 7.56 | 6.25 | 0.00 | NA | -17.3 | | -19.3 |
| NAIC Growth GRF c | C | 11.27 | 10.60 | NA | NA | -5.9 | NA | -0.4 |
| PrgrssvRgtFd PGF | N | 10.47 | 8.50 | 0.04 | 18 | -18.8 | e | -12.8 |
| RoyceFocus FUND | O | 6.59 | 5.62 | 0.13 | 262 | -14.7 | .34e | 8.3 |
| RycMcroCap OTCM | O | 11.14 | 9.40 | -0.10 | 209 | -15.6 | 1.72 | 10.2 |
| RoyceValTr RVT | N | 15.92 | 14.05 | -0.25 | 2205 | -11.7 | 1.57e | 14.7 |
| SalomonSBF SBF j | N | 13.45 | 12.32 | 0.02 | 1036 | -8.4 | 1.90e | -20.7 |
| SmallCapFd MGC | N | 11.29 | 10.21 | 0.04 | 20 | -9.6 | 2.05e | -10.1 |
| SourceCap SOR | N | 50.52 | 58.75 | 1.25 | 39 | 16.3 | 4.60a | 31.5 |
| TriContl TY | N | 22.16 | 19.55 | -0.04 | 663 | -11.8 | 3.13e | -10.6 |
| ZweigFd ZF | N | 7.59 | 8.06 | 0.01 | 933 | 6.2 | .72 | -12.4 |
| **Specialized Equity Funds** | | | | | | | | |
| ASA ASA c | N | 21.74 | 18.30 | 0.05 | 334 | -15.8 | .60 | 32.2 |
| GntlFdCan g CEF cl | A | 3.40 | 3.46 | -0.01 | 147 | 1.8 | .01g | 17.6 |
| CohnStrsAdvtg RLF | N | 12.95 | 14.85 | 0.90 | 521 | 14.7 | 1.26 | NS |
| CohenStrsTR RFI | N | 12.68 | 12.95 | -0.10 | 113 | 2.1 | .96a | 18.8 |
| Dundee Prec Mtls DPM.A cy | T | 13.23 | 9.05 | NA | .NA | -31.6 | NA | NA |
| FstFnlEd ,FF | N | 14.07 | 11.87 | 0.03 | 70 | -15.6 | .10 | 30.5 |
| GabelliMlti GGT | N | 9.37 | 8.27 | -0.08 | 115 | -11.7 | 1.56e | -21.6 |
| GabelliUt .GUT | N | 7.34 | 9.06 | 0.05 | 78 | 23.4 | .72 | 29.4 |
| H&Q Hlth HQH | N | 30.88 | 24.72 | 0.42 | 193 | -19.9 | 4.78e | -12.3 |
| H&Q LifeSci HQL | N | 26.08 | 20.80 | 0.40 | 429 | -20.2 | 3.93e | -13.9 |
| HnckJ BkOpp BTO | N | 10.00 | 7.98 | 0.05 | 899 | -20.2 | .77 | 16.4 |
| JohnHanckFnl JHFT | O | 17.19 | 13.85 | 0.00 | .35 | -19.4 | 2.64e | 22.3 |
| LCM Intnt FND | A | 2.92 | 2.53 | 0.07 | 11 | -13.4 | .26e | -61.0 |
| meVC DrprFshr MVC | N | 15.42 | 9.27 | 0.09 | 523 | -39.9 | .34 | -16.6 |
| Munder @Vantage | z | 6.83 | NA | NA | NA | NA | NA | NA |
| PeteRes PEO | N | 26.79 | 24.64 | 0.04 | 141 | -8.0 | 1.74e | -5.4 |
| Seligman New Tech | z | 11.24 | NA | NA | NA | NA | NA | NA |
| Seligman New Tech II | z | 9.42 | NA | NA | NA | NA | NA | NA |
| Tuttis TUX | A | 11.42 | 11.85 | -0.01 | 5 | 3.8 | 1.30e | 19.8 |

| STOCK (SYM) | EXCH | NAV | CLOSE | NET CHG | VOL 100s | PREM /DISC | DIV | 52 WK MKT RET |
|---|---|---|---|---|---|---|---|---|
| Italy Fd ITA | N | 7.90 | 6.77 | 0.04 | 36 | -14.3 | 7.67e | -25.3 |
| JapanEquity JEQ c | N | 5.82 | 5.22 | 0.03 | 89 | -10.3 | j | -25.4 |
| JapanOTC JOF | N | 6.88 | 5.96 | 0.06 | 336 | -13.4 | .82e | -13.0 |
| JF China JFC | N | 7.55 | 6.08 | 0.08 | 18 | -20.5 | | -17.1 |
| JF India JFI c | N | 8.19 | 6.48 | 0.10 | 88 | -20.9 | 1.47 | -17.5 |
| KoreaEqty KEF | N | 3.25 | 2.65 | 0.04 | 238 | -18.5 | | -1.4 |
| KoreaFd KF | N | 12.63 | 10.10 | -0.01 | 2326 | -20.0 | .19e | 6.6 |
| KoreanInvFd KIF | N | 6.22 | 6.01 | 0.01 | 9 | -3.4 | | 26.5 |
| LatAmEq LAQ | N | 13.50 | 10.89 | -0.01 | 18 | -19.3 | .17e | -10.9 |
| LatAmDiscv LDF | N | 10.37 | 8.32 | 0.02 | 80 | -19.8 | .04e | -15.3 |
| MalaysaFd MF | N | 4.46 | 3.45 | 0.00 | 521 | -22.6 | | -17.6 |
| MexEqIncoFd MXE c | N | 8.40 | 7.71 | 0.00 | NA | -8.2 | .62 | -11.9 |
| MexicoFd MXF | N | 19.36 | 16.84 | 0.14 | 537 | -13.0 | .18e | 9.3 |
| MS AfrInv AFF | N | 8.78 | 7.10 | 0.00 | 61 | -19.1 | .33e | -3.5 |
| MS Asia APF | N | 8.70 | 6.77 | 0.02 | 580 | -22.2 | .19e | -25.3 |
| MS EmMktFd MSF | N | 9.04 | 7.08 | 0.11 | 115 | -21.7 | 2.31 | -23.2 |
| MS India IIF | N | 9.86 | 7.68 | -0.02 | 75 | -22.1 | 2.47e | -4.3 |
| MS EstEur MNE | N | 15.30 | 12.24 | 0.32 | 170 | -20.0 | j | -10.9 |
| NewGrmnyFd GF | N | 7.50 | 5.90 | 0.08 | 268 | -21.3 | .08 | -41.2 |
| ROC TwnFd ROC | N | 4.16 | 3.55 | 0.05 | 604 | -14.7 | .37e | -34.0 |
| ScddrNwAsia SAF | N | 9.37 | 7.49 | 0.01 | 27 | -20.1 | 2.02e | -21.2 |
| SingaporeFd SGF c | N | 5.91 | 4.65 | 0.01 | 67 | -21.3 | j | -27.1 |
| SoAfricaFd SOA | N | 11.31 | 8.68 | 0.03 | 142 | -23.3 | .30 | -16.2 |
| SpainFd SNF | N | 7.85 | 8.81 | 0.11 | 61 | 12.2 | 1.13e | -7.3 |
| SwissHelvFd SWZ | N | 12.84 | 10.49 | 0.02 | 169 | -18.3 | 1.49e | -16.7 |
| TaiwanFd g TWN | N | NA | 9.25 | 0.30 | 392 | NA | | -27.4 |
| TemplChinaFd TCH cl | N | 9.26 | 7.65 | -0.05 | 48 | -17.4 | .18e | 12.0 |
| TempltnDrgn TDF | N | 8.46 | 6.95 | 0.10 | 302 | -17.8 | 1.03e | 3.2 |
| TemplMktFd EMF a | N | 7.96 | 7.10 | 0.10 | 731 | -10.8 | .10e | -1.8 |
| TempltnEmrg TEA cl | N | 10.60 | 8.65 | 0.03 | 50 | -18.4 | .59e | 2.3 |
| TempltnRus TRF cl | N | 14.13 | 14.00 | 1.00 | 407 | -0.9 | e | 5.1 |
| TempltnViet TVF | N | 7.55 | 6.03 | 0.02 | 18 | -20.1 | j | 2.5 |
| Thai Capital TF c | N | 1.59 | NA | NA | NA | NA | NA | NA |
| ThaiFd TTF | N | 3.02 | 2.70 | -0.07 | 49 | -10.6 | .02e | -19.5 |
| Third Canadian THD cy | T | 17.36 | 13.60 | NA | NA | -21.7 | NA | -0.0 |
| TurkishFd TKF | N | 4.18 | 4.58 | -0.10 | 104 | 9.6 | 3.23e | -47.9 |
| United Corps Ltd UNC cy | T | 60.18 | 36.60 | NA | NA | -39.2 | NA | 21.8 |
| ZSevenFd ZSEV | O | 4.23 | 4.25 | -0.05 | 3 | 0.5 | .26e | -46.4 |

| STOCK (SYM) | EXCH | NAV | CLOSE | NET CHG | VOL 100s | PREM /DISC | DIV | 12 MO YIELD |
|---|---|---|---|---|---|---|---|---|
| **U.S. Govt. Bond Funds** | | | | | | | | |
| ACM IncFd ACG | N | 8.55 | 8.67 | 0.08 | 2132 | 1.4 | .84 | 9.3 |
| ACM OppFd AOF | N | 8.15 | 9.05 | 0.00 | 17 | 11.0 | .72a | 8.2 |
| EIS Fund EIS c | N | 18.53 | 16.70 | 0.00 | 8 | -9.9 | 1.05e | 6.1 |
| MFS GvMkTr MGF | N | 7.38 | 6.68 | 0.00 | 515 | -9.5 | .40 | 6.7 |
| MSDW Gvtln GVT | N | 9.80 | 9.80 | 0.01 | 500 | -6.1 | .54 | 6.0 |
| ScudderGvt KGT | N | 7.53 | 7.14 | -0.05 | 308 | -5.2 | .48 | 7.0 |
| **U.S. Mortgage Bond Funds** | | | | | | | | |
| AmIncmFd MRF c | N | 9.13 | 8.65 | -0.07 | 23 | -5.3 | .66 | 7.3 |
| AmSelPort SLA c | N | 13.41 | 13.30 | -0.04 | 157 | -0.8 | 1.20 | 8.1 |
| AmStrat ASP c | N | 12.70 | 12.59 | 0.09 | 145 | -0.9 | 1.14 | 8.1 |
| AmStratll BSP c | N | 13.20 | 12.58 | 0.05 | 480 | -4.7 | 1.14 | 8.5 |
| AmStratIII CSP c | N | 12.53 | 12.10 | 0.00 | 440 | -3.4 | 1.05 | 8.6 |
| BlkrkAdv BAT c | N | 11.77 | 11.17 | 0.06 | 251 | -5.1 | .60 | 5.5 |
| BlkRkBrd BCT c | A | 15.92 | 14.30 | 0.00 | 17 | -10.2 | .75 | 6.0 |
| BlkrkIncTr BKT c | N | 8.05 | 7.21 | 0.03 | 2105 | -10.4 | .56 | 8.1 |
| BlkrkInv BQT c | N | 9.66 | 9.32 | 0.05 | 584 | -3.5 | .40 | 4.9 |
| BlkrkStrTrm BGT c | N | 9.85 | 9.74 | -0.01 | 236 | -1.1 | .38 | 4.7 |
| Hyperion02 HTB c | N | 9.82 | 9.58 | 0.01 | 140 | -2.4 | .01 | 1.6 |
| Hyperion05 HTO c | N | 10.01 | 9.74 | 0.05 | 193 | -2.7 | .55 | 5.0 |
| HyperionFd HTR c | N | 9.24 | 8.45 | 0.02 | 1379 | -8.5 | .87 | 10.3 |
| NationsGov03 NGI | N | 10.33 | 10.00 | -0.01 | 135 | -3.2 | .44 | 4.5 |
| NationsGov04 NGF | N | 10.45 | 10.06 | 0.00 | 682 | -3.7 | .47 | 4.6 |
| PIMCO Comrcl PCM c | N | 13.62 | 14.27 | 0.27 | 122 | 4.8 | 1.13a | 9.3 |
| TCW/DW 02 TRM | N | 10.79 | 10.55 | 0.00 | 203 | -2.2 | .48 | 4.5 |
| TCW/DW 03 TMT | N | 11.11 | 10.62 | 0.06 | 912 | -4.4 | .56a | 5.4 |
| 2002Target TTR c | N | 14.67 | 14.56 | 0.06 | 77 | -0.7 | .66a | 4.7 |

# EXPLANATORY NOTES

a-The NAV and market price are ex dividend. b-The NAV is fully diluted. c-NAV is as of Thursday's close. d-NAV is as of Wednesday's close. e-NAV assumes rights offering is fully subscribed. f-Rights offering in process. g-Rights offering announced. h-Lipper data has been adjusted for rights offering. j-Rights offering has expired, but Lipper data not yet adjusted. l-NAV as of previous day. o-Tender offer in process. v-NAV is converted at the commercial Rand rate. w-Convertible Note-NAV (not market) conversion value. y-NAV and market price are in Canadian dollars. All other footnotes refer to unusual circumstances; explanations for those that appear can be found at the bottom of this list. NA signifies that the information is not available or not applicable. NS signifies fund not in existence of entire period. Source: Lipper

## Table 16-2 (*cont.*)

| STOCK (SYM) | EXCH | NAV | CLOSE | NET CHG | VOL 100s | PREM /DISC | DIV | 12 MO YIELD |
|---|---|---|---|---|---|---|---|---|
| ♠ProspctSt PHY | N | 3.12 | 4.28 | 0.00 | 615 | 37.2 | .90 | 20.1 |
| PutnmMgdYld PTM | N | 8.61 | 9.19 | 0.14 | 115 | 6.7 | 1.07 | 12.6 |
| SalomonHIF HIF | N | 9.27 | 10.24 | 0.14 | 52 | 10.5 | 1.20 | 13.3 |
| SalomonHIF II HIX | N | 10.04 | 10.76 | − 0.04 | 632 | 7.2 | 1.38 | 14.2 |
| ♠ScudderHigh KHI | N | 5.47 | 6.98 | 0.03 | 156 | 27.6 | .81 | 12.4 |
| SrHighInc ARK | N | 5.51 | 5.37 | − 0.02 | 463 | − 2.5 | .75e | 14.2 |
| ♠VnKmHiInc VIT | N | NA | NA | 0.00 | 309 | NA | .56 | 12.3 |
| ♠VnKmTrII VLT | N | 4.74 | 5.68 | 0.13 | 98 | 19.8 | .74 | 12.4 |
| ZenixFd ZIF | N | 2.98 | 3.66 | − 0.03 | 219 | 22.8 | .56 | 16.7 |
| **Other Domestic Taxable Bond Funds** | | | | | | | | |
| ACM MgdDlr ADF | N | 6.54 | 7.73 | − 0.01 | 377 | 18.2 | 1.02 | 13.3 |
| ACM MgdInco AMF | N | 4.60 | 4.66 | 0.00 | 487 | 1.3 | .51 | 12.4 |
| AllmrST ALM | N | 10.89 | 10.33 | .10 | 152 | − 5.2 | .73m | 7.6 |
| Bexil BXL | A | 11.93 | 10.60 | 0.00 | NA | − 11.1 | .96 | 9.6 |
| ProspectSt CNN cl | N | 6.72 | 6.72 | − 0.02 | 31 | 0.0 | .72m | 12.1 |
| ♠ColonIntmk CMK | N | 8.85 | 8.14 | − 0.06 | 63 | − 8.0 | .79 | 10.5 |
| ♠CrSuisInco CIK | N | 4.82 | 5.36 | 0.03 | 880 | 11.2 | .72a | 13.5 |
| DufPhipsBnd DUC | N | 13.60 | 13.35 | − 0.01 | 203 | − 1.8 | 1.02 | 7.8 |
| FrnkInMulti FMI | N | NA | NA | 0.00 | 121 | NA | .67a | 8.6 |
| ♠HnckJ IncSec JHS | N | 16.39 | 14.90 | − 0.06 | 127 | − 9.1 | 1.04f | 7.1 |
| ♠HnckJ Invst JHI | N | 21.41 | 19.50 | 0.01 | 46 | − 8.9 | 1.36f | 7.2 |
| ♠LncInNtlInco LND c | N | 13.23 | 12.35 | 0.34 | 175 | − 6.7 | 1.00e | 7.3 |
| MassMuInv MCI | | NA | 25.00 | 0.00 | 55 | NA | 1.88a | 12.0 |
| MassMuPrt MPV | | NA | 9.95 | 0.00 | 142 | NA | .96a | 15.1 |
| MFS Charter MCR | N | 9.17 | 8.32 | 0.07 | 1080 | − 9.3 | .60m | 8.5 |
| MFS Intermd MIN | N | 7.47 | 6.83 | − 0.02 | 972 | − 8.6 | .44m | 7.0 |
| MFS MultInco MMT | N | 6.52 | 6.05 | 0.01 | 862 | − 7.2 | .47m | 9.1 |
| NationsBal NBM | N | 10.35 | 9.70 | − 0.14 | 214 | − 6.3 | .44 | 4.5 |
| OppenMulti OMS | N | 8.31 | 8.07 | 0.01 | 278 | − 2.9 | .75m | 16.3 |
| PutnmMstInco PMT | N | 6.78 | 6.50 | − 0.10 | 569 | − 4.1 | .58 | 9.7 |
| PutnmMstIntrm PIM | N | 6.58 | 6.18 | − 0.05 | 1013 | − 6.1 | .54 | 9.98 |
| PutnmPrem PPT | N | 6.53 | 6.13 | 0.02 | 859 | − 6.1 | .54 | 10.0 |
| RCM Stratg RCS | N | 11.40 | 11.10 | 0.01 | 563 | − 2.6 | .89a | 9.4 |
| ♠ScudderMulti KMM | N | 7.85 | 8.07 | 0.04 | 240 | 2.8 | .93a | 13.2 |
| ♠ScudderStratIn KST | N | 11.53 | 11.80 | − 0.20 | 112 | 2.3 | 1.20 | 13.5 |
| USLIFE Fd UIF | N | 8.56 | 8.08 | 0.08 | 61 | − 5.6 | .68 | 8.8 |
| ♠VnKmIncTr VIN | N | 6.60 | 6.76 | 0.02 | 96 | 2.4 | .55 | 8.6 |
| ♠ZweigTotFd ZTR | N | 6.67 | 7.28 | 0.03 | 1103 | 9.1 | .65m | 10.4 |
| **World Income Funds** | | | | | | | | |
| Abrdn AP IncFd FAX | A | 4.67 | 4.10 | − 0.01 | 5609 | − 12.2 | .54 | 13.6 |
| AbrdnCmwlthFd FCO a | N | 9.87 | 9.05 | 0.03 | 672 | − 8.3 | .84 | 9.3 |
| AllncWrld AWG | N | 9.76 | 10.52 | − 0.19 | 148 | 7.8 | 1.32 | 12.9 |
| AllncWrld II AWF | N | 9.65 | 9.98 | 0.03 | 1685 | 3.4 | 1.38 | 12.0 |
| BlkrkNoAm BNA c | N | 11.38 | 10.39 | 0.09 | 216 | − 8.7 | .75 | 7.5 |
| ♠Drsdnr RCM DSF | N | 6.87 | 6.66 | − 0.02 | 364 | − 3.1 | .72 | 10.7 |
| EmergMktFlt EFL | N | NA | 11.70 | − 0.20 | 20 | NA | 1.47 | 13.7 |
| EmergMkt II EDF | N | 10.48 | 11.77 | 0.02 | 238 | 12.3 | 1.65 | 14.2 |
| EmergMktInco EMD | N | 12.07 | 12.75 | 0.15 | 39 | 5.6 | 1.65 | 13.5 |
| GlblHiInco GHI a | N | 14.31 | 13.11 | − 0.09 | 445 | − 8.4 | 1.61e | 12.1 |
| ♠GlblIncoFd GIF | A | 5.65 | 5.30 | 0.00 | 7 | − 6.2 | .57 | 10.9 |
| GlblIncFd GDF | N | 9.97 | 11.78 | 0.18 | 199 | 18.2 | 1.42 | 12.7 |
| MS EmMktDebtFd MSD | N | 8.04 | 7.28 | − 0.01 | 184 | − 9.5 | .84 | 15.2 |
| MS GlblOpp MGB | N | 7.13 | 7.16 | 0.11 | 142 | 0.4 | 1.13e | 15.5 |
| SalomonWld SBG | N | 9.68 | 9.99 | 0.04 | 354 | 3.2 | .88a | 10.0 |
| SlmnWldInco SBW | N | 12.34 | 13.36 | 0.05 | 101 | 8.3 | 1.42a | 13.9 |
| ScddrGlblFd LBF | N | 5.77 | 5.25 | − 0.05 | 141 | − 9.0 | .70 | 11.9 |
| StrtGlblInc SGL a | N | 12.06 | 11.45 | 0.06 | 269 | − 5.1 | 1.21e | 10.9 |
| TemplIncoFd TEI | N | 11.04 | 10.68 | 0.07 | 436 | − 3.3 | 1.24a | 12.7 |
| TemplGlbGvt TGG | N | 6.44 | 6.19 | 0.02 | 254 | − 3.9 | .48 | 8.2 |
| TemplGlob GIM | N | 6.94 | 6.60 | 0.01 | 1617 | − 4.9 | .54 | 8.2 |
| **National Muni Bond Funds** | | | | | | | | |
| ACM MuniSec AMU | N | 12.08 | 12.88 | − 0.08 | 47 | 6.6 | .87 | 6.9 |
| AmMuniInco XAA c | N | 14.95 | 13.84 | 0.08 | 41 | − 7.4 | .84f | 5.8 |
| AmMunTrmTr2 BXT c | N | 10.73 | 10.70 | 0.00 | NA | − 0.3 | .62 | 6.9 |
| AmMunTrmTr3 CXT c | N | 11.24 | 11.05 | − 0.05 | 39 | − 1.7 | .57a | 5.4 |
| ApexMunFd APX | N | 9.40 | 9.13 | 0.08 | 199 | − 2.9 | .60e | 6.6 |
| BlkrkMuni08 BRM | N | 17.17 | 15.73 | − 0.04 | 272 | − 8.4 | .80 | 5.0 |
| BlkrkMuni BMT | N | 11.15 | 10.60 | 0.04 | 115 | − 4.9 | .58 | 5.5 |

| STOCK (SYM) | EXCH | NAV | CLOSE | NET CHG | VOL 100s | PREM /DISC | DIV | 12 MO YIELD |
|---|---|---|---|---|---|---|---|---|
| PutnmMunOpp PMO | N | 13.35 | 13.47 | 0.01 | 474 | 0.9 | .91a | 6.7 |
| PutnmTxF PMH | N | 13.77 | 13.26 | 0.01 | 26 | − 3.7 | .86 | 6.6 |
| ♠ScudderMuni KTF | N | 12.09 | 11.62 | − 0.01 | 433 | − 3.9 | .72 | 6.3 |
| ♠ScudderStrat KSM | N | 12.01 | 11.88 | 0.03 | 141 | − 1.1 | .75a | 6.3 |
| ♠SeligQual SQF | N | 14.31 | 12.60 | − 0.01 | 4 | − 11.9 | .67 | 5.7 |
| ♠SeligSel SEL | N | 11.92 | 10.53 | − 0.02 | 23 | − 11.7 | .61 | 5.9 |
| ♠VnKmAdvII VKI | A | 14.65 | 12.93 | 0.01 | 103 | − 11.7 | .79 | 5.7 |
| VnKmAdvtg VKA | N | 16.67 | 14.35 | − 0.02 | 101 | − 13.9 | .83 | 5.5 |
| ♠VnKmInv VIG | N | 9.95 | 8.65 | − 0.01 | 10 | − 13.1 | .49 | 5.8 |
| ♠VnKmMun VMT | N | 10.01 | 8.80 | 0.02 | 634 | − 12.1 | .53 | 5.9 |
| ♠VnKmOpII VOT | N | 14.80 | 13.18 | − 0.15 | 197 | − 10.9 | .81 | 5.8 |
| ♠VnKmOpp VMO | N | 17.45 | 15.70 | − 0.01 | 203 | − 10.0 | .97 | 5.7 |
| ♠VnKmMunTr VKQ | N | 15.95 | 13.64 | − 0.09 | 340 | − 14.5 | .82 | 6.0 |
| ♠VnKmSelect VKL | A | 13.74 | 12.37 | − 0.03 | 18 | − 10.0 | .76 | 6.0 |
| ♠VnKmMuniTr VKS | N | 14.66 | 13.23 | − 0.03 | 168 | − 9.8 | .82 | 5.4 |
| ♠VnKmInsMun VIM | N | 16.88 | 15.05 | − 0.05 | 134 | − 10.8 | .86 | 5.7 |
| ♠VnKmInvGrd VGM | N | 17.37 | 14.91 | 0.02 | 211 | − 14.2 | .88 | 5.9 |
| ♠VnKmValMuni VKV | N | 15.55 | 13.80 | 0.01 | 215 | − 11.3 | .83 | 5.7 |
| **Single State Muni Bond** | | | | | | | | |
| BlkrkCA2008 BFC | N | 17.20 | 15.50 | − 0.03 | 1130 | − 9.9 | .77 | 4.8 |
| BlkRkCA RAA | A | 15.28 | 15.55 | 0.00 | 2 | 1.8 | .79 | 5.0 |
| BlackRock CA Mun BFZ | A | 14.38 | 14.75 | NA | NA | 2.6 | NA | NA |
| BlkrkFla2008 BRF | N | 16.28 | 15.18 | 0.01 | 27 | − 6.8 | .75 | 4.9 |
| BlkRkFL RFA | A | 15.44 | 14.25 | 0.00 | NA | − 7.7 | .80 | 5.5 |
| BlackRock FL Mun BBF | N | 14.11 | 14.75 | NA | NA | 4.5 | NA | NA |
| BlkRkNJ RNJ | A | 14.80 | 13.88 | 0.00 | NA | − 6.2 | .73 | 5.4 |
| BlackRock NJ Mun BNJ | N | 14.10 | 14.87 | NA | NA | 5.5 | NA | NA |
| BlkrkNY2008 BLN | N | 16.64 | 15.59 | 0.01 | 1 | − 6.3 | .75 | 4.8 |
| BlkRkNY RNY | A | 15.24 | 14.27 | 0.12 | 23 | − 6.4 | .82 | 5.9 |
| BlackRock NY Mun BNY | N | 13.91 | 14.40 | NA | NA | 3.5 | NA | NA |
| BlkRkPA BPS | A | 15.22 | 14.08 | − 0.11 | 41 | − 7.5 | .82 | 5.7 |
| ♠ColCAInsMun CCA | A | 15.99 | 16.51 | 0.13 | 72 | 3.3 | 1.04f | 5.4 |
| ♠ColNYInsMun CNM | A | 15.77 | 14.35 | 0.00 | NA | − 9.0 | .82 | 6.0 |
| DreyfCAMun DCM | A | 9.14 | 8.52 | 0.10 | 20 | − 6.8 | .46 | 5.6 |
| DreyfNYMun DNM | A | 9.38 | 8.74 | 0.14 | 66 | − 6.8 | .48a | 5.6 |
| EtnVncCA MIT CEV | A | 14.67 | 14.00 | − 0.10 | 173 | − 4.6 | .84f | 5.0 |
| EtnVncFL MIT FEV | A | 14.53 | 12.67 | − 0.06 | 30 | − 12.8 | .81f | 5.2 |
| EtnVncMA MIT MMV | A | 14.27 | 13.90 | 0.00 | 2 | − 2.6 | .83f | 5.1 |
| EtnVncMI MIT EMI | A | 14.65 | 13.15 | 0.06 | 56 | − 10.2 | .78f | 5.1 |
| EtnVncNJ MIT EVJ | A | 14.05 | 13.29 | − 0.01 | 66 | − 5.4 | .83f | 5.2 |
| EtnVncNY MIT EVY | A | 14.40 | 14.04 | 0.01 | 35 | − 2.5 | .84f | 5.2 |
| EtnVncOH MIT EVO | A | 14.21 | 13.83 | − 0.03 | 8 | − 2.7 | .79f | 5.2 |
| EtnVncPA MIT EVP | A | 14.32 | 12.84 | 0.00 | NA | − 10.3 | .72 | 5.5 |
| ♠GrnwchCA GCM | A | 14.32 | 14.00 | 0.02 | 2 | − 2.2 | .62 | 4.3 |
| MA HlthEdu MHE | A | 13.55 | 13.87 | 0.00 | 2 | 2.4 | .80 | 5.5 |
| MN MuniInco MXA c | A | 14.88 | 14.46 | 0.11 | 15 | − 2.8 | .85f | 5.2 |
| MN MuniTrml MNB c | A | 10.71 | 10.48 | 0.00 | NA | − 2.1 | .59 | 5.6 |
| MN MuniTrm MNA c | N | 10.44 | 10.45 | 0.02 | 75 | 0.1 | .61a | 5.6 |
| MSDW CaIns IIC | N | 15.04 | 14.25 | 0.03 | 108 | − 5.3 | .78 | 5.3 |
| MSDW CaQty IQC | N | 14.82 | 13.25 | − 0.10 | 38 | − 10.6 | .69 | 5.2 |
| MSDW InsCa ICS | N | 15.97 | 15.11 | − 0.01 | 6 | − 5.4 | .75 | 5.1 |
| MSDW NY Qty IQN | N | 14.78 | 13.18 | 0.09 | 51 | − 10.8 | .69 | 5.4 |
| MuniHldgCA MUC | N | 15.17 | 14.37 | − 0.07 | 539 | − 5.3 | .82e | 5.7 |
| MuniHldgFL MFL | N | 15.14 | 14.12 | − 0.01 | 351 | − 6.7 | .81e | 5.7 |
| MnHdgs MI Ins II MDH | N | 17.06 | 15.97 | NA | NA | − 6.4 | NA | 5.7 |
| MuniHldgNJ MUJ | N | 14.72 | 13.22 | − 0.03 | 288 | − 10.2 | .75e | 5.5 |
| MuniHldgNYIns MHN | N | 15.44 | 14.10 | 0.09 | 723 | − 8.7 | .79e | 5.7 |
| MuniyldAZ II MZA | A | 14.13 | 13.06 | − 0.17 | 49 | − 7.6 | .68 | 5.7 |
| MuniyldCAFd MYC | N | 15.18 | 15.00 | 0.00 | 302 | − 1.2 | .96f | 5.6 |
| MuniyldCA MIC | N | 14.86 | 14.23 | 0.08 | 183 | − 4.2 | .76e | 5.4 |
| MuniyldCA II MCA | N | 15.38 | 14.30 | 0.07 | 67 | − 7.0 | .81a | 5.7 |
| MuniyldFL Fd MYF | N | 14.70 | 13.97 | 0.01 | 92 | − 5.0 | .79e | 5.8 |
| MuniyldFL Ins MFT | N | 14.84 | 14.15 | 0.05 | 63 | − 4.6 | .90f | 5.6 |
| MuniyldMI Fd MYM | N | 14.86 | 13.80 | − 0.07 | 3 | − 7.1 | .79e | 5.9 |
| MuniyldMI ins MIY | N | 15.71 | 14.16 | − 0.04 | 151 | − 9.9 | .81e | 5.8 |
| MuniyldNJ Fd MYJ | N | 14.99 | 14.43 | − 0.12 | 178 | − 3.7 | .96f | 5.8 |
| MuniyldNJ Ins MJI | N | 15.12 | 14.82 | 0.05 | 35 | − 2.0 | .94f | 5.4 |
| MuniyldNYIns MYN | N | 14.91 | 13.94 | 0.02 | 309 | − 6.5 | .83f | 5.6 |
| MuniyldPAIns MPA | N | 15.07 | 15.00 | 0.04 | 198 | − 0.5 | .83e | 5.7 |

positions, although some funds charge an exit fee, the amount of which may depend on how long the fund shares have been held. Such companies are open-ended because they have no fixed number of shares although some funds do close themselves to further purchases by new investors when they become un-wieldly to manage or when the managers perceive a lack of investment oppor-tunities to which new cash may be devoted. Open-end funds are called **mutual funds**.

Open-end funds are not publicly traded on exchanges. Rather, a person who wishes to invest in a mutual fund deals directly with the fund itself and receives newly issued shares. When a person decides to liquidate an interest in such a fund, the investor again contacts the mutual fund and arranges to have the shares redeemed. Mutual funds are sold directly by the fund or through brokers who receive part of the sales load if one is charged.

The obvious advantage of an open-end fund is that because the fund itself agrees to redeem shares at net asset value, there can be no discount. When closed-end funds trade at significant discounts, enterprising speculators have sometimes purchased large amounts of the shares on the open market and then successfully forced the closed-end fund to amend its articles of incorporation to become an "open-end" fund (thereby automatically eliminating the discount from net asset value).

Table 16-3 is an excerpt from the *Wall Street Journal* showing quotations for many mutual funds. In this table, "NAV" stands for net asset value per share; because there is no market trading in open-end fund shares, there are no share price quotations as is the case with closed-end funds. The heading "Inv Obj" refers to the investment objectives of the fund; a key to investment objective abbreviations appears in Table 16-4. The next five columns show percent returns for the indicated periods including both increases in NAV and distributions (which may be the form of dividends or capital gains realized by the fund). In each case, these figures assume reinvestment of any distributions. The letters appearing adjacent to the return figures are in essence grades com-paring the performance of the fund over the indicated period with other funds of the same objective. An A indicates a fund in the top one-fifth, while an E indicates a fund in the bottom one-fifth. The column headed "Max Init Chrg" shows the sales load for the fund, as explained below. The column headed "Exp Ratio" (expense ratio) shows the percentage of the fund value that is paid for management fees and promotional expenses on an annual basis. This number includes only asset-based charges; it does not include direct expenses such as brokerage commissions. Some mutual fund charts also show a **turn-over ratio** for the portfolio, that is, the number of times per year that the en-tire portfolio is bought or sold. This number is quite useful to investors in determining how actively the fund is managed and to what extent the man-agers attempt to pick stocks or follow a buy and hold strategy.

Until relatively recently, the fees that mutual funds charged were strictly regulated by the SEC. There were two types of funds: **load funds** and **no-load funds**. A **load** is an additional charge imposed when one invests in the fund. It is sometimes called a **front-end load**, because it is usually imposed on the purchase of the mutual fund shares. Historically, the load was about 8 percent above the net asset value for small investments, and decreased gradually for larger investments. Load funds can be easily identified from Table 16-3 as the ones showing a number other than zero for maximum initial charge. Load funds are heavily advertised and recommended by brokers who receive a commission from the load. For example, the AAL Mutual A funds in Table 16-3 are all load funds. An investment in one of these funds would need to increase in value by at least 4 percent plus annual expenses shown in the last column before an investor could break even.

No-load funds are funds that offer to sell shares at net asset value. They are sold without extensive advertising and usually without the intervention of a broker, so that the investor has to locate the desired investment and contact the manager of the no-load fund directly. Many investment advisers recommend that investors invest in no-load funds suitable for their investment needs in order to avoid paying the sales load. However, the actual investment performance of the two types of funds does not unambiguously indicate that this strategy leads to a higher net return.

The SEC has relaxed the rules relating to sales charges, and many mutual funds have switched to more complex pricing structures. Many funds have reduced their front-end loads but have imposed a **back-end redemption charge** or **exit fee** on redemptions occurring within a specified period after the investment is made. In addition, SEC Rule 12b-1 allows mutual funds to deduct certain marketing and distribution costs directly from assets; in effect this imposes the costs of distribution (**12b-1 fees**) on existing fund holders rather than on new investors. Funds adopting this practice in Table 16-3 are marked with a "p." With a variety of costs being imposed, some in a hidden manner without complete disclosure, the comparison of costs between alternative mutual fund investments is treacherous, and the formerly sharp line between load and no-load funds has become blurred to some extent.

Table 16-3 shows that mutual fund managers create "families" of mutual funds, each with their own investment objective. The goal is to provide a fund that meets the investment objectives of numerous diverse groups of investors with different short-term and long-term goals. Most fund families permit free transfer of investments from one fund in the family to another fund in the same family without service charge. In this way, the manager hopes to retain control over investment funds even when the goal of the investor changes because of changes in individual circumstances.

Most mutual funds are actively managed. That means the fund manager shifts investments aggressively in order to maximize the return to investors. The usual yardstick for performance is whether the fund exceeds the market performance of one of the broad market averages, usually the Standard & Poor's 500 stock index. The efficient capital market hypothesis suggests that fund managers cannot hope to beat the market averages consistently, and in fact most mutual funds have not been able to consistently exceed these market averages. One study in the late 1970s showed, for example, that 90 percent of the managed funds fared worse than the Standard & Poor's 500 index over a 10-year period.

Table 16-3

# MONTHLY MUTUAL FUND REVIEW

| NAVS | FUND | INV | TOTAL RETURN & RANK †ANNUALIZED | | | | | MAX INIT | EXP |
|---|---|---|---|---|---|---|---|---|---|
| 10/31 | NAME | OBJ | OCT | 1 YR | 3 YR† | 5 YR† | 10 YR† | CHRG | RATIO |
| | **AAL Mutual A** | | | | | | | | |
| 4.79 | AggGrth p | LG | +0.4 | −47.8 E | NS .. | NS .. | NS .. | 4.00 | NA |
| 11.55 | Balance p | BL | +2.4 | −6.4 B | +4.6 B | NS .. | NS .. | 4.00 | 1.09 |
| 10.24 | Bond p | IB | +1.7 | +14.7 B | +6.3 D | +7.0 C | +6.6 E | 4.00 | 0.81 |
| 29.20 | CGrowth p | LC | +2.9 | −21.9 B | +3.0 A | +11.9 A | +12.2 B | 4.00 | 0.91 |
| 12.33 | EqInc p | EI | +1.6 | −12.5 D | +1.8 C | +7.2 D | NS .. | 4.00 | 0.92 |
| 6.28 | HiYBdA | HC | +3.0 | −0.5 B | −1.6 D | NS .. | NS .. | 4.00 | 1.00 |
| 8.16 | Intl p | IL | +2.4 | −32.5 D | −4.4 D | −1.7 E | NS .. | 4.00 | 1.36 |
| 7.20 | LgColdxll p | SP | +1.7 | −26.2 E | NS .. | NS .. | NS .. | 4.00 | NA |
| 11.58 | MidCap p | MC | +3.9 | −23.2 D | +8.2 D | +6.5 D | NS .. | 4.00 | 1.14 |
| 9.03 | MidCpldx t | MC | +4.2 | −13.6 B | NS .. | NS .. | NS .. | 4.00 | NA |
| 11.43 | MuniBd | GM | +1.3 | +11.4 A | +4.7 B | +6.2 A | +6.7 B | 4.00 | 0.73 |
| 12.71 | SmCap p | SC | +7.6 | −5.4 C | +13.4 B | +8.9 C | NS .. | 4.00 | 1.53 |
| 9.15 | SmCpldx p | SC | +5.1 | −8.6 D | NS .. | NS .. | NS .. | 4.00 | NA |
| 9.47 | SmCapVal p | SV | +6.0 | NS .. | NS .. | NS .. | NS .. | 4.00 | NA |
| 3.47 | TechStk p | TK | +15.7 | −61.0 C | NS .. | NS .. | NS .. | 4.00 | NA |
| | **AAL Mutual B** | | | | | | | | |
| 4.72 | Aggress t | LG | +0.4 | −48.4 E | NS .. | NS .. | NS .. | 0.00 | NA |
| 11.49 | Balance t | BL | +2.2 | −7.3 B | +3.6 B | NS .. | NS .. | 0.00 | 2.03 |
| 28.16 | CGrowth p | LC | +2.8 | −22.7 B | +1.9 B | NS .. | NS .. | 0.00 | 1.88 |
| 12.31 | EqInc p | EI | +1.5 | −13.4 D | +0.7 D | NS .. | NS .. | 0.00 | 1.99 |
| 6.28 | HiYBdB p | HC | +2.9 | −1.3 B | −2.3 D | NS .. | NS .. | 0.00 | 1.73 |
| 7.99 | Intl p | IL | +2.3 | −33.2 D | −5.5 E | NS .. | NS .. | 0.00 | 2.53 |
| 10.91 | MidCap | MC | +3.8 | −24.1 E | +6.9 D | NS .. | NS .. | 0.00 | 2.46 |
| 12.13 | SmCap p | SC | +7.5 | −6.4 C | +12.3 B | NS .. | NS .. | 0.00 | 2.56 |
| 3.42 | TechStk t | TK | +15.5 | −61.5 C | NS .. | NS .. | NS .. | 0.00 | NA |
| | **AAL Mutual Inst** | | | | | | | | |
| 10.24 | Bond | IB | +1.8 | +15.0 A | +6.7 B | NS .. | NS .. | 0.00 | 0.39 |
| 29.25 | CGrowth | LC | +2.9 | −21.6 A | +3.4 A | NS .. | NS .. | 0.00 | 0.54 |
| 7.28 | LgColdx | SP | +1.5 | −25.4 D | NS .. | NS .. | NS .. | 0.00 | 0.20 |
| | **AARP Invst** | | | | | | | | |
| 15.81 | 21Cent | SG | +9.4 | −39.6 E | NS .. | NS .. | NS .. | 0.00 | 1.19 |
| 16.92 | Balanced | BL | +2.1 | −12.5 D | NS .. | NS .. | NS .. | 0.00 | NA |
| 41.91 | CapGr | LG | +5.5 | −35.0 B | +0.5 C | +9.3 B | +10.5 C | 0.00 | 0.90 |
| 15.44 | GNMA | MT | +1.3 | +12.3 C | +6.9 B | +7.1 C | +6.5 D | 0.00 | 0.73 |
| 21.27 | Global | GL | +0.4 | −18.4 B | NS .. | NS .. | NS .. | 0.00 | NA |
| 19.55 | GroInc | LC | +2.4 | −23.6 B | NS .. | NS .. | NS .. | 0.00 | NA |
| 19.92 | HlthCare | HB | +3.0 | −17.5 C | NS .. | NS .. | NS .. | 0.00 | NA |
| 12.92 | Income | AB | +2.1 | +11.8 E | NS .. | NS .. | NS .. | 0.00 | 0.91 |
| 35.82 | Intl | IL | +1.2 | −28.5 C | NS .. | NS .. | NS .. | 0.00 | NA |
| 23.89 | LgCoGro | LG | +3.1 | −38.5 D | NS .. | NS .. | NS .. | 0.00 | 1.05 |
| 22.61 | LgCoVal | LV | −1.1 | −16.9 D | NS .. | NS .. | NS .. | 0.00 | NA |
| 9.23 | MgdMuni | GM | +1.1 | +11.0 A | NS .. | NS .. | NS .. | 0.00 | NA |
| 11.04 | PthwyCnsv | MP | +1.9 | −5.7 B | NS .. | NS .. | NS .. | 0.00 | NA |
| 11.85 | PthwyGro | XC | +1.9 | −22.2 C | NS .. | NS .. | NS .. | 0.00 | NA |
| 14.10 | S&P500 | SP | +1.8 | −25.3 C | NS .. | NS .. | NS .. | 0.00 | NA |
| 10.83 | ShtTmBd | SB | +0.9 | +10.0 D | NS .. | NS .. | NS .. | 0.00 | NA |
| 17.00 | SmCoStk | SC | +5.9 | −4.7 B | −0.3 E | NS .. | NS .. | 0.00 | 1.74 |
| 13.92 | TechInn | TK | +13.3 | −65.7 D | NS .. | NS .. | NS .. | 0.00 | NA |
| | **ABN AMRO Funds** | | | | | | | | |
| 4.98 | AsiaTiger | PR | +5.1 | −30.0 C | −7.9 E | −14.9 E | NS .. | 0.00 | 1.76 |
| 4.99 | BlrIntDvl | IL | −1.4 | −31.9 D | −9.2 E | −2.4 E | NS .. | 0.00 | 1.18 |
| 10.77 | CCM Balan p | BL | +3.8 | −13.4 D | +5.2 B | +10.7 A | NS .. | 0.00 | 1.05 |
| 10.34 | CCM BondI | IB | +1.9 | +13.4 C | NS .. | NS .. | NS .. | 0.00 | NA |
| 10.34 | CCM Bond N | IB | +1.9 | +13.1 D | +6.9 B | +7.4 B | NS .. | 0.00 | 0.76 |
| 20.45 | CCM GrI | LG | +5.5 | −25.8 A | NS .. | NS .. | NS .. | 0.00 | NA |
| 20.38 | CCM Gr N | LG | +5.5 | −26.0 A | +4.2 A | +12.2 A | NS .. | 0.00 | 1.07 |
| 11.11 | CCSmCpVal p | SV | +2.0 | +7.6 C | NS .. | NS .. | NS .. | 0.00 | 1.40 |
| 10.76 | Gwth | LG | +4.6 | −36.5 C | −4.1 D | +4.3 D | NS .. | 0.00 | 1.03 |
| 11.44 | IntlEq | IL | +2.3 | −32.4 D | −5.7 E | +0.5 D | NS .. | 0.00 | 1.31 |
| 7.90 | LatinAm | LT | +1.9 | −30.9 E | +1.8 D | −1.6 D | NS .. | 0.00 | 1.73 |
| 16.49 | M&C BalanN | BL | +2.4 | −6.3 B | +4.0 B | +9.9 A | NS .. | 0.00 | 1.13 |
| 22.43 | M&C Gro N | LC | +2.3 | −17.4 A | +1.9 B | +10.8 A | NS .. | 0.00 | 1.03 |
| 11.72 | SmCp | SG | +6.9 | −16.9 A | +7.2 D | +5.0 C | NS .. | 0.00 | 1.15 |
| 15.67 | TalonMdCpN p | MV | +7.0 | +3.4 C | +13.7 B | +11.9 C | NS .. | 0.00 | 1.30 |
| 9.39 | Value | XV | −1.3 | −19.6 E | −1.5 E | +5.3 E | NS .. | 0.00 | 1.06 |
| 17.55 | VeredAggGro N | SG | +0.3 | −10.1 A | +38.6 A | NS .. | NS .. | 0.00 | 1.40 |
| | **AFBA 5Star Funds** | | | | | | | | |
| 10.46 | Balanced | BL | +3.6 | −6.4 B | +5.1 B | NS .. | NS .. | 0.00 | 1.06 |
| 11.69 | Equity | XC | +4.6 | −22.8 C | +5.6 B | NS .. | NS .. | 0.00 | 1.06 |
| 12.60 | USA Gbl | XC | +8.1 | −19.8 B | +8.8 A | NS .. | NS .. | 0.00 | 1.06 |
| | **AHA Funds** | | | | | | | | |
| 8.53 | Balan | BL | +0.9 | −8.0 B | +6.9 A | +10.6 A | +11.3 A | 0.00 | 0.46 |
| 14.07 | DivrEq | XV | +0.4 | −16.4 E | +6.1 B | +12.5 B | +14.1 B | 0.00 | 0.16 |
| 10.57 | Full | AB | +2.3 | +14.3 B | +7.2 A | +7.9 A | +7.8 B | 0.00 | 0.31 |
| 10.69 | Lim | SB | +1.0 | +11.2 B | +6.9 A | +6.9 A | +6.3 C | 0.00 | 0.24 |
| | **AIM Funds A** | | | | | | | | |
| 8.68 | Agrsv p | MG | +4.8 | −40.5 C | +7.0 C | +3.8 D | +14.4 A | 5.50 | 1.04 |
| 8.59 | AsianGr p | PR | +5.0 | −19.5 A | +4.1 B | NS .. | NS .. | 5.50 | 1.92 |
| 24.99 | Bal p | BL | +3.6 | −20.0 E | +2.2 C | +6.9 C | +11.2 A | 4.75 | 0.96 |
| 25.53 | BasicVal p | XV | +2.0 | −8.2 C | +15.0 A | +14.2 A | NS .. | 5.50 | 1.32 |
| 11.22 | BlChp p | LG | +4.0 | −35.1 B | −2.2 C | +7.7 C | +10.9 B | 5.50 | 1.19 |
| 14.69 | CapDev p | MC | +2.0 | −21.8 D | +9.8 C | +9.0 C | NS .. | 5.50 | 1.28 |
| 10.46 | Chart p | LG | +4.4 | −38.8 C | −2.3 C | +5.9 D | +8.9 D | 5.50 | 1.06 |
| 19.72 | Const p | XG | +5.7 | −43.1 C | +1.6 C | +4.0 D | +11.1 C | 5.50 | 1.08 |
| 7.62 | DentTred p | XG | +8.1 | −50.5 D | NS .. | NS .. | NS .. | 5.50 | 1.50 |
| 6.32 | DevMkt p | EM | +6.0 | −28.5 E | −4.9 E | −12.5 E | NS .. | 4.75 | 1.87 |
| 5.46 | EmrgGrth p | MG | +15.9 | −45.4 D | NS .. | NS .. | NS .. | 5.50 | 1.68 |
| 9.77 | Euro p | EU | +4.0 | −42.4 E | −8.1 E | −0.7 E | +3.0 E | 5.50 | 1.68 |
| 16.52 | EuroDev p | EU | +3.3 | −30.0 D | +8.5 A | NS .. | NS .. | 5.50 | 1.69 |
| 12.58 | GlAgGr | GL | +4.7 | −38.9 E | +1.7 C | +1.1 D | NS .. | 4.75 | 1.65 |
| 20.40 | GlFinSer p | SE | −0.3 | −17.0 E | +13.8 A | +14.5 A | NS .. | 4.75 | 2.00 |
| 14.58 | GlGr p | GL | +3.6 | −41.2 E | −4.1 E | +2.7 D | NS .. | 4.75 | 1.62 |
| 29.93 | GlHltCr p | HB | −1.6 | +10.9 A | +22.3 B | +17.5 B | +13.0 C | 4.75 | 1.73 |
| 9.05 | GlInc p | WB | +2.5 | +8.6 C | +1.7 D | +3.6 C | NS .. | 4.75 | 1.25 |
| 7.96 | GlInfra p | GL | +2.4 | −48.0 E | −7.1 E | −3.5 E | NS .. | 4.75 | 2.00 |
| 10.58 | GlRes p | NR | +7.2 | −13.4 E | −1.1 E | −8.2 E | NS .. | 4.75 | 2.00 |
| 7.41 | GlTelecm p | TK | +14.2 | −71.2 D | −14.9 E | −6.8 E | NS .. | 4.75 | 1.63 |
| 10.36 | GlTrend p | GL | +2.9 | −20.1 B | +7.6 A | NS .. | NS .. | 4.75 | 2.00 |
| 16.16 | GlUtil p | UT | −0.4 | −30.5 E | +1.5 C | +7.6 C | +8.6 D | 5.50 | 1.03 |
| 8.76 | HiIncMuA p | HM | +1.1 | +9.1 A | +1.3 E | NS .. | NS .. | 4.75 | 0.55 |
| 4.57 | HYld p | HC | +2.2 | −12.9 E | −8.8 E | −4.2 E | +4.0 E | 4.75 | 0.93 |
| 6.71 | HYldII p | HC | +3.3 | −14.0 E | −1.8 D | NS .. | NS .. | 4.75 | 1.00 |
| 6.91 | Inco p | AB | +2.5 | +6.9 E | +1.5 E | +4.2 E | +6.6 E | 4.75 | 0.95 |
| 9.40 | IntGov p | IG | +2.1 | +12.6 E | +5.6 E | +6.8 D | +6.4 D | 4.75 | 0.98 |
| 14.45 | IntlEq p | IL | +2.4 | −28.0 C | −2.2 C | +2.0 C | NS .. | 5.50 | 1.44 |
| 12.40 | IntVal p | IL | +2.2 | −19.8 A | −2.4 C | NS .. | NS .. | 5.50 | 1.54 |
| 10.45 | LimM p | SU | +0.8 | +9.7 D | +5.8 D | +6.0 D | +5.6 D | 1.00 | 0.54 |
| 10.95 | LrgCpBV p | LV | +0.6 | −8.7 A | NS .. | NS .. | NS .. | 5.50 | 1.25 |
| 8.82 | LrgCpGr t | LG | +5.8 | −50.3 E | NS .. | NS .. | NS .. | 5.50 | 1.58 |
| 8.83 | LrgCpOpp | LG | +0.8 | −33.4 B | NS .. | NS .. | NS .. | 5.50 | 2.34 |
| 22.19 | MdCpEq p | MC | +3.9 | −6.6 A | +18.0 A | +10.9 B | +14.7 A | 5.50 | 1.37 |
| 16.12 | MdCpOpp p | MG | +4.0 | −30.7 B | NS .. | NS .. | NS .. | 5.50 | 2.08 |
| 8.58 | MidCpGr p | MG | +10.7 | −40.3 C | NS .. | NS .. | NS .. | 5.50 | 1.63 |
| 8.08 | Muni p | GM | +1.1 | +8.0 E | +3.9 D | +5.0 D | +5.9 E | 4.75 | 0.85 |
| 3.36 | NewTech p | TK | +15.1 | −61.9 C | NS .. | NS .. | NS .. | 5.50 | NA |
| 13.24 | RealEst p | SE | −2.9 | +11.9 A | +9.6 B | NS .. | NS .. | 4.75 | 1.61 |
| 15.25 | SelEqty p | XG | +3.1 | −43.4 C | +4.0 C | +7.7 B | +9.4 D | 5.50 | 1.07 |
| 8.77 | SmCpEq p | SC | +3.8 | −10.2 D | NS .. | NS .. | NS .. | 5.50 | NA |
| 22.49 | SmCpGr p | SG | +8.1 | −35.8 D | +22.2 A | +15.1 A | NS .. | 5.50 | 1.13 |
| 12.49 | SmCpOpp p | SG | +7.0 | −18.5 A | +33.9 A | NS .. | NS .. | 5.50 | 1.47 |
| 8.63 | Strat p | GT | +2.7 | +2.1 E | −0.1 E | +1.1 E | +6.2 D | 4.75 | 1.21 |
| 9.35 | Summit I | XG | +5.5 | −49.5 D | −1.9 D | +5.9 C | +9.8 C | 0.00 | 0.72 |
| 11.36 | TFInt | IM | +0.9 | +9.0 C | +5.1 A | +5.7 B | +5.9 C | 1.00 | 0.41 |
| 10.13 | Valu p | LC | +2.5 | −24.9 C | +1.7 B | +9.1 B | +13.2 A | 5.50 | 1.00 |
| 6.35 | ValueII p | XG | +3.8 | −33.5 A | NS .. | NS .. | NS .. | 5.50 | NA |
| 12.65 | Weing p | XG | +1.8 | −47.4 C | −6.9 E | +2.8 D | +7.1 E | 5.50 | 1.03 |
| | **AIM Funds B** | | | | | | | | |
| 8.45 | Agrsv t | MG | +4.8 | −40.9 C | NS .. | NS .. | NS .. | 0.00 | 1.86 |
| 8.38 | AsianGr t | PR | +5.0 | −19.9 A | +3.3 B | NS .. | NS .. | 0.00 | 2.67 |
| 24.91 | Bal t | BL | +3.6 | −20.6 E | +1.4 D | +6.1 D | NS .. | 0.00 | 1.73 |
| 24.61 | BasicVal t | XV | +1.9 | −8.8 C | +14.2 A | +13.5 A | NS .. | 0.00 | 1.97 |
| 10.87 | BlChp t | LG | +3.9 | −35.6 B | −2.9 D | +6.9 C | NS .. | 0.00 | 1.88 |
| 14.10 | CapDev t | MC | +2.0 | −22.3 D | +9.0 C | +8.2 D | NS .. | 0.00 | 1.99 |
| 10.18 | Chart t | LG | +4.4 | −39.1 D | −3.0 D | +5.1 D | NS .. | 0.00 | 1.80 |
| 18.89 | Const t | XG | +5.6 | −43.5 C | +0.8 D | NS .. | NS .. | 0.00 | 1.85 |
| 7.50 | DentTred t | XG | +7.9 | −50.9 D | NS .. | NS .. | NS .. | 0.00 | 2.17 |
| 6.26 | DevMkt t | EM | +6.1 | −28.8 E | −5.5 E | NS .. | NS .. | 0.00 | 2.47 |
| 5.40 | EmrgGrth t | MG | +15.6 | −45.8 D | NS .. | NS .. | NS .. | 0.00 | 2.37 |
| 9.29 | Euro t | EU | +4.0 | −42.8 E | −8.7 E | −1.4 E | NS .. | 0.00 | 2.33 |
| 16.07 | EuroDev t | EU | +3.2 | −30.5 D | +7.7 A | NS .. | NS .. | 0.00 | 2.39 |
| 11.97 | GlAgGr t | GL | +4.7 | −39.2 E | +1.1 C | +0.6 E | NS .. | 0.00 | 2.19 |
| 19.71 | GlFinSer t | SE | −0.4 | −17.4 E | +13.2 A | +13.9 A | NS .. | 0.00 | 2.50 |
| 14.00 | GlGr t | GL | +3.4 | −41.5 E | −4.6 E | +2.1 D | NS .. | 0.00 | 2.16 |
| 28.02 | GlHltCr t | HB | −1.7 | +10.3 A | +21.7 B | +16.9 C | NS .. | 0.00 | 2.23 |
| 9.05 | GlInc t | WB | +2.4 | +8.1 C | +1.1 D | +3.0 C | NS .. | 0.00 | 1.75 |
| 7.61 | GlInfra t | GL | +2.3 | −48.3 E | −7.6 E | −4.0 E | NS .. | 0.00 | 2.50 |
| 6.96 | GlTelecm t | TK | +14.1 | −71.3 E | −15.3 E | −7.3 E | NS .. | 0.00 | 2.13 |
| 10.23 | GlRes t | NR | +7.1 | −13.9 E | −1.6 E | −8.7 E | NS .. | 0.00 | 2.50 |
| 10.16 | GlTrend t | GL | +2.8 | −20.4 B | +7.1 B | NS .. | NS .. | 0.00 | 2.50 |
| 16.10 | GlUtil t | UT | −0.5 | −31.1 E | +0.8 C | +6.8 D | NS .. | 0.00 | 1.80 |
| 8.77 | HiIncMu t | HM | +1.0 | +8.2 B | +0.5 E | NS .. | NS .. | 0.00 | 1.30 |
| 4.58 | HYld t | HC | +2.1 | −13.5 E | −9.5 E | −4.9 E | NS .. | 0.00 | 1.69 |
| 6.71 | HYldII t | HC | +3.2 | −14.6 E | NS .. | NS .. | NS .. | 0.00 | 1.75 |
| 6.92 | Inco t | AB | +2.6 | +6.2 E | +0.7 E | +3.4 E | NS .. | 0.00 | 1.71 |
| 9.42 | IntGov t | IG | +2.0 | +11.7 E | +4.8 E | +6.0 E | NS .. | 0.00 | 1.74 |
| 13.78 | IntlEq t | IL | +2.3 | −28.5 C | −3.0 D | +1.2 C | NS .. | 0.00 | 2.18 |
| 10.86 | LrgCpBV t | LV | +0.5 | −9.2 A | NS .. | NS .. | NS .. | 0.00 | NA |
| 8.67 | LrgCpGr t | LG | +5.6 | −50.6 E | NS .. | NS .. | NS .. | 0.00 | 2.24 |
| 8.74 | LrgCpOpp t | LG | +0.9 | −33.9 B | NS .. | NS .. | NS .. | 0.00 | NA |
| 20.53 | MdCpEq t | MC | +3.8 | −7.2 A | +17.2 B | +10.2 C | NS .. | 0.00 | 2.02 |
| 15.89 | MdCpOpp t | MG | +3.9 | −31.2 B | NS .. | NS .. | NS .. | 0.00 | 2.83 |
| 8.45 | MidCpGr t | MG | +10.6 | −40.7 C | NS .. | NS .. | NS .. | 0.00 | 2.32 |
| 8.09 | Muni t | GM | +1.0 | +7.2 E | +3.1 E | +4.2 E | NS .. | 0.00 | 1.61 |
| 3.33 | NewTech t | TK | +14.8 | −62.2 C | NS .. | NS .. | NS .. | 0.00 | NA |
| 13.27 | RealEst t | SE | −3.0 | +11.0 B | +8.8 B | NS .. | NS .. | 0.00 | 2.37 |
| 13.95 | SelEqty t | XG | +3.0 | −43.8 C | +3.2 C | +6.9 C | NS .. | 0.00 | 1.84 |
| 8.70 | SmCpEq t | SC | +3.7 | −10.9 D | NS .. | NS .. | NS .. | 0.00 | NA |
| 21.48 | SmCpGr t | SG | +8.0 | −36.3 D | +21.3 A | +14.3 A | NS .. | 0.00 | 1.88 |
| 12.03 | SmCpOpp t | SG | +6.9 | −19.1 A | +32.9 A | NS .. | NS .. | 0.00 | 2.22 |
| 8.65 | Strat t | GT | +2.7 | +1.5 E | −0.7 E | +0.4 E | NS .. | 0.00 | 1.86 |
| 9.61 | Valu t | LC | +2.5 | −25.5 C | +0.9 B | +8.2 C | NS .. | 0.00 | 1.77 |
| 6.30 | ValueII t | XG | +3.6 | −33.9 A | NS .. | NS .. | NS .. | 0.00 | NA |
| 11.86 | Weing t | XG | +1.7 | −47.7 C | −7.6 E | +2.0 E | NS .. | 0.00 | 1.78 |
| | **AIM Funds C** | | | | | | | | |
| 8.45 | Agrsv t | MG | +4.8 | −40.9 C | NS .. | NS .. | NS .. | 0.00 | 1.86 |
| 8.37 | AsianGr t | PR | +4.9 | −19.9 A | +3.4 B | NS .. | NS .. | 0.00 | 2.67 |
| 24.95 | Bal p | BL | +3.6 | −20.6 E | +1.4 D | NS .. | NS .. | 0.00 | 1.73 |
| 24.61 | BasicVal t | XV | +1.9 | −8.8 C | NS .. | NS .. | NS .. | 0.00 | 1.97 |
| 10.87 | BlChip p | LG | +3.9 | −35.5 B | −2.9 D | NS .. | NS .. | 0.00 | 1.88 |
| 14.09 | CapDev t | MC | +2.0 | −22.3 D | +9.0 C | NS .. | NS .. | 0.00 | 1.99 |
| 10.20 | Chart t | LG | +4.3 | −39.2 D | −3.0 D | NS .. | NS .. | 0.00 | 1.80 |
| 18.88 | Const t | XG | +5.6 | −43.5 C | +0.8 D | NS .. | NS .. | 0.00 | 1.85 |
| 7.50 | DentTred t | XG | +7.9 | −50.9 D | NS .. | NS .. | NS .. | 0.00 | 2.17 |
| 5.40 | EmrgGrth t | MG | +15.9 | −45.8 D | NS .. | NS .. | NS .. | 0.00 | 2.37 |
| 16.09 | EuroDev t | EU | +3.2 | −30.5 D | +7.7 A | NS .. | NS .. | 0.00 | 2.39 |
| 11.98 | GlAgGr t | GL | +4.7 | −39.2 E | +1.1 C | NS .. | NS .. | 0.00 | 2.19 |
| 19.71 | GlFinSer t | SE | −0.4 | −17.4 E | NS .. | NS .. | NS .. | 0.00 | 2.50 |
| 14.01 | GlGr t | GL | +3.5 | −41.5 E | −4.6 E | NS .. | NS .. | 0.00 | 2.16 |
| 28.03 | GlHltCr t | HB | −1.7 | +10.3 A | NS .. | NS .. | NS .. | 0.00 | 2.23 |
| 6.96 | GlTelecm t | TK | +14.1 | −71.3 E | NS .. | NS .. | NS .. | 0.00 | 2.13 |
| 16.10 | GlUtil t | UT | −0.5 | −31.0 E | +0.8 C | NS .. | NS .. | 0.00 | 1.80 |
| 4.57 | Hyld p | HC | +2.1 | −13.6 E | −9.5 E | NS .. | NS .. | 0.00 | 1.69 |
| 6.90 | Inco t | AB | +2.4 | +6.0 E | +0.7 E | NS .. | NS .. | 0.00 | 1.71 |
| 9.39 | IntGov t | IG | +2.0 | +11.7 E | +4.8 E | NS .. | NS .. | 0.00 | 1.74 |
| 13.79 | IntlEq t | IL | +2.3 | −28.5 C | −3.0 D | NS .. | NS .. | 0.00 | 2.18 |
| 12.12 | IntVal t | IL | +2.2 | −20.5 B | −3.1 D | +3.1 B | NS .. | 0.00 | 2.32 |
| 8.67 | LrgCpGr t | LG | +5.6 | −50.6 E | NS .. | NS .. | NS .. | 0.00 | 2.24 |
| 8.73 | LrgCpOpp t | LG | +0.8 | −33.9 B | NS .. | NS .. | NS .. | 0.00 | NA |
| 20.51 | MdCpEq t | MC | +3.8 | −7.2 A | NS .. | NS .. | NS .. | 0.00 | 2.02 |
| 15.89 | MdCpOpp t | MG | +3.9 | −31.2 B | NS .. | NS .. | NS .. | 0.00 | 2.83 |
| 8.45 | MidCpGr t | MG | +10.6 | −40.7 C | NS .. | NS .. | NS .. | 0.00 | 2.32 |
| 3.33 | NewTech t | TK | +14.8 | −62.2 C | NS .. | NS .. | NS .. | 0.00 | NA |
| 13.25 | RealEst t | SE | −3.0 | +11.1 A | +8.8 B | +6.4 E | NS .. | 0.00 | 2.37 |
| 13.93 | SelEqty t | XG | +3.0 | −43.8 C | +3.2 C | NS .. | NS .. | 0.00 | 1.84 |
| 21.47 | SmCpGr t | SG | +8.1 | −36.3 D | NS .. | NS .. | NS .. | 0.00 | 1.88 |
| 12.05 | SmCpOpp t | SG | +6.9 | −19.1 A | NS .. | NS .. | NS .. | 0.00 | 2.22 |
| 9.62 | Valu t | LC | +2.4 | −25.5 C | +0.9 B | NS .. | NS .. | 0.00 | 1.77 |
| 6.30 | ValueII t | XG | +3.6 | −33.9 A | NS .. | NS .. | NS .. | 0.00 | NA |
| 11.87 | Weing t | XG | +1.7 | −47.8 C | −7.6 E | NS .. | NS .. | 0.00 | 1.78 |
| | **AMF Funds** | | | | | | | | |
| 9.97 | AdjMtg | MT | +0.6 | +7.0 E | +6.1 D | +6.0 E | +5.6 E | 0.00 | 0.48 |
| 9.83 | IntMtg | MT | +1.1 | +11.6 D | +6.7 C | +7.1 C | +6.7 C | 0.00 | 0.51 |
| 10.75 | ShtUSGv | SU | +0.8 | +9.7 D | +5.9 D | +6.2 C | +6.1 C | 0.00 | 0.51 |
| 10.83 | USGvMtg | MT | +1.3 | +12.0 C | +6.8 C | +7.3 B | +6.8 C | 0.00 | 0.52 |
| | **AMIDEX Mutual Funds** | | | | | | | | |
| 7.76 | 35 p | IL | +6.3 | −57.1 E | NS .. | NS .. | NS .. | 0.00 | 2.20 |
| 6.02 | 35A p | IL | +6.4 | −57.3 E | NS .. | NS .. | NS .. | 4.00 | 2.20 |
| 5.94 | IsraelTech t | TK | NN | NN .. | NN .. | NN .. | NN .. | 0.00 | NA |
| 9.38 | **API Gr fp** | GL | +4.0 | −29.2 C | −0.3 D | +3.3 D | +6.8 D | 0.00 | 2.42 |
| | **ARK Funds** | | | | | | | | |
| 13.09 | Balanced | BL | +3.2 | −14.1 D | +7.2 A | +11.5 A | NS .. | 0.00 | 0.90 |
| 13.04 | BalancedA p | BL | +3.3 | −14.1 D | +7.1 A | +11.3 A | NS .. | 4.75 | 1.01 |
| 13.02 | BalancedB | BL | +3.3 | −14.8 D | +6.3 A | NS .. | NS .. | 0.00 | 1.77 |
| 16.54 | BlChpEqA p | LC | +2.9 | −25.0 C | +1.9 B | +10.7 A | NS .. | 4.75 | 1.08 |
| 16.27 | BlChpEqB p | LC | +2.8 | −25.6 C | +1.1 B | NS .. | NS .. | 0.00 | 1.83 |
| 16.57 | BlChpEqI | LC | +3.0 | −24.9 C | +2.0 A | +10.9 A | NS .. | 0.00 | 0.97 |
| 14.79 | CapGr | LG | +4.7 | −34.0 B | +6.8 A | +14.0 A | NS .. | 0.00 | 1.00 |
| 14.36 | CapGrB p | LG | +4.5 | −34.6 B | +5.9 A | NS .. | NS .. | 0.00 | 1.86 |
| 14.63 | CapGrwthA p | LG | +4.6 | −34.1 B | +6.7 A | +13.8 A | NS .. | 4.75 | 1.11 |
| 6.59 | EmMktEqA p | EM | +4.9 | −28.6 E | −5.1 E | −12.2 E | NS .. | 0.00 | 1.85 |
| 8.85 | EqIdxA p | SP | +1.7 | −24.7 A | 0.0 A | NS .. | NS .. | 4.75 | 0.50 |
| 8.87 | EqIdxI | SP | +1.7 | −24.5 A | +0.3 A | NS .. | NS .. | 0.00 | 0.25 |
| 9.72 | EqInc | EI | −1.9 | −13.7 D | +1.2 C | NS .. | NS .. | 0.00 | 0.98 |

Table 16-3 (*cont.*)

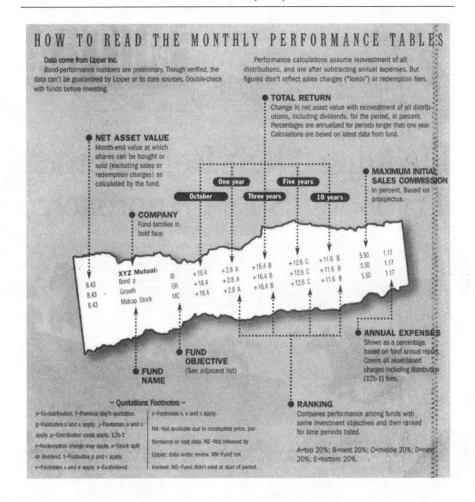

Table 16-4

## MUTUAL-FUND OBJECTIVES

Categories compiled by The Wall Street Journal, based on classifications by Lipper Inc.

### STOCK FUNDS

**Emerging Markets (EM):** Funds that invest in emerging-market equity securities, where the "emerging market" is defined by a country's GNP per capita and other economic measures.

**Equity Income (EI):** Funds that seek high current income and growth of income through investment in equities.

**European Region (EU):** Funds that invest in markets or operations concentrated in the European region.

**Global Stock (GL):** Funds that invest in securities traded outside of the U.S. and may own U.S. securities as well.

**Gold Oriented (AU):** Funds that invest in gold mines, gold-oriented mining finance houses, gold coins or bullion.

**Health/Biotech (HB):** Funds that invest in companies related to health care, medicine and biotechnology.

**International Stock (IL) (non-U.S.):** Canadian; International; International Small Cap.

**Latin American (LT):** Funds that invest in markets or operations concentrated in the Latin American region.

**Large-Cap Growth (LG):** Funds that invest in large companies with long-term earnings that are expected to grow significantly faster than the earnings of stocks in major indexes. Funds normally have above-average price-to-earnings ratios, price-to-book ratios and three-year earnings growth.

**Large-Cap Core (LC):** Funds that invest in large companies, with wide latitude in the type of shares they buy. On average, the price-to-earnings ratios, price-to-book ratios, and three-year earnings growth are in line with those of the U.S. diversified large-cap funds' universe average.

**Large-Cap Value (LV):** Funds that invest in large companies that are considered undervalued relative to major stock indexes based on price-to-earnings ratios, price-to-book ratios or other factors.

**Midcap Growth (MG):** Funds that invest in midsize companies with long-term earnings that are expected to grow significantly faster than the earnings of stocks in major indexes. Funds normally have above-average price-to-earnings ratios, price-to-book ratios and three-year earnings growth.

**Midcap Core (MC):** Funds that invest in midsize companies, with wide latitude in the type of shares they buy. On average, the price-to-earnings ratios, price-to-book ratios, and three-year earnings growth are in line with those of the U.S. diversified midcap funds' universe average.

**Midcap Value (MV):** Funds that invest in midsize companies that are considered undervalued relative to major stock indexes based on price-to-earnings ratios, price-to-book ratios or other factors.

**Multicap Growth (XG):** Funds that invest in companies of various sizes, with long-term earnings that are expected to grow significantly faster than the earnings of stocks in major indexes. Funds normally have above-average price-to-earnings ratios, price-to-book ratios, and three-year earnings growth.

**Multicap Core (XC):** Funds that invest in companies of various sizes with average price-to-earnings ratios, price-to-book ratios and earnings growth.

**Multicap Value (XV):** Funds that invest in companies of various size, normally those that are considered undervalued relative to major stock indexes based on price-to-earnings ratios, price-to-book ratios or other factors.

**Natural Resources (NR):** Funds that invest in natural-resource stocks.

**Pacific Region (PR):** Funds that invest in China Region; Japan; Pacific Ex-Japan; Pacific Region.

**Science & Technology (TK):** Funds that invest in science and technology stocks. Includes telecommunication funds.

**Sector (SE):** Funds that invest in financial services; real estate; specialty & miscellaneous.

## Table 16-4 (*cont.*)

**S&P 500 Index (SP):** Funds that are passively managed and are designed to replicate the performance of the Standard & Poor's 500-stock Index on a reinvested basis.

**Small-Cap Growth (SG):** Funds that invest in small companies with long-term earnings that are expected to grow significantly faster than the earnings of stocks in major indexes. Funds normally have above-average price-to-earnings ratios, price-to-book ratios, and three-year earnings growth.

**Small-Cap Core (SC):** Funds that invest in small companies, with wide latitude in the type of shares they buy. On average, the price-to-earnings ratios, price-to-book ratios, and three-year earnings growth are in line with those of the U.S. diversified small-cap funds' universe average.

**Small-Cap Value (SV):** Funds that invest in small companies that are considered undervalued relative to major stock indexes based on price-to-earnings ratios, price-to-book ratios or other factors.

**Specialty Equity (SQ):** Funds that invest in all market-capitalization ranges, with no restrictions for any one range. May have strategies that are distinctly different from other diversified stock funds.

**Utility (UT):** Funds that invest in utility stocks.

### TAXABLE BOND FUNDS

**Short-Term Bond (SB):** Ultra-short Obligation; Short Investment Grade Debt; Short-Intermediate Investment Grade Debt.

**Short-Term U.S. (SU):** Short U.S. Treasury; Short U.S. Government; Short-Intermediate U.S. Government debt.

**Intermediate Bond (IB):** Funds that invest in investment-grade debt issues (rated in the top four grades) with dollar-weighted average maturities of five to 10 years.

**Intermediate U.S. (IG):** Intermediate U.S. Government; Intermediate U.S. Treasury.

**Long-Term Bond (AB):** Funds that invest in corporate- and government-debt issues in the top grades.

**Long-Term U.S. (LU):** General U.S. Government; General U.S. Treasury; Target Maturity.

**General U.S. Taxable (GT):** Funds that invest in general bonds.

**High-Yield Taxable (HC):** Funds that aim for high current yields from fixed-income securities and tend to invest in lower-grade debt.

**Mortgage (MT):** Adjustable Rate Mortgage; GNMA; U.S. Mortgage.

**World Bond (WB):** Emerging Markets Debt; Global Income; International Income; Short World Multi-Market Income.

### MUNICIPAL DEBT FUNDS

**Short-Term Muni (SM):** California Short-Intermediate Muni Debt; Other States Short-Intermediate Muni Debt; Short-Intermediate Muni Debt; Short Muni Debt.

**Intermediate Muni (IM):** Intermediate-term Muni Debt including single states.

**General Muni (GM):** Funds investing in muni-debt issues in the top-four credit ratings.

**Single-State Municipal (SS):** Funds that invest in debt of individual states.

**High-Yield Municipal (HM):** Funds that invest in lower-rated muni debt.

**Insured Muni (NM):** California Insured Muni Debt; Florida Insured Muni Debt; Insured Muni Debt; New York Insured Muni Debt.

### STOCK & BOND FUNDS

**Balanced (BL):** Primary objective is to conserve principal, by maintaining a balanced portfolio of both stocks and bonds.

**Stock/Bond Blend (MP):** Multipurpose funds such as Balanced Target Maturity; Convertible Securities; Flexible Income; Flexible Portfolio; Global Flexible and Income funds, that invest in both stocks and bonds.

In recent years, there has been a strong trend toward **index funds** that are not actively managed but hold a portfolio that is structured so that it closely mimics the mix of stocks in one or more broad market indexes. An index fund may be attractive to sophisticated investors, because it involves significantly less trading than a managed fund, and brokerage commissions, investment advice, and other costs are therefore significantly reduced. The tremendous growth in mutual funds in recent years is in part the result of the increased use of index funds by pension plans and other institutional investors who are seeking only a market level return on their investments.

## §16.6 Exchange Traded Funds (ETFs)

An **exchange traded fund** (ETF) is an index representing a basket of stocks that are traded on the Exchange throughout the day, much as though it were a single stock. When trading ETFs, investors have the advantage of trading a diversified basket of stocks that reflect the performance of an industry sector, style, or region as a single security. The first ETFs were publicly traded in December 2000.

Several index funds have been traded over the counter for some time, including funds with such exotic names as FT SE/XiahuaChina25 or Nasdaq 100 Index Tracking Stock (using the symbol "QQQ"), the S&P Depository Receipts ("SPY") and DJIA IndustrialDIAMONDS ("DIA"). The first two exchange-listed index funds are the S&P Global 100ETF and the NYSE sponsored S&P Global 100Index.

A table of exchange traded funds appears in the *Wall Street Journal*. See Table 16-5.

## §16.7 Unit Investment Trusts

A **unit investment trust** is usually a vehicle for fixed income investments, particularly municipal bonds, though some unit investment trusts may hold mortgage-backed securities and corporate bonds. A unit investment trust has a fixed portfolio of securities, all with the same or similar maturities. They are "unmanaged" in the sense that they invest in a portfolio of securities and hold them until they mature or are called for redemption. Unit investment trusts have fixed life spans that vary from 1 to 30 years. When the unit investment trust receives payments of principal or interest, the amounts are paid to the investors and not reinvested. Unit investment trusts are created by a sponsor, usually a brokerage firm. Units are sold publicly and the sponsor usually maintains a secondary market so that investors may sell their investment before maturity.

Unit investment trust units are sold on a dollar price basis that includes a sales charge of 3 to 5 percent. The longer an investor holds the trust units, the lower the impact of the sales charge on the yield. Many unit trusts invest in diversified portfolios, while others concentrate on single-state issues that offer income that is double or triple tax-exempt for residents of those states. (**Double**

Table 16-5

# EXCHANGE TRADED PORTFOLIOS

Includes Exchange-Traded funds and HOLDRs
Friday, November 9, 2001

## AMEX

| YTD %CHG | 52 WEEKS HI | LO | STOCK (SYM) | DIV | YLD % | VOL 100S | CLOSE | NET CHG |
|---|---|---|---|---|---|---|---|---|
| + 9.8 | 113.64 | 79.50 | DJIA Diam DIA | 1.59e | 1.7 | 25616 | 96.31 | + 0.08 |
| + 78.1 | 44.88 | 2.41 | B2B Int HOLDRs BHH | .26e | 6.7 | 1145 | 3.90 | + 0.03 |
| + 25.0 | 195 | 92.51 | Biotch HOLDRs BBH | .03e | ... | 15884 | 127.80 | – 1.00 |
| – 61.8 | 66.44 | 13.16 | BrdBnd HOLDRs BDH | .08e | .5 | 1049 | 17.41 | + 0.03 |
| – 36.1 | 98.25 | 48.80 | Europe HOLDRs EKH | 1.40e | 2.2 | 7 | 62.75 | – 0.45 |
| – 35.7 | 92 | 26.30 | IntArc HOLDRs IAH | .13e | .4 | 89 | 37.01 | + 0.10 |
| – 14.6 | 80.25 | 23.90 | Intrnt HOLDRs HHH | | ... | 369 | 33.10 | + 0.65 |
| – 71.3 | 44.44 | 4.59 | IntInfr HOLDRs IIH | | ... | 1690 | 6.35 | + 0.29 |
| – 19.5 | 86.63 | 52 | Mkt2k HLDRs MKH | .99e | 1.6 | 225 | 60.87 | – 0.02 |
| – 37.7 | 98.85 | 41.81 | OilSvc HOLDRs OIH | .36e | .6 | 12011 | 59.15 | + 2.00 |
| – 12.6 | 115.88 | 84.32 | Pharm HOLDRs PPH | 1.43e | 1.4 | 2842 | 99.85 | – 0.30 |
| – 10.6 | 127 | 95 | RegnlBk HOLDRs RKH | 2.98e | 2.8 | 16 | 107.26 | – 0.36 |
| – 10.3 | 100.90 | 70 | Retail HOLDRs RTH | .27e | .3 | 405 | 87.25 | + 0.05 |
| – 17.2 | 65.60 | 27.31 | Semi HOLDRs SMH | .05e | .1 | 36502 | 40.58 | – 0.17 |
| – 36.1 | 97.94 | 28.15 | Sftwre HOLDRs SWH | .06e | .1 | 2563 | 40.75 | + 0.55 |
| – 16.4 | 64.63 | 43.03 | Telcom HOLDRs TTH | .90e | 2.0 | 256 | 44.62 | + 0.46 |
| – 20.5 | 121.56 | 87.89 | Util HOLDRs UTH | 3.47e | 3.6 | 2537 | 96.10 | + 0.70 |
| – 28.9 | 99.63 | 50.60 | Wrls HOLDRs WMH | 1.38e | 2.3 | 432 | 60.04 | + 0.12 |
| – 13.5 | 59.10 | 40.41 | iShrDJUSEn IYE | .47e | 1.0 | 119 | 47.56 | + 1.26 |
| – 5.5 | 43.28 | 30 | iShDJUSBM IYM | .76e | 2.1 | 619 | 37.05 | + 0.08 |
| – 8.2 | 64.50 | 41.40 | iShDJUSCCy IYC | .29e | .6 | 117 | 51.10 | + 0.02 |
| – 1.1 | 44.51 | 38.32 | iShrDJUSCNC IYK | .53e | 1.2 | 186 | 42.98 | + 0.31 |
| – 10.7 | 104.22 | 73.15 | iShrDJUSFin IYG | 1.54e | 1.7 | 15 | 88.24 | – 0.26 |
| – 15.0 | 73 | 52 | iShrDJUSHlth IYH | .29e | .5 | 320 | 61.15 | + 0.05 |
| + 0.3 | 86.15 | 70 | iShrDJUSRE IYR | 3.83e | 5.0 | 175 | 76.14 | – 0.27 |
| – 16.2 | 67.78 | 43.25 | iShrDJUSTot IYY | .55e | 1.1 | 344 | 51.55 | – 0.04 |
| – 25.9 | 89.75 | 63.15 | iShrDJUSUtil IDU | 2.33e | 3.5 | 95 | 65.81 | + 0.20 |
| – 11.1 | 90 | 65 | iShrDJUSFi IYF | 2.12e | 2.7 | 92 | 77.38 | – 0.37 |
| – 59.4 | 62.88 | 8.23 | iShrDJInt IYV | .16 | 1.3 | 354 | 12.56 | + 0.44 |
| – 20.6 | 49.94 | 29.63 | iShrDJUSTc IYZ | .78e | 2.5 | 70 | 30.82 | + 0.26 |
| – 31.3 | 111.06 | 36.45 | iShrDJTch IYW | | ... | 252 | 51.25 | + 0.49 |
| – 2.6 | 95.12 | 72.70 | iShrSP400V IJJ | 1.17e | 1.4 | 367 | 83.26 | – 0.16 |
| – 10.4 | 78.53 | 60.90 | iShrRu3000V IWW | 1.33e | 1.9 | 24 | 68.65 | – 0.18 |
| – 26.3 | 75.50 | 43.30 | iShrMSEMU EZU | .68e | 1.3 | 126 | 53.99 | – 0.02 |
| – 19.6 | 76.94 | 41 | iShrRu2000G IWO | .12e | .2 | 597 | 51.60 | – 0.27 |
| + 0.4 | 129.65 | 102.90 | iShrRu2000V IWN | 2.19e | 1.9 | 285 | 116.12 | – 0.73 |
| – 23.4 | 63.55 | 32.65 | iShrRu3000G IWZ | .13e | .3 | 65 | 39.69 | – 0.58 |
| – 23.7 | 80.50 | 45.52 | iShrSPEu350 IEV | .80e | 1.4 | 186 | 58.49 | + 0.08 |
| – 10.9 | 86.02 | 58.50 | iShrSP600G IJT | .66e | .9 | 136 | 69.87 | – 0.37 |
| – 1.1 | 86.58 | 66.35 | iShrSP600V IJS | .92e | 1.2 * | 185 | 76.14 | + 0.33 |
| – 4.7 | 10.06 | 7.50 | iShrMSAusy EWA | .22e | 2.4 | 241 | 9.05 | + 0.01 |
| – 8.9 | 8.70 | 6.69 | iShrMSAus EWO | .14e | 2.0 | 6 | 6.89 | – 0.02 |
| – 32.4 | 19 | 8.40 | iShrMSBra EWZ | .64e | 5.7 | 113 | 11.15 | + 0.15 |
| – 24.9 | 15.19 | 8.70 | iShrMSCan EWC | .37e | 3.7 | 24 | 10.05 | – 0.05 |
| – 26.5 | 25.24 | 14.50 | iShrMSFra EWQ | .05e | .3 | 62 | 18.14 | – 0.16 |
| – 27.9 | 20.60 | 10.35 | iShrMSGer EWG | .19e | 1.3 | 479 | 14.05 | ... |
| – 27.0 | 12.44 | 6.85 | iShrMSHK EWH | .24e | 2.9 | 160 | 8.40 | + 0.15 |
| – 30.0 | 23.13 | 12.25 | iShrMSIta EWI | .31e | 2.0 | 85 | 15.84 | – 0.06 |
| – 24.9 | 13.25 | 7.77 | iShrMSJpn EWJ | e | | 4172 | 8.31 | – 0.16 |
| + 17.1 | 16.13 | 10.32 | iShrMSSK EWY | .10e | .7 | 48 | 14.34 | + 0.29 |
| – 14.1 | 5.88 | 3.85 | iShrMSMay EWM | .06e | 1.4 | 83 | 4.35 | ... |
| + 1.4 | 17.35 | 11 | iShrMSMex EWW | .18e | 1.3 | 68 | 13.50 | – 0.09 |
| – 25.3 | 23.85 | 13.20 | iShrMSNth EWN | .28e | 1.7 | 64 | 16.94 | – 0.01 |
| – 33.7 | 7.13 | 3.81 | iShrMSSng EWS | .15e | 3.5 | 243 | 4.31 | + 0.11 |
| – 11.5 | 26.15 | 16 | iShrMSEsp EWP | .16e | .8 | 21 | 20.29 | – 0.40 |
| – 25.1 | 17.75 | 10.55 | iShrMSSwi EWL | .09e | .7 | 86 | 12.59 | + 0.04 |
| – 15.2 | 18.56 | 11.90 | iShrMSUK EWU | .27e | 1.8 | 160 | 14.95 | + 0.12 |
| – 30.6 | 20.69 | 8.85 | iShrMSSwe EWD | .05e | .4 | 56 | 12.40 | – 0.26 |
| – 22.4 | 14.44 | 6.51 | iShrMSTaiwn EWT | e | | 116 | 8.20 | – 0.06 |
| – 7.4 | 46.45 | 32.19 | iShrDJUSChm IYD | 1.15e | 2.9 | 89 | 40.35 | – 0.15 |
| – 16.7 | 60.63 | 37.40 | iShrDJUSInd IYJ | .44e | .9 | 55 | 47.05 | – 0.10 |
| – 22.3 | 40.10 | 22.70 | iShrsGS Netwkng IGN | | ... | 123 | 30.85 | + 0.20 |
| – 22.1 | 52.55 | 28.45 | iShrsGS Sftwr IGV | | ... | 3 | 40.80 | + 0.55 |
| – 9.3 | 79.95 | 44.89 | iShrGS Smcdtor IGW | | ... | 693 | 65.89 | + 0.53 |
| – 8.6 | 66.69 | 34.75 | iShrGSchsTch IGM | | ... | 332 | 48.76 | – 0.14 |
| – 15.4 | 109.30 | 61 | iShrsNasBioTch IBB | | ... | 5396 | 85.50 | – 1.99 |
| – 16.1 | 77.24 | 49.55 | iShrRu1000 IWB | .74e | 1.3 | 209 | 58.92 | + 0.07 |
| – 10.2 | 61.62 | 47.30 | iShrRu1000V IWD | .81e | 1.5 | 797 | 53.90 | + 0.14 |
| – 10.9 | 73.95 | 52.80 | iShrRuMidGrth IWP | .01e | ... | 95 | 65.92 | – 0.05 |
| – 7.4 | 60.10 | 47.50 | iShrRuMid IWR | .16p | ... | 12 | 54.75 | – 0.25 |
| – 4.7 | 79.40 | 64.52 | iShrRuMidVlu IWS | .30e | .4 | 8 | 72.96 | – 0.71 |
| – 22.6 | 80.16 | 40.25 | iShrRu1000G IWF | .29e | .6 | 1615 | 50 | + 0.16 |
| – 15.2 | 79.83 | 51.80 | iShrRu3000 IWV | .60e | 1.0 | 10431 | 61.43 | + 0.13 |
| – 8.7 | 103.80 | 73.50 | iShrRu2000 IWM | 1.21e | 1.4 | 2107 | 87.40 | – 0.30 |
| – 9.2 | 109.55 | 79.10 | iShrsSP400 IJH | 1.10e | 1.2 | 243 | 93.79 | – 0.04 |
| – 18.9 | 58.73 | 38.10 | iShrSPTSE6U IKC | .91e | 2.2 | 3 | 42.15 | + 0.70 |
| – 14.9 | 81.84 | 48 | iShrsSP500G IVW | .47e | .8 | 217 | 58.06 | + 0.24 |
| – 14.4 | 67 | 46.30 | iShrSP500V IVE | .96e | 1.8 | 558 | 54.24 | – 0.06 |
| – 15.2 | 143.56 | 85.25 | iShrSP400G IJK | .55e | .5 | 58 | 105.05 | – 0.15 |
| – 14.3 | 144.28 | 94.25 | iShrsSP500 IVV | 1.43e | 1.3 | 1156 | 112.60 | + 0.43 |
| – 4.7 | 118.29 | 88.25 | iShrsSP600 IJR | 1.65e | 1.6 | 241 | 103.05 | – 0.10 |
| + 1.4 | 90.04 | 76.08 | iShrsCohen&St ICF | 3.14e | 3.9 | 121 | 81.05 | – 0.63 |
| – 35.4 | 84.13 | 27.20 | NASDAQ100 QQQ | | ... | 726434 | 37.73 | – 0.02 |
| – 14.1 | 144.30 | 93.80 | SPDR SPY | 1.44e | 1.3 | 154569 | 112.72 | + 0.12 |
| – 8.8 | 100.80 | 71.50 | SPDR Mid MDY | .71e | .8 | 9205 | 86.06 | – 0.32 |
| – 1.8 | 24.63 | 17.05 | SPDR BscInd XLB | .94e | 4.5 | 92 | 21.04 | + 0.06 |
| – 9.5 | 30.81 | 21 | SPDR ConSvc XLV | .09e | .4 | 192 | 24.67 | – 0.15 |
| – 11.1 | 28.88 | 22.52 | SPDR ConStpl XLP | .31e | 1.2 | 230 | 25.39 | + 0.06 |
| + 0.8 | 29.35 | 20 | SPDR CycTrn XLY | .24e | .9 | 124 | 25.80 | – 0.14 |
| – 17.6 | 34.90 | 22.37 | SPDR Engy XLE | .48e | 1.8 | 6299 | 27.35 | + 0.52 |
| – 12.8 | 30.66 | 21.15 | SPDR Fncl XLF | .30e | 1.2 | 2636 | 25.72 | – 0.17 |
| – 17.4 | 32.66 | 20.40 | SPDR Indu XLI | .36e | 1.4 | 156 | 25.82 | – 0.09 |
| – 24.9 | 44.66 | 17.62 | SPDR Tch XLK | | ... | 9031 | 23.53 | – 0.09 |
| – 13.7 | 34.55 | 27.60 | SPDR Utils XLU | 1.16e | 4.1 | 459 | 28.64 | + 0.18 |
| – 13.4 | 85.06 | 55.30 | sTrackDJGlTitn DGT | .72e | 1.1 | 21 | 66.65 | – 0.38 |
| – 27.9 | 87.31 | 40 | sTrackDJLCapG ELG | .09e | .2 | 38 | 52.70 | ... |
| – 9.8 | 138.16 | 109.37 | sTrackDJLCapV ELV | 2.22e | 1.8 | 11 | 123.21 | – 0.45 |
| – 21.2 | 96.16 | 51.20 | sTrackDJSCapG DSG | | ... | 18 | 63.32 | – 0.58 |
| + 3.3 | 132.65 | 105.25 | sTrackDJSCapV DSV | 3.04e | 2.5 | 9 | 121.66 | – 0.63 |
| – 13.3 | 98.89 | 68.30 | sTrackFort500 FFF | 1.07e | 1.3 | 665 | 80.17 | + 0.19 |
| – 33.5 | 81.19 | 24 | sTrackFort e50 FEF | | ... | 37 | 33.06 | – 0.96 |
| – 28.0 | 95.56 | 34.96 | sTrackMSHTch35 MTK | | ... | 45 | 48.40 | + 0.32 |
| – 56.7 | 56.25 | 7.55 | sTrackMSInt MII | | ... | 10 | 12.08 | + 0.13 |
| + 1.6 | 126.70 | 109.70 | sTrackWlshREIT | 2.88e | 2.5 | 42 | 113.69 | – 0.31 |
| – 11.1 | 118 | 86.80 | VanguardTot VTI | .60e | .6 | 1037 | 102.08 | + 0.22 |

## NYSE

| YTD %CHG | 52 WEEKS HI | LO | STOCK (SYM) | DIV | YLD % | VOL 100S | CLOSE | NET CHG |
|---|---|---|---|---|---|---|---|---|
| – 15.7 | 73.70 | 48.20 | iShrSP100Gbl IOO | .57e | 1.0 | 22 | 58.77 | + 0.40 |

## CBOE

| YTD %CHG | 52 WEEKS HI | LO | STOCK (SYM) | DIV | YLD % | VOL 100S | CLOSE | NET CHG |
|---|---|---|---|---|---|---|---|---|
| – 15.8 | 76.13 | 47.72 | iShrsSP100 CBOE OEF | .15p | ... | 420 | 57.97 | + 0.40 |

# MITTS

Composite Regular Trading
Friday, November 9, 2001

## AMEX

| STOCK | SYM | VOL 100s | LAST | CHG |
|---|---|---|---|---|
| MerLySPDR06 | GWM | 20 | 9 | + 0.08 |
| MerLySemi | SME | 10 | 8.85 | – 0.25 |
| MerLyBbd07 | BDM | 17 | 7.55 | ... |
| MerLyNikkei | NML | 20 | 8.65 | ... |
| MerLyIntrnt07 | IHM | 1 | 7.72 | – 0.13 |
| MerLyRus04 | RUM | 63 | 10.44 | – 0.07 |
| MerLyBio07 | BHM | 25 | 9.25 | – 0.15 |
| MerLySPMI06 | MPF | 57 | 9.01 | + 0.11 |
| MerLyDJ06 | MDJ | 44 | 9.05 | – 0.07 |
| MerLyNik07 | MLJ | 10 | 8.15 | + 0.05 |

| STOCK | SYM | VOL 100s | LAST | CHG |
|---|---|---|---|---|
| MerLyGlbl04 | GMM | 1 | 8.92 | – 0.08 |
| MerLyNik05 | MLN | 67 | 9.50 | + 0.03 |
| MerLyNASD07 | MNM | 2 | 8.25 | ... |
| MerLyNikMI06 | NKM | 48 | 8.30 | – 0.18 |
| MerLyNikMI02 | MNN | 104 | 9.66 | – 0.09 |
| MerLyMai11 06 | FUM | 110 | 8.93 | – 0.07 |
| MerLySP05 | MLF | 2169 | 10.25 | – 0.07 |
| MerLySP06 | FML | 134 | 9.09 | + 0.07 |

## NYSE

| STOCK | SYM | VOL 100s | LAST | CHG |
|---|---|---|---|---|
| MerLySP07 | IEM | 1 | 11.20 | – 0.15 |
| MerLySP02 | MIM | 61 | 13.66 | – 0.09 |
| MerLyNik02 | JEM | 126 | 9.75 | + 0.06 |
| MerLyvSP 05 | MIJ | 45 | 10.25 | – 0.12 |

tax exempts are issues exempt from federal and state income taxes; triple tax exempts are issues exempt from federal, state, and city income taxes.) Single-state issues may lack the protection that wider diversification provides. Some unit investment trusts may contain bonds that are less than investment grade or are in default so that, as with all investments, some preliminary investigation is desirable.

Unit investment trusts are attractive investments for small investors, because they permit the investment of modest amounts in a diversified or predictable portfolio. Because bonds held by unit investment trusts may be callable, advertised high yields are not guaranteed. It is likely that older high-yielding securities will in fact be called before they mature, thereby reducing the yield available on the balance of the investment.

Because unit investment trusts are unmanaged (that is, there is no trust-level trading of portfolio securities), they have very low expenses. The median management fee for a conventional no-load fund is about 1.2 percent, whereas the median fee for a unit investment trust is about 0.2 percent.

Although these trusts typically impose sales charges and have limited life, in many cases investors who hold their units until maturity may roll them over into a new unit investment trust for a reduced fee.

## §16.8 Real Estate Investment Trusts

A real estate investment trust (REIT) is not strictly an investment company, but is similar in some respects. REITs invest in real estate and not in securities. They compete directly with investment companies for the small investor's dollars, because they provide a fair amount of instant diversification in relatively conservative real estate investments and a return that is typically competitive with or higher than mutual fund returns. A number of REITs are publicly held; about 85 of them are publicly traded on securities exchanges. As a result, interests in REITs are easy to buy and sell, and they provide the benefits of owning real estate without management responsibilities.

REITs have had a checkered career. In the 1970s and 1980s, they were sometimes formed to serve as tax shelters or to develop and construct commercial real estate ventures that usually failed. The form that is popular today is called an equity REIT and usually functions as a conservative manager of completed income-producing properties. Such a REIT may own 15 or 30 properties in a number of different communities. Although the managers take a cut of the income, the yield on well-managed REITs is attractive given the yields generally available on other conservative investments. If a REIT distributes substantially all its income to its investors, it is treated as a conduit in exactly the same way as investment companies are.

## §16.9 Hedge Funds

A hedge fund is in essence a private investment company. The typical hedge fund is a limited partnership with no more than 99 investors or with only investors with a net worth of $3,000,000 or more. Under federal law (the Investment Company Act of 1940), a fund with more than 100 investors must register and comply with an array of regulations unless the investors are qualified high net worth individuals or institutions. Thus hedge funds are often limited to 99 investors (and presumably one general partner) precisely to avoid such regulation.

The name comes from the hedging strategies pursued by the early funds. The original hedge fund, set up in the 1940s, invested half in long positions and half in short positions in an effort to minimize risk. Today, hedge funds are used more as a way to gain leverage, that is, as a way of using borrowed funds to augment the investment pool. Similar practices are severely restricted for registered funds. Federal law prohibits a registered fund from effecting short sales (with unimportant exceptions). Federal law also specifies that a registered company may have no more than a 1/2 debt/equity ratio. In contrast, hedge funds have been able to achieve leverage of 10/1 or even 100/1. One of the concerns about the proliferation of hedge funds is that through leveraging they are able to control a large percentage of the trading in important markets. Indeed, in 1999 a highly leveraged hedge fund, Long Term Capital Management, failed, and some feared that the entire world financial system might collapse without government intervention.

Although hedge funds are largely exempt from SEC regulation, they do in many cases fall within the jurisdiction of the Commodities Futures Trading Commission (CFTC), because their investments in commodities (such as stock index futures) qualify them as commodities pools. The CFTC has, however, routinely granted exemptions from its rules for hedge funds.

Hedge funds typically require a large investment ($500,000 or more) from each investor and offer limited withdrawal privileges. The managers of the fund usually take a large percentage of gains (often as much 20 percent) as their compensation. Managers often receive no compensation unless there are gains, and in many cases carryover losses must be made up before any compensation may be paid (the "high water mark" rule). Most hedge funds seem to be quite conservatively managed (as one might expect of a fund with very wealthy clients) and seem on the average to beat the broader market by a few percentage points. Because hedge funds are unregulated, those who run them are beyond the SEC's supervisory jurisdiction.

## §16.10  Risk in Mutual Funds

Mutual funds provide instant diversification for the small investor at relatively nominal cost. The major problems with the small investor's use of this investment vehicle are, first, the difficulty of ascertaining the actual cost of alternative mutual fund investments, and second, the bewildering variety of different families of funds, and the equally bewildering variety of funds with varying investment objectives within each family.

Although one of the primary reasons for investing in a mutual fund is diversification, some funds pursue a strategy of minimal diversification. These funds invest in 35 to 50 stocks, rather than the typical 200 to 500, on the theory that fund managers can more easily follow the stocks in the portfolio and structure the portfolio better in terms of overall performance.

Risk is arguably the most important factor for an investor to consider when choosing an investment, but it is often difficult to determine the risk level of a specific mutual fund, although most funds are sufficiently diversified so that there is little risk from any individual stock. But every fund carries some level of market risk. If it is mostly invested in well-established companies, fund values will tend to move by the same or even lesser percentages than broad-based market indexes. If the fund is invested in smaller and younger growth companies, the value of a share in the fund will usually exhibit wider swings than the market as a whole. An investor has little to go on other than the fund name and announced strategy (both of which tend to be unreliable) and the raw listing of stocks in the portfolio (which is typically subject to a 60-day delay).

Attempts to quantify mutual fund risk have been controversial, with much disagreement about what to quantify. A particular fund may have low risk by one measure but high risk by another.

A domestic stock fund may have considerable volatility. But then the question arises how to measure volatility risk. One possibility is standard deviation, a statistical measure that blends the probability of price swings with their size to give a single figure (usually stated in percentage form) that is roughly equal to price changes that may be experienced two-thirds of the time. In other words, standard deviation provides a measure of what might be called normal price swings.

Another possible measure of a fund's risk is its **beta coefficient**. The beta coefficient is a measure of the tendency of the fund to move with changes in some benchmark index. Thus, a fund with a beta of 1.0 moves by the same percentage as the market, whether up or down. A fund with a beta of 2.0 moves twice as much, and a fund with a beta of 0.5 moves half as much. For example, if the S&P 500 is up by 2 percent on a given day, a fund with a beta of 2.0 should be up by 4 percent, while a fund with a beta of 0.5 should be up by 1 percent. The same relationship should hold on the downside.

With both standard deviation and beta, an open question is the period of time over which one looks to see how the fund has performed. Proposals have focused on one year and five years, while one of the major mutual fund rating agencies prefers three years. The period of time chosen may lead to very different answers, which is why fund managers tend to use several different time periods when they attempt to assess risk. Of course, there is no reason that several results not be disclosed to investors. But it is unclear how an investor should interpret information that a fund has a beta of (say) 2.0 over the last five years but only 1.0 over the last year. Such information could indicate either that the fund has become more conservative or that the fund contains a few stocks that during the past year moved against the market.

One way to deal with the problem of changing fund risk is to require mutual fund prospectuses be updated monthly. Presumably, risk measurement would then be based on the portfolio as it stands on the date of filing. That is, a mutual fund would be required to calculate what its performance in prior periods would have been if it had held the stocks in its current portfolio during those earlier periods. The problem with this disclosure, however, is that a fund that seeks to buy distressed stocks that have fallen dramatically in price on the theory that they are now undervalued would appear to be very risky, even though the drop in price occurred before the fund's acquisition. On the other hand, if the acquired stocks fell in price at a time when the rest of the market was rising, inclusion of such stocks in the fund's portfolio could make the fund appear to be quite conservative. And various possible combinations of these effects could lead to any result in between.

One major mutual fund rating agency, Morningstar, uses six different factors to assess fund risk: stock concentration, sector concentration, standard deviation, beta, p/e ratio, and highest monthly loss. But these factors do not capture all forms of risk. For example, one manager confided that he was overconcentrated in stocks of companies with large amounts of debt and that as a result the fund had performed poorly because investors unexpectedly began to shun such companies.

With mutual funds, one cannot always trust the label. Popular words— "growth," "value," "aggressive growth," and "balanced"—do not have precise definitions and portfolios described by any of these terms may include a variety of different securities with widely varying risk and yield characteristics. "Growth" typically refers to shares whose earnings are expected to grow faster than average over time, while "value" refers to shares that are attractively priced on the basis of traditional value measures such as dividend yield, price-earnings (P/E) ratios, or price-to-book values. However, many "growth" funds have extensive holdings of income-producing stock, while "value" funds may have shares that are very "pricey" based on traditional measures. A person who desires a "low risk" investment may inadvertently end up with a fund that has a much higher degree of risk than expected. One "balanced" fund, for example, has an average P/E ratio as high as 33 and a price-to-book ratio of 11 to 1. These are astronomical numbers when compared with the S&P 500 with a P/E ratio of 19 and a price-to-book ratio of 3.8 to 1. A "balanced" fund, one would think, would be relatively similar to the S&P index.

Although there is no express legal requirement that a mutual fund be accurately named, each fund must state its avowed investment policy in its articles of incorporation. Statements of purpose can be quite general and can leave a lot of wiggle room. One worry about mutual fund investing is whether a fund will in fact pursue the strategies that are implicit in its name or that are stated (or suggested) in sales literature. On the other hand, it is entirely possible that a fund manager may in good faith decide that the announced strategy is imprudent at some point. A too-tightly worded statement of purpose may prevent the manager from serving investors well. In an effort to deal with these concerns, eight large mutual fund managers, acting through the Investment Company Institute (ICI), the industry's trade association, have developed a two-page fund profile to be distributed in tandem with the fund prospectus.

## §16.11 Mutual Fund Investment Strategies

Practically speaking, it makes little sense for a small investor to worry about past fund performance. Theory suggests that picking a fund based on past performance is rather like trying to predict the next flip of a coin on the basis of past flips. Several long-term studies of mutual fund performance have shown that funds do not beat the market any more often or consistently than one would expect as a matter of statistical chance. This is not, however, an especially surprising finding. The "market" is, after all, nothing more than the traders who compose it. Thus, the idea that on the average one will do about the average is to be expected. The efficient market theory, therefore, does not imply that no fund will ever beat the market several years in a row. Rather, it simply means that the number of funds that do so will be about what one would expect at random. This may be one reason why fund managers set up several funds with different focuses. The more funds one has under management, the better the chances that one will significantly outperform the market and then can be used to promote sales in future years.

If the investor ignores performance, however, what should the investor consider? The answer is that when choosing a mutual fund, the single most important consideration, after deciding the level of risk one wants, is the amount of fees and expenses. Such information is readily available in the financial press and through brokerage houses.

As discussed above, there are essentially four types of fees that a mutual fund may charge: a sales load, an exit fee, a management fee, and a 12b-1 fee. The first two are direct charges to investors, while the latter two are charges borne by the fund. In addition, the fund pays brokerage commissions on individual trades. Some indication of the extent of these expenses can be found in the fund's turnover ratio. Most funds turn over their portfolios about once a year, but some funds turn over two or more times in a year. A few have turnovers of less than once a year. Other things being equal, a fund with low turnover is likely to perform better than one with high turnover under the efficient market theory.

Some brokerage firms charge exit fees upon the transfer of funds from one mutual fund family to another or from one brokerage firm to another. A common complaint about these fees is that brokers do not disclose their existence when persuading the investor to make the initial investment.

A number of former no-load funds now levy exit fees, marketing fees, distribution fees, and low loads of perhaps 3 percent. Nevertheless, many true no-load mutual funds still exist. Exit fees should be distinguished from sales loads. In many cases, exit fees are charged only if the investor redeems within a relatively short period of time. Thus, the fee may work to the advantage of investors by discouraging redemptions and allowing the fund manager to invest more funds in longer-term investments rather than in cash. Moreover, in some cases exit fees are added to the fund and not paid to the manager or broker (as sales loads are). For the investor who is prepared to hold a fund investment for the long haul, exit fees may therefore actually increase return.

Mutual funds often offer investors a choice as to how fees are to be paid: either a traditional front-end load or an exit fee coupled with a 12b-1 fee drawn from annual earnings. The choice between the two will depend on how long the investor wants to stay in the investment.

For example, a fund might offer Class A shares with a 6.5 percent upfront load, or Class B shares with no upfront load, but a one percent 12b-1 fee plus a declining exit fee that begins at 4 percent. In the long run, these should come out to about the same thing, but there may be a significant difference in the short run. The following table, based on a $10,000 investment and assuming a 10 percent return, shows how this might work:

### Value of Shares if Redeemed at Year-End

| Year | Class A<br>(6.5% front end load) | Class B<br>(1% 12b-1 fee plus<br>4% declining exit fee) |
|---|---|---|
| 1 | $10,285 | $10,459 |
| 2 | 11,314 | 11,514 |
| 3 | 12,445 | 12,674 |
| 4 | 13,689 | 13,949 |
| 5 | 15,058 | 15,351 |
| 6 | 16,364 | 16,725 |
| 7 | 18,221 | 18,222 |
| 8 | 20,043 | 19,853 |

In this example, the hefty upfront charge applied to Class A shares means that the Class B shares are $174 ahead of the Class A after one year if the fund shares are sold at that time. The advantage of Class B continues for seven years. After that time the continuing 12b-1 charge pushes the Class B share permanently below the Class A shares.

As a rule of thumb, if a fund has a front-end load of 4.5 percent or less, it is usually cheaper to pay the load than a one percent 12b-1 fee. For investors that cash out early, it is usually cheaper to pay the 12b-1 charge than a 5 percent or more front-end load, unless there is a heavy exit fee in addition to the 12b-1 charge. When Rule 12b-1 was originally approved, the assumption of the SEC was that these charges would permit more selling effort, more growth in the size of funds, and a concomitant reduction in fees. Everything has happened as expected, except the reduction in fees.

Similar considerations of fees and expenses should be paramount in choosing a variable annuity. (As discussed in the earlier chapter on annuities and retirement plans, annuities are a close substitute for mutual funds.) Variable annuity operating expenses tend to be somewhat higher than expense ratios for mutual funds, but this difference results at least partly from the fact that a variable annuity also carries a death benefit. Moreover, a variable annuity grows tax free, while gains on a mutual fund may be reduced by taxes, although usually only to the extent of distributions. Sales and redemption charges in the insurance industry also tend to be higher than sales loads and exit fees in the mutual fund industry. Moreover, comparative information is very difficult to come by for insurance companies, in part because they are regulated state by state. The *Wall Street Journal* runs a weekly listing of prices, returns, and operating expenses for most major variable annuities.

In addition to fees and expenses, however, another very important factor in choosing an insurance company is the adequacy of its capitalization. Until recently, this information was not assembled in any standardized fashion, but a uniform formula for calculating the risk-based capital ratio has now been promulgated by the National Association of Insurance Commissioners for use in determining when state regulators should step in to "rehabilitate" an ailing company. Ironically, insurers have generally been forbidden from disclosing this information themselves, because state regulators have been concerned that it will be used to persuade consumers that insurers are somehow safer than they really are. The information is available, however, through private advisory services and some public rating firms.

Because of the way they are organized, mutual funds, including both open-end and closed-end funds do not have the risk of undercapitalization that goes with insurance companies. A mutual fund holds its investments in trust for the investor-shareowners, and there is no commingling of investments for other purposes (e.g., underwriting the insurance component of a whole life policy). Moreover, an open-end mutual fund is required to pay out the net asset value of a share (less any redemption fee) on demand. On the other hand, this potential for cash outflow on demand may lead an open-end mutual fund to keep more of its funds in cash. Closed-end funds that may only be liquidated by selling shares to other investors in a secondary market such as the NYSE need not worry about cash-outs. But such funds usually trade at less than their net asset value.

Because many mutual funds are sold through brokers, conflict of interest problems may arise. Specifically, brokers may be tempted to recommend that investors buy the funds that carry the highest commissions or that they sell one mutual fund and buy another in order to generate additional commissions. The practice of churning mutual funds to generate commissions is sometimes referred to as **twisting**, and because of the high sales loads that some funds carry, it can be a greater drain on return than conventional churning of individual stocks. As a general rule, trading can only rarely be justified in connection with a mutual fund or other less risky investment precisely because they are less risky and therefore tend to change in price less than individual stocks. On the other hand, when an investor decides to switch from (say) a growth strategy to an income strategy, then switching mutual funds may make sense.

The decision whether to invest through a mutual fund or in individual stocks appears to be significantly related to the generation in which one grew up. Babyboomers seem to prefer investing through funds, whereas their parents appear to prefer individual investing. It is unclear what "Generation X" will turn out to prefer. But if trends hold, investment dollars will generally flow into funds and out of individual accounts.

Individual investors often diversify among different classes or categories of investments in order to achieve a blended risk and return combination and to minimize the effects of a decline in value of any one category of investment. A plausible balanced portfolio for an investor with capital in the range of $100,000 might include 25 percent in riskless insured investments, 25 percent in long-term bonds or mutual funds specializing in longer-term bonds, 40 percent in conservative stocks with some growth potential, and 10 percent in individual growth stock or strongly growth-oriented mutual funds. These percentages may change significantly, of course, with specific investment goals and with changes in economic conditions. A relatively young investor, for example, may have a larger percentage in growth stocks and a smaller percentage in lower-yielding long-term bonds or bond funds.

Finally, it is unclear that it makes sense to diversify among mutual funds. To the extent that the investor mixes mutual funds of differing objectives (i.e., with differing risks), all that one is doing is creating some sort of blended return for a unique level of risk. It is unlikely that a small investor will be able to fine-tune risk at this level on any rational basis. To the extent that the investor mixes mutual funds with similar investment objectives in hopes of gaining more diversification, it is doubtful that diversification makes much difference beyond 200 to 300 different stocks. Moreover, because many funds are indexed to the market (either fully or largely), it is unclear whether one does in fact gain any additional diversification. In many cases, the different funds will have invested in the same underlying stocks and other instruments so that the net result of diversifying among funds will simply be the multiplication of record-keeping headaches for the investor. On the other hand, if the strategy is to construct a customized portfolio using **sector funds**, that is, to invest industry by industry or country by country rather than company by company, then purchasing several mutual funds may make sense. Moreover, to the extent the investor can costlessly move among mutual funds with differing investment strategies, it is possible to play one's hunches about market movements without penalty unless, of course, one guesses wrong. But if one wants to invest in managed funds, it may make sense to diversify among funds to some extent in order to reduce the risk that one fund manager may pursue a particularly disastrous strategy or may diverge from the fund's announced strategy.

## §16.12  Money Market Funds

One type of mutual fund that is extremely popular is the money market fund. This investment device is the virtual equivalent of an uninsured savings account. The development of this type of mutual fund is a good illustration of the problems of government regulation when faced with free market forces. For many years the United States government regulated the maximum interest rates that commercial banks and savings and loan associations could pay on savings accounts. The maximum rate was 5½ percent. This created no real problem until the early 1980s, when competitive interest rates rose to 12 percent or higher in some areas. At first, regulated banks and savings and loan associations were overjoyed, as they paid 5½ percent interest on deposits which they could lend out at rates as high as 15 or 16 percent. That joy proved to be very short-lived, however, as mutual fund managers, investment banks, and brokerage firms devised a new type of mutual fund that promised market rates of interest for depositors in a virtually risk-free investment. All at once, the regulated banks and savings and loan associations were faced with a severe liquidity crisis as millions of savers withdrew funds from regulated savings accounts in order to invest them in these new accounts. The federal government quickly realized that if these long-standing financial institutions were to survive at all, they would have to be permitted to compete effectively with the new-fangled money market funds for savings. Thus, the development of the money market fund was the cause for deregulation of bank interest rates in the early 1980s. The competitive bank and savings and loan programs that were developed in response to the money market fund are described in the following section.

A money market fund is a mutual fund that invests only in short-term, virtually riskless investments. These funds bear names such as "cash management accounts" or "liquid assets funds." Most money market funds are very large, with hundreds of millions or billions of dollars of assets. They invest in such items as negotiable bank certificates of deposit issued by large commercial banks, bankers' acceptances, commercial paper, short-term time deposits with foreign banks, and U.S. treasury notes and bills. Investments are usually in units of at least $10,000,000, and often in amounts of $100,000,000 or more. Because all of these investments have very short maturities, measured in days rather than months or years, the risk of default or collapse is very low. Money market funds may also have specialized portfolios to a limited extent. Some funds invest solely in short-term tax-exempt municipal anticipation notes or similar securities in order to provide a tax-exempt yield on a pure money market fund investment. Of course, the yield on tax-exempt funds is significantly lower than the yield on taxable money market funds.

One unique aspect of money market funds is that the trading unit is one dollar and earnings are reflected not by increases in the value of the trading unit but by adding more trading units to the account. The result is that an investor who holds, for example, 3,456 shares of a money market fund thinks in terms of having a deposit of $3,456. Additional trading units are added to the fund in proportion to its size in one dollar units. Depositors are permitted to write checks on the account without limitation, although small checks under $100 are usually prohibited. Whenever a check is presented, the required number of trading units are redeemed into dollars. The whole arrangement is indeed very close to a bank account. Although money market funds are not insured against loss by the United States government, investment advisers generally view these investments as cash equivalents, given the gilt-edged nature of the investments that form the portfolios of these funds and the short maturity periods.

Nevertheless, in 1990, a major publicly held company, Integrated Resources, defaulted on its commercial paper, leaving two money market funds facing potential losses that could have reduced the net asset value of a share below one dollar. In both cases, the parent companies immediately rushed in to make up the losses, leaving the money market funds' record of never having lost money intact. The immediate consequence was that money market funds upgraded the quality of the commercial paper in their portfolios. The secondary consequence was that issuers of commercial paper with lower credit ratings found it increasingly difficult to raise working capital by issuing commercial paper. Several other money market funds also might have **broken the buck** (often because of investments in derivatives), but they were propped up by their sponsors with infusions of cash. One small money market fund that broke the buck went out of business in 1994, paying investors a little over $0.90 per share. (The fund dealt exclusively with a partnership of banks that owned the fund.) Government-only funds invest exclusively in securities issued by the

United States government and its agencies. An extremely risk-averse investor might consider investing in one of these funds because the risk of default is virtually eliminated. The significance of breaking the buck lies in the fact that most investors treat such funds as equivalent to a checking or savings account.

## §16.13 Insured Money Market Accounts and Certificates of Deposit

Interest-bearing deposits in commercial banks and savings and loans institutions are virtually riskless investments to the extent they are insured by the Federal Deposit Insurance Corporation (FDIC). The maximum deposit currently covered is $100,000. Banks and thrifts now offer a variety of different accounts; the two most widely used are a traditional **passbook account** that pays perhaps 4 percent per year and requires no minimum balance, and an account with a minimum balance (often $2,000) that pays floating interest rates that generally depend on market interest rates. The latter type of account may be called a **money market account**, a **money market checking account**, or a variety of other names that emphasize that it provides a floating interest rate based on market rates; it is the traditional banking institutions' response to the money market fund described in the previous section. Usually a depositor is entitled to write a limited number of checks on the account without penalty or service charge. Some institutions may also provide free transferability from a money market account to a checking account at the same institution, or vice versa. Some accounts provide an automatic periodic transfer of excess funds in a checking account to a money market account. This is called a **sweep**. Traditional checking accounts are non-interest-bearing and excess funds should not be deposited in them.

Banks and savings institutions also offer competitive interest rates on **certificates of deposit** (**CDs**) that pay somewhat higher interest rates than on passbook or money market accounts. CDs are usually issued in round-number denominations such as $1,000, $5,000, $10,000, and larger amounts. Interest rates on larger-denomination CDs may be somewhat higher than on smaller denominations. A CD differs from a traditional interest-bearing savings account in that the investor agrees to leave the specified amount with the bank for a specified period (e.g., one month, six months, a year, or longer). Withdrawals before the expiration of the period are usually permitted subject to a forfeiture of a substantial portion of the interest otherwise earned.

When investing sums in excess of $100,000, the federally insured bank account or CD does not provide protection against a partial loss in the event of bank failure. Although bank failures may seem to be a remote possibility, when dealing with large sums of money even remote risks should be avoided. If the amount involved is not too large, complete protection can be obtained by making separate $100,000 deposits in different insured institutions or in accounts under different names in a single institution.

When the amount is so large that it is unwieldy to break it into $100,000 units, there are alternative investments that are either riskless or carry such slight risk of default that they are viewed as riskless. These investments include Treasury bills or notes and high-quality **commercial paper**. Commercial paper is unsecured debt maturing on a specific day in the future no more than nine months from the date of issue. Commercial paper that large finance companies or major industrial corporations issue is also generally viewed as a risk-free short-term investment. The yield is somewhat higher than on Treasury bills, which are entirely risk-free.

A similar investment is a **bankers' acceptance**—a short-term interest-bearing note whose payment has been guaranteed by a major commercial bank. Acceptances arise out of commercial transactions, usually large international sales transactions. Payment may also be guaranteed by the parties to the underlying transaction and possibly by a lien on the goods themselves. Like high-quality commercial paper, bankers' acceptances are generally viewed as risk-free; the yield is also somewhat higher than on Treasury bills.

A person investing very large sums of money on a short-term basis (over $100,000) may consider a **repurchase agreement** (**repo**). A repo is a loan structured as a sale; a bank "sells" an investor riskless securities—usually Treasury instruments—while simultaneously agreeing to buy them back at a later date for a higher price. The difference in price represents interest to the investor. Repos may be overnight transactions or may continue for as long as a year.

Repos are widely used to avoid the risk of bank failure on investments in excess of $100,000. The theory is that if the bank fails while a repo is open, the customer simply keeps the securities sold to it. In this kind of transaction, it is therefore important that the securities involved be in some way set aside for the investor, usually through a third-party escrow account. The investor should also get a list of the securities sold, including certificate numbers. Otherwise, a bankruptcy trustee or receiver may later argue that the transaction was actually an unsecured loan. Repos generally earn somewhat more than banks pay on insured CDs for the same period.

A **reverse repo** is a repo from the standpoint of the dealer who is seeking to borrow securities in order to sell them. A dealer wishes to sell securities it borrows when it anticipates a price decline so that it can replace the securities at a lower price. In other words, it wishes to engage in a short sale of the securities that are the subject of the transaction.

During periods of low interest rates, the returns available on bank CDs may fall to unusually low levels because of the relative lack of competition for such funds. Most who invest in CDs do not move quickly from bank to bank or to other investments, and banks may have much less need for CD funds during low-interest periods. Thus banks may cut the rates they offer for these funds more than the amount rates are falling in the broader market.

At the very least, one should check the rates being offered at several banks before **rolling over** a CD (i.e., before redepositing the principal in a new CD upon maturity of the old CD). Many financial publications publish the highest rates being offered around the country, so one is not limited to local banks. In addition, many securities firms sell **brokered CDs**. The securities firm negotiates with a bank to offer an attractive interest rate in exchange for the securities firm's finding depositors. The securities firm in effect sells participations in these CDs that often pay higher returns than those available to individuals at a bank.

Although many brokered CDs are insured by the FDIC, some investments in brokered CDs may be part of a larger CD that may be partially uninsured.

Other relatively safe investments include short-term bond funds, tax-exempt funds, conservative stock funds, and money market funds. Although these investments are not guaranteed, they carry very low levels of risk because of the quality of the issuers and because of diversification. Generally speaking, bigger funds are better than smaller funds in that a smaller fund may suffer a rash of withdrawals that requires the fund to dispose of its better-quality securities.

When investing in a bond fund it is important to check the fund's **duration**. Duration is a measure of the average length of time over which the bonds in the fund will mature. The longer a fund's average duration, the more sensitive the fund is to interest rate changes. A short time to maturity means that the prospect of principal repayment looms relatively large in valuing the bond. The point is that the longer the period until maturity, the more important the present value of the periodic payments becomes. Thus if interest rates in the economy rise, the value of a longer-term fund will fall more quickly than the value of a similar shorter-term fund. A fund with a longer duration is therefore riskier than a fund with a shorter duration.

Another source of higher returns in periods of low interest rates is lending to family members who otherwise would borrow funds from a bank or other commercial source. Investing, after all, really is lending sums of money to banks or other firms. If a family member has a genuine need and is responsible, why not cut out the middle person? The lender should be able to get a higher rate than a bank would pay on a deposit, and the borrower should be able to get a lower rate than a bank would charge for interest. This same idea leads many small business owners to lend money to their businesses (although in the context of business, there may be additional tax considerations depending on the legal form of the business). The idea of intrafamily lending and borrowing as a substitute for investing assumes that family members will charge and pay interest at or near market rates. It is not uncommon to feel that charging interest is for the commercial world and not something that family members should insist on or expect. But if an intrafamily loan is prompted by a family member's need for an investment opportunity and benefits the borrowing family member, such feelings are irrational and unrealistic. If such feelings cannot be overcome, however, it is better to stick to commercial sources.

An intrafamily loan may take the form of a home equity loan, which allows the borrower to deduct interest payments for tax purposes. Presumably, an intrafamily home equity loan may be set up even if a commercial home equity loan is already outstanding. The only limitation is that the total amount outstanding may not exceed the purchase price of the house plus improvements. Of course, such a loan would need to be junior to any existing commercial loan. That is, such a loan would need to be secured by a third mortgage if there is a first mortgage and another home equity loan outstanding.

When making an intrafamily loan, it is particularly important to follow the formalities for tax purposes. Following formalities is also important because in the event of the borrower's bankruptcy, it is more likely that the loan will be respected as a bona fide claim and not merely as an effort to divert assets.

Moreover, the parties are more likely to respect the relationship if it is formalized. In the case of a home equity loan, it is important to check the terms of the senior mortgages to be sure that additional borrowing is allowed. If it is not, such a loan may constitute an event of default and trigger a demand for payment of the first mortgage.

## §16.14 Individual Investing

Despite the wide variety of investment services and products available, many small investors continue to manage their own portfolios. Indeed, statistics indicate that roughly half of all securities are held and traded by individual investors. Although the purchase of mutual fund shares is generally sound advice for the small investor, it is possible to build a portfolio with reasonable diversification and minimum transaction costs by investing, say, $50,000 in 20 round lots of unrelated stocks trading for about $25 each and by scrupulously resisting the temptation to trade.

Is this worth the effort, given the easy availability of mutual funds? Probably not for most investors if one includes the value of the investor's time. But there are several reasons why managing one's own portfolio, with or without the help of an investment adviser, may make sense for some investors. For one thing, an individual investor may be able to take on more risk (through margin borrowing or otherwise) than can be had through a mutual fund. It is possible, however, to buy mutual funds on margin through some brokerage houses. Moreover, the investor can often achieve a higher level of tax deferral simply by buying and holding growth stocks, although such a strategy also increases risk. Taxes may also be minimized by careful timing of sales of gainers and losers, so that during any given tax year, capital gains roughly equal capital losses. Presumably, mutual funds also seek to balance gains and losses to minimize taxes for their investors, though it is obviously impossible for a fund to adjust for other aspects of an individual's tax situation.

Other advantages of individual investing include control over investment strategy and the ability to invest based on one's own views or insights into particular segments of the market. By managing one's own account, the expenses that go with investing in mutual funds can be avoided. Although individual investors generally pay commissions that are higher than those paid by mutual funds, it is unwise to trade in an effort to beat the market anyway. In addition, it is always possible to minimize commissions by using a discount broker when it is necessary to trade for tax planning or portfolio balancing purposes. Moreover, mutual funds sometimes pay higher commissions than necessary in exchange for **soft-dollar** services such as customized investment advice that is sometimes of dubious value. (Indeed such services are sometimes conveniently offered to fund managers at attractive resort locations or on a cruise.)

Perhaps more important than commission rates is the frequency of trading (or **turnover**). An informal review of no-load growth funds suggests that a turnover rate between 100 and 200 percent is quite normal. Moreover, many fund managers engage in **window dressing** or selling off stocks that have performed poorly just before the end of a reporting period in order to eliminate those stocks from the portfolio as reported to shareholders. In other words, some funds may choose to sell at a low price just to avoid controversy.

The individual investor may also enjoy increased flexibility in trading. Large funds necessarily hold large blocks of shares in individual companies and often cannot trade quickly, because the market reacts to big trades. It has been suggested that mutual funds vastly understate trading costs, because calculations routinely ignore the price effect of trading. For example, in one reported case, speculators sold short stocks held by a large mutual fund that had announced that it was almost fully invested, because it was thought likely to liquidate some of its holdings.

A related worry about mutual funds is that they may be overdiversified. A little diversification goes a long way. Studies indicate that 20 different stocks are enough to eliminate virtually all company-specific risk as long as the stocks are spread among industries. A fund that is invested in 500 different stocks cannot follow all of these stocks as closely as a fund that holds only 50 stocks. Moreover, funds that grow very large may be forced to buy riskier securities at the fringes in order to maintain portfolio balance. Also, if a large fund were to experience significant withdrawals, it might well choose to sell the most liquid (and presumably safest) securities first (on the theory that such sales will entail the smallest losses), even though the effect is to increase the risk in the fund. These tactics led to the closing of one money market fund. There is no reason that a similar dynamic could not befall a stock fund.

Finally, advocates argue that if diversification makes sense, more diversification makes more sense, and that one should therefore diversify globally over a wide variety of investment types. But academic studies have raised questions about the wisdom of global diversification, at least in down markets, because foreign markets tend to follow U.S. markets when prices fall. As for diversifying among more widely differing investments, such a strategy does not permit fine-tuning of risk. If everybody invested in a portfolio of everything, everyone would enjoy the same return. But clearly some investors are willing to take more risk for more return. In short, the logic of diversification can be taken too far, and there must be some point at which further diversification makes no sense.

Although the advantages of individual investing may seem marginal, on balance it appears that an investor who holds a diversified portfolio and refrains from trading except when absolutely necessary to balance the portfolio or to gain tax advantages may do better over the very long haul than the typical mutual fund investor.

Many brokers and financial planners advise investing a specific amount at regular intervals, say, $100 every pay period. This strategy is called **dollar cost averaging**. This plan may protect the investor from the dangers of investing large amounts at a market peak and failing to invest at a market trough. Dollar cost averaging each month results in the investor buying more shares when prices are low and fewer shares when prices are high.

Although regular investing may be a good way to discipline oneself to save, the advantages of dollar cost averaging are more psychological than real.

469

Indeed, academic studies have found that an investor would do better most of the time by putting all available funds into the market at once rather than spreading the investments out over time. Thus, if one finds that for one reason or another it is necessary to invest a large sum of money, it is better to invest it all immediately. If one desires to invest in the stock or bond market but wants to take one's time deciding precisely how, one may buy stock index or bond futures to lock in current market levels.

Individual investing is a broad concept and a wide variety of arrangements may be made with brokers regarding how one's account is handled. Moreover, there are many different kinds of brokerage houses, ranging from full-service firms to no-frills discounters. A full-service brokerage house offers research and investment advice, whereas the no-frills discounter does not. A full-service house may also offer other benefits. For example, if the firm has an investment banking department that underwrites offerings, an investor who has an account at that firm may be offered shares in these offerings, whereas investors at other firms may only be able to buy in the secondary market at higher prices.

When opening an account, NASD rules require a brokerage house to obtain certain information from the investor that is designed to help determine the customer's sophistication, investment goals, and capacity to bear risk. With respect to risk, the broker will want to know (quite legitimately) about income, net worth, dependents, and other personal factors. Similar information may be required if the customer wishes to trade in different securities (such as options) or to open a margin account.

Most full-service brokerage houses offer both **discretionary accounts** and **nondiscretionary accounts**. A discretionary account allows the broker to order trades without consulting with the investor. Discretionary accounts are increasingly rare and probably undesirable in a world in which independent investment advisers are readily available. Retaining an investment adviser (who typically charges a percentage fee based on the size of the account being handled) will often more than pay for itself in saved commissions and fees at the brokerage level. Moreover, an investment adviser and a broker will monitor each other's recommendations and may thus avoid problems that might arise with an individual account manager acting alone, such as overtrading an account or investing in high-commission, high-risk securities. It is a good idea when opening an account to read and retain a copy of all forms executed in connection with the account. These forms explain the customer's rights and obligations in great detail, and establish a record of the customer's investment goals that may be crucial if a dispute later arises about the handling of the account.

## §16.15  Commission Rates, Best Execution, and Churning

The hazards of individual investing should not be underestimated. Individual investors pay much higher commission rates than mutual funds do, and commissions often are not clearly stated on monthly statements or confirmation slips. A large institutional investor may pay as little as one cent a share, whereas an individual investor making a $10,000 trade may pay $8 to $10 at a discount broker or as much as $200 at a full-service broker. In all fairness, however, the trade at the discount broker may not be at the best possible price, so the overall difference in price may be less dramatic than first appears.

With respect to OTC stocks, many brokers charge a commission even for stocks in which they make a market. In addition, when individual investors purchase or sell OTC stocks and bonds, they usually pay the ask price when they buy and receive the bid price when they sell, while institutional investors can usually negotiate a price between the quotes. In other words, individual investors do not get **best execution**.

The same is increasingly true of NYSE stocks. Stocks listed on or after April 19, 1979, may be traded away from the exchange, a practice called **off-board trading**. This trading has led to the development of competing market makers who actively seek "order flow" and sometimes pay a small finder's fee to referring brokers for orders sent to them rather than to the exchange floor. The practice is known as **payment for order flow**. As with ordinary OTC orders, these orders are executed at (rather than between) the quotes (which is why market makers are willing to pay for referrals). In early 1995, the SEC reacted to payment for order flow by adopting a rule requiring disclosure in investor trade confirmations of the aggregate referral fees that the broker receives but did not require disclosure of the fee that the specific trade generated.

Although quotes are readily available for stocks (so that one can at least know what the spread is), it can be difficult to find out what the spread is for bonds. Most bonds are bought and sold in-house by brokerage firms. Moreover, trading in bonds tends to be more one-sided. Investors usually buy and hold bonds, and thus brokerage houses tend to sell many more bonds than they buy.

The SEC has taken steps to encourage exchange trading of bonds, but it is unclear whether a significant exchange-based market will develop. Brokers often tout bonds they are offering as being commission-free, but clearly they have no reason to sell products that do not make them money somehow. Thus, it is virtually never the case that one can immediately sell a bond back to the broker for the full price paid. The difference may be thought of as either a spread or a commission, but as far as the investor is concerned it is the same thing—a transaction cost.

In the end, inferior execution may not be that big a problem for most individual investors. A ten-cent difference on a $20 stock is 0.5 percent, which, given average gains for stocks over the long haul, will be recouped in less than a month. Nevertheless, the difference is just another way that trading costs mount up for the individual investor.

One of the most common problems experienced by individual investors is excessive trading or **churning**. Most brokers are compensated solely by commissions on trades actually made. Although most brokerage houses pay their salespeople a modest salary for a year or so during training or when starting out, most houses pay no base salary at all thereafter. Thus, a broker makes money only if customers trade. To be sure, it is always up to the customer in the end whether to trade (except in the case of a discretionary account), but investors often place trust in their brokers and follow their advice quite blindly (in some cases seemingly ignoring the commissions that are subtracted from their accounts).

Many brokerage firms have responded to the danger of churning by their brokers by offering so-called wrap accounts to customers who engage in active trading. With a wrap account, an active trader may pay a fixed fee periodically instead of commissions on individual trades.

## §16.16 Investment Advice

In addition to churning, another danger of individual investing is the difficulty of obtaining reliable advice about investments. Many investors who choose to maintain their own portfolio do so because they think a good broker will occasionally have access to nonpublic information, or at the very least will learn of material information before the market price reflects the news. Trading on inside information is clearly illegal if disclosure of the information constitutes a breach of fiduciary duty. Although an investor who merely gains the benefit of inside information without reason to know that advice is based on it probably will not be held liable, the risk to the broker and the brokerage house is considerable. One should therefore be skeptical about any hint that information is ahead of the market and should always ask oneself why such information is offered. Often, the answer will be that the broker is simply trying to generate a trade and a commission.

As a practical matter, there is virtually no way for a small investor to be ahead of the market with respect to new information. Companies routinely discuss developments by conference call with brokers and analysts. The result is that the market almost always adjusts to information before it can filter down to the investor on the street. Even if the information is relatively fresh, it is unlikely that one can act fast enough if the broker is required to consult with the investor. Indeed, it is unlikely that a broker who is authorized to act alone can act with enough speed to capture much of a benefit. In any event, the hazards of letting the broker act alone probably outweigh the occasional benefit.

Whatever the value of potential access to better information, there are numerous forces at work that compromise the quality of information that is available to individual investors. As a matter of law, brokers are limited to making recommendations only for investments for which they have a **reasonable basis**. In practice, this requirement means that a given brokerage firm will be limited in the stocks that its brokers may recommend by the list of stocks for which the firm has a current research report. And because of potential liability to investors, most brokerage firms are quite vigilant in enforcing this limitation. This does not mean, of course, that an investor cannot buy or sell a stock that the brokerage firm does not follow. It only means that the investment advice that one may expect to obtain from the firm is limited to the securities that the firm follows.

Brokerage firms often recommend stocks in which they make a market or for which they are serving as an underwriter or in which they have a substantial inventory. Another factor to consider in evaluating advice is that analysts often own the stocks they tout. Thus, they have an incentive to see that others buy the same stock. On the other hand, it may be a good sign that an analyst has confidence in the advice. Although brokers are prohibited from **front-running**, that is, trading ahead of a customer order that is expected to affect the market, it is not now illegal to buy ahead of one's own recommendation, though short-term trading by investment advisers without disclosure of the practice to clients may be a violation of federal securities law.

Finally, it is important to understand the point of view of the analyst. Some analysts focus on underlying value (**fundamentals**), while others focus on market forces (**technical factors**). In one incident reported in the *Wall Street Journal*, analysts at a single firm using different methods simultaneously recommended buying and selling the same stock.

## §16.17 The Suitability Rule

In addition to the requirement that the broker have a reasonable basis for recommending a security, stock exchange and NASD rules require a broker to recommend only investments that are suitable for an investor's personal circumstances and investment goals. What is suitable for an investor depends both on the amount of risk that an investor can afford to take as well as the amount of risk that the investor wants to take. Violations of the **suitability rule** are clearly grounds for discipline of the broker. Many arbitration panels have found violations of the rule to justify compensation to aggrieved investors. And at least one state court has found a violation of the suitability rule (together with state law fiduciary duty) when a broker failed to ensure that a customer account was sufficiently diversified.

Despite the suitability rule, brokers may tend to recommend securities that for one reason or another are unsuitable for the investor. Riskier securities generally carry higher commissions, markups, spreads, and discounts, which means that both the broker and the house make greater profits from selling riskier rather than safer investments. There also have been numerous examples of brokers overselling in-house products.

## §16.18 Investing in Initial Public Offerings

Evidence indicates that on the average, **initial public offerings** (IPOs) of stock outperform the market on a risk-adjusted basis. In other words, an investment in an IPO is more likely to show a profit than other stock investments of comparable risk. In many cases, the increase in price of such offerings is dramatic. Thus, it is not surprising that investors are anxious to purchase such shares and are miffed when they cannot get in on such deals.

There are complex forces at work in the IPO market that cause it to behave as it does and that carry significant risks for investors. One of the reasons that IPOs tend to be underpriced is that the investment bankers who **underwrite** (distribute) IPOs have a keen interest in seeing the stock sold quickly (seeing the stock go **out the window** in the argot of Wall Street). In most cases, underwriters purchase the offered stock from the issuer and resell it, a practice that is known as a **firm commitment** underwriting. Thus, the underwriter must ordinarily keep what is not sold. Initial prices therefore tend to be set on the low side. Moreover, in a **fixed-price offering**, which is the most common practice, the price must be set so as to satisfy the most reluctant investor. It is also important that a public offering indeed be public, that is, widely distributed. Perhaps more important, if the price of the stock goes down in the aftermarket, investors may sue under the strict liability provisions of the Securities Act of 1933. Finally, for a variety of reasons, owners and managers of the company going public prefer that the price of the stock increase after the offering, even though it may mean that they receive less for the stock in the first place.

As one might expect, investment banks are under intense pressure to allocate IPO bargains to their best customers. Thus, one reason that many investors cannot get in on such deals is that investment banks may have allocated all their shares to customers with whom they have had long relationships and to influential persons whose favor they seek. Indeed, it is these relationships that enable investment banks to assure issuers that their stock will indeed go out the window on a timely basis. On the other hand, customers may sometimes be asked to invest in less attractive stocks if they wish to continue to receive desirable opportunities to invest in the future.

Investment bankers also do not want customers to whom they sell IPO shares to immediately resell the shares into the market for a quick profit. This practice is known as **flipping**, and tends to cause the price to fall before the issue can be fully marketed. It also injures the reputation of the investment bank and conceivably may give rise to liability under the federal securities laws. Thus, investment bankers want assurance that investors will keep the stock allocated to them for a decent interval. The implicit threat may be that if the stock is flipped the recipient will not be offered IPO shares in the future. Indeed, one sometimes hears complaints from persons who were allocated shares in an IPO that they are being subtly coerced into keeping the shares longer than they would prefer.

## §16.19  Penny Stocks

Generally speaking, a **penny stock** is a low-priced high-risk stock that is sold through brokerage houses specializing in such issues. The rule of thumb is that a penny stock is a stock that sells for less than five dollars per share. But the difficulty in defining a penny stock is apparent from SEC rules, which define penny stocks by defining nine categories of what they are not.

The problem with penny stocks has not so much been with the stocks themselves as with the firms through which they are sold. Thus, SEC rules relating to penny stocks are directed to brokerage houses. They require special disclosures by the brokerage house to their customers in connection with the risk, firmness of price quotations, and compensation. They also require special disclosures be made to investors in periodic account statements and the preservation of information with regard to the firm's sales staff. The rules also provide for exemptions for firms whose business is not primarily in connection with penny stocks and for certain limited offerings.

The SEC has also adopted special rules to deal with **blank check offerings** of stock. A blank check offering is an offering to raise funds for purposes to be determined. SEC rules provide that funds raised from a blank check offering must be placed in escrow until the offering is completed and until business assets accounting for at least 80 percent of the funds have been acquired. The definition of penny stock includes all blank check offerings without regard to price.

Broker-dealer firms that sell penny stocks are often called **boiler rooms** or **bucket shops**. They usually rely on **cold calling**, that is, calling potential customers with whom the firm has no prior relationship in an effort to sell the stock of the day. These firms may engage in high pressure sales tactics designed to sell a stock. Individual employees of boiler rooms often move from firm to firm as one operation is shut down and another opens up, or the firms themselves disband after a stock has been sold and then re-form under a new name to sell a new stock.

# THE BUSINESS OF LAW

## §17.1 Introduction

Many of this book's readers are law students who plan to make their living and their careers in the practice of law after they graduate and, of course, pass the bar examination. This chapter is intended to give these readers insight into the complexities and realities of modern law firms. Many readers doubtless have a vague understanding of the economics of the practice of law in the modern era. They know, for example, that lawyers try cases, give advice, and become criminal lawyers or prosecutors. They also know that lawyers charge fees for rendering these services and that, presumably, clients willingly pay fees for these services. Even though they realize that most law school graduates work in law firms, and that they probably will do so as well, they may not have any idea what a modern law firm is like. In a sense, this chapter is designed to acquaint them with their future employers.

It is uncommon today for a freshly minted lawyer simply to hang out his shingle and begin practicing as a solo attorney. That is usually a recipe for slow starvation since potential clients are usually unwilling to trust the management of significant legal matters to an untried lawyer. A very common pattern today is that a law student will work for a law firm over one or more summers while in law school and then be invited to join the law firm as a full-time associate after she has graduated and passed the bar. After several years working as an associate she will be promoted to partner. If so, she may remain in that firm for the balance of her professional career. More likely, however, she will change firms several times during her career.

Of course, not all law students follow this route. Some may decide to become employees of federal, state, or local governments. Many of these agencies provide training for recent law school graduates. Some may decide to become in-house attorneys working as an employee of a corporation. Many large companies have substantial legal staffs and do much of their legal work in-house. However, as discussed below, this avenue is rarely open to a newly minted attorney. Some may decide to go into other areas, such as banking or finance, and not practice law at all. This chapter, however, deals only with law students who decide to practice law in law firms that predominantly handle business matters for large clients. It does not consider directly the lawyer who wishes to end up being chief executive officer of a large corporation or manager of a division or subsidiary of such a corporation. It also does not discuss the solo practitioner, an attorney who joins a two- or three-person practice in a rural area, or a lawyer who specializes in non-business areas such as family law, adoption, divorce, criminal law, and the like, whether or not that lawyer is with a major firm. The lawyer that is discussed in this chapter is engaged primarily with business and commercial matters within a firm. Indeed, that is usually where the bread comes from that fuels the modern law firm.

Typically, an associate will remain in that status for five to eight years working under the careful tutelage of an experienced attorney. During this period, she will gradually be given greater responsibility and discretion. After her years as an associate, she may be made a partner. Many modern law firms have two or more gradations of partners, but in any event she becomes a permanent member of the firm. If she does not make the grade to become a partner, the firm may arrange for her to join a less demanding firm. More likely, however, she will simply be let go and cast adrift to find another job as best she can. In times of full employment for lawyers she may be able to work as a **contract lawyer** for solo practitioners or small law firms that have need for temporary legal assistance. In the very worst scenario, she may be unable to find any law-related job and must find some other work to put bread on the table.

Most newly minted lawyers today obtain employment with large commercial firms based in large and medium-sized cities. These firms are much larger than the law firms of forty years ago. The largest may have more than 1,000 lawyers located in ten or more American cities with branch offices in another half-dozen cities in foreign countries. Further, they do a wide variety of commercial and transactional work, including litigation, governmental relationships, transactions with foreign manufacturers, business litigation, business formation, public offerings of securities, and the like. Most partners in large firms today specialize in specific business areas. While some lawyers in modern firms may specialize in family law, adoption, divorce, estate planning, criminal law, and the like, the core of the firm's practice is business and commercial matters.

Before describing these modern firms, it is useful to consider first the interesting question of how lawyers add value to commercial transactions. This chapter then discusses the traditional law firm of the 1960s and 1970s and how it has evolved into the modern megafirm of the twenty-first century. The chapter then discusses the boom period that existed from late 1999 through early 2001, and the bust that occurred very unexpectedly thereafter. It is quite possible, of course, that this bust will end within a relatively short period of time and a new recovery will be underway when a current reader opens this book.

## §17.2 How Lawyers Add Value to Business Transactions

Modern business transactions involve numerous actors, including attorneys, accountants, investment bankers, and corporate officers and employees. What do attorneys do for which clients happily pay so handsomely? It seems clear that they must add value in some way, since otherwise businesses would not be willing to pay for their services. But what do they add? And what happens when a deal goes sour in part because of something the lawyer did or failed to do?

Very little has been written about how lawyers create value in their transactional roles. One thing that lawyers do in connection with business transactions is to render a formal legal opinion that the transaction when completed will have certain legal consequences. However, formal legal opinions are very limited in scope, relating to noncontroversial matters such as whether the documents, when executed, will have specific effects on title, whether shares of stock contemplated to be issued will be validly issued, fully paid, and nonassessable, and so forth. This role is so limited, however, that it hardly explains the fees that are charged and happily paid.

One important role of lawyers is to translate deals and issues into the precise language of the law so that transactions are memorialized as accurately as possible, and risk and uncertainty are reduced. It is a fact of life that transactions are negotiated in a world of imperfect information and significant transaction costs. Lawyers may create value by reducing this uncertainty; for example, they may suggest that the parties enter an agreement that is subject to specific contingencies. They may suggest that one party make certain specific representations dealing with information in its control but not known to the other party. They may also narrow areas of uncertainty. One party may offer a representation that "seller has no reason to believe" that a certain situation exists; the other party may wish greater security, and the lawyer suggests that the phrase be modified to say *after diligent investigation* seller has no reason to believe" the situation exists. Lawyers also may suggest that teeth be put into the agreement through a promise by the party with more reliable information to indemnify the other if the information turns out to be inaccurate.

Lawyers may also provide reputational benefits. A buyer of a business may refuse to accept a legal opinion from an in-house lawyer or from an unknown law firm. However, it may readily accept and rely upon an opinion by a lawyer from a prestigious national law firm. Such opinions are so common that they have a name, "comfort letters" or "cold comfort letters." In effect the lawyer from the national law firm is lending his reputation to assure that the transaction is an acceptable one.

Finally, lawyers also create value by reason of their specialization in certain areas of the law. Securities regulation is a classic example. The principles and rules in this area are complex and arcane. A company planning to sell shares to the public for the first time will probably have to make changes in its structure, its formal documents, and its financial structure. The advice of a skilled lawyer in this area may be essential if the client is successfully to go public as planned.

## §17.3  The Traditional Law Firm of the 1960s

In roughly 1960, the traditional law firm was a general partnership in which all partners shared the benefits and burdens of the law practice. Under well-established partnership principles, each partner was personally liable for all obligations of the partnership, including malpractice claims arising from actions of associates or other partners, and claims based on partnership contracts. However, malpractice was not a major concern; lawyers were rarely sued for malpractice, and many firms did not even bother to carry malpractice insurance, which was then incredibly inexpensive in contrast to present premiums.

By modern standards, traditional law firms of the 1950s and 1960s were small. A large firm might have 30 or so partners and 10 or 15 associates; a medium-size firm was one with perhaps 12 or 15 partners and associates combined. Firms usually had only a single office (although some firms had small branch offices in other cities, particularly if a major client had offices in that city). All the partners in a firm knew each other personally and typically prided themselves on acting civilly and with respect toward each other. The firm structure was usually informal; many firms did not have written partnership agreements, and in effect decisions were made through a committee, by a trusted senior partner, or by some form of consensus of all the partners. When partnership decisions needed to be made, it was easy to fit all the firm's partners around a single table. When the decision involved who should be promoted from associate to partner, all the existing partners would have had at least some contact with and personal knowledge about each candidate.

Law firms during this period were almost entirely male. There were very few female law school graduates to begin with, but as a matter of policy, most firms simply declined to interview or hire female lawyers. These firms believed that their clients would refuse to accept a female lawyer in a professional relationship. Justice Sandra Day O'Connor of the United States Supreme Court has graphically described that the only jobs she was offered after graduating from law school in the early 1950s were secretarial ones.

There was great stability in firm membership. There was relatively little lateral movement by lawyers from one firm to another, and a person elected to be a partner in an established partnership reasonably expected to spend his entire productive career with that firm. As long as the partner remained productive, he could expect to receive a fair share of the partnership income; if his billings temporarily declined (e.g., because of ill health), the firm might carry him until he recovered.

In these traditional firms of the 1950s and 1960s, there was a fair amount of specialization among lawyers. The country lawyer or lawyer in general practice who did not hesitate to represent clients no matter what area of law was involved had largely disappeared from major law firms by World War II. Although most lawyers had areas of specialization, it was not uncommon for an individual lawyer to feel comfortable representing clients with problems in several quite different legal areas (e.g., taxation, antitrust, and securities law). As the legal system was becoming more complex during this period, however, lawyers generally found it increasingly difficult to retain proficiency in several different areas, and therefore there was a tendency to narrow areas of practice and increase the degree of specialization.

Firms generally had established relationships with specific clients that were treasured and cultivated. These relationships were often of long standing and based on a firm lawyer also serving as the general counsel of the business. When a single business relied on more than one firm, each firm's areas of responsibility were generally clear-cut and there was little or no competition among the firms. These relationships were usually based on a handshake or on oral understandings.

The firm typically did not commit in advance to a price for its services on specific matters; a new client might be advised of each lawyer's normal billing rate, but the amount of time to be spent was not normally estimated or established in advance. If the matter was complex, the firm might request an **advance**, a substantial payment against which time spent on the matter would be billed. If the advance was exhausted (or nearing exhaustion), the firm might request an additional advance or, quite possibly, defer further billing until the matter was completed. The amount actually billed after the work was completed was decided by the firm and the lawyer with responsibility for the matter. The bill typically stated that it was for services rendered without any itemization of costs, charges, or identification of who actually performed the work. The size of the bill might be based on the amount of time spent, but more subjective factors were also common: the lawyer's assessment of value of the result achieved, the complexity of the matter, and what fee the matter will bear. Of course, billing disputes occurred from time to time, but they were not very common. When they did occur, disputes were usually negotiated out as both firm and client recognized the importance of the continuing relationship. Lawyers were encouraged to keep time records, but sometimes these important records were skeletal or fragmentary, and some lawyers prided themselves on never keeping time records and billing on the basis of what they believed their services were worth.

Traditional law firms did not have formal retirement policies for aging lawyers. A partner might continue to practice until his seventies, or even longer, although as age limited his skills, other partners might suggest that he should retire or accept "of counsel" status, which was a gentle way of being told he no longer was carrying his share of the firm. Upon retirement, the senior lawyer usually became of counsel and the firm might maintain an office for his use or provide him with secretarial assistance. A lawyer who was of counsel might come in to the office one or two days a week to pick up his mail, and usually maintained some contact with the remaining partners. Firms generally did not have retirement plans that provided direct financial benefits for the aging lawyer. Rather, each lawyer was expected to make whatever financial provision he desired for his retirement during his productive years with the firm. Because partners were viewed as self-employed, they were not eligible for social security benefits.

This picture of the traditional law firm remained reasonably accurate throughout the 1960s, although the trend toward specialization continued and many law firms grew steadily during this period, reaching a size much larger than had been previously known. The development of the megafirm with hundreds of lawyers, however, can be traced to events that became dominant in the 1970s and 1980s.

## §17.4 The Transition from the 1960s to Today

The very large law firm of today bears little resemblance to the typical firm of the 1960s. For example, Skadden, Arps, Slate, Meagner & Flom, L.L.P., the second largest American firm, in 2001 had 335 partners and 1,347 associates. It had a total of 1,704 lawyers, with its principal office in New York City and ten offices in other American cities plus foreign offices in London, Paris, Brussels, Hong Kong, Frankfurt, Tokyo, Toronto, Beijing, Singapore, Vienna, Moscow, and Sydney, Australia. It is difficult to imagine how a firm of this size could evolve within a couple of decades from the typical firm of the 1960s.

In one sense, the growth of large law firms of today is simply a function of the increased amount of legal work that is available and the increased specialization that has occurred. More litigation and law-related work requires more lawyers. The 1970s and 1980s were boom times for lawyers and law firms. Law-related work increased rapidly in part due to increased governmental regulation of business. These were boom times in the American economy, and the need for legal services increased along with business activity generally.

The growth during this period took a different form from earlier periods. Historically, a growth in legal business was reflected by the creation of new law firms, often spin-offs from existing law firms. The growth in legal business during the 1970s and 1980s was met by law firms growing to meet the increased demand. Rather than spinning off new firms, law firms increased the number of partners and associates in firms. Firms, furthermore, did not hesitate to open new offices under their own names in various cities in order to serve the needs of established clients that were themselves opening plants or other facilities in distant cities. As international business boomed, American law firms opened offices in their own names in a variety of foreign countries in order to serve the international operations of their American clients. The numbers of partners in large law firms increased dramatically.

Firms also discovered that it was profitable to grow by increasing the number of associates. As the demand for legal services grew, firms found that the costs of new associates could be multiplied and passed on to clients without objection. A common practice of firms was to bill time for associates at three times their actual salary and cost of fringe benefits: one-third for the associate, one-third for administrative costs, and one-third for the partners. Under this regime, the ratio of associates to partners increased rapidly, from 1:1 (or less) in the traditional firm of the 1960s to 3:1 or 4:1, or higher in a few instances. Growth in the number of associates simply meant greater profits for the firm and its partners. Firms thus had every incentive to grow rapidly by increasing the number of associates relative to the number of partners, a process known as leveraging.

Not surprisingly, many associates remained with their firms and became partners. As law business continued to increase, firm size and firm income grew dramatically.

Law schools were obviously affected by these developments. As word spread about the salaries new lawyers were commanding, schools began to receive a flood of additional applications for admission. At about the same time, jobs were tightening in traditional academic areas. Many of the best and the brightest, including many young persons with master's or doctor's degrees in traditional areas, decided to go to law school. Recent college graduates decided to give up the idea of traditional employment in business or in academia and become lawyers. As the demand for lawyers increased, new law schools were opened and class sizes in existing schools were increased. Law schools became more selective in their admission policies, and the quality of the average graduate improved. Law practice was obviously remunerative and growing; a legal career was extremely attractive; and law business and law practice was booming. During this period, the government developed guaranteed student loan programs that permitted many law students to finance virtually their entire legal education through loans on which principal payments began only after graduation. The booming market for young lawyers alleviated any concern about repayment of these loans, and many law students took advantage of these generous programs.

The 1980s were salad days for law firms, for partners, for associates, and for law schools. Legal services were a major growth industry. Firms expanded, and reexpanded; salaries and benefits for associates continued to rise; associates were hired with a view toward future growth as much as present needs. Firms created expensive summer internship programs for law students completing their first and second years of law school to encourage them to join the firm upon graduation. Firms that were growing rapidly committed themselves to additional expensive office space to ensure space for future expansion. Indeed, the growth of legal services was a contributing factor to the boom in new office space in many cities during the 1980s; law firms were viewed as desirable tenants, and their commitments to rent space helped the financing of many speculative new buildings.

In the early 1990s, this balloon was punctured by a brief recession that occurred quite unexpectedly. The demand for legal services abruptly and unexpectedly failed to continue to grow; law firms found themselves overstocked with lawyers and expensive office space that they could not use. Some of the more overextended firms laid off new associates, an action that was unheard of previously. Some firms paid new hires a bonus not to come as an associate or as a summer intern. Almost immediately, the tightening of the market for legal services had consequences for law school graduates and students. Although new jobs did not dry up completely, they did become more difficult to find and more competitive; education loans suddenly became potentially burdensome; and many individuals reconsidered the decision to apply to law school. Virtually overnight, the market for legal services changed from a seller's market to a buyer's market.

During this period, control over the pricing of legal services largely shifted from being under the virtually complete control of the firm. Large and sophisticated clients began to shop among law firms for the best and cheapest legal services, and firms competed directly and vigorously for legal business. This spirit of competition directly affected the personal relationships within law firms; the feeling of permanence and lifetime commitment on the part of partners that existed in the traditional law firm of the 1970s was replaced by an emphasis on production and rain-making (i.e., bringing in client business).

These dramatic changes in law firms and the roles of lawyers did not occur overnight. However, with the benefit of hindsight, it is clear that the changes did occur very rapidly and unexpectedly. The early 1990s was a period of continued experimentation by law firms as they adjusted to new and quite different economic conditions. The pattern during this critical period was similar to the boom and bust periods that periodically occurred in the real estate and securities markets. Competition for high quality associates became particularly intense, and salaries increased to then previously unheard-of levels—virtually doubling to as much as $85,000 per year in the largest firms—as firms competed to attract the strongest and best graduates.

## §17.5  Training of Associates

In the 1970s, as now, a newly minted member of the bar that was invited to join a law firm began as an employee of the firm and not a partner—he was an associate. This status involved both an apprenticeship and a probationary period. The associate learned how to practice law by watching and assisting the experienced partners; at the same time, the partners evaluated the ability of associates in terms of whether they should be made a partner (i.e., whether the associate should ultimately be admitted to the firm as a partner and share the risks and benefits of that firm's practice).

The training process usually involved extensive mentoring. At first, a partner or senior associate very closely supervised the work of the associate, who gradually would be given more discretion and authority. One important aspect of this program was exposing the associate to real life situations. A litigation associate would accompany the experienced partner to depositions and the courtroom. He would assist the litigation partner in interviewing witnesses and preparing the case for trial, but primarily he was there to learn. He later would be permitted to handle simple depositions and routine litigation matters on his own. A transactional associate would be exposed to complex transactions by working with the partner on real transactions, although the partner himself was fully capable of handling the task on his own. In this way, the associate would learn how to register a securities offering for an initial public offering (IPO) or prepare a complex contract for the purchase or sale of a business that would protect the client's needs and goals. Although it was not always obvious to the client, an important aspect of this process of training young lawyers was that the client paid for a major part of the training of the young associate, because the ultimate fee included the services of both the supervising lawyer and the associate.

Many firms had formal rotation programs for new associates to acquaint them with the areas of firm practice. An associate might thereafter have a voice in which department or area of practice he wished to specialize in.

A new lawyer typically could expect to remain an associate for 6 to 10 years, depending on the tradition in the specific law firm. If he seemed clearly unqualified to become a partner, he might be terminated in the first year or so of his employment with the firm; otherwise, he was virtually assured of employment until the partnership decision was made. Toward the end of this period, the associate's duties were similar to those of a partner. He was expected to handle most matters on his own and begin to develop his own client base. He might serve as a mentor for new associates. It was not uncommon for an associate who was not offered a partnership position to have spent nearly a decade with the firm. He was a skilled and trained lawyer. The firm might help to place him with a client's legal office or with a smaller or lesser firm, or simply cast the associate loose to find a new job on his own. In the traditional firm, it was up-or-out with a vengeance; if one did not make partner, one was gone. There was no middle ground for the young lawyer.

By today's standards, associates did not have to work very hard. An associate might bill 1,600 hours during a year; that figure reflects, of course, that associates did not bill for every hour they were present in the firm's offices. Today, many firms expect an associate to bill at least 1950 hours per year, and in periods of heavy workloads associates may bill 2200 hours per year, or more. Some firms have created "bonus programs" to encourage associates to increase their billing hours. These programs, also known as sweat equity programs, generally are offered only when the firm is having difficulty keeping up with its current business, given the firm's current manpower.

## §17.6 Growth of In-House Legal Counsel Departments

Before describing law firms in the twenty-first century, it is helpful first to sketch the relationship between lawyers who are employed by their corporate clients and the law firms that represent the clients.

As corporations developed and grew in size, it quickly became clear that the corporation had need for continuing legal advice and legal representation. As late as the 1960s, it was common for a large corporation to have historical connections with a specific law firm that did (or oversaw) virtually all the corporation's significant legal activities. All of the important legal work of the corporation was in fact handled by or under the direction of the favored law firm or a favored specific partner in the firm. These relationships continued over long periods; often, one or more partners of the law firm were also members of the board of directors of the corporation and, if the corporation employed a lawyer as general counsel, that person was often a partner in the law firm or had prior association with the firm. Sometimes, the firm maintained office space within the corporate offices, or vice versa. These arrangements have not entirely disappeared; they are sometimes found today in smaller businesses, and occasionally in larger ones as well.

By the 1950s, most large corporations had created not only the office of **general counsel** or **chief legal officer** (CLO)—who was a full-time employee of the corporation—but also skeletal legal staffs to assist the general counsel. However, these staffs were almost always small and handled only the most routine legal matters. For example, they might be involved in the preparation of minutes of meetings of the board of directors, the preparation of simple patent applications and routine contracts, the closing of real estate transactions, and the searching of titles of potential oil and gas leases. More substantial legal matters were handled by lawyers from the outside law firm.

In this setting, the outside law firm handled virtually all of the interesting, challenging, and significant legal work (and a great deal of the routine work as well). That firm also was regularly involved in selecting specialized or local counsel, when that was felt to be necessary, and overseeing the performance of these attorneys. The internal legal staff had little challenging work and was often viewed as the backwater of the legal profession. This view of the position of the inside legal staff was widely shared by partners and associates of the dominant law firm. Indeed, the law firm might place associates who did not make partner on the client's inside legal staff in order to cement the continuing relationship and at the same time provide a suitable spot for the junior attorney where he could do little harm. Even with the upgrading of the internal legal staffs (described below) that has occurred in recent years, a tinge of this old attitude may continue to exist on the part of some lawyers today, but to the extent it still exists, that attitude is quite mistaken.

The systematic upgrading of internal legal staffs in terms of quality, size, and prestige was largely fueled by the same economic considerations that affected law firms. During the 1970s, large corporations faced an explosion of regulatory activity and products liability litigation. During the period, the corporate general counsel and the favored law firm were not only forced to become familiar with new regulatory requirements but also increasingly to practice preventive rather than reactive law. The lawyers found themselves increasingly involved in the establishment and monitoring of legal compliance systems or participating in corporate planning discussions about future economic activities so that legal problems could be anticipated and prepared for. Initially, virtually none of this important work could be trusted to the inside legal staffs as they were then constituted.

As the quantity of legal work increased with the burst of regulatory and litigation activity in the 1970s and 1980s, the bills for legal services that law firms submitted to corporations grew dramatically. The additional work also contributed to the rapid expansion of law firms during this period. However, during the same period, many corporations found that there was an urgent need to control costs. They were facing increased domestic and foreign competition as well as problems caused by rapid technological change and government regulation. Control over costs through improved efficiency, downsizing, and outsourcing seemed essential if the corporation was to thrive. Cost-conscious corporate executives quickly realized that legal costs were getting out of hand, and the most obvious way to reduce these costs was to improve the capability of the inside legal staff to handle more matters and, incidentally, to reduce the need for the services of expensive outside lawyers.

Upgrading the capability of inside legal staff is not very different from upgrading the capability of an independent law firm. Imaginative general counsel must be hired to increase the size of the legal staff and improve its quality. Salaries must be improved; systematic attempts must be made to attract more competent lawyers and train them, in much the way associates in law firms are trained, and to give them more challenging work. As legal costs continued to rise, more and more corporations decided to improve the quality of their internal legal staffs.

Many outside law firms initially welcomed this trend because at the time legal business was booming, and the improved internal staff freed the firm's partners, associates, and paralegals from more routine matters. However, the development of substantial in-house legal staffs quickly strained traditional relationships with outside law firms. Inside counsel was not only doing work that previously had been done profitably by associates at the law firm, but also were taking over work that previously justified the investment of significant time by individual partners.

To consider the most extreme scenario, picture a senior partner of a law firm in the 1970s with a historic relationship with a corporation that has only a tiny internal legal department. That partner was in an enviable position. He had the confidence of both the management and the individual members of the board of directors. For many years, the firm had handled virtually all the corporation's legal work, although much of it was routine and delegated to senior associates. Now, a new inside general counsel is appointed specifically to reduce overall legal costs by moving work to an increasingly sophisticated internal law department and giving isolated pieces of work to less-costly law firms. Assume that one major source of legal work involves the regular and routine acquisitions of smaller firms by the corporation in order to obtain desired locations or desired products. Such a program is traditionally a major source of profitable legal business for law firms. The first step by the new general counsel is the assignment of a newly hired inside lawyer to assist the outside firm in one or more acquisitions. After a few transactions, the outside firm is told that the inside lawyer is now in overall charge of acquisitions and will report directly to the general counsel; the law firm is assured that it will be consulted if any unusual problems arise. Gradually, inside counsel entirely take over most of the acquisitions work, and eventually most deals are handled entirely without the assistance of the outside firm so that the amount of its business noticeably declines.

If one puts oneself in the position of the senior partner of the outside firm in this scenario, it is easy to see why there might be some bitterness and friction. The outside firm has in effect trained the inside lawyer to take over a portion of that firm's business. If this pattern recurs in other areas of specialized work, such as managing litigation, tax, and securities regulation, relationships may become increasingly strained. Perhaps the senior partner of the firm with historic connections with the client may try to return to the good old days, by getting the general counsel fired or at least having her responsibilities cut back. Generally, such efforts did not succeed, because the inside general counsel had effectively reduced the cost of legal services without any noticeable diminution in quality. Indeed, efforts to undermine the position of the general counsel may strain the traditional relationship even further, because the basis for the unhappiness of the senior partner and the outside firm is fully understood by top management, who cannot be expected to be sympathetic.

Once the historic ties between law firm and client were loosened and the independence of inside counsel firmly established, it was common for the corporation, through its general counsel, gradually to shop legal work with other firms in an effort to obtain the best legal services at the best price. As a result, historic ties declined further.

Today, most large corporations routinely place outside legal work with several different law firms. Many corporations, of course, still have close historical connections with specific law firms that provide a substantial amount of continuing legal work for the corporation, with legal fees running into the hundreds of thousands or millions of dollars per year. It is clear, however, that this pattern is not what it was a generation or so ago. Inside staff has responsibility for many substantive matters, often including the handling of litigation that in an earlier era would have been routinely handled by outside counsel. If legal fees have increased, it is because the corporation's need for legal services of the type now provided by outside counsel has increased.

As inside counsel become increasingly involved in placing legal work with competing law firms, they necessarily become directly involved in fee arrangements. The traditional method of billing of course is based on hourly rates for the lawyers involved. Inside counsel may view straight hourly billings with skepticism, because it encourages over-staffing of a job and padding of bills. Inside counsel may therefore seek to limit the number of lawyers assigned to the work, establish a maximum number of hours that the client will be billed — (so-called **capped billing**) — or insist that only certain specific lawyers be assigned the work. These controls quickly spelled an end to the once-common practice within firms of assigning inexperienced lawyers to a project as part of their learning experience. The cost of training new lawyers no longer could be transferred to clients.

As inside counsel have developed alternative sources for legal services, creating competition among law firms, a variety of novel billing techniques have developed that permit direct comparisons of fee proposals by different firms: **fixed fees, capped fees, volume discount arrangements** (particularly for recurring litigation issues), **incentive billing** (with fees for successful outcomes higher than for less successful ones), **value billing, task billing, partial contingency fees, blended rates,** and so forth.

The development of sophisticated inside counsel has increased the competition among law firms as inside counsel have attempted to obtain needed expert outside legal services at the best price.

## §17.7 A Snapshot of the Modern Large Law Firm

At this point it is useful to describe a typical large, big city law firm today and contrast it with the traditional firm existing a generation or so ago.

*Size.* The most visible difference between law firms of today and those of the 1970s is that most modern law firms are behomeths—several hundred partners scattered in offices around the world and perhaps a thousand or more lawyers altogether. The size of the Skadden Arps firm has been described previously. In 2001, the nation's third largest firm, Jones, Day, Reavis & Pogue, headquartered in Cleveland, had 476 partners and 976 associates with branch offices in thirteen other cities. The nation's fiftieth largest firm, Proskauer Rose, LLP of New York had 151 partners and 395 associates. The hundredth largest firm, Preston, Gates & Ellis, LLP, based in Seattle, had 183 partners and 163 associates in eight American cities and an outpost in Hong Kong. The two-hundredth largest firm, Hodgson, Russ, LLP, of Buffalo, New York had 96 partners, and 97 associates in five American cities. The two-hundred-fiftieth largest firm, Verner Lipfert, Bernhard, McPherson & Hand, Chartered, of Washington, D.C., had 75 partners and 57 associates. A "midsized" firm today is not clearly defined, but it is certainly one with 100 or more lawyers.

These large firms provide full service for their clients in many legal areas, from employment law to complex litigation, from estate planning to structuring complex corporate transactions. They may analyze the legal, economic, and social implications of doing business in Mexico under the North American Free Trade Agreement (NAFTA) or the risks of opening a new plant in Mongolia or Russia. The increase in size and diversity of law firms is largely a result of the need to provide services for large publicly held businesses over a wide range —to ensure that a large volume of regular legal business will continue to come the firm's way. Mid-size and smaller firms, in contrast, tend to be **boutiques**, specializing in litigation or in one or more areas of law but not providing the full breadth of services provided by the very large firm.

*Relations among partners.* One consequence of size is that the close personal relationships among partners that generally existed in firms in earlier years have largely disappeared. Large firms today tend to be impersonal. It is not uncommon for many partners in a large firm to know neither the names nor the faces of many of their co-partners. Firm retreats in which all partners spend a few days with each other may be necessary simply to introduce partners to each other! The size and impersonality of very large firms has changed the motivations of both partners and associates. A sense of loyalty to the firm has diminished; money is the important thing. If a firm falters, why take a chance that things will get better? Leave, if you can.

*Departmentalization and specialization.* Law practice in a large firm is a series of specialized practices. A firm may provide full-service coverage for its clients, but it is impossible for a single lawyer to remain current on developments in many legal areas today. Large firms are divided into groups or sections based on areas of specialized practice. One group of lawyers may form the intellectual property group; other groups will specialize in transactional work, commercial litigation, estates and trusts, environmental law, and so forth. Lawyers in one specialized area may have little contact or interchange with lawyers in other areas. Although a partner working in the intellectual property section, for example, may not know the partners working in the litigation section, she will know and work closely with the other lawyers in the intellectual property section. These relationships may extend to other intellectual property specialists in other offices of the law firm. In other words, friendships and loyalty may exist at the department level across widely separated offices. When a new associate is hired by a firm, he is usually assigned to a section, and thus is involved in a specialty from the outset. Many firms, however, permit new associates to transfer from one specialty area to another within limits in order to find a slot for the associate in which he is happiest.

*Increased mobility of individual partners.* In contrast with the situation forty or fifty years ago, it is unusual today for a lawyer to spend a lifetime in a single firm. Partners come and go. Many lawyers today have been partners in two or three different firms, and expect that they will move again. Successful partners may feel little compulsion to remain with a firm when faced with an attractive offer from a competing firm if many of his co-partners are not known to him. Success today tends to be measured by developing clients who are personally loyal to the partner and who may be expected to go with her if the partner decides to seek greener pastures. What counts today are mobile or portable billings.

Partners may decide to leave a firm for a variety of reasons. They may become dissatisfied with their present firm for some reason and cast about openly for another connection. They may feel that their personal compensation does not adequately reward the amount of business they bring in. Or there may be real or imagined personal slights. Dissatisfaction may also be more general. They may find the institutional and centralized structure of the firm too confining. Or they may simply feel restless and that it is time to move to a new environment.

Today, lawyers who are rainmakers or those who have developed a valuable specialization often receive unsolicited proposals to change firms. A successful partner may be approached by a **head hunter** who proposes that greener pastures may be found in a competing firm. Such a proposal is itself flattering, and it is not surprising that in an era of great mobility a successful lawyer might seriously consider a lateral move even if he is not unhappy in his present position.

It is also not uncommon for a whole section of partners and associates practicing in a specialized area, such as white collar crime or intellectual property, to move in a single group to a different firm. It is as though a whole minifirm decided to move to greener pastures. When the rainmakers in the section decide to go, the partners and associates that largely service the clients may decide to go also. A firm that loses one or more sections or groups of partners may find itself critically wounded by the defections and unable to continue as a separate viable entity as other partners and sections also decide to bail out.

*The attractiveness of small firm practice.* Partners in a large firm may find themselves increasingly constrained by the economics and politics of large firm practice. A much smaller firm appears to be an attractive alternative. This disaffection may lead an entire section or group to split off to form a small, specialized firm on its own. Sometimes, one or two mobile partners may themselves decide to form a new firm and hire junior lawyers from outside. The attractiveness of a smaller firm is that the senior partners will be in control of their own destinies. They will be both manager and rainmaker. They may feel that their operating costs will be lower in a small firm, and therefore they will be able to capture more of the revenue their services and contacts provide. These spin-off firms may continue to have good relations with the parent firm and cooperate on specific matters.

*Formal partnership agreements.* Another consequence of firm growth is that all large firms today have carefully drafted partnership agreements. Forty or fifty years ago some law partnerships did not have formal partnership agreements at all. The default provisions of state partnership statutes are designed basically for the small firm; they are simply not adequate to resolve the many practical problems that arise in large law firms with hundreds of partners and associates. There must be clear rules about mandatory retirement policies and what happens upon the death of a partner. There must be express authority to expel a nonperforming partner, a management structure that is binding upon all partners, and so forth. With hundreds of partners, a firm simply cannot rely on the good faith and good sense of individual partners to work out problems as they arise. It is interesting that although a large firm may have one or more partners that specialize in partnership law, including drafting of partnership agreements for large law firms, the firm will usually retain an outside law firm to prepare its partnership agreement. This avoids possible later legal attacks on the terms of the partnership agreement, avoids the appearance of conflict of interest, and ensures that provisions have been objectively developed.

*Limitation of Liability.* As the number of lawyers in a firm increases, the probability that claims of malpractice will be made by unhappy clients also increases. Large firms always carry substantial amounts of malpractice insurance but, given the magnitude of many matters handled by large law firms, there is always some risk that a claim may exceed the amount of insurance available. Of the two hundred largest law firms in 2001, roughly two out of three have elected to be limited liability partnerships, eliminating the risk that innocent partners may have personal responsibility for misconduct by other partners or associates. A few firms have elected to be professional corporations or professional associations, but the LLP election is overwhelmingly the most popular way to assure protection for innocent partners.

*Centralization of management.* Management of a large firm is centralized in a **management committee** or in a single **managing partner**, or very commonly in both. The general partners as a group typically have only minor roles in large law firm management; they may be entitled to vote on major questions (such as the selection of members of the management committee or the managing partner or whether a specific partner should be expelled). When general partners do have the power to vote on an issue, votes are usually weighted by sizes of partnership interest (although some partnership agreements provide for the common law rule of counting votes on a per capita basis). Decisions may be based on a majority vote or, depending on the issue involved, on the affirmative vote of some higher percentage. Unanimity is not required (to avoid opportunistic vetoes). Management participation rights of general partners in a law firm, in short, are similar to rights of limited partners in a limited partnership or shareholders in a corporation.

Day-to-day management of the firm is vested in the managing partner (sometimes the officer is called chairman or executive director or given a similar title), and important decisions are made by the management committee. Typically, the managing partner has grown up in the law firm, is imbued with knowledge of the firm's culture and manner of operation, and is respected by the rainmakers. The managing partner is also usually a relatively senior partner in the firm, although some managing partners are comparatively young; the confidence of partners generally is more important than the age of the managing partner. A few firms have experimented with nonlawyer managers who have formal management training and experience, but these experiments have generally not been very successful. The managing partner must ensure the smooth internal working of the firm. She has the responsibility of running a business that involves hundreds of lawyers and a support staff that may number in the thousands. The managing partner must ensure that the secretarial and support staff, office space, computer equipment, and the like, are adequate for the size of the operation. She must ensure that the firm's cash flow is adequate and that lines of credit are available to carry the firm over rough spots, that billings are made promptly and systematically, that conflicts of interest are avoided (a major problem in large law firms), that confidentiality rules are understood and followed, that internal personnel clashes are resolved, fees appropriately negotiated with major clients and fee disputes resolved; and so forth. The managing partner may also be involved in a variety of personnel problems, discussions with underperforming or unhappy partners, the promotion of associates, and so forth. The managing partner is the official spokesperson for the firm, and normally will be involved in, or at least aware of, discussions with major potential clients and negotiations with possible lateral hires.

The position of managing partner is a high visibility and prestigious position in most firms. The job may be particularly attractive and glamorous during periods of firm growth but may become much less attractive when the managing partner has to face unpleasant problems of downsizing, negotiation with powerful clients who feel that they should have a greater voice in the setting of fees, and dealing with rainmakers who may have large egos and little inherent loyalty to the firm. It is a time-consuming job, and some successful partners have been reluctant to assume these responsibilities for fear that their personal practices may suffer if they devote most of their time to internal matters. For this reason, some firms prefer to select as managing partners lawyers who are close to retirement and who do not expect to return full-time to practice when their managerial stint is completed.

The management committee is the ultimate source of partnership authority and decisions. It usually consists of senior partners from various offices and sections or departments of the firm. Members are typically selected by a vote of the partners. It may meet regularly to review firm operations and the performance of the managing partner or irregularly to resolve specific issues that have arisen.

In addition to firm-wide officers, firms with multiple offices usually designate office managers for each office. These may be known as branch or office managing partners; their duties relate to staff management within the office, billing supervision, partner and personnel counseling within that office, and so forth.

*Slicing up the pie.* The large law firm is, of course, a business. To be successful, it must keep its lawyers who perform essential services happy, particularly the lawyers who consistently generate business for the firm, the rainmakers. Perhaps no topic is more sensitive, more controversial, and the subject of greater talk and speculation within law firms than the compensation of individual partners. The method of determining each partner's slice of the pie varies widely from firm to firm. At one extreme is the you-eat-what-you-kill approach, tying compensation closely to total billings by individual partners. At the other extreme is the lock-step in which all partners with the same seniority receive the same size slice without regard to their productivity. A somewhat similar alternative is straight percentages: A partner with a 1.775 percent interest in the partnership receives 1.775 percent of the net profits. These are extremes; much more common are arrangements that provide a standard draw based on seniority or other factors plus a year-end distribution that is based on some weighting of the two basic variables: rainmaking and billings. These year-end bonuses may provide a major portion of the total annual compensation of partners.

Firms that have a discretionary compensation system may take a variety of subjective factors into account in the compensation decision. These factors include overall service or benefit to the firm, future potential, protection of morale of other partners, actions that place the firm in a favorable public light, and client satisfaction (i.e., providing the greatest benefit to clients at reasonable prices, thereby improving the long-term relationship with specific clients). Once a firm moves away from a mechanical calculation of compensation, a critical issue becomes who makes the decisions. Most of these firms have a **compensation committee** whose members may not be eligible for discretionary bonuses. The managing partner and management committee may perform this function in some firms. If a compensation committee is used, it is essential that that committee work closely with the managing partner and the management committee, because if there are inconsistent policies followed by the management committee and the compensation committee, the individual partners will almost certainly follow the money rather than the managers.

A partner who brings an important client to a firm may legitimately expect a reward for doing so. This reward would be over and above the services he or she performs for that client during the year. This **finding bonus** may continue for several years. However, if other lawyers primarily provide services to the client and the client remains with the firm, the continuation of the finding bonus becomes increasingly questionable, because it is likely that the lawyers actually performing the work explain why the client has remained with the firm.

Associates in large law firms are usually compensated on the basis of a schedule that is based exclusively on years of service. However, associates who provide exceptional service may receive special bonuses, or be moved up in the chain of seniority and be made partners well before their peers.

*The expulsion of partners.* At one time, the ultimate goal of every associate was making partner. Acceptance into the partnership was a virtual lifetime guarantee of security of employment and income. No longer. Partners who are marginal producers are quickly pruned. Law firm agreements typically provide for expulsion of partners by a decision of the management committee and, often, a vote of the partners. Firms do not hesitate to exercise this power when a partner is perceived as resting on his oars, just not fitting in, or having made a mistake that has cost the firm an important client. This point was vividly made to one of the authors when a junior partner in a major Chicago firm complained that the only lawyers in his firm that had any job security were associates in their third, fourth, and fifth years (before the partnership decision was made). Although this junior partner was primarily responsible for the preparation of witnesses in massive products liability litigation, he felt he had less job security as a partner than did the associates (who were, after all, mere employees).

*Mandatory retirement.* Law firms also need to address the problem of retirement of aging partners. Many firms have a mandatory retirement age, often preceded by a period of reduced activity during which the partner is expected to gradually reduce her practice and transfer continuing clients to younger members of the firm. The critical age may be set at 60 or even younger. Firms also have formal retirement plans, typically of the defined contribution variety. At an earlier time, some firms experimented with unfunded defined benefit plans, but these plans effectively imposed the obligation to fund senior partners' retirement on younger partners who were at the height of their earning power. Some younger partners decided to migrate to other firms to avoid the reduction of their compensation necessitated by the payments to retired partners under the firm's retirement plan.

*The changing roles of associates.* In the modern law firm, associates do much of the routine work within law firms. That is as true today as it has been in the past. Historically, most associates could realistically expect that they will eventually be promoted to the partnership level if their work is satisfactory. That is not necessarily true today. Firms may hire more associates than they can realistically expect to make partner. The expectation is that some will drop by the wayside, not work out as hoped, or be lured away by other firms.

The volume of work within the firm at the time the partnership decision must be made is a prime determinant of whether the firm will promote associates, lay them off, defer the final decision for another year or so, or offer them permanent associate status. In modern firms, there is usually a fair amount of natural attrition of associates. The average attrition rate in large firms in 1999 was 18.5 percent; it increased in the boom year of 2000 to 23.64 percent, and then declined significantly in 2001 (as the job market tightened) to 15.97 percent.

The number of associates employed by a firm may vary dramatically over periods of time depending on the workload of the firm. As business activity expands, associates may be added in the corporate and transactional areas; as recession looms, associates in those areas may be laid off or transferred while the number of associates working in the litigation and bankruptcy areas may grow. Some firms seek to keep a ratio of roughly three or four associates for each active partner; however, the variations over time and among firms are so great that such a number is not very meaningful. If the availability of routine legal work declines and clients begin to closely monitor law firm billing, firms may find that it is not practicable to maintain the current level of associates. Individuals may be laid off and the number of new associates hired may be reduced. In 2001, many large firms had more partners than associates presumably because of the decline in business and the reduction in the number of new hires. In particularly lean years, some large firms may completely withdraw from the associate market, planning to grow through lateral rather than new hires. Conscious decisions by many firms in 2001 to reduce the ratio of associates to partners obviously resulted in significantly fewer jobs being offered to law school graduates in 2001 than were offered in each of the years 1997 through 2000.

From the standpoint of training and promotion of associates, firms naturally prefer to transfer a portion of their cost to clients by assigning associates to work on client matters. As cost controls imposed by clients have tightened, however, this opportunity has declined. The mentoring that now occurs is primarily at the cost of the firm itself, and the investment that firms have in individual associates has therefore increased significantly. Firms have also found that the old up-or-out rules of the past are often no longer in the best interests of the firm because of the amount firms have invested in the training of associates. A variety of retention policies have been developed for valuable associates who will not become partners. For example, some firms have moved to a three-step rather than two-step progression to full partnership; in addition, firms have created permanent nonpartner positions so that their investment in associates who fail to make partner is not totally lost.

Another major factor that has influenced law firm policies with respect to associates is the increase in the number of female law school graduates, from practically zero in the 1960s to 50 percent (or more) in law schools today. Firms have found it necessary to develop maternity and child-raising policies to permit the retention of female associates who are juggling child-raising and a legal career. Even so, the attrition of female associates in most law firms is higher than for their male counterparts, and there are many fewer senior partners who are female than one would expect simply from the number of female associates hired in the last decade.

Some firms in large cities have experimented with joint or cooperative training of associates, particularly in litigation and transactional skills. Young associates from participating firms may be expected to attend intensive several-day seminars conducted by leading trial lawyers from various firms. The seminar may involve role-playing, mock depositions or cross-examinations, and work on actual transactions. Whether this cooperative effort will succeed, given the competitiveness among firms, remains to be seen since the tab for this training is entirely borne by the firms and not by clients.

*Income and equity partners.* Clients not unnaturally prefer to have partners rather than associates handle their legal matters. There is some incentive, therefore, to shorten the probationary period for associates and designate younger lawyers as partners so that they are able to deal directly and effectively with clients. At the same time, their production and experience may not justify their sharing in firm income to the same extent as more experienced partners. Even though they are called partners, their compensation may continue to be largely based on salary and annual bonus.

In an effort to accommodate these conflicting goals, many firms have created a two-tier partnership status: **Equity partners** are the senior partners who own the firm and share predominantly in its success or failure, while **income partners** are the younger lawyers who do not share in the business risk of the law firm and who receive a salary plus a year-end bonus in much the same way senior associates previously did. Income partners have some of the benefits of partnership. They may attend firm meetings, serve on most firm committees, and be given information about the firm's economic picture. However, they do not share in losses or in profits (except to the extent of a bonus) and may not serve on the significant firm committees that deal with management and compensation. Customarily, an income partner is ultimately promoted to equity partner, but some income partners may remain in that status throughout their legal careers.

Firms that have elected to practice as professional corporations or limited liability companies may create a similar two-tier system, with shareholders and senior shareholders. One LLC firm describes persons who are basically income partners as **participating associates**, a neutral phrase that may be used without regard to the legal form adopted by the law firm. Some firms have not formally created two-tier partnership tracks, but reach the same result by internal rules.

*Permanent associates.* In addition to the creation of the intermediate status of income partner, some firms have abandoned the up-or-out rule for associates and have tried to recoup their investment in training costs by retaining associates indefinitely. If an associate has shown ability in one or more specialties, but is not viewed as potentially of partner caliber, particularly in terms of rainmaking, he or she may be offered a permanent position in the firm on a salaried basis. The title of these lawyers may be **senior attorney** or **senior counsel**, although some may be called simply **staff attorney** and others may be given the more prestigious title of **of counsel**. These positions may be either part-time or full-time. Female attorneys with extensive child-care obligations may elect this status with the expectation that they may later be moved into an equity partnership position when their family responsibilities make full-time work feasible.

The number of nonpartner, nonassociate lawyers in major firms is not great. Among the largest firms in 2001, Akin Gump (with 350 partners and 447 associates, for example, had 65 "other" lawyers. Holland & Knight (with 740 partners and 488 associates) had 228 "other" lawyers. A somewhat smaller firm, Lane Powell of Seattle (with 104 partners and 43 associates) had 29 in the "other" category. Many firms decline to reveal the number of nonpartner, nonassociate lawyers in their employ, and those that list "other" employees do not specify what role they play.

## §17.8 Law Firm Alternatives: Solo Practice and Contract Lawyers

Many law students choose a legal career based on stories of high salaries and numerous job opportunities. There was a major decline in law firm hiring both at the end of the 1980s and in 2001. Many graduates entering the job market during these periods of decline suffered a rude shock when no immediate job offers were received. The shock was particularly severe for students who had borrowed funds for their legal education and faced the prospect of repaying the loans without any immediate source of income. Of course, legal jobs did not dry up totally. Honor graduates from the more prestigious law schools continued to find jobs, but students in the bottom half of their graduating classes, particularly those graduating from less prestigious law schools, faced disaster.

What should a new lawyer do if he fails to locate a job at a law firm despite a major and continuing effort extending over several months? Of course, one could give up the idea of practicing law and go into business management, open one's own business, or go back to school to study something else. These are not necessarily bad ideas, because many persons in positions of responsibility in government and business have law degrees although they never practiced. Of interest here, however, are the avenues by which a recent graduate can practice law although no firm is willing to offer him an immediate job. It is always possible that one might find employment in a smaller firm (or possibly with a lawyer in solo practice who wishes to reduce his workload) in a large city or a small community. In addition, there are two avenues by which one can obtain practical experience that might open up job opportunities as lawyers in the future: solo practice and working as a temporary or contract lawyer.

A lawyer who has passed the bar may always hang out his shingle and begin the practice of law without any significant prior experience (except perhaps working at a law firm for a summer while in law school). This is undoubtedly doing it the hard way in today's specialized environment, although at one time it was an accepted method of starting a practice, particularly in smaller communities.

As a general proposition today, a young lawyer should spend some time in an apprenticeship under the oversight of a more experienced lawyer before striking out on his own. Legal apprenticeship is a practical necessity today because law schools generally do not try to teach law students the mundane and nitty-gritty details of practicing law and representing clients. A recent law school graduate may not know where the courthouse is, to use a common expression. The McCrate Report, prepared a few years ago by the American Bar Association, has recommended that law schools provide more detailed and practical training, but that is not very likely to occur in the foreseeable future.

In considering solo practice, lawyers quickly realize that they will starve if they do not have clients. Some cities have programs that permit lawyers to sign up to represent indigent criminal defendants for a modest fee; however, that is bare subsistence, at best. One must get paying clients to survive. Unfortunately, one is not likely to get many clients simply by opening an office and waiting for walk-in clients. One typically has to "network" to get paying clients who largely select lawyers based on recommendations from other people, or on the basis of family, personal, or neighborhood ties. It is possible to survive as a solo practitioner with little or no experience, but it is very difficult.

Another possible avenue is to seek a series of temporary positions with lawyers or law firms who need immediate assistance to handle their current workload but who are not in a position to take on a permanent hire. A person obtaining such a position is called a **contract lawyer.** The development of contract lawyering appears to be a recent phenomenon. The idea is basically simple. Typically, a placement agency offers to supply qualified lawyers to law firms or solo practitioners for a fee. The lawyers are employed by the placement agency, which is responsible for taxes, withholding, and other employment-related matters. The success of this business obviously depends on there being a supply of unemployed qualified lawyers and a need by law firms for temporary assistance. Many lawyers who fail to find employment with a firm, and who do not wish to test the rigors of solo practice, have found that serving as a contract lawyer provides a bridge into more traditional law practice. Contract lawyers are also called **temps** or **temporaries.**

From the standpoint of successful solo practitioners and small law firms, temps are attractive because they permit temporary or seasonal needs for lawyer services to be met without making permanent hires. Firms faced with additional work that may be temporary today are well aware of the over-staffing problems that occurred at the end of the 1980s. A typical situation is a firm with a major case that hires temps to perform more or less routine legal services in connection with the case while permitting its partners and associates to handle higher-paying work. A decision to hire temps may also be prompted by on-staff illness, maternity leaves, special projects, or seasonal increases in workload, as in tax firms during March and April. Solo practitioners with a litigation practice may use temps exclusively to assist them, overseeing their work but paying the placement agency a relatively small amount for the services being provided.

A temp may end up working for several months under the supervision of an experienced lawyer on a specific case. Not only does the temp learn the ropes of legal practice but also she may be offered a permanent job at a later time. Even where no permanent offer is forthcoming, the temp has gained valuable experience as well as entries on one's resume and possible letters of recommendation. The attractiveness of becoming a temp does not lie in the salary, which usually is on an hourly basis and may not significantly exceed the salary of paralegals. However, some income is always better than no income, and the experience of being a temp may well lead to a job in the future, either directly or through recommendations.

The use of temporary lawyers may create ethical and legal issues both for the contract lawyer and the employing firm or solo practitioner. If a temp works under the direction of a lawyer or law firm for an extended period, the question may arise whether the temp has in fact become an employee for tax and unemployment compensation purposes. Ethical issues may also arise, but the practice of using temporary lawyers is so new that the full ramifications have not been explored. Obviously, a temp who has worked on one side of a case should not accept temporary employment with the other side to work on the same case. But all sorts of ethical issues short of this extreme situation can readily be envisioned.

## §17.9  The Boom Years of Law Practice: 1998-2000

The profitability of large law firms obviously depends on the business cycles of the economy in general and of the legal profession in particular. During good years, large law firms have been very profitable indeed. The years 1998 and 1999 were such years while the year 2000 was a transition year, and, as discussed below, 2001 was a bust.

The "high tech" boom involved two areas of intense activity that produced immense amounts of capital investment and large amounts of legal work in the 1998-2000 period. The first was the telecom boom, the upgrading of the telephone system in the United States. The Telecommunications Act of 1969 had deregulated the telephone industry and swept away rules limiting competition. In a highly competitive environment, start-up firms were created to develop wireless communication and nationwide broadband systems that entailed investments approaching one-half trillion dollars between 1997 and 2000. The second major area was computerization, the creation of networks, the Internet, and electronic communication in general. This area, quickly dubbed the "dot.com" industry, received more publicity but involved a smaller aggregate dollar investment than telecommunications. Hundreds of new publicly held companies were formed in these two industries in a relatively brief period.

Venture capital firms are modern vehicles that arrange for capital to flow into new enterprises. They provide seed capital for start-up companies, and then arrange for initial public offerings after the start-up has attracted a following. During boom periods, the time between the creation of a new start-up and its making a public offering of its stock was only about nine months. When the start-up goes public, the venture capital firm usually recoups its entire initial investment while retaining a substantial preferred stock position; it then reinvests the funds in a new start-up to repeat the process. During 1998 and 1999, stock prices of both telecommunication and dot.com firms increased rapidly, creating many instant millionaires and attracting investments from relatively unsophisticated members of the public. It has been estimated that the internal rate of return for venture capital firms during this period was about 54 percent per year.

While start-ups could raise large amounts of money very easily, they sometimes had difficulty finding talented individuals to develop the contemplated products. Furthermore, many of these firms were not close to being profitable under conventional accounting standards. One measure of the success of these firms was the "burn rate," the speed with which the corporation was using up its original invested capital. A decline in the burn rate was viewed as a highly optimistic indication of future success, which tended to lift the price of the stock.

During 1999 and 2000, West Coast law firms had more business than they could handle. For example, in late 1999 seven Silicon Valley law firms were working on IPOs for 334 companies. Over the previous two years, the same firms had successfully taken public more than 500 new companies, many of them high tech. The future appeared so bright that law firms increased both the number and compensation of lawyers, associates, and summer interns.

On January 1, 2000, the firm of Gunderson Dettmer Stough Villeneuve Franklin & Hachigian ("Gunderson Dettmer") a highly profitable firm with headquarters in Menlo Park, California, stunned the legal world when it announced that it was raising salaries for first-year associates from $100,500 per year to $145,000 plus a guaranteed $20,000 first-year annual bonus. At that time Gunderson Dettmer was a firm of about 90 lawyers concentrating on three "high tech" areas: (1) information and communication technology, (2) medical/ life/science/health care, and (3) consumer/retail products and services. Firms across the country were stunned but generally responded by increasing their entry level salaries for associates and summer interns. They felt they had little choice because if they failed to increase entry level salaries they would lose their most desirable potential associates to the high-flying high tech firms.

The pressure for salary increases continued to be particularly intense in California during the year 2000. Despite some early indications that the boom may have been slowing, the firm of Brobeck, Phleger & Harrison located in San Francisco announced the following salary scale for associates in 2001:

> 1st year: $135,000 plus bonus up to $35,000
> 2nd year: $145,000 plus bonus up to $46,000
> 3rd year: $160,000 plus bonus up to $52,000
> 4th year: $175,000 plus bonus up to $57,000
> 5th year: $195,000 plus bonus up to $60,000
> 6th year: $205,000 plus bonus up to $60,000
> 7th year: $215,000 plus bonus up to $60,000
> 8th year: $225,000 plus bonus up to $60,000

These high salaries for associates were not limited to California, though that state was the leader. The reaction across the country was varied. Salaries of associates depend in part on the location of the principal offices of the law firm. In 2001, large New York firms generally started first-year associates at $125,000 ($10,000 below the leading West Coast firms) while a leading Philadelphia firm started associates at $100,000 plus a guaranteed bonus of up to $1,500. A leading Minneapolis firm paid first-year associates $90,000, while a Kansas City firm started associates in the $76,000 to $83,000 range. Ranges varied for firms competing in the same city. In Boston, for example, Foley, Hoag & Eliot started associates at $135,000 while Testa Hurwiz & Thibaeault started its associates at

$150,000. If these firms had California offices, however, they faced strong pressure to offer competitive salaries to associates in various offices.

How could law firms afford to pay such princely salaries to inexperienced lawyers? The explanation is simple: at the time law firms were swimming in profits and it appeared that the good times would continue indefinitely. That is well illustrated by The National Law Journal on August 6, 2001 (at the beginning of the collapse of the dot.com market), that listed "profits per partner" in the year 2000 for a dozen of the largest law firms in the United States. A sampling indicates that senior partners in law firms did not go hungry in 2000:

> Cooley Godward, Palo Alto, California—$905,000 per partner
> Coudert Brothers, New York—$390,000 per partner
> Davis Polk & Wardwell, New York—$1,740,000 per partner
> Dorsey & Whitney, Minneapolis—$370,000 per partner
> Latham & Watkins, Los Angeles—$900,000 per partner
> Jenner & Block, Chicago—$410,000 per partner
> Locke Liddell & Sapp, Dallas—$435,000 per partner
> Orrick Harrington, San Francisco—$750,000 per partner
> Shearman & Sterling, New York—$1,350,000 per partner
> Stroock & Stroock & Lavan, New York—$685,000 per partner
> Weil, Gotshal & Manges, New York—$1,025,000 per partner

Presumably junior partners received less than the per-partner average while senior partners received more.

While these numbers may seem princely to both law students and law professors, they should be put into perspective. They are modest when compared with the compensation of chief executive officers of publicly held corporations during the 2000-2001 period. Precise comparisons are difficult because executive compensation usually has several components: salary, long-term compensation, stock options, restricted stock, long term incentive plans, and the like. However, law firm partners were not in the same salary league. In the year 2000, John Reed, the retiring CEO of Citigroup was paid a salary of $5.4 million and had additional long-term compensation of $287.6 million, for a total compensation of $293 million. The CEO who ranked twentieth in compensation in the year 2000 was Jeffrey Skilling of Enron, who was paid an aggregate $72.5 million in compensation. Taking all the CEOs of publicly held reporting companies as a group, the *average* compensation of chief executive officers was $13.1 million in a single year.

Unfortunately, many areas of legal practice did not share in the wealth that was being distributed to partners in large law firms. In the year 2000, newly hired prosecutors at the state level began at the $40,000-$50,000 level, while many public defenders began to work at the high $30,000 level. Law clerks in state Supreme Courts began work in the $35,000 to $60,000 range while state judges were paid in the $100,000 to $150,000 range. The salaries of federal judges ranged from Chief Justice Rehnquist's salary of $186,300 down to United States magistrates and bankruptcy judges who were paid in the $133,000 range. Law professors also did not share in the wealth. Full professors teaching in state law schools (almost all of whom had more than ten years' teaching experience) were mostly in the $125,000 to $175,000 range, but there were exceptions in both directions, depending on specific states. The University of Wyoming, for example paid full professors $89,857 and beginning assistant professors $62,064. Law school deans had salaries generally above $175,000, though again there was great variety. These data are based on information provided by state law schools; salary figures for deans and professors in many of the most prestigious private law schools are not available.

## §17.10 The Year of The Bust: 2001

The first small indications that the high tech bubble was slowing down appeared in the latter part of 2000. These first indications were not taken seriously by many senior partners in highly successful law firms. They remembered the brief slowdown that occurred in the late 1980s and early 1990s, and presumably believed that any decline would be brief and would not affect long-term growth. Firms therefore saw no reason to change their plans for 2001, including the number of new associates and summer interns that had been promised jobs and the compensation levels for associates that were based in part on the Brobeck Phleger salary scale that had previously been announced to become effective for the year 2001.

The full magnitude of the decline in business gradually became apparent in the spring and summer of 2001. The decline was first evident in the telecom area but rapidly spread to dot.coms, as well. Start-ups that had not developed viable and profitable businesses found that the cash window had closed almost overnight and that the companies were no longer viable. The collapse spread quickly from company to company, and shareholders lost billions of dollars. In one telecom area, competitive local exchange carriers, $140 billion had been invested but companies quickly ran out of cash, found themselves unable to raise additional cash, and simply defaulted on planned projects. It has been estimated that 95 percent of the $140 billion invested in this one part of the telephone communications industry was irretrievably lost.

Another datum indicating the extent of the collapse is that between 1997 and 2000, telecom companies had, in the aggregate, raised close to a half trillion dollars. On November 18, 2001, the *New York Times* stated that the decline in the value of these companies was "one of the most spectacular investment debacles ever. Bigger than the South Sea bubble. Bigger than tulipmania. Bigger than dot.bomb. The flameout of the telecommunications sector when it is over will wind up costing investors hundreds of billions of dollars." In 2001 alone, defaults by telecommunication companies constituted 56 percent of all industrial defaults.

The collapse in the computerization/Internet area was not as severe as in the telecom area but followed the same path. Many start-up firms found that there was no way to continue in business without additional capital and there simply was no way to raise that capital. When they closed their doors, lessors and creditors—typically suppliers of hardware, office equipment, computers, and the like—repossessed physical assets, leaving the dot.com with liabilities, a business plan, but no assets.

Of course, a limited number of telecom and dot.com firms survived, considerably chastened. These companies had business plans that enabled them to be profitable despite the general decline in the high tech area.

In several instances, venture capital firms that originally took failing start-ups public resumed control over the companies in an effort to recover some part of their investment. Basically, the venture capital firm selected and installed its own person as CEO, directing her to recover as much as she could from the liquidation of the business. Since the venture capital firm originally acquired a preferred stock position (while public investors received common stock), any cash that was recovered went to the venture capital firm. The public shareholders typically lost their entire investment. Nevertheless, venture capital firms in the first six months of 2001 had a net loss of 18 percent of their invested capital.

These events unexpectedly reduced the manpower needs of law firms. Firms that had agreed to hire a full complement of summer law clerks at then-current salary levels found that they were significantly overstaffed and did not have enough work to keep all of its associates busy.

One group of lawyers who were immediately injured by the high tech collapse were partners and senior associates that had left their law firms to become general counsel of high tech firms that subsequently failed. Since many law firms were overstaffed, the chances of such an attorney returning to his old firm were not good.

The business collapse described above did not occur instantaneously; rather, its enormity gradually became apparent in the summer and fall of 2001. A first indication of trouble occurred on February 14, 2001, when Dewey Ballantine, a major New York firm, announced it was laying off 10 to 15 associates from its Manhattan office. However, the firm spokesman "denied the economy was a factor" and explained that the layoffs were a result of a slowing down of the "firm's associate attrition rate."

In August 2001, a National Law Journal survey showed that law firm profits were declining rapidly from the record year of 2000. Interviews with some large firms indicated that the level of compensation of associates would not increase in the immediate future, but that firms did not intend to roll back salary levels.

The magnitude of the collapse became apparent when it was revealed that the law firms that had been involved in 350 initial public offerings during 2000 were working on a total of only 10 IPOs in the spring of 2001.

As summer associates and interns began to arrive at large law firms, it was apparent that there was not enough work to support them. Firms generally honored their basic commitment to summer interns and delayed a reduction in the number of permanent associations. However, as business declined, the inevitable result was layoffs at many firms. After the September 11 terrorist bombing, the New York office of Shearman & Sterling announced that it was laying off about 10 percent of its associates with the explanation that the firm can no longer maintain "a boom economy work force in a weak economy that has further deteriorated since September 11." Estimates of total layoffs since the terrorist attack on September 11, 2001 run as high as 400 associates across the country.

Some firms initially adopted other approaches. For example, one California firm, the Venture Law Group, reduced starting pay for associates by 33 percent in the fall of 2001. It also told 13 associates to report in January 2002, rather than early fall 2001. However, in October, the same firm decided to lay off 10 lawyers and 22 staff members, and to delay indefinitely the starting date for its first-year associate class. At the same time one small Chicago firm advertised for additional business on the ground that its billing rates were low because it did not pay associates $125,000 to start. In November 2001, Brobeck, Phleger offered a voluntary separation plan to associates who worked in the transactions area and who would bill less than 1300 hours in 2001. If they agreed to leave at year-end, they would be paid roughly five months' salary, their health insurance would be continued through April 15, 2002, and they would be entitled to outplacement counseling. If they decline, they may be subject to termination. Associates in the litigation and securities sections were not offered this option, since work in those areas had not declined as significantly as in the transactions area.

There also have been reports of firms withdrawing apparently firm offers to summer interns or starting associates for the year 2002. In some instances, firms have withdrawn offers only to law students from less prestigious schools.

The terrorist attack on September 11, 2001 accelerated the decline in firm business. The period after Labor Day is normally an active period for law firms, following a natural slow-down of activities that occurs over the summer. However, after the attack on the World Trade Center, law business virtually ceased for about a week. Law firms in or near the World Trade Center were of course closed, but reverberations were much broader. The level of business around the country declined in part from shock and disbelief that unthinkable events had actually occurred. Deals that appeared to be firm either stalled or were withdrawn under the "material adverse change" clauses that are common in substantial contracts. Securities markets not directly affected were thrown into turmoil and share prices declined abruptly.

Several firms have announced plan changes following September 11. A Philadelphia firm announced that it would drop its summer program and restock its staff as necessary by hiring laterals from other firms. Also at risk were associates from earlier years who had been promised permanent jobs with the law firm. Brobeck, Phleger offered to maintain full health insurance and other benefits for lawyers who agree to take unpaid sabbaticals or to accept part-time work of less than three days a week. Brobeck, Phleger also announced it was reducing reimbursements for nonbillable meals, travel, entertainment, messenger service, overnight mail, and business retreats. These developments were independent of the layoffs of associates described above.

The severity of the business decline was doubtless increased by the events of September 11, 2001. Recovery, however, will undoubtedly eventually occur. Whether or not the optimism and effervescence of the boom period will return, however, remains to be seen. As this is written near the end of 2001, it seems unlikely.

# ◆ MASTER WORD LIST